Introduction to Private Equity, Debt and Real Assets

Founded in 1807, John Wiley & Sons is the oldest independent publishing company in the United States. With offices in North America, Europe, Australia and Asia, Wiley is globally committed to developing and marketing print and electronic products and services for our customers' professional and personal knowledge and understanding.

The Wiley Finance series contains books written specifically for finance and investment professionals as well as sophisticated individual investors and their financial advisors. Book topics range from portfolio management to e-commerce, risk management, financial engineering, valuation and financial instrument analysis, as well as much more.

For a list of available titles, visit our website at www.WileyFinance.com.

Introduction to Private Equity, Debt and Real Assets

*From Venture Capital to LBO,
Senior to Distressed Debt,
Immaterial to Fixed Assets*

Third Edition

CYRIL DEMARIA

WILEY

This edition first published 2020

© 2020 John Wiley & Sons Ltd.

Registered office
John Wiley & Sons Ltd, The Atrium, Southern Gate, Chichester, West Sussex, PO19 8SQ, United Kingdom

For details of our global editorial offices, for customer services and for information about how to apply for permission to reuse the copyright material in this book please see our website at www.wiley.com.

Wiley publishes in a variety of print and electronic formats and by print-on-demand. Some material included with standard print versions of this book may not be included in e-books or in print-on-demand. If this book refers to media such as a CD or DVD that is not included in the version you purchased, you may download this material at http://booksupport.wiley.com. For more information about Wiley products, visit www.wiley.com.

Designations used by companies to distinguish their products are often claimed as trademarks. All brand names and product names used in this book are trade names, service marks, trademarks or registered trademarks of their respective owners. The publisher is not associated with any product or vendor mentioned in this book.

Library of Congress Cataloging-in-Publication Data

Names: Demaria, Cyril, author.
Title: Introduction to private equity, debt and real assets : from venture
    capital to LBO, senior to distressed debt, immaterial to fixed assets /
    Cyril Demaria.
Other titles: Introduction to private equity
Description: Third edition. | Hoboken : John Wiley & Sons, 2020. | Includes
    bibliographical references and index.
Identifiers: LCCN 2020004378 (print) | LCCN 2020004379 (ebook) | ISBN
    9781119537380 (hardback) | ISBN 9781119537410 (adobe pdf) | ISBN
    9781119537373 (epub)
Subjects: LCSH: Private equity.
Classification: LCC HG4751 .D46 2020 (print) | LCC HG4751 (ebook) | DDC
    332.6—dc23
LC record available at https://lccn.loc.gov/2020004378
LC ebook record available at https://lccn.loc.gov/2020004379

Cover Design: Wiley
Cover Image: © oxygen/Getty Images

Set in 10/12pt SabonLTStd by SPi Global, Chennai, India

Printed and bound by CPI Group (UK) Ltd, Croydon, CR0 4YY

C9781119537380_211223

John Donne wrote that 'No man is an island entire of itself'. I am indebted to my family and my friends for their constant support, their kindness and their gentle nudges. This book is dedicated to them.

Contents

Acknowledgements

I thank Sarah Debrand for her kind assistance in helping me put this new edition together. Her inputs, patience, kindness and reactivity were very much of help. Thank you.

I also thank the Emerging Markets Private Equity Association, and specifically Jeff Schlapinski and Sabrina Katz, for kindly providing me with crucial data.

About the Author

Since 2017, Cyril Demaria has been a Partner and Head of Private Markets at Weller-shoff & Partners, in Zurich. The company is an independent research and advice company to institutional investors and family offices. He is also the General Partner and President of Pilot Fish, created in 2009, which manages a series of venture capital funds for family offices and high net worth individuals. Prior to his current role, Cyril Demaria was in charge of private markets research at the Chief Investment Office of UBS Wealth Management from 2014 to 2016. From 2009 to 2012, he co-founded and was Partner and Chief Investment Officer at Tiaré Investment Management AG, a Zürich-based wealth and investment management company. Prior to that, he created a multi-strategy fund of funds focused on environmental matters. He was also an Associate in private equity funds of funds, a Portfolio Manager responsible for private equity fund investments at a French insurance group where he managed 27 investments totalling EUR 60 million in private equity funds and funds of funds. As Head of Corporate Development at Externall (Paris), he managed four asset acquisitions and raised debt financing. He started his career in a hybrid venture capital and fund of funds firm (San Francisco, Paris).

A French and Swiss citizen, Cyril Demaria holds a BA in Political Sciences from the Institut d'Etudes Politiques (Lyon), a Master's in Geopolitics applied to Money and Finance (Paris), a Master's in European Business Law (Paris), is a graduate from HEC (Paris) and holds a PhD from the University of St Gallen.

An Affiliate Professor at EDHEC, he also lectures at EADA (Barcelona), as well as universities and business schools. He collaborates regularly as an expert with Invest Europe, France Invest and the Swiss Private Equity and Corporate Finance Association. He is the author of:

- *Développement durable et finance* (Maxima, 2003).
- *Introduction au private equity* (Revue Banque Editeur, 2006, 2nd edn 2008, 3rd edn 2009, 4th edn 2012, 5th edn 2015, 6th edn 2018) – foreword by Xavier Moreno (former President of the AFIC, Managing Partner of Astorg Partners).
- *Profession: business angel – Devenir un investisseur providentiel averti*, with M. Fournier (Revue Banque Editeur, 2008) – foreword by Claude Bébéar (Chairman of the Board of Axa, Chairman of the think tank Institut-Montaigne).
- *Le marché, les acteurs et la performance du private equity suisse*, with M. Pedergnana (SECA, 2009, 2nd edn 2012) – foreword by Patrick Aebischer (President of the Ecole Polytechnique Fédérale de Lausanne).

He can be reached at: cyril.demaria@pilot-fish.eu, +41 79 813 86 49.

Introduction

The initial version of this book was born as an exercise of pedagogy in a sector which was largely uncharted: private equity. I wrote then that it was the direct result of 'my experience of reading the available literature and my recurring lack of satisfaction regarding their ability to combine so as to formulate an articulate theory'. I was obviously not the only one. The success of the abridged French version of this book (Demaria, 2006, 2008, 2010, 2012, 2016 and 2018), of which the first edition as well as the updated reprints were each sold out within less than a year, tends to confirm it. The second edition was also translated into Spanish, Portuguese and Mandarin, reaching an even wider public.

Things have changed. First, there are now multiple books on private equity, at times highly opiniated (Phalippou, 2017). This is a positive development, as we all collectively need multiple sources of information of high quality. Many academics from different disciplines, as well as finance practitioners, have also tried to contribute to public enlightenment, often with considerable success. Highly acclaimed academics, such as Josh Lerner, Antoinette Schoar and Paul Gompers in the USA, or Per Stromberg, Tim Jenkinson and Douglas Cumming in Europe, are a few of a growing academic community extending our knowledge of this difficult and largely misunderstood part of a broader category of finance called 'alternative assets'. Private equity has benefitted from their efforts tremendously. There have also been honourable attempts to paint a portrait of private equity by famous and reputable practitioners, such as The Institute of Chartered Accountants of England and Wales (ICAEW).

However, one of the recurring criticisms made notably to many academic works is that they often remain prisoners of ill-adapted theoretical frameworks. Using toolboxes designed for analysing quantitative data, these frameworks soon reveal their limitations. The discrepancies which can be observed between research by academic authors and empirical observations by practitioners are a testimony to their inadequacy. There are constant gaps between the findings of the former and the facts as reported by the latter. Multiple sources rehash outdated content (at times biased), trying to valiantly maintain an illusion of coherence – with some dogmas coming from the analysis of listed markets. Many concepts, such as efficient markets and the measure of risks through volatility, are inadapted. This should now be clear and acknowledged – notably as they are not even relevant for listed markets.

It is time to devise new instruments, a task long overdue. Private equity cannot be turned simply into equations as is done for hedge funds. It requires specific tools, for example to analyse its performance, risk and liquidity. Indeed, acknowledging that liquidity is not a risk but a variable of private equity investing and thus supporting specific analyses should now be straightforward. The consequences of this acceptation are that there are three dimensions to analyse systematically, instead of two. This notably changes the framework to analyse the source of value creation in private equity specifically, where there is no such thing as an 'illiquidity premium' (a concept only applicable in fixed income).

Second, the sector has grown very fast and morphed multiple times. To say that private equity is moving fast is an understatement. We try to keep up with these fast-paced changes, which is why this third edition goes beyond a simple update. Private equity has become part of a larger sector, often referred to as 'private markets', 'private capital' or 'private finance'. In previous editions, we presented what is now distinctly identified as 'private debt' and 'private assets' as part of the private equity universe. They are now autonomous, and we have amended this book to take this into account. This third edition will therefore include developments on private debt and private real assets. We will also describe in more detail how funds work and how to analyse them. To be more complete, we will also include the analysis of a start-up. We have chosen to look at each piece of the private markets puzzle and recognise that they somehow do not form a harmonious and clear picture.

0.1 A MOVING TARGET

A confusing terminology

Private equity is constantly being redefined. Establishing a typology of transactions is thus especially tricky, notably when there is semantic confusion. One of them is the confusion between 'private equity' and 'leveraged buy-out' (LBO) in the USA, where they are used interchangeably. LBO is dedicated, as we will see, to the transfer of ownership (a buy-out) of a company, with the additional twist that the buyer uses debt for the acquisition (hence the leverage). Though LBOs represent the great majority of investments made in private equity in developed markets, they are just one of the components of private equity. The American confusion comes from the fact that LBO has a bad reputation there and the expression was in substance blacklisted. Associated historically with asset stripping, this reputation is now contaminating the expression 'private equity'. Warren Buffett, himself described by Burton Malkiel[1] as a 'quasi private equity investor'[2] (Kaczor, 2009), classified LBO managers as being 'porn shop operators', and the semantic confusion between private equity and LBO as 'Orwellian'.

Because of its constantly changing nature, the expression 'private equity' often covers only part of its field of action. Indeed, the 'private', which refers to 'unlisted', element is no longer decisive; nor is that of 'equity'.

---

[1] Author of 'A random walk down Wall Street', former Governor of the American Stock Exchange, Professor of Economy at Princeton University.

[2] '[...] *Question: I suppose that you have met with Warren Buffett?*

B. Malkiel: Yes. He is a brilliant man, a brilliant businessman. But he does not only buy and sell shares as usual asset managers do: buy undervalued securities and resell them when they are overvalued. Warren Buffett said "the ideal duration of share holding is forever." All his great successes, starting with the Washington Post, were to buy companies, and incidentally help them, notably by having a seat at the Board [...]. When one of his investments in Salomon Brothers did not work, he became CEO for a certain time. [...]

Question: As a private equity manager somehow?

B. Malkiel: You can indeed almost consider Warren Buffett as a private equity manager [...]'. (Our translation.)

Not just 'equity'

Stating that *'private equity' is (just) 'equity'* is a mistake. From this assumption, it might also be assumed that private equity may be analysed validly with the tools used for public equities. This has so far been proven wrong: the timeframe, the risks, the skills required and the returns associated with private equity investments differ substantially from those associated with public equities.

The defining feature is the **value creation**, which is the result of the implementation of a plan by the management on behalf of the owner(s) of the company, also referred to as 'investor(s)'. A focus on value creation also applies to the more recent segments of the private markets universe, such as private debt and private real assets. Investors analyse companies and assets to assess their plans for development (or restructuring in specific cases). In the case of specific private debt strategies such as direct lending, although the 'governance' is structured through debt contracts, investors monitor the implementation of the plan and act in case of significant deviation from it.

Not necessarily 'private'

To implement this plan efficiently, the company benefits from being private. Some companies, such as Dell in 2013, can be delisted to undertake significant changes. In this example, Silver Lake Partners and Michael Dell acquired the company for USD 24.4 billion to take it private and launch a stream of acquisitions, such as EMC for USD 67 billion in 2015.

Therefore, if it is not 'equity', then 'private' could appear as defining the sector. Once again, this has been proven wrong: although private, that is non-listed assets, companies and assets can implement plans more easily, some private equity investors also operate on the stock exchange. For example, in the case of a private investment in public entities (PIPE), investors inject significant capital in profitable and growing listed companies in what is usually described in private equity as 'growth capital'. Other investors execute their private equity investment with a listed structure, such as a Business Development Company (BDC) or Special Purpose Acquisition Company (SPAC).

The common and defining feature of these investments in private or public entities is their long **holding period**: the average 3 to 5 years during which the company is held by the investor in private equity. This is necessary to implement the plan referred to above to create value. This differentiates, for example, private equity investors from activist investors. The latter belong to the hedge fund world and borrow some of the tools from the private equity box to apply them to listed companies. Their holding periods are shorter than in private equity.

More than private equity: the emergence of new 'private market' segments

The criteria of value creation and long holding periods support the identification of additional segments in private markets. Private debt has long been in the shadow of private equity. After all, two of the oldest strategies in the book are focusing on convertible debt: mezzanine debt and distressed debt. They are 'quasi private equity', in a way. Mezzanine debt is often associated with the acquisition of a company through LBO, by providing some of the debt for that purpose. Distressed debt aims at acquiring the debt of an ailing company under bankruptcy procedures and taking control of it by converting this debt into equity. However, their risk–return profiles differ significantly from private equity strategies. The emergence of direct lending (also known as senior lending), consisting of financing companies through plain vanilla debt ('senior debt') without the intervention of a bank, gave a critical mass to the private debt sector. It is now on the radar of investors, along with mezzanine and distressed debt. These two strategies themselves, being rather established, have also morphed and extended their reach. For example, mezzanine debt has been rebranded as 'unitranche debt' to provide a more flexible and comprehensive financing solution to borrowers in a context of low interest rates. Distressed debt has extended its reach to 'non-performing loans', as cases of distressed companies have been rather far apart in a benign macro-economic environment supported by very low interest rates since the crisis of 2007–2009. However, banks hold loans granted up to 2007 which are under-performing and are therefore an attractive target for distressed debt specialists.

Private real assets have also become another sub-category of the private markets universe. Investors invest in real estate, infrastructure and natural resources through equity (private equity real assets) or debt (private debt real assets). They apply a value creation plan to them over a rather long holding period ranging from 3 (energy) to 7 years (infrastructure and timberland).

0.2 A CONSUBSTANTIAL LACK OF INFORMATION

Private means little, if any, information

Operating in the non-listed world has one consequence: a *recurring lack of information*. Private companies and assets provide only scarce information, for two reasons. First, there is no regulatory obligation to provide any. Investors and private companies generally have no obligation to report the details of their activities, except in some jurisdictions. Second, producing this information is expensive and time consuming. It is sometimes disproportionately expensive compared to the size and revenues of small and medium-sized businesses or assets, which are the core targets of private market investors. Most of them have limited reporting capacity and do not, for example, have real enterprise resource planning (ERP) software. Their financial indicators (if any) are at best basic, and analytical accounts are already seen as 'advanced management'.

Before investing, investors often have to generate, collect, structure and analyse the information themselves. This is one of the defining features of their activity, to mitigate the asymmetries of information between the insiders (the sellers of a company or an asset, for example) and them, the outsiders. During the investment, one of the challenges of the investor is to be fully informed and on time, notably to make sure that the plan is executed (Jensen, 1989, 1997) – and if not, that corrective measures are implemented. One of the challenges is that the management of the companies or the assets produces the information and might have different interests. Investors therefore face the initial and ongoing challenge to foster the alignment of interests between the management (their 'agents') and themselves (the 'principals'). This is in essence what private markets investing really is: **setting up and enforcing actively a governance framework, based largely on self-generated information in order to implement a plan to create value materialised upon the exit of the investment** (its sale or listing on the stock exchange, for example).

Information on private markets is collected and communicated scarcely, heterogeneously and unsystematically

A lack of information on private companies and assets translates into a general lack of information on private markets. Our analysis, which is based on websites of most of the information providers on private markets, demonstrates it: information is non-systematic, scarce, expensive and difficult to gather (see Table 0.1). This will remain

TABLE 0.1 Sources and categories of information in private equity

			Geographical coverage						Performance (benchmark) of general partners by strategy														Activity		Source Type			Funds
			USA	Europe	MEA	Lat. Am.	APAC	Afr.	VC	Growth	LBO	Mezz.	Distr. debt	Senior debt	Private RE	F. of funds	Infra.	Energy	Secondaries	Timberland	Farmland	Index	Prim. Mark.	Sec. Mark.	LP/GP back office	Voluntary	FOIA & public data	# covered
Database providers	Fund and deal data level	PitchBook	P	P	P	P	P	P	P	P	P	P	P	P	P	P	P	P	P	P	P	–	P	P	–	YES	YES	42 618
		VentureSource (Dow Jones)	P	P	–	P	P	P	P	P	P	P	P	P	P	P	P	P	P	P	P	F	P	–	–	–	YES	35 000
		CEPRES	P	P	"ROW"		P	"ROW"	P	P	P	P	P	P	P	P	P	P	P	P	P	F	P	P	YES	–	–	6 400
		MergerMarket	P	P	P	P	P	–	P	P	P	P	P	P	P	P	P	P	P	P	P	F	P	–	–	YES	YES	10 400
	Fund level data	AVCJ	–	P	P	–	P	–	P	P	P	P	P	P	P	P	P	P	P	P	P	F	P	–	–	YES	YES	12 000
		Preqin	P	P	P	P	P	P	P	P	P	P	P	P	P	P	P	P	P	P	P	F	P	P	–	YES	YES	36 000
		EurekaHedge	P	P	P	P	P	P	–	–	–	–	–	–	P	–	P	P	P	P	P	–	P	P	–	YES	YES	8 200
		PEI Connect	P	P	P	P	P	P	–	–	P	P	P	P	P	P	P	P	P	P	P	–	P	P	–	YES	YES	30 000
		Bison	P	P	P	P	P	P	P	P	P	P	P	P	P	P	P	P	P	?	?	F	P	P	YES	YES	YES	6 200
		Cobalt	BASED ON BISON AND HAMILTON LANE DATA – Platform powered by both Bison and Hamilton Lane																									
		eFront Pevara	P	P	P	P	P	P	P	P	P	P	P	P	P	P	P	P	P	?	?	F	P	P	YES	–	–	3 900
	Direct deal data	Dealogic	P	P	P	P	P	–	P	P	P	?	?	P	?	–	P	P	?	?	?	F	P	P	?	?	?	
		S&P Capital IQ	P	P	P	P	P	P	P	P	P	P	P	P	P	–	P	P	?	?	?	–	P	P	?	?	?	
		Zephyr (Bureau van Dijk)	P	P	P	P	–	–	P	P	P	?	P	P	?	–	?	?	?	?	?	F	P	P	–	–	YES	
		Cliffwater	P	–	–	–	–	–	F	F	P	–	P	P	P	–	P	P	?	?	?	F	P	–	?	YES	?	
	Fund and deal data	EMPEA	–	P	P	P	P	P	–	P	P	P	P	P	P	P	P	–	–	–	–	F	P	–	–	YES	YES	3 200
Internat. and regional associations	Fund level data	ILPA	BASED ON CAMBRIDGE ASSOCIATES DATA																									
		Invest Europe	–	F	–	–	–	–	F	F	F	F	F	F	F	F	F	–	–	–	–	F	F	–	YES	–	–	8 000
		LAVCA	–	–	–	P	–	–	P	P	P	P	–	–	P	–	P	–	–	–	–	F	F	–	–	YES	?	?
		NVCA	F	–	–	–	–	–	F	F	F	–	–	–	–	–	–	–	–	–	–	F	F	–	–	YES	YES	?
Universities	Fund level	PCRI	P	P	–	"ROW"	–	–	F	F	F	–	–	–	–	–	–	–	–	–	–	–	F	–	YES	–	YES	38 641
	Direct deal	CMBOR	–	P	–	–	–	–	–	–	P	–	–	–	–	–	–	–	–	–	–	–	P	–	YES	YES	–	

(continued)

TABLE 0.1 (*Continued*)

		Geographical coverage						Performance (benchmark) of general partners by strategy														Activity		Source Type			Funds
		USA	Europe	MEA	Lat. Am.	APAC	Afr.	VC	Growth	LBO	Mezz.	Distr. debt	Senior debt	Private RE	F. of funds	Infra.	Energy	Secondaries	Timberland	Farmland	Index	Prim. Mark.	Sec. Mark.	LP/GP back office	Voluntary	FOIA & public data	# covered
	Cambridge Associates	P	P	P	P	P	P	P	P	P	P	P	P	P	P	P	P	P	P	P	F	–	–	YES	YES	–	7 420
	Thomson VentureXpert	The database has been discontinued and replaced by an access to Cambridge Associates via Thomson Eikon																									?
Intermediaries & gatekeepers	Burgiss	P	P	"ROW"	P	–	P	P	P	P	P	P	P	P	P	P	P	P	–	P	–	P	P	YES	–	–	?
Fund level data	Hamilton Lane	P	P	"ROW"	P	–	P	P	P	P	P	P	?	P	P	P	P	P	–	–	–	P	P	YES	YES	YES	?
	StepStone	P	P	P	P	?	P	P	P	P	P	P	P	P	P	P	P	?	?	?	–	–	–	YES	YES	–	?
	State Street	–	–	–	–	–	–	–	–	–	–	–	–	–	–	–	–	–	?	?	F	–	–	YES	YES	?	?
	Greenhill	Global						–	–	–	–	–	–	–	–	–	–	–	–	–	–	F	–	–	?	?	?

Note 1: 'F' refers to free offering, 'P' refers to paying offering and 'M' refers to member access only. 'MEA' refers to Middle East. 'Lat. Am.' refers to Latin America. 'Afr.' refers to Africa. 'APAC' refers to Asia-Pacific. 'Mezz.' refers to mezzanine debt. 'Distr. debt' refers to distressed debt. 'RE' refers to real estate. 'F. of funds' refers to funds of funds. 'Infra.' refers to infrastructure. 'Prim. markets' refers to primary markets. 'Sec. markets' refers to secondary markets.

Note 2: Voluntary means that clients have accepted to give information on their own funds (LPs or GPs) in exchange for free access to data, for example.

Note 3: LP/GP back-office means that operators have access to data from clients.

Note 4: 'FOIA' (Freedom of Information Act) means that the information is not available directly from public websites. It must be requested by American interested parties. We have grouped it with public information data.

Note 5: Most of the sources offer some form of free index and a paying access to detailed data.

Note 6: S&P Capital IQ is a platform included in the S&P Global Market Intelligence offering. It has to be differentiated from S&P Global, S&P Global Ratings, S&P Global Platts and S&P Dow Jones Indices.

Note 7: Preqin and PitchBook provide some form of free data based on their granular and detailed paying offering.

Note 8: The majority of professional associations (such as Invest Europe and ILPA) do not provide performance data but only activity data. However, some national associations (such as France Invest) provide both.

Note 9: EMPEA covers all emerging market regions. Farmland and Timberland strategies are included in real assets and there is no separate asset class for impact investing, but they are considering this strategy.

Note 10: Preqin also covers hybrid funds and co-investments.

Note 11: MergerMarket's data includes information from Unquote.

Note 12: VentureSource provides an index based on venture capital transactions, not fund performance.

Source: Author, based on public information, private discussions and correspondence. As of December 2018. For clarity, the table does not include data from national/local professional associations.

as such for the foreseeable future. It is highly unlikely that there will be a 'pure and perfect information context' any time soon for non-listed companies and assets – which happen to make up 99% of the total number of companies in a given economy.

This lack of information notably contributes to the frequent gaps between research and the facts highlighted above, and that theoretical models ill-adapted to private markets are still much in use. These models have been tested on larger sets of data on stock exchanges and have proven some form of relevance and robustness at a certain time.

Consequences of lack of information: simplifications

This lack of available information has resulted in some *methodological simplifications*. For example, observers assimilate casually the findings for a part of the sector (e.g., large LBOs operated on listed companies) as a general rule for the entire activity of LBOs. This is proven wrong regularly. Small and medium-sized companies are bought out by different investors, with substantially different financing techniques and investment purposes.

Another simplification is to assimilate the private market sector with private market funds. Even though funds (intermediaries which will be presented in the course of this book) are probably a good indication of the trends in the sector, they certainly do not sum up private market activity. Fund managers have organised themselves in rich and powerful national (such as the British Private Equity and Venture Capital Association or France Invest) and regional associations (such as Invest Europe and the American National Venture Capital Association), which tend to hide the existence of other players.

For example, business angels play a significant role in financing start-ups. Also known as angel investors, they are the very first individuals willing to support an emerging venture. They are largely as yet unknown, while venture capital funds, which do the same, tend to take the limelight. Corporations, endowments, foundations, high net worth individuals, state-owned structures, banks, insurance groups and other economic players are also making direct investments which are not necessarily observed by the associations mentioned above, and therefore remain largely unbeknownst to the public. The fact that these investors are below the radar significantly contributes to the lack of information affecting private markets.

For the purpose of this book we will essentially refer to the activity of funds and fund managers as this is the most documented. However, whenever possible, we will provide additional information to give some perspective to the developments.

Long-term perspectives in terms of information

In the long term, information is expected to slowly increase for at least three reasons. The first is *regulatory*. European (Alternative Investment Fund Manager Directive (AIFMD), Solvency II Directive), American (Foreign Account Tax Compliance Act (FATCA), Volcker Rule, Dodd–Frank Act) and international (Basel III and IV Agreements, pension and insurance regulations) regulations have introduced new obligations which have a direct impact on private markets. They can be summarised as follows: always faster (insurance groups request quarterly reports within 45 to 60 days after closing of the quarter), always more comprehensive (*CalPERS vs. San Jose Mercury News* kick-started the movement in 2002) and always more objective (AIFMD, with third-party valuations of private companies and assets) information has to be provided to fund investors. Regulators, such as the American Securities and Exchange Commission (SEC), have also started to investigate the practices by fund managers and ask for more information. To gain time and provide this level of detail, adopting a state-of-the-art IT system is necessary for fund managers. Some of the information patiently gathered will therefore be more readily available and possibly communicated to the larger public if the pressure to do so increases.

The second reason is that fund managers engage more frequently in *fundraising* (and communication). They have to document the activity of theirs funds permanently and in an ongoing fashion. Fund investors themselves require an increasing quantity and quality of information from fund managers.

The third reason is *operational risk management*, a new risk for an asset class which is used to small teams managed as boutiques. The downfall in 2018 of The Abraaj Group, created in 2002 and the largest Middle Eastern private market fund manager with USD 13.6 billion of assets under management, has emphasised the need to conduct thorough due diligence on fund managers. Cases of potential conflicts of interest in these 'asset management houses' (as large private equity fund managers describe themselves) will dramatically increase as they operate in various interconnected sectors (private real estate, distressed debt, LBO, private investments in public entities, etc.), but also potential insider trading cases as LBOs are increasingly targeting listed groups. This should argue in favour of advanced monitoring and reporting systems to protect general partners themselves in case of legal procedures.

One of the consequences of more information: more fees

The logical consequence of this quest for more information is that management fees,[3] which are at the heart of the relationships between fund managers and fund investors, will paradoxically not decrease – at least in the short term. The reason is related to the ramp-up of IT system expenditure (to catch up with regulations and investors' requirements), the weight of regulations (financially and time-wise) and the need for extensive track records of fund managers (notably due to the quasi-impossibility of creating captive firms in banks and insurance companies going forward). These factors will push towards mergers of fund managers and increase barriers to entry to new fund managers in private markets. The balance of power will hence stay on the side of existing fund managers – whether good or not – and the fees will thus continue to be set by fund managers to their own advantage.

0.3   BENIGN NEGLECT, MALIGN CONSEQUENCES

Lack of information and simplifications have significant consequences. First, pseudo-information such as 'rumours' or 'reputation', that is to say noise in scientific terms, has filled the information gap. Second, even academic findings are not put into perspective by the larger public. Public action plans are taken to correct supposed market imbalances, and are often ill-adapted and there is a growing antagonism between the different parts of the private equity system for that reason.

Low information can translate into bad conclusions

Thus, we know what we do not know. This is an important piece of information in itself. *Statistics of private equity performance and activity should be read with caution.* They are often the result of periodical polls of private equity fund managers, answering

---

[3]This expression, as well as most of the other technical terms and expressions, is defined further on in the book, as well as in the Glossary.

on a voluntary basis. These figures are unaudited; they cover a different sample of funds over time depending on the answer rate, and are applicable in any case to only a portion of the private equity industry. Though this information is interesting and of use, it is crucial to always remember that it only reflects a part of the reality. For example, European countries regularly record low volumes of financing of start-ups *by venture capital funds*. Read too fast, this information might lead public authorities to conclude that there is a lack of capital available. However, in many countries funds are crowded out by other sources of private financing, such as business angels or family offices. These investors are below the radar of statistics and therefore are not accounted for in activity statistics. Laments about a European 'lack of start-up capital' have become an ingrained and recurring thought, difficult to rationally analyse.

Bad information often translates into (bad) public policies

As a consequence, the French (2007) and British (2009) governments have been focusing on start-ups at seed stage, because according to public statistics, venture capital funds have not been investing in them sufficiently.[4] This was perceived as a market imbalance which had to be corrected (somehow, rightfully, but only in specific cases; see Lerner, 2009, p. 9 and Chapter 3).[5] Whether true or not, this gap in financing has been targeted by a set of measures heavily financed by the taxpayer. Another example is to be found in federal venture capital funds of funds in the USA and the UK (2009). Innovation America and the National Association of Seed and Venture Funds (NASVF) suggested the setting up of a USD 2 billion fund of funds dedicated to supporting business angels and funding public programmes. This would be an extension of the Small Business Administration (SBA) programme, which has experienced difficulties in staying afloat.

Unfortunately, the *track record of public initiatives* (Lerner, 2009)[6] *and funds of funds is bad* (Arnold, 2009b), notably because of the proximity with local political agendas which affect public investment structures (Bernstein, Schoar & Lerner, 2009), whether they are sovereign wealth funds or funds of funds. In the UK, state-backed venture capital funds have under-performed by comparison with their commercial counterparts. The returns of the latter (2002–2004) were 7.7%, whereas UK VC funds (commercial and public) of the same vintage were 1.7%. An excess of capital in the UK would explain these dismal results.

0.4 KNOWING THE DEVIL TO CIRCUMVENT IT

This book will (unfortunately) not be able to completely avoid the above-mentioned traps of simplification and lack of information. I am a prisoner of the same constraints my peers have had to deal with. Part of the value of this book, if there is one, could be

---

[4] Other examples include the Small Business Investment Company Program (USA, 1960s), Building on Information Technology Strengths (Australia, 1999), BioValley (Malaysia, 2005); see Lerner (2009).

[5] Lerner demonstrates that innovation is linked to growth, as it optimises the use of inputs.

[6] 'The Small Business Investment Company was poorly designed initially, with counterproductive requirements, and then implemented inconsistently' (p. 9) and 'the argument that *governments* can effectively promote entrepreneurship and venture capital [...] is a much shakier assumption' (p. 10).

that it was written with these limits in mind. This gives the content a critical perspective which could thus highlight its originality.

A unique dynamic framework of analysis to capture a fast-paced evolution

The second reason why this book differs from the rest lies in its approach to private equity financing as a cycle, and not a static body of financial practices. Two factors motivate this approach:

- *Private equity has been attracting an ever increasing amount of capital* over the course of the last three decades (from roughly USD 100 billion under management in 1990 to USD 3 trillion in 2018, according to Preqin).[7] This capital inflow has contributed to changing the dynamics of the sector, its structure, its practices and its influence on the overall economy over the course of only six to seven business cycles (that is to say, on average 3 years of economic growth and 2 years of recession). The source of this inflow, notably pension funds, has also exposed the private equity sector to exogenous influences as its visibility has increased (we will of course come back to this later).
- *Private equity players are constantly innovating and at a fast pace.* This innovation potentially explains the persisting gaps between the academic literature and the daily activities of practitioners, as the scientific body struggles to catch up with the pace of innovation. Unfortunately, the lack of available data does not help the work of the scientific community.

Because private equity is evolving constantly and rapidly, it can only be captured partially by a single book. For that reason, dear reader, this book will focus on identified trends and on practical and theoretical dialogue; and it will draw some hypotheses to guide you towards an understanding of upcoming events.

This third edition integrates feedback

I encourage feedback in that regard. This third edition takes into account the comments that I have gathered directly – or indirectly. Some readers have expressed their satisfaction[8] (seven out of ten comments on the Amazon website, when the two editions are combined). Others asked for further reading suggestions.[9] Even though this book offers a Bibliography, I include references in the text leading to specific material, helping readers to deepen their knowledge in certain areas.

---

[7] According to the same source, the assets under management of private markets ('private capital' for Preqin) reached USD 4 trillion as of end 2018. These figures are merely global estimates and essentially gather amounts managed by funds.

[8] 'I'm not an investment banker, and bought this to get an insight into Private Equity [PE] to approach potential investors to buy a business. For me, this book was very insightful, and it had loads and loads of information. The guy gives you all kinds of trends and comparisons between PE & other investments in graphs and numbers, and this will help you loads if you're in PE sales or business brokerage, for it definitely gives you excellent tools to approach potential investors, especially ones who might doubt the PE field after the last crisis. Sometimes it gets too detailed in comparing the US's PE with Europe's PE, and sometimes you might get lost, but you definitely can't go wrong with this book. Great book.' Amazon.com, Comment Mazahreh, 17/10/2010.

[9] Amazon.com, Comment M. Rivera Raba, 19/8/2010.

One of the criticisms of the book has been its emphasis on historical perspectives and the lack of business cases and practical elements.[10] Indeed, Chapters 1 and 2 draw conclusions from past experiences – and some readers loved it.[11] One of the most interesting books about venture capital (Lerner, 2009) is actually purely built on past experiences and the reasons for their successes and failures. My initial idea was to underline what helped to shape a vivid private equity environment, and what are the prerequisites for finding it in a given region or country. However, I did not explicitly state this. I hence added elements about emerging markets (and how they match this background) to put the history in perspective. The addition of private debt and private real assets to this third edition is the vindication that this historical approach was not only interesting, but necessary. Thanks to it, it is possible to understand the emergence of these two sectors, in the footsteps of private equity, that is out of a long series of public–private partnerships.

However, the subsequent five chapters and the conclusion are not about history, but rather document and debate the state of the private equity market. To try to increase the reader's satisfaction, I have co-developed with Rafael Sasso a business case about a private equity investment in a listed company based in an emerging market (Kroton Educacional SA) by a major private equity investment firm (Advent International). I have also added, as much as possible, documents which can be operationally used to raise money from private equity funds, or to form funds.

Cartoons have either been praised[12] or heavily criticised[13] by readers as a mere distraction. To please more conservative readers, I have removed them (hence promoting the first edition to 'collector' status).

My writing style seems to polarise the readership: some readers like it,[14] others do not.[15] I decided to stick with it. First, changing it could be very artificial, and hence make the experience of reading this book painful. Then, because the criticism of not being structured around 'clear and concise arguments, and a math-like structure'[16] is precisely what motivates this book: it *cannot* be structured in a maths-like argumentation (see points 1 and 2 above). As for a lack of clear and concise arguments, I believe that this book is actually quite factual given the lack of information already highlighted (see point 2 above).

---

[10]'... but no in depth information on how to form or run a private equity [sic]', Amazon.com, Comment Brandon Dean, 11/5/2011.

[11]'This is an ambitious and much needed book, but could be better executed. In its first chapters, Introduction to Private Equity helps the newcomer get his/her head around the concept of private equity. The first chapter is the best: through the example of Christopher Columbus, the reader builds a basic intuition for private equity. From this lofty and creative beginning, the next chapters describe the basic structure of limited partners, general partners, and companies. It also describes the basic categories of venture, growth, and LBOs. Simple graphs and light-hearted cartoons reinforce concepts [...].' Amazon.com, Comment Shouvik Banerjee, 18/4/2011.

[12]Amazon.com, Comment Ioannis Akkizidis, 22/9/2010; Comment Andreas Jäk, 12/7/2010; Comment Shouvik Banerjee, 18/4/2011.

[13]Amazon.com, Comment HBS2011, 20/9/2010.

[14]Amazon.com, Comment Ioannis Akkizidis, 22/9/2010.

[15]Amazon.com, Comment Kristoffer Buus, 5/12/2011.

[16]Amazon.com, Comment Kristoffer Buus, 5/12/2011.

Overall, I will try to keep in mind some of the suggestions, such as: emphasising more the purpose of each chapter, differentiating more country-specific principles and country-specific features, keeping one message per graph and trying to get better graphs in black and white.[17] This book will be structured to identify the critical elements that have shaped the private equity industry (Chapter 1) and which remain necessary for those countries willing to establish this industry (Chapter 2). Once these founding parameters have been analysed, we will see how the private equity sector is organised as an ecosystem (Chapter 3) centred on the entrepreneur and the lifecycle of companies (Chapter 4). In that respect, the investment process and the entire private equity activity is based on interpersonal relationships and on arm's-length interactions (Chapter 5). These conclusions will allow us to distinguish the trends and fads affecting an activity in 'teenage time' (Chapter 6), before examining the responsibilities (Chapter 7) that the sector will have to handle. The Conclusion (Chapter 8) will provide some prospective analysis.

This third edition has been significantly increased, revised and developed. It notably integrates elements about new trends, as well as practical documents. It also includes elements about past (and now defunct) trends, some of which have been confirmed and look to be on the verge of institutionalisation.

REFERENCES

Books and Booklets

Demaria, C. (2006, 2008, 2010, 2012, 2015, 2018) *Introduction au Private Equity* (RB Editions, Paris), 1st, 2nd, 3rd, 4th, 5th, 6th edns, 128 pp.

Lerner, J. (2009) *Boulevard of Broken Dreams, Why Public Efforts to Boost Entrepreneurship and Venture Capital Have Failed – and What to Do about It* (Princeton University Press, Princeton, NJ), 229 pp.

Phalippou, L. (2017) *Private Equity Laid Bare* (CreateSpace Independent Publishing Platform), 205 pp.

Newsletters and Newspapers

Arnold, M., 'State-led venture capital lags behind rivals', *Financial Times*, 5 August 2009.

Kaczor, P., 'Les indices n'ont pas été décevants', *L'Agefi*, 16 November 2012.

Papers and Studies

Bernstein, S., Lerner, J. and Schoar, A. (2009) 'The investment strategies of sovereign wealth funds', Harvard Business School Working Paper 09–112, 53 pp.

Jensen, M. (1989, rev. 1997) 'Eclipse of the public corporation', Harvard Business School, 31 pp.

---

[17] Amazon.com, Comment Shouvik Banerjee, 18/4/2011.

PART I

What are Private Equity, Private Debt and Private Real Assets?

Capitalism is a highly dynamic system in which corporations have to constantly anticipate market needs and shifts. The pace of change has seemingly increased, notably with a wave of deregulation and liberalisation in the 1970s and 1980s. Conglomerates and monopolies were forced to focus and broke up into smaller entities. These focused entities then started to merge to create significant players in their markets. New companies were created to address emerging needs.

However, the sources of financing were not particularly adapted at that time. Indeed, whenever a company needed financing, two solutions came to mind: the stock exchange and bank loans. The stock exchange provides a limited solution. It provides only access to additional funding for medium- and large-sized companies that meet specific criteria (sales figures, total of balance sheet, minimum number of years of existence, etc.). Newborn start-up companies did not qualify.

Nor did they take out a loan to fund their early growth or later engage in cross-border development and acquisitions. The conditions for taking out a loan are strictly defined. Risks are assessed through a scoring system, through which banks compare the situation and project of a company with past projects from similar companies. If past projects were not successful, such as funding young companies, or too complex to have been financed, such as a cross-border acquisition, then the financing is declined. Even if the project fits the criteria of the scoring system, the company still must prove its ability to pay back the bank in fixed instalments. For that it must demonstrate its ability to generate stable and strong cash flows, and also have limited debts. It also has to provide some form of collateral for the loan. If the loan is not paid, the bank will seize the assets pledged as collateral, sell them and hence get paid back thanks to the proceeds of this sale. This assumes that the value of the collateral is high enough to cover the debt, the interests due and the cost of the procedure.[1]

If neither the stock exchange nor banks finance business creation and development, then who, or what, does? Where does the money come from to finance the transmission or take-over of family companies, for example? Or to restructure an ailing business? To help a business further focus and optimise its operations and financial structure? From 'private markets' for that matter, that is to say, 'private equity', 'private debt' and 'private real assets'.

Private equity supports companies at every stage of their development, from inception (seed capital), to early-, mid- and late-stage development (venture capital), growth (growth capital), transfer of ownership (LBO) and restructuring (turn-around capital). Interestingly, banks were some of the first institutions to engage in this type of activity through their 'merchant banking' activities.

Private debt finances companies where banks do not. Lending is actually being reshaped. This movement started with the switch in the USA from an economy essentially supported by banks to an economy supported by financial markets.[2] It has slowly permeated other countries, notably in Europe. Under the pressure of regulations (such as the Basel III Agreements), and as a consequence of the last financial crisis, banks have been retreating from specific financing operations, such as lending to small and medium-sized businesses. This has paved the way for the rise of 'non-bank finance companies': direct lending. If companies engage in operations which cannot be scored or which go beyond the usual daily activity, they have to resort to this type of financing. Some projects, such as mergers and acquisitions, require more flexible forms of financing than a standard loan. Subordinated debt, such as mezzanine financing, can support this type of project. In specific jurisdictions, such as the USA and the UK, acquiring an ailing business to restructure it becomes easier under the bankruptcy procedure. This is the purpose of distressed debt investing.

As companies had to refocus, they had not only to master the delicate equilibrium between equity and liabilities, but also work on the structure of their assets. They started to dispose of real estate, infrastructure, energy and other assets, sometimes to rent them back (in a sale-and-lease-back operation, for example). Management teams have often associated an asset-heavy balance sheet as a slow-moving target for more agile competitors. These assets represented a reserve of value that could be monetised to engage in acquisitions or to refocus the firm further. As these assets were sold to private real-asset specialists, dedicated strategies emerged to handle these assets in whatever shape and state, ranging from plain vanilla, or even trophy assets, to derelict ones.

Private equity represents the bulk of private markets, with 60% of the documented private market funds activity, private real assets representing 25% and private debt 15%. It will therefore be at the centre of this book, while addenda will be made whenever possible to include private debt and private real assets. We will therefore start by explaining private equity as an economic driver (Chapter 1), to then include its further developments (Chapter 2).

---

[1] For example, in Spain there has been a debate since, after the 2007–2009 crisis, loans are not covered if assets have depreciated. Thus, borrowers have lost their assets pledged as collateral and still owe money to the banks.

[2] According to *The Economist* (15 December 2012), in the USA, banks are responsible for 25–30% of total lending. In Europe, 95% of total lending comes from commercial banks.

CHAPTER 1

Private Equity as an Economic Driver
An Historical Perspective

*C*olumbus: scientist, entrepreneur and venture capitalist
After 7 years of lobbying, Christopher Columbus convinced the Spanish monarchs (Ferdinand II of Aragon and Isabella I of Castile) to sponsor his trip towards the West. His 'elevator pitch' must have been the following: 'I want to open a new and shorter nautical route to the Indies in the West, defy the elements, make you become even more powerful and rich, and laugh at the Portuguese and their blocs on the Eastern routes.'

Columbus probably did not know at that stage that he was structuring a venture capital operation. But indeed he was, as his project combined these elements: it was an entrepreneurial venture financed by external investors, presented a high risk of failure, with a high return potential and barriers to entry protecting a competitive advantage.

These elements form, at various degrees, the common ground for all private equity deals (venture capital, growth capital, leveraged buy-out, etc.). Another element lies in the 'private' characteristics of the deal negotiated privately between the parties: before the advent of the stock exchange, each deal was on non-listed companies or projects.

Even though it is difficult to imagine whether, and how, Columbus did his risk–return calculation when assessing the viability of his project, we can assume that the risks borne by the operation were identified and that there was a plan to mitigate them – or at least light enough candles in church! The risks were high, but not unlimited (thus distinguishing his venture from pure gambling).

The prospect of reaching the Indies gave quite a good sense of what could have been the return on investment for the financial sponsors: the Spanish monarchs and the private investors from Genoa. Not only did the potential return exceed by far that which a conventional investment could provide, but the new route had a potentially disruptive impact on international commerce, giving the newborn unified Spanish Crown a much needed mercantile boost.

Private equity has always existed . . . only in a different form than today
This example illustrates the fact that private equity has always existed, in one form or another, throughout history. Examples of historical buy-outs are more difficult to identify, hence the focus of this chapter on venture capital. Buy-outs transfer majority

ownership in exchange for cash and are generally friendly. Typically, buy-outs are conducted with insider knowledge. They have only recently started to become important, as they require sophisticated financial markets and instruments.

Historically, large buy-out operations were 'barters', with a strong real-estate/commercial focus. This involved mainly swapping countries or towns for other ones. The state today known as New York was swapped by the Dutch West Indies Company (WIC) for Surinam, a plantation colony in northern South America, in 1667 (Treaty of Breda).[1] This turned out to be a bad deal.

Modern private equity emerged from large macro changes (and still requires them to emerge)

The emergence of private equity as a dynamic financial tool required the interplay of (i) a supportive social, legal and tax environment, (ii) adequate human resources and (iii) sufficient capital. Together, these three conditions developed slowly until they reached the current level of professionalism and formalism which characterises private equity.[2] The clear identification and separation of the three conditions forming the 'private equity ecosystem' has been a continuous process, which is still under way.

The purpose of this chapter is to identify the key elements distinguishing private equity from other categories of investment. Private equity financing in the early days of venturing was an intricate mix of public policy, entrepreneurship and financing. The quest of European monarchs for greater wealth and power is emblematic for this mix, pooling public and private resources in order to identify and exploit sometimes remote resources (see Section 1.1).

Public policies, entrepreneurship and financing became less complex and slowly gained autonomy. The public interest and policies were separated clearly from the King's personal interest and will. Once the basic legal and tax framework had been established and adapted to the alterations in social and economic factors, the entrepreneur emerged as the central figure of the private equity ecosystem (see Section 1.2).

Private equity investors developed a capability to identify them, providing capital and key resources to help with their venture and get their share of success. By gaining this know-how and expertise, those investors contributed to further professionalisation, developing strategies to mitigate risks and optimise returns (see Chapter 2).

---

[1] In 1626, Peter Minuit, then Director General of the WIC, acquired the island of Manhattan from the Indians and began constructing Fort New Amsterdam. In 1664, owing to commercial rivalry between the Dutch and the English, an English fleet sent by James, Duke of York, attacked the New Netherlands colonies. Being greatly outnumbered, Director General Peter Stuyvesant surrendered New Amsterdam, which was then renamed in honour of James. The loss of New Amsterdam led to the Second Anglo-Dutch War of 1665–1667. This conflict ended with the Treaty of Breda, under which the Dutch gave up their claim in exchange for Surinam.

[2] Lerner (2009) states: 'often, in their eagerness to get the "fun stuff" of handing out the money, public leaders neglect the importance of setting the table, or creating a favorable environment' (p. 12): universities and government laboratories, adapted tax and legal policies, education (see Section 4.1 for further developments) and a favourable exit environment.

1.1   POOLING INTERESTS TO IDENTIFY AND EXPLOIT SOURCES OF WEALTH

The fundamental objective of any rational investor is to increase his wealth.[3] Private equity offers investors the opportunity to finance the development of private companies and benefit from their eventual success. Historically, the *raison d'être* of those companies has been to identify and control resources, thereby developing the wealth of venture promoters by appropriation.

Private equity operations require a sponsor

The main financial sponsor might have been a political leader, who would legally and financially ease the preparation and the execution of the venture for the benefit of the Crown and himself. The control of resources and the conquest of land motivated the launch of exploration ventures (a). Companies were created to support political efforts,[4] thereby guaranteeing the demand for their product in exchange for their participation in a public effort to build infrastructures, create a new market and more generally encourage commerce and the generation of wealth. They could leverage public action (b). Apparently, conflicts of interest did not ring any bells at that time.

Private equity operations are symbiotic with public initiatives

Often, private investors were complementing this public initiative, convinced by the pitch made by a person combining technical competence and know-how, with a vision and genuine marketing talent. This person would be identified nowadays as an entrepreneur – or the precursor of televangelists, when the marketing presentation becomes a 7-year sermon, in the case of Columbus.

1.1.1   Identify, Control and Exploit Resources

The quest to master time and space has given birth to pioneering public and private initiatives, bearing a substantial risk but also a potentially high reward. This reward was usually associated with the geographical discovery of new resources (land control) and/or effectiveness (new routes to the Indies, for example), allowing a better rotation of assets and improving the returns.

High risk, high return potential

Columbus's project supported a *substantially higher risk* than the equivalent and usual routes to the East. This project was deemed to be possible thanks to progress in navigation and mapping, and some other technical and engineering discoveries. In that respect, Columbus's expedition was emblematic of the technological trend, as well as being political, religious and scientific; all of which he mastered so as to present his project.

---

[3]Selectively, some investors may add secondary items on their agenda, which can vary from gaining a foothold in the market/in a given company (corporate investors), to monitoring technical progress, achieving social recognition and other specific issues. However, viable investment programmes usually put financial returns at the top of their list (at least in order to achieve self-sustainability within a certain period of time).

[4]As a result, still today, public 'programs geared toward going to nascent entrepreneurs may instead end up boosting cronies of the nation's rulers or legislators' (Lerner, 2009, p. 11).

The risks taken by Columbus were of two different kinds:

(i) Initial validation of theoretical assumptions, with substantial risks linked to the transition from a theoretical framework to an operational process.[5] Columbus's prediction of the diameter of the Earth (3700 km instead of 40 000 km) proved wrong, but his venture was successful in the sense that he reached an unknown new continent. This kind of outcome (refocusing the 'research and development (R&D) effort' towards a different outcome) occurs in start-up companies financed by venture capital even today. Hopefully, not all venture-backed companies have a CEO who under-evaluates the effort to be produced by a factor of 10.

(ii) Execution of the four successive trips, with the presence of favourable winds and currents, the correct calculation of the time spent at sea with embarked supplies, navigation hazards (storms), morale of the crew and other operational aspects. Operational risks are generally financed by later-stage venture capital and expansion investors.[6]

For all of the above reasons, Columbus's project was *innovative* in many respects. It was guided by ambition and a vision. It was designed to test concretely the validity of a certain number of theories, which would be of great reward if Columbus touched Indian ground after journeying to the West.

The *high return potential* was related to Columbus's calculations, according to which the new nautical route could save a substantial amount of time (and risk) to reach the Indies, despite the Portuguese land bloc. The return potential would be earned not from the initial trip itself, but from opening a new route for future trips to gather expensive goods (mainly silk and spices) and bring them back to Europe.

Another key element was that this new nautical route would have paved the way to developing a number of other new ventures using the route to gain other valuable goods. Columbus's success would not have been a one-time pay-off, but the source of recurring and long-term income.

A long-term investment, protected by a favourable legal environment

The time horizon of the trip was calculated in months, which represents a *long-term investment*, and the pay-off would have been calculated in years. This represents another element that qualifies Columbus's trip to the West as a private equity project.

Protection by the Spanish monarchs *of this advantage*, by giving a legal right to the private sponsors of the project to the use of this new route (the historical equivalent of the current 'barriers to entry' in a given market), was a crucial element of the evaluation of the return on investments. Columbus was promoted to the status of 'Admiral of the Seas' by the Spanish monarchs, and then to Governor once he succeeded in his venture. This meant that he just had to sit and wait for the profits to come, after making this initial breakthrough.

---

[5] Today, this would qualify as a transition from 'research and development' mode to 'go to market' mode.

[6] This is an early illustration of a phenomenon that would become Johnson's '10/10 Rule' (Johnson, 2010): a decade to build a new platform, and a decade to find a mass audience (or exploitation).

As an additional incentive, Columbus would have received a share of all the profits made via this nautical route. More specifically, Columbus asked, aside from the titles and an official charge, for a 10% share of the profits realised through the exploitation of the route to the West. He had option rights to acquire one-eighth of the shares of any commercial venture willing to use the nautical route that he had opened. This kind of financial incentive (percentage on profits realised and the equivalent of stock options; in private equity this incentive is called carried interest) is often used to reward the management of a company, should it reach a certain number of targets.

In that respect, the dispute about the reward to be granted by the monarchs of Spain to Columbus after his journeys, as well as the difficulty of providing a quick and easy return for the Genoese investors (as there was little gold to find on the Caribbean Islands), is another point comparable with typical private equity operations, an outcome different from that originally planned. Some disputes in recent years between creators and managers of Internet start-ups and their financial backers prove that this still happens today – and, just like back then, in the courts.

Pooling of resources

This pooling of the energies and resources of an entrepreneur (Columbus), of Genoese private investors (representing 50% of the pool of money) and of the Spanish monarchs as a sponsor syndicate for the project is another criterion for its qualification as a private equity project. Its commercial purpose, even if not exclusive in this example, is another.

Still not a template for modern venture capital . . . but not too far from it

Columbus's venture, however, stands out as different from a typical private equity investment. He benefitted from political and legal support that would not be sustainable in an open and fair trade market today – or at least not so openly provided.

However, national states are still largely involved today in venture capital. Fundamental research is largely financed by public sources (Mazzucato, 2015), notably for military purposes. Moreover, applications of this fundamental research are also funded by public contracts for start-ups. The US Small Business Act of 1958 is an example, reserving a proportion of public procurement to small and mid-sized businesses. These start-ups can also be financed by public funding, either indirectly or directly. Indirectly, the European Investment Fund invests public funds in venture capital funds. At the federal level, the USA invested in Small Business Investment Corporations dedicated to finance small and mid-sized non-listed companies. Equivalent programmes have been set up in the UK, France and other countries. Directly, In-Q-Tel is a not-for-profit venture capital fund notably funded by the Central Intelligence Agency in the USA. Other countries such as France, or regions such as Belgium's Wallonia, have direct investment programmes in non-listed firms.

The Italian investors were 'hands off' in the project. However, Columbus convinced them and enrolled the providers of the three ships in his venture. This implies that even if there was no equivalent of a 'lead investor' and 'investment managers' (see Chapter 2) to look after Columbus's project, the monitoring was done according to historical standards, that is to say: on site, day-to-day and probably with vigorous debates about the option of continuing and taking the risk of wreckage or worse; or returning and saving both fleet and crew.

1.1.2 Leverage Public Policies and a Favourable Business Environment

Even if Columbus's project was driven by religious and commercial purposes, the political ambitions of the Spanish monarchs were the key factor triggering public commitment.[7] Governmental, and more generally public, support is instrumental in contributing to the emergence of private equity ventures by funding fundamental research, financing key infrastructures and creating a favourable environment for the development of ventures. However, private equity projects which qualify as such, and which have served public policies, are limited in number – and public programmes alone are not sufficient.[8]

1.1.2.1 The Separation of Public and Private Financing as a Key Element of the Emergence of an Autonomous Private Equity Sector

This stems from the fact that with the separation of the King as a public body and the King as a private person, projects were no longer financed by public subsidies. The specific convergence of interest that had allowed Columbus to set up his project increasingly became a rarity.

The increased control of the use of public money, a greater focus on fair trade and the official ambition to let market forces act as far as possible in favour of private and public interests have played a significant role in the limitation of the state's direct intervention in private equity projects. This, however, does not mean that this role has totally disappeared: it has evolved (Mazzucato, 2015) towards the establishment of an appropriate legal and tax framework, as well as more complex intervention, mixing public contracts and the active management of public money. Lerner (2009) confirms that 'policymakers face [today] the challenge of having to consider many different policies. It is often unclear how proposed changes will interact with each other. There is no clear "instruction manual" that explains which changes will have the desired effects.'

1.1.2.2 The Transformation of Public Intervention: Setting up a Legal and Tax Framework

With progress in commerce, transportation and techniques, entrepreneurs could reach a higher number of clients, as well as producing in quantity and more capital-intensive goods. To follow this trend, and finance the investments needed, the entrepreneur often had to seek outside financing, and thus set up a formal company, with agreements, contracts and partnerships with third parties.

To enforce these conventions, a legal and tax framework has to be in place and respected. One of the most ancient examples of a legal framework is known as the Code of Hammurabi, King of Babylonia (1792–1750 BC; see Gompers & Lerner, 2006). This set of 285 laws was displayed in public places to be seen by all, so that it could be known and thus enforced. This Code liberated the commercial potential of the Babylonian civilisation, notably *paving the way for the creation of partnerships – and hence later of private equity partnerships*. Until then, most companies were initiated and run by families. Financial support at that time often came from personal or family wealth,

---

[7]Interestingly, as noted by Lerner (2009): 'the critical early investments have not been made by domestic institutions but rather by sophisticated international investors' (p. 12).
[8]'Far too often, government officials have encouraged funding in industries or geographic regions where private interest simply did not exist' (Lerner, 2009, p. 13).

and/or from guilds that helped their members set up their venture after being admitted as a member.

With partnerships, Mesopotamian families could *pool the necessary capital to fund a given venture, spreading the risk.* However, these ventures were not financed by equity investment. Capital infusion mostly took the form of loans, which were sometimes secured by the pledge of a man's entire estate, with his wife and children considered a part of it. If he defaulted on payments, his family would be sold into slavery to pay his debts (Brown, 1995). Lending to support risky ventures with significant collateral was still current practice as recently as the 16th century, as described by Shakespeare in *The Merchant of Venice* (where the borrower/venturer puts a pound of his flesh, in effect a portion of his heart, as collateral to the loan). This was the equivalent of what private debt could finance today, although with different collateral.

In that respect, the Code of Hammurabi initiated the distinction between the entrepreneur and the financier, with the distinction between equity and debt, the creation of collateral for the debt and the privileges attached to loans (such as priority of reimbursement in the case of liquidation of the company).

1.1.2.3 The Transformation of Public Intervention: Infrastructure Financing

However, this legal and tax support may not have been sufficient for the emergence of private equity. Besides law, other public actions are usually geared to helping entrepreneurs, directly or indirectly, and create favourable conditions that nurture the creation of companies. However, as mentioned by Lerner (2009): 'for each effective government intervention, there have been dozens, even hundreds, of failures, where substantial public expenditures bore no fruit'. As a result, direct help, because of its cost to the public budget and the distortion in competition that it introduces, tends to be confined and to give way to a more indirect mode of intervention. This indirect mode of intervention had already been identified and used by Hammurabi, who, aside from being a military leader, invested in infrastructures in order to foster the prosperity of his empire.

During his reign, he personally supervised navigation and irrigation plans, stored grain against famine and lent money at no interest to stimulate commerce. Broad wealth distribution and better education improved standards of living and stimulated extra momentum in all branches of knowledge, including astronomy, medicine, mathematics, physics and philosophy (Durant, 1954). In that respect, the liberation of private energy and the symbiotic relationship between public and private investments greatly rewarded the King for his action. This interaction with the private sector might be a test for modern programmes: if the public initiative does not act as a catalyst or indirect support, then the programme might simply not be relevant.

Indeed, public initiatives and private equity financing are still acting in an intricate way in many respects, but the relations between these two spheres have evolved towards autonomy of the private real asset sector (in the specific case of infrastructure) and a more 'hands-off' approach in public intervention. As a result, public intervention is creating the backdrop for private equity, paving the way for a subtler interaction, combining contracting, incentives and soft regulations.

This does not necessarily lead to a frictionless cooperation. Norway provides a recent example. In 2011 and 2012, ExxonMobil, Total, Statoil and Royal Dutch Shell sold their 48% stake in Glassled, a gas pipeline operator based in Norway, to a consortium of investors: Allianz, UBS, Abu Dhabi Investment Authority and Canada Pension

Plan Investment Board. The Norwegian state owns the remainder through state-owned firms. In 2013, it unilaterally decided to cut the transportation tariffs for gas transiting through the pipelines by 90%. The consortium estimated its lost revenues as USD 1.8 billion by 2028 and sued the Norwegian state, as they saw the change in regulation as illegal. The lawsuit was rejected in 2015 by the first regional court, in 2016 by the Court of Appeal and in 2018 by Norway's Supreme Court (Elliott, 2018).

1.2 CHAMPIONING ENTREPRENEURSHIP

However, this favourable legal and tax environment is useless if the social acceptance of risk and innovation is low. The entrepreneur is the embodiment of this acceptance, as the individual willing to take the initial risk of creating and/or developing a venture. As such, he is therefore central in the private equity landscape. Without him, private equity does not have any reason to exist (see Section 1.2.1). However, private equity needs very specific entrepreneurs and companies to finance. The role of the entrepreneur is to implement a plan and support the creation of value (for example, by converting product/service innovation into business successes), and therefore generate a financial return (see Section 1.2.2). Entrepreneurship acts as a transformer of disparate elements in a venture, making it blossom and become an attractive fruit. As a metaphor, private equity could be described as an ecosystem in itself (see Section 1.2.3).

1.2.1 No Private Equity without Entrepreneurs

The figure of the entrepreneur is at the centre of the private equity universe. He is the one who can transform inputs into something bigger than the sum of the elements taken separately, which are time, capital, work, ideas and other elements. What distinguishes the entrepreneur from other workers is his ability to innovate (at large), to take risks and to create and manage a company. However, not all entrepreneurs are able to manage a company successfully.

What makes private equity attractive is the reasonable and proven prospect of getting a substantially higher reward than on the traditional financial markets (i.e., listed stocks or bonds). This reward is the counterpart of a risk that would not be borne by the rest of the financial system (banks, individuals and other sources of capital). Thus, private equity-backed entrepreneurs are in fact a small portion of the pool of entrepreneurs that are active in any given country.

Company creation and disruptive innovation

The chief image of the entrepreneur is the 'company creator'. This individual is guided by a vision, often supported by an innovation. The emblematic entrepreneur financed by venture capital investors is building a company willing to capitalise on a 'disruptive innovation', which could radically change a market or create a new branch of a given industry. James Watt (1736–1819) is probably the incarnation of this category.

This Scottish mathematician and engineer improved the steam engine, set to replace water and muscle power as the primary source of power in use in industry (Burstall, 1965). Created in 1689 to pump water from mines, steam power existed for almost a century, with several cycles of improvement, before the steam engine made a breakthrough. In 1774, James Watt introduced his disruptive 'Watt steam engine', which could be used not just in mining but in many industrial settings. Using the steam engine meant that a factory could be located anywhere, not just close to water. Offering a dramatic increase in fuel efficiency (75% less consumption), the new design was retrofitted to almost all existing steam engines in the country.

Serial entrepreneurs: a cultural or universal phenomenon?

Another figure which has emerged over time is the 'serial entrepreneur', an emblematic figure in the USA which has still to appear in the rest of the world. This is probably related to different cultural contexts and levels of social fluidity. Thomas Edison (1847–1931) invented and developed many important devices, such as the light bulb, the phonograph and the stock ticker. He patented the first machine to produce motion pictures and planned the first electricity distribution system to carry electricity to houses (Bunch & Hellemans, 2004). 'The Wizard of Menlo Park' was one of the first inventors to apply the principles of mass production to the process of invention. One of the most prolific inventors, Edison held more than 1000 patents at one stage.

In 1878, Edison convinced several investors, such as John Pierpont Morgan, Lord Rothschild and William Vanderbilt, to invest USD 300 000 in the creation of the Edison Electric Light (EEL) Co., and to fund his experiments with electric lighting in return for a share in the patents derived from his research. JP Morgan continued to support the growing company by acquiring shares and backing the company's merger with EEL's main competitor, the Thomson-Houston Electrical Company. This merger resulted in the creation of General Electric (Frederick Lewis, 1949).

Gompers, Kovner, Lerner and Scharfstein (2010) state that there is a persistence of performance in entrepreneurship. An entrepreneur who has already been 'successful' (an initial public offering or take-over of his company has happened) has a 30% chance of succeeding (21% for an emerging entrepreneur and 22% for an entrepreneur who tried and failed).

They hence develop *specific skills, which are critical*. This is important, because some of these entrepreneurs will retire once their success is fulfilled (which is a net loss for the economy), and others will become business angels (see Chapter 4) and hence provide experience and expertise to other entrepreneurs (some sort of 'entrepreneurial spill-over effect').

These repeat entrepreneurs have also developed a *reputation*, associated with success. That might be crucial as suppliers, clients and recruits would then be willing to do business with these successful entrepreneurs. Once again, this reputation might be 'portable' to start-ups which are financially supported by a successful entrepreneur turned business angel.

Nursing ideas (laboratories) and nursing companies (incubator and entrepreneur-in-residence (EIR) programmes)

Not every entrepreneur is able to come up with an idea ready to be produced. Inventors and developers sometimes hatch their ideas in a laboratory and can develop them before spinning off, but most are developing new products and technologies in their garages or other more casual places. To help support their efforts, some venture capital funds have developed 'entrepreneur-in-residence programmes'. Once an idea has matured, investors can take an early lead on the development of the company and get a greater share in the company in exchange for their past efforts. Other companies provide 'incubators' or 'business accelerators'. EIR, incubator and business accelerator programmes provide facilities, support and at times capital to entrepreneurs with interesting ideas.

One of the most famous 'entrepreneurs in residence' was probably Leonardo da Vinci (1452–1519). As well as being an inventor, he was also a sculptor, architect, engineer, philosopher, musician, poet and painter. These activities generated substantial investment opportunities, either for mercantile or patronage purposes. Da Vinci met 'investors' who aspired to both, such as Ludovico Sforza, Duke of Milan, in 1482. Da Vinci wrote a letter to the Duke in which he stated that he could build portable bridges; that he knew the techniques of bombardment and the engineering of cannon; that he could build ships as well as armoured vehicles, catapults and other war machines. He served as principal engineer in the Duke's numerous military enterprises and was also active as an architect. He spent 17 years in Milan, leaving after the Duke's fall in 1499.

Under the Duke's administration, Leonardo designed weapons, buildings and machinery. From 1485 to 1490, Leonardo produced studies on multiple subjects, including nature, flying machines, geometry, mechanics, municipal construction, canals and architecture (designing everything from churches to fortresses). His studies from this period contain designs for advanced weapons, including a tank and other war vehicles, various combat devices and submarines.

These examples are provided by way of illustration, to show the continuity with the figures of entrepreneurship currently backed by venture capital throughout history. Da Vinci was probably more interested in research than entrepreneurship, but the 'entrepreneur in residence' model that is active in the Silicon Valley today finds its roots in the Italian financial and political support of exceptional men who were able to make breakthrough discoveries.[9]

Interestingly, the model of 'entrepreneur in residence' was developed in Europe throughout the Middle Age and the Renaissance, but did not manage to survive after the European Revolutions. It was only in the USA that EIR programmes managed to gain a hold. This is linked to the fact that most of these entrepreneurs in residence are serial entrepreneurs, which are still a rarity in the rest of the world.

The 'incubator' model (the most famous examples being Idealab, CMGI, Internet Capital Group and Softbank) failed. It re-emerged under the form of 'business accelerators', such as Y Combinator and TechStars in the USA. Somehow, these incubators or business accelerators tend to emerge as early signs of venture capital bubbles. The number of incubators grew from 15 in 1999 to 350 in 2000 (Singer, 2000; *The Economist*, 2000), while business accelerators grew from 4 in 2007 to 579 in 2016 (Gust, 2016), confirming this impression. The National Business Incubation Association[10] declares 2200 members in 62 countries (75% are in the USA).

The main criticism addressed to incubators and business accelerators is that they fall into the same trap as venture capital funds in the USA (see Chapter 4 and the 'broken'

---

[9]Indeed, according to Johnson (2010), location contributes to the success of an entrepreneur: 'the average resident of a metropolis with a population of five million people was almost three times more creative than the average resident of a town of a hundred thousand.' Big cities make their residents more innovative than residents of smaller ones.

[10]www.nbia.org.

American venture capital model): they do not work on major breakthroughs, instead aiming at 'flavour of the month' start-ups (Internet business-to-consumer start-ups in 2000, applications for mobile phones in 2012, fintechs in 2016) with a quick return. They spend little on the ventures, sprinkling money and making a lot of investments, hoping for the best to come out of this pool. They also focus on fundraising and helping entrepreneurs polish their speeches to convince investors (the 'elevator pitch'), instead of thoroughly challenging their plans and ideas. Their value creation is therefore limited.

In fact, finding capital is only one of the challenges of entrepreneurs in a more comprehensive picture that starts with a self-assessment of their own capacities, delegation, business planning and then financing (Trinomics, 2018). Their main challenge is to communicate their innovation, spread the word on their vision and thus convince their partners (employees, managers, financial backers, bankers, clients, providers, etc.) that they are able to lead the company to the next stage and transform their young venture into a business success.

1.2.2 Converting Ventures into Business Successes

Value creation is closely related to innovation, but not exclusively. Indeed, there is value creation in leveraged buy-outs (LBOs) by boosting companies through a significant and durable increase of sales, operational improvements or some other area of company improvement.

However, innovation financing provides us with a template illustrating the logic behind private equity.

In order to be able to deliver a consistent and high level of returns, a private equity firm has to focus on value creation and develop specific expertise that is applied to a certain type of innovation (Guerrera & Politi, 2006). There is innovation either in the product or in the service companies deliver (innovation by destination); or else in the processes they engineer (innovation by processing); in the way they contribute to structure their market (strategy innovation); or in the way they are managed (financial and management innovation).

Technological or managerial innovation: a basis for private equity

In the process of mastering space and time, entrepreneurs have discovered breakthrough technologies and invented new ways of communication. The infant equivalent of venture capital was instrumental in financing the development and deployment of these new technologies. An example of this public action helping to convert innovation into business success lies in the support provided to Galileo Galilei (1564–1642) by the Medici family, and especially Cosimo de Medici.

Galileo's achievements included demonstrating that the velocities of falling bodies are not proportional to their weight; showing that the path of a projectile is a parabola; building the first astronomical telescope; coming up with the ideas behind Newton's laws of motion; and confirming the Copernican theory of the solar system. Galileo translated his scientific knowledge into various technologies. In 1598, Galileo developed a 'geometric and military compass' suitable for use by gunners and surveyors. For gunners, it offered, in addition to a new and safer way of elevating cannons accurately, a way of computing quickly the charge of gunpowder for cannonballs of different sizes and materials. In about 1606, Galileo designed a thermometer, using the expansion and contraction of air in a bulb to move water in an attached tube.

In 1609, Galileo capitalised on the invention of the telescope (a patent for which was denied to a Flemish designer, Paolo Sarpi, a friend of Galileo) and lobbied the Venetian government against purchasing the instrument from foreigners, since Galileo could at the very least match such an invention. By then, Galileo had improved upon the principle of the telescope. The Venetian government subsequently doubled his earnings, even though Galileo felt that the original conditions were not honoured (Kusukawa & MacLean, 2006).

However, public intervention itself does not provide the support necessary to create and develop a company and follow it through every step of its life. This is where private equity's intervention is fundamental. Galileo and da Vinci could have greatly benefitted from their inventions, if they could have created companies to exploit them. Columbus's wealth was built on his project to go West, which was probably as risky and theoretical in its reach as the discoveries and inventions of the two Italian geniuses. What distinguishes them from Columbus is the fact that they were treated as civil servants, receiving a salary and some additional resources for their work. Columbus's travels were financed to the extent of 50% by Genoese investors willing to benefit from the new nautical route.

The necessity of entrepreneurial talent and enlightened financial support

Converting a disruptive innovation into a commercial success therefore requires not only an entrepreneurial talent, but also some additional competences and resources that only private equity investors can provide. This is not only capital, but also an ability to help tailor a company project to a viable reach and ambitious goals. The expertise of the private equity investor is thus often used in the shadow of the entrepreneur himself. An illustration of this comes from the partnership between Matthew Boulton and James Watt. The innovations of Watt would never have seen daylight without the ever-cheery Boulton, who funded the venture and took a share of the patent rights, even if Watt almost gave up on the project several times.

The responsibilities were clearly distributed: Watt was the inventor and Boulton provided the management experience and the capital. This is one of the first examples of a successful venture by a duo combining entrepreneurship and innovation on one side, and finance and operational management on the other. The *separation of the entrepreneurial from the investment manager function* is a key landmark in the emergence of the private equity sector as such. This separation was missing from Columbus's project to transform it into a complete commercial success.

The entrepreneurial and financial relationship: a fruitful tension

The impact of this separation is not theoretical: it changes the way an idea can be converted into a commercial success dramatically. Offering a very high increase in fuel efficiency for what was a minor design change, Watt's new design for the steam machine was soon retrofitted to almost all of the steam engines in the country. Watt's design used about 75% less fuel than the most established steam engine at that time: the Newcomen engine. Since the changes were fairly limited, Boulton and Watt licensed the idea to existing Newcomen engine owners, taking a share of the cost of fuel they saved.

Ten years after Boulton and Watt entered formally into partnership (and after Boulton invested GBP 40 000, taking all the financial risks on his own), the venture began to produce the expected returns. In 1800, the two partners retired from business, now extremely wealthy, and handed over to their sons, Matthew Robinson Boulton and James Watt Jr. This configuration, even though illustrating the separation between investors and entrepreneurs, would be considered unusual now. First, because the investor did not cash out from the company but rather adopted a long-term approach and was willing to stay in the company as long as possible (this approach is actually close to the approach of family offices, managing fortunes and businesses from an inter-generational perspective). This implies a perfect alignment of interests between the entrepreneur and the investor, which may not be the case nowadays, as investors usually sell their stake in companies after 3 to 5 years. Closed-end funds are usually created for 10 years, and they must manage to invest and divest from the companies within this timeframe (this will be developed and explained later in this book).

The fact that the company that Boulton and Watt created broke even after 10 years would not disqualify the company from being financed by private equity investors. Investors would probably sell their stake prior to that, either by listing the company (which is what happens for biotechnology companies – even if they are not profitable, for example) or by selling it to competitors, who would be able to generate economies of scale and benefit from the growth prospects of the company. What is unusual, however, is that the entrepreneur and the investor managed to focus on this venture without making a living out of it for a long time. The rule of risk diversification and the necessity to generate returns early would not allow an investor to invest 100% of his time in a given portfolio company, or wait for such a long time before getting a return.

This is probably because Boulton was investing his own money, and private equity investors today invest as professionals (fund managers) the money they have collected from third parties (fund investors). This is another source of possible misalignment of interests. The pressure from fund investors to generate stable and consistent returns above a certain threshold stems from the fact that these fund investors have to deliver a return to their shareholders (corporations), or be able to cash in at least under a certain time constraint, with a given risk–return profile (banks, insurers).

This pressure is then transmitted along the investment value chain to the fund and its managers. These managers have to deal with these constraints and thus exert pressure on the managers of companies to deliver the expected returns within a given timeframe. This pressure should, however, not be perceived as negative.

As seen with the historical examples, the fact that Columbus and Watt had some investors on their side also helped them to get results and stay focused on the outcome. The delicate equilibrium to be maintained between innovation and the strategy to go to market with this innovation is probably the key differentiator between aborted companies and successful but meteoric successes on the one hand; and long-standing and growing companies on the other. The investor must not only have genuine know-how and talent to support the entrepreneurs, but also challenge them and guide them towards the market. Even though big corporations have financial and technical know-how, very few have the expertise to nurture innovation and bring it to market. This means that private equity has its own specificities that are not only difficult to replicate, but also to copycat outside of a given ecosystem.

1.2.3 Entrepreneurship and Private Equity Form a Specific Ecosystem

The separation of the roles of entrepreneurs and investors, associated with the emergence of partnerships, has paved the way towards a better collaboration between the financial and the entrepreneurial worlds. Not every partnership was built under the same conditions as the template-like Watt–Boulton relationship. Most of the time, partnerships have to be established between entrepreneurs and investors who did not know each other prior to the contact, leading to a potential investment from the investor in the projected venture of the entrepreneur.

Entrepreneurial and financial frictions: the exit scenario

Aside from these conditions, the existence of *exit strategies* from a given investment is crucial for professional investors. If an investor chooses to back an entrepreneur, he usually does it with a certain roadmap in mind. Entrepreneurs can afford to spend all the time necessary to lead a venture to succeed, their own expectations and the money available being the only limit. This means that, theoretically, an entrepreneur with a company generating positive income could continue to run it for a very long time (possibly until retirement).

Investors have a given timeframe to make an investment and get the return from it, as their activity is usually to generate profits and redistribute them. In that respect, the presence of an active private equity sector is determined by the existence of exit scenarios, that is to say, opportunities to sell investments to third parties. According to Bain (2019), based on Dealogic data, LBO funds recorded 1146 exits valued at USD 378 billion in 2018. This has to be compared to 1063 exits valued at USD 366 billion in 2018 (Bain, 2018). Figure 1.1 provides a perspective over time of exits for LBO funds worldwide.

Pitchbook (2019) states that for the USA alone, 1049 LBO exits accounted for USD 365 billion in 2018 and 1253 exits for USD 365 billion in 2017. As a matter of comparison, Pitchbook (2018) counted 1265 venture capital exits in 2017, valued at USD 67 billion in 2017.

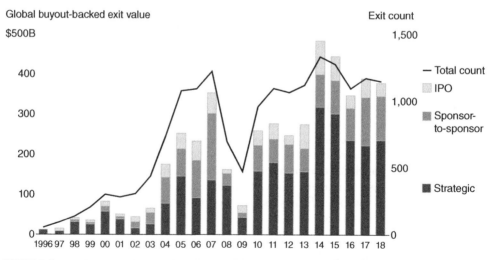

FIGURE 1.1   Evolution and breakdown of global LBO-backed profitable exits, by value
Source: Bain (2019), based on Dealogic data. Excludes bankruptcies.

These exit scenarios are usually:

- A profitable trade sale of the investment to another company or private equity group (also known as 'mergers and acquisitions' or 'strategic acquisitions'). Trade sale is the main exit route in private equity, and usually represents 50–70% of all exits. As a matter of illustration, in 2017, Pitchbook (2018) counted 72.5% of profitable (that is excluding failures) venture capital exits as acquisitions by a third party. In some sectors this exit scenario may prove to be difficult, given the concentration of the number of players (antitrust regulations) or the nature of the sector (banks and insurers are sometimes barred from take-over by foreign players, and must comply with specific regulations preventing certain operations).
- A sale to another financial investor is the second most frequent scenario, representing around 15–25% of all exits. This happens in the case of an LBO following a previous one (a 'secondary leveraged buy-out'), and increasingly from venture capitalists to LBO investors. In 2017, Pitchbook (2018) counted 18.5% of profitable venture capital exits as a sale to an LBO fund.
- A listing on the stock exchange, offering to the private equity investor the opportunity to sell his stake on the market. This stock exchange must exist, offering a minimum liquidity and attractive listing conditions, including adapted regulations. This exit route is less frequent and represents 10–20% of all exits. It represented 22.5% of profitable LBO exits in the USA in 2018 and 30% in 2017, according to Pitchbook (2019). It represented 9% of profitable venture capital exits in 2017 (Pitchbook, 2018).
- A sale to the management, which is rare as this means that the management must structure a private equity operation with its own capital (otherwise, this operation would fall within the trade sale scenario). This, however, could happen in the event that a venture-backed company becomes profitable. As it is debt free, the management could try to structure a management buy-out (MBO) to acquire the stake of the investors in the company, if no other exit scenario is offered.
- End of activity, bankruptcy or sale of remaining assets, thus a failure. This exit path is more common in venture capital than in other segments of the private equity market. This non-profitable type of exit accounts for 30–70% of venture capital exits overall. It is compensated by the fact that successes are also more rewarding in absolute terms. In LBOs, this represents 5–10% of all exits.

The stock exchange: useful indicator, overbearing influence

One of the first historical examples of a professional exit from a private equity-like operation was the introduction of the company created initially by Thomas Edison. In 1896, General Electric was one of the original 12 companies listed on the newly formed Dow Jones Industrial Average, and is the only one remaining from that time today. This listing allowed its investors to exit from their investments and realise a profit. However, this exit route is an exception as most of the exits in private equity are trade sales with longer holding periods for companies.

The rise of private equity as a financial tool for funding companies has been enabled by the growth of the stock exchange. Private equity could find not only an exit path for financing on the stock exchange, but also a source of opportunities such as corporate spin-offs, or delisting companies, and even taking parts of public companies.

As we will see (Chapter 4), the influence of the stock exchange can also be overwhelming. As it is a major source of information to establish the value of private companies, and as it is also an important (even if numerically minor) source of exits, private equity tends to adopt some of the behaviours specific to the stock exchange. This results in over-valuations, over-confidence, booms and busts, as we will see later in this book.

Private equity has also influenced the way business is done. More specifically, it contributed to create a *true entrepreneurial ecosystem*, with booms and busts, and a process of 'creative destruction', as described by Joseph Schumpeter. This process bears a certain risk and it is the role of professional private equity investors to manage this risk, mitigate it and generate a return that is commensurate with this risk. Chapter 2 will explore this question in more detail.

1.3 CONCLUSION: AN ATTEMPT AT A DEFINITION

So far, the Introduction and this chapter have identified the main elements that are necessary for the emergence of a private equity sector. Private equity, and private markets in general, are non-traditional ways of financing. They thus qualify as 'alternative investments', characterised (Mercer Management Consulting, 2012) 'by expectations of enhanced return opportunities, diversification, and lower levels of liquidity'.

We draw the following definition: a private market investment is '(i) a negotiated investment at arm's length in equity or debt for (ii) a long holding period, bearing (iii) specific and significant risks, and (iv) generating hopefully high returns (v) on behalf of qualified investors (vi) to create value by implementing a plan and supporting entrepreneurs'. This definition is an attempt to pin down a sector in constant evolution. There are multiple other ones. For Mercer Management Consulting (2012), private equity's purpose is to 'improve returns relative to public equity markets [and] access new sources of alpha' (that is, performance). Private equity hence differentiates itself from hedge funds (speculative funds using financial leverage targeting liquid assets and applying to them specific strategies, often using options and financial derivatives) and 'exotic assets' (sometimes called 'alternative alternatives'; see Blessing, 2011) such as commodities, collectables and asset-based lending.

1.3.1   A Negotiated Investment at Arm's Length

A private market investment involves an arm's-length negotiation and transaction. Although the process of private market investing might start off as a competition, such as for example an auction, there is a stage of this process where the potential investor gets some sort of exclusivity. As seen in the Introduction, generating information about the company or the asset is a lengthy and expensive process, called 'due diligence' and explored further in Chapter 5. Therefore, the investor willing to bear the costs of this process has to validate that there is a significant chance of reaching an agreement with the seller. The exclusivity ensures this.

Therefore, there is no hostile acquisition in private markets, even in the case of the delisting of a company. To access and generate the information, cooperation from the seller is necessary. The negotiation is a discovery process, which leads to adjustments to the price of the transaction. It is an ongoing process until the final transaction.

There are exceptions to this rule. It could be possible that multiple consortia of investors compete until the very end of an auction process, or of a start-up investment. Likewise, a hostile take-private could also potentially be possible. However, these remain exceptions to an established rule, which has different consequences in private equity, private debt and private real assets investing.

1.3.1.1 In Equity: Preferred Returns and/or Increased Control over Decisions (Private Equity)

To address the increasing complexity of deal structuring and funding requirements, better master the risks inherent in their investments and calibrate the anticipated returns, private equity investors innovate constantly. Thanks to negotiated arm's-length transactions, investors can assess carefully and rather precisely their risks. Their investment may take the form of capital increases (venture capital, expansion capital), the replacement (leveraged buy-out) and even the reconstitution (turn-around capital) of the company's capital.

In venture and growth capital, investors negotiate specific rights for their investments with company managers, such as preferred returns and/or an increased control over decisions. These rights are negotiated in shareholders' agreements and grant investors such rights as additional voting rights attached to their shares, priority preferential profit, to match a predefined multiple of their initial investment in the event that the business is sold. They can also use other instruments such as stock options to achieve specific targets in terms of risk mitigation or return optimisation.

In transfer of ownership, whether of healthy companies through an LBO or of ailing ones through turn-around capital, the analysis of risks leads to the design of different instruments. In the case of LBOs, it is about fine-tuning the use of debt to acquire the company. For that purpose, investors execute scenarios to reach the optimal level and structure of debt. The aim is that the interests and the debt can be repaid thanks to the dividends paid by the acquired company, even in the advent of adverse conditions. This can also lead to the set-up of private insurance mechanisms ('warranties'), granted by the seller to the buyer of the company if a risk has been identified but cannot easily be mitigated. Warranties could also be applied in the case of the acquisition of an ailing company by a turn-around investor, although usually the price paid for the asset is the main variable of adjustment. In specific cases, the seller of the distressed business will in effect pay the buyer to take over the business.

1.3.1.2 In Debt: Additional Cover for the Risks Entailed by the Investment (Private Debt)

Some investors prefer to reduce the relative risk of their investment, even if it means reducing their potential performance. This is how investment in convertible debt emerged, with less risk than an investment in pure equity: mezzanine debt is repaid *in fine*, often associated with options to convert them into the company's shares under certain conditions. This particular kind of debt is riskier than ordinary debt, since it is subordinated to the priority payment of other loans, so-called 'senior' or 'junior', 'second lien' or subordinated by senior to the mezzanine debt. The payment of subordinated debt depends therefore on the complete success of the deal. This justifies a higher interest rate and the creditors' participation in the possible success of the business thanks to options to convert the debt into capital. Venture lending is the equivalent of mezzanine debt for venture capital and growth capital deals. It is quite common in the USA but still rare in Europe. Mezzanine debt is the counterpart of LBO investing, with theoretically a higher risk protection. Likewise, with venture debt and venture capital.

Distressed debt is another form of convertible debt. Investors acquire at a significant discount some of the debt of an ailing business undergoing a bankruptcy procedure. The intensive due diligence executed by the investors allows them to assess the value of the assets of this business. Thanks to this analysis, the investor is able to assess the worst-case scenario: the liquidation value of the business. If selling the assets of the company in the turn-around fails, the investor should be able to at least recoup his investment. The due diligence also supports business planning. The best-case scenario entails setting up a plan with the management of the firm, submitting it to the bankruptcy court and converting some of the debt into equity to take control of the firm. In the process, the previous owners are eliminated ('washed out') and the debt of the ailing business is reduced to a manageable level. Investors usually inject some cash into the business to support its restructuring. If the plan is successfully implemented, distressed debt investors can sell the business and make a profit. Distressed debt is the counterpart of turn-around capital, with supposedly higher risk protection.

Direct lending also implies negotiation at arm's length. The purpose is to finance operations that would normally not fall in the purview of banks. Investors actively assess the plan of the management and its chances of success. Unlike banks, which rely on a scoring system, direct lending investors apply the equivalent of a due diligence process. The information is often generated at the expense of the borrower, at the request of the investor. The duration, interest rate, amount of debt and covenants are tailored to each case and are the risk mitigation instrument used by the investor. The borrower is a healthy, profitable and growing company with a transformative approach. In that respect, direct lending is the counterpart of growth capital.

1.3.1.3   To Acquire Assets: Combining Equity and Debt Instruments (Private Real Assets)

Many companies have been reducing the size of their balance sheet, and in the process sold assets. States have privatised real estate, infrastructures and natural resources. When assets change hands, it is at arm's length, as they require a careful analysis from the buyer. Some of these assets are plain vanilla: up to the highest standards, well maintained and requiring minimal management efforts. They still have to be assessed and priced. Others require more or less extensive improvements, a change of purpose (from office to residential use in real estate, for example) and other managerial efforts. The due diligence can be extensive and require multiple months of effort. Private real asset investors usually combine equity and debt instruments to acquire these assets, along the lines described before. The purpose is to combine variable levels of income and capital gain, the latter depending on the successful implementation of a transformation plan. Some investors specialise in providing private equity for real assets, and a few others private debt for real assets. The latter is a fairly small and recent activity.

1.3.2   A Long Holding Period

Irrespective of which type of financial instrument is used, private equity investments are usually held for 3 to 7 years. Private debt investments range from 4 to 8 years. Private real-estate investments are held for 3 to 10 years or more. At the early stage of its investment in a given business, the private equity investor must evaluate when and how it will liquidate this investment. As we shall see in Chapter 4, this is due to a contractual requirement: funds are created for 10 (maximum 12) years.

1.3.3   Implying Specific and Significant Risks

These investments bear specific and significant risks (Chapter 3), as they target businesses and assets in special situations – such as creation or restructuring, for example. This is the intrinsic risk of each of the segments of this asset class. Furthermore, they are subject to the cyclical nature of private markets as an emerging asset class, and to the general business cycles.

1.3.4   With High Expected Returns

As compensation for the risk borne by investors, return expectations are higher (Chapter 3) than those from comparable investments in listed securities.

1.3.5   Undertaken on Behalf of Qualified Investors

Given the lifetime of a private equity fund (usually 10 years), the risk borne by this type of deal, the long holding period of investments and the need to diversify investment among several funds to apply a sound investment policy, the great majority of private market funds are subscribed by institutional investors, that is to say pension funds, insurance companies, banks or even endowments in the USA (Chapter 3).

1.3.6   To Create Value by Implementing a Plan and Supporting Entrepreneurs

There is no private market investment without a plan to significantly change a company or an asset and, most of the time, without entrepreneurs. In the case of private real assets investing, entrepreneurship is more confined to project management, but there is still a creative undertaking associated with the set-up of a plan. As confirmed by Monitor Group (2010),[11] entrepreneurship is first and foremost a local phenomenon. Accordingly, private markets investing is mostly a local activity.

Monitor Group notably states that public policies address with varying success the challenge of supporting entrepreneurship. Actions range from cutting the administrative burden, to setting up incubators or improving access to venture capital. Nevertheless, a few topics remain neglected: promoting the entrepreneurial spirit (values, attitudes and motivation), developing skills, setting up a fully functional financing framework (seed investing and business angels, as well as IPOs) and taxes. The impact varies strongly, as shown in Figure 1.2.

---

[11] www.compete.monitor.com/App_Themes/MRCCorpSite_v1/DownloadFiles/NED_report_final.pdf.

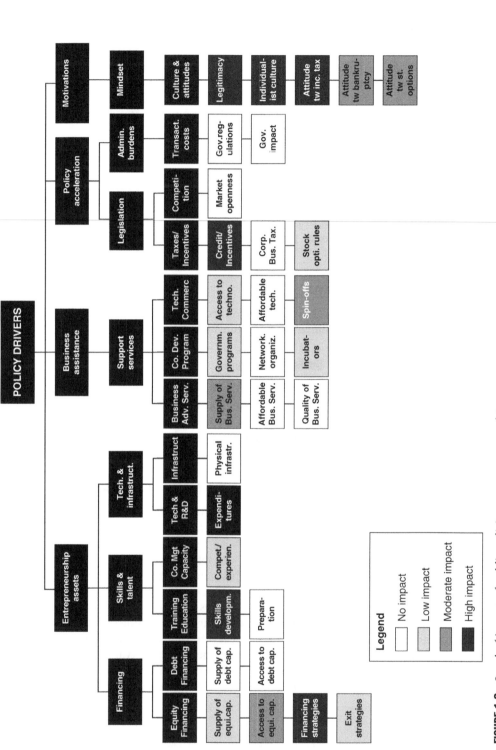

FIGURE 1.2 Level of impact of public policies on entrepreneurship
Source: Monitor Group (2010).

Entrepreneurship is one of the most powerful supports for economic growth and prosperity in a global modern economy. Few factors have as much impact on the emergence of innovation, job creation and the contribution to a dynamic and competitive economy as entrepreneurship. The 'creative destruction' described by Joseph Schumpeter is fuelled by waves of innovation driven by entrepreneurs.

Entrepreneurship is the creation and management of new companies, often through the discovery of new opportunities or market needs on existing markets. Entrepreneurship leading to fast growth, transforming whole economies and industries, is specific. It is based on innovation, that is to say the successful commercialisation of products and services based on new ideas. It is driven by individuals gifted with specific competences, characteristics and capacities, as illustrated in Figure 1.3.

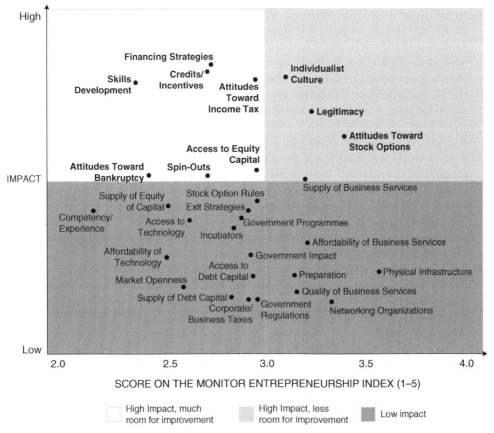

FIGURE 1.3 Relation between policies (and their impact) and the Monitor Group entrepreneurial index
Source: Monitor Group (2010).

According to Monitor Group, for a given amount invested, the entrepreneur produces innovations of better quality and with a higher efficiency than large companies. Four models of entrepreneurship have been identified by the consulting group:

1. The '*classical*' model, illustrated by Silicon Valley: in this high-tech entrepreneurship model, the intellectual property developed by university or governmental laboratories is commercialised thanks to the help of venture capital investors. This system has worked for Boston and Route 128 in the USA, and Cambridge in the UK. In general, this model is effective when connected to research of world-class level. The presence of a close financial centre is necessary, as well as a culture of cooperation between the academic and the professional sectors (which is difficult to achieve). Due to the success of this model, many initiatives have been undertaken to replicate it, often without success (Lerner, 2009).

2. The '*anchor firm*' model: ventures emerge from a company either through spin-offs or the departure of experimented employees, who have identified a business opportunity and decide to pursue it independently. The relationship between the new venture and the anchor firm is more symbiotic than competitive, as the latter often acts as the first client (more than a source of financing). This is why this model usually gives birth to a cluster of companies. More than creating companies against the former employer, entrepreneurs collaborate with it. This applies to more traditional locations such as the north-west of Saudi Arabia, Vancouver (Canada) or the triangle of research in North Carolina (USA). This is the model that is the easiest to replicate, notably in developed countries.

3. The '*event-driven*' model: a major industrial or economic event drives a significant number of unemployed individuals to launch their own company or to leave the sector. Due to a sudden influx of qualified people, the launch of new companies becomes possible, such as in the case of San Diego (USA) at the end of the Cold War, Washington DC (USA) or South Korea after the crisis of 1997. Israel could also qualify under this model after its foundation, and the arrival of a million individuals after the fall of the USSR.

4. The '*local hero*' model: a local entrepreneur, who started from scratch, has succeeded and gained international exposure, hence creating vocations among other entrepreneurs. This was the case for Medtronics (which invented the first personal pacemaker) and Minneapolis (USA), Microsoft in Washington (USA) and Wipro in Bangalore (India).

The models can be combined and are rarely identified as 'pure models'. HP, Apple, Google and Intel are anchor companies in the Silicon Valley.

This definition provides the opportunity to discuss some of the socio-economic consequences that have emerged with the rise of the private equity sector. For example, in the USA serial entrepreneurs appeared because of the fixed maximum term of investments and high expected returns. Slowly, entrepreneurs have begun to specialise in certain roles – such as the creation, development, internationalisation, restructuring or turn-around of companies. This list is not exhaustive.

Chapter 2 will take a closer look at the structuring of the private equity sector, the emergence of its key elements and its dynamics. This will be done through an analysis of recent history.

REFERENCES

Books and Booklets

Blessing, S. (2011) *Alternative Alternatives* (Wiley, Chichester), 242 pp.

Brown, D. (1995) *Mesopotamia: The Mighty Kings (Lost Civilizations)* (Time-Life Books, New York), 168 pp.

Bunch, B. and Hellemans, A. (2004) 'Thomas Edison', in *History of Science and Technology* (Houghton Mifflin Harcourt, Boston, MA), 784 pp.

Burstall, A. (1965) *A History of Mechanical Engineering* (MIT Press, Cambridge, MA), 456 pp.

Durant, W. (1954) *The Story of Civilization, Vol. 1 – Our Oriental Heritage* (Simon & Schuster, New York).

Frederick Lewis, A. (1949) *The Great Pierpont Morgan* (Harper & Row, New York), 306 pp.

Gompers, P. and Lerner, J. (2006) *The Venture Capital Cycle* (MIT Press, Cambridge, MA, 2nd edn), 581 pp.

Johnson, S. (2010) *Where Good Ideas Come From: The Natural History of Innovation* (Riverhead Books, New York), 326 pp.

Lerner, J. (2009) *Boulevard of Broken Dreams, Why Public Efforts to Boost Entrepreneurship and Venture Capital Have Failed – and What to Do about It* (Princeton University Press, Princeton, NJ), 229 pp.

Kusukawa, S. and MacLean, I. (2006) *Transmitting Knowledge: Words, Images, and Instruments in Early Modern Europe* (Oxford University Press, Oxford), 274 pp.

Mazzucato, M. (2015) *The Entrepreneurial State* (PublicAffairs, Philadelphia, PA), 260 pp.

Mercer Management Consulting (2012) *The Roles of Alternative Investments*, 18 pp.

Newsletters and Newspapers

Elliott, S., 'Norway's Supreme Court rejects appeal over Gassled natural gas transportation tariff reduction', S&P Global Platts, 28 June 2018.

Guerrera, F. and Politi, J., 'Flipping is a flop for investors', *Financial Times*, 19 September 2006.

Singer, T., 'Inside an Internet incubator', *Inc. Magazine*, 1 July 2000.

The Economist, 'Hatching a new plan', 10 August 2000.

Papers and Studies

Bain, Global Private Equity Report 2018, 2018, 80 pp.

Bain, Global Private Equity Report 2019, 2019, 88 pp.

Gompers, P., Kovner, A., Lerner, J. and Scharfstein, D. (2010) Performance persistence in entrepreneurship, *Journal of Financial Economics*, No. 96, pp. 18–32.

Gust, Global Accelerator Report 2016 (http://gust.com/accelerator_reports/2016/global/, last accessed 21/4/2019).

Monitor Group, Paths to Prosperity, 2010, 88 pp.

Pitchbook, 2018 Annual VC Liquidity Report, 2018, 12 pp.

Pitchbook, 2019 Annual US PE Breakdown, 2019, 15 pp.

Trinomics, The Entrepreneur's Guide to Growing and Financing Innovative Energy Technology Companies, 2018, 45 pp (https://ec.europa.eu/energy/sites/ener/files/documents/building_the_investment_community_for_innovative_energy_entrepreneurss_guide_0.pdf, last accessed 21/4/2019).

Modern Private Equity –
A French Invention?

Human needs have increased and diversified throughout history. Public and private efforts have strived to answer these needs. Private efforts evolved substantially, notably with the agricultural and industrial revolutions. The latter gave birth to start-up companies. Some of these companies were financed by their founders ('bootstrapped'). Others collected capital from outside sources, notably from venture capital.

Venture capital itself became more formal as entrepreneurship developed, with the launch of dedicated structures and funds. In the early stage of modern and formal venture capital, the entrepreneur, the investment manager and the investor emerged as clearly distinct figures. Modern venture capital, in particular, oversaw the differentiation between the capital provider (the investor) and the investment manager.

The professionalisation of private equity investors

By pushing the differentiation of roles further, the different actors of the venture capital industry paved the way for its professionalisation. Investors monitor and control investment managers. They essentially adopt a 'hands-off' approach, by delegating the work to the investment manager. Investment managers select ventures, designing plans with entrepreneurs, monitoring and controlling the investments. Entrepreneurs build the ventures, implement plans, structure and effectively run the companies.

Each venture is unique and entrepreneurs, to a large extent, learn by doing. This effort is a constantly renewed process, for each venture and each entrepreneur. Over time, investment managers accumulate knowledge by investing in different ventures. Their knowledge is a permanent feature that they can offer to help entrepreneurs. The extent of this knowledge can include changing the management of the companies they have invested in. To do this, they have to develop their own methodology and a philosophy of investment. This became possible as investors gave them the resources and opportunity to fully dedicate their time to venture investing.

Europeans were at the forefront of this initiative. Just as Columbus was a European individual discovering America, it was a European going to the USA who would formalise modern venture capital after World War II: the French General Georges Doriot. He initiated this effort in 1946 (Gupta, 2004). It was not a lone one: in 1945, the Bank of England and major British banks decided to form the Industrial and Commercial Finance Corporation to finance small and medium-sized companies. It then raised external money after 1959, and became 3i in 1983, which listed on the London Stock Exchange in 1994.

However, Doriot focused on start-ups instead of the general fabric of small and mid-sized businesses affected by the retreat of bank lending. This made his effort unique. Does this mean that modern venture capital is a French invention? The word 'entrepreneur' certainly is, and in many respects France had the assets to thrive in venture capital. Nevertheless, it is in the USA – at Harvard Business School – that the 'father of modern venture capital' Doriot created, with Ralph Flanders and Karl Compton, the American Research and Development Corporation (ARD). As we will see in this chapter, the ARD became home to many successful venture capital investments, the most emblematic being the Digital Equipment Company (which later merged to form Compaq, which eventually merged with Hewlett Packard).

The right venture capital mix – for the USA

The legal framework, even if it is important and nice to have, is *not enough* to guarantee the success of investment structures *if the economic and social environment is risk averse*. David Landes, an economic historian, states that 'if we learn anything from economic development, it is that culture makes almost all the difference' (*The Economist*, 2009). In that respect, IHS Global Insight found that in the USA, in 2005, venture capital-backed companies represented almost 17% of the national GDP and 9% of private sector employment (*The Economist*, 2009). The specific American *culture* is a success factor of its venture capital industry, but not the only one.

Indeed, emerging markets, despite their social and cultural eagerness to take risks, are still lacking some fundamental factors such as *the rule of law and its effective application* and *fair business practices* – including the application of economic policies and regulations. To this effect, *adapted economic policies* (see Chapter 1 and Mazzucato, 2015) and *openness to immigration* are important too (see Lerner, 2009 on the importance of expatriates, and Chapter 4 of this book). These developments are crucial for building a long-standing private equity environment, and benefitting from its impact.

The rush to private equity in emerging markets, notably China, over the course of the last two decades has anticipated this evolution. However, the local context has still to catch up. This assumes that adopting the American socio-economic model is the target. This can be debated. The US venture capital industry is born of the local context and adapted to it. Each country is different and does not necessarily have to develop a venture capital industry to succeed in innovating. Japan and South Korea offer alternative models to the venture capital industry in financing innovation successfully, both being champions in terms of R&D and having given birth to waves of technological innovation.

2.1 USA: THE FOUNDRY OF MODERN PRIVATE EQUITY

In many respects, the industrial revolutions before the 20th century belonged to the categories described in Chapter 1, that is to say innovation combining political and financial sponsors. Railroads, canals and other infrastructure projects belong to this category. However, *the intricate mix of political and private interests led to financial scandals* which were increasingly incompatible with the democratisation of Western societies. The Panama Canal project offers an example of a major financial bribery scandal in France, combining public and private interests in a toxic mix. Europe gave birth to multiple other scandals of this kind.

2.1.1 The Strict Separation of Public Policies and Public Financing

To avoid further scandals, the application of public policies was separated from public financial backing, thus introducing controls in the management of public finances. This is the case, for example, in the creation of the War Finance Corporation in 1918 by the American Congress. Originally set up to support the war-related industries, the WFC was converted to support agricultural and railroad industries (Cendrowski, Martin, Petro & Wadecki, 2008).

2.1.2 The Separation of Public Endeavours and Private Efforts; the Subsequent Support of the Former for the Latter

This initiates the *tradition of public support to private companies which are serving a public interest* (see notably Mazzucato, 2015). The Reconstruction Finance Corporation, set up in 1932 in the USA, is another example. The Second World War gave birth to another initiative. In 1942, Congress created the Small War Plants Corporation (SWPC), which, as its name states, was dedicated to small companies. This is the first initiative which recognised the *need to help entrepreneurs and small businesses for the sake of national and public interest.*

This help was of a financial, educational and legal nature. Not only did the SWPC set the trend for financing through loans to small businesses, but later the Office of Small Businesses also created educational programmes. During the Korean War, small businesses could apply for certification entitling them to participate in requests for proposals from the government. This paved the way for the creation of the Small Business Administration in 1953.

2.1.3 Governmental Input: SBA, DARPA and ERISA

The creation of an *administration which was specifically formed to promote and protect the interests of small businesses* is a manifestation of the early awareness of this category's importance for companies in the USA. Interestingly, one of the main activities of the SBA was to provide *educational programmes and financial assistance* to entrepreneurs. In many respects, the administration placed the ability to grow businesses at the centre of its policy.

To support entrepreneurs further, and go beyond public support, Small Business Investment Companies (SBICs) were created in 1958.[1] This is the unofficial date of birth of the modern venture capital industry in the USA. Hence, 'the government played a critical role in shaping Silicon Valley', though 'with a "stop and start" pattern of

---

[1] Draper, Gaither & Anderson was the first venture capital limited partnership, formed in 1958 (Draper, 2011). Kleiner, Perkins, Caufield & Byers was one of the early players, set up in 1972, which shaped Silicon Valley and the venture capital industry (Perkins, 2008, pp. 108–109).

government funding' over two decades, hence debunking 'the myth of "instant industrialization"' (Lerner, 2009, pp. 34, 8 and 33, respectively).

SBICs were a result of the statement by the Federal Reserve saying that 'in simplest terms, the small business could not get the credit... needed to keep pace with technological advancement' (Cendrowski, Martin, Petro & Wadecki, 2008). This statement remains true, and the 2007–2009 financial crisis made it even more obvious when suddenly, liquidity dried up for small and medium-sized companies. By promoting access to public markets and orders for small and medium-sized businesses, the SBA has been supporting not only the birth but also the growth of young companies – something that Europe still needs.

New technologies were at the core of the SBIC initiative, and access to public markets was necessarily a major support to help small companies innovate and compete with larger businesses. In the context of the Cold War, *armament and defence industries had the lion's share of public expenses – and hence led the way in R&D*. The Defense Advanced Research Projects Agency (DARPA) was leading the American effort to gain the technological advantage over the USSR. Created as 'ARPA' in 1958, the agency represented an answer to the launch of Sputnik in 1957. It was renamed DARPA in 1973, and gave birth to major technological innovations such as hypertext, computer networks and the graphical user interface.

The switch from infrastructure and equipment budgets to defence had a significant impact on entrepreneurial thinking. This shows just how much not only the provision of business ideas, but also a market for them (even a small or highly specialised one), is important. The separation of political decisions from public funding was the first step towards the transformation of public action. Increasingly, public–private cooperation was expected, notably because public budgets had reached their limits. Public intervention was hence situated on the incentive side, with help for start-ups and early venture capital firms; or on the market side, with the equivalent of an 'affirmative action' for public orders in favour of small businesses.

Not every public initiative was in favour of the venture capital industry. The 1970s saw a strong market downturn, when IPOs were scarce and many investors could not realise their investments. Private equity investments suffered under these conditions and their returns were significantly affected. The financial downturn led Congress to vote in the Employee Retirement Income Security Act (ERISA) in 1974, to prevent pension fund managers from taking excessive risks. Private equity being seen as a high risk/high return investment, in 1975 pension funds halted their investments (venture capital funds raised USD 10 million that year). In 1978, ERISA was clarified to explicitly enable pension fund managers to invest in private equity.

The fourth element helping the entrepreneurial ecosystem was the *change in capital gains tax rate*, from 49.5 to 28% (later decreased to 20%). One way to help venture capital firms raise funds was to show promising net returns – and lowering the tax impact had an immediate and visible effect on the bottom line for institutional and private investors.

In the space created by direct and explicit public intervention, a new set of actors – such as universities, spin-offs from large groups and professional venture capitalists – emerged slowly.

2.1.4   Universities, Defence and Disruptive Innovation

Doriot, a former member of the military, was teaching at Harvard and decided to set up his investment structure there in 1946. The *location* had a *significant impact* on the activity and success of ARD. Doriot chose the *USA*, where he had emigrated to, and not France, where he could have returned to. He then chose *Harvard* to create ARD, and did not reproduce his initiative at INSEAD – the top European business school that he co-founded in 1957.

Indeed, ARD's best investment was a company created by two Massachusetts Institute of Technology (MIT) engineers: the Digital Equipment Corporation (DEC). MIT and Harvard are located in the same Boston area, which helps to create a solid network of relations. DEC's IPO in 1970 was a landmark of what venture capital could achieve in the new technologies, having funded an emerging start-up and leading it towards the stock exchange.

Doriot's legacy

The success of Doriot's initiative lies in the development of the venture capital industry, fuelled notably by the stock exchange boom in the 1960s. Some teams, which were created by former ARD executives, could generate their own track record. In that respect, the *educational aspects of Doriot's approach and of the SBIC system*, as well as the strong ties to the university system, could give birth to an even more dynamic centre on the US West Coast, with Silicon Valley. The strength of Silicon Valley lies in its ties to local industry giants, which are more diversified than around Boston and less dependent on military contracts.

The *relationships between universities and venture capital are strong*, not only to feed VC firms with a strong and qualified deal flow, but also to invest in them. The alumni network is a very valuable asset that VC firms can tap into in order to expand their portfolio companies, recruit talent, evaluate opportunities, recommend investments and more generally provide a wealth of goodwill to the universities and their partners.

As *universities have contracts with the defence industry*, notably in R&D, VC firms are strongly connected to this sector as well. The US government has its own structure (In-Q-Tel), but VC firms are keen on financing *technologies which will eventually have a civil application*. The most advanced model in that respect is Israel. This country of 8.7 million inhabitants (as of 2017) counts 1212 investment structures active locally, with 162 funds and 8005 active high-tech companies according to the IVC Research Center in 2019. These companies are connected to the Israeli defence industry in many respects, notably in IT protection (e.g., Check Point Software Technologies, listed on the NASDAQ), communication (ICQ, acquired by AOL and then Mail.Ru Group), geo-localisation (Waze, acquired by Google), computer vision (Mileye, acquired by Intel) and semiconductors (Mellanox, acquired by NVIDIA).

The Israeli market is small and its local sources of financing remain limited. As a consequence, a specific Israeli VC model emerged. International treaties historically facilitated the transfer of Israeli start-ups to the American market. These companies were re-incorporated as local US companies once they had reached pilot/prototype mode. The strategy was then to invite US VC funds to finance the 'go-to-market' stage and eventually list the company on the NASDAQ, for example. US VC fund managers identified the opportunity to finance local start-ups early by opening an office in Israel, and sourcing local opportunities directly. They could then support their growth and development in the USA at a later stage.

Public and private initiatives have propelled Israel ahead of innovation through *education*, and in the universities in particular. Promising students achieve a graduate degree, do their mandatory military service (where they can work over 2 to 3 years on high-level technology) and then return to civilian life with a significant theoretical and practical background. They are even allowed to keep the intellectual property of the innovations which they have developed while in the army. They are then ready to create a start-up, which is financed through the VC firms based in Tel Aviv.

Israel has the highest ratio of PhDs, engineers and scientists per person in the world – with very influential institutions in the IT sector and medical industries, such as Technion – the Israel Institute of Technology (*The Economist*, 2009). *Instead of replicating* the American venture capital industry, *Israel has developed its own model* and integrated it when needed in the American framework *to create synergies*. This is a radically different approach from the European perspective.

2.1.5 Challenges

Despite its successes, ARD was mainly the creation of one man and had to merge with Textron in 1972, when Doriot retired. This difficulty in managing the transition from the founding partners of a private equity fund manager to the next generation is a recurring problem in the private equity industry, which is largely dominated by individual personalities to this day. But in the case of ARD, it was also linked to a *structural rigidity*: ARD was still an old-fashioned structure in its legal organisation (Hsu & Kenney, 2004). There was no formal separation between the capital to invest and the capital spent on operations (which is very often the case for *evergreen* holding companies; see Chapter 4). Corporate governance was greatly limited by corporate law, which is not designed adequately for controlling investments.

To address the inadequacy of the corporate structure, investment managers turned to the fund structure (Draper, 2011, Chapter 2), and notably the *limited partnership*, which was more attractive than a typical industrial holding structure for many reasons. First, the limited partnership *separated the capital providers (fund investors) and the capital managers (fund managers)*. Then, the limited partnership was setting a *limit to the life of the investment structure* without forcing fund managers out of activity. The limited partnership was also *distributing profits*, which were *taxed differently* – and particularly at a lower level than dividends. By separating investment management by the fund managers from capital provision by the funds, it was possible to audit the two structures on a stand-alone basis and check if management was done according to contractual fund regulations (the limited partnership agreement).

The 1960s supported the emergence of the venture capital industry. The boom of the US stock exchange supported this growth, confirming the success of VC investments. The same decade witnessed the emergence of the LBO industry. The take-over of the Orkin Exterminating Company, by Lewis Cullman and his team in 1964, was probably the first LBO in history (Cendrowski, Martin, Petro & Wadecki, 2008). Therefore, the modern private equity industry was born after the Second World War, and its growth was accelerated by a series of legal and regulatory changes, notably the liberalisation of the financial sector in the 1980s.

The great American challenge: intellectual property laws

Nevertheless, despite this rapid development, the private equity industry faces multiple challenges in the USA. Its legal and tax system is complicated and burdensome. The sanctions are difficult to predict and evaluate, notably for product liabilities through punitive damages. Its patenting system is a source of regular litigation which is holding back innovation, and also over-protecting patent holders.[2]

Intellectual property is a major issue when it comes to innovation, investment and returns. It is especially difficult to strike the right balance between the reward of innovation and the excessive protection of minor improvements. Even worse, the patenting system can be used unfairly to protect a collective innovation or a technological element which is necessary for an industry and could later be used against an innovator. This can substantially decrease or annihilate the returns on investments.

Intellectual property rights do not create any value by themselves. They provide protection for the production of goods or services. The processing remains necessary in order to realise the investments made in intellectual property. In that respect, unused patents which are later activated in order to sue companies are a major problem when venture capitalists want to finance incremental innovation (which is their core activity).

The increasing costs associated with starting up

Another challenge which is associated with venture financing in the USA is the *increasing cost of building a start-up*. This is counter-intuitive, especially since the concept of 'lean start-up' (Ries, 2011) has given birth to a movement aiming to build rapidly and at low cost IT start-ups launching so-called 'minimal viable products'. According to this movement, start-ups can then adjust their products (or services) based on the reception by clients and – if necessary – change their business model. The reality is, however, much more nuanced. First, this theory could only potentially be applicable to non-critical products and services. For example, medical technologies, infrastructure services and mission-critical software are not adapted to minimal viable products. Even if, in the short term, this approach appears less expensive, it can prove more expensive overall. Preparation and planning are expensive, but avoid loss of time and capital by testing. In an open environment, trying and testing means that competitors can learn from failed attempts. The start-up which did not succeed will require even more resources to deal with this legacy and catch up with the competition benefitting from spill-over effects, that is learning from the innovation of others.

Not only are fixed investments costly, whether in the short or mid term, but also variable expenses (office space, salaries, etc.). The centres of competence – such as Silicon Valley and the Boston area – are a determining factor in the success of start-ups,

---

[2]This system has given birth to 'patent trolls', hoarding patents to sue companies which could infringe them. For the first time in US history, they filed in 2012 the majority (61%) of US patent lawsuits according to Colleen Chien, Law Professor at Santa Clara University, compared to 45% in 2011 and 23% in 2007. 35% of start-ups which have raised between USD 50 and 100 million have been sued on a patent, as well as 20% of those which have raised USD 20 to 50 million. The ratio of demands (some of them settled before reaching the lawsuit stage) to lawsuits runs between 100:1 and 307:1 (McBride, 2012).

notably because they attract talent and can benefit from the local socio-economic environment. However, the struggle to attract and retain scarce talent, and have sufficient space, pushes operational costs ever higher. The logical solution would be to delocalise start-ups, and set them up in less costly areas. The problem is that venture capital financing is first and foremost a local activity. Funds usually finance companies in their region, notably thanks to syndication with like-minded co-investors. Fund managers need to interact frequently with entrepreneurs, often informally. This is not the case for LBO investors, who usually target companies nationwide.

Venture capital models and their limits

The US venture capital model has been experiencing four cumulative challenges, resulting in a questioning of this very model after the crash of IT investments in 2000. First, the amounts raised by existing and emerging venture capital fund managers increased very quickly. This had an impact on the valuation of the portfolio companies, which as a consequence has increased as well. Second, the cost of creating a company in the USA was increasing comparatively faster due to the scarcity of talent and space in the right location. Third, the exit scenarios of VC investors relied increasingly on IPOs, which eventually failed to materialise. Finally, the returns dropped significantly as a consequence of the first three effects. This led to a rather long period of mediocre venture capital fund returns after 2001. Post-crisis investments proved to be much more profitable, breeding a new cycle, and one could arguably wonder if the situation in 2019 is similar to the one experienced in the run-up to the crash of 2000. This would lead to another contraction and an extended period of mediocre returns, during which the valuation and investment excesses leading to the crash are cleaned up from the portfolios of venture capital funds.

Israel benefits from a relative cost advantage by nurturing early-stage ventures and transferring them at a later stage to the USA. This model, which has been at the origin of major successes described above, led to the description of Israel as a 'start-up nation' (Senor & Singer, 2010). However, this model relies on three fundamental pillars: a significant public effort in the defence industry; a need for technologies in application of this military effort; and an ability to transfer successful start-ups to the USA to grow them. The latter depends on bilateral US–Israel treaties and agreements, which can change due to political and diplomatic factors. The American and Israeli 'venture capital models' are therefore highly contingent on broader efforts and public initiatives.

2.2 EUROPE: ADAPTING A SUCCESSFUL MODEL OR CREATING ITS OWN?

Inventing a 'European Silicon Valley' has been the dream of many countries. The candidates were numerous in the UK, France, Germany, Scandinavia and the rest of the world (see Lerner, 2009). However, this dream has never materialised, despite public policies promoting this model and public funds supporting those policies.[3] The advent

---

[3] Lerner (2009) provides in his chapter 9 a list of sensible recommendations for public programmes which are probably the best demonstration of the 'dos and don'ts' of private equity public programmes.

of the *European Union* (EU), and the perspective of a *pan-European market,* renewed the conviction that Europe could compete by applying locally a successful model from abroad. However, Europe diverges from the USA and Israel. Culture plays a major role in the process of innovation. Risk-prone populations in California and Israel cannot be compared to the somewhat more risk-averse populations in Europe.

This triggers two possible alternative conclusions. One alternative is that Europe may not need the equivalent of an American or Israeli 'venture capital model'. Like Israel, Europe has a cost advantage in terms of talent and space, and it is also innovating. According to the 'Innobarometer 2016 – EU business innovation trends' report (European Commission, 2016; latest version available as of 2019), two-thirds of EU companies have introduced at least one innovation between January 2013 and February 2016: 40% introduced new or significantly improved goods or services, 34% new or significantly improved organisational methods; 33% new or significantly improved market strategies; and 30% new or significantly improved processes.

This is happening with the current organisation of the venture capital industry in Europe. Local venture capital firms are eagerly trying to spot opportunities. However, funds are merely built and invested on a national basis. This could trigger an issue in terms of efficient venture capital allocation on an EU scale. Given the role of venture capital in the growth of countries, this allocation is important in order to foster economic growth for the next 15 to 20 years.

The second alternative conclusion is, therefore, that Europe needs an organised pan-European venture capital industry. This remains to be carefully justified and proven. Assuming that it is so, the EU has to transform four specific local features into competitive assets, as Israel did for itself. The first feature is that the *risk aversion of its population* differs from that in the USA and Israel. This has multiple consequences. One is that the resilience of start-ups might be higher, once entrepreneurs have launched, than in more entrepreneurial countries. Another is that European entrepreneurs might innovate in different parts of the international value chain, for example incrementally in business-to-business solutions. Major successes are often business-to-consumer companies which have been listed on the stock exchange. However, this is a very small proportion of the overall innovation of national economies. Instead of trying to 'disrupt' markets and compete head to head with Israeli and American start-ups, European entrepreneurs, but also other less visible ones such as the Japanese and South Koreans, might have adopted strategies and business models more symbiotic with the current economic environment. Capital needs might diverge significantly in that context, and require less venture capital.

The second feature is that Europe welcomes a *lower pool of immigrants creating start-ups* than the USA. It cannot count on the integration of foreign entrepreneurs. Europe can, however, count on home-bred entrepreneurs, who constitute a significant cohort of talent. Nevertheless, immigrants in the USA were largely instrumental in leading the efforts of the country in business-to-consumer innovation.

This is notably due to the third feature, which is a fragmented European market. Despite the efforts undertaken to create an integrated and harmonised market, consumption habits, languages, regulations, borders and cultures limit the launch of pan-European products and services in a simple way. However, the USA also has a mosaic of state and local regulations and Israel does not have a large market either. Therefore, the lack of a true pan-European market is a limiting factor but cannot alone be seen as the main difference from the USA and Israel. Nevertheless, the Innobarometer 2016 notes that 65% of survey responses mention that the market is dominated by established competitors, posing problems for the commercialisation of innovative goods and services. A lack of financial services is also mentioned (58%), as well as the cost and complexity of meeting regulations and standards (57%) and a lack of human resources (49%), especially with marketing (28%), technical (24%) and financial (22%) skills.

The fourth factor is a lack of direction for industry. Europe has a limited industrial policy, though some agendas have emerged – for example, to promote specific research industries (Horizon 2020 being one). European companies mention increased public support, notably to train their staff in the promotion and marketing of innovative goods and services, as a possible significant impact on their activity (29%). Public support in accessing or reinforcing selling online (26%) and participating in conferences, trade fairs and exhibitions (24%) came next.

These specific European features are deep-rooted. There is no simple way to change them in order to transpose a foreign model. The question is therefore: does Europe need a different model than today and if so, to achieve what target? This question is actually relevant for other countries or regions willing to explore the idea of developing their own venture financing model of innovation, with the risks of costly failure that this entails (Lerner, 2009).

2.2.1   Government Input: Legal Changes, Tax Rebates, Infrastructures and Pan-EU Market

European start-up costs remain relatively low, notably when the quality/cost ratio of infrastructures and education systems are factored in, compared to Silicon Valley. Talent is available, as well as space, at a much cheaper price. IPOs remain until now a rarity in Europe for venture-backed start-ups. Trade sales (also known as 'strategic acquisitions' by corporations) are the main exit paths for venture investors. As a result, European start-ups appear to be more attractive.

A welcome adoption of the limited partnership framework

Modern venture capital sectors in Europe were initiated by major changes generated by the *adoption of the equivalent of the limited partnership/general partnership structure*. The UK has its local (e.g., British and Scottish) versions of the US structure. France adapted this framework to its local law by creating the Fonds Commun de Placement à Risque (FCPR), which later became the Fonds de Placement en Capital Investissement (FPCI). Switzerland also created its own version, as did Luxembourg with the Special Investment Fund (SIF) and the Restricted Alternative Investment Fund (RAIF). In Spain, the law regulating venture capital entities recognises the fund and fund manager structure by allowing 'the issuance of shares of classes other than the general class of the company, provided that any preferential treatment received by its holders and the conditions for access [of] such treatment is adequately reflected in the bylaws of the company'.[4] One of the motivations was to offer to local venture capital firms the same

---

[4] Article 26.5 of Law 22/2014, of November 12, which regulates (among others) venture capital entities.

advantages as off-shore structures. In many respects, *European countries have set a specific tax framework for capital gains*, as well as a defined term in order to encourage investors to invest in venture capital firms.

Despite the adoption of the best legal practices from the USA, which is an unusual move on a European scale, the venture capital industry has only recently emerged as a significant private equity actor, able to attract international limited partners. The reason is that until 2000, the performance of American venture capital funds looked significantly more attractive than for European ones. The 2000 market crash, which chiefly affected IT start-ups and therefore the venture capital sector, reset the comparison. European venture capital managers gained rapidly in experience and expertise, and their returns are now fairly comparable (Figure 2.1). However, European venture capital funds still raise only a fraction of that gathered by American funds, thus triggering the recurring question of a potentially harmful imbalance for the European economy; or of a different model of financing.

The double-edged impact of the pan-European common market

The EU economic and financial union opened a larger market not only to local European companies with significantly lower barriers, but also to foreign companies with a local subsidiary. As local companies in Europe were cheaper than in the USA, and American start-ups were more often listed, fast-growth companies in the USA could buy their passport to the EU with very attractive conditions. Yahoo, eBay and other major companies emerged from the 1997–2003 cycle and entered the EU in this way. The same applied to VC investments. The first pan-European venture capital firms were coming from the USA and directed their main focus at late-stage investments, such as IDG Ventures, Benchmark Capital (now Balderton) and other famous general partners from Silicon Valley. One of the ways to learn the workings of the European markets

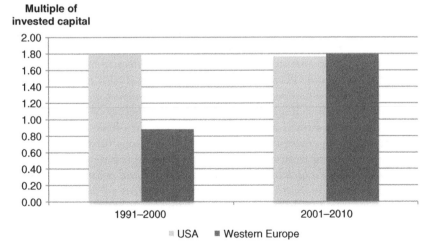

FIGURE 2.1   Performance of venture capital funds in the USA and Western Europe before and after the dotcom crash.
Source: Author, based on Cambridge Associates data. Performance is measured in USD for US VC funds and EUR for Western European funds. Funds are gathered by their year of creation (vintage year).

was to tag along with local players and identify promising potential acquisitions for an American champion.

In that respect, US venture capital fund managers have demonstrated their capacity to adapt, and their pragmatism. While the investment rationale in Israel was to bring innovation to the larger American market, in Europe it is to help local players to conquer their neighbouring markets and offer a development platform for potential US buyers. If there is a pan-European VC model to start to analyse, it is therefore the one developed by foreign investors willing to capitalise on European opportunities.

National attempts to nurture a 'European' venture capital industry

Europe has deployed a *wealth of initiatives to create a viable venture capital sector*. Each *nation* has adopted some ideas coming from the USA, such as the limited partnership and the SBIC system, to generate national support for its start-ups. These initiatives were difficult, tortuous and costly – and above all remained first and foremost essentially national. The UK has imposed itself as the leading European market, thanks notably to its early listing of venture capital vehicles – such as 3i in 1994. Capitalising on this, as well as on the influence of its financial centre, its cultural and linguistic proximity to the USA and a tradition of innovation, the UK became the place of choice for the creation of a private equity structure. Regional or pan-European LBO fund managers have elected London as the main location for their headquarters. This role will have to be re-evaluated as the UK exits the EU, and the terms of future cooperation remain to be explicitly defined.

France tried to go its own way, combining public initiative with semi-private financing. The Sociétés Régionales de Développement (SDRs) were created in 1955 to nurture local ventures and help them grow on a national scale. Even though this was a very costly initiative, which eventually failed, it was an occasion for the French venture capitalists and LBO investors to acquire their know-how and thus prepare for the emergence of independent funds (some of them being initially transatlantic structures, such as Sofinnova and Apax France).

The UK and France even went a step further, *enabling retail investors to participate in venture capital vehicles*. The UK created Venture Capital Trusts (VCTs), which are trusts created to invest in start-ups, eventually listed on effective launch. France developed the Fonds Commun de Placement dans l'Innovation (FCPI) to invest in start-ups and then the Fonds d'Investissement de Proximité (FIP) to invest in regions in a broader range of private companies. Regarding the returns, the success of these retail vehicles remains to be carefully assessed and benchmarked, but they have attracted significant amounts of capital to an emerging sector. One of the reasons for this attractiveness is that retail investors benefit from tax rebates when they contribute to these funds.

The major hurdles of a lack of proper stock exchange and common legal standards

Without a *financial market of reference* (the equivalent of the NASDAQ) to list the most promising venture-backed companies, European start-ups lack one of the most promising and lucrative exit venues for investors. The risk–return profile for European venture capital investors is thus different than in the USA: start-ups are smaller, aim to bring to the market less disruptive and more incremental innovation, eventually leading to a trade sale. In that context, venture capital investors can only invest a limited amount viably, to help develop their portfolio companies. Indeed, to generate a significant multiple of investment, start-ups have to be capital efficient and target a limited number of national markets. This skews portfolio construction and the investment strategy of European venture capital investors.

Despite EU legal convergence, *national laws remain an entry barrier on the national markets*. Therefore, the start-ups target first and foremost their national markets (see Figure 2.2). One example is the patenting system, which is still very expensive and burdensome in the EU.[5] Another example is the lack of common practices in corporate law, even though the European corporation (societas europaea, SE) has existed officially since 2001 and was adopted by member states progressively. However, the main reason for the slow growth of European companies is the problem of expanding sales into other European countries, the biggest challenge being the differences in language and culture.

Since Europe has a certain legacy, its innovating processes are the result of a common cultural background and national differences. A large part is hidden from the statistics and clear identification, notably because venture capital financing was for a long period of time the business of rich families (family offices), corporations, public finances (directly or indirectly), banks (directly or through captive structures) and not least, personal connections. Depending on the national specificities, and aside from the independent venture capital firms, some of the sources of financing dominate others: corporate venturing and family offices in Switzerland; public finances and corporations in France; banks and corporations in Germany; family offices and personal connections in Italy; family offices and corporations in Scandinavia, state and regional public bodies together with family offices in Spain, and so on.

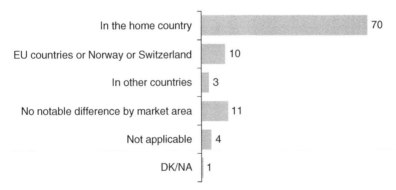

FIGURE 2.2 Location of companies' lead markets
Source: EU Innobarometer 2009.

---

[5]The system has, however, evolved significantly in 2012 towards a pan-European patenting system. Though the details are still in the making, the cost of patenting for a European protection could fall from EUR 36 000 to roughly EUR 5000 thanks to a mutual recognition of patents within the EU, and the restriction of the valid languages to three (see, among others, Barker, 2012).

2.2.2 National Champions, Information Technologies and Incremental Innovation

However, the *role of large corporations remains crucial for innovation in Europe*: they innovate more, notably if they are larger and are part of a group of companies (see Table 2.1). Corporate giants have a tradition of *spinning off* some of their business units, notably innovative ones. Corporations might give birth to innovative ideas which are difficult to develop internally. Reasons might be that these ideas do not fit with the corporate strategy, or that they are too resource consuming. Corporates let these innovative outfits grow out of their perimeter, while possibly retaining a stake in them.

Companies could invest directly in start-ups out of their balance sheet, but this could possibly have a negative impact on these start-ups for multiple reasons. First, a start-up directly financed by a corporation could be seen as part of the corporation itself. Competitors of that corporation could be wary of working with the start-up. Then, a start-up might fret that the corporation would gain undue advantage by sitting

TABLE 2.1 'Has your company introduced any [...] innovation since January 2012?'

	At least one innovation	No innovation at all
EU 28	72%	28%
Company size		
1–9 employees	70%	30%
10–49 employees	79%	21%
50–249 employees	89%	11%
250+ employees	95%	5%
Sectors		
Manufacturing	76%	24%
Retail	74%	26%
Services	72%	28%
Industry	64%	36%
Part of a group		
Yes	83%	17%
No	70%	30%
Company turnover in 2014		
≤ 100 000 EUR	61%	39%
> 100 000 to 500 000 EUR	71%	29%
> 500 000 to 2 million EUR	78%	22%
> 2 million EUR	82%	18%
Company turnover since 2012		
Risen by 5% or more	80%	20%
Remained approximately the same	68%	32%
Fallen by 5% or more	67%	33%

Source: European Commission (2015).

on the start-up's Board, notably if the corporation wants to enter this market. Another objection is that the corporation might apply a bureaucratic and burdensome reporting process to the start-up, akin to those applied to subsidiaries and business units, thus weighting down their agility and nimbleness while adding up costs.

Some corporations have therefore set up *corporate venturing programmes* to maintain a foothold in the fields of innovation. Corporate venture capital (CVC) consists for corporations to invest in start-ups while keeping them at arm's length. Lerner (2009) has detailed the challenges when setting up such programmes and the motivations of corporations, which range from financial returns to exposure to new ideas and concepts, strategic alliances and generating opportunities for future acquisitions, once these start-ups are proven.

Some of these negative features associated with direct corporate investments still apply to CVC investments, notably in terms of reputational association and reporting requirements, but they are reduced. Start-ups accept CVC investments to fund them, and also because corporations are *crucial customers* for start-ups in EU markets where access to public orders is difficult and means having 3 to 5 years of existence and profitable activity. If 56% of corporations in the EU won a contract of public procurement (see Figure 2.3), the value of these contracts would represent only 39% of the total value of public procurement between 2009 and 2011 (see Figure 2.4).

Even worse, the administration is highly averse to innovative products and services. This attitude is reducing the interest of start-ups in applying for the grant of such contracts (see Figure 2.5).

As a result, large corporations earn the lion's share of these public procurements (see Figures 2.3 and 2.4 below). Teaming up with large corporations can open access to

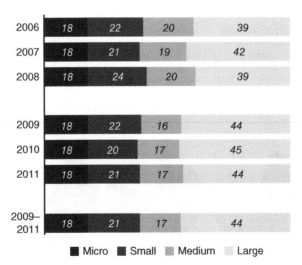

FIGURE 2.3 EU-27 SMEs' share of public contracts won, by number of contracts (%)
Note: percentages may not add up to 100 due to rounding (margin of error ±0.9–1.3%)
Source: PWC, ICF GHK and Ecorys (2014).

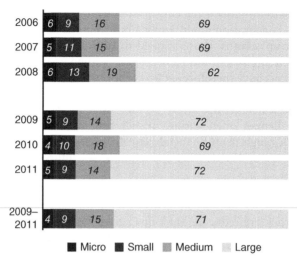

FIGURE 2.4   EU-27 SMEs' share of public contracts won, by aggregate value of contracts (%)
Note: percentages may not add up to 100 due to rounding (margin of error ±1–1.4%)
Source: PWC, ICF GHK and Ecorys (2014).

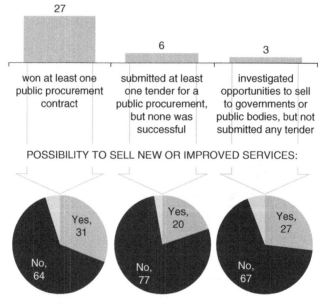

FIGURE 2.5   Innovation in public procurement
Source: EU Innobarometer 2009.

public procurements for start-ups. Large corporations are also usually *located in each and every significant national EU market*, which is very helpful for a small company setting foot abroad. Opening subsidiaries in the EU continental markets is complex, owing to the difficulty of opening bank accounts, setting up shop, understanding the legal and tax system, as well as local corporate and business practices. Having close partnerships with a large corporation is hence a factor of success in Europe, which may not be that important in the USA.

European start-ups have to adapt to the local innovation process, in each country, and in the EU overall. Either a start-up designs a product/service which is complementary to the business lines of a corporate giant, or its product/service is an input for a corporate giant. This means that in any case, the start-up will be active in the same sector as these corporations: for example, biopharma in Switzerland, infrastructures in France, mobile networks in Scandinavia, or services in the UK.

The industrial revolution in the information technologies area has changed the landscape slightly. Europe now benefits from high-quality telecommunications infrastructures, and the advent of the 'information age' has opened doors to start-ups willing to set up shop in their national countries despite the lack of obvious tradition and expertise in that sector. The reason is that the IT industry has become the glue inside and between companies. Roger McNamee has summed up this perspective (AlwaysOn, 2005):

The 1990s were characterized by three gigantic waves of applications, [that] every enterprise in the developed world adopted at the same time . . . We're now between big waves, with the next huge opportunity [coalescing] around enterprise web services that require creating best practices . . . People don't even know what the business processes are yet, so I think we're going to spend . . . money where it's mostly build rather than buy. As a consequence, that money gets fragmented and spread over this really wide array of things.

This opens up a *wide perspective for European start-ups*, as suddenly it is not the size that matters so much, but rather the ability to adapt to customers' needs and local specificities. In fact, the impact of the IT revolution still varies widely from one industry to another. Information-intensive sectors, such as the travel industry, have been completely redesigned, with airlines reporting that 90% of their bookings are now done online. However, labour-intensive industries are still largely unaffected, but should be targeted by the next corporate and consumer IT trend. Pervasiveness, existing infrastructures to be leveraged and the need to automate business processes will probably spread IT further through the economy, creating new opportunities in traditional sectors while adapting IT to these sectors' needs. As a result, European venture capital will have its fair share of *challenging evaluations of investment opportunities*. The distinctions between industries will start to blur, and corporate giants are developing activities designed to adapt to this change. The difficulty for venture capitalists is to adjust to this change by financing those start-ups which can provide them with the necessary products and services, while going beyond a niche market.

Europe has imposed its *leadership in many industries*, such as automobiles and transport, aerospace and defence, and healthcare (see Figures 2.6 and 2.7). These industries are innovation intensive, but the output of the R&D tends to be less noticed by

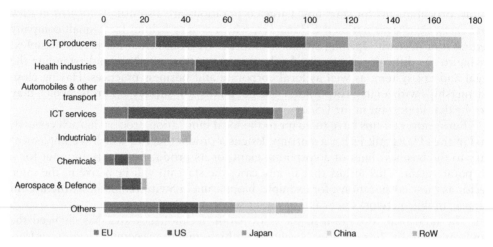

FIGURE 2.6   R&D investment by 2500 representative companies by industry and main country/region (€ billion)
Source: European Commission (2017).

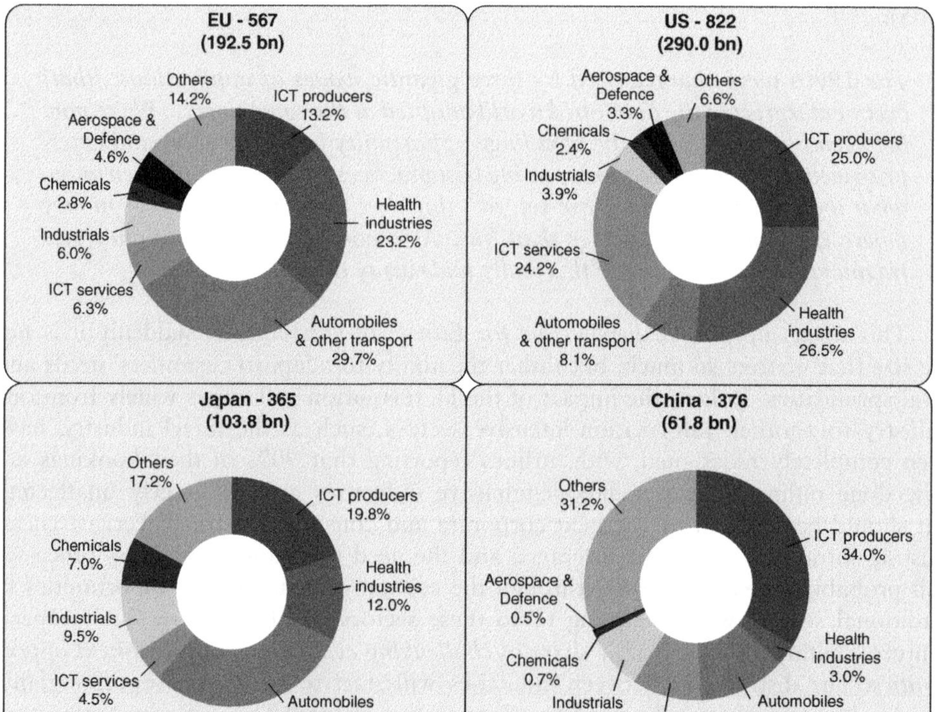

FIGURE 2.7   R&D shares of industrial sectors within main country/region (number of companies represented, R&D amounts)
Source: European Commission (2017).

the larger public. They also require less venture capital investments. This can feed a general misconception of Europe as 'falling behind', with the USA outcompeting any nation bar China. In fact, China is still a smaller country in terms of innovation (see Figures 2.7 and 2.8). If the USA is indeed outcompeting in terms of ICT R&D expenses (Figure 2.6), this is less or not true in other industries.

Europe is leading the pack in various labour-intensive industries, such as transport, energy and healthcare, which are willing to integrate IT, organise the virtualisation of their production, differentiate themselves from their competitors and provide their customers with innovative products. Its core competence notably lies in *incremental innovation*, which increases the value of an existing product or service, following the pace of the national champions in their developments. Even though less visible, the incremental innovations are the source of regular and long-term economic growth. This competence in incremental innovation could explain why Europe has caught up with the USA in the domain of innovation (see Figure 2.9). Companies in the USA are less likely to have introduced new or significantly improved services between 2012 and 2015

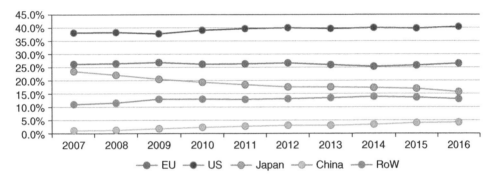

FIGURE 2.8 Evolution of R&D shares of main regions over 2007–2016
Source: European Commission (2017).

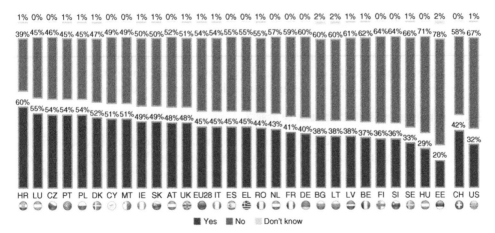

FIGURE 2.9 'Has your company introduced new or significantly improved services since January 2012?'
Source: European Commission (2015).

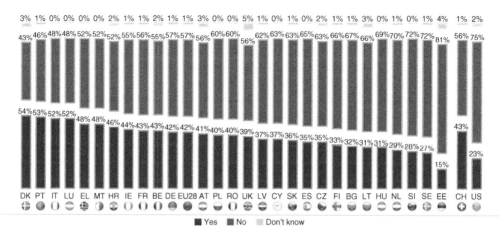

FIGURE 2.10 'Has your company introduced new or significantly improved goods since January 2012?'
Source: European Commission (2015).

when compared to those in the EU (32% vs 45%). This is also true for goods (23% vs 42%, see Figure 2.10), processes (17% vs 32%), organisational methods (26% vs 38%) and marketing strategies (26% vs 36%).

As a consequence, the compared risk–return profiles of American and European venture capital firms are relatively different. While American venture capital firms aim at realising some of their investments through an IPO, and hence focus on a limited number of start-ups, European venture capital firms are growing a larger panel of start-ups at a more moderate speed and try to avoid losses.

2.2.3   Challenges

In many respects, Europe has reached a first level of maturity in the professionalisation of its venture capital market. However, the situation is variable. The UK, France and Scandinavia are the most advanced markets, with active and numerous venture capital firms. Other markets lag behind (see Figure 2.11).

The challenge is hence a double one: offering a way for lagging markets to catch up with the most advanced markets; and developing a European platform in order to gain further competitive advantages and leadership in certain industries.

2.2.3.1   A Fragmented Market: Obstacle or Asset?

Building an active European venture capital sector, notably in seed and late-stage financing, implies the lowering of the barriers of intervention at the late stage in order to build pan-European champions at a cost equivalent to American champions. As for seed investments, it is necessary to rely on national (or even local) initiatives as they are the closest to needs, with control of the cost of capital – notably when it comes to public financing.

However, fragmented markets can also be an advantage. Companies are partially protected up to a certain stage from competition by national barriers (language, law, etc.). Those able to colonise European markets are solid and have proven their ability to thrive in adversity. Fragmented markets are also a way to test the ability of the product

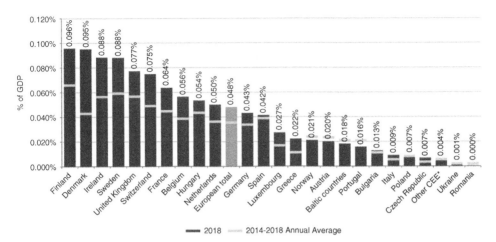

FIGURE 2.11 Venture capital investments as a percentage of GDP, by location of the portfolio company
Note: *Other CEE consists of Bosnia-Herzegovina, Croatia, Macedonia, Moldova, Montenegro, Serbia, Slovakia and Slovenia
Source: IMF, World Economic Outlook Database (GDP), EDC, Invest Europe (2018).

or service to fit the needs of very different customers. The difficulty for venture capital investors comes from the different staging of the financing of start-ups. Financing is quite linear in the USA, with increased sizes and increased valuations at each round, but Europe shows a different profile. National companies are deemed to follow the same trend, but will be rather less successful. Future pan-European or international companies need a second wave of financing rounds. This usually lengthens the holding period for initial investors (seed and early-stage rounds of financing) and dilutes their ownership (hence reducing their financial returns).

In many respects, the emergence of a true European venture capital market will be linked to an active direct secondary market. National investors should be allowed to exit when a company reaches a certain level of maturity, in order to preserve the viability of the venture capital value chain, without hampering the development of portfolio companies. Companies that were introduced to the stock exchange prematurely have had trouble with growing and succeeding. Allowing early investors to exit, while continuing to enlarge the company privately, is an important step to enable Europe to challenge the USA.

2.2.3.2 A Strong Risk Aversion

The common conception about Europe is that it lacks the entrepreneurial spirit which characterises the USA. David Landes states that countries 'can build as many incubators as [they] like, but if only 3% of the population want to be entrepreneurs, as in Finland, [they] will have trouble creating an entrepreneurial economy' (*The Economist*, 2009). However, the situation may not be as obvious as common sense might dictate.

Finland is in the top five of the most innovation-friendly countries in the EU, according to the EU rankings (see Figure 2.12). The Finnish public authorities have thus built an environment which is adapted to their own citizens: Finland benefits from the most advanced entrepreneurial environment in Europe (see Figure 2.13). Analysing

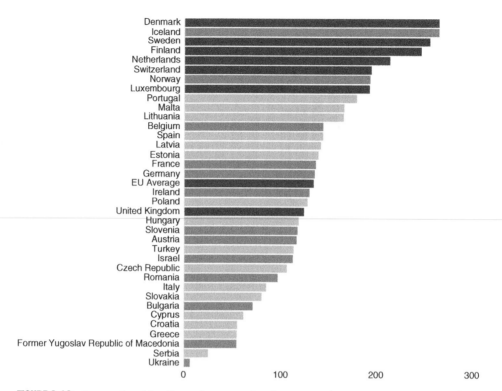

FIGURE 2.12   Innovation-friendly environment (performance relative to EU in 2010 as of 2017)

Note: the darkest shade (initially dark green) refers to 'innovation leader', then (initially light green) 'strong innovator', then (initially light brown) 'modest innovator' and finally (initially yellow) 'moderate innovator'. 'EU Average' was initially blue.

Source: European Innovation Scoreboard (online interactive tool), 2018.

the success of a given country (e.g., Finland) by applying the criterion of the level of entrepreneurial activity may be misleading if this criterion is applied indiscriminately to each country without taking into account its specificities.

Put differently, the notion of success in entrepreneurship may differ radically depending on the country, as much as the type of private equity investment strategy (see Table 2.2). It is not the case that a country is risk averse compared to another one, where its population does not want to take certain risks, but may be more eager to take others. As mentioned before, on the European continent, corporate venturing and the role of national champions (such as Nokia in Finland) determines the capacity of entrepreneurs to grow activities in symbiosis with their privileged partners. The size of markets also limits growth: meteoric successes such as in the USA are less likely to happen in economies with a few million citizens.

Moreover, European entrepreneurs may not want to grow their companies fast in order to sell them, but more slowly and durably to pass them on to the next generation. That implies there will be a path to sustainable growth which will be set by the owner-manager over the course of several decades, whereas in the USA it is more frequent that the owner-manager gives control to an external manager and eventually sells

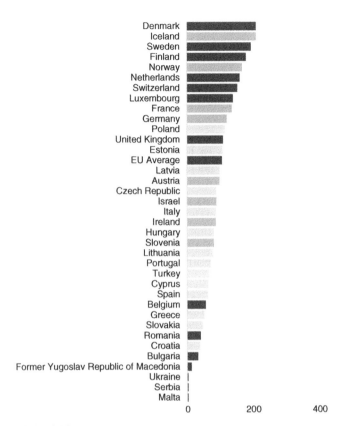

FIGURE 2.13 Opportunity-driven entrepreneurship (performance relative to EU in 2010 as of 2017)
Note: the darkest shade (initially dark green) refers to 'innovation leader', then (initially light green) 'strong innovator', then (initially light brown) 'modest innovator' and finally (initially yellow) 'moderate innovator'. 'EU Average' was initially blue.
Source: European Innovation Scoreboard (online interactive tool), 2018.

TABLE 2.2 Risks and returns of private equity investments

	Direct investment in individual businesses	Investment in one or several funds	Investment in a group of funds
Number of businesses in portfolio	1–5	15–20	Around 300
Level of diversification	Low	Medium	High
Expected return	Very high	High	High
Risk of default	Very high	Low	Minimal

his venture (maybe in order to create another one). Serial entrepreneurs are hence more frequent in the USA than in Europe: 35% versus 15% according to Axelson and Martinovic (2015), for whom this explains a difference in performance between Europe and the USA. Their study applies specifically to venture capital-backed start-ups. One should be wary of generalising the conclusions.

Indeed, if serial entrepreneurs are a factor of success for start-ups for a given economy, this is not necessarily the only reason for outperformance. First, because success (or failure) in building a company may not constitute a useful experience for building another venture. The reason is that each entrepreneurial venture is different from the previous one (as well as the conditions in which it is created), and a replication of the know-how may not be possible in smaller geographical markets. Moreover, having a long-term owner-manager may be more positive for the company: choices are made for the longer term, and this team will create more value in the long than in the short term.

Serial entrepreneurship implies that the owner-manager will leave the company after a rather short period of time (5 to 7 years). This means that US ventures have to bear costs such as recruitment, opportunity and changes. This also means that a US venture supports higher risks than European ones when top management is at stake. These costs are not borne by a European company whose founding team stays on in the long term; even though that does not necessarily mean that the venture will be more successful.

2.2.3.3   A Lack of Immigration

The education system may be part of the difference. Whereas the US education system is focused on practical knowledge and specialisation, European systems provide individuals with a broader background and an ability to learn by themselves. This kind of knowledge is useful in tackling changing conditions, reacting rapidly to unexpected events and coping with a lack of competence (notably as the population is less mobile in Europe).

It also creates a certain *stickiness in the economic and entrepreneurial environment.* Individuals will be less easily enticed to start a radically new venture if their education has convinced them that they are unlikely to succeed without a certain number of factors that need to be acquired at the beginning of the venture. In that respect, their versatility is also a limiting factor: European entrepreneurs are able to anticipate obstacles and to integrate them mentally. However, this cultural and educational background which has been transmitted to European entrepreneurs helps their ventures to achieve a better relationship with their environment, to integrate and also participate in it.

If Europe wants to improve its ability to create disruptive innovations, to go beyond the usual mental, social and cultural barriers that its system conveys, *it has to change its immigration policy and open its frontiers to would-be entrepreneurs.* In 2009, 52% of American start-ups were founded by immigrants, as opposed to 15% 10 years before (*The Economist*, 2009). In 2016, the figure was 30%, as opposed to 13.3% in 1996 (Fairlie, Morelix & Tareque, 2017). The immigration policy of a given country demonstrates not only its will to benefit from an inflow of outsiders, but also that it is ready to accept and promote them. For national outsiders, this gives the signal that the country is prepared to give underdogs a chance, which in turn may trigger some competition and the motivation to succeed, despite the lack of initial assets. According to the Global Startup Ecosystem Report 2018 (Startup Genome, 2018), 20% of the world's tech start-up founders were immigrants, while immigrants make up roughly 4% of the world's population.

Immigration is closely related to education. Because the universities in the USA are highly regarded, foreigners want to graduate and launch a venture so as to capitalise on their knowledge and their own experience there. Foreigners will compensate for the lack of local knowledge and immigrants do not fear failure. Europe has therefore to increase its attractiveness, perhaps by setting a different focus. It could promote its public research, and perform a fair selection process based on the capability of the candidates, and not their money or ability to succeed in languages and pre-formatted tests. In many respects, immigrants dream of living 'the American dream' and work harder and take greater risks.

2.2.3.4   What Will be the Next Source of Innovation in Europe?

Public and private research is determining the success of European venture capital. The *recurring lack of funding of universities' research* is often mentioned as one of the main reasons for the lack of new ideas and ventures. This supposed lack of funding is mainly a myth. The amounts invested in R&D per country do not appear to be a major issue, as some European countries are leading the way in terms of the amounts spent on R&D (see Figure 2.14).

In fact, the most important factors are *how this innovation is generated* and, even more importantly, *how it is spread across the economy*. For economies to grow through innovation, what matters is technology transfer. Fundamental and applied research needs relays to be transformed into innovative products and services. Venture capital is one of them, and enables entrepreneurs to bring theoretical and practical innovation to the merchant economy. Venture capital is combined with other relays between laboratories and project teams, such as technology transfer units within universities, and then from project teams to start-ups, such as incubators and accelerators.

European public research still lacks a systematic approach to technology transfer, though some progress has been made. The approach is largely bespoke and

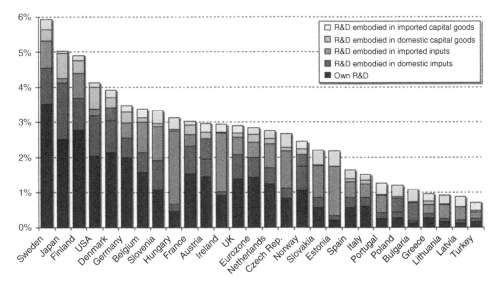

FIGURE 2.14   Percentage share of total R&D content in the national economies
Source: Europe Innova Synthesis Report 2008.

decentralised. Some countries, such as Germany with the Fraunhofer Society or France with the Institut National de Recherche en Informatique et en Automatique (INRIA), are leading the way. Combined with a relative lack of appetite for risk, this approach leaves Europe with potentially unexploited potential in terms of innovation.

Moreover, European universities do not have a leadership which is able to aggregate a critical mass of scientists and venture capital. Each nation is replicating the same system as its neighbours, with limited synergies. Cooperation in university research is improving in Europe, under the aegis of the European Commission and its programmes, but there is no clear unique centre of competence for any given discipline.

This fragmentation of its university landscape is a challenge for Europe, notably because the next waves of innovation are at the convergence between industrial sectors such as IT and biotechnologies; nanotechnologies and other sectors; new materials and other sectors. The need to set up multi-disciplinary teams is not only academic, but also physical, with a common campus and facilities to set up project teams and launch forward-looking projects.

As a consequence, European innovation remains largely invisible. This does not mean that there is no innovation, however. Europe grants a larger amount of patents per year (see Figure 2.15) than any other country or region, with the contribution by each country varying. The ownership of intellectual property developed in universities – and who has the right to benefit from innovation – has to be clear, notably to help entrepreneurs exploit intellectual property. In that respect, university spin-offs are easier to manage when the team is from one institution with a clear sector of intervention, falling into only one category.

The relative degree of innovation of these patents and their exploitation remains to be analysed. A first indicator could be the revenues generated from abroad by these patents (see Figure 2.16). Switzerland and The Netherlands are outliers, but it is still

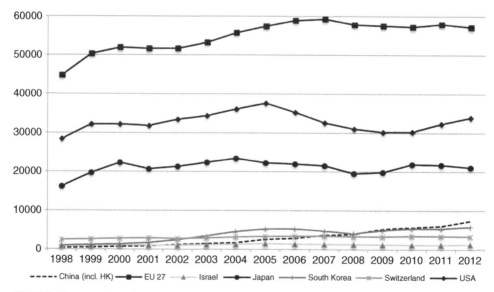

FIGURE 2.15   Number of patents according to the residence of the inventors, by priority year. Patents all applied for at the EPO, USPTO and JPO
Source: OECD, Patent Database 2019.

Country	Weight in GDP	Score (2013)	CAGR (2006-13)	Lead/Gap to EU-28 CAGR	Trendline (2006-13)
EU-28		0.64%	9.6%	**N/A**	
Cluster 1	9.3%	0.03	18.3%	12.5	
Cluster 2	29.5%	0.01	9.0%	3.3	
Cluster 3	61.2%	0.00	−17.6%	−23.4	
Cluster 4	N/A	N/A	N/A	N/A	
Cluster 1					
NL	4.5%	3.72%	17.5%	11.7	
CH	3.6%	3.07%	8.6%	2.8	
IE	1.2%	2.23%	28.8%	23.1	
Cluster 2					
FI	1.4%	1.38%	16.8%	11.1	
LU	0.3%	1.29%	5.3%	−0.5	
SE	3.0%	1.08%	1.7%	−4.0	
IS	0.1%	0.90%	:		
HU	0.7%	0.89%	10.6%	4.9	
DE	19.5%	0.77%	18.6%	12.8	
DK	1.8%	0.71%	1.8%	−3.9	
BE	2.7%	0.64%	8.2%	2.4	
Cluster 3					
UK	14.1%	0.46%	−3.0%	−8.7	
FR	14.6%	0.43%	6.7%	0.9	
AT	2.2%	0.25%	7.4%	1.7	
IT	11.1%	0.19%	18.2%	12.4	
CZ	1.1%	0.13%	17.3%	11.5	
NO	2.7%	0.08%	−11.7%	−17.4	
RO	1.0%	0.07%	−13.2%	−18.9	
ES	7.1%	0.07%	−0.3%	−6.1	
PL	2.7%	0.05%	8.0%	−2.3	
EL	1.2%	0.00%	−100.0%	−105.8	
MT	0.1%	0.00%	−100.0%	−105.8	
PT	1.2%	0.00%	−100.0%	−105.8	
SK	0.5%	0.00%	−100.0%	−105.8	
BG	0.3%	0.00%	0.0%	−5.8	
EE	0.1%	0.00%	0.0%	−5.8	
HR	0.3%	0.00%	0.0%	−5.8	
CY	0.1%	0.00%	0.0%	−5.8	
LV	0.2%	0.00%	0.0%	−5.8	
LT	0.2%	0.00%	0.0%	−5.8	
SI	0.2%	0.00%	0.0%	−5.8	
ME	0.0%	0.00%	:		
MK	0.1%	0.00%	0.0%	−5.8	

Note: Provisional: EU-28 (2011-2013); 2013 (BE, BG, CZ, DK, DE, EE, IE, FR, HR, IT, CY, LV, LT, LU, HU, MT, NL, AT, PL, PT, RO, SI, SK, FI, SE, UK, NO, ME, MK); EL (2011-2013); ES (2012, 2013).
Potential outlier: 2013 (DE, NL).
Eurostat country flags have been retained in the EU-28 aggregate.
Exception to reference year: 2012 (NL, IS, CH).
Exception to reference period: 2006-2012 (NL, CH); CZ (2009-2013); RO (2008-2013).
Data unavailable: AL, RS, TR, BA, IL, FO, MD, UA.
(:) = missing data.

FIGURE 2.16   Licence and patent revenues from abroad (% of GDP): 2006–2013
Source: Eurostat's ERA Monitoring Handbook 2016.

possible to see that some countries have a better ability to transform innovation into ventures than others.

As a consequence, European innovation is largely incremental, business-to-business and focused. This is probably why Europe does not necessarily generate large business-to-consumer IT companies. It does have its own large companies such as SAP, Nokia, Ericsson, Dassault Systems and Sabre, but these companies essentially address business needs. There are exceptions, such as Net-a-Porter, Spotify and Skype (now part of Microsoft), but the focus largely remains on heavy technology adopted by corporate customers.

2.3 CONCLUSION: EMERGING MARKETS, BUILDING CASTLES ON SAND?

In many respects, private markets are close to a 'gold rush' situation. Capital raised by private equity funds reached an all-time high in 2017 (see Figure 2.17), notably due to a significant increase in the amounts collected by private equity funds. Private equity funds collect roughly 50–60% of the total capital collected by private market funds; private real asset funds come next with 30–40%; private debt funds come last with 10–15%.

Note: the amounts in this figure do not match those in Figure 2.18, as Preqin appears to have restated the number of funds and amounts raised in its 2019 publication.

In the case of private equity, a smaller number of funds collected a larger aggregated amount (Figure 2.18). The average fund size has thus increased. The trend is driven by

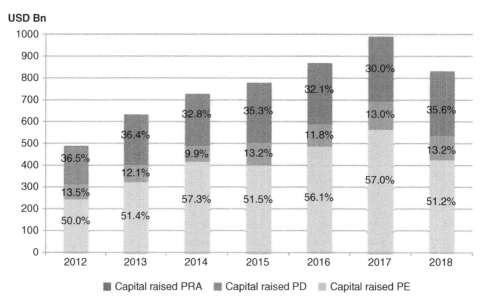

FIGURE 2.17 Global private equity, private debt and private real assets fundraising (2012–2018)
Source: Author, based on Preqin (2019).

USD Bn

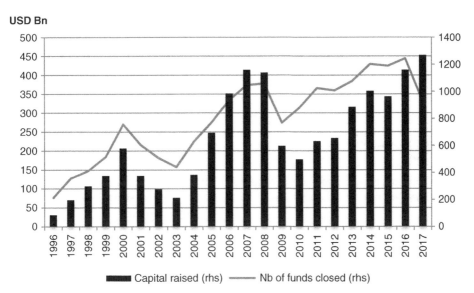

FIGURE 2.18 Global private equity fundraising (1996–2017)
Source: Author, based on Preqin 2018.

funds dedicated to mega LBO operations (targeting companies with an entreprise value above USD 5 billion), which have seen their size increase significantly.

Note: the amounts in this figure do not match those in Figure 2.17, as Preqin appears to have restated the number of funds and amounts raised in its 2019 publication.

The amounts collected remain largely allocated to developed markets (Figures 2.19 and 2.20), North America representing roughly 56% of the amounts collected in 2018 by private equity funds and Europe 21%. Asia represented 19% and the rest of the

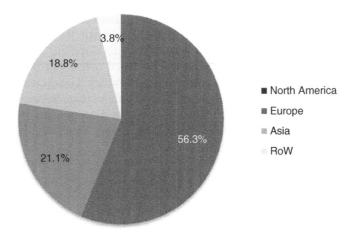

FIGURE 2.19 Regional distribution of private equity
fundraising, by amounts collected (2018)
Source: Author, based on Preqin 2019.

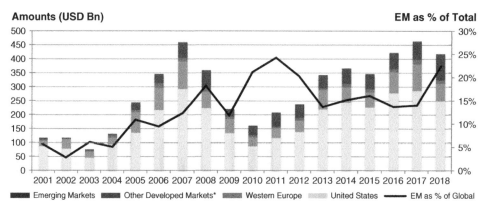

FIGURE 2.20 Private markets fundraising by region, by amounts collected
Source: Author, based on EMPEA 2019.

world 4%. When looking at the number of funds created, the percentages are respectively 54%, 17%, 21% and 8%. An inflexion point seems to have been reached in 2007. Between 2001 and 2006, emerging markets funds represented between 3% (2002) and 11% (2005) of the total raised globally. From 2007 to 2018, the proportion was 12% (2007 and 2009) to 24% (2011).

Interestingly, the proportion increased between 2009 and 2013, while the amounts raised globally decreased significantly. The logical conclusion is that emerging markets funds capitalise on a more resilient base of investors. This could be explained by a relative home bias of emerging fund investors allocating to local private market funds. Assuming that this explanation is true, it means that emerging markets funds can count on a local investor base deploying around USD 25 to 35 billion, and an international base which is more fickle and can deploy up to USD 55 to 65 billion in emerging markets.

This is particularly visible in Table 2.3. African private markets funds collected USD 1.1 billion in 2009 and USD 4.5 billion in 2015. Between these two extremes, the continent seems to attract roughly USD 2.5 to 3 billion worth of capital every year. One could assume that local investors and international development agencies constitute the bulk of the recurring capital, and that international investors come in punctually, possibly when foreign fund managers launch a local strategy. The same reasoning seems to hold for CEE and CIS after 2008: amounts collected fluctuate between USD 0.9 and 2.2 billion, with an exception in 2012 (USD 5.2 billion). Assuming that these variations are partially due to exchange-rate fluctuations, it seems that local funds collect regularly around USD 1.5 to 2 billion every year.

Emerging markets need time to structure their private equity sectors

This chapter and Chapter 1 have drawn multiple conclusions about the importance of transparency, the rule of law, economic policies, of universities and large corporations, as well as culture. Unfortunately, many emerging markets do not qualify to be elected as markets where a professional venture capital firm could be active. Davidoff (2010) provides a few examples in Russia (39th in the IESE private equity country

TABLE 2.3 Private markets fundraising by region (2001–2018, USD billion)

Year	2007	2008	2009	2010	2011	2012	2013	2014	2015	2016	2017	2018
Africa	2.27	2.87	1.06	2.31	2.50	2.75	1.89	3.67	4.50	2.48	2.28	2.90
Emerging Asia	26.40	40.66	15.60	19.06	35.58	29.76	31.03	35.58	38.46	45.26	53.00	78.27
CEE and CIS	9.87	5.90	1.50	1.10	2.16	5.20	1.63	2.00	0.93	1.66	1.23	1.56
Latin America	5.66	5.85	3.00	8.58	9.20	6.31	5.99	11.47	8.86	4.52	4.53	9.21
Middle East	5.06	2.38	0.67	0.85	0.36	0.23	0.89	0.96	0.26	0.45	0.20	0.09
Multi-regions	7.50	7.85	3.97	2.00	0.74	3.83	5.19	1.67	2.54	3.38	3.63	0.90
Emerging markets	56.75	66.52	28.79	33.89	50.54	48.08	46.63	55.35	55.56	57.75	64.87	92.93
Global	459.66	359.81	219.58	160.44	207.91	237.87	341.57	365.99	346.74	422.19	463.34	418.12

Source: EMPEA 2019.

attractiveness index[6] ranking), China (18th), Thailand (27th) and Indonesia (37th), but also South Korea (24th) and Australia (a developed market, ranked 7th in the IESE index).

Japan (5th in the IESE ranking[7]), South Korea and South Africa (36th in the IESE ranking), which are close to Europe in terms of legal and economic development, are still looking for the development of their own venture capital activity. Unfortunately, as demonstrated so far in this book, this is not know-how that can be exported, but needs to be grown locally through the nationally most active and innovative economic agents. As a result, the intentions of investors in terms of allocation to emerging markets remain fairly cautious (see Figure 2.21). The most attractive region is Asia (see Figure 2.22 and Table 2.3).

Following these conclusions, it is highly unlikely that private equity in European, African and Latin American emerging markets will grow into an established and professional activity (i.e., up to the standards of the USA and Europe) in less than a generation. It took 40 years for the USA to reach that result, and 30 for Europe to catch up. It looks very unlikely that emerging markets will achieve the same standards (notably legally and culturally) in less than two decades (at least).

---

[6]The IESE ranking (https://blog.iese.edu/vcpeindex/ranking/) provides insights about the attractiveness of different countries. The basis is 100 (USA), and the other countries are positioning themselves on the basis of different criteria against this reference. Though scoring can be criticised, as the USA is far from being the perfect place to invest in private equity, it shows how fund managers can expect to invest in other countries compared to the leading country in the sector. Comparison has its virtues, notably as this chapter and Chapter 1 are providing guidelines and background about how to build a viable sector. This is how each nation will be able to build a viable and long-lasting private equity ecosystem (see Part II).

[7]Despite a low entrepreneurship level – see Karlin (2013) (http://knowledge.wharton.upenn.edu/article.cfm?articleid=3145, last accessed 7 January 2013).

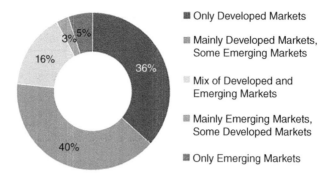

FIGURE 2.21   Private equity investors' intentions for targeted markets in the next 12 months, as of November 2018
Source: Preqin (2019).

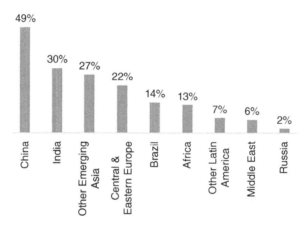

FIGURE 2.22   Investor views on emerging markets presenting the best opportunities in private equity, as of November 2018
Source: Preqin (2019).

Two generations will probably be necessary for the most advanced strategies (such as turn-around, distressed debt and LBO[8]), given the fact that Europe, despite its high level of development, needed so much time to create a professional venture capital activity, as well as a full LBO ecosystem. Moreover, Europe benefits from a diversity of situations from which nations and the EU can learn and develop their own model. This is not necessarily the case for other emerging markets. Not surprisingly, indeed, it is growth capital which is dominating the investment landscape in emerging markets

---

[8]Which are only really visible in Japan, South Korea and Australia, according to Cumming and Fleming (2012).

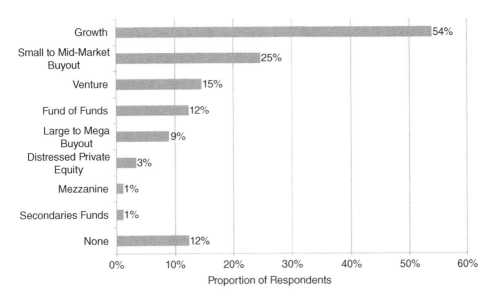

FIGURE 2.23 Investors' perspectives on the most attractive strategies in Asia
Source: Preqin 2012.

(see Figure 2.23). Venture capital dominates the intentions of investors (70% for emerging markets-based investors and 64% for developed markets-based investors, according to Preqin, 2018b), followed by growth capital (67% and 42%, respectively) and buy-out (41% and 59%, respectively). The majority of investors plan to maintain their current allocation (58–64% depending on the location of fund investors), while 30–36% plan to increase it (Preqin, 2018b); 6–7% plan to decrease it.

Current situation in emerging markets: the first boom – and bust?

One could argue that emerging markets have been attracting a lot of attention and commitments, and have given birth to significant investments (see Table 2.3 above). This is not necessarily the proof that these markets are adequately structured and are working efficiently. As Lerner (2009) states about the Chinese venture capital sector: 'the boom in the late 1990s and the early 2000s was largely fuelled by investors in the United States and Western Europe, who were attracted to the tremendous growth potential of the Chinese market despite the immaturity of the sector and lack of experience of venture professionals.'

Hence, if the intervention of international investors is one of the structuring aspects of the building of a viable private equity sector (see Chapter 1), it can backfire. Power (2012) states that even if Asia continues to attract attention (18.8% of allocations of international investors in 2018, compared with 17.9% in 2010), it is because of high return expectations. There is a direct and strong link between historical returns and current exposure in emerging markets (see Figure 2.24).

Indeed, if the returns on investments are not up to expectations (see Table 2.4) because deal opportunities are fewer or too expensive (see Natarajan, 2012 for China),

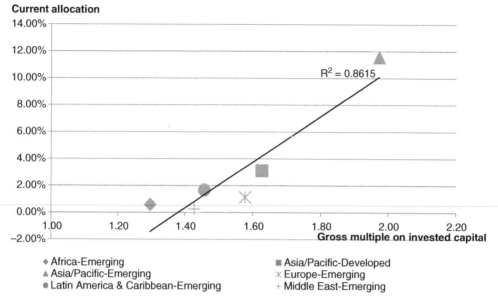

FIGURE 2.24   Current allocation to emerging markets and gross multiple on invested capital of emerging market funds
Source: Author, based on Cambridge Associates data (as of Q2 2018).

TABLE 2.4   Chinese private equity IRRs by year when the deal was struck

Year	%
1998	−5.9
1999	−8.3
2000	16.1
2001	8.2
2002	8.6
2003	21.3
2004	32.6
2005	31.3
2006	25.9
2007	5.2

Source: Centre for Asia Private Equity Research (*The Economist*, 2010).

and exits are more difficult because the local IPO market has shut down (see Deng, 2012[9] for China), international investors (which are often regional, see Figure 2.25 for Asia) can shift their focus to a market rather fast (see Table 2.3).

----

[9] Quoting notably the Centre for Asia Private Equity Research.

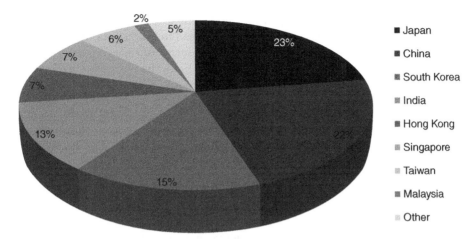

FIGURE 2.25 Breakdown of Asia-based investors by location
Source: Preqin 2012.

That potentially leaves the local initiatives without fuel (see Figure 2.26 for Latin America, for example). It is hence very important to pace this capital inflow and at the same time structure the market by taking the decisions necessary to face future busts and instabilities of commitments of international investors prone to fads and fashions in investing (notably on emerging markets) and to a herd mentality (the 'BRICs' leitmotiv has proved to be a powerful lemmings-to-the-cliff-like direction in that respect). Indeed, some countries (such as China, Mexico, Brazil, Colombia and Chile) have started to

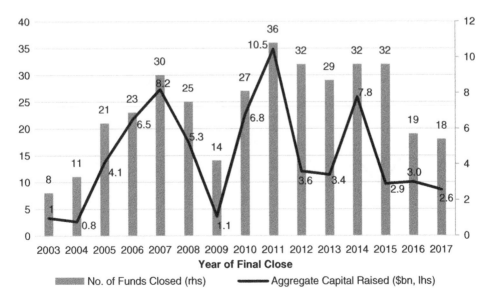

FIGURE 2.26 Fundraising in Latin America (2003–2017)
Source: Preqin 2012, 2018.

direct their own resources (notably pension funds and sovereign wealth funds money) towards their national markets (with the risks attached to this lack of diversification).

Recurring obstacles to a modern private equity sector in emerging markets

According to Preqin (2018b), private equity funds in emerging markets have collected on average USD 82.7 billion per year between 2008 and 2017. The lowest amount was in 2009 (USD 31 billion) and the highest in 2014 (USD 120 billion). There are multiple obstacles to the emergence of a modern private equity sector in emerging markets. The first is the importance of political sponsors, which are still much too significant. There are additional limiting factors which require attention, some of which are detailed below.

2.3.1 Emerging Asia

Preqin (2018b) counts 2809 fund managers active in Asia, and 640 local fund investors. On average, USD 65.8 billion was raised by 394 funds during the period 2008–2017 (Figure 2.27). There was an average of 271 growth and buy-out deals done for an average amount of USD 23.3 billion between 2008 and 2017, and 2040 deals in venture capital done for an average amount of USD 25.9 billion over the same period. Emerging Asia is increasingly a tale of two 'markets': China and the rest of Asia. According to a LAVCA and Cambridge Associates (2018) survey, China was the most attractive emerging market, with 6% of respondents finding it not attractive and 66% attractive. As a matter of comparison, Southeast Asia was not attractive for 10% of respondents and attractive for 50% of respondents. India was not attractive for 11% of respondents and attractive for 49%.

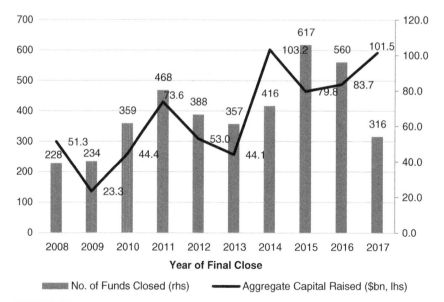

FIGURE 2.27 Fundraising in Emerging Asia (2003–2017)
Source: Preqin 2018.

- China (18th in the IESE ranking) has a strong level of political commitment in business, with red tape, lack of transparency and a high level of corruption. The country has received a lot of attention (notably regarding the set-up of local venture capital firms). However, Power (2012) states that a study from Pricewaterhouse-Coopers 'found a combination of corruption, government interference, and a lack of transparent financial information costs investors an average of 50 percent of the value of the deal'. Regulations are a maze, difficult to understand and the bureaucracy is unpredictable and difficult to handle (Knowledge@Wharton, 2011). The court system is weak and unreliable (Knowledge@Wharton, 2011). Fake accounting scandals have already been hitting China, and the innovation potential of local start-ups is deceptive. Local start-ups are often replicating innovation from abroad and adapting it to cater specifically to local needs (Bain, 2019b). The Chinese government itself decided to tighten the rules on private equity investments (Bain, 2019a), possibly to rein in what Bain describes as a 'bubble' (Bain, 2019b). Aggregate capital raised by Chinese funds (including Taiwan) increased from roughly USD 30 billion in 2013 to USD 93 billion in 2017 (Preqin, 2018a) and USD 13 billion in 2018 (Weiland, 2019).
- India (28th in the IESE ranking) has a democracy with nepotism, red tape and also a high level of corruption (see Kurian & Zachariah, 2012: 'India is possibly the least attractive of the emerging private equity markets', due to lower growth, poor corporate governance and bad returns). It has to deal with its regulations, tax regime and overall 'impossible government' (David Bonderman, TPG capital founder, quoted by Kurian & Zachariah, 2012). 'China may have similar woes but investors have seen profits there' (Rahul Basin, of Baring Private Equity Partners, quoted by Kurian & Zachariah, 2012). As a result, the country attracts between USD 1 (2014) and 3.6 (2017) billion, with an average around USD 2.3 billion every year (Preqin, 2019).

2.3.2 Latin America

Preqin (2018b) counts 382 fund managers active in Latin America (including the Caribbean), and 184 local fund investors. On average, USD 4.7 billion was raised by 26 funds during the period 2008–2017 (see Figure 2.26 above). There was an average of 78 growth and buy-out deals done for an average amount of USD 4.1 billion between 2008 and 2017, and 113 deals in venture capital done for an average amount of USD 494.9 billion over the same period. According to a LAVCA and Cambridge Associates (2018) survey, Latin America was the second most attractive region after China, with 7% finding it not attractive and 64% attractive.

- Brazil appeared for a while as the main Latin American magnet for private market investments. According to EMPEA (2018), from USD 1.6 billion raised in 2006 by private market funds, the total reached USD 3.8 billion in 2008. 2009 saw a sharp reduction to USD 0.9 billion, followed by a strong rebound in 2010 (USD 3 billion raised) and 2011 (USD 7.3 billion). This was the peak. Since then, the country has suffered from a relative disaffection, notably due to macro-economic factors. Average amounts raised yearly are roughly USD 2.4 billion, with a minimum of USD 0.7 billion in 2016 and a maximum of USD 4.4 billion in 2014. Investments amounted on average to USD 2.7 billion, with a high point in 2012 at USD 4.6 billion and a low point in 2015 at USD 1.9 billion. The investment activity remains dynamic, and Brazil remains the largest private markets market in Latin America, but the country ranks only 54th on the IESE private equity attractiveness index. The reason is that valuations of companies are high, infrastructures are lacking, inflation is lingering, regulations are very complex, bureaucracy is burdensome, and overall the political context remains far too present in the economy – and volatile. Another concern is that 70% of start-ups are replicating innovation from abroad, hence raising concerns about the capacity of the country to breed disruptive start-ups (Sreeharsha, 2012). This led to very contrasting views on Brazil by fund investors. According to a LAVCA and Cambridge Associates (2018) survey, 23% of respondents to a survey thought that the risk–return profile of Brazilian private equity was getting worse, while 45% thought that it was improving. These are both the highest figures among all Latin American countries.

- Mexico (42nd in the IESE ranking) is the second market for private equity in Latin America. It accounts for 22% of investments in the region. According to Amexcap, private market funds raised USD 4.3 billion in 2016. This has to be compared to USD 152 million in 2008 and USD 2.1 billion in 2015 (Goebel, Arangua, Valadez & Gonzalez, 2019). The country counts 177 active fund managers (of which 119 are local). USD 2.7 billion was invested in 2016 through 269 transactions (USD 6.5 billion in 2015 through 238 transactions) and as of October 2017, the dry powder was estimated to be USD 25 billion. Mexico is not spared by critics. It 'has a great economy, but there are very few things to buy [there]' for David Rubenstein, Founder and CEO of The Carlyle Group (Primack, 2012). The local business culture and the perspectives of Mexican entrepreneurs on control and governance are notably targeted by the comments. According to a LAVCA and Cambridge Associates (2018) survey, 6% of respondents to a survey thought that the risk–return profile of Mexican private equity was getting worse, while 32% thought that it was improving.

- Colombia (40th in the IESE ranking) has rapidly become the third most dynamic market in Latin America. USD 12 million was raised by private equity funds in 2014, 102 in 2015, 106 in 2016 and 49 in 2017 (Padilla & Arango, 2019). 111 private equity funds are active. Since then, amounts have regularly increased to reach USD 4.4 billion in 2014. This success is notably related to the political stability and some structural changes,[10] but this is only the start. Twenty funds are active (for a total of assets under management of USD 2.2 billion – including natural resources, which are normally not within the scope of private equity). The challenges (notably cited by Boscolo, Shephard & Williams, 2013)[11] are the limited track record of funds, a rather small number of potential transactions (Mexico suffers from the

---

[10]Decree 964 (2005), which established minority shareholder rights and introduced more transparency in corporate governance. Decree 2175 (2007) created in effect the local equivalent of limited partnerships (*fondos de capital privado*) and allowed pension funds to invest up to 5% of their assets in local private equity funds.

[11]http://knowledge.wharton.upenn.edu/article.cfm?articleid=3154.

same difficulties), the lack of awareness of private equity from entrepreneurs[12] and exits which remain difficult. Nevertheless, the Colombian government has launched a programme to promote and develop the sector in Colombia (Bancoldex Capital) and issued new regulations in 2018 to align private equity fund practices with international standards.[13] According to a LAVCA and Cambridge Associates (2018) survey, 4% of respondents to a survey thought that the risk–return profile of Colombian private equity was getting worse, while 38% thought that it was improving. This made it the most attractive country of the region.

2.3.3 Emerging Europe (CEE and CIS)

Preqin (2018b) counts 413 fund managers active in Emerging Europe, and 62 local fund investors. On average, USD 5.9 billion was raised by 25 funds during the period 2008–2017 (Figure 2.28). There was an average of 96 growth and buy-out deals done for an average amount of USD 4.6 billion between 2008 and 2017, and 141 deals in venture capital done for an average amount of USD 386.8 billion over the same period.

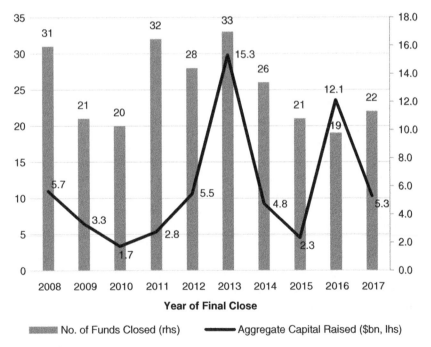

FIGURE 2.28 Fundraising in Emerging Europe (2003–2017)
Source: Preqin 2018.

---

[12]See also Blohm, Fernandes and Khalitov (2013, http://knowledge.wharton.upenn.edu/article
.cfm?articleid=3153).
[13]Decree 1984 (2018).

- One of the most promising emerging markets is probably Central Europe, due notably to the convergence with EU law, the close connections with other EU economies and the development of an active private equity market. However, its slow growth brings it closer to Latin America than Asia in terms of attractiveness for fund investors, with average amounts raised between 2010 and 2018 of EUR 0.7 billion. Though entrepreneurship lags behind Western Europe, exceptions such as Skype (based in Estonia but founded by a Swede and an Estonian) have promoted venture capital as a potentially winning strategy. Poland represents the largest private equity market in the region, usually followed by Hungary, Czech Republic and Romania. The Baltic countries regularly appear high as recipients of private equity investments.
- Russia is not spared by the critics (Primack, 2012). For David Rubenstein, it 'may be attractive to visit as a tourist, but it's very difficult to make a lot of money there' (hence, the environment, legal, tax and political issues are criticised). Geopolitical and political tensions, notably between Russia and the USA, have further reduced the attractiveness of the country. Western sanctions on Russian representatives and companies have sent a signal to potential funds investors. The indictement by local Russian courts of an American national leading for Baring Vostok, one of the most established Russian private equity firms, has sent chilling signals in the private equity community. According to a LAVCA and Cambridge Associates (2018) survey, Turkey, Russia and CIS were the least attractive markets for private equity, with 19% of survey respondents seeing them as very unattractive, 39% as unattractive and 4% as attractive.

2.3.4 Africa and the Middle East

Preqin (2018b) counts 532 fund managers active in Africa and the Middle East, of which 73 are in North Africa, 202 in the Middle East and 257 in Sub-Saharan Africa. The region counted 248 fund investors. On average, USD 1.9 billion was raised by 17 African funds during the period 2008–2017 (Figure 2.29). The figures were respectively USD 1.2 billion and 8 funds in the Middle East (Figure 2.30). There was an average of 77 growth and buy-out deals done locally between 2008 and 2017, and 42 deals in venture capital over the same period. In the Middle East, the figures were respectively 19 growth and buy-out deals with an average value of USD 577 million, and 25 venture capital deals with an average value of USD 148 million. The region struggles to attract attention. A LAVCA and Cambridge Associates (2018) survey shows that 49% of respondents find Sub-Saharan Africa not attractive and only 15% attractive. As for the Middle East and North Africa, the figures were respectively 42% and 9%.

There are multiple reasons for this disaffection. First, political influence and a volatile environment have not helped local private equity operators. Second, restrictions on ownership in some countries, as well as red tape and bureaucracy have also limited operations. Even if local GDP growth has often been strong for a prolonged period of time, a relative lack of investment opportunities and a difficult environment for exits have also restricted the development of private equity.

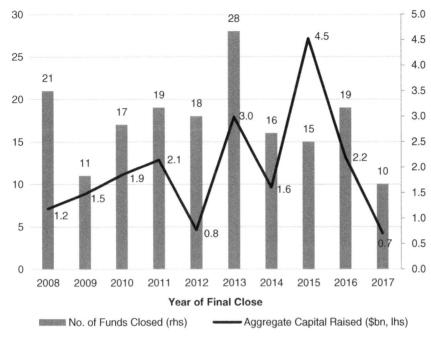

FIGURE 2.29 Fundraising in Africa (2008–2017)
Source: Preqin 2018.

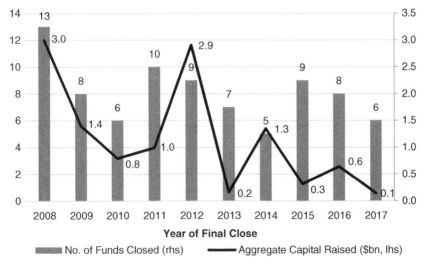

FIGURE 2.30 Fundraising in the Middle East (2008–2017)
Source: Preqin 2018.

REFERENCES

Books and Booklets

Cendrowski, H., Martin, J., Petro, L. and Wadecki, A. (2008) *Private Equity: History, Governance and Operations* (Wiley, Chichester), 480 pp.

Draper, W. (2011) *The Start-up Game* (Palgrave Macmillan, New York), 261 pp.

Gupta, U. (2004) *The First Venture Capitalist* (Gondolier, Calgary), 240 pp.

Lerner, J. (2009) *Boulevard of Broken Dreams, Why Public Efforts to Boost Entrepreneurship and Venture Capital Have Failed – and What to Do about It* (Princeton University Press, Princeton, NJ), 229 pp.

Mazzucato, M. (2015) *The Entrepreneurial State* (PublicAffairs, Philadelphia, PA), 260 pp.

Perkins, T. (2008) *Valley Boy* (Gotham Books, New York), 289 pp.

Ries, E. (2011) *The Lean Startup: How Today's Entrepreneurs Use Continuous Innovation to Create Radically Successful Businesses* (Penguin Books, London), 336 pp.

Senor, D. and Singer, P. (2010) *Start-Up Nation: The Story of Israel's Economic Miracle* (Little, Brown & Co., New York), 320 pp.

Newsletters and Newspapers

AlwaysOn, 'Build rather than buy – competitive advantage', 12 January 2005.

Barker, A., 'Europe votes for a single patents system', *Financial Times*, 11 December 2012 (www.ft.com/intl/cms/s/0/cf2e8746-439e-11e2-a68c-00144feabdc0.html#axzz2GFV9QgeJ, last accessed 29 December 2012).

Blohm, M., Fernandes, A. and Khalitov, B., 'Entrepreneurship in Colombia: "Try fast, learn fast, fail cheap"', Knowledge@Wharton, 2 January 2013.

Boscolo, R., Shephard, B. and Williams, W., 'The private equity landscape in Colombia', Knowledge@Wharton, 2 January 2013.

Davidoff, S., 'Private equity looks abroad, but may be blind to the risks', DealBook, *New York Times*, 21 December 2010.

Deng, C., 'Finding an exit from China gets harder', *The Wall Street Journal*, 24 July 2012.

Karlin, A., 'The entrepreneurship vacuum in Japan: why it matters and how to address it', Knowledge@Wharton, 2 January 2013.

Knowledge@Wharton, 'Risky business: private equity in China', 26 January 2011.

Kurian, B. and Zachariah, R., 'Global investors put Indian private equity story on hold', *The Times of India*, 26 July 2012.

McBride, S., 'US patent lawsuits now dominated by "trolls" – study', CNBC, 10 December 2012.

Natarajan, P., 'China's private equity market sees fewer deal options', *The Wall Street Journal*, 15 October 2012.

Power, H., 'Is bigger better?', *Private Equity International*, March 2012.

Primack, D., 'Carlyle's Rubenstein: where we're not investing', The Term Sheet, *Fortune*, 12 December 2012.

Sreeharsha, V., 'Brazil steps up investments in overlooked tech start-ups', DealBook, *New York Times*, 5 December 2012.

The Economist, 'Special report on entrepreneurship', 14 March 2009.

Weiland, D., 'Chinese private equity funding hit by sharp downturn', *Financial Times*, 15 March 2019.

The Economist, 'Barbarians in love', 25 November 2010.

Papers and Studies

Axelson, U. and Martinovic, M. (2015) 'European venture capital: myths and facts', London School of Economics, 61 pp.

Bain (2019a) India Private Equity Report 2019 (www.bain.com/insights/india-private-equity-report-2019/).

Bain (2019b) Spotlight on Private Equity in China: The Case for Caution (www.bain.com/insights/private-equity-china-global-private-equity-report-2019/).

Cumming, D. and Fleming, G. (2012) 'Barbarians, demons and hagetaka: a financial history of leveraged buyouts in Asia 1980–2010', Working Paper, SSRN 2008513, 36 pp.

EMPEA (2018) 'The shifting landscape for private capital in Brazil', EMPEA Brief, May, 12 pp.

European Commission (2015) Innobarometer 2015 – The Innovation Trends at EU Enterprises Report, Flash Eurobarometer 415, 200 pp.

European Commission (2016) Innobarometer 2016 – EU Business Innovation Trends Report, Flash Eurobarometer 433, 209 pp.

European Commission (2017) The 2017 EU Industrial R&D Investment Scoreboard, 118 pp.

Fairlie, R., Morelix, A. and Tareque, I. (2017) The 2017 Kauffman Index of Start-Up Activity, 52 pp.

Goebel, H., Arangua, H., Valadez, A. and Gonzalez, M. (2019) The Private Equity Review, Mexico (8th edn), June (https://thelawreviews.co.uk/edition/the-private-equity-review-edition-8/1190961/mexico).

Hsu, D. and Kenney, M. (2004) 'Organizing venture capital: the rise and demise of American Research & Development Corporation, 1946–1973', Working Paper 163, 51 pp.

Invest Europe (2018) European Private Equity Activity – Statistics on Fundraising, Investments and Divestments, 72 pp.

LAVCA and Cambridge Associates (2018) Latin American private equity Limited Partners Opinion Survey, 12 pp.

Padilla, H. and Arango, P. (2019) The Private Equity Review, Colombia (8th edn), June (https://thelawreviews.co.uk/edition/the-private-equity-review-edition-8/1190924/colombia).

Preqin (2018a) Special Report: Asian Private Equity & Venture Capital, 24 pp.

Preqin (2018b) Special Report: Private Equity in Emerging Markets, 16 pp.

Preqin (2019) Preqin Markets in Focus: Private Equity & Venture Capital in India, 12 pp.

PWC, IFC GHK and Ecorys (2014) 'SMEs' access to public procurement markets and aggregation of demand in the EU', 170 pp.

Startup Genome (2018) Global Startup Ecosystem Report 2018 – Succeeding in the New Era of Technology, 242 pp.

PART II

The Private Markets Ecosystem

Private markets have to be seen as an ecosystem. They are built on the interaction of fund investors and fund managers, the latter being in charge of deploying the capital in companies (Chapter 3). Private markets cover the cycle of development of companies, and provide solutions for all their activities (including in difficult times for example, Chapter 4). Focusing on private equity, at the core of the sector are human relationships and trust. The process of investing is based on building this trust and these human relationships, notably in dealing with information asymmetries (Chapter 5).

CHAPTER 3

Private Markets

A Business System Perspective

We are all investors in private markets (see Section 3.1), even though not necessarily directly and consciously. Financial institutions ('institutional investors') collect money from each individual through various channels such as, for example, insurance premiums or pension savings (Davidoff, 2012). They redistribute this capital inflow in the financial system, and notably to non-listed companies.

The money invested is usually split and allocated between different categories of investment ('asset classes'), in order to benefit from the risk–return profile of each category of investment. The expectations of private market investors with regard to the risk and return of their commitments vary according to their industry of origin; the source of the money they invest; and their economic and regulatory constraints. For that reason, financial institutions are themselves not necessarily investing directly in private markets. They have delegated the management of their non-listed investments to professionals (agents), on their account (principals). Evaluating the performance of these fund managers can be tricky and sometimes corresponds more to a leap of faith than a scientific risk–return calculation (see Section 3.2).

3.1 WE ARE ALL INVESTORS IN PRIVATE MARKETS

Institutions (such as banks, insurers and pension funds); companies; individuals and possibly other for-profit or non-profit organisations (such as endowments, foundations and associations) are the main sources of capital for private markets.

Non-institutional investors are high net worth individuals (HNWIs). These individuals, because of their personal wealth, are considered as informed and aware of the risks borne by the selection of private market funds. They can delegate the management of their assets partially or in total to private banks or family offices. These groups select funds for them.

Retail investors represent less than 10% of capital collected in Europe. They can invest in listed private equity vehicles ('evergreen' funds or holding companies) or funds specifically designed for retail investors, such as VCTs in the UK or FCPI and FIP in France. In the USA, private market funds are not accessible to retail investors. The only option is to invest directly (see Section 3.1.1.1) in private companies or through listed structures such as Business Development Companies (BDCs) or Special Purpose

Acquisition Companies (SPACs), which are in essence listed holding companies of private assets or companies.

For the purpose of this book, we will focus on institutional fund investors (i.e., insurance groups, pension funds and banks) that we will call at times 'limited partners' (LPs), and fund managers that we will call at times 'general partners' (GPs).

3.1.1 Sources of Capital

Sources of capital are split along three dimensions. First, investors can be *constrained* by regulations or *unconstrained*. Insurance groups, pension funds and banks belong to the first category. Family offices, which manage the wealth of families, HNWIs, as well as companies, belong to the second category. In between are foundations and endowments, which are largely unconstrained investors, with an obligation to spend a certain amount of their gain every year to keep their tax-exempt situation. Governmental agencies and sovereign wealth funds being public entities, their constraints can be very variable.

Second, investors can delegate their investments or execute themselves. For example, insured individuals and future pensioners delegate their investments. HNWIs can delegate or execute their investments themselves, as mentioned above.

Third, investors can have access to the full spectrum of investment opportunities or not. In Figure 3.1, investors have access to funds of funds, funds and private companies, because regulations deem them sufficiently sophisticated. In practice, many investors do not invest directly in private companies, as this requires a high level of expertise and significant resources, and involves a significant level of risk.

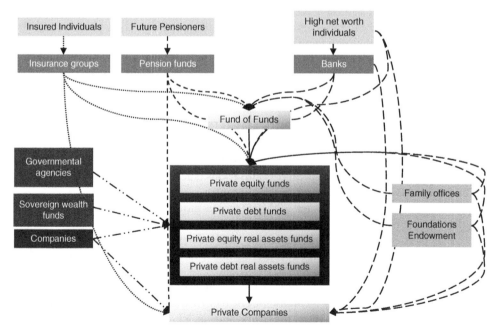

FIGURE 3.1 Capital sources and actors in the private markets value chain
Note: 'PE' refers to private equity, 'VC' refers to venture capital, 'LBO' refers to leveraged buy-out
Source: Demaria (2006, 2008, 2010, 2012).

Investors have three main channels to invest directly or indirectly in non-listed companies (Figure 3.1): directly (Section 3.1.1.1), through funds (Section 3.1.1.2) and through funds of funds (Section 3.1.1.3).

Western institutional investors allocated 4.6% of their assets under management to private equity in 2007. This proportion fell back to 3% in 2009 and grew to 3.6% in 2011 (Russell Research, 2012). On average, European pension funds allocated 3.7% of their assets under management to private equity in 2010 according to Preqin. As of 2018, allocations ranged from 0.4% to 3% globally, depending on the type of investor, according to Preqin (Figure 3.2).

The main absents of this ranking are banks. Their prudential ratios[1] ('Basel III ratios') are proving unfavourable to private equity. The same reasoning has been applied to insurance groups in Europe (Solvency II Directive). The method to compute their solvency ratios has increased the risk weighting associated with private markets investing. Over the course of the last decade, private markets have experienced a switch in sources of financing from banks and insurance groups to pension plans (see Introduction).

3.1.1.1   Direct Investments in Private Companies (thus Being at the Same Investment Level as Private Equity Funds)

Increasingly, investors, and notably retail investors (individuals), are tempted to invest their savings directly in non-listed companies (this trend is hence not reflected in the

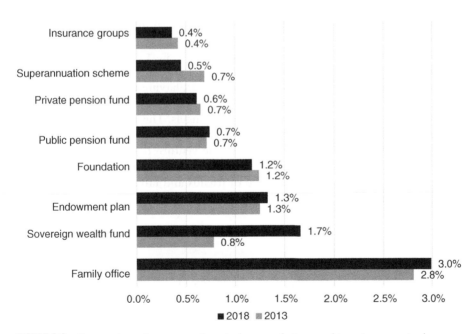

FIGURE 3.2   Proportion of aggregated capital currently invested in private equity by investor type
Source: Preqin 2018.

---

[1]The amount to be kept by banks in their balance sheets to cover their risks.

statistics gathered by professional organisations, as they track only their members' activity, that is to say institutional investors and fund managers). Crowdfunding, which connects individuals with companies willing to raise capital, is one venue for direct investment. Business angel clubs are another. Some countries (such as France and the USA) have set up tax incentives to help individuals to invest directly in non-listed businesses (see Chapter 4).

Though these initiatives might fill a vital economic need for these private companies, the risks involved in direct investing may be under-estimated (Davidoff, 2012).[2] In fact, investing in companies which have a very low level of transparency, where corporate governance has to be negotiated directly with other stakeholders, where investment monitoring has to be proactive, systematic and organised in advance requires expertise, know-how, time and resources. Individuals might be ill-equipped to undertake these tasks alone – hence their initial protection by law to undertake certain kinds of risky investments. The delays associated with the legalisation of crowdfunding in the USA have illustrated the difficulty in balancing the protection of individuals and their desire to invest in very risky businesses.

In contrast, investment professionals have the time, the experience and the expertise necessary to generate a deal flow of quality and analyse investment opportunities. To do so, a private markets investor must not only have some visibility and look actively for investment opportunities, but also have the relevant network. Such an investor must also have the financial means to manage the due diligence and invest. He must perform a complete and thorough analysis of investment opportunities and review the risks and potential return of the investment. Finally, the investor must be able to contribute actively to the development of his/her investments.

Investing directly in non-listed companies (notably start-ups) should be limited as much as possible to experienced investors. They often have operational experience and sector/functional expertise. Some wealthy individuals, having been successful in industry or in services, can coach entrepreneurs willing to create their companies, or help newly formed companies, thus becoming business angels. This is how individuals[3] were able to be part of the success story of Google, for example.

Most of the time, entrepreneurs invest in the venture they lead. In the case of a start-up company, the founding team puts in the initial capital to launch the operations ('bootstrapping'), sometimes with the help of friends and family ('love money'). Their stake is usually then diluted at every round of financing, as new investors put in money and receive shares in the company.

---

[2]'Retirement funds are being used increasingly for anything but retirement. Instead 401(k)s and individual retirement accounts are becoming money pots used to invest in business start-ups, speculate in gold and buy private equity investments. [...] The downside [...] is that there is no money for retirement if the business fails. And there is evidence that most of these businesses do fail. [...]'

[3]Andy Bechtolsheim, co-founder of Sun Microsystems and Vice President at Cisco Systems, and Ram Shriram, former President of Junglee and Vice President of Business Development at Amazon .com.

When it comes to organising the transfer of ownership of a company through an LBO (see below for an illustration), the management of the company can be part of the investors' syndicate, sometimes for a significant amount and even at par with the financial investors. This is the case when the LBO is an MBO, that is to say when the team of the company is structuring the operation and has contacted investors to help them fund the operation. In some cases, an MBO is operated by the management alone. In that specific case, the MBO is 'unsponsored'. If a fund or a financial institution is involved, the MBO is 'sponsored'.

Direct investments are probably the riskiest method of private equity investing, with prospects for the highest return. The rate of failure depends on the nature of the operation. Start-ups generally have a very high rate of mortality, whereas LBOs and growth capital are considered less risky.

3.1.1.2   Invest in a Private Markets Fund

Private markets funds are created in order for investors to delegate investment management to professionals, fully dedicated to this task, who can theoretically identify the best opportunities, negotiate the best deals and help companies grow. Some 'generalist' funds offer investors the opportunity to cover most of the investment spectrum of private equity, with an 'all-in-one' logic. In that respect, managers invest in a combination of venture capital, expansion and LBO opportunities. Even though attractive at first sight, this strategy has been declining as it suffers from multiple hurdles.

Indeed, investing in private equity is a long-term process, where experience is gained patiently and expertise accumulated on the ground. Teams are often of limited size and the personal network of team members determines the success of the fund. This is why the best funds specialise in certain kinds of operations, such as in Europe: Index Ventures Partners in venture capital; CVC or EQT Partners for LBOs. Some funds even focus on industrial sectors: Francisco Partners focus on technological LBOs in the USA; Sequoia Capital focuses on IT venture capital (in the USA for its main VC fund). Being a generalist fund manager requires competing with a large panel of specialised fund managers, which is very difficult.

In Europe, funds can be pan-European, such as Accel Europe or Balderton Capital Europe for late-stage venture capital; Permira and BC Partners for large LBOs. However, given the specificities of local markets, teams often cover regional or local markets, such as Scottish Equity Partners focusing on venture capital in the UK; or MBO Partenaires dedicated to small buy-outs in France. Halder, in Germany, covers mid-market buy-outs for the German-speaking countries (i.e., Austria, Germany and the German-speaking part of Switzerland). Being a generalist fund requires an expensive infrastructure, with local offices and teams.

Some fund managers have developed a branding strategy, seeking to replicate a successful positioning abroad (Sequoia Israel, Sequoia China); or diversifying into other operations (Sequoia Growth Capital) than their traditional positioning. Other fund managers, such as Blackstone, Apollo, KKR or Carlyle, have converted themselves into 'private equity houses', to invest funds dedicated to real estate, hedging, infrastructure and private debt (see Figure 3.3 and *Financial Times*, 2010).

Pure players (i.e., those focused on venture capital or LBO) are riskier if they have a very narrow focus. To select them, the fund investor must have an intimate knowledge

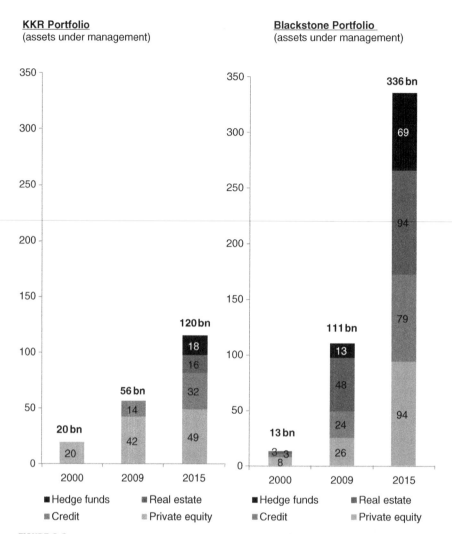

FIGURE 3.3 Structure of assets under management at KKR and Blackstone
Source: Favaro and Neely (2011); author.

of the industry where the fund is active. This can prove very tricky, if the fund investor wants to invest in venture capital, covering environment, IT, biotechnologies and other specialised sectors. To establish expertise in all of these areas of investment, fund investors have to put in a significant amount of resources.

The difference between diversified funds and specialised funds is thus determined according to the amount to be invested by the fund investor and its investment strategy. Given the necessity to diversify between a minimum of at least 5 to 10 funds, if a fund investor does not have more than EUR 20 to 30 million to invest, it could be an adequate strategy to invest in diversified funds covering the full spectrum of private markets and thus diversify only the operational risk, leaving it to the fund manager to diversify industry- and sector-wise.

3.1.1.3 Invest in a Fund in Charge of Selecting the Top Specialised Private Market Funds (Funds of Funds)

Funds of funds (see Section 4.4.1) provide investors with access to shared expertise. They can theoretically diversify their investments geographically, gain access to top investment opportunities and benefit from the support of specialists in their private equity investments. Technically, funds of funds are at the border between private equity and asset management. HarbourVest and Partners Group, for example, offer fund of funds programmes to institutional investors.

Fund of funds programmes can include the opportunity for their investors to co-invest with the programme in private equity funds, and sometimes even in underlying direct investments. This grants investors access to opportunities at limited or lower cost, with the possibility for investors to tailor their risk exposure and possibly increase their return. However, funds of funds themselves add a layer of costs and fees.

Some intermediaries, called gatekeepers, select funds for investors and build specific programmes for them ('mandates' or 'segregated accounts'). These gatekeepers can also manage funds of funds, but create segregated accounts for investors willing to invest EUR 25 million or above. These programmes are designed to provide a specific exposure to certain risks for the client. Hamilton Lane or Cambridge Associates are examples.

The main difference between fund of funds managers and gatekeepers is that the former are usually putting their own money into the product they manage (at least 1% of the fund size is committed by its manager – some fund of funds managers do not commit 1% of the size of their funds, however). Gatekeepers are pure advisors and thus their incentive is limited to a service provider's commitment to quality, and officially does not go to performance generation. However, as these advisors' mandates are usually renewed regularly, performance is taken into account in the renewal of the mandate.

3.1.2 Private Equity Investment Rationale

Any investor willing to allocate part of their capital to private equity is doing so for two reasons: diversification and return enhancement.

Volatility is irrelevant to measure risk

Financial theory often measures risk as the volatility of the price of an asset. As private market assets are not listed, this means that price variations are far and apart. This means that either private markets are low-risk investments, or that volatility is irrelevant to measure the risk of investments. The temptation would be to 'rebuild' the equivalent of a volatility of the price of private market assets. Some attempts have been made in this approach, by so-called 'desmoothing' private market prices. This is far from being convincing for multiple reasons.

First, this approach considers that the only way to approach investing is the framework developed for listed assets. This is not demonstrated. Listed assets offer a specific feature to investors: the ability to sell their assets fairly fast, assuming that there are buyers. This is often referred to as 'liquidity'. This feature fluctuates over time, depending on market conditions, and has a cost. One could argue that the standard framework is in fact private markets, with mandatory active investing and mid- to long-term horizons, and that stock exchanges are an exception on which assets are monitored, traded often and thus priced regularly.

Second, listed assets are subject to artificial volatility, notably due to the fact that there is a contagion of asset price movements. Regardless the intrinsic value of an asset, any significant piece of information will affect its price simply because other assets move. This means that risk is probably overstated on stock exchanges. This is particularly true as volatility considers that any movement, including when prices are trending upward, is a risk.

Third, taking volatility as a measure of risk and trying to force private assets into this framework assumes that the stock exchange is a valid monitor of asset prices. It is in fact a rough and imperfect proxy. Listed assets can change hands out of the stock exchange, for example on dark pools. Moreover, if an asset has to be sold in full, its price is going to diverge significantly from the market capitalisation, which is a product of the price per share multiplied by the number of shares. The reason is that premiums and discounts apply, depending whether the owner is a majority or minority shareholder; if this shareholder has specific rights; and depending on the context of the transaction.

Sources of risk: theory

The logical conclusion would be that volatility is not a relevant measure of risk in investments. A better and more relevant measure of risk is a combination of the *probability* and the *amounts lost* given a loss of capital. Another would be the *probability of missing a target return within a specific timeframe*, or the *probability of a missed payout*. These approaches are closer to a value-at-risk framework, and thus adapted to combine statistical and probabilistic data.

However, many investment portfolios are built with volatility as a measure of risk. As private market assets fluctuate less than listed assets, they show a low correlation with them. For example, private equity funds invest in mostly non-listed companies, and because their investment cycles are substantially longer (on average 3 to 5 years, as opposed to less than 6 to 12 months for a given fund investing in listed companies), private equity funds have created their own cycles, which last more or less for 5 years. These cycles are not correlated directly to the evolution of the stock exchanges index. They appear as an immediate source of risk reduction for investors building portfolios of different assets, listed and not listed.

Private market funds are nevertheless connected with listed markets, at least for two reasons. First, *valuations of assets* are often made in reference to the valuation of listed assets. This is done when an investment is made (at entry), and then regularly when the investment is held and reported on. Second, *exits* from investments ('divestments') are mainly trade sales or IPOs. If stock exchanges are depressed, public companies will make fewer acquisitions or will negotiate lower valuations.

Private markets are also affected by *macro-economic factors*. One of them is interest rates, in two ways: large companies usually borrow money to make acquisitions from private market funds. The higher the interest rates, the more difficult it is for a company to transform an acquisition from a private market fund into a profit, thus pushing down the price they offer. Interest rates also affect transfer of ownership through LBOs, as they condition the impact of the financial leverage in the deal. The higher the interest rate, the more difficult it will be for an LBO fund to generate the expected performance with the assets, as transfers to lenders will be significant.

Another macro-economic determinant is *GDP growth*. Acquired companies have to grow and gain value, and be an attractive potential target for future acquirers. It is easier to grow as a firm if the overall economy itself is growing. Private market strategies are affected differently by GDP growth. For example, venture and growth capital capitalise on a strong economic growth. LBO funds thrive in more challenging environments, when companies have to change and reinvent themselves. Distressed debt (see Chapter 4) is performing well when acquiring sound businesses challenged by recessions, restructuring them and selling them when the economy has recovered. These investment strategies are a source of diversification for investors, as they are potentially a support to build an 'all weather' portfolio, that is to say, a portfolio of investments which performs regardless of the macro-economic conditions.

Diversification to reduce risk: practice

In practice, private markets provide risk diversification at portfolio level for multiple reasons: they provide an exposure to a wider range of industries and geographical locations than listed stocks. They also offer access to companies and assets at different stages of maturity, and in different situations, ranging from inception to turn-around. Thus, risk reduction is mainly driven by the fact that fund managers are active owners.

A wider range of sectors of investment

Private markets provide an access to *new sectors of investment*. Venture capital offers an exposure to emerging sectors, such as information technologies, nanotechnologies, clean technologies, biotechnologies, financial technologies, new materials and other areas of innovation. These sectors often do not count listed companies among the ranks of their actors, except for conglomerates with R&D capacities in these sectors. Hence, venture capital offers a diversification vector in emerging areas. LBOs cover a wide area of sectors, sometimes targeting industry sectors which are not – or only imperfectly – covered by the stock exchange. Examples range from very narrow industries, difficult to understand by non-specialists in chemical industries, aerospace and pharmaceuticals, to unloved sectors such as funeral homes and undertaking, tobacco, gambling or mining.

A diversified set of regions of investments

Diversification is also geographical. Private market fund managers target emerging markets with sufficient maturity to offer exit perspectives. Instead of targeting local listed companies, which can prove to be very tricky and difficult to manage, it could make sense for an investor to invest on the mid to long term in an emerging country with an experienced team in buy-outs, for example. Some local funds are sponsored by established groups to set up their operations in Central Europe, India, China and some other markets.

A broad range of maturity of investments

The maturity of investments can also vary. Private markets offer the opportunity to invest in high-growth companies through venture capital, growth capital and small to mid-market buy-outs. LBOs provide access to companies willing to re-engineer their operations (for example, moving out of hardware to go to software), implement a new strategy (moving from selling software licences to cloud-based software), shift their business model (moving from a software subscription to computing as a service), acquire providers or distributors and consolidate part of the value chain, diversify or refocus, internationalise their operations and many more activities. Distressed debt provides access to companies in trouble, with a prospect of turning them around. In contrast, the stock exchange accepts companies exceeding a minimum turnover threshold, a certain number of years of existence and generally showing a certain degree of maturity.

Return enhancement: fund selection

The source of risk diversification with private market funds can also be a source of return enhancement. By targeting less efficient markets, investors can benefit from the value created by professional fund managers analysing, selecting, investing, managing, monitoring and exiting from private companies and assets. The source of diversification and value creation is thus not immediately synonymous with lower returns.

However, investing in multiple funds can lead an investor to revert to the average performance of private market funds, due to simple arithmetic. If an investor has superior fund selection skills, then a diversification through the selection of multiple funds should not lead to recording an average performance. Figure 3.4 illustrates this theory with funds of funds. Capital Dynamics generated this application by using a Monte Carlo simulation based on investment multiples. By selecting 30 funds, a fund of funds increases significantly the probability of reaching a multiple of 1.5 to 2.

According to Capital Dynamics, contrary to financial theory for listed markets, private equity fund selection increases the overall anticipated return substantially. This is explained by the persistence of the performance of top private equity fund managers over time (Kaplan & Schoar, 2003). The selection operated by fund of funds managers does not converge towards a private equity index, but leads to a positive selection, thanks to systematic selection in the best half of the sample, as illustrated in Figure 3.4.

However, a Monte Carlo simulation assumes that specific parameters are met by a given sample, such as a normal distribution of the data points. This is not the case in private markets. Moreover, very few investors have developed superior fund selection skills. As a consequence, the actual distribution is the one recorded in Figure 3.5. Direct investments in US start-ups are risky, with a 30% chance of losing the whole amount invested in a start-up. The reward potential is also significant, with a 25% chance of generating a multiple on investment of 5 or more. There is no normal distribution

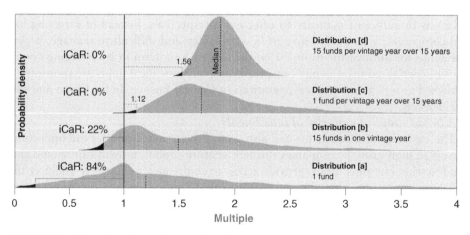

FIGURE 3.4 Diversification reduces risk and increases return
Sample: 1755 American funds
Source: Capital Dynamics analysis based on Venture Economics data up to 30 June 2007 including European and US funds as well as VC and buyout funds with vintage years 1983 to 2003 (2,699 funds), Monte Carlo Simulation with random selection.

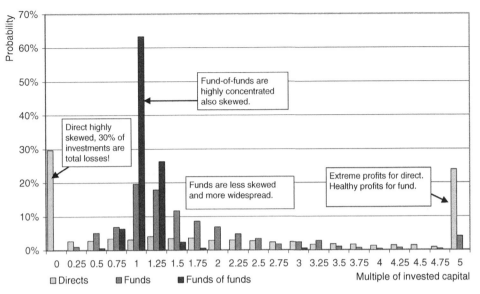

FIGURE 3.5 Dispersion of returns of direct investments, funds and funds of funds
Sample: 5000 direct US investments, 300 European VC funds and 618 funds of funds
Source: Weidig and Mathonet (2004), based on Thomson VentureXpert data; Wellershoff &
Partners, based on Cambridge Associates data.

of direct investments. This means that a Monte Carlo simulation is irrelevant in this
context. This also means that only active investors can thrive: investing a lot in multiple
companies will not revert to an obvious average, as there is none.

Funds are also not following a normal distribution. They are skewed towards higher
returns, with a 'fat tail' on the right of multiple 1. This is a visible illustration of the
ability of fund managers to create value and to limit losses. There is no fund generating an absolute loss. Funds of funds are theoretically tools for both diversification and
improved portfolio returns, a rare occurrence in finance. However, they are not evolving
as planned by Capital Dynamics. The reason might be the combination of three factors:
the impact of fees, which are reducing the performance of funds of funds; a fund selection capability which is inferior to that described by Capital Dynamics; and a statistical
effect related to the high number of underlying investments, which ultimately dilute the
returns of high-performing funds.

Given the increase in transparency in private markets over time, the role of funds
of funds has changed as we anticipated in previous editions of this book. The fact that
fund managers' performance is increasingly known reduces their edge as savvy private market fund investors. Moreover, diversification can be achieved by fund investors
alone, thanks to a better understanding of this asset class and the performance of fund
managers. As funds of funds do not necessarily deliver a better-adjusted risk–return
portfolio, they had to evolve or disappear (see Section 4.4.1). One of the main evolu-
tions has been funds of funds co-investing directly in private companies with the funds
they invest in. This reduces the weight of fees on the capital invested. It also provides
them with the opportunity to overweight the potential winners among their underlying

investments. This assumes that funds of funds managers are able to access systematically and identify potential winners.

Return enhancement: active ownership

One of the most common mistakes made when assessing performance in private equity is to compare the evolution of listed securities indexes (DJIA, S&P 500, FTSE, etc.) with the median or average performance of private market funds. These comparisons, however tempting they may be, lead to considerable confusion, prejudicial to the understanding of private equity.

First, *listed securities indexes are based on an arbitrary selection of stocks*. They often include the securities of large companies which are sufficiently liquid. This is very different from private equity, which is a less liquid asset class (compared to the market in listed securities), financing mainly growing small and medium-sized businesses.

Second, *the indexes of listed securities are an anti-selection of securities* – they are 'hands off'; that is, they are not managed actively. By contrast, private markets investing is based on the concept of 'hands-on' selection and management (which explains the structures exhibited in Table 3.1).

There is no passive management as such in private markets. However, mention should be made of listed private equity indexes, like those created by LPX or JP Morgan. On this basis, exchange traded funds (ETFs) were created. Investors can use passive management tools to target the underlying assets: a selection of listed fund management companies akin to banks or asset managers. They do not offer a direct and clear exposure to the wide array of private companies and assets owned by private market funds.

In fact, listed private equity stocks can serve as early indicators of upcoming venture capital and LBO bubbles. They are popular when markets peak and get disproportionately sanctioned when markets tank (see Figure 3.6). There are multiple reasons for this:

- Listed private equity stocks effectively provide access to intermediaries: fund managers. Their health relies on their ability to collect new funds and execute transactions. Most of the management fees collected are redistributed to their employees.
- These structures are less transparent than most of the listed structures, as their performance fees depend on the evolution of private companies and assets that are difficult to understand, and on which there is limited to no information.
- Information on these structures tends to be limited to the minimum set by regulations, which are designed for other types of businesses.

TABLE 3.1   Structures of private equity funds

	Venture capital	Mid-sized LBO	Large LBO	Fund of funds
Fund size	€100 million	€300 million	€3000 million	€500 million
Number of investments	15–20	10–15	5–10	>20
Number of employees	10	20	75	25
Management fees	2.5%	2.0%	1.5%	1.0%
Management fee per employee	€250 000	€300 000	€600 000	€200 000
Management fees (per year)	€2.5 million	€6 million	€45 million	€5 million

Source: Demaria and Pedergnana (2009, 2012).

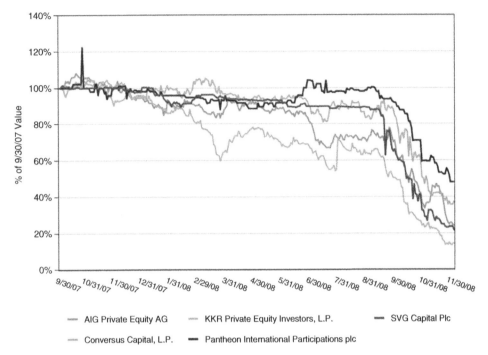

FIGURE 3.6 Publicly listed private equity performance
Source: Cogent Partners 2008.

▪ As they are fairly small structures, bundled with larger financial institutions in indexes, they are not specifically covered by analysts and are not well understood.
▪ They are thinly traded, because of their size, the lack of transparency and the fact that they are largely misunderstood.

Third, *market trends on the stock exchange remain largely independent of those in private equity*. Notably, the performance of stock pickers is known almost immediately, while that of private equity investors has to be computed and annualised after the sale of portfolio companies. This means that short-term analyses (below 3 to 5 years' horizon) are meaningless.

Finally, indexes do not reflect average market performance, but represent a proxy of it. It is tricky to compare the performance of an index with average private equity performance. Strictly speaking, a set of emblematic private equity transactions should be selected according to the criteria applied for stock exchange indexes and then compared with the latter. This would draw potentially fruitful comparisons, assuming that the selected private equity transactions could be a proxy for the private equity market's behaviour.

Returns in private equity and their persistence

There is nevertheless a method to compare the performance of private market funds with the performance of listed indexes: the Index Comparison Method (ICM), also more commonly referred to as Public Market Equivalent (PME). This method is explained further in Section 3.3. According to this method, private equity funds theoretically offer an enhanced return, compared to stock funds or exchange-traded funds (ETFs). Rouvinez (2007) states that private equity delivers a performance of 300 basis points higher than the returns from the listed sector. Hence, though there is still much academic debate, the main conclusion (Higson & Stucke, 2012) so far is that private equity outperforms stock exchange indexes (notably the S&P 500) by 500 to 800 basis points. As regards direct investment in companies, annual returns are approximately 12–20%. If the performance of mutual funds is between 6% and 10% in the long term, the targeted performance of private equity investments for institutional investors is situated between 11% and 15%.

As much as private equity has attracted capital (from an estimate of USD 100 billion in 1990 to USD 1.7 trillion in 2011 and USD 3.2 trillion in 2018 according to Preqin), its marginal returns have declined. According to a JP Morgan (2007) study, prior to the crisis, fund investors expected their private equity investments to generate a 12.6% net return in the long term. According to Coller Capital's Global Private Equity Barometer of Winter 2017–18,[4] 82% of fund investors expect to achieve annual net returns of 11% or more across their private equity portfolio over the next 3 to 5 years. Only 17% of them expect to reach net returns of 16% or more. 60% of fund investors expect returns to further decline as the private equity market matures.

Investors pay specific attention to past performance because, unlike in other areas of finance, it matters due to a phenomenon known as the 'persistence of performance of fund managers'. Kaplan and Schoar (2005) were the first to document the persistence of performance of private equity fund managers.[5] Sensoy, Wang and Weisbach (2014) note that 'private equity performance continues to outperform public markets on average' over 1999–2006, as they did in 1991–1998, despite the general maturing of the industry. Korteweg and Sorensen (2015) note that the persistence of performance remains factually true for high and low performers.

Fund selection skills, already referred to above, are of high importance as performance persists. An increased maturity of the asset class makes it even more critical. Sensoy, Wang and Weisbach (2014) describe the maturing of the PE industry as translating into narrower gaps of performance between top- and bottom-quartile funds.

As the dispersion has narrowed and fund managers have started to deploy strategies to optimise their internal rates of return, the analytical framework of the academic literature has shifted and does not account for these strategies. Therefore, a fund manager can drop (or upgrade) from one quartile to another without actually losing ground in terms of value creation and performance generation. Performance persistence might look as if it is declining on the basis of a quartile analysis (Braun, Jenkinson & Stoff,

---

[4]Coller Capital, Global Private Equity Barometer, Winter 2017–18, 12 pp (www.collercapital .com/sites/default/files/Coller%20Capital%20Global%20Private%20Equity%20Barometer%20 Winter%202017-18.pdf). Sample is 110 fund investors in PE funds, 40% of which are based in North America, 40% in Europe and 20% in Asia-Pacific.
[5]Robinson and Sensoy (2013) confirmed it, while Harris, Jenkinson and Stucke (2012) find that it declined for LBO fund managers after 2000. However, this is debated. Li (2014) found, for example, that LBO fund managers exhibit a stronger persistence of returns than VC fund managers. However, Harris, Jenkinson and Kaplan (2014) found additional evidence of persistence of performance of VC fund managers and a drop in persistence for buy-out funds after 2000.

2013; Harris, Jenkinson & Kaplan, 2014; Korteweg & Sorensen, 2015), but might in fact have persisted by other measures.

The nature of the fund investor and its performance

The fact that fund investors exhibit, depending on their skillset and resources, an ability to generate outperformance thanks to their asset allocation (Swensen, 2009) and their fund manager selection (see Introduction) proves that the persistence of returns of fund managers remains a fundamental feature of private market investing. Looking at the underlying deals of LBO fund managers (only), Braun, Jenkinson and Stoff (2017) conclude that there is a persistence of returns due to features of specific fund managers, and that it has declined over time. They attribute this to the maturing of the LBO sector, the commoditisation of financial and operational engineering instruments used in this area, as well as the move of professionals between GPs (or forming new ones). They also state that the increasing level of auctions has wiped out a large portion of proprietary deal flow, as well as competition for deals that have led to increased valuations (and lower valuations as well as lower persistence).

Beyond that common-ground risk–return approach, each category of investor has its own criteria and expectations, which can differ substantially from one to another. The source of funds invested by LPs conditions the expected return and the volatility accepted. In that respect, *family offices, HNWIs, university endowments and foundations* have an approach towards private equity which tends to target absolute returns. They thus tend to overweight venture capital in their asset allocation in private equity. HNWIs who have sector expertise and want to be involved in the underlying asset companies' life sometimes act as consultants, Board members or even executives.

Private equity is increasingly seen as a source of returns, which could help pension funds to balance their long-term liabilities. Indeed, academics (Lerner, Schoar & Wang, 2008) have stated that Ivy League American university endowments have generated a significant portion (roughly 45%) of their returns from private equity[6] and hedge funds – though the study covers only 2002–2005. Yale and Harvard have allocated more than 15% of their assets under management to this asset class. They currently allocate more than 25% of their assets to private markets.

Insurance groups take a different approach. The money they collect through insurance premiums may theoretically be recalled at any time to reimburse damages. Statistically, insurance groups estimate more or less – for a given instance of damage – which percentage of the sums collected will be called in a given year. They can infer how much can be invested in the short, mid and long term. To avoid swings in the premium they charge to insured people year on year, insurance groups have to keep a certain amount of money in their accounts (solvency ratios). They have developed expertise to retain potential gains in their balance sheet; mobilising them when a big event occurs requires a massive payout.

Not surprisingly, insurance groups like the bottom of the J in the 'J-curve' (see below), as this is a way to register immediate (even though theoretical) 'losses' and thus

---

[6]This might be related to their strong connection with their alumni network. An illustration of the strength of this connection is visible at www.cbinsights.com/blog/venture-capital/university-entrepreneurship-report.

keep non-taxed profits in their accounts to face potential future payouts. Insurance groups are thus interested in fund placements with a predictable cash flow profile and, if possible, avoid big distributions in a given year as these profits would be taxed and may not be mobilised for future payouts. Insurance groups are hence regular investors in LBOs and growth capital, in order to use the 'J-curve' continuously at its optimal pace. The mid to large groups have also developed in-house expertise to build and operate funds of funds in order to align the J-curve profile of these products with their own needs. They may not regard absolute returns as their main target.

Banks have developed expertise in selecting funds, structuring products and offering their expertise to third parties. Banks have to comply with solvency ratios, as defined by the Basel III Agreements. Some banks have created funds in-house, such as LBO funds, as they have the expertise to invest capital and also structure debt. However, this has given rise to a number of potential conflicts of interest (see Section 3.2.3 and Chapter 7), not only between the role of lender and investor of a given bank in the same deal, but also between its role as lender/investor and advisor. Most of the investment banks have spun off their private equity activities, as they were willing to keep their role of advisors (which additionally does not require any prudential capital to cover risks). A few have set up co-investment funds in order to participate in a large consortium of acquisition, where their interests as investors and their advisor role are aligned.

Since there has been a favourable interpretation of the 'prudent man' rule in the USA, the UK, but also in emerging markets such as Latin America, private equity is part of the asset allocation of *pension funds*. These pension funds are placed in the delicate situation of collecting money regularly from future pensioners for a given time, with a definite date from which they will have to pay out pensions for an indefinite term. They are thus investing in the long term, targeting the highest return possible, with the constraint that they have to face some long-term demographic trends which are in most developing countries increasing the number of pensioners with a limited number of net contributors to pension plans. Pension plans will thus have to recycle more actively their capital under management.

Even if this allocation sometimes remains rather modest (notably in Latin America), due to the time needed to deploy the capital allocated, it is the relative lack of information about the asset class which has limited the allocations so far.

Private equity fund managers' performance is usually based on two indicators: the multiple of investment and the internal rate of return. A third indicator has emerged progressively: the public market equivalent. In the case of a pension fund, these financial indicators are a minor component of the overall calculation to decide whether or not to invest with a given fund. Among the multiple other elements of information, two categories can be drawn: the hidden costs associated with being a universal owner and the hidden costs associated with private equity investments.

The hidden costs associated with being a universal owner

An illustration of the specific situation of pension plans lies in their status of 'universal owners', for some of them (Hawley & Williams, 2007). This category of fund investors already faces the future challenges that most of the others will have to deal with: their asset pool is so large that excluding certain assets from their portfolio increases the risks supported without any corresponding return potential. The large public and private pension funds in the USA and Europe are in this category. As are sovereign wealth funds (SWFs), even though they do not have the same constraints as pension funds in terms of asset allocation (Bernstein, Lerner & Schoar, 2009).

For these investors, it is *difficult to beat the benchmark* as they are technically influencing the market quite heavily every time they move. This is why they have focused their efforts on influencing the management of the companies they are investing in (notably on the stock exchange); adopted a proactive approach to climate change questions and corporate governance; and targeted alternative investments early on, in order to benefit from the high return potential that they can deliver.

In private markets, universal owners are important fund investors. They not only *provide a high level of capital*, but also play the *role of a signal* to other investors: if CalPERS invests in a given fund, it is because this fund has been through the thorough due diligence procedures of the pension fund and is thus of a certain quality.

One of the questions that universal owners face in finance is that once a company enters their private markets portfolio, there is a high chance that it will then be transferred to another compartment of their portfolio (such as listed equities). Once a private equity fund, for example, divests one of its portfolio companies, there is a high likelihood that it will sell it to a listed company or list it on the stock exchange – where universal owners are also heavily involved financially.

As such, the permanence of these companies in the portfolio of universal investors is not necessarily a problem as long as they create value and continue to grow. As a matter of fact, *private market funds act as an accelerator of the rotation of financial assets* in their portfolio.

The problem comes when private market funds adopt behaviours which are detrimental to other financial stakeholders, such as:

1. *Quick flips*[7] (Henry & Thornton, 2006), which consist of LBO funds to buy a company with a high leverage, keep it in their portfolio for 1 to 2 years, and then resell it. The problem with this practice is that fund managers usually do not have the material time to create value. The *costs generated* by the buy and sell strategy, *as well as the fees collected are not compensated by the value created* – regardless of the profit that the fund generated itself. In that respect, for universal owners, this corresponds to an *impoverishment* as the reward for the fund manager does not correspond to value creation. *Universal owners, just like the economy, are net losers in that case.*

2. *Leveraged recapitalisations* (also referred to as '*dividend recaps*'), which consist of increasing the initial leverage of acquisition of a portfolio company by an LBO fund and distributing the difference between the new leverage and the old. Unless the company has greatly outperformed its business plan, and the fund manager

---

[7]See Winfrey (2012) and *Private Equity International* (2012), illustrating the case of the acquisition of Norcast Wear Solutions in 2011 by Castle Harlan. The Swiss group Pala sold Norcast in 2011 to Castle Harlan in a secondary LBO for USD 190 million. Seven hours later, the business was sold to Bradken (an industrial conglomerate listed in Australia) for AUD 202 million (hence a USD 27 million profit for Castle Harlan). Pala sued Bradken and Castle Harlan. Bradken might, however, have had sound reason for using Castle Harlan as a finder (see Aidun & Dandeneau, 2005).

contributed greatly to its success, leveraged recapitalisations are actually a danger-ous operation. Not only do they *increase the overall risk of the LBO by reapplying leverage during an investment, they also reduce the incentive of the fund manager to outperform.* The reason for this reduced incentive is that usually leveraged recap-italisations are done to refund the capital investment of the fund (and possibly distribute an anticipated profit) with the difference between the new and the old debt. The fund locks in its performance at the time of the recapitalisation. What-ever the performance of the deal after, it will be higher in terms of internal rate of return (IRR, see Section 3.3.1). *As a matter of fact, leveraged recapitalisations are stopping the clock* of the investment, and offer an option to the fund to boost its IRR artificially.

3. *Successive LBOs* (also refereed to as '*secondary LBOs*' or '*subsequent LBOs*'), which could also be a net loss for universal owners, even if they materialise by way of a profit at the fund level for the primary, secondary, tertiary, and so on LBO fund. Universal owners have to bear the costs of the creation of a fund, as well as the cash management costs while the fund invests, the investment costs (including due diligences and possible aborted deals costs), the fees of the fund manager, the divestment costs, the carried interest on the performance and the cash management costs once the distribution is operated. For every LBO, this is the impressive list of costs that a fund investor has to support to hopefully get a return.

   It is hence easy to understand that once a fund A sells a portfolio company to a fund B, which both belong to the same fund investor, it is very difficult to offset these double costs for that which materialises in fact only by a valuation of the company at market price! The company will remain an underlying portfolio company for the universal owner, but in the process it will have cost the owner a significant amount.

4. *Delisting/relisting*, which is another example of potentially costly LBO operations. Delisting a company requires taking over the company (usually at a premium over its stock price, generally of 30% or more) to acquire a certain percentage of its capital under a time constraint, to legally squeeze out the remaining minority share-holders and finally to delist it. The LBO fund manager usually tries to relist it later, as this is the best way of making a profit, given the costs associated with the delist-ing and the price paid for the portfolio company. This listing is also expensive, and involves a certain number of risks, given the fact that listings depend on the general situation of the economy and the evolution of the financial markets. In that respect, delisting/relisting has very high risk. Some successes – such as Seagate Technology, a disk drive manufacturer – illustrate the motivation of such opera-tions. Silver Lake acquired the company in 2000 for USD 2 billion (Poletti, 2006), and introduced it in 2002 on the stock exchange with a market capitalisation of roughly USD 5.8 billion.

In addition to these costs, a universal investor has to factor in *friction costs*. Assum-ing that a universal investor is investing on the stock exchange and in private markets, the friction costs appear every time the business changes hands and the universal owner has to bear these costs. These costs notably include placement, mergers and acquisitions (M&As), IPOs and any other intermediary costs.

The worst case is probably when the costs related to the *asymmetry of information* kick in and result in a bad M&A operation. An example is the acquisition of Skype by eBay, with a write-off from the latter of USD 1.7 billion. A universal owner who owned eBay stocks and had been investing in a venture capital fund which financed Skype would not only have supported all the costs associated with venture capital investing, the cost of uncalled capital and the opportunity costs, but also the friction costs (investment banking fees) and the ultimate loss associated with the eBay excesses in the Skype acquisition.

Another example is the Vonage IPO (see General Conclusion, Chapter 8), where a universal owner who was invested in Vonage through a fund dedicated to primary issue investments and previously through a venture capital fund supporting the company would have seen a 90% write-off on the stock price. Here, in addition to all the costs listed before, the universal owner would have supported the IPO costs and possibly the mutual fund costs.

To justify these costs, LBO fund managers have to focus on real value creation and at a level which can justify all these opportunity and operational costs for fund investors. They also have to maximise the performance of their investments, which is not necessarily the case. According to Cao and Lerner (2006), most LBO fund managers sell their portfolio companies 6 to 12 months too early. The difference in performance is significant, because if the funds had kept these portfolio companies longer, they could have gained on average 18% more of the value of their investment. If the IRR of the fund could have decreased with the additional time spent holding the firm, the absolute performance would have been better and even greater for the fund investor, as it lowers the friction costs. In that respect, fund investors have to make a full cost analysis when they compare their venture/growth/turn-around capital fund investments with their LBO fund investments.

Under the crude light of this list of costs associated with investing along the equity value chain, a few conclusions come to mind. The first conclusion is that analysing the performance of private equity funds with only IRR and the multiple of investments (see Section 3.3.1) of these funds is pretty much irrelevant: *the value creation is what matters*. This can be assessed by the analysis of the performance of the asset after divestment and the analysis of the situation of the companies before and after each private equity investment.

The second conclusion is that *institutional investors should set a (realistic) return target for their investments in private equity* and sanction not only the under-performance *but also the over-performance* (notably IRR-wise). A high rate of rotation of assets can actually harm the overall returns of an institutional investor: it increases the cost of uncalled capital,[8] the opportunity and friction costs. The return target should be calculated as a trade-off between the overall costs supported all along the investment chain by the universal investor and the extra return generated by each intervention.

The third conclusion, which is counter-intuitive, is that *private markets funds should be designed to actually last longer*. Prior to the crisis, it took 7 years for a

---

[8] As explained below, private market funds deploy the capital they collected progressively, as investment opportunities arise. This means that some of the capital remains 'uncalled' until investments materialise. This uncalled capital bears some costs for fund investors, as it has to remain available at rather short notice and can only be invested in short-term money instruments bearing minimal interest, if any.

company to go from inception to the stock market at least (and recently on average 12 years) in Europe. This means that a universal owner willing to decrease the cash management, opportunity, friction and asymmetry of information costs should encourage venture capitalists to build longer-term funds and increase their holding periods.

Universal owners also have a high interest in changing the economics of the private markets sector, as the returns are expected to follow a decreasing trend in the mid term. It is in their interest to act on the fees and costs associated with operations, notably in the LBO area. That also means that the incentive structure of the fund manager should be drastically reviewed. Beyond the current debate on the level of fees paid to fund managers, the real challenge is to design an incentive system which better aligns the interests of the fund manager and the interests of the fund investors. An accrued carried interest for every increment of investment multiple generated, combined with a cap on management fees (or budget), would be a first step in the right direction.

Large institutional investors have already started to adjust, notably by buying stakes in GPs with whom they have invested considerable amounts. This allows them to gain a share of the management fees without forcing the fund managers to lower these fees (notably through the application of the 'most favoured nation' clause). Other investors have requested the setting up of co-investment programmes or asked fund managers to set up segregated accounts with their own specific fees. One of the issues is that co-investing does not guarantee access to the best investment opportunities. Segregated accounts might lead to a form of adverse selection, that is to say, investors get access to deals which are less attractive.

So, the trend is towards pre-defined budgets (see McCrum & Schäfer, 2012) and progressive carried interest (which grows with the realised performance), and away from percentages of assets under management. Fund managers will need to align themselves with that trend if they are to attract fund investors. However, the best are already attracting too much capital and will continue to set up conditions which are favourable to them. The result could be a dual system of private equity fund management.

The hidden costs associated with private equity

De facto, private equity has the possibility to finance a company throughout its life, from inception to turn-around and even beyond (see Chapter 4). Private equity funds bear a lot of direct and indirect costs, which can be categorised as set-up costs, management costs, due diligence costs and carried interest (see Section 3.2.2). Usually, private equity fund managers communicate on returns net of these fees, which are already substantial. Unfortunately, the list does not end here (it could notably include funds of funds or consultants' fees).

For fund investors, additional costs have to be factored in. The first is the *cost of uncalled capital* (cash management): once committed to a fund, the capital can be called at any time by the fund manager of a private market fund. The amount committed can meanwhile be technically deployed somewhere other than on the money market, but the lack of visibility on capital calls makes it difficult to properly time the rebalancing (and the corresponding sales on the public equity market, for example). Investors who have ventured to put the uncalled capital to work in hedge funds instead of money markets have suffered from dramatic liquidity issues during the 2007–2009 crisis.

Then come the *opportunity costs*: the fact that fund investors cannot plan the distribution from most private market funds means that some cash will stay idle (or on the money market) until it finds a new place. The fact that the amounts distributed in private equity, for example, are usually substantial magnifies the opportunity costs. This should notably be factored in when private equity funds show a high IRR and low multiple of investments: the rotation of assets is hence accelerated but not necessarily optimal for fund investors, who will see the benefit of this high IRR depleted by the lack of opportunities to reinvest it at the same level of return.

Beyond risk and return: liquidity, the third dimension of private markets investing

Private markets add another dimension to the usual risk–return arbitrage of asset selection: time/liquidity. The timeframes considered, the timing of investments and the weighting of venture capital, LBOs and other private equity strategies can significantly affect the overall performance (see Table 3.2) of private market investors.

However, for pension fund managers, the perspective is different. Given the long investment horizon of pension funds, longer time-to-liquidity horizons are not a risk, but merely the third dimension of the usual risk–return approach. Indeed, private equity has proven that its returns are less volatile than listed equity indexes (Figure 3.7). In that respect, the stock exchange presents an additional risk, compared to private equity returns, that has to be factored in according to the lessons of the 2007–2009 crisis.

One illustration of the consequences of this additional risk was the '*denominator effect*' that long-term investors had to face during 2008 and 2009. Long-term investors usually formulate their asset allocation as a percentage of their total assets under management. If the total of assets under management varies downwards (notably due to heavy discounts on the stock exchange), and private equity does not (due to the lower volatility of the asset class, as shown in Figure 3.7), then there is an apparent over-commitment to private equity ('the denominator effect').

Unless asset allocations are evaluated over 3 to 5 years, investors have then to divest to match their target allocation – or temporarily increase their private equity allocation (a strategy which was adopted by some US pension funds). The secondary market for stakes in private market funds is not large (about 8–10% of the total size of private market funds) and provides limited liquidity. Private market fund stakes are usually negotiated at a discount (between 10% and 30% of the net asset value of the fund) due to the lack of transparency of funds. Moreover, it is estimated that 6 to 7 years from

TABLE 3.2 Average net private equity fund IRR by type of fund investor

Type of investor	Entire sample	Time period		By region (1991–2003)		
		1991–1998	1999–2003	USA	Europe	Rest of the world
Funds of funds	14.62%	20.39%	13.00%	13.64%	14.77%	22.39%
Public pension	14.55%	19.26%	10.94%	14.27%	18.29%	17.48%
Corporate pension	15.05%	16.40%	14.47%	13.29%	18.83%	13.44%
Banks	16.85%	14.38%	17.91%	10.70%	21.97%	18.21%
Insurances	18.26%	23.77%	15.85%	16.38%	20.79%	17.64%
Endowments	16.00%	24.42%	12.26%	16.01%	18.62%	8.05%
Family offices	14.60%	19.50%	12.49%	14.33%	20.18%	–3.60%
Government agencies	11.80%	8.09%	14.66%	–2.19%	4.80%	19.36%
Total	14.88%	19.44%	12.46%	14.28%	16.52%	16.68%

Source: Hobohm (2010).

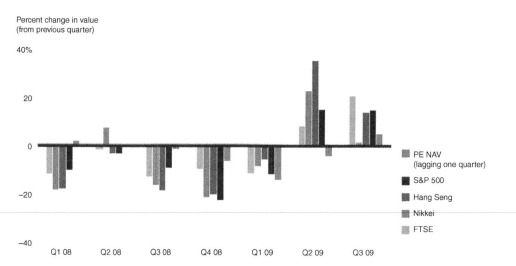

FIGURE 3.7 Comparison of evolution of market indexes and of the net asset values of private equity
Source: Bain (2010), based on Preqin and Bloomberg.

inception are necessary to evaluate realistically the potential performance of a given 10-year private equity closed-end fund.

What does this mean for pension fund managers? Liquidity being the third dimension of investing in private equity, either pension fund managers should decide to rethink the way their asset allocations are assessed (e.g., by adopting a longer term than a yearly timeframe); or they should pre-plan for a liquidity solution. Before the crisis, some sovereign funds – such as Temasek in Singapore – decided that instead of selling their private equity assets, they could securitise them. This solution has proven successful and could show the way for pension funds, when their programmes have reached a certain maturity.

These investment practices are not mutually exclusive. For example, pension plans can invest directly in companies in their neighbourhood, through funds based in the same country as themselves; and through funds of funds in order to address a lack of expertise (investing abroad) and sometimes a lack of resources. However, in many respects funds remain the best way to invest in private markets.

3.2 ORGANISATION AND GOVERNANCE OF PRIVATE EQUITY FUNDS

The relatively deceptive performance of their direct private equity investments has led institutional investors to give mandates to intermediaries. They have therefore focused on the selection of funds and funds of funds. However, these ways of reasoning are not mutually exclusive: institutional investors can invest in funds of funds to cover sectors and/or regions, owing to lack of expertise or financial resources; and funds in order to focus on certain strategies and benefit from direct co-investment opportunities. This requires know-how in evaluating and selecting funds, which is done in the context of structural imperfection of information and low availability of data.

3.2.1 Private Equity Fund Managers are Financial Intermediaries

Private market funds are usually created for a 10-year lifespan, with some exceptions. In the case of private debt funds providing plain vanilla debt to corporations (direct lending), funds are usually created for 8 years. In the case of funds of funds, the lifespan is usually 13 years, and infrastructure funds last 15 years. These 10 years are then subdivided into an investment period (generally of 5 years,[9] with a possible extension of 1 year) and a divestment period[10] (the remaining 5 years, with a possible extension of 2 to 3 years). Funds are advised by the fund manager (a 'general partner' if it is a limited partnership, or a 'management company' for other fund structures), which is comprised of the professionals ('principals') in charge of analyses and investment recommendations. The management team is hence permanent, whereas the funds are investment tools created for a pre-determined amount of time.

The fund manager is usually the only one to have a legal personality, as the funds do not have it. This means that funds are tax transparent: they do not pay taxes. Fund investors pay taxes themselves on the potential profits made by the funds, assuming that they are not tax exempt. There are exceptions, for example if the management manager and the fund are blended in a single structure such as a holding company. Listed vehicles or Luxembourg SICARs are an example. Another is open-ended funds, also called 'evergreen'. These structures pay taxes, and fund investors have to compute those taxes, possibly claiming them back, in their operations.

The distinction between funds and fund managers provides a strict separation between analysis and reporting functions on the one hand, and investment functions on the other. The alignment of interests between the fund managers and fund investors is theoretically fostered by the contribution of the fund manager, being at least 1% of the fund size, and currently above 3% according to Preqin. The assumption that a contribution from the fund manager to the fund increases the alignment of interests with fund investors is widely debated, owing to the agency costs (Tirole, 2005). In particular, it is clear that fund managers can collect back their contribution to the fund thanks to significant management fees. A 1% contribution to a fund can usually be recouped in 6 to 9 months of activity. A contribution of 3% can be recouped in 9 to 24 months. Another source of alignment of interests lies in the set-up of a performance fee ('carried interest', see below).

Fund managers raise the capital for the funds that they create in one or multiple steps (a 'closing'). The number of closings varies from one to four or even five, depending on the track record of the fund manager, the quantity of capital sought, the level of appetite of fund investors and other specific factors related to the fundraising strategy of a fund manager. A fundraising period lasts from a few weeks to 18 or even 24 months. After a fund holds its final close, it does not admit new investors. Fund investors commit to the fund by signing a subscription agreement, a document materialising their adhesion to the fund regulations.

Fund investors have little or no room for negotiations, as fund managers usually do not want to change significantly the terms and conditions of the fund, nor their investment strategy. Fund investors own the fund and mandate the fund manager to

---

[9]It can be 3 years in the case of direct lending funds and funds of funds.
[10]Also referred to as 'harvesting period', at times.

operate the fund. Fund investors can therefore theoretically change the fund manager if they wish to do so. Fund investors can do that for a cause, and sometimes without cause (through a 'no fault divorce clause'). They usually have to gather a qualified majority (most of the time with a qualified majority, and sometimes by a unanimous decision bar the fund manager itself). These rules are defined by the fund regulations (see Template 2 as an example for a limited partnership). In practice, fund investors rarely change the fund manager, which has the upper hand in terms of negotiations and power.

Fund managers are in charge of investing the capital they managed, by analysing investment opportunities, filtering them and negotiating the terms of the investment. They then call the capital from the investors to make the investment. Once the investment is made, the fund managers are in charge of monitoring it, controlling the execution of the plan and taking all the necessary action to generate a return on the investment. They are in charge of reporting, that is communicating regularly to the fund investors on the situation of the funds that they manage for them. Then, the fund managers are in charge of disposing of the investments (exit through a trade sale, an IPO, a sale to another investor or possibly a liquidation) and distributing the proceeds of this disposal.

What happens if a fund has not sold all of its assets at the end of its lifespan? Four main options can be explored. First, most of the fund regulations plan extensions. Private equity funds can usually be extended twice a year, sometimes at the discretion of the fund manager and sometimes upon a vote from the fund investors (at the simple or qualified majority). Second, it is possible to try to sell the remaining assets of the fund at all costs, on the direct secondary market or even for a symbolic euro to the management of the assets in portfolio.

Third, it is possible to restructure the fund to transfer its assets to a new fund in a so-called 'GP-led restructuring'. In this case, the fund manager of the current fund which is reaching the end of its lifespan creates a new fund, whose purpose is only to acquire the assets of the old fund. The fund investors in the old fund are offered the choice to be transferred to the new fund, or to get cash. New investors in the new fund would replace the exiting ones and thus provide the cash to pay them out. The new fund is created with the idea that the assets are valuable but would not be sold in good condition at that time. Although this scenario appears to be a win–win situation, it creates a conflict of interest. The buyer and the seller of the asset are the same fund manager. Setting an objective price to transfer the assets from the old fund to the new one is therefore difficult. For example, let's imagine that the transfer is done at the current net asset value (NAV). Exiting investors from the old fund might argue that the price is too low and does not reflect the full value of the assets, as fund managers tend to value the assets in the portfolio conservatively. New investors might argue that the price is too high as assets are traded at a discount on the secondary market. This could pave the way to litigation.

Fourth, and this is the most frequent scenario: fund managers continue to manage the fund beyond the term set by the fund regulations (including the extension period). There is usually no sanction for doing so, and the alternative for fund investors (selling at a discount or for a symbolic euro) is unsavoury. Therefore, funds can last 15 or 20 years, far beyond the expected lifespan at their launch. This is particularly true for venture capital funds which hold significant zombie firms.

3.2.2 Incentives and Fees

Figure 3.8 provides an overall perspective of the cash flows for private market funds.

Fund investors and the fund manager commit capital to the fund. The sum of the commitments is the fund size.

The compensation of the fund manager is called a 'management fee' and is paid by the fund for the services provided (advice, analyses, fund management and reporting). This fee is generally 1.25%[11] to 2.5%[12] per year for a direct investment fund (around 0.5–1% per year for a fund of funds), depending on the fund size. This fee is calculated on the fund size[13] during the investment period, and usually on the NAV of the portfolio once the investment period has ended.

The NAV of a fund is computed by the fund manager to provide fund investors with the best estimate possible of the value of the assets in the portfolio. This 'fair value'[14] has to reflect realistically the current value of the assets as if they were to be sold as of date.

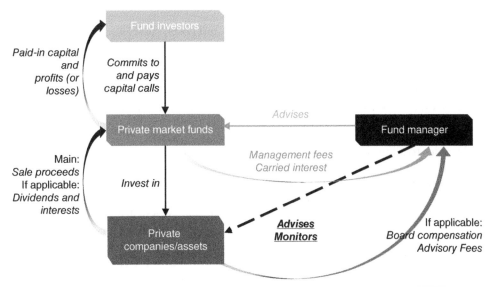

FIGURE 3.8 Cash flows of private market funds
Source: Demaria (2006, 2008, 2010, 2012).

---

[11] For example, for funds exceeding USD 10 billion of funds size (committed capital).

[12] For example, for small funds of less than USD 50 million of funds size.

[13] The basis of calculation can vary, but is usually the committed capital (i.e., the fund size) or at times the capital invested during the investment period and the net asset value of the fund (i.e., the residual value of the fund) during the divestment period or at times on the committed capital with a declining scale. In the latter case, management fees decrease from 1.5% to 1.25% per year, then 1%, 0.75% and so on. Management fees are usually collected by the fund manager quarterly in advance.

[14] Defined as 'the price that would be received to sell an asset in an orderly transaction between market participants at the measurement date', 'in the principal market or in its absence the most advantageous market for the asset'.

The International Private Equity and Venture Capital Valuation Guidelines (IPEV),[15] defined and endorsed by major professional private equity associations, provide some guidance to fund managers on how to compute the value of the assets in a portfolio. As of December 2018, the IPEV define the following methods to value an asset: a market approach, using multiples of aggregates such as sales or EBIT(D)(A), industry valuation benchmarks or available market prices (also known as listed comparables); an income approach (discounted cash flows); and a replacement cost approach (net assets). The results have to be adjusted according to specific factors, such as the nature of the instruments used and the rights (such as veto, multiple votes and liquidation preferences) conferred by these instruments. In the EU, the valuation exercise has to be done independently either by a third party or within the fund manager by a department working independently.

Increasingly, management fees are debated, as they substantially dent the net results of fund investors. Some fund managers, such as Bain Capital, have started to offer different mechanisms – such as a lower management fee and higher carried interest (see next paragraph for a definition).[16]

Moreover, the fund supports additional fees and costs, such as:

■ An initial set-up cost, generally 1% of total fund size[17] (at most).
■ Fund administrator and custodian fees, if applicable, generally 0.05–0.1% per year.
■ Operational costs, which can vary substantially, and cover audit, legal and expertise fees, as well as due diligence expenses for new investments. Should these new investments not be materialised, these expenses are lost ('abort fees').

In order to align the interests between fund investors and fund managers, the latter are entitled to a performance fee called 'carried interest' (or 'carry') of generally 20%[18] (5–10% for funds of funds) on the profit generated. Some fund managers have indexed their carried interest on the progression of certain performance metrics.

For example, if a fund does not generate an IRR higher than 10%, the carried interest is 0%; if the fund generates an IRR between 8% and 12.99%, the carried interest is 10%; if the IRR is between 13% and 16.99%, the carried interest is 15%; if the IRR is between 17% and 19.99%, the carried interest is 20%; if the IRR is between 20% and 24.99%, the carried interest is 25%; if the IRR is above 25%, the carried interest is 30%. This can lead to some biases, since the IRR as a metric is not immune to heavy criticism (see Section 3.3.1.2[19]). The alternative would be to use multiples of invested

---

[15] www.privateequityvaluation.com/.
[16] According to Primack (2012a), the three options available for limited partners in Bain Capital Fund XI were:

■ Market standard: 1.5% management fee, 20% carried interest, 7% preferred return.
■ 1% management fee, 30% carried interest, 7% preferred return.
■ 0.5% management fee, 30% carried interest, no preferred return.

[17] This can go up to 3% for retail funds such as FPCI and FIP in France.
[18] Some fund managers charge lower carried interest, for example in senior debt or timberland. Some fund managers with the best performance charge 25% or even 30% of carried interest.
[19] And Kocis, Bachman, Long and Nickels (2009), Chapters 7, 9 and 11.

capital or a public market equivalent to set the thresholds and ensure the best alignment of interest.

However, to provide a guaranteed return for the risks taken by the investors, which are higher than the risks taken by the fund managers, it is a general business practice that fund investors are entitled to a preferred return rate ('hurdle rate') which usually varies between 6% and 8%. The pro-rata of this preferred return is then usually paid to the fund manager ('catch-up'), if the performance is sufficient and if the fund regulation plans for it. Beyond this, the allocation of performance is done along the rule defined by the carried interest.

Therefore, the sequence is as follows (see Figures 3.9–3.11): first, the capital is committed and invested. Then, the committed capital is fully repaid, and the hurdle rate is distributed to the fund investors (if the fund regulations planned it) – for example 8%, then the catch-up which is 25% of the hurdle rate[20] and then 80% of performance to the fund investors and the carried interest of 20% to the fund managers. This sequence can be operated according to two different approaches: the European and the American waterfall.

The European waterfall, which is adopted by more than 80% of funds worldwide, disposes that the sequence should be applied at the fund level. Before any profit is distributed to the fund manager, the fund manager has to fully repay the fund to fund investors, and the hurdle rate (if any) too. The advantage of this approach is that it is prudent and any profit distributed is acquired definitely. However, this means that the fund manager has to wait usually 6 years or more until the distribution of a catch-up (if any) and carried interest.

The American waterfall, which is adopted only by the very best fund managers who can impose it on fund investors, disposes that the sequence applies deal by deal. If an investment was sold, the fund manager has to repay the capital used for this investment, make sure that the hurdle rate is cleared and then distribute the profit along the lines of the carried interest clauses. This approach enables the fund manager to collect the carried interest earlier. However, it also implies that in the advent of a subsequent investment leading to a loss, the fund manager would have to repay the carried interest collected to compensate for the loss. This is the 'claw back' clause. The fund manager therefore has to make sure to keep enough of the carried interest collected from early divestments to repay any loss appearing later.

Figure 3.9 shows the composition of a fund at its creation. Usually, the fund manager commits 1% (sometimes more[21]), while fund investors commit the rest.

Figure 3.10 shows the breakdown of the fund investment and expenses during the investment period. The fund pays fees to the management company and supports

---

[20]The catch-up rebalances the distribution to the fund manager. If the carried interest is 20%, it means that the fund manager should collect one-fifth of the profit of the fund. If the hurdle rate was fully distributed to the fund investors and the fund manager has to catch up with this distribution, the fund manager is entitled to collect one-quarter of the amount distributed as a hurdle rate. After the payment of the hurdle rate and the catch-up, the fund investors have been paid 8% and the fund manager 2%, which are respectively 80% and 20% of the sum distributed so far.

[21]According to industry statistics from Preqin and MJ Hudson, in 2018 the average was around 3% of the fund size, some teams providing 1% and others committing up to 15%.

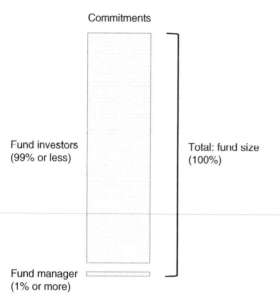

FIGURE 3.9   Cash structure of a fund at creation stage
Source: Author.

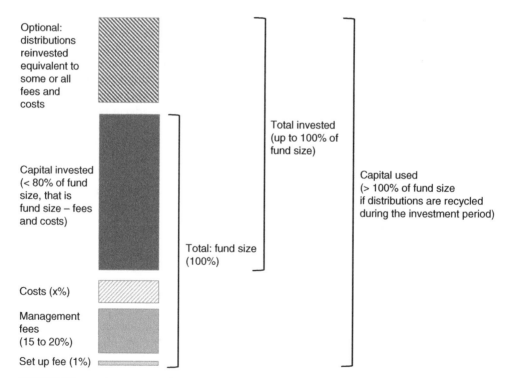

FIGURE 3.10   Cash structure of a fund during the investment period
Source: Author.

expenses (audit, legal, etc.). This amount is thus not invested, unless a provision entitles the general partner to recycle part of the proceeds of the funds invested to reach 100% of the fund size as a total invested.

Figure 3.11 shows the breakdown of the fund repayment in the case of a European waterfall. As an example, we assume that the fund doubled its size (EUR 100 million), which means that the amount invested will generate enough profits to compensate for the burden of the fees and deliver EUR 100 million in profits.

Some fund managers are entitled to receive fees, commissions and other income paid by portfolio companies in relation to their active role in backing the management teams

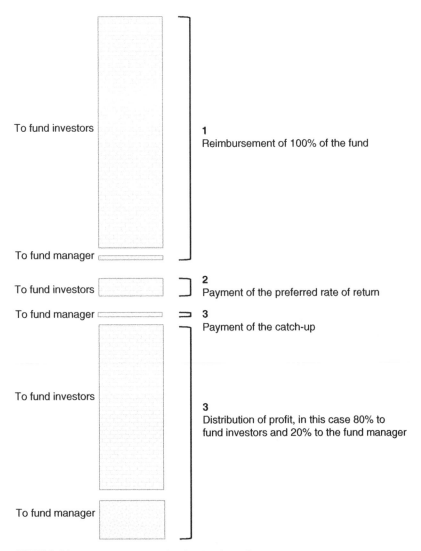

FIGURE 3.11 Cash structure of a fund at liquidation stage
Source: Author.

of portfolio companies.[22] Most of the fund regulations (limited partnership agreements) in Continental Europe provide that these fees are paid to the fund, in part[23] or fully, and not the fund manager. Technically, the fund manager collects them and reduces proportionally the amount charged to the fund as management fees in what is known as a 'fee offset' mechanism. This is logical as the management team is de facto already paid for this service.

Whatever the treatment of these amounts, it is important that they are declared to the investors. Charging consulting or other fees to portfolio companies paves the way for conflicts of interest (see Section 3.2.3). Fee retrocessions may not be as widespread in American funds, but the tide might be changing. Already, some teams voluntarily retroceded these sums partially or in total. Regulators are increasingly favourable towards the idea of establishing clear rules as regards these fees. Since 2015, the SEC has been actively enforcing a strict interpretation of fund regulations[24] when it comes to the payment of fees from portfolio companies to fund managers[25] and their affiliates.[26]

3.2.3 Conflicts of Interest

The separation between funds and the fund manager offers, theoretically, a number of guarantees as to the initial good faith of the management team. However, the fund manager is not immune from conflicts of interest. Fund regulations set rules to minimise – and if possible avoid – such conflicts of interest.

The limited partnership agreement (LPA, see Template 2), which regulates the relations between limited partners (fund investors) and the general partner (fund manager), provides a basis for governance. Investors have, theoretically, the right to participate, up to a certain level, in the governance of the fund they have invested in. However, practically, most of the time investors have no say once they have signed the LPA. The rights of limited partners are hence merely bound to be informed by the general partner, usually on a quarterly basis, and with an audited annual report. An annual general meeting of the fund allows limited partners to obtain a more precise view of portfolio companies and the development of fund investments.

The fact that some fund managers keep the list of their investors confidential limits the exchange of information between investors and hence the practical exercise of governance rights. It is therefore important that investors are formally represented within

---

[22] However, this definition is particularly large and can encompass, for example, a private jet.
[23] Usually at least 80% of them, the rest going to the fund manager.
[24] See notably Anderson, Gray, Browder and Tincher (2019).
[25] As a matter of example, KKR was fined USD 30 million in 2015 for misallocating broken deal expenses. TPG Partners was fined USD 12.8 million in 2017 for taking accelerated monitoring fees in case of exit of portfolio companies. The Blackstone Group was fined USD 39 million for not properly disclosing them in 2015 and Apollo Management USD 52.7 million in 2016 for the same reason. WL Ross was fined USD 10.4 million in 2016 for failing to disclose certain fee allocation practices and THL Managers USD 5 million for the same reason in 2018. First Reserve Management was fined USD 3.5 million for failing to disclose conflicts of interest related to fees and expenses in 2016 and Yucaipa Master Manager USD 3 million for the same reason in 2018.
[26] As an example, KKR's affiliate Capstone refunded fees charged to portfolio companies in 2015, having failed to properly disclosed them.

the fund's governance mechanisms. However, their role is usually only to advise the fund manager, through an Advisory Board, about the resolution of potential conflicts of interest. Fund investors are not more active due to the nature of fund investing and the shield from responsibilities that funds provide to investors. It is necessary that the fund rules, written by the fund manager and negotiated with the investors, nevertheless provide a clear framework of practice and reporting. Regulators, such as the SEC in the USA and the European regulators in Europe, increasingly monitor private market fund regulations and ensure that they comply with general regulations, that they are effectively applied and that they respect a certain level of fairness.

The lack of transparency – even for fund investors – of private market funds has raised some questions, notably in the USA. The San Jose Mercury News has asked public pension funds to disclose the details of the performance of their private equity fund investments. This triggered a trial where the court ordered these public pension funds (such as CalPERS and MassPRIM) to comply with their disclosure duties and apply the Freedom of Information Act (FOIA). In effect, this unleashed a wave of publications and communications, which has significantly improved the public's information about private markets.

However, fund managers are resisting disclosure and transparency. They have been fairly successful so far, as private markets remain today a largely opaque world. Some fund managers, seeking to prevent any further publication of information as regards their portfolio, have excluded public pension funds and other fund investors potentially subject to FOIA provisions from their investors list. Their reasoning is that this legal decision may not be limited, in the future, to the disclosure of the aggregate performance of the fund. Courts may decide that it is mandatory to disclose information with regard to portfolio companies. Fund managers do not want to disclose such information and try to keep it as confidential as possible, notably to avoid giving an unfair advantage to the competitors of their portfolio companies, but also the potential buyers. This also keeps fund investors in the dark and limits their ability to benchmark funds.

So far, Europe and the rest of the world have not shown any movement towards mandatory disclosure. The disclosure debate has illustrated the difficulty of obtaining information, even as regards the performance of funds. This applies not only to investments and performance, but also to fees and compensation schemes.

The most frequent source of conflicts of interest concerns income to the fund manager where the fund investors are not participating (i.e., fees and costs, see above). Other sources of conflict of interest can be linked to:

- The *simultaneous management of multiple vintages of funds*[27] ('parallel funds' treatment), which raises the question of the allocation of investment opportunities to this or that fund under management. This conflict of interest can be managed by establishing a priority as to the oldest vintage, or setting up a pro rata allocation for funds of the same vintage.

---

[27]This conflict of interest is close to the one which arises when there are co-investment mechanisms: should the general partner allocate as a priority the amounts of the fund it manages to the investment opportunity, or should it offer the opportunity to the limited partners entitled to co-invest? At a fund of funds level, this conflict of interest arises when allocating portions of highly coveted private equity funds between mandates (or segregated accounts) managed for some limited partners, and funds of funds managed by the general partner.

- *Reinvestment in a portfolio company already belonging to a fund* managed by a given fund manager. Other funds managed by this fund manager may be considered 'natural investors', as this fund manager knows the company and has done the investment work already. This is called 'cross investment' in venture capital (subsequent rounds of investments) and 'deal recycling' in LBOs (when a fund sells a company to another fund), and could lead to favouring one group of fund investors or another. The valuation of the company would be decided by the fund manager who is at the same time on the seller side with one fund and on the buyer side with another. This is why cross investments and deal recycling are generally excluded in fund regulations (LPAs).
- The *maximisation of the revenues* derived from the management of the fund and its portfolio companies. For example, companies with no real chances of success ('zombie' companies) can be held in the portfolio to maximise the management fees in the divestment period (which are generally indexed on the residual value of the fund), or to charge additional fees.
- The *valuation* of the companies of the fund *to show flattering performance*. Not (or under-) provisioning investments can help to produce artificially high unrealised performance. These high unrealised performances can help to raise new funds, and also to calculate high management fees in the divestment period. In that respect, the transition of valuation methods from historical costs to the fair market value opens up large debate. By valuing portfolio companies thanks to listed comparables ('comparable method') and the intrinsic performance of companies ('discounted cash flows'), the fund manager manages the information – even though it is audited. In that respect, auditors certify the method used, not the end result. Even if some private equity associations encourage the adoption of the fair market value (see above) as a reference to establish NAVs, some fund managers have decided to stick to the historical costs method, at times with good reason. The historical cost is deemed more conservative and less volatile, but also potentially less accurate. This approach might be more relevant for start-ups, distressed businesses and unusual situations. In order to preserve fund investors' interests, the European AIFM Directive has set the rule that a third party should produce a valuation of the portfolio of private equity funds (see above). Whether this rule will clarify the situation and improve the fund investors' information remains to be proven.[28]
- Technically, a third-party valuation is what happens with the prospect of a secondary sale. Potential buyers of a fund stake on the secondary market make a bid

---

[28] As a matter of fact, most of the fund managers apply different valuation techniques to comply with the requests of the wide range of their fund investors. Some fund managers provide a 'conservative view', a 'fair view' or a 'best estimate' and their own expected outcome (or high end value) for the fund's portfolio. This blurs even more the picture of the valuation of funds. As the quarterly and annual reports are the main communication channel between the fund investors and managers, fund investors have to face a difficult task: choosing a value for their investments. Adding a fourth valuation will just increase the 'noise' for the fund investors, as the third party will only have the same amount of information as the fund investors to produce a valuation by construction. Hence, the intervention of a third party will add to the operational costs of a private markets fund without any substantial benefit for the fund investors. The fact is that this value can only be determined for certain when the fund has been liquidated, that is to say at the end of its lifespan.

which is then 'the market price', the reference of negotiations between the exiting investor and the potential new entrant.

- The *time allocation* of the fund managers to the various funds under management. It is in the fund investors' interest to assess the time commitment of the management team for existing funds and how it will be allocated going forward.
- *Carried interest* not being sufficient to motivate a fund manager to deploy its best efforts to manage a fund. A portfolio which is valued below its cost, and for which the efforts deployed by the fund manager could only lead to recovering the fund's initial size and eventually paying the preferred rate but no carried interest, may lead the fund manager to deploy only minimal effort to service this fund. The fund investors' range of action is unfortunately restricted in that respect:
    - Either the portfolio is considered a low-expectation investment and *written off* by the fund investors, who might legitimately walk out of their relationship with the fund manager for further fundraising.
    - Or the fund manager can *renegotiate the terms of the fund management* and set up a new incentive structure on the basis of the current NAV as the cost, and thus calculate the carried interest above this threshold. This comes at a cost for the fund investor, as the fund manager will apply its incentive structure even if the fund is not fully reimbursed. It is thus in the best interest of the fund investors to take pre-emptive action and to make sure that the fund is managed actively and proactively by the fund manager in order to avoid this situation. Experienced fund managers, thanks to long-established know-how and expertise, can avoid this situation and cut their losses or take a turn-around approach early in the investment management to avoid a downward spiral in the valuation of their portfolios.
- *The fund manager mastering the fund information.* The information of fund investors is fully controlled by fund managers, who provide quarterly and annual reports. These documents possibly open the way for action by investors, but the level of details and the time lag in their production dull the potential for action. Fund investors must be diligent in their analysis and may ask for a 'fairness opinion' in order to guarantee that the value of the fund reflects its real value (with all the limits associated with a third-party valuation).

3.2.4 Power, Checks and Balances

Fund investors have by definition a confined role in private market funds.[29] They delegate management to a fund manager, only controlling and eventually sanctioning the latter. It is thus in their best interest to *define the limited partnership agreement as precisely as possible* and negotiate clauses that may be necessary for a good relationship over the course of the life of the fund, that is to say 8 to 15 years plus possible extensions.

Moreover, it is important that fund investors go beyond the written rules of the limited partnership to create an *interpersonal relationship* with the fund manager. Being part of the Advisory Board is one of the ways to be more involved in the life of a fund,

---

[29]Though fund investors are 'limited partners', they are 'not powerless' (*Private Equity International*, 2012).

even though the number of seats is limited and often reserved for professionals who could prove useful for the operational life of the fund.

The sanction of a given general partner relies more on the *possibility of the opportunity to invest in the next fund* than trying to change the course of the current investment made with it. The interaction between fund investors and managers lies in a constructive dialogue, the purpose of which is to assess the evolution of portfolio companies. Fund investors can then compute their own valuations and decide whether or not they want to proceed with the next generation of funds.

Hence, it is in the fund investors' best interests to *closely monitor* the evolution of the fund and provide the fund manager with *feedback* and possibly *advice*. There is still a high gap in expectations and resources between fund investors and managers. Most fund managers still consider fund investors as pockets of money, without any additional resources to provide. This can be true, but it is in the fund manager's best interests to assess if they can go beyond and possibly identify potential clients or partners for their portfolio companies in their pool of limited partners. The increased level of professionalism of fund managers and fund investors has led to an *improved quality of dialogue*, which can only benefit both parties. However, the changes in the balance of power – depending on whether the market is more in favour of fund investors (in the case of recession, when investors are wary of putting more capital to work in the industry) or fund managers (in the case of expansion, when money flows are exceeding the absorption capacity of private market funds) – make it *difficult to really establish a consensus on practice*. The legal pressure for more disclosure and possibly regulation, coming from the USA, also has some adverse effects. Some fund managers have increased their transparency, but the industry consensus is that too much publicity can only harm the business. It is thus in the best interests of fund investors to understand what is at stake with every fund manager and establish a specific means of communication.

In the private markets industry, conflict, especially before the court, is highly inadvisable. Not only will this destroy the ability to work on subsequent funds, but it also damages relationships which are meant to last many years. This is also why the replacement of a fund manager is rare and mostly a last resort. In this event, fund investors have to identify a new fund manager and negotiate with it the management of an existing portfolio. This is not only a lengthy and difficult process, but also a costly one, as the new fund manager has to be motivated to turn around a portfolio and generate new and profitable investments.

To make their investment choices, investors must, however, establish some criteria, reflecting their priorities and measuring the performance of their investments with regard to these criteria in order to manage the uncertainty related to private equity investments (see Section 3.3).

3.3 MEASURING PERFORMANCE, MANAGING RISKS AND OPTIMISING RETURNS

One of the main difficulties in assessing the interest that an investor may have in investing in private equity is to evaluate the performance of private equity funds. Figures are not disclosed publicly and there is no real benchmark to compare the performance of the funds.

This means that performance has to be evaluated in an uncertain context (a), combining lack of information with different measurement rules. However, more than finding the 'right' performance measure for funds, limited partners may be more interested in understanding the nature of the performance generated, aligning their risk–return profile with those of the underlying funds, thus optimising their returns (b).

3.3.1 Measuring Performance in an Uncertain Context

There is no infallible way to evaluate the performance of a private equity team. The performance of a fund is generally evaluated according to two criteria: (i) the multiple of investment (total value to paid-in, or TVPI) and especially the realised multiple of investment (calculated through the distributed to paid-in, or DPI); and (ii) the IRR. A third criterion is gaining ground: the public market equivalent (PME). These measures of performance can be presented net or gross of fees. Only the net measures of performance (i.e., after the payment of all fees and carried interest) are of interest to the investor. However, this can introduce a bias as regards the size of the fund. In fact, the smaller the fund, the higher the impact of fixed costs will be and the net performance will show degradation compared to its peer group.

3.3.1.1 The TVPI is the Ratio between the Current Value of a Given Asset (a Company or a Portfolio, for Example) and the Price Paid for it

The net multiple of investment (MOIC), also known as TVPI, reveals the global performance of an investment fund. The net multiple of investment is calculated as follows:

- It is necessary to add all the proceeds from portfolio companies, including their sale, transferred to the fund (the 'distributed'). If assets are still in portfolio, then the net asset value (the 'residual value') is used.
- Then the costs supported by the fund (including fees) and the carried interest paid to the team are deducted.
- The total of these two operations is then divided by the amount invested in the company.

It is therefore possible to compute a DPI ratio and an RVPI, the sum of which is the TVPI.

Positive aspects

The ratio allows investors to know how much they gained for each euro invested. It is cash-on-cash and factual, and difficult to manipulate (except the RVPI). This ratio is important to determine the absolute value creation generated by a given investment. In order to benchmark the performance of an investment with the TVPI, it is important to obtain the net values, after fees and carried interest. This is the only way to have a homogeneous sample and truly assess the performance of an investment.

This measure of performance is easy to calculate at investor level (cash in/cash out), but is far from being perfect.

Limits

The TVPI does not take into account the impact of time on the investment, which is why it has to be combined with an IRR analysis. It also does not take into account the context of investments, and has thus to be combined with a PME analysis. It is difficult to compare and analyse quantitatively, and in particular it is not risk-adjusted. Finally, it takes into account the capital effectively invested (not the committed), which has significant consequences for institutional investors (see below).

As for the valuation of a fund

The multiple is not reliable if the fund is still active, as it is exact only once the fund has been liquidated and all the fees have been paid, that is to say at the term of the 8 to 15 years of the fund's lifespan. The valuation is difficult when it is necessary to estimate performance during the activity of the fund (before the term), as a part of the portfolio is still not liquidated. The intermediate valuation of the fund is thus determined by the choices of the management team as to the value of the unrealised portfolio. Valuation techniques condition the perception of investors as to the performance of the fund. Some teams may find an incentive to maintain active 'zombie' companies in order to produce attractive (even if unrealised) returns during fundraising (see above).

It is thus necessary to look at other ratios, such as the DPI, which gives an idea of the realisation of the performance, and the RVPI, which is the portion of the performance which has not yet materialised.

As for the amounts invested

When an investor commits to pay a certain amount to a fund, he does not pay the total of the commitment upon his signature. Rather, it is the fund manager who calls portions of the commitments as needed by the investments of the fund and the management fees paid to the team. This means that in the majority of cases, an investor will commit to a certain amount, but technically will not pay 100% of it owing to the early distributions of some of the first investments. By reinvesting these early payments, the investor usually pays only 60–80% of his commitment net of the distributions. However, a commitment is translated for an institutional investor by a portfolio of capital which is immobilised in prudential (banks) and solvency (insurance groups) ratios.

To truly account for the total return of a private markets fund investment, it is necessary to add to the multiple of investment the product of the unpaid commitments which are put into liquid placements, and then to deduct the cost of capital as revealed by prudential and solvency ratios.

This question is not truly valid for individual investors and funds of funds. Individuals do not have to observe prudential or solvency ratios as such (they only have to keep some assets liquid in order to meet their liabilities). Funds of funds are in fact buffers between private market funds and institutional investors, thus smoothing the flows and diversifying the risks. In that respect, the absence of prudential treatment of funds of funds opens a debate. Funds of funds have been under-privileged by the Basel II and Basel III Agreements and the solvency regulations, even though one of their main features has been to eliminate the perspective of default from reimbursement in private equity (Weidig & Mathonet, 2004). The multiple of investment is a useful tool for measuring performance, but does not take into account the impact of time on the performance of an investment. Notably, given the fact that the capital calls are made as needed, and as distributions are made according to the sale of portfolio companies, a given multiple can express different investment realities.

A lower multiple, but executed over a short time, can be more interesting than a higher multiple over a long period of time. However, this implies that investment opportunities deliver a constant return over time and that there are no transaction costs or costs of opportunity (which is not true in practice).

In that respect, and all things being equal otherwise, evaluating the performance of small multiples over short periods, or high multiples over long periods, has to be appreciated within the function of the total of the costs involved in each scenario, and also the risk involved. Appreciations can diverge between institutional investors, some being more attentive to the absolute performance (i.e., a high multiple, with a lower sensitivity to the time dimension, such as pension funds) and others to the relative performance (i.e., a lower multiple, but served over shorter periods of time).

3.3.1.2   The IRR is Calculated through a Formula which Factors in the Impact of Time on a Given Investment

The annualised IRR is calculated by taking into account the quarterly cash flows, and then the eventual residual value of the fund at year end (as audited) is added. It is the rate at which the NPV of cash inflows equals the NPV of cash outflows.

The IRR formula is as follows:

$$\text{Discount rate} = \text{flow of year } n/\text{flow initial year}^{1/n} - 1$$

The IRR complements the multiple analysis method, in the sense that it provides for a better comprehension of the nature of the performance of a fund. The impact of the time dimension is obvious on the return, as shown in Table 3.3 and Figure 3.12, but also on the genesis of the performance.

Positive aspects

The IRR is useful for comparing the ability of a fund manager to put capital to work and organising the rotation of its assets. However, a high IRR may not be proof of excellent performance. It has to be combined with the TVPI to assess how the fund manager has created the value. In that respect, the *holding period* of a given investment is useful information, to truly understand the involvement of the fund manager in a company and whether it has had the time and opportunity to take a constructive approach. Some fund managers may be tempted to sell companies quickly in order to generate a high IRR, even though additional and substantial value could have been created through a longer holding period. Giving priority to the IRR emphasises the quick exit of investments, even at the expense of the better performance of the investment (*Financial Times*, 2005).

TABLE 3.3   IRR derived from the multiple and the length of investment

Year	Multiple											
	1.25×	1.5×	1.75×	2×	2.5×	3×	3.5×	4×	5×	6×	8×	10×
2	12	22	32	41	58	73	87	100	124	145	183	216
3	8	14	21	26	36	44	52	59	71	82	100	115
4	6	11	15	19	26	32	37	41	50	57	68	78
5	5	8	12	15	20	25	28	32	38	43	52	58
6	4	7	10	12	16	20	23	26	31	35	41	47
7	3	6	8	10	14	17	20	22	26	29	35	39
8	3	5	7	9	12	15	17	19	22	25	30	33
9	3	5	6	8	11	13	15	17	20	22	26	29
10	2	4	6	7	10	12	13	15	17	20	23	26

Source: Coller Capital.

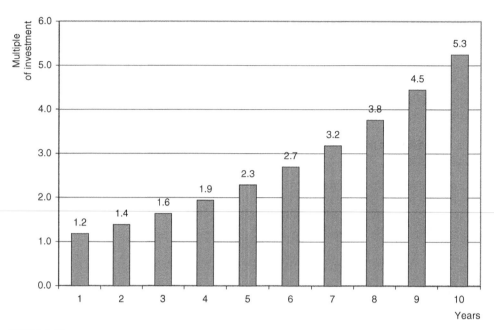

FIGURE 3.12 Investment multiple necessary to get an IRR of 18%, depending on holding period by the fund (expressed in years)
Source: Author.

This is not intrinsically negative, however this kind of operation is difficult to reproduce over time and as a recurring *modus operandi* (this is a major point of the due diligence of limited partners, as illustrated in Template 3). The IRR is important when the investor wants to evaluate the intrinsic performance of a management team, and especially its aptitude for reproducing performance. Investment pacing and exit timing are crucial, especially when it is a matter of maximising performance. In that respect, IRR is one of the most useful elements of information in understanding performance, but not the only one.

Rapid exits from investments do not open the way for the investment teams to prove their capacity for value creation. Central Europe is an example of this: privatisation and company restructuring have offered numerous opportunities in cable, telephony and other infrastructure industries (energy, water). Some private equity funds have shown impressive IRR, although perhaps temporarily. It is difficult to analyse this performance, as this source of opportunities has mostly dried up. Investment teams have to prove themselves in a different context, and by other means than just structuring attractive investment projects. This is where the evaluation of the performance is key.

Depending on their risk aversion and return expectations, investors may place the emphasis on TVPI or IRR as their main indicator of performance. Funds which are targeting high IRRs may apply a strategy targeting a higher rotation rate of assets, but this means that the fund manager has to identify good-quality opportunities for investment more frequently. This may not be the case, and some investors would rather stay with longer-term investments, but generate higher absolute returns.

Limits

The IRR suffers from multiple limits,[30] notably because the formula was developed to compare simple investment projects. It assumes, for example, that any distribution can be reinvested at no cost at the same level of return. This is not the case in private markets. It also suffers from some of the same issues as the TVPI, as it does not take into account the context of the investment (the PME does, see below). It only takes into account the capital effectively invested (not just committed). The IRR is not risk-adjusted and is difficult to compare and analyse quantitatively.

The IRR can be manipulated in case of delayed capital calls or quick distributions. This is particularly true when fund managers use lines of credit (also known as 'equity bridge financing'). The principle is that when a fund makes an investment, the fund manager borrows the corresponding capital from a specialised lender. The capital is called from fund investors, usually after a delay. This is when the IRR starts to be computed. By using a credit line, a fund manager in effect boosts the IRR of the investments. In Europe, most of the credit lines are limited by the AIFM Directive to a maximum of 12 months (otherwise, funds can be requalified as 'leveraged funds', as hedge funds are, and are submitted to a higher level of regulatory control). Assuming that an LBO deal is done for an average of 4 years in developed markets, this means that the capital of fund investors is for 25% less time. This could look attractive, except that the capital unused costs money to institutional fund investors, sitting idle on their balance sheet and costing them money under prudential and solvency ratios. There is a significant cost of opportunity, but also a lower absolute return collected ultimately as these credit lines cost interest to funds. Therefore, fund managers can boost their IRR and reduce their performance with these instruments. They can also appear as performing better than their peer group if they are compared exclusively on the basis of the IRR of their funds. Some fund managers go to the extent of using credit lines to anticipate the exit of a portfolio company, to stop the IRR formula sooner and give it a further boost.

Besides a voluntary manipulation, IRRs can be boosted by the simple order of cash flows. If two funds have the same investment multiple of 2.75×, but one records its best deal first and the less good one after and the other records the deals in the exact reverse order, then the first fund will have a much better IRR than the second. In our example (Table 3.4), the first has a 54% IRR and the second a 29% IRR. The modified IRR (MIRR) can help solve this issue, as it considers each cash flow as starting in year 1 and computes an explicit reinvestment rate. In our example, with a reinvestment rate of 0%, the MIRR for the two funds stands at 16%. However, the MIRR for private market funds would require benchmarks with a common reinvestment rate, which is difficult to gather. They are thus more difficult to compare.

3.3.1.3   The PME Provides Context to Private Market Investments

The PME replicates the cash flow pattern of a private markets fund by buying an index of listed (or unlisted) assets when the fund draws down capital, and selling the index when the fund disposes of assets. The PME can be computed as an IRR or a TVPI.

---

[30] For a detailed criticism and analysis of the IRR, see Kocis, Bachman, Long and Nickels (2009), Chapters 7, 9 and 11.

TABLE 3.4   IRR derived from the multiple and the length of investment

	Fund I	Comments		Fund II	Comments
Year 1	−10	*Investment 1*	Year 1	−10	*Investment 2*
Year 2	0		Year 2	0	
Year 3	0		Year 3	0	
Year 4	40	*Sale deal 1*	Year 4	15	*Sale deal 2*
Year 5	−10	*Investment 2*	Year 5	−10	*Investment 1*
Year 6	0		Year 6	0	
Year 7	0		Year 7	0	
Year 8	15	*Sale deal 2*	Year 8	40	*Sale deal 1*
TVPI	2.75×		TVPI	2.75×	
IRR	53.53%		IRR	29.25%	

Source: Author.

Positive aspects

The PME is the only performance measure which can take into account the context of investment. The performance of the index used as a comparison point provides a perspective on the actual value creation by the fund manager. A perfect PME would in fact match each cash inflow with the corresponding cash outflow to benchmark each investment, but most PME calculations blend the flows to benchmark a fund. Another positive aspect of the PME is that it eliminates the question of the duration of investments, which otherwise prevents a like-for-like comparison between an IRR and the annual performance of an index of listed assets.

Limits

However, the PME presents multiple limits. First, it is at times difficult to find an index to benchmark specific private market investment strategies. For example, start-ups in emerging sectors might not have any comparable listed competitors (and thus no index to track them). Benchmarking companies in difficult situations is also difficult, as bankrupted or quasi-bankrupted companies might have been excluded from the stock exchange. As for real assets, the question is even more challenging as listed entities are usually companies operating the assets, not the assets themselves.

The PME also has its own methodological limits. In particular, the formula requires a careful application when a fund is not fully liquidated. Indeed, it is possible to oversell the index: the fund distributing proceeds usually does not communicate how much is a refund of the original investment and how much is the profit (or the loss) distributed. Thus, the observer has to compute a pro-rata of the distribution versus the remaining NAV to regulate the distributions, as explained by Rouvinez (2003).

The PME also does not solve the fact that it is not risk-adjusted, and takes into account the capital invested (not committed).

3.3.2   Managing Risks and Optimising Returns

Performance is generally realised over the 5 to 7 years following the launch of a fund, as shown by the curve in Figure 3.13. The profile of a private equity fund is thus very specific: *the J-curve.*

The investment period of a fund is generally 5 years, and the first portfolio companies are sold 3 to 4 years after the launch of the fund. This fund must support the

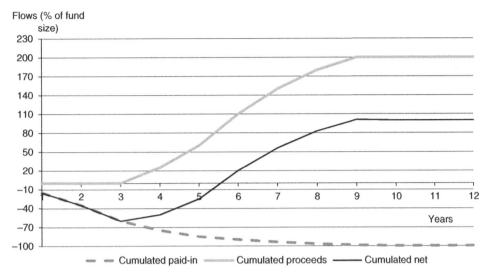

FIGURE 3.13   Simplified cash flow curves of an LBO fund
Source: Demaria (2006, 2008, 2010, 2012).

management fees and initial investments without any revenues. Cash flows are thus at first negative; then, as investments bear fruit, the curve slowly turns around and the fund reaches the break-even point. On the graph, break-even is reached after year 5. At this date, the initial exits (and eventual additional revenues) will theoretically have compensated the investment costs and amount invested. Then, the subsequent exits will compensate further fees and costs associated with the remaining exits and portfolio liquidation.

TVPI and IRR are used mostly to compare the performance of portfolios built by fund managers for funds. In order to compare the performance, funds are sorted by vintage year.[31] The vintage of a fund is given by the date at which it holds its initial closing. In order to compare properly the performance of a fund, it is also necessary to obtain its net return figures. It is also necessary to determine which geographical zone the fund covers, what type of financing is provided (VC, LBO, mezzanine, etc.), what the industry is (IT, biotech, consumer goods and services, etc.) and other features. Some databases provide the net performance of comparable funds by strategy, region, vintage year and industry. This can substantially reduce the sample to benchmark the fund, and eventually lead to the conclusion that there is no benchmark for a given fund.

Performance analysis: beyond TVPI and IRR

It is thus in the best interest of the fund investors to analyse the details of the performance of a fund, investment by investment. The main target of fund investors,

---

[31] The vintage year of a closed-end private markets fund refers to the year of its creation. This can be open to debate: it is the date of its first closing (that is, the date at which the fund manager decided to effectively create it legally with a minimum critical mass of capital), the date of its first investment (which is when effectively the fund is active) or the date of its final closing (when the fund will not admit any new investor). Depending on the data source, one of the three possible dates is retained.

while assessing the past performance of a fund, is to identify whether and how the fund manager can reproduce this performance with the subsequent generation of funds.

The difficulty lies in the fact that there is no uniform method of analysing the content of a portfolio, and it is also difficult to assess whether the success or failure of a company is the result of external factors or investment management. Most of the time, it is a combination of factors and it is difficult to assess exactly what has happened. A given portfolio may have shown mediocre performance, but given the market conditions and the structure of this portfolio, the general partner may have done an exceptional job.

Confronted with the same market conditions, fund managers may react very differently. Some teams will focus on their best companies and try to bring them to the top. Others will focus on ailing companies and try to mitigate the losses as far as possible. Ideally, fund managers should simultaneously support their 'star' companies and work with the difficult ones to find a way out. Most of the time, scarcity of time and resources does not allow them to do that.

Experience is thus paramount in evaluating the performance of fund managers and in determining with which team it makes sense to invest. Hence, determining whether the concentration of performance on a limited number of deals is normal (venture capital) or not (growth capital) is a matter of understanding the dynamics of each market segment. It is also crucial to ascertain the market timing and whether an under-performing portfolio was the victim of a crash (VC in IT in 2000–2003, LBO in 2007–2009) or bad investment decisions (over-allocation to Internet start-ups, over-leverage to acquire companies).

Qualitative analysis

Another factor lies in the analysis of the performance generated deal by deal. For an LBO, the profit generated can come from the progression of its turn-over (sometimes through acquisitions), from its operational improvement, from the leverage effect, from the increase of multiple paid (multiple of EBIT or EBITDA) for a company and some other additional factors. It is in the best interests of the fund investor to understand what was driving the generation of profit.

In that respect, past performance is just one element of information required to take the decision to invest in a new fund. Fund investors have first and foremost to assess what is the positioning of a team, what are its core strengths and its leverage to create value. This applies not only to past portfolio management, but also to reference calls and ascertaining the market sentiment towards a team. This feedback will often be heterogeneous, but will help fund investors to understand the distinguishing features of a team and whether it fits within their expectations.

In many respects, the fund manager is in a state of permanent fundraising. To maintain an optimal investment capacity, an active presence on the market and an ability to manage investment opportunities, it must in fact maintain a permanent investment period. To reach that capacity, the fund manager will raise a fund on average every 2.5 to 3 years. By doing so, it will be able to make the investment periods of the funds it manages coincide. De facto, fundraising for the next generation of funds starts only 3 years after closing a given fund. Fund managers are thus constantly preparing the next fundraising, as it takes on average 9 to 12 months to close a fund, and pre-marketing efforts start a year before officially opening a fund to subscriptions. Most of the fund regulations plan that in order to raise the next generation of a fund series, a fund manager must have deployed at least 70% of the latest generation to date.

Even though institutional investors consider that experience and track record are the most important elements when selecting a private equity fund, they must be able to evaluate the performance of a team without having the full picture of its investment success.

The challenge for fund managers is to find the right fund size. In the aftermath of the 2007–2009 crisis, it appeared that fundraising became very challenging and some funds were smaller than the previous generation. More recently, fund sizes have been growing very fast, and the frequency of fundraising increased substantially, due to the appetite of fund investors for private market funds and the returns they deliver. Academic studies have since then shown that the optimal size for funds is situated between USD 150 and 300 million for venture capital funds and between USD 300 and 500 million for mid-market LBO funds (see Figure 3.14).

As market conditions are constantly evolving, fund investors have to evaluate the market where the analysed funds are active, as well as the capacity of the general partner to identify investment opportunities, structure investments, manage them and sell the portfolio companies with a substantial profit. They can be supported in that process by funds of funds managers and gatekeepers.

Fund investors' due diligence

Fund investors willing to allocate capital to private equity need to invest a significant amount of resources to assess the teams and have to do so regularly and over a long period of time. It is therefore in the interests of a new entrant to team up with established teams such as funds of funds (for small amounts to be invested) and gatekeepers (for amounts above EUR 25 to 50 million), to help them understand the market dynamics and set up their investment strategy.

Even though this represents a cost, fund investors will benefit greatly from the experience of seasoned professionals, with a good knowledge of the market, teams and past

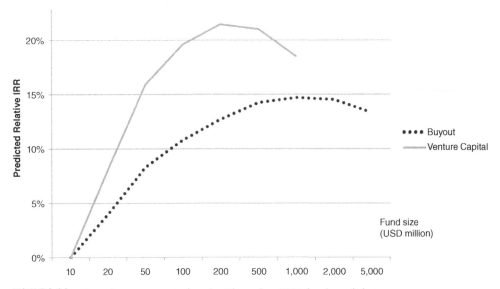

FIGURE 3.14 Size of venture capital and mid-market LBO funds and their returns
Source: Lerner, Leamon & Hardymon (2012).

performance. They could also benefit from opportunities such as secondary sales and other offerings which are not spread widely across the market.

To understand the nature of the performance generated by a fund, fund investors are granted access to documents: the due diligence package. This set of documents presents the past activity of the fund manager; its investment strategy and eventually the changes made to adapt to market conditions; the projected fund and its strategy; the composition of the team; its positioning on the market; its competitive advantage; its analysis of market conditions and investment opportunities; as well as other factors useful to help fund investors understand the investment opportunity. These documents are usually drafted by the fund manager, sometimes with the help of a placement agent. The latter is an outsourced fund placement organisation, helping fund managers identify potential fund investors and supporting them in selling the fund to these investors.

Regardless of the intrinsic quality of these documents, and in order to manage the risks accordingly, fund investors have set up procedures, sometimes with due diligence questionnaires that have to be filled in by fund managers willing to raise funds. These questionnaires are questionable, as they represent a lot of paperwork and do not really provide an insight into the investment opportunity. This has led fund managers to criticise pension funds and funds of funds as bureaucratic investors, generating paperwork in order to justify their fees and jobs.

Most of the private equity specialists have their own due diligence procedures, with supporting documents (see a sample in Template 3). As private equity is a small world, it is necessary to cultivate good relationships with placement agents, as well as with other intermediaries of the private equity ecosystem. This is particularly useful while assessing emerging management teams. This informal part is important, as the composition of general partners can change and team dynamics are important in understanding the nature of the risk and the generation of performance.

To compare a fund with its peers, it is necessary to identify its sector of investment, the geographical area covered, the vintage year and the investment strategy. To determine its intrinsic performance, and by extension the quality of its management team, it is then necessary to compare its IRR and multiple (net, once fees and costs have been deducted). This performance analysis is only indicative of potential performance for the future (Kaplan & Schoar, 2003) if the investment team has remained stable and if it did not change its investment strategy radically, if its geographical market has not changed and if its sectors of investment have not been changed.

While for market finance past performance does not constitute an indication of future performance, it is not the same in private equity. In fact, multiple scientific studies have shown that the performance of an investment team is stable over time, owing especially to its quality, its capacity to attract interesting investment opportunities and support the emergence of serial entrepreneurs. All of these factors, once combined, create an environment which is favourable to the reproduction of high-level performance.

Volatility of performance

The absence of a stable and coherent evaluation framework gives rise to many questions, because to choose between the different sets of assets available (stocks, bonds, private equity, commodities, hedge funds, fine art, etc.) it is necessary to have a basis for comparison (see Figure 3.15).

Figure 3.16 illustrates the case of US LBO and mezzanine funds. This illustration has to be used with caution for three reasons. First, the 20-year horizon provides

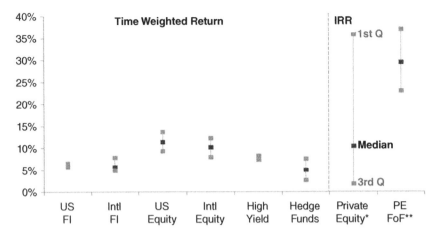

FIGURE 3.15 Return and volatility comparisons between different asset classes (1995–2005)
* Venture capital and leveraged buy-out funds tracked by Venture Economics of the vintage 1995
** Funds of funds invested in venture capital and leveraged buy-out tracked by Venture Economics of the vintage 1995
Source: Capital Dynamics, FI, P&I, Bloomberg, Venture Economics.

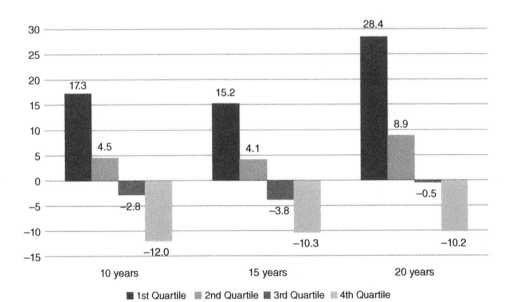

FIGURE 3.16 Annualised returns of US LBO and mezzanine funds by quartile, over a 10-year, 15-year and 20-year time horizon (%, as of 30 September 2011)
Source: Credit Suisse, VentureXpert, IDC 2011.

elements of information on historical conditions which are no longer valid: the market was less mature and fund managers could exploit higher market inefficiencies. Second, the picture was taken in 2011, that is to say a little after the 2008–2009 crisis, and might still affect the performance figures. Third, the 10-year horizon is only partially reliable as it captures funds which are still active and whose assets are conservatively valued.

Nevertheless, the figure is interesting as it shows the dispersion of performance. Depending on the quartile considered, this performance measured with the IRR (with all the caution associated with this metric, see above) varies dramatically. The volatility of fund performances from one vintage year to the other is high too. These phenomena should be taken into account to properly assess the risks associated with the performance of private equity funds and funds of funds.

Moreover, adding to the difficulties of fund investors, accessible data is partial and not communicated systematically by fund managers (see the Introduction). The performance calculation itself differs depending on the structures. Investors have thus to manage their investments with such uncertainty that the data itself is subject to interpretation.

The question of the correlation between the evolution of private markets and general market evolution remains open. An attempt was made by Mackewicz & Partners (2004), who estimated it to be around 0.6, but depending on the nature of the investments made and the method of analysis applied, the results vary between 0.3 (hence no proven correlation) and 0.9 (a very high correlation). The correlation is low when venture capital investments are concerned, and increases with the maturity of companies where growth and LBO funds invest.

According to Cambridge Associates' data, investors in private equity (venture capital, growth capital and mezzanine) funds of vintage years 2000 to 2009 (so realised or largely realised) would have recorded, if they could have invested in all the funds worldwide, pro-rata of the size of these funds, a 10.9% IRR net, which is a 1.69× multiple. As a matter of comparison, a PME with the MSCI World would have generated a 6.3% IRR and a 1.35× multiple. A PME with the S&P 500 would have generated an 8.4% IRR and a TVPI of 1.54×. This sample over-weights the impact of the Internet bubble and the financial crisis. A 1995–2009 sample provides an 11.9% IRR and a 1.69× multiple, with a PME (MSCI World) of respectively 5.8% and 1.32×. The PME S&P 500 shows respectively 7.6% and a 1.48× multiple.

However, the main difference with the stock exchange lies in the disparity of performance between the best teams and the rest of the market. Investors must be especially selective in order to identify the best investment teams and get high returns while still achieving a sufficient diversification of their portfolio.

Investing in the best funds, which are managed by the top-quartile investment teams, is the best way to guarantee the lowest correlation with the market and get high returns. However, except for a small number of fund managers, offering funds that are difficult to access because they are over-subscribed, it is difficult to identify which funds will be best in the future. Funds of funds try to provide for their investors access to the best funds and an optimal diversification, but their added value remains to be proven beyond diversification. The net performance of funds of funds of vintage years 2000 to 2009 is 8.9% for a multiple of 1.64×, and a PME MSCI World of 6.8% and a multiple of 1.45×. As for the PME S&P 500, the figures are 9.4% and 1.71×. The figures are similar for the vintage years 1995–2009, with an IRR of 8.6%, a multiple of 1.61×, a PME MSCI World IRR of 6.4% and a multiple of 1.42×, and a PME S&P 500 IRR of 8.4% and a multiple of 1.64×.

The generation of performance for each fund has to be reviewed carefully, in order to understand what the knowledge and experience of each member of the general partner is, what the investment pace was, what the successes and losses were, what the analysis of these events is and how they can be reproduced/avoided going forward.

3.4 PITFALLS AND CHALLENGES

Assessing fund managers' investment discipline

As described above, fund managers have the upper hand in negotiations with fund investors. This is related to their high past performance and the relative persistence of returns of fund managers. The temptation of fund managers is therefore to maximise their income, notably by *increasing their fund sizes*. The logic is that the intensity of the work is the same whether for a small or a large investment, but the income increases a lot in terms of management fees and carried interest if the fund size increases.

However, the downside of this reasoning is significant for fund investors. If the intensity of the work is the same, the expertise changes a lot. There is a direct link between fund size and average investment size. A team usually does 10 to 25 deals with a given fund, depending on the number of team members. If the fund size is USD 100 million and the team plans to make 10 investments, the average investment size should be around USD 8 million (10 times USD 8 million plus the costs and management fees equalling USD 100 million). If the fund size increases to USD 250 million, then the average investment size should be USD 20 million. Larger investments require a different skillset to assess the opportunities, but even more importantly to create value. In the first case, if the team is composed of venture specialists, they are likely to make early-stage investments, that is to say, when start-ups emerge and work through their early recruitments, prototypes and initial launch of a product or a service. In the latter case, they will focus on supporting these companies with commercialisation, industrialisation and structuring, or even internationalisation. This requires a very different network, know-how, expertise and ultimately governance skillset from the investor.

The second consequence of an increase in fund size is that the competition is intensifying for larger deals. The number of opportunities is not significantly affected by the capital on offer (the demand), but by the sources of deals (the supply): macro-economic disruptions, repositioning of conglomerates and delistings are driving the supply of large and mega LBOs, for example. Regardless the capital on offer, these deals are intermediated and will be executed in one way or another. Having more funds competing for these deals ultimately leads to a price increase. The competition also increases because corporations compete to acquire the same companies, but also large fund investors such as sovereign wealth funds and pension funds. The playbook of large LBOs has become increasingly well known, and somehow commoditised.

The temptation of fund managers' diversification

To meet what appears to be a *commoditisation of large LBOs*, successful fund managers have been tempted to *diversify their sources of income*.[32] Initial attempts were not very successful, when LBO fund managers dipped their toes into Internet start-ups, investing at the turn of the millennium to get extra performance. As these investments soured, the fund managers decided to focus on the 'core deals' in their track records when they went back to the market to raise their next fund. They excluded Internet investments from their track record, as they officially no longer belonged to their investment strategy. Whether this is justified or not is a matter of assessment by fund investors. In fact, this warrants an enquiry as regards the discipline applied by the team and its ability to learn from these mistakes and avoid them in the future.

More recently, fund managers have branched out in other strategies. As they have been managing funds with an increased size, especially in a large LBO, some of them (Blackstone, KKR, the Carlyle Group, Apollo) have launched private real-estate funds, private debt funds, but also funds of funds, private equity energy funds or hedge funds, often with mixed success. Their brand has been used to convince investors that they could reproduce the success from their core strategy in other areas. The results can be disappointing: the level of fees is high (as the brand is supposed to command it), but the performance is not necessarily as high as with a pure player. The reasons are that the team launching the new strategy might have a lower risk appetite to avoid damaging the brand with risky deals, and the best fund managers do not need the brand of an established one out of their sector of activity. Therefore, emerging teams sponsored by an established fund manager might not have the same credentials as pure players and thus not perform as well.

One of the questions that fund investors may ask is whether this diversification guarantees the best *alignment of interests*, as not only are these private equity powerhouses deriving more management fees and could thus be less attracted by generating profits for the funds, but this could also multiply the risk of conflicts of interest. When an LBO firm is not only active on the capital, but also on the debt side, sometimes managing LBO and mezzanine funds, one could infer that *should a deal go bust*, there could be difficult arbitrage decisions to take for the fund manager. The Advisory Board in that respect is useless, as they are attached to a given fund but not to the fund manager itself – and, in any case, they rarely have a veto and sanction power. The analysis of failed deals is an important element of analysis for a fund investor, not only to understand the context and actions of the fund manager, but also what experience and know-how the fund manager has gained out of it.

To justify their diversification, LBO powerhouses are claiming that this diversification is exploiting *synergies* between their different lines of business and provides fund investors with additional expertise at no extra cost that would otherwise be out of reach and lead to less efficient investment decisions. Even though this logic can be sustained to some extent, the synergies between hedge funds and private equity activities are expected to be limited. This is probably why Soros Group (hedge funds) and

---

[32]The saturation of the institutional investor's market for large and mega LBO funds has indeed pushed some general partners to explicitly target the retail market. This might prove that this segment of the market has reached a certain maturity and will evolve towards concentration, and/or a reduction of management fees or a specialisation towards specific strategies, sectors or geographies.

Towerbrook (private equity) have split: the synergies between the two lines of business of George Soros were essentially limited to back-office economies of scale and limited exchanges of information with regard to deals which could be done.

This movement has also highlighted a debate before the 2008–2009 crisis: the *convergence between private equity and hedge fund activities*. Even though large LBO funds are more active on the listed stock exchange, overtaking groups and applying their techniques to extract values out of them, the logic of hedge fund investing and private equity investing differs substantially. Some hedge funds have played the free-rider strategy, taking pre-emptively substantial stakes in under-valued, mismanaged companies and hoping for LBO firms to take over these businesses and make the necessary improvements, thus benefitting from their work. Over the course of the last few years, hedge funds have been large investors in private debt and were also co-investors in private equity deals. These were illiquid investments for relatively liquid funds and triggered some difficulties in case of investor redemptions.

Aside from this overlap, hedge fund investing is based on arbitrage and market movements. Some hedge fund managers called 'activist investors' have tried to apply private equity techniques to listed groups, with variable levels of success. The idea is to take a significant minority ownership in a listed group, for example 5%. The next step is to contact the management to undertake some changes in the strategy and management of the company. If the management does not reply to the satisfaction of the activist, then the latter wages a public campaign of communication to gather the support of other investors for his plan. Then, there is a request to change the composition of the company's Board so that the activist can get access to it, ultimately affecting the governance of the group and possibly changing the management. The main difference between activism and LBO investing is that the first uses public scrutiny to push his agenda, while the latter uses the full control of the Board and the confidentiality of private ownership to make changes.

The convergence of hedge funds and private equity funds may be observed on another level, which is the *fund structure*. Private equity fund managers envied hedge fund managers their annual profit sharing, while hedge fund managers envied private equity managers their 10-year lock-up period. Private equity funds are blamed by fund investors for the necessity to commit to a 10-year vehicle with limited exit scenarios. This is a potential issue for investors in need of capital, which is even more extended with funds of funds (often created for 13 to 16 years). Hedge funds resolve this issue thanks to a liquidity clause, after a lock-up period. However, this works to the extent that investor redemptions are limited, far and apart.

A solution to the stickiness of private equity fund stakes was illustrated through the promotion of SPAC vehicles and BDCs in the USA. SPAC vehicles are created as trusts which have to be approved as to their strategy and investment purpose by their trustees. Once the trust is set up, the SPAC becomes a publicly listed vehicle and its shares can be sold by the owners at will (with a liquidity mechanism organised by its promoter).

Jenkinson and Sousa (2009) have raised concerns about the viability of SPACs, noting that more than half of approved deals immediately destroy value (notably because 'the extreme incentives faced by the SPAC founders create corresponding conflicts of interest'). BDCs have seen their values plummet by 20% after the crisis (Kahn, 2011), hence joining the listed private equity sector in its recurring fight against the discount on NAV which affects most listed private equity assets.

Golden Gate Capital proposed a solution by creating an evergreen fund with annual profit sharing. This could lead to a wave of innovation in the structure of private equity vehicles, thus extending further the frontiers of liquidity.

Assessing the emerging or transitioning fund managers

As each fund is a radically new structure, the only permanent element to be assessed is the fund manager. This can prove to be tricky in two situations: during a *generational change* in the team and with an emerging fund manager. When old members of a fund manager retire, the consequences can be radical, as deal sourcing and execution are strongly related to the personal and interpersonal skills of each member of the team. This transition has thus to be prepared and managed carefully, but there is no guarantee that the successors will be able to reproduce the same quality of network and know-how accumulated over the years. Fund managers have thus to determine the quality of each member of the fund manager, as well as the value of the fund manager as a firm – its image, reputation and whether it will withstand the departure of key members.

Emerging fund managers have been recognised as generating significantly higher performance than their established peer group by academic studies (Lerner, Schoar & Wang, 2008), but with a higher dispersion of returns (thus a higher fund manager selection risk). However, evaluating fund investment proposals from newly formed fund managers remains a difficult task. Unless this fund manager is a spin-off from an existing group, with a track record and a history of collaboration between the partners, the team will be difficult to assess. Fund investors can check the background and individual track record of each team member, as well as their quality, through interviews. However, this does not provide an extensive view of their capacity to work as a team and to develop the skillset necessary to truly source, execute and exit from private equity deals.

The overlooked importance of operational risk

Aside from the evaluation of the quality of the fund manager itself, fund investors face an *operational risk*, as the structure set-up is important for guaranteeing that the fund will be operated according to market standards and with a professional approach. This is why emerging fund managers sometimes place themselves under the umbrella of a group which becomes its '*sponsor*', thus providing good-quality infrastructure and back office for the fund manager.

Given the difficulty of assessing emerging fund managers, fund investors may be tempted to go only for established firms raising new funds. However, it is not only successful existing firms that are courted by an increasingly high number of potential fund investors, thus reducing the access of new investors to this pool; but virtually every single fund can declare to be 'top quartile' or 'top decile', depending on what pool of funds is being considered as the benchmark.

Club deals

As the private equity sector becomes more professional, investment discipline has emerged as a key criterion. In large LBOs, sellers are almost systematically launching *auctions* in order to dispose of their assets. This has led fund managers to team up in 'club deals', especially to target very large companies, in order to spread the risks of a given operation and avoid unnecessary competition. These *consortia* have led to an investigation by the SEC in the USA on the grounds that this could be perceived as anti-competitive practice (Lattman, 2011, 2012; Lattman & Lichtblau, 2012). So far the SEC has dismissed some of these accusations; others remain to be proven (Primack,

2012b). The practice of club deals has receded nevertheless, notably after the crisis of 2008–2009.

This raises questions about their *proprietary deal flow*. Another difficulty lies in the analysis of their value creation, as private equity firms acting as a consortium will claim that the success of a deal will be closely linked to their action alone. The influence that private equity groups can have on very large companies remains to be assessed during the due diligence, notably by interviews with the management teams of portfolio companies.

Co-investments

Instead of structuring club deals, fund managers have been teaming up with their fund investors, offering them to co-invest with the fund. This practice has drawn significant attention. Fund managers like the idea, to avoid the accusation of cartellisation of collusion with their competition. They can still acquire a firm which is bigger than their usual bite size. In the process, they can reward their larger fund investors – or convince new ones to join in the next fund by offering them a flavour of what they do.

Fund investors like the idea of co-investing as they can then reduce the overall fees and costs that they support. Though fund investors still have to invest in the fund (and thus support the costs and fees), they can save some of these costs when investing directly next to the fund. In practice, co-investing is not free (some fees and carried interest might still apply) and might be restricted in volume (e.g., for one dollar invested in the fund, the fund investor can co-invest one dollar). Co-investing can be challenging, as the fund investor gets a rather short window of time to invest, when the fund manager has done all the due diligence and has to decide the amount to invest in the deal. The fund investor then has to decide, and has limited or no chance to do his own analysis. The liabilities attached to a direct investment, as co-investment is, also have to be carefully weighted.

The SEC has also started to investigate the practice of co-investments, as it sanctions fund investors who do not co-invest and rewards unduly those who do. Indeed, when a fund manager analyses an investment opportunity, he ultimately charges the fund for the cost of doing so. These costs are, whether the deal happens or not, paid by the fund. A co-investor would not pay the costs associated with a deal which ultimately did not materialise, and might pay a small share of the costs associated with doing a deal. This imbalance penalises pure fund investors and triggered the investigations of the regulator.

Is co-investing worth the trouble? Aside from the fact that it increases the direct exposure and thus the risk of the fund investors doing it, there is a significant risk of adverse selection: the fund manager does not guarantee a systematic acess to all the investment opportunities. A fund investor might not have access to the best one. If he does, he might not have the resources to take a timely and informed decision. Overall, academic and empirical studies have shown that co-investing does not deliver higher returns than fund investing (Fang, Ivashina & Lerner, 2015).

Increased competition for deals and costs

Auctioning and increased competition, including from industrial groups, have raised the number of broken deals (hence *break-up fees*), thus accumulating costs for funds without any investment to recoup them. Auctions are pushing private equity groups to be more aggressive and raise their prices. The leverages being applied are increasing, and are sometimes too aggressive to be supported by lenders. This can lead to *failed auctions*, paving the way for a typical private equity negotiation with exclusivity and arm's-length negotiation. It is thus in the limited partners' interest to understand the exact sourcing of investments and how it was negotiated.

Increased concentration risk for fund investors

Club deals and co-investments are making it difficult for fund investors to diversify. A fund investor can hope that a fund will deliver a profit by compensating bad investments with good ones. A fund investor selecting multiple funds increases his chances of avoiding or minimising losses. However, funds investing in club deals reduce the diversification effect. A fund investor tempted to co-invest also effectively reduces his chances of diversifying. To address this risk, fund investors have to carefully craft their investment programme (see Section 3.5).

3.5 SETTING UP AN INVESTMENT PROGRAMME: PORTFOLIO CONSTRUCTION

3.5.1 The Confluence of Bottom-up and Top-down Perspectives: Portfolio Construction

Investors willing to invest in private markets have to reconcile two approaches: a *top-down* vision and a *bottom-up* approach (for further elements, see the introduction to Demaria, 2015). Fund investors make scenarios about the future and look at the past to assess how financial assets behaved under specific conditions. Based on this, they develop an investment strategy which is translated into an allocation to different assets, ranging from listed stocks and bonds to private markets. On this basis they have a top-down vision from private markets, assigning to them an expected level of risk (for further elements, see Demaria, 2019 and Demaria *et al.*, forthcoming) and thus a corresponding level of returns, based on their aptitude to stay invested for a specific time (duration). Then, they scout for fund investment opportunities which could match their vision: they scout the market and filter the opportunities. When confronted, the top-down and bottom-up approach led to the construction and management of private market fund investments.

3.5.1.1 Bottom-up Risks

So far, we have covered in this book some of the risks born by fund investors from a bottom-up perspective. Fund investors have to assess fund managers and their fund investment proposals (Template 3 provides a due diligence list). This is the manager selection risk. A good understanding of the private markets universe (see Chapter 4) supports the analysis of fund investors, who have to understand what is available or not. Some of their desired strategies might not exist, such as LBOs in emerging markets due to a lack of affordable leverage in markets with high inflation; or distressed debt investments out of the USA and the UK due to a lack of appropriate bankruptcy legislation. Mapping the market is therefore a significant effort and requires resources and time. Fund investors follow a step-by-step process (Figure 3.17), sourcing the funds, selecting them, negotiating some terms (whenever possible) and monitoring them, to then start the same process again when the fund manager raises the next funds.

3.5.1.2 Top-down Risks

Fund investors have to integrate private equity cycles and macro-economic shifts (see Section 3.1), that is to say, adopt also a *top-down* perspective. Among the risks that fund investors have to contend with are:

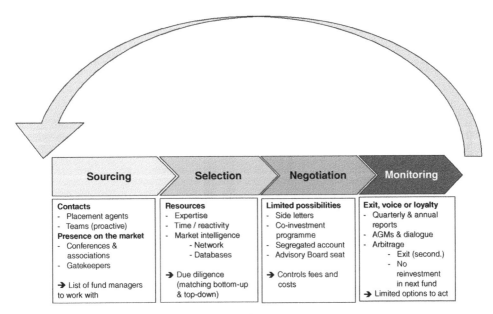

FIGURE 3.17 The process of fund investing and monitoring
Source: Author.

- Market risks – risks of losses due to adverse movements of macro-economic variables such as interest rates in the case of LBOs, or foreign exchange rates in the case of emerging market investments.
- Liquidity risks – investors in private market funds might not be able to liquidate their positions easily and rebalance portfolios.
- Commitment risks – investors might not be able to answer capital calls due to liquidity shortage.
- Contagion risks – fund investors might be affected by the inability of their peers investing in the same given fund to answer a capital call (hence potentially missing an investment and reducing the diversification provided by the fund).
- Capital loss – investors take the risk of losing capital with their private market investments. Figure 3.18 provides an illustration with private equity funds of funds.

Moreover, fund investors have limited tools to actively manage their private market portfolios and rebalance their allocations. The only two options are the secondary market for fund stakes, to invest and sell opportunistically, and co-investments to over-weight some private market assets.

3.5.1.3 Programme Costs

Fund investors not only support the fees and costs billed to the funds they invest in by fund managers, but also specific costs. They have to set up and run their private markets investment programme and therefore support operational costs. They also support opportunity costs when private market funds distribute proceeds from their investments. Fund investors usually have to wait until a new fund is formed and calls the capital. Evergreen funds embed these opportunity costs. They support the costs of the

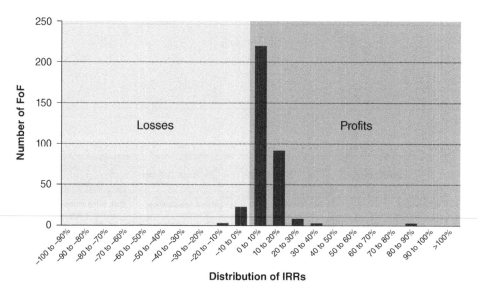

FIGURE 3.18   Distribution of private equity funds of funds by IRR bracket
Source: Wellershoff & Partners, Cambridge Associates 2017. Data as of June 2016.
Sample of 346 funds.

capital committed but not yet called, which is another form of opportunity cost. This capital can be called on short notice (usually 10 to 30 days).

3.5.1.4   Portfolio Construction

The confrontation of the top-down and bottom-up approaches gives birth to an investment programme (Figure 3.19). The output is a grid which will be matched by upcoming funds being raised over the next 5 to 7 years, to diversify not only along the list of criteria in Figure 3.19, but also across vintage years to avoid an ill-timed exposure. As a matter of fact, fund investors should not try to time their investments in private equity markets (Brown *et al.*, 2019). The behaviour of private markets and their different sub-segments is particularly difficult to predict, just like the behaviour of financial markets such as the stock exchange. Hence, to properly build a programme, it is necessary to deploy at least over 5 years when setting up a programme, and then regularly invest on a yearly basis to keep the exposure constant.

This means that to appreciate the success or failure of a private equity programme, it is necessary to wait a certain amount of time. Figure 3.20 shows that, for example, programmes still in the J-curve (5 years' duration) exhibit no performance, and that this performance appears as the programme matures.[33]

Investing in private equity is hence a long-term project, to invest with fund managers in a succession of at least two to three funds, which should avoid the temptation of

---

[33] However, a survivorship bias in the data (i.e., only successful limited partners continued beyond a certain duration with their private equity endeavours, which means that the performance of long-term programmes might reflect only the performance of the most successful limited partners) might blur the interpretation of the performance of programmes of 30 years' duration.

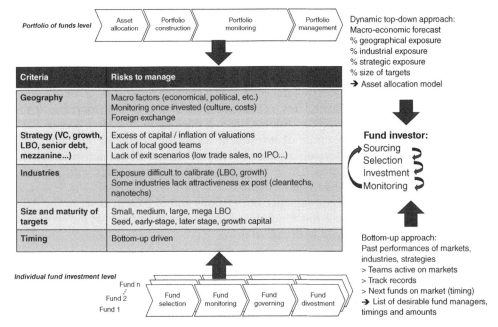

FIGURE 3.19 The dynamic of the construction of an investment programme in private markets
Source: Author.

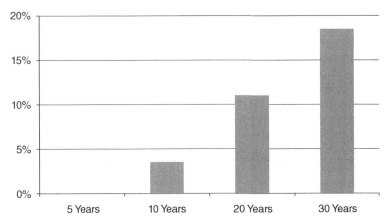

FIGURE 3.20 Relationship between the age of a private equity programme
and the net IRR of the programme
Source: Lerner, Schoar and Wongsunwai (2007).

arbitrage and opportunistic behaviours. Recession years are, for example, a source of high LBO performances. This means that fund investors have to select fund managers during boom times to prepare for the worst. To do so, they first need to thoroughly understand how fund managers invest (Chapter 5), how they source their opportunities, operate their analysis and create value in their portfolio companies (see sample of due diligence analysis in Template 3).

It is only with this intimate knowledge of the specific dynamics of private markets that an institutional investor can evaluate opportunities and take risks by backing, for example, emerging teams or by investing in funds with original strategies. In fact, the traditional method of evaluation of teams with a track record and a stable market does not apply in the latter case. This could be a marker to determine whether a given investor, fund of funds manager or gatekeeper is just tagging along with other investors or is able to create value. This relates to another specificity of private markets: at the heart of its activity, its logic and functioning, there is the human being (see Section 3.2). Human relationships, the aptitude of investment teams for evaluating managers and to find the right people to develop a business are paramount. These activities are the daily work of investment teams. These very same human relationships will make the difference between good and bad performance.

This performance is the consequence of decisions and of a context set in the past. It will be difficult to reproduce this kind of performance in the future, as the economic environment will have changed with regard to:

- aversion to risk of the stakeholders in the private equity ecosystem
- financing costs
- leverage effect
- stability of the economy.

3.5.1.5 Specific Constraints

This programme is also determined by the specific constraints that any fund investor would have to comply with. Some investors have only operational constraints. Foundations and endowments have to spend a certain amount per year to retain their tax-exempt status. Family offices and HNWIs might require a specific payout for their expenses.

Some fund investors have to comply with regulatory constraints, hence limiting them in their ability to allocate to some strategies for example (for more details, see the introduction to Demaria, 2015). Pension funds might have restrictions on the volume they can allocate to a private markets fund programme. Insurance groups might be restricted in the duration of their investments. Banks might have to handle the solvency costs associated with specific strategies. Regulators assign scores to assets depending on the duration and the capital at risk, and banks and insurance groups have to apply these scores (unless they can show statistically that they diverge from this generic score in their investments).

As a consequence, the performance of fund investors can vary significantly (see Figure 3.21; for further elements, see Hobohm, 2010). This performance depends notably on their appetite for certain categories of funds. Depending on the vintage and the market segment selected, performance can be very volatile. For example, endowments were eager to invest in venture capital funds (whose performance was stellar between 1992 and 2001), whereas banks are traditionally keen on investing in LBO funds. Timing hence has consequences on performance. Supporting emerging general partners and strategies was one of the success factors of endowments and foundations in the USA (see Section 3.3.4). The access of endowments to unique resources – such as a network of alumni – is critical (Lerner, Schoar & Wang, 2005). The tolerance for failure and the relative freedom granted to the investment team in the selection of private equity funds, as well as a certain flexibility in the investment policy, could also be other explanatory factors.

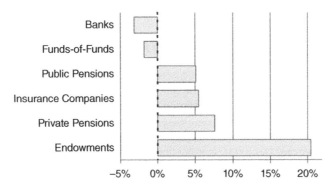

FIGURE 3.21 Performance of limited partners in the USA, according to their nature (%, 1992–2001)
Source: Lerner, Schoar and Wongsunwai (2007).

REFERENCES

Books and Booklets

Demaria, C. (2006, 2008, 2010, 2012, 2015, 2018) *Introduction au Private Equity* (RB Editions, Paris), 1st, 2nd, 3rd, 4th, 5th, 6th edns, 128 pp.

Demaria, C. (2015) *Private Equity Fund Investments* (Palgrave Macmillan, Basingstoke), 276 pp.

Demaria, C. and Pedergnana, M. (2009, 2013) *Le marché, les acteurs et la performance du private equity suisse* (SECA Editions), 1st, 2nd edns.

Demaria, C., Debrand, S., He, R., Pedergnana, M. and Rissi, R. (2000) (forthcoming) *Asset Allocation and Private Markets* (Wiley, Chichester).

Hobohm, D. (2010) *Investors in Private Equity, Theory, Preferences, Performances* (Springer Gabler, Wiesbaden), 199 pp.

Kocis, J., Bachman, J., Long, A. and Nickels, C. (2009) *Inside Private Equity, The Professional's Handbook* (Wiley, Hoboken, NJ), 262 pp.

Lerner, J., Leamon, A. and Hardymon, F. (2012) *Venture Capital, Private Equity, and the Financing of Entrepreneurship* (Wiley, New York), 464 pp.

Tirole, J. (2005) *The Theory of Corporate Finance* (Princeton University Press, Princeton, NJ), 640 pp.

Newsletters and Newspapers

Davidoff, S., 'The risks of tapping your retirement fund for an alternative use', DealBook, *New York Times*, 30 October 2012.

Favaro, K. and Neely, J., 'The next winning move in private equity', *Strategy + Business*, Summer 2011, Issue 63.

Financial Times, 'Lex: Internal rate of return', 1 June 2005.

Financial Times, 'Private equity groups diversify', 20 December 2010.

Henry, D. and Thornton, E., 'Buy it, strip it, then flip it', *Business Week*, 7 August 2006.

Kahn, R., 'Please don't freeze in August', *PEHub Wire*, 19 August 2011.

Lattman, P., 'Judge widens antitrust suit against private equity firms', *New York Times*, 8 September 2011.

Lattman, P., 'Private equity industry attracts S.E.C. scrutiny', *New York Times*, 12 February 2012.

Lattman, P. and Lichtblau, E., 'E-mails cited to back lawsuit's claim that equity firms colluded on big deals', *New York Times*, 10 November 2012.

McCrum, D. and Schäfer, D., 'Investors urge equity funds to reveal budgets', *Financial Times*, 23 January 2012.

Poletti, T., 'Going private starts to make sense', *San Jose Mercury News*, 10 April 2006.

Primack, D., 'Bain Capital raising USD 8 billion', *Fortune*, 30 May 2012a.

Primack, D., 'Conspiracy theories', *Fortune*, 11 October 2012b.

Private Equity International, 'When a flip too quick?', 9 November 2012.

Winfrey, G., 'Mining company sues Caste Harlan', *Private Equity International*, 6 June 2012.

Papers and Studies

Aidun, C. and Dandeneau, D. (2005) 'Is it possible to sell a portfolio company for too much?', Private Equity Alert, Weil, Gotshal & Manges, November, 3 pp.

Anderson, J., Gray, E., Browder, J. and Tincher, J. (2019) 'SEC enforcement against private equity firms in 2019: year in review', Willkie Farr & Gallagher, Client Alert, March 1, 7 pp (www.willkie.com/~/media/Files/Publications/2019/03/SEC_Enforcement_Against_Private_Equity_Firms_in_2018_Year_in_Review.pdf).

Bain (2010) Global Private Equity Report, 76 pp (https://www.bain.com/insights/global-private-equity-report-2010/).

Bernstein, S., Lerner, J. and Schoar, A. (2009) 'The investment strategies of sovereign wealth funds', Harvard Business School Working Paper 09-112, 53 pp.

Braun, R., Jenkinson, T. and Stoff, I. (2017) 'How persistent is private equity performance? Evidence from deal-level data', *Journal of Financial Economics*, **123**(2), pp. 273–291.

Brown, G., Harris, R., Hu, W., Jenkinson, T., Kaplan, S. and Robinson, T. (2019) 'Can investors time their exposure to private equity?', Kenan Institute of Private Enterprise Research Paper No. 18-26 and SSRN Working Paper 3241102, 38 pp.

Cao, J. and Lerner, J. (2006) 'The performance of reverse leveraged buyouts', Boston College, Harvard University and National Bureau of Economic Research, 48 pp.

Demaria, C. (2019) 'Measuring private markets risks in practice', Wellershoff & Partners, 22 pp.

Fang, L., Ivashina, V. and Lerner, J. (2015) 'The disintermediation of financial markets: direct investing in private equity', *Journal of Financial Economics*, **116**(1), pp. 160–178.

Harris, R., Jenkinson, T. and Kaplan, S. (2014) 'Private equity performance: what do we know?', *Journal of Finance*, **69**(5), pp. 1851–1882.

Harris, R., Jenkinson, T. and Stucke, R. (2012) 'Are too many private equity funds top quartile?', *Journal of Applied Corporate Finance*, **24**(4), pp. 77–89.

Hawley, J. and Williams, A. (2007) 'Universal owners: challenges and opportunities', *Corporate Governance: An International Review*, **15**(3), pp. 415–420.

Higson, C. and Stucke, R. (2012), 'The performance of private equity', Working Paper, Coller Institute of Private Equity, London Business School, 49 pp.

Jenkinson, T. and Sousa, M., 2000 'Why SPAC investors should listen to the market', Unpublished Working Paper, University of Oxford, SSRN 1331383, 35 pp.

JP Morgan Asset Management (2007) The Alternative Asset Survey 2007, 40 pp.

Kaplan, S. and Schoar, A. (2003) 'Private equity performance: returns, persistence and capital flows', MIT Working Paper 4446–03, 46 pp.

Korteweg, A. and Sorensen, M. (2015) 'Skill and luck in private equity performance', SSRN Working Paper 2419299, 69 pp.

Lerner, J., Schoar, A. and Wang, W. (2005) 'Smart institutions, foolish choices? The limited partners performance puzzle', Harvard University, 58 pp.

Lerner, J., Schoar, A. and Wang, J. (2008) 'Secrets of the academy: the drivers of university endowment success', Harvard Business School Finance Working Paper No. 07-066, MIT Sloan Research Paper No. 4698-08, 39 pp.

Lerner, J., Schoar, A. and Wongsunwai, W. (2007) 'Smart institutions, foolish choices: The limited partner performance puzzle,' *The Journal of Finance*, **62**(2), pp. 731–764.

Li, Y. (2014) 'Reputation, volatility and performance persistence of private equity', Federal Reserve Board of Governors, Working Paper, 56 pp.

Mackewicz & Partners (2004) 'Institutional investors and their activities with regard to the alternative asset class private equity: An empirical European survey', 84 pp.

Robinson, D. and Sensoy, B. (2013) 'Do private equity managers earn their fees? Compensation, ownership and cash flow performance', *Review of Financial Studies*, forthcoming and NBER Working Paper 17942, 50 pp.

Rouvinez, C. (2003) 'Private equity benchmarking with PME+', *Venture Capital Journal*, 43(8), pp. 34–39.

Rouvinez, C. (2007) 'Looking for the premium', *Private Equity International*, June, pp. 80–85.

Russell Research (2012) Russell Investments' 2012 Global Survey on Alternative Investing, 18 pp.

Sensoy, B., Wang, Y. and Weisbach, M. (2014) 'Limited partner performance and the maturing of the private equity industry', *Journal of Financial Economics*, 112(3), pp. 320–343.

Swensen, D. (2009) *Pioneering Portfolio Management* (Free Press, New York), 408 pp.

Weidig, T. and Mathonet, P.-Y. (2004) 'The risk profile of private equity', QuantExperts/European Investment Fund, 33 pp.

CHAPTER 4

The Universe of Investment

Private markets belong to the world of finance, even though they remain far from being only a financial asset class. The analysis of the universe of investments shows the specific nature of private markets: they are the only financial technique able to follow a company or an asset through each of the steps of its existence, from inception to turn-around. Moreover, whether in the investment process, the methods of investment or investment monitoring, what distinguishes private markets is the importance of the qualitative analysis over quantitative data. In that respect, human intervention is really the core component of private markets (see Chapter 5).

Private markets investing finances private (that is, not listed on the stock exchange) companies or assets through the provision of debt and/or capital (Figure 4.1). Private markets investing targets the full range of equity and liabilities of a private company or asset, by providing equity, convertible debt and debt. Equity investments in private companies are classified as 'private equity', debt provision to private companies as 'private debt', and capital and debt provided to finance private assets as 'private real assets' investments.

Figure 4.1 shows a series of instruments to invest in private markets. These instruments can be a source of innovation. For example, convertible debt combines features associated with debt (for risk management) and equity (for performance generation) investment instruments. These instruments can be adjusted to specific investment cases, but rely on the existence of an adequate and enforceable legal environment (see Chapters 1 and 2). Other private market instruments, notably in the real asset sector, are rather recent and some are still in the making.

As we will see, the border between different sectors of investment is porous. For example, in business restructuring, it is often possible to acquire the equity of a company (turn-around capital) for a symbolic amount, or some of its debt to later convert it into capital (distressed debt). Convertible debt itself is at the border between equity and debt investments. Some assets listed at the time of investment will eventually be acquired and delisted ('public to private' LBO). Companies financed by private equity can eventually be listed. In some cases, such as private investments in public equities (PIPE[1]), a company financed by private equity is and will remain listed. These companies tend to be small or mid-sized and show very low (or even no) volumes of daily

---

[1] See Section 4.1.2 for further elements of PIPEs.

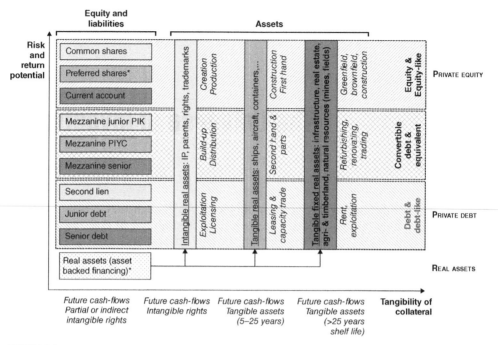

FIGURE 4.1   Private markets: instruments and landscape
Source: Author.

share trading. In many respects, these 'listed' companies are comparable to their private equivalent.

To mitigate risks, different investment instruments can be used (Figure 4.2). For example, private equity investors can use common and preferred shares, depending on the result of their analysis of a company. Preferred shares can embed different political and economic rights. These rights are negotiated between investors, depending on their perception of the risks and profit potential offered by the investment opportunities. As a result, shares are not necessarily equivalent and fungible: some are potentially worth a lot more than others, depending on the realisation (or not) of certain events, for example.

Therefore, investors have a large choice to fine-tune the design of their instruments according to their needs and the analysis of investment opportunities. This was not always the case. For a long time, instruments were limited to equity and some form of debt instruments.

Figure 4.2 shows that at the higher end of the risk spectrum, debt strategies are non-existent. Debt has to be serviced through the payment of interests (even if they can be deferred), the repayment of the principal (which can be deferred as well) and the establishment of a claim on a solid collateral. This is not applicable to companies at seed stage.

Besides direct active ownership, there are tools to invest with relatively hands-off approaches and without intermediaries – such as equity crowdfunding and crowdlending. Both focus on the financing of start-ups by any retail or professional investor via a website or an electronic platform. These two investment channels are restricted to

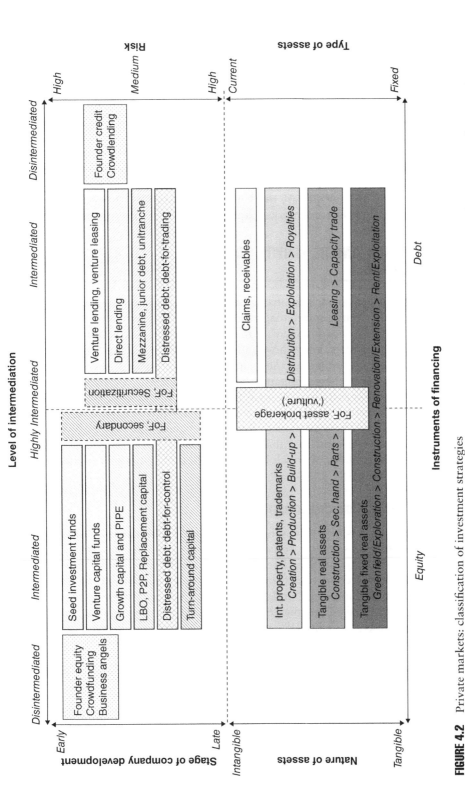

FIGURE 4.2 Private markets: classification of investment strategies

Note: this panorama does not include direct active investments by investors themselves. 'Sec.' refers to 'secondary'. 'PIPE' refers to 'private investments in public entities'. 'P2P' refers to 'public-to-private'. 'Int.' refers to 'intangibles'. 'FoF' refers to 'funds-of-funds'

Source: Author.

projects of rather small size, relatively easy to assess and understand by investors, who do not undertake thorough checks and analyses (so-called 'due diligence'). These two investment instruments are recent and largely unproven. In particular, the lack of strong corporate governance rules, associated with light investor protection rules, limited information requirements, limited (or no) monitoring and control cast a large shadow on them. The viability of these instruments will be tested when the financed companies face the strains of an economic recession and have to tackle its challenges.

Our estimate, based on Cambridge Associates and Preqin databases, is that private equity represents 55–60% of the private markets fund investment universe, private debt 18–20% and private real assets 25–28%. The USA accounts for 67%, Europe 20% and the rest of the world 13% of private markets fund investments. Private equity funds represent roughly 5% of the total market capitalisation of listed companies.

4.1 PRIVATE EQUITY: VENTURE, GROWTH, LBO AND TURN-AROUND CAPITAL

Private equity funds can finance companies at virtually each and every stage of their development. Private equity fund managers aim to solve specific issues affecting companies, which should significantly increase their value. Investors support entrepreneurs with capital, advice, contacts, know-how and expertise. They act as a sparring partner in the governance of the companies they support. To capture this upside, fund managers acquire part or all of these companies before implementing the plan, and then sell their stake when the company has executed the plan and its value has increased. Two main types of operations are executed by private equity funds: capital increases and transfers of ownership. These two operations can be combined in specific strategies. Database provider Preqin estimated that as of December 2017, private equity funds managed over USD 3 trillion, of which USD 1.1 trillion of committed capital was not yet invested ('dry powder').

4.1.1 Venture Capital: Financing Company Creation

Even though the USA has historically been seen as the birthplace of modern venture capital, and therefore as setting a certain template for would-be investors and fund managers abroad, each country has developed its own version of venture capital. Venture capital funds finance companies from inception (seed capital) to prototyping (early stage), industrialisation (mid-stage) and commercial launch, until they reach profitability or are acquired or listed on the stock exchange (late stage, also known as expansion). Venture capital represents roughly 19% of the private equity funds investment universe, and 11% of the private markets investment universe.

4.1.1.1 Venture Capital Investment Targets

Venture capital is the main provider of financing for the creation and early development of a specific kind of company. These companies bear strong technological risks, high R&D expenses and often important investments in equipment, intellectual property and more generally fixed assets.

Venture capital is synonymous with healthcare and life sciences (LS) and information technologies (IT) investments (Figure 4.3), essentially in the USA and Western

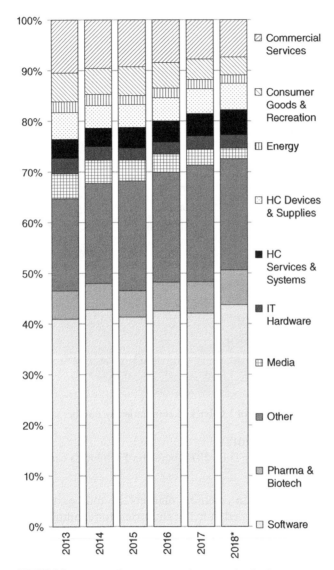

FIGURE 4.3 Global financing trends to VC-backed companies by number of deals and by sector
* As of 31 December 2018
Source: KPMG Venture Pulse 2019, based on PitchBook's data as of 31 December 2018.

Europe (Figure 4.4). Other sectors have at times challenged this supremacy, such as clean technologies and nanotechnologies, but the two former sectors of investment still form the bulk of investments. However, no sector succeeded in establishing a significant footprint which would be large enough to establish a cluster equivalent to the Israeli or American ones.

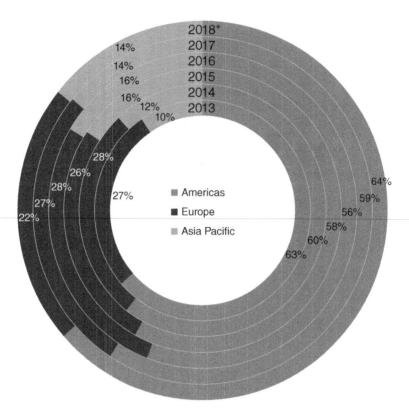

FIGURE 4.4 Financing of VC-backed companies by number of deals and by region
* As of 31 December 2018
Source: KPMG Venture Pulse 2018, based on PitchBook's data as of 31 December 2018.

Investment opportunities in emerging markets are only partially covered. In fact, independent funds are still needed in many countries, for example in Eastern and Central Europe. As a consequence, many entrepreneurs emigrate to developed countries to bring their innovation to market, thus impoverishing their home market. Some start-ups catering to specific local needs cannot be delocalised and struggle to emerge. The need to develop clusters of innovation, with a full financing chain, is an important step in establishing a vibrant entrepreneurial scene. Multiple factors have to be combined to establish successful clusters (see previous chapters).

Elements necessary to a healthy venture capital sector

As much as any other private equity strategy except large and mega LBOs, venture capital investors are generally active in a specific geographical area, defined by a common business culture and a specific set of rules. What is specific for venture capital investors is that they need one or multiple centres of industrial expertise. It is important that investors communicate and understand management teams on a common cultural basis (*The Economist*, 2009). As a consequence, the type of culture (see Table 4.1) also influences the nature of the investments and the type of companies financed in a given country.

TABLE 4.1 Typology of European socio-cultural environments with regard to innovation

Rigid socio-cultural environment	Closed socio-cultural environment	Strong socio-cultural environment
Czech Republic	Austria	Belgium
France	Cyprus	Denmark
Hungary	Germany	Estonia
Lithuania	Greece	Finland
Latvia	Spain	Ireland
Portugal	Italy	Luxembourg
Slovakia	Malta	The Netherlands
	Poland	Sweden
		Slovenia
		United Kingdom

Source: Europe Innova Synthesis Report 2008.

Three elements appear as essential to support the innovation capacity of a given country: support for fundamental research; an efficient process to support knowledge and technology transfer; and an environment adapted to company creation in innovative sectors.

Invest Europe (formerly known as EVCA, 2010) has listed factors which, at the macro-economic level, could help to increase the dynamism of venture capital markets:

(i) First, fight the fragmentation of European stock exchanges, which is currently partially solved thanks to the mergers at Euronext–NYSE and further movements in Europe (SIX Swiss Stock Exchange–Oslo Stock Exchange). However, the stock exchange landscape remains rather fragmented and hostile for a pan-European listing of promising start-ups.

(ii) Broaden the tax breaks associated with small and medium-sized businesses (SMBs), which is a European problem in general.

(iii) Reduce the barriers to international investment in venture capital.

(iv) Reduce the administrative, social and tax burden on start-ups (see Figure 4.5), notably by adopting measures adapted to their situation. This type of measure (e.g., thanks to a tax refund on R&D expenses in France[2]) helps companies to postpone the impact of certain expenses or refund certain R&D expenses. However, not all tax incentives are fruitful or positive. They can introduce distorted incentives, and moral hazard.[3]

(v) Provide an efficient, clear and integrated system to protect intellectual property.

(vi) Revise international accounting standards and adapt SMBs. This element is just as important to understand the reading, understanding and communication between investors and leaders.

---

[2] Crédit Impôt Recherche.

[3] Lerner (2009) states that 'a study of the French scheme [OSEO-Garantie] finds that the probability that a small business borrower goes bankrupt in the four years after taking out a loan goes from 9 percent if the loan does not have a government guarantee up to a stratospheric 21 percent if it does' (p. 80).

(vii) Revise the regulation on financial risks. Basel II & III Agreements, the European Solvency II Directive and a few more regulations are hampering allocation of assets to venture capital. These regulations, even if adopted at the supra-national level, can be modified and adjusted by national and pan-European regulations.

(viii) Integrate the commercialisation in the programmes financing SMBs. In fact, most public efforts have been aimed at supporting R&D, but commercialisation is a crucial factor which has to be supported. The competition from incumbents being very strong, SMBs need support to commercialise their attractive products.

(ix) Avoid conceiving public intervention in the form of constraints and restrictions (see Figure 4.5). This is in line with what we have seen in Chapters 1 and 2. It has substantial consequences: 'private equity funds that were active in nations with well-operating legal systems had an average return multiple [...] 19 percent better than the typical fund established in that subclass and that year, while those in other countries had a multiple 49 percent worse than the benchmark' (Lerner, 2009, p. 95).

Entrepreneurship: resistances and myths

Resistances to entrepreneurship might also be fuelled by myths surrounding these endeavours. Wadhwa (2011)[4] debunks some of them, by recalling the following facts:

- *Technology entrepreneurs are seasoned executives.*[5] Contrary to the belief that the typical American technology entrepreneur is in his 20s, 'Duke University's 2009 survey of 549 company founders found that the average and median ages of these

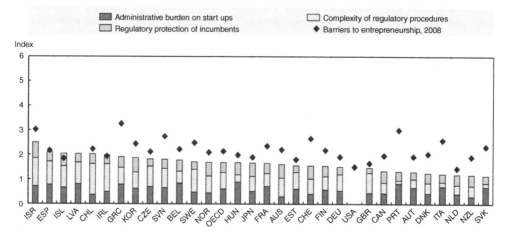

FIGURE 4.5   Barriers to entrepreneurship in 2008 and 2013, including administrative burden to start-ups
Note: 0 = least restrictive, 6 = most restrictive. For the USA, the 2013 observation is not available
Source: OECD 2017.

---

[4]www.boston.com/business/technology/articles/2011/08/02/when_it_comes_to_tech_ entrepreneurs_and_their_successes_legends_abound.
[5]The myth of the 'young entrepreneur' is rather powerful, see Pfanner (2012).

founders was 40. Twice as many were older than 50 as were younger than 25, and 43.5 percent had two or more children'.

■ *Entrepreneurs are made entrepreneurs, not born as such.* 52% of the entrepreneurs were the first in their families to start a business. Only 39% had an entrepreneurial father and 7% an entrepreneurial mother. Only 25% started in college.

■ *Higher education is correlated with success.* The myth of the 'college dropout' is just that – a nice bedtime story. American-born founders of engineering and technology firms tend to be well educated. 'On average, companies founded by college graduates have twice the sales and workforce of companies founded by people who did not go to college. Surprisingly, attending an elite university doesn't provide a significant advantage in entrepreneurship. What matters is the degree.'

■ *Venture capital follows innovation, it does not 'make' it.* Less than 5% of venture capital goes to early-stage companies, which take the risk of developing innovative products. 'The reality is that venture capital follows innovation.'

Cultural resistance is illustrated by Bradshaw (2012), describing the American attitude (embracing risks and being eager to grow something large) and the British attitude (cautiously managing cash, mitigating the downside as much as possible and limiting the success target to something achievable). These statements have been made so often, that they are almost ingrained in the collective psyche. As stated by Needleman (2012) and confirmed by the OECD (Figure 4.6), US entrepreneurship has stabilised after a decline in 2008–2011. It increased substantially in the UK after 2009 (Figure 4.6).

The US venture capital model and its consequences

Although it is true that the American economy benefits from specific assets, assuming that there is only one way to success ('shooting for the sky') is misleading. Surowiecki (2011) explains that part of the American success in breeding successful start-ups comes from 'venturesome consumers' (from the retail and the corporate sectors). In business-to-consumer information services, Americans are often ready to embrace technology – and effectively behave as beta-testers of free services – which gives the economy an edge in productivity: 'in that sense, [the American] culture of innovation depends on consumers as much as on entrepreneurs.' Though that might be true for some business-to-consumer innovation, it might not be applicable for business-to-business innovation, notably related to infrastructures and standards. The USA, having dealt with multiple standards in mobile phones, is still today lagging behind Japan and Europe. They ignored text messaging, mobile instant messaging and other consumer innovations for a long time. They are also lagging behind South Korea and Europe for Internet broadband adoption and fibre-to-the-home (FTTH).

There are actually multiple models for entrepreneurial success. The American model focuses on 'lean ventures',[6] dedicated to business-to-consumer services, with a limited capital consumption at early stage[7] and then with massive needs as the company grows and needs to attract users at scale. The aim is to be listed on the stock exchange or sold for large sums. Shooting at the sky requires large amounts to invest, and thus an IPO or

---

[6]Schonfeld (2011).

[7]Arrington (2010) hence describes the pressure of 'super angels' (business angels who turned into fund managers) to find the next 'big thing' and the subsequent valuation increase of the start-ups, reaching USD 4 million pre-money (i.e., before capital increase) at the seed stage.

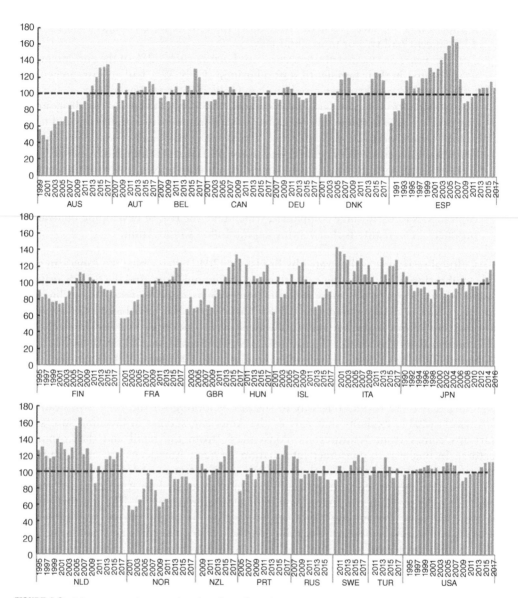

FIGURE 4.6   New enterprise creation in selected countries
Note: number of new creations in 2012 is 100
Source: OECD 2018.

large acquisition for a return on investment. Western European start-ups focus on less
visible business-to-business IT, with the target of reaching profitability and then being
sold to a trade buyer at a valuation between EUR 50 and 150 million.

    Israel's model of venture capitalism

    According to KMPG's Venture Pulse, in 2017 more than USD 250 billion was
invested in venture capital globally (Figure 4.7). The USA collected USD 130 billion
(up from USD 83 billion in 2017), Europe USD 24 billion and Israel USD 4.7 billion.

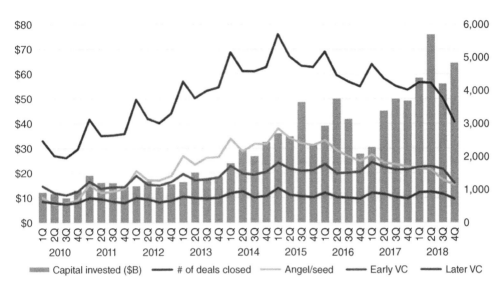

FIGURE 4.7   Global venture financing by volume and number of deals
Source: KPMG Venture Pulse 2019.

Bloch, Kolodny and Maor (2012) state that over the course of 2003 to 2011, VC firms have invested USD 11 billion in Israel's high-tech companies, USD 45 billion in Europe, USD 26 billion in China and USD 7 billion in India. According to these authors, 'there is much more to Israel than technological know-how. It is a small, highly networked country with a high concentration of educated workers. Interdisciplinary skills are common, and most workers are multilingual.' This is a clear example of a specific model of a venture capital cluster which has emerged as an original template.

Start-up financing has been closely related to military technology developments in Israel. Gladwell (2011) (quoting Dima Adamsky) illustrates how countries have adopted innovation, with the example of the adoption of the 'Revolution in Military Affairs' (RMA), which 'refers to the way armies have transformed themselves with the tools of the digital age'. According to Gladwell, 'Adamsky begins with the simple observation that it is impossible to determine who invented RMA. The first people to imagine how digital technology would transform warfare were a cadre of senior military intellectuals in the Soviet Union, during the nineteen-seventies. The first country to come up with the high-tech systems was the United States. And the first country to use them was Israel, in its 1982 clash with the Syrian Air Force.' This applies to the Internet technologies which were partially invented in the USA (Internet protocol) and Europe (World Wide Web), and later put in practice by start-ups in the USA, Israel and Europe.

Gladwell states that these are 'three revolutions, not one, and Adamsky's point is that each of these strands is necessarily distinct, drawing on separate skills and circumstances. The Soviets had a strong, centralised military bureaucracy, with a long tradition of theoretical analysis. But they didn't do anything with it, because centralised military bureaucracies with strong intellectual traditions aren't very good at connecting word and deed'. This statement applies to a lot of innovations, either coming from public (CERN) or private (Xerox PARC) research centres.

Which model of venture capital would be adapted to this type of innovation context (which mostly describes Continental Europe, Russia and Japan)? Darcy, Kreamer-Eis, Debande and Guellec (2009) tried to address this concern by describing the conditions necessary for a technology transfer[8] from public institutions to the private sector. They describe notably three options: spin-out (which does not fit with the risk-averse culture in Europe and even more public research labs), collaboration between universities and the private sector (which so far has failed to be widely adopted) and IP licensing (which looks more promising but lacks a platform to match offer and demand).

'The United States', continues Gladwell, 'has a decentralized, bottom-up entrepreneurial culture, which has historically had a strong orientation toward technological solutions. The military's close ties to the country's high-tech community made it unsurprising that the US would come with the technological applications derived from this analysis'.

Finally, Israel's 'military culture grew out of a background of resource constraint and constant threat. In response, they became brilliantly improvisational and creative'. However, 'as Adamsky points out, [Israel's] military built around urgent, short-term "fire extinguishing" is not going to be distinguished by reflective theory' (Gladwell, 2011).

This explains notably, in a context of more or less permanent macro-economic crisis in Western Europe and more recently after 2007 in the USA, why Israel's 'innovation model' has been praised; as well as being difficult to generalise and adopt in different economies.

The European emerging model of venture capitalism

The model of growth in Europe is one constrained by multiple currencies, languages, laws, business practices and cultures. Staging the growth of start-ups progressively and differently than in the USA, with a continent-wide market, hence makes sense.

Exceptions, such as Skype or Spotify, exist but do not invalidate the conclusion that if a business model is effective, it will be replicated in other countries and multiple companies will co-exist on the European market, hence producing a healthy and durable competition (which might be lacking on the American market, with the consequences attached thereto).[9]

Europe has competitors for Google (in Russia: Yandex), for eBay (in the German-speaking countries: Ricardo), for Yahoo (in Germany: Gmx), for LinkedIn (in Germany: Xing). Discounting these successes would ignore some of the lessons born of these start-ups, which have capitalised on different know-how and might actually outlast some of their American counterparts.

The reassuring conclusion of these initiatives is that '"quality," [psychologist Dean] Simonton writes, is "a probabilistic function of quantity". Simonton's point is that there is nothing neat and efficient about creativity. "The more successes there are," he says, "the more failures there are as well"' (Gladwell, 2011).

Hence, there is not yet any European venture capital model, but a series of national initiatives that might lead to a syncretic one: venture capital is structured around clusters

---

[8]'From invention and IP generation to business concept, proof-of-concept phase and first customers' (p. 9).

[9]Alleged or legally proven anti-competitive behaviours (Microsoft, Google, Amazon), individual privacy mishandling (Facebook, Google), predatory practices (Facebook).

in the UK, with leading universities at the core of innovation. In France, certain sectors are privileged, owing to political choices manifest in tax breaks. Swiss venture capital shows specificity: corporate venturing is a major source of start-up financing.

Maybe tapping into the Israeli potential would be a start, as they are lean start-ups adapted to a small market and with international potential. This is the suggestion of Bloch, Kolodny and Maor (2012), notably in semiconductors, telecommunications, medical devices, water treatment and agriculture – all sectors where Europe has assets to develop and capitalise on while collaborating with Israeli start-ups.

The models highlighted by Bloch, Kolodny and Maor (2012) are:

- A typical partnership to share risks and pool resources.
- Investing in local start-ups.
- Setting up a corporate venture capital arm.
- Establishing an incubator in Israel.
- Establishing local R&D centres.
- Acquiring a local start-up.

These six options are actually a way to learn and adapt innovation to local conditions. They might be a template for other models of venture capitalism.

Other 'models' of venture capitalism: the Chilean initiative

What emerges from different initiatives to build a venture capital industry is that it is expensive and needs long-term commitment, significant funding and cooperation between multiple actors of the innovation and venture capital industry.

The spill-over effect of these efforts (whether successful or not) is actually part of the building of the venture capital ecosystem. These externalities, as economists call them, will coalesce, transform their surroundings and something close to a venture capital cluster will start to materialise. Some countries, such as Chile (*The Economist*, 2012a), have started rather pragmatically by trying to attract the immigrant entrepreneurs turned down by the USA (notably due to a restrictive visa policy).

'Start-Up Chile' hence selects promising start-ups, provides roughly USD 25 000 (pre-seed) and/or USD 80 000 (seed stage) and a visa for 1 year. Between 2010 and 2012, around 500 companies and 900 entrepreneurs from 37 countries have applied. The aim was to have supported 1000 companies by the end of 2013. In 2019, the programme declared to have supported 1616 start-ups (54.5% of which were still active at that time) and more than 4500 entrepreneurs from 85 countries.

The programme has attracted attention, but will it create a self-sustaining venture capital industry and notably push local nationals to start their own ventures? At least the cultural context seems to evolve, as companies apply more to seed financing, universities start to explore innovation centre set-ups, newspapers cover more start-ups and, above all, there is experience and know-how sharing, as well as coaching with local entrepreneurs.

As noted by *The Economist* (2012a), there is still a need for more venture capitalists, more innovative entrepreneurs and – more worryingly – the idea that this Chilean platform might then lead them to Silicon Valley. Administrative burdens, a rigid bureaucracy and a punitive bankruptcy regime are also slowing down the efforts of Start-Up Chile.

Overall, this initiative might succeed if – like that of Singapore – it lasts (it took 30 years to build Silicon Valley). As long as it lasts, 'when you have a bunch of smart people with a broad enough charter, you will always get something good out of it,' Nathan Myrhvold, formerly a senior executive at Microsoft, argues. 'It's one of the best investments you could possibly make – but only if you choose to value it in terms of successes. [...] Innovation is an unruly thing. There will be some ideas that don't get caught in your cup. But that's not what the game is about. The game is what you catch, not what you spill' (Gladwell, 2011).

The Economist (2012c) states that 'economic theory suggests four main reasons why firms in the same industry end up in the same place. First, some may depend on natural resources [...]. Second, a concentration of firms creates a pool of specialised labour that benefits both workers and employers [...]. Third, subsidiary trades spring up to supply specialised inputs. Fourth, ideas spill over from one firm to the next.'

Wilson (2012) explains that most would-be clusters (Bangalore in India, Shanghai's high-tech centre, Seoul's Digital Media City) never reached their goals: 'most efforts to create clusters focus on one or two elements [...] which do not make a difference unless they add up to sustainable serial innovation. To generate one groundbreaking technological development after another, innovation must be embedded within long-lived social institutions and networks. Four different sectors must be linked together: government, business, civil society (non-profit organisations) and academia'. This environment then does not need hazardous coincidences: it nurtures constant sparks of innovation.

For Wilson, three measures are crucial to support the collaboration between these four sectors:

(i) Building cross-sector networks that are richer, more diverse and more deliberately structured than in the past.
(ii) Leaders should continually reform their organisations, to create an innovation climate, adjusting incentives and organisational structures to reward creativity and collaboration.
(iii) Leaders should invest in talented, innovative individuals, attracting, retaining and empowering the right mix of people who can foster serial innovation.

The last recommendation is actually the crucial point in the case of Start-Up Chile. Is this country, culturally, linguistically and religiously homogeneous, able to retain and 'empower' individuals who came opportunistically? That would mean serious frictions among the local population (as differences are often rejected), and serious efforts to develop a multi-cultural, multi-linguistic and rich environment for an 18-million-strong country, geographically isolated and stretched along the Andes. In its list of potential hubs which could catch up with Silicon Valley and Israel, New York, London and Berlin are mentioned by *The Economist* (2012c) because they are bigger and livelier, and therefore more attractive to young people; and they have a wider pool of industries and hence skills on which companies can draw.

4.1.1.2 Actors and Structures

Seed financing or bootstrapping, that is the question
According to the Monitor Group (2010), 52% of entrepreneurs declare that there is sufficient capital for high-growth companies, but only 37% agree with the statement that there is enough capital to launch companies. A study of Invest Europe (EVCA, 2002) states that 95% of the entrepreneurs surveyed would not have been able to launch

TABLE 4.2 Sources of equity capital in the USA

Sources of capital for private companies	Start-up stage	Growth stage
Founder's own savings	Yes	Maybe
Friends and family	Yes	Yes
Angels (wealthy individuals)	Yes	Maybe
Professional VC investors	Yes	Yes
SBICs (USA only)	Maybe	Yes
Corporations	No	Maybe
Employee stock ownership plans	No	Maybe
Public stock offering	No	Yes
Personal and business associations	Maybe	Maybe
Commercial banks (debt)	No	Yes
Savings & loans (debt – USA only)	No	Maybe
Life insurance companies (debt)	No	Maybe
Commercial credit companies (debt)	No	Yes
Factors (debt)	No	Yes
Leasing companies (debt)	Maybe	Yes
Public programmes, R&D programmes	Maybe	Maybe
Tax shelters	Maybe	Maybe
Foundations	Maybe	Maybe
Supplier financing	Maybe	Maybe

Source: Yale School of Management; author.

their companies without venture capital[10] (or that they would have grown much more slowly). 60% state that their companies would not exist without venture capital.

The sources of capital for start-ups are rather limited (see Table 4.2). Most of the funding for entrepreneurs comes from their own savings, their friends and family, and their network. It is only after demonstrating a certain capacity to reach crucial milestones that the circle of potential financial backers will get larger.

Hence, start-ups usually raise capital in stages, as it helps to break down the amounts required into smaller portions and helps entrepreneurs to reduce the dilution of ownership attached to fundraising (see Table 4.3).

Bootstrapping

As explained by Karbasfrooshan (2012), *bootstrapping* (i.e., self-financing by entrepreneurs) is tempting in order to preserve control and ownership. However, giving away portions of the company (or eventually even giving up control) 'shines a light on another reality of value creation: you have to ensure that others want to see you succeed and prosper, and the only way to do that is to hand out equity; as John Doerr says "no conflict, no interest"'. In that respect, a Board of Directors helps when it is time to make tough decisions.

---

[10]This is a recurring problem, as Lerner (2009) states: 'By the time of the Great Depression of the 1930s, there was a widespread perception that the existing ways of financing fast-growing young firms were inadequate. Not only were many promising companies going unfounded, but investors with high net worth frequently did not have the time or skills to work with young firms to address glaring management deficiencies' (p. 36).

TABLE 4.3 Stages of financing for a typical IT firm

Venture milestone	Amount invested	Type of investor	New investor owns (%)	Post-money valuation (USD)	Founder owns (%)*	Founder value (USD)
Initial seed start-up	25 000	Founder	100	25 000	100	25 000
Product R&D	75 000	Family	35	215 000	65	140 000
Product testing	150 000	Friends	15	1 000 000	55	550 000
Shipping product	300 000	Angel	10	3 000 000	50	1 500 000
Expansion round	2 000 000	VC firm	33	6 000 000	33	2 000 000
Late-stage round	5 000 000	VC firm	25	20 000 000	25	4 000 000
Go public (IPO)	10 000 000	Public	20	50 000 000	20	10 000 000

* Assuming no further investment than the initial one by the founder.
Source: Yale School of Management; author.

Having small amounts of cash also 'forces entrepreneurs to tackle issues head-on and generate real solutions'. However, there is no room for adjustments in case of obstacles (either difficulties or faster growth than expected). The fact that entrepreneurs are perpetually fundraising (having raised too little or no money to start the company) means that they are being permanently distracted.

Reputation is another problem. Not raising money might actually hurt the business: 'while you may score extra points for building a large business despite being bootstrapped, you don't actually score many points for running a small business if you have avoided venture capital, even though 99.9 percent of VC-funded companies wouldn't exist or last as long as yours if they didn't have VC funding to rely on.'

Seed financing

Seed financing is dedicated to help transform an idea into a company. Before becoming very fashionable, seed investing was one of the least favoured areas of investment, because the survival rate of companies is rather low and returns are usually generated over the course of more than 5 years. The fact that Europe offers different opportunities for growth, compared to the USA, has an impact on emerging companies. Innovation tends to be adopted more slowly at the beginning, but accelerates strongly – sometimes outpacing the USA, as was the case with mobile phones or Internet broadband. This explains why seed investments need longer to take off. There is a wide area of political and economic experimentation opened up here.

Some countries have tried to gather certain key elements in 'campuses' (UK), 'technoparks' (Switzerland) and 'pôles de compétence' (France) to try to replicate the Boston and Silicon Valley clusters. These key elements are usually a source of knowledge (Oxford, Cambridge, ETHZ, EPFL, Stanford, Harvard), solid infrastructures, a qualified and diversified pool of human resources, a qualified and seasoned pool of capital and an entrepreneurial spirit (see Chapters 1 and 2 to further understand the importance of these factors).

According to Lerner (2009), 'on average a dollar of venture capital appears to be three to four times more potent in stimulating patenting than a dollar of traditional corporate R&D' (p. 62). On average, 46 jobs have been created in the companies which have answered the survey, after capital injection.

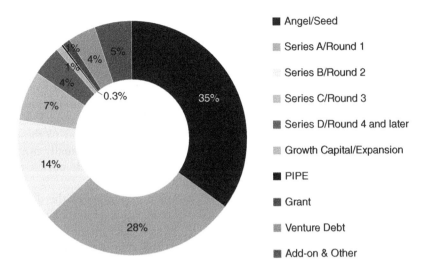

FIGURE 4.8 Breakdown of the number of venture capital deals by stage in 2018
Source: Preqin 2019.

Business angels and crowdfunding

If venture capital finances innovative start-ups, it is business angels which are considered as the key elements of seed investment. As illustrated in Figure 4.8, they represent roughly 15–35% of the rounds of financing in venture capital, by deal number. Without them, many of the investment opportunities offered to venture capital funds would simply not exist. In volumes, the cumulated amounts invested by business angels are much smaller (Figure 4.9).

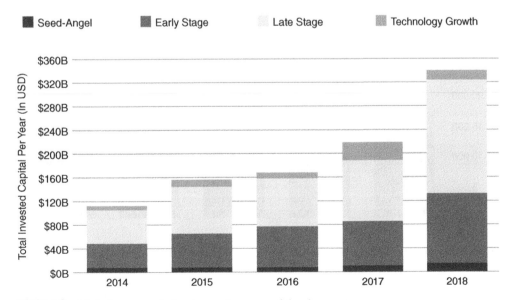

FIGURE 4.9 Global venture deal volumes, by stage of development
Source: Crunchbase 2018.

Seed capital is crucial as it shapes the future company. As illustrated in Figure 4.10, funding has remained fairly strong after the financial crisis of 2009. This is good news, as a dearth of financing might simply put the venture financing value chain under threat (the alternative being 'bootstrapping', see above).

It even accelerated further in 2018. This in fact might be a source of concern. The market for venture financing is driven by the number of investment opportunities which match specific criteria: a management of quality, a viable business model, a product or service which fits a real and significant market need. We will refer to these below as 'viable ventures'. The market for venture capital investments is usually not (or just marginally) driven by the offer of capital. Two scenarios are possible in case the offer and demand for venture capital are not balanced.

First, there is a scenario where the offer of capital is inferior to the demand. As seen in previous chapters, the number of new ventures tends to be fairly stable over the mid-term. In case of recession, the scarcity of jobs on offer might drive individuals to launch a freelance activity. These freelancing activities are not the target for venture capital investments. Nevertheless, the number of viable investments to be funded by venture capital might exceed the amounts on offer. The reason might be that investors are more risk averse given the macro-economic environment, that they are already fully invested, or that they lost capital due to the recession. Some promising ventures might not get financed, but these are an exception. Most might raise less capital than initially expected. In that case, they will set interim milestones to reach and raise their capital in multiple stages.

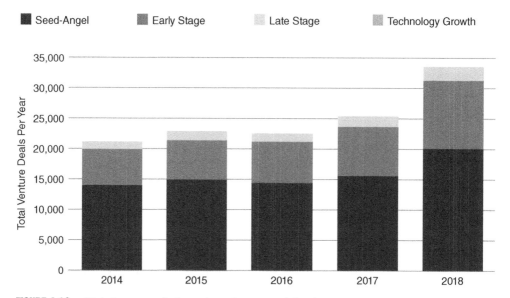

FIGURE 4.10 Global venture deal numbers, by stage of development
Source: Crunchbase 2019.

Second, there is a scenario where the offer of capital exceeds the natural demand. This is the case where investors are over-confident or have no other attractive opportunities to invest. The consequences are stark, as:

- Some non-viable ventures might get financed, thus leading to subsequent losses. This means that investors might leave the venture financing market altogether, or that the amounts lost will have to be reconstituted to be invested in the next generation of start-ups. Indeed, investors tend to reinvest the capital of past successes (and sometimes the capital gains as well) into the new opportunities. Rebuilding investment capacity takes time.
- An excess of capital might finance too many start-ups vying for the same market. This means that the competition is very high from early on. Not only will start-ups not be able to set a higher price for early adopters as they would normally do to build their business viably, but they might also have to launch a price war from the start. As the market eliminates the weaker players, the amounts needed by start-ups to survive in this context increase substantially: they have to last and gain market share when weaker competitors disappear. The return on the total invested decreases correlatively. Moreover, recouping the amounts invested is more challenging, as customers get used to the low prices and might not agree to a price increase later on.
- An excess of capital might also give the wrong incentive to viable ventures. They might collect capital more easily and increase the amounts raised (see Figure 4.11 as a recent illustration). This excess of capital collected will relieve the pressure of making the most efficient use of it, wasting some capital. As capital providers will compete to invest in start-ups, valuations will increase. For a given amount, the productivity of the use of capital will not only be lower, but the investor will get a smaller share of the company. This will contribute to depressing the returns of investors, as valuations at exit (essentially trade sales) might not follow the same path. Figure 4.12 provides a comparison point with Figure 4.11: the number of exits has been fairly stable over time and the amounts (with the exception of Q3 2018) did not change substantially. In Q2 2018, the average exit was for around USD 124 million. It was around USD 146 million in Q2 2019, a 16% increase. As a matter of comparison, the average size of seed and angel rounds increased by 60% year on year (it increased by 42% in 2018).

It is a common mistake to assume that a lack of economic dynamism is due to a lack of innovation, which itself is due to a lack of entrepreneurship, which is due to a lack of capital. Public authorities are regularly convinced to lavish their national start-ups with taxpayers' money. Unfortunately, these efforts are doomed to fail. The market is driven by a number of viable opportunities which are *structural*, and thus require legal, social, cultural and economic changes. Capital will flow to opportunities if the conditions are ripe and if *governance rights* are properly set, thus leading to profits and a virtuous venture financing circle. Any excess of capital, notably from public sources, will in effect generate significant losses but also depress the returns generated by viable ventures.

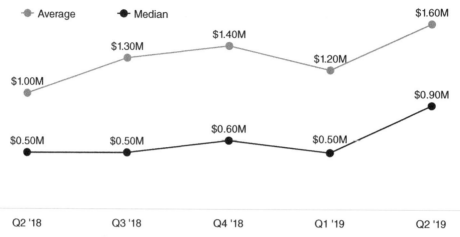

FIGURE 4.11   Seed and angel round size globally
Source: Crunchbase 2019.

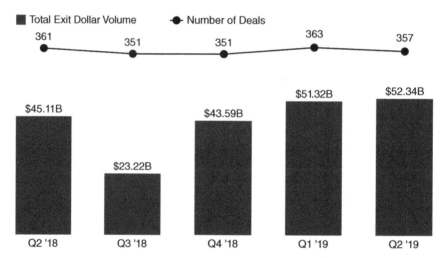

FIGURE 4.12   Acquisitions of venture-backed companies globally
Note: dollar volumes are aggregated from transactions with known dollar
amounts. For most mergers and acquisitions, dollar amounts are not disclosed
Source: Crunchbase 2019.

As the best deals are supposed to compensate for the losses in a venture portfolio, this
means that ultimately an excess of capital might push the sector of venture capital in
collective losses. Institutional investors will then stop to invest in venture capital funds.
Viable ventures will find it even more difficult to find capital. This was clearly the case
in Europe after the bubble and crash of the late 1990s and early 2000s. The European
venture capital funds struggled for a long time to raise capital, and local start-ups had
to be much more efficient in their consumption of capital. As a result, European venture
capital performance outpaced America for the following decade.

A recurring issue for business angels and bootstrapping is their isolation, notably if they venture out of IT. Start-ups are financed in multiple rounds, helping them to reach the next milestone and stage of development. For that, investors have to team up and syndicate their investments as the company grows. They notably syndicate their start-up investments with professional venture capital investors, which are specialised in terms of geographical localisation, industry, but also stage of development. The consequence is that, for example, even if a promising company in renewable energies in a tertiary city in an emerging market gets seed financing from local business angels, it might simply not find any further venture financing. Cleantechs collect very limited amounts globally, and essentially in industrial clusters in developed markets.

Industrial clusters with a critical mass of activity and financing are crucial (see previous chapters). This means that innovation in other sectors than IT is either driven by corporations, or bootstrapping. This does not bode well for the growth of these other sectors, and their innovation, in particular if they are capital intensive.

Business angels

Business angels are a catalyst for the emergence of small structures from ideas and business plans. They help entrepreneurs to structure their ideas, develop them professionally, gather initial capital and key human resources, and identify their early business partners. In that sense, they are closest to the original spirit of venture capital, where 'profitability was a goal of the effort [...] but were not the overriding purpose of the [venture capital] firms. Instead, they were depicted as a necessary part of the process' (Lerner, 2009, p. 37).

These business angels are usually former entrepreneurs or executives who turned out to be HNWIs. As illustrated in Figure 4.13, they are a phenomenon which is

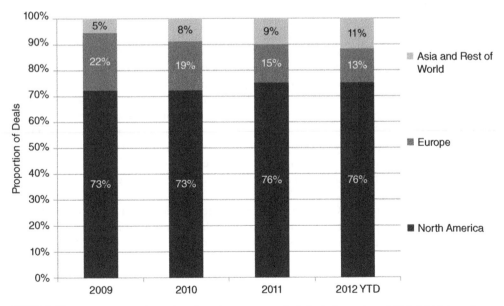

FIGURE 4.13 Proportion of angel and seed venture capital deals by region: 2009–2012 (as of September 2012)
Source: Preqin 2012.

TABLE 4.4 Typical amounts of start-up capital required

Amount (USD)	Proportion (%)
Less than 10 000	29
10 to 25 000	26
26 to 100 000	19
101 to 500 000	17
500 000 to 1 000 000	5
Over 1 000 000	4

Source: Yale School of Management.

essentially American. They are necessary to a healthy venture capital sector. Some countries, such as the USA and France, have recognised their importance, by entitling these individuals to specific tax breaks if they invest (or reinvest) in unlisted companies.[11]

According to the Center for Venture Research[12] (University of New Hampshire), business angels invest on average USD 22–23 billion per year in the USA. In 2018, USD 23.1 billion was invested by 334 565 business angels in 66 110 companies. These figures are remarkably stable and essentially the same in 2011.

The average deal size is roughly USD 300 000 to 350 000. Indeed, most of the start-ups require small amounts of capital (see Table 4.4).

In 2018, 15% of exits were at a loss (in 2011, 24% of exits were bankruptcies) and more than half were by merger or sale (54% were mergers and acquisitions in 2011). Sectors financed were healthcare (23%), software (20%), retail (13%), biotech (9%), financial and business (8%), industrial and energy (6%), among others. In 2011, sectors of investment were software (23%), healthcare and medical devices (19%), industry and energy (13%), biotech (13%), IT services (7%) and media (5%).

Equity crowdfunding and ICOs: not such a good idea after all

At the junction of the retail investment market, the Internet and seed capital is crowdfunding. Internet platforms have emerged to help match start-ups (often in seed stage) willing to raise money and/or sell their first products from/to individuals. The concept has gained traction with the voting in of the Jumpstart our Business Start-Ups Act in the USA in April 2012, which was in effect legalising the concept of mass marketing private placements of the equity of start-ups to the public (donation-based, reward-based and lending-based initiatives are compliant with the regulations). The SEC has issued rules to implement the legal recommendations in 2015,[13] and regularly revises and adjusts them.[14]

Initial coin offerings (ICOs) are a disintermediated version of an equity crowdfunding offering. An entrepreneur or a company issues a document (a 'white paper') detailing their ambition and for which they raise capital. In exchange for this capital, 'tokens' are

---

[11]France has even created specific investment vehicles for these individuals, such as the Société unipersonnelle d'investissement à risque (SUIR), which do not seem to have taken off.
[12]http://wsbe.unh.edu/cvr?page=1.
[13]www.sec.gov/news/pressrelease/2015-249.html.
[14]www.sec.gov/smallbusiness/exemptofferings/regcrowdfunding.

created and can be further exchanged on a public or private individual ledger maintained by the entrepreneur or the company. These tokens have variable attributes, some of them being a simplified version of a security with no governance rights or representations.

Though highly lauded by the entrepreneurs (who see a cheap and hassle-free source of financing at hand), by individuals (who imagine investing in the next emerging Google or Facebook through these platforms) and politicians (who see a way to bridge the seed financing gap without dealing with difficult questions of taxation and business angel status), this solution might not be as optimal at it seems.

First, because this is 'dumb equity'. Most of the value created by business angel (Kerr, Lerner & Schoar, 2011) and venture capitalists comes from their involvement in the ventures, by providing advice, expertise and networks, but also by controlling the management of a company, sometimes supplementing it or replacing it. Crowdfunding platforms do not provide Board members to start-ups, and in effect leave the crowd of investors without any power to negotiate the terms of investments, monitor efficiently their investment and take action.

Second, because crowdfunding gives the wrong impression that investing is cheap, easy and could lead to great rewards. Playing the lottery is all of these things – but it's not investing, even though the risk is high (see Davidoff, 2012b). In effect, the organisation of annual general assemblies and dealing with the legal correspondence and procedures might consume in postage and organisation a significant portion of the money collected from the crowd investors. Investing requires time-consuming and expensive due diligence, which is necessary to take an informed decision. Business angels themselves have to go through this painful process to negotiate their rights (though not necessarily always reaching the expected result, see *The Founding Member*, 2011).[15]

Third, because if regulations have so far protected – and increased this protection of – retail investors, there must have been a reason. This reason is that they lack the expertise of being qualified/accredited/professional investors. By removing the 'barriers' or protections of individuals (after trying to categorise the venture capital industry as a source of systemic risk, see Freeman, 2009), to let them commit in highly 'illiquid' and high-risk ventures might sound quite illogical.

Instead of amending the ill-conceived Sarbanes–Oxley regulations, which are burdensome and do not deliver the expected protection, soften the barriers to entry to the stock exchange and hence review the problem of company financing and the participation of retail investors (with an appropriate risk return to their financial profile), the American legislator has put them in the highest-risk investment category and waived

---

[15]In fact, one of the practices of business angels has been to use convertible debt to invest in start-ups. The reasoning was that this tool, designed for bridge financing (i.e., short-term loans of 12 to 18 months to prepare the next round of financing) would benefit the entrepreneurs (it is cheap to organise and structure and does not involve any discussion on the valuation, which can be postponed to round A) and the investors like it because they have seniority over equity in a debt-free company. However, if the next round does not happen on time (which is quite frequent due to delays in fundraising, or in reaching milestones), the debt matures and companies can be forced into bankruptcy. As there are no assets (hence no collateral), investors lose their money and entrepreneurs are forced to give up. This tool, which looks attractive, can actually have rather dreadful consequences. This is just one illustration of the difficulty in calibrating an investment in a start-up by qualified/accredited investors.

the patiently elaborated protection designed for stock exchanges – which crowdfunding platforms are[16] (focusing on primary placements). Some of the largest frauds of the 2007–2009 period were Ponzi schemes (which were tested on a large scale in the 1920s), to which professional investors succumbed. How could retail investors see clearly through opaque emerging start-ups without thorough due diligence, and protect themselves from the risks they would have identified through due diligence without any negotiating power (Schonfeld, 2012)? The Jellyfish tank case (Jeffries, 2012) is just one example of why crowdfunding is deemed to be a future source of problems.

One might argue, though, that crowdfunding has always existed in one way or another, notably when people started cooperative companies; or when people financed the emerging company of one of their neighbours or family members (the 'fools, friends and family' category). First, cooperative companies empower everyone to be not only a business owner on an equal footing with anyone else, but also systematically part of the business decisions. To put it differently, there is no founder and no management shares; no specific rights, notably because cooperatives do not have shares. Everyone is strictly equal and the management of the cooperative is not aiming at liquidity or profit.

Then again, people financing a start-up from a neighbour are actually not the crowd, but people who actually know this person (more or less) on a personal basis. Due diligence is replaced by an intimate knowledge of the individual, his/her background, family, behaviours ... The background check does not have to be done, because it is immediate and capitalised over the year informally. There is no such thing in case of crowdfunding, where total strangers are dealing with one another.

Some crowdfunding platforms argue that they select projects before admitting them for fundraising. Regardless of the fact that their interests lie with the fundraiser (who will pay them a commission in case of success), the due diligence of the crowdfunding platform will never replace the expertise of a business angel or a venture capitalist.

At the end of the day, the risk of crowdfunding is that it will be receiving projects which have been rejected by other sources of 'smart capital' (adverse selection), notably because entrepreneurs are aware of what professional investors bring to the table (and are ready to give up ownership and control and to cope with diplomacy in exchange for that); or are judged too expensive by professional investors (me-too business-to-consumer start-ups tend to exhibit this feature).

Indeed, most of the profits over the last venture capital cycle have been made in the business-to-business sector, with companies addressing technical issues in semiconductor design, in storage (virtualisation, big data management, cloud computing), in software design and automation, and other specific areas that retail investors fail to grasp properly. Biotechnologies, clean technologies, new materials, medical technologies and a large portion of the economy will in effect remain out of reach of this financing technique. However, the legal precedent of loosening the protection of retail investors will have long-lasting and resounding consequences, which might be on the scale of the abrogation of the Glass–Steagall Act in the 1990s and the consequences attached to it in terms of systemic risk.

---

[16]As confirmed by the fine that the SEC imposed on SharesPost for trading shares of private companies (see Linley, 2012; Rappaport & Eaglesham, 2011).

Private placement platforms: also not such a good idea

Another initiative might have resounding consequences: the advent of private placement platforms[17] such as Nyppex, SecondMarket and SharesPost (see Gelles, 2010). Although their fortunes have dwindled with the official listing of Facebook and Zynga (which made the bulk of the transactions on these platforms – Facebook accounted for two-thirds of transactions on SecondMarket, according to Dembosky, 2012),[18] and hence might reduce the risk of major problems, the concept itself cast a shadow over the idea of venture capital secondaries.

By in effect trying to replicate the stock exchange to allow shares to be traded between qualified/accredited/professional investors, these platforms have actually accredited the idea that selling a stake in a private company is necessarily a matter of a liquidity event. It should not be.

Actually, solving the problem of venture investing is dealing with a growing gap between the time horizon to develop a start-up successfully and bring it to maturity (on average 9.4 years in 2010, according to Knowledge@Wharton, 2010)[19] and the time horizon of a venture capitalist (between 3 and 7 years). By staging investments, venture capitalists have paved the way for specialisation of their activity according to the maturity of a company. The next steps would be to offer them an exit as soon as they have done their work, that is to say, bringing a given company successfully to the next milestone (or development stage).

Historically, the rule was that venture investors should all stay invested together until a liquidity event happened. That would align the interests of historical shareholders (who have an intimate knowledge of the company) and the newcomers (who have a very limited knowledge of it). This was also related to the fact that financial resources were scarce, as the venture capital industry was still very small.

This is no longer the case: venture capital funds can reach the size of a billion, and the due diligence capacities have increased thanks to the expertise of the teams, the documentation routinely produced by start-ups (thanks to affordable software) and the due diligence specialists available on the market. Hence, secondaries are not only possible, but they should be encouraged, though not through platforms (see Patricof, 2009 for an examination of the consequences of the emergence of the Nasdaq on the IPO market and the race towards size and subsequent dearth of IPOs in recent years).

Arm's-length transactions, between professionals who know each other, have built a sound reputation and can demonstrate achievements as owners of a given business are actually what define a healthy secondary transaction. Eliminating the 'middle man' or the process of due diligence does not make sense: if auctions in LBOs are highly documented and require extensive due diligence in mature, stable and documented

---

[17]The equivalent of private placement platforms for ICOs is each of the individual public ledgers dedicated to each ICO through which they are exchanged.

[18]In effect, Goldman Sachs has closed its 'GSTrUE' (Goldman Sachs Tradable Unregistered Equity OTC Market) which was specialised in trading 144a securities. Launched in 2007, notably to trade soon-to-be-listed shares of general partners such as Oaktree and Apollo, it was closed in 2012 (see Lattman, 2012). That did not prevent dark pools from launching their own initiatives (Demos, 2011).

[19]Anecdotal evidence suggests that this time did change significantly since then: https://about .crunchbase.com/blog/startup-exit/.

businesses, it does not seem logical to imagine that start-ups can waive the costly, tortuous and painful but necessary acquirer due diligence.

4.1.1.3 Venture Capital Funds

Venture capital funds represent the large majority of formal start-up financing (Figure 4.14). The USA has shaped the modern limited partnership structure in many respects. It also realised early on that in order to set up a dynamic venture capital industry, it had to involve public money either through direct contribution to the funds (through its SBIC programme), or by granting their portfolio companies a certain access to public investments (through the Small Business Administration Act).

European approach: the attraction of retail venture capital

Similarly, European countries have either tried to promote investment vehicles by giving them special tax treatment,[20] or by encouraging them through public seed programmes.[21] According to Invest Europe (EVCA, 2009), nations rank differently as to venture capital investments than for the overall private equity sector. The UK and France are leading the European rankings. This leading position of the UK and France as to European investments tends to show that this sector needs to be nurtured by adapted regulations, taxation and more generally by a favourable 'ecosystem'. Venture capital

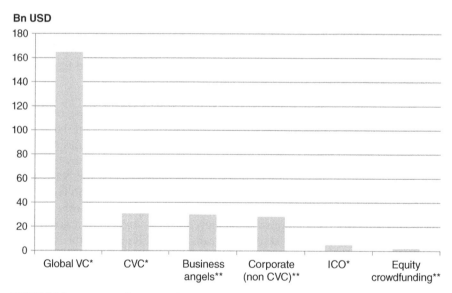

FIGURE 4.14   Sources of start-up financing
* Figures for 2017
** Figures for 2015
Source: Wellershoff & Partners, CB Insights, WBAF, ACA, Foro Excala, ABAN, Arabnet, Crowdexpert, EBAN, Massolution and Coindesk.

---

[20] Venture Capital Trusts in the UK, Fonds Communs de Placement dans l'Innovation in France.
[21] The Netherlands, France, Germany and Belgium have set up an equivalent of the American SBIC programme at different stages.

investors are generally specialised not only by sector, but also according to the maturity of the companies they are backing. Switzerland comes fourth as to corporate venturing and sixth as to venture capital investments.

VC gathers *captive investment structures*, which belong to banks or insurers, and *independent teams*. These captive structures are mostly European and continental.[22] This is related to the fact that retail investors can invest in VC retail funds with tax rebates. Distributing these products means having access to a wide network, such as banks or postal ones, for example.

On and off... and on: corporate venturing

Corporate venturing[23] is another form of captive team,[24] where companies provide capital to invest in emerging companies. The interest of large corporations in venture capital is driven by industrial synergies (29% of investors) and financial gains (50% of investors). For 21% of investors, synergies and financial gains are of equal importance. For entrepreneurs, corporations can bring expertise, knowledge, know-how, contacts, services and knowledge of the industry which might be beneficial.

Corporate venturing capital (CVC) efforts have mainly been a succession of 'stop and go', owing to the fact that corporations tend to sacrifice these units during cost-cutting programmes and launch them when they feel rich – which usually means at the highest point of a business cycle. Between 2000 and 2009, more than 350 corporate venturing programmes were launched (40% of which have been active for 3 years or more). According to Bielesch *et al.* (2012), there are more than 750 programmes active worldwide. 1466 programmes were counted by the Global Corporate Venturing website in 2018. The number of new CVC firms investing for the first time increased from 64 in 2013 to 264 in 2018 (CB Insights, 2019). CVC programmes have ramped up their global activity from USD 10.6 billion invested in 1029 deals in 2013 to USD 53 billion in 2740 deals in 2018 (CB Insights, 2019).

In 2013, North America dominated CVC programmes, with 64% of the deal share by continent. Asia represented 19%, and Europe 16%. In 2018, the figures were 41%, 38% and 17%, respectively. This allowed some emerging markets such as China to catch up with developed markets, with 29 deals representing USD 0.3 billion in 2013 and 351 deals representing USD 10.8 billion in 2018. As a matter of comparison, Japan started with 70 deals and USD 0.1 billion in 2013 and reached 317 deals representing USD 1.4 billion, while the figures for India were, respectively, 18 deals for USD 0.1 billion and 71 deals for USD 1.8 billion. These figures have to be put in perspective, however: only the disclosed numbers are accounted for by CB Insights. The reality might differ substantially from reported figures.

The interest of corporations does not stop at arm's-length initiatives. Some corporations invest directly off their balance sheet. In fact, the number of deals done directly

---

[22]Though Asia might have developed its own version, financed by conglomerates, listed groups and sovereign wealth funds.

[23]For more information, see www.globalcorporateventuring.com.

[24]Intel Capital, Siemens Ventures, GV (ex Google Ventures), Salesforce Ventures, Maersk Ventures, Porsche Ventures, SNCF Ecomobilité Partenaires, Novartis and Swisscom Ventures are a few examples. Sometimes, corporate venturing efforts can be jointly delegated to an independent team (such as with Iris Capital in France, which has welcomed Publicis and Orange as leading LPs in 2012).

increased from 729 in 2013 to 3820 in 2018, largely overtaking the CVC deals (912 and 2177, respectively, as seen above). Some corporations have a dual approach, investing via a CVC programme and off their balance sheet. They participated in 117 investments in 2013 and 563 in 2018.

The drawbacks of accepting a direct investment in a corporation or CVC investment are that the start-up might actually be identified with the group and find it difficult to work with companies which are either competitors or steering away from the group. Moreover, the group can change its strategy and the start-up might end up in a sector which is no longer strategic (hence cutting the financial and operational support at a critical time). The corporation can also choose to adopt a different technology, and hence compete directly with the start-up it has initially chosen to invest with. Start-ups can also take the risk that corporations are either too intrusive in their management, or tempted to peep into their proprietary knowledge and technology.

Indeed, 'looked at through historical data, corporate venturing's role in supporting entrepreneurs has been relatively limited. They participated in 16 percent of the overall number of venture capital deals in 2013 and 23 percent in 2018. Given their often short-term lives and interest in deal-making at the end of an economic cycle, corporate venturing units have had a reputation for being fickle and "dumb" money' (Haemmig & Mawson, 2012). Corporate venturing is essentially aimed at revenue generative (pre-profit) companies (or companies with a current product or service being developed), which means that these programmes are a basis to fund potential partners (or as a secondary purpose, for a potential acquisition at a rather attractive price). Indeed, CVC deals are larger than the typical VC deal, implying that they are active at a later stage of development of start-ups. However, this is changing as the number of CVC programmes investing in seed rounds was 111 in 2013 and jumped to 332 in 2018.

Bielesch *et al.* (2012) state that the endeavours of corporate venturing programmes are deemed to last beyond a cycle, as they complement the R&D efforts of corporations and gain access to new technologies and business models (somehow outsourcing this effort to partners) and help to penetrate fast-growing emerging markets. This is confirmed by the fact that corporate venturing programmes are first and foremost co-investing, notably to forge cross-industry networks. They hence cover a wider industry spectrum than typical VC investors.

According to the manager of the corporate venturing arm of LG Electronics, Mike Dolbec (quoted in Haemmig & Mawson, 2012), there are three stages of the corporate venture capital model:

(i) Investing in a third-party fund. It does not deliver on the corporation's expectation. It does not provide deep insight and perspective, nor with deal flow.
(ii) Setting up a local office in Silicon Valley, staffed with people whose careers have been in the company (or were recently recruited).
(iii) Hiring Silicon Valley people, experienced venture investors with previous operating experience.

The issue with the third model lies in incentives management. It is difficult to promise (or even calculate) 20% of the upside of corporate venturing investments, as this would disrupt radically the pay policy in the company.

The classical model reborn: independent teams

Independent teams have thus been thriving, sometimes starting as captive teams and slowly acquiring independence as their track record was being built. Teams generally have a sector focus (IT, LS, clean techs, new materials) and very often even specialise in various sub-segments (telecommunications, semiconductors, software, mobile technologies, infrastructures for IT, for example). Geographically, teams focus on a region. If a firm covers multiple regions, they open local offices and share knowledge and expertise. This is the case for Sequoia Capital, which has opened offices in Israel and China.

4.1.1.4   Operational Activities

Venture capital appears as one of the most emblematic forms of private equity investments (see Figure 4.15). Because of its simplicity, it is historically one of the first to have appeared. VC investors acquire a stake in a company in the form of equity. They often pool their efforts and build an *investment syndicate*, which usually reinvests as long as the company develops and shows some promising outcome. Venture capital investors usually have different expertise and know-how. As they syndicate and attract outsiders, they can offer a richer network and pool of competences.

The dynamics of syndication vary depending on the sector considered. We can differentiate industries with:

- A high level of diversification and a moderate level of syndication, such as IT industries.
- A moderate level of diversification and a moderate level of syndication, such as non-IT industries, medical and life sciences, as well as semiconductors.
- A low level of diversification and a moderate level of syndication, such as communications and media, as well as biotechnologies.

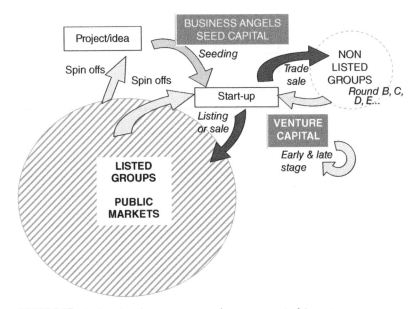

FIGURE 4.15   Lifecycle of a company and venture capital investments
Source: Demaria (2006, 2008, 2010, 2012).

Beyond capital, venture capital provides 'soft capital' which is necessary to mitigate the risks. Being able to find customers for pilot projects, or to attract key human resources in the company, or just qualified lawyers and auditors, can be crucial. As the returns in private equity are highly volatile, competences which could substantially reduce the overall risk appear as a must-have (see Figure 4.16). This is why VC investors team up with some of their natural competitors, sometimes even building so-called 'club deals' where they invite other investors.

Moreover, VC investments are made through successive rounds of financing. This means that an investor who specialises in early start-up investments will plan to reinvest at least twice the amount of his initial investment in the same company. Capital deployment is very progressive and is deemed to be stopped if the company fails to reach the next stage of development.

4.1.1.5 Challenges

Venture capital's unique dispersion of returns and its sources

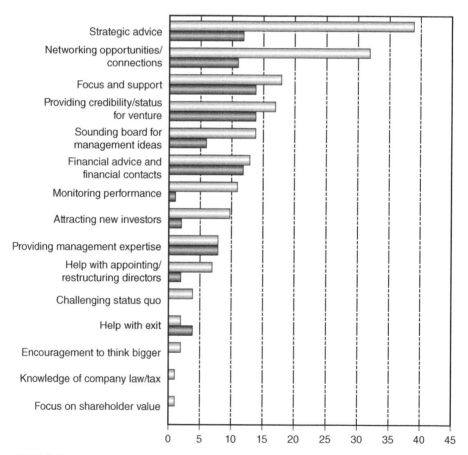

FIGURE 4.16 Most important contribution of a venture or growth capital investor (except capital)
Note: dark grey, growth capital; light grey, venture capital
Source: NUBS/EVCA (2002).

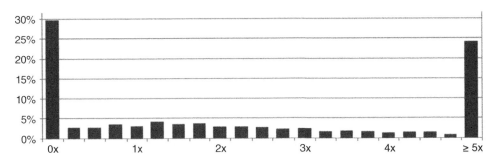

FIGURE 4.17 Dispersion of returns in venture capital
Source: Weidig and Mathonet (2004).

The dispersion of returns in venture capital (see Figure 4.17) might be difficult to understand. It is in the nature of VC investing to see a significant proportion (if not the majority[25]) of the portfolio companies fail. The reasons for these failures are quite numerous:[26] beyond betting on the wrong innovation (LCD vs MEMS in routers), sector[27] or standard (AAC vs MP3 in music), the market might be too small (satellite telephones), not solvent (cures for rare diseases in poor countries), or support only one or very few contenders (satellite radio, social networks).

It might also be that the technology aged faster than expected due to another innovation, or that the innovation was introduced too early for the market to pick up, or was copied by a bigger company with more marketing power. Beyond that, the operations might have failed to produce a reliable product or service (despite promising pilots or beta tests), the management team might have split because of strategic disagreements, some may have died prematurely. The reasons which lead portfolio companies to a dead end form a never-ending list.

Venture capital and valuations

Even if the company succeeds in building a viable product/service, with a sufficiently large market, with an effective position on it, addressing solvent customers and growing, it does not necessarily translate into a profit for venture capitalists. Not only do the valuations at entry and exit matter a lot to generate profits (some successful companies started in 1997–2000 and were financed at very high valuations, and were later sold at a loss despite being profitable and growing rapidly), but also the exit path matters (IPOs are more lucrative and some investments were made with this exit in mind – to finally end up being acquired by a corporation for a much lower price).

Even though in expansion, venture capital has witnessed business cycles, one of the most emblematic being the 1998–2003 cycle. The crash of 2000 can be analysed as an excess of available capital compared to the absorption capacity of the market:

---

[25]75% according to Shikhar Gosh, quoted by Gage (2012).

[26]They are summed up by Tyejee and Bruno in Lerner (2009, pp. 51–52).

[27]'Venture capital investors' mission is to capitalize on revolutionary changes in an industry, and the well-developed sectors often have a relatively low propensity for radical innovation' (Lerner, 2009, p. 60). However, it is difficult to identify which 'new sectors' to invest in (healthy pet food, personal medical diagnostics) and which 'traditional sectors' will still benefit from innovation (e.g., health records and health management).

there were not enough innovating projects which corresponded to the VC investment philosophy. This led to some form of introspective analysis, on whether the VC model is 'broken' (Mulcahy, Weeks & Bradley, 2012)[28] or not (Demaria, 2012;[29] Primack, 2012a). Smaller funds were raised as the industry suffers from a certain lack of attractiveness, notably due to disappointing performance while the excesses of 1998–2003 were being mopped up. Since then, venture capital has recovered, and large funds have been raised and deployed again.

Another VC boom was fuelled by the 'Internet social media' start-ups (*Financial Times*, 2011b). Faccbook, Groupon, Twitter and the like raised USD 5 billion in the first semester of 2011 (Reuters, 2011), the largest amount invested since the USD 55 billion deployed in 2000. A potential bubble was created (*The Economist*, 2010), with 'concept' companies being chased by potential investors, and strong herd investment behaviour and very high valuations for companies which were still private and with no revenues.[30] The lack of revenues has encouraged high valuations (Bilton, 2012): '"It serves the interest of the investors who can come up with whatever valuation they want when there are no revenues", explained Paul Kedrosky [. . .]. "Once there is no revenue, there is no science, and it all just becomes finger in the wind valuations."'

The crash happened in 2012 after Zynga, Facebook and Groupon went public, and the aftermath was limited to the Internet social media this time. One of the differences of this 2007–2012 boom and crash is that it was truly international, with very high valuations for Russian, Chinese, Indian and European concept companies. As Reuters (2011) states: 'In [. . .] 1999 through 2001, the VC industry sank USD 96.4 billion into web start-ups alone, with more than 80 percent of that [. . .] in the United States [. . .]. Of 10 755 VC deals over that run, 7174 took place in the US market. Not so today. Of the more than USD 5 billion of VC money invested so far in 2011, just USD 1.4 billion has been deployed in US start-ups [. . .]. Roughly three quarters of the 403 deals have taken place overseas.'

Just like the previous one, that crash did not affect each company the same way. Some were winners, others did not fare so well. Facebook was valued above USD 100 billion while being private vs USD 60 billion at the end of 2012; Groupon above USD 15 billion vs USD 4 billion at the end of 2012 (*The Economist*, 2011). The first went public, with initial difficulties, and then started its ascendancy to multiply its price per share by six over the course of 7 years; the second is trading at 10% of its peak price per share at the time of writing.

Europe is still spared from this kind of difficulty as the market does not seem to have reached maturity yet – but exhibits problems of its own as a lot of its VC funds do not seem to reach the critical mass required to have attractive returns and hence be really viable (see notably Kelly, 2011, who confirms that Europe lacks this critical mass and a mature venture capital ecosystem).

Venture capital exits: IPO or not?

Beyond this list of failed companies or loss-making investments, some of the portfolio companies will pay off handsomely and compensate for the losses of the rest of the

---

[28] www.kauffman.org/uploadedfiles/vc-enemy-is-us-report.pdf.
[29] www.pehub.com/176010/is-enemy-fact-us/.
[30] YouTube, FriendFeed, Zite, Hot Potato, Beluga, GroupMe, TweetDeck, Dodgeball, Instagram.

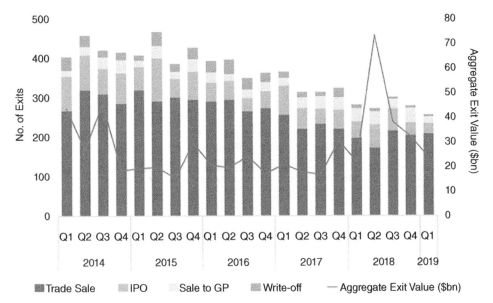

FIGURE 4.18 Exit paths for VC investors, broken down by type of exit
Source: Preqin 2019.

portfolio. This happens with successes such as Google, Yahoo, Cisco and other listed companies. They are the most famous investments from venture capitalists, but they are also exceptions (see Figure 4.18).

However, IPOs are very lucrative exit paths. Indeed, when the 'IPO window' is closed (as happened in 2009, see Figure 4.19), venture capitalists, even if breeding successful companies, can generate sometimes rather mediocre returns due to the fact that none of the 'stars' of their portfolio could gather the returns able to lift the portfolio performance up to the usual standards of return for the risks supported by investors (Waters, 2010).

VC investors hence rely on access to stock exchanges such as the Nasdaq for their biggest successes. In Europe, there is no real equivalent, even though the AIM and Alternext are trying to rise to this status. In fact, European venture capitalists rely on large groups to acquire their portfolio companies. Kelkoo, which was financed by SGAM, Banexi and Innovacom, was acquired by Yahoo. Skype was acquired by eBay, and later Microsoft. Some – such as Iliad or Tableau Software – went public successfully, but still appear as exceptions. This is related to the fact that the time horizon of a fund is rather constrained and that portfolio companies may not grow fast enough to reach the stage where they could safely become listed.

Depending on the evolution of the stock exchange mergers, the London AIM could become the stock exchange of reference for European, and even American, companies (Braithwaite & Demos, 2011). British regulation is lighter than American regulation,[31]

---

[31] www.londonstockexchange.com/companies-and-advisors/aim/aim/aim.htm.

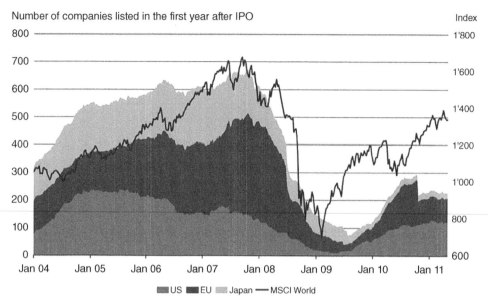

FIGURE 4.19   Evolution international IPOs
Source: Crédit Suisse, IDC, Bloomberg 2011.

although there are multiple options to go public in the USA.[32] American regulation, and notably the Sarbanes–Oxley Act, has in fact considerably increased the duties of listed companies in the USA, hitting large groups and small and medium-sized capitalisations indiscriminately.

As languages and business cultures are close to each other, the AIM is an attractive alternative.

This stock exchange needs the critical mass of listings that could promote it to the status of a genuine European listing platform for European growth companies (which is lacking, as can be seen from Figure 4.20). The competition from other stock exchanges (notably Asian, and among them Hong Kong) hampers these efforts.

Figure 4.21 shows that overall there is a low rate of entrepreneurial activity in high-income economies, as individuals have the choice of accepting jobs and have to face high competition if they start a business. However, Canada and the USA still record levels above 15%. Israel positions itself around 12%, a level that only the Slovak Republic and The Netherlands approach.

---

[32] Going public is mostly for big companies with a market value of above USD 100 million. SEC Regulation S-B offers a simplified procedure for companies with a value of USD 20–50 million to sell stock to the public. Sometimes large private offering procedures are close to public ones: Small Company Offering Registration (SCOR) to offer to the public USD 1 million or less with very light procedures; SEC Regulation A to sell up to USD 5 million to the public at low requirements (costs are usually USD 75 000–125 000). SEC Regulation D, which is an alternative to a venture capital round, with offerings to the public.

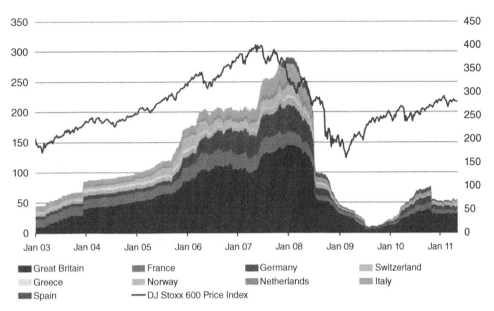

FIGURE 4.20 Evolution European IPOs
Source: Crédit Suisse, IDC, Bloomberg 2011.

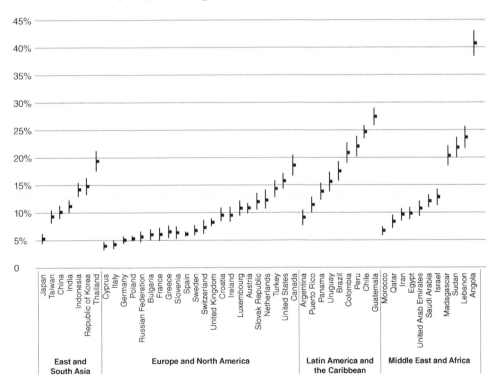

FIGURE 4.21 Total early-stage entrepreneurial activity (TEA) rates among 18–64-year-olds
Source: Global Entrepreneurship Monitor 2018.

Entrepreneurship as a career choice, as well as the status of entrepreneurs once successful, plays a significant role in the decision to start up a business (Figure 4.22). There is a direct link between the perception of entrepreneurship as a good career choice and the actual act of starting up.

The most important social and cultural dimension for private equity remains the readiness of the population to take risks. A look at the age pyramid, and at the social and economic structures, shows differences between Europe, Israel and the USA. However, the latter two show a strong dynamism in entrepreneurship and risk acceptance. This is where the European political initiative would have the highest impact: not only as to financing fundamental research, but also by promoting risk acceptance (or reducing the fear of failure), even if this means finding a specific model of generation and support for spin-offs as a first step.

The education system is another determining factor in the promotion of entrepreneurship, and the generation of vocations. It helps to train and prepare future entrepreneurs, and helps talents to emerge, notably by favouring initiatives and confrontation of risks in a controlled environment (to later face real-world risks).

Culture plays a significant role in entrepreneurship (Chapter 2), but it is not the only determining factor. Indeed, with the right assets, a county might be able to attract foreigners willing to start a company. Foreign-born entrepreneurs are a major source of successful companies in Silicon Valley, to the point that the cap put on visas for IT workers in the USA regularly makes the headlines of national media. In Europe, a significant portion of independent workers are of foreign extraction. The attractiveness of an economy, as well as its openness to skilled foreign entrepreneurs, is a crucial factor

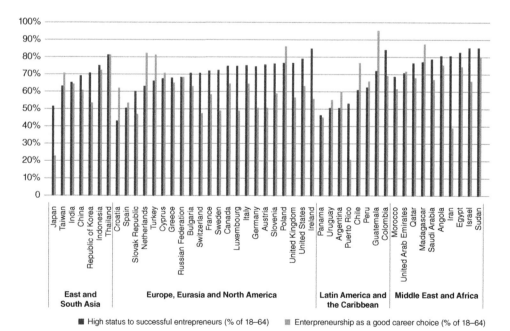

FIGURE 4.22 Societal attitudes about entrepreneurship and the status of entrepreneurs among 18–64-year-olds
Source: Global Entrepreneurship Monitor 2018.

to foster innovation and the creation of start-ups. Europe still has significant progress to make.

4.1.1.6 Limits

Not every young company needs seed or venture capital. In that respect, Microsoft was only marginally venture backed. Its development was essentially financed through its commercial agreement with its first client (IBM). The same statement applies to Google: even though financed by VC funds, it raised only two rounds of financing. In contrast, Federal Express had to raise multiple rounds of financing to support its development in the 1970s, at a time when venture capital was very scarce. The capital intensity of its business explains this need.

There is therefore no real strict rule as to VC investments, just as there is no clear border between venture capital and growth capital.

4.1.2 Growth Capital: Financing Companies' Expansion

Though probably the most ancient form of private equity investments, growth capital is not easy to identify. Often it gets confused with venture capital (notably late-stage VC, which can finance cash-flow-positive companies, or even profitable companies). It can also overlap with small and mid-sized LBOs, notably when the LBO goes along with a capital injection. According to Cambridge Associates and Preqin, GC represents roughly 12% of the PE fund investment universe (6% of the PM universe), although this amount appears rather low.

4.1.2.1 Growth Capital Investment Targets

Nevertheless, growth capital is generally associated with the financing of strong-growth companies (see Figure 4.23), which are usually profitable. These companies need capital to finance their development, increase their production capacity, support a sales effort or develop internationally. Growth capital is therefore focused on growth financing, helping companies which are not able to get loans either because of their size, their financial record or because banks are still deeming them too risky.

4.1.2.2 Actors and Structures

Interestingly, most of the LBO fund managers declare that they are growth capital investors as well, thus blurring the border between the top end of growth capital and the low end of LBO. It is therefore difficult to identify the specialists in this area, even though it appears to be the leading sector in certain countries such as Spain and Switzerland. Growth capital also acted as replacement capital (i.e., buying out the owners of a business) for a long time, before the LBO became well known and investors and banks were sophisticated enough to import it (through owner buy-outs, or OBOs).

LBOs do not provide any capital to a company, as it is just a way to manage a transition of ownership. So, if an LBO fund manager is willing to inject capital into a company, that operation will be growth capital. This also applies to PIPEs, which can either be the acquisition of blocks of shares (secondary purchases on the stock exchange) and/or growth capital operations made through the acquisition of new shares (primary purchase on the stock exchange).

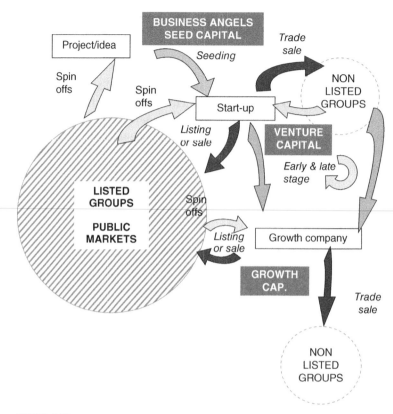

FIGURE 4.23   Lifecycle of a company and growth capital
Source: Demaria (2006, 2008, 2010, 2012).

Pure growth capital funds may have different targets. Some emanate from industrial groups, with a strong mid-market focus and an industrial perspective. 21 Investimenti, in Italy, is an emanation of the Benetton family and has even set up a sister company in France (21 Central Partners). Others are part of the offering of a private equity team, such as Ardian (ex-Axa Private Equity), which has developed multiple lines of products.

There are also many captive teams. Banks find a logical development in private equity through growth capital. Given the credit history that they are registering continuously with their corporate clients, they are able to better evaluate the risks associated with capital injection – thus offering an alternative to simply refusing a loan. Banks have a natural deal flow coming from their commercial activities. These are usually small proximity funds for regional (Zurcher KantonalBank in Switzerland, Institut de Participations de l'Ouest[33] in France) or national banks (BNP Paribas Développement in France).

4.1.2.3   Operational Activities

Growth capital funds take minority and sometimes majority stakes in companies, mostly through capital increase. These companies are not indebted (or at very modest levels), as they need all of their resources available in order to finance their

---

[33]Now part of Crédit Industriel et Commercial (CIC).

development. They are usually not a competitive target for an LBO, as they cannot service the acquisition debt and can be subject to unstable revenues depending on their ability to capture market shares or to enter a new market. This relative lack of attractiveness explains the comparatively small size of assets under management (Figure 4.24) and has probably spared growth capital the consequences of the VC bubble which burst in 2000–2001; and of the LBO bubble in 2008–2009.

4.1.2.4 Challenges

Growth capital is another historical version of private equity, as it is a somewhat simple investment method. One of the features of growth capital is that it does not need a complex financial ecosystem to exist, unlike VC or LBO financing – which both imply the existence of specialised financial actors. The importance of growth capital, on a given private equity market, can be one of the indicators of the maturity of this market. The higher the share of private equity operations it represents, the less mature is the market in many respects.

In fact, the main competitors of growth capital are banks, able to take more risks in their lending policies; stock exchanges, able to welcome smaller companies and to finance their development policies; and corporations, willing to take over promising relays of growth.

However, growth capital could be subject to a renewed surge, owing to multiple factors. The Basel II and III Agreements will lead to restrictions on bank loans for risky (i.e., mostly small and medium-sized) companies. Stock exchanges should normally offer alternatives, but suffer from the fact that the cost to list is increasing, owing to stricter regulation, and the fact that a company needs to be recommended by analysts when they have to raise capital or debt. Investment banks have been reducing their financial research departments, as they are less and less able to recoup research costs through

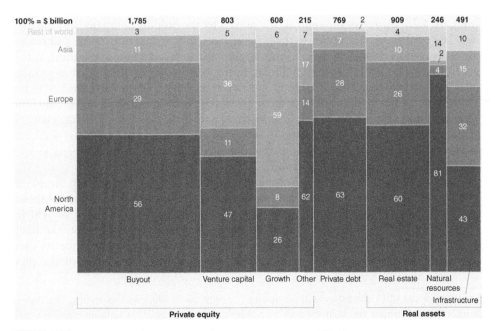

FIGURE 4.24   Private markets assets under management as of 2018
Source: McKinsey and Preqin 2019.

their brokerage fees. This means that small and medium-sized companies, which are not as actively traded as 'blue chip' companies, have experienced increasing difficulties in attracting attention.

In fact, some companies are de facto in the 'listing twilight zone': they are unable to raise capital or debt through the markets, and they cannot delist alone because it is too costly. These companies offer opportunities for growth capital funds (through PIPEs or delisting) willing to take them over and support their development.

4.1.2.5 Limits

Growth capital investments are probably the least risky in the private equity sector, as the companies are mostly profitable (or are soon to be) and growing. The return is theoretically also less attractive, as these companies are already valued with the inclusion of their growth perspective. They are still an attractive investment as they offer relative security to the investor compared to LBOs and venture capital, and the return is still higher than on the stock exchange.

4.1.3 LBOs: Financing Companies' Transfer of Ownership

LBOs are the result of financial innovation: the use of financial, legal and tax levers to buy a company (or multiple companies in the case of leveraged build-up, or LBU – see below). The purpose of an LBO is to manage and finance the transfer of ownership of a company by using a combination of capital and debt. The sale process can be at arm's length or competitive (through an auction), as illustrated in Chapter 5.

The buyer of the company[34] will borrow against future cash flows generated by that company (which is also the collateral of the debt). For that purpose, the targeted company has to generate substantial and stable cash flows. The amount borrowed by the buyer can reach up to 60–80% of the price of the company, depending on the characteristics of that company. The rest is provided by the buyer under the form of equity.

Figure 4.25 illustrates the central role played by the holding company and the cash flows. The bank lends the money to the holding company, whose only asset (and reason to be) is the ownership of the target. This implies a structured finance operation, which is very specific as it is not a traditional loan. In the example of Figure 4.25, a mezzanine fund is part of the structuring. This fund is between the bank and the LBO fund, whether we look at the seniority of the debt or the share of the profits received. A mezzanine fund invests via convertible debt. It first gets interest, and if the structuring is successful, it will also get a share of the profit generated upon sale of the company. In Figure 4.25, the operation is a management buy-out as the management of the target company invests in the holding along with the LBO fund.

Thanks to this mechanism, the company bought out will pay dividends to the owner (the holding), which in turn will repay the debt and the interest. The collateral (guarantee) of the debt of the holding company is the shares of the companies bought by the holding. If the structuring fails and the holding cannot repay the debt, the bank will become the owner of the company. The company bought out pays for its own acquisition. Depending on the success of the operation and the impact of the final

---

[34]To structure the LBO, the buyer will set up one (or multiple holding) company(ies). The buyer will inject capital under the form of equity in a holding company. This holding company will borrow from banks or specialised credit institutions (such as mezzanine funds, see below). The total collected will allow the holding to acquire the target company from the seller.

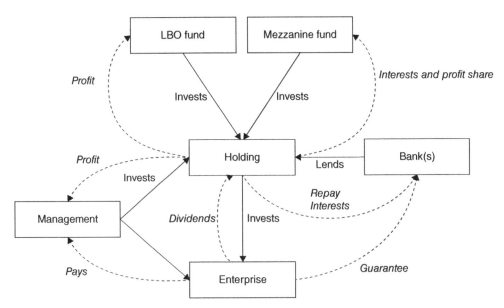

FIGURE 4.25 Example of management buy-out structuring
Source: Demaria (2006, 2008, 2010, 2012).

ownership by an LBO fund, the value of the company will grow and it will finally be sold to repay the debt, the capital and to generate a profit.

LBOs are essentially operated in developed markets (see Chapters 1 and 2), as this type of operation requires rather low interest rates and thus low inflation rates. It also requires an adapted tax and legal framework, as well as an efficient enforcement of legislation and court decisions. Moreover, it requires specialised actors and a certain level of sophistication from investors and lenders. According to Cambridge Associates and Preqin, LBOs represent roughly 69% of the PE fund investment universe (38% of the PM universe).

4.1.3.1 LBO Investment Targets

LBO targets and purpose
  LBO fund managers target profitable companies which have:

(a) Either a specific ownership problem to solve – succession/inheritance, retirement, divorce of owners, exiting co-owner; and/or
(b) A specific project to put in place – structuring[35] (process overhaul), modernisation, acquisitions/consolidation (horizontal by buying competitors; vertical by colonising the value chain), restructuring/divestments, internationalisation, outsourcing/insourcing (production, sales, R&D), see Figures 4.26 and 4.27.

---

[35] Kocis, Bachman, Long and Nickels (2009) state 'the central goal of buyout is to discover means to build [...] value. In many cases, this work has included refocusing the mission of the company, selling off noncore assets, freshening product lines, streamlining processes, and often, replacing existing management. A happy conclusion to this disruptive process is that the company reinvigorated, brought public [...] or sold at a profit to a strategic buyer' (p. 9).

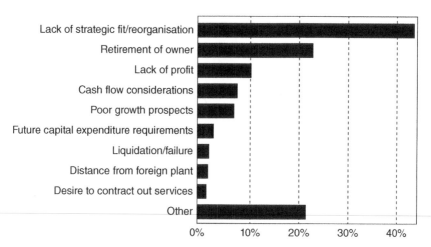

FIGURE 4.26 Reasons for launching an LBO on a company
Source: CMBOR/EVCA 2001.

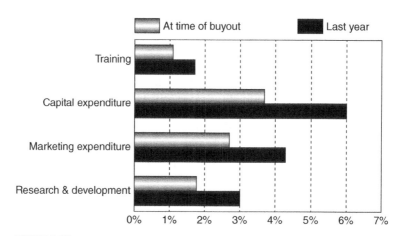

FIGURE 4.27 Type and proportion of expenses (as a percentage of sales) at time of LBO and after
Source: CMBOR/EVCA 2001.

LBO investments are usually done through majority ownership (notably to benefit from the tax leverage, see Section 4.1.3.3). Minority ownership in a buy-out is possible, however; notably in the case of replacement capital (e.g., to facilitate the exit of a current owner – a case of owner buy-out – see below), or on emerging markets where the leverage is not accessible and legislation prevents the control of local companies by foreign owners.

Most LBOs are based on the assumption of buying a company at a certain price, executing a given strategy in 2 to 5 years, and reselling the company at a higher price at the end of the holding period (either to another company/group, or to another financial investor).

Types of LBOs

There is a wide range of ways to structure an LBO, with different levels of risk attached to each of them. The level of risk increases with the number of moving parts.

- The less risky LBO is probably *owner buy-out*. The case arises when a co-owner wants to sell a stake in a company. The other owner(s) will acquire the company and will borrow money to acquire the stake of the seller. This happens when, for example, three brothers own an industrial paint company and one of the three wants to sell his shares. If the other two do not have the money, they will structure the LBO to replace the exiting current brother (and slowly refund the loan with the results of the company). It can also happen when two married people own a company jointly, and then divorce. If one of the two newly divorced individuals wants to keep the firm, an OBO might help to pay for the other part of the firm and help the second individual to exit. As all else remains equal, and there is limited or no asymmetry of information involved (as the co-owners are supposed to have the same level of information), the risk for the buyers is limited. This risk is, however, real – as the buyers use debt for the acquisition. OBOs can fail when the debt increase is not matched by an operational plan to significantly improve the performance of the company. A value creation has to match the added risk. If a fund is involved, this is a 'sponsored' OBO, if not, then the OBO is 'unsponsored'.
- An alternative is *management buy-out*, a leveraged buy-out which is led and substantially backed financially by the current management team of the company. This happens when the owner retires or a company divests, and the management of the company decide to lead the acquisition of the company. Sometimes, the team is the majority shareholder in the equity structuring part of the deal. In terms of risk, an MBO is at par with an OBO. The management is actually more informed than the non-executive owners of the state of the company. However, they might have less of a controlling perspective and might struggle to split their roles between management and governance, with conflicting views to handle. The risk profile of an MBO is therefore different from that in an OBO, but not necessarily higher. An MBO can be sponsored or unsponsored.
- The standard LBO is an *institutional buy-out* (sometimes referred to simply as 'LBO', as this is the template of the operation): a fund (or group of funds) identifies a company for sale and acquires it thanks to the tax, financial and legal leverages. This happens when an owner (who is not a manager) retires and has no interest in staying on as an owner; or when a company divests from certain sectors. It is called an 'institutional' buy-out because the leader of the acquisition is the fund itself. The risk is higher as the historical owner(s) leave(s), and some of the corporate network, memory and culture disappears.
- A *leveraged buy-in* (LBI) is when a fund acquires a business and has to immediately change or significantly overhaul the management. This happens when manager-owners leave the firm. The risk is higher as not only does the company lose its governance, but also its operational memory and know-how. Usually, a transition period is planned to facilitate the transfer of knowledge.
- A *management buy-in* (MBI) is a company take-over by an outside management team. This is riskier than a standard LBI, as the management faces the same issues

as in an MBO, with the added hurdle of discovering the company in terms of operational management, while setting up the governance. An MBI can be sponsored or unsponsored.

▪ A *leveraged build-up* (LBU) is structured to buy a company (the 'platform' company) and then later make additional acquisitions (the 'add-on(s)') to consolidate a sector and become an industry leader. This is probably the riskiest form of LBO, as the level of failure in mergers and acquisitions is significant. As the company operates these acquisitions under the constraint of repaying a significant debt and serving the interests, any mishap in delivering on the synergies will put the operation at risk.

Many combinations are possible, depending on the involvement of the management and its origin (insider or outsider). For example, a buy-in management buy-out (BIMBO) is an LBO which involves the entire – or parts of the – current management team and managers from the outside.

4.1.3.2 Actors

LBO has been growing at a fast clip. Correlatively, actors have started to specialise – depending on the size of the companies targeted, the type of value creation programmes implemented, and sometimes by industries.

LBO deal sizes and categories

Expected LBO deal sizes determine LBO fund sizes. Fund managers have developed specific skillsets to address the most frequent issues faced by their portfolio companies. These issues are largely conditioned by the company size. As a given fund will operate 15 to 25 deals, the fund size is fairly easy to compute, by multiplying the average expected deal size by the expected number of deals in the fund, plus the sum of the management fees and other ancillary costs. When a deal fits the skills of a fund manager but is too large for the fund, then it is syndicated (as explained above, by structuring a club deals with competitors, or a co-investment with fund investors).

Deal sizes are segregated into small, mid-, large and mega LBOs. Unfortunately, the definition has evolved over time, and differs depending on the geographical region considered. Cambridge Associates defines the brackets as follows. Small LBO funds have a size of USD 350 million or less, mid-sized LBO funds have sizes above USD 350 million to a billion, large LBO funds are above USD 1 billion to 3.5 billion, and mega LBO funds have a size above USD 3.5 billion. At times, the mid-market is split between 'lower mid-market' and 'higher mid-market', the frontiers of which vary, but could be set at USD 350–500 million and then USD 500 million–1 billion.

Small and mid-sized LBO fund managers target local companies, with the aim of supporting them in their build-up (external growth through acquisitions), launching new products or services, facing an ownership transition, the structuring and professionalisation of their operations, and overall grow to the next stage. Small and medium-sized LBOs are often much closer to growth capital than large or mega LBOs. Not only is the financial structuring simpler, but the managerial and entrepreneurial questions are also much more important. Though large and mega LBO fund managers also support build-ups, they focus on refocusing companies, operational improvements, and at times value chain integration.

Small LBO fund managers have a local to national reach. Mid-sized specialists have a national or regional reach. Large and mega LBO fund managers have a wider reach, covering the USA or Western Europe. Some of them have a global approach. Mega fund managers often have a global reach.

When modern private equity was still nascent, some fund managers were until recently doing venture capital, growth capital and medium-sized LBOs within the same fund. This model, which was once applied on a national basis by Apax and on a European scale by 3i, has disappeared as teams specialised. It re-emerged as fund managers started to host separate teams each responsible for a specific strategy. For example, Ardian counts a fund of funds activity, a secondary team, an LBO team and a growth capital team.

Listed LBO *fund managers*

Some LBO fund managers are listed (Blackstone, Apollo and Carlyle, notably) and others have initially listed their funds (KKR, which later merged with the fund and relisted in New York). These groups are mainly active in the segment of very large international buy-outs (above the billion-dollar threshold). To invest in certain countries, they can cooperate with local investors. The American KKR has co-invested in France with the local LBO investor Wendel to buy Legrand (a EUR 1.4 billion operation in 2004).

Wendel itself is listed in France, just like 3i in the UK. These structures are in fact close to being holding companies, combining the investment structure and the manager into one unit.[36] They do not have a planned lifetime (unlike most private equity funds). However, not all very large and large buy-out actors are listed: in the USA, Bain Capital and TPG are still private. Goldman Sachs is one of the few captive players owned by a bank. BC Partners and Permira, headquartered in the UK, specialise in very large buy-outs all over Europe and are private managers of unlisted private equity funds. On the continent, PAI Partners follows the same path.

There are multiple reasons for listing funds. One of them is to avoid constant fundraising and spending time on road shows in order to convince prospective fund investors. Another is to be free from the pressure to sell a company in a given timeframe, and thus be able to time the exit of a given investment better.

However, these benefits also have drawbacks. The fund manager has to publish a great deal of information on his portfolio and he must also be ready to bear market scrutiny. Also, a listed structure can only raise funds in good times, when capital is abundant and when, furthermore, the valuations of portfolio companies are high. The value of the shares of the listed structure is significantly below the net asset value of its portfolio, 30–40% below in good times, 50–70% in difficult times. The market usually punishes the lack of perceived transparency in the structure.

Listed fund managers offer a way to set a price for fund manager stakes owned by exiting staff members, such as the founders or leading managing partners. As they own a

---

[36]Other examples include Berkshire Hathaway in the USA, Softbank in Japan, Eurazeo in France, Gimv in Belgium or Investor AB in Sweden.

significant portion of the company, it is necessary to evaluate it. A listing provides a valuation and a way out. It is also useful to determine a price in order to set a stock option plan for promising staff members without immediately diluting the current partners.

Whether listed fund managers will be able to keep alive the 'partnership spirit' which made them successful remains to be seen. In fact, very few private banks in the past, which were built on a similar model, could resist the listing effect – which dilutes responsibilities, attracting managers more than real partners and eventually kills the long-term perspective and corporate cultures which promote trust and loyalty.

Independent and captive LBO teams

Fund managers can be independent (they are owned by their executives), captive (they are owned by an external group such as Goldman Sachs, Metlife or Google) or fully integrated in a structure (the LBO teams of some Canadian pension funds such as CPPIB or OTPP).

Independent teams are probably the most efficient, as they are free from conflicts of interest that could hamper the efforts of *captive teams* from banks. Potential conflicts of interest are one of the reasons why investment banks and commercial banks have decided to spin off their LBO teams, even if they remain involved as fund investors and sometimes as non-executive shareholders of the fund manager.

Independent teams have developed specific know-how which can lead them to syndicate, even though they could structure a deal perfectly alone. They have complementary skills which could prove to be useful in a given operation, requiring, for example, complex structuring and streamlining operations. Some teams are specialised in MBOs, others in minority LBOs or other specific operations. LBOs managed through a syndicate of funds are generating higher returns (Guo, Hotchkiss & Song, 2008).

The specific case of replacement capital

Replacement capital is dedicated to the partial transfer of ownership. This strategy provides an exit to a shareholder in a company that is not itself for sale. This approach is probably more frequent in emerging markets, as the equivalent of an unleveraged buy-out of a significant ownership in a firm. In that respect, it is a secondary transaction, as existing shares change hands. The buyer of these shares negotiates specific minority rights with other shareholders and notably an exit scenario. This strategy is often counted in statistics of LBO operations as the skillset is rather similar in replacement capital and usually operated by the same funds.

4.1.3.3 Operational Activities

Tax leverage

Depending on the local tax laws, the structuring of an LBO generally targets a certain ownership percentage. This ownership percentage (98% of ownership in Switzerland, 95% in France, 90% in the UK, for example) grants the fund manager the option to consolidate the financial statements of the holding and the target. As the holding does not have any other purpose than holding the shares of the target, it is a source of deficit due mainly to its interest payments. Through the consolidation, the holding can add its structural losses to the profits of the target, and hence reduce the taxes that are paid.

This is called *tax leverage*: the LBO is somehow 'subsidised' pro rata in relation to the losses generated by the holding.

Financial leverage

The second leverage effect is *financial*. It is attributed to two cumulative phenomena:

1. The reduction of the debt of the holding company thanks to the payment of the target. The target company is acquired thanks to a debt contracted by the holding. As the target company is profitable, it is distributing dividends. These dividends are used to pay down the debt of acquisition and the related interests. As time goes by, the debt of acquisition is reduced to nil. This is theoretical, because often the maturity of the debt of acquisition goes beyond the average holding time of the portfolio company by the fund (via the holding company). In fact, the holding period spans from 3 to 5 years on average, whereas the maturity of the debt is often 6 to 8 years. This means that part of the debt of acquisition is then refunded at exit time thanks to the proceeds of the sale (or sometimes, the holding of the acquisition gets listed and the debt is then continued and paid by the company as usual until its term). Nevertheless, the debt is refunded thanks to the payments of the target, in the process increasing the value of the equity injected in the holding.

2. The difference between the cost of debt of the holding and the dividend yield of the target. If the dividend yield of the target is higher than the cost of debt, then the holding pockets the difference, often to refund the debt (or to distribute an anticipated profit).

The risk linked to the financial leverage will evolve over the course of the following years. The highest level of risk is at the beginning of the investment, as the financial leverage is the highest. Fund managers pay specific attention to this period of time, and set up a precise plan (the 'first 100-days plan' and pre-plan corrective measures if something does not go according to plan). The risk decreases with the debt as time goes by, except in the case of a dividend recapitalisation. This mechanism consists of re-leveraging the deal, using the extra debt as an early profit distributed to the fund (and thus the fund investors).

Legal leverage

The third leverage is *legal*. The structuring gives to the owner of the holding full control of the governance and the Board. If a fund solely owns 100% of the holding, then in effect the fund manager has the capacity to control very narrowly the execution of the LBO strategy by the management (in effect, it can go to the point of replacing the management if needed). If the holding is owned by private equity funds and the management of the company, then the situation changes and the legal leverage might be less effective. Nevertheless, it is very unusual that a fund (or a group of funds) does not own the majority of the holding to be able to exercise their political rights in the most efficient way.

Structuring

The maximum amount which is borrowed is not fixed in advance. It depends first and foremost on the cash flows generated by the target. It depends then on cost of debt (the interest rate), and on the appreciation of the risks of the LBO by the lender. Four dimensions are thus involved: the amount borrowed, the cost of the debt, the duration and the legal guarantees (the 'covenants'), providing the lender with information instruments to monitor the debt.

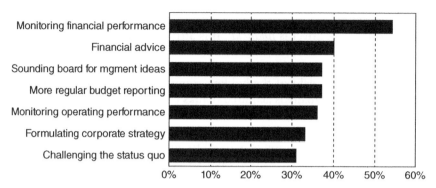

FIGURE 4.28 Contributions of LBO investors after investing
Source: CMBOR/EVCA 2001.

LBO deals are usually structured by one fund, which can then invite other funds to co-invest with the lead investor ('club deals'). Some LBO funds are dedicated to minority investments (either as part of an LBO consortium or as providers of replacement capital, see above). Consortia of acquisition are frequent when the target reaches a certain size, notably if it is listed. Each fund manager brings its connections and know-how to participate in the take-over offering (this has led to some accusations of collusion and anti-competitive behaviours, see above).

Value creation

LBOs are often accused of being a source of 'asset stripping', where companies are acquired to be dismembered and sold in small pieces. Though these operations were frequent in the 1980s, it is unlikely to be the case today. Figure 4.32 later shows that far from squeezing resources from portfolio companies, LBO investors actually increase the capital expenditures (i.e., investments), marketing expenditures and R&D of their portfolio companies.

Figure 4.28 exhibits the type of value creation that an LBO investor provides to its portfolio company. Not surprisingly, the financial performance comes first, but financial advice, bouncing ideas and contributing to the strategy, increasing the scrutiny of operations and finances (presumably to take action) are part of the value creation. Basically, an LBO challenges the status quo in a firm, to find sources of value creation and materialise them to sell a company at a higher price.

The fact that the exit scenario implies a higher price means that it is very unlikely that the LBO operation will have as its sole purpose the exercise of a financial leverage (though that can happen). The future buyer of the company must buy an asset which has grown in value for him (hence sometimes the divestment projects, to focus a company on a specific market and make it compatible with the strategy of a conglomerate). This growth in value can be driven by a growth in sales (e.g., launching a new product/service or tapping the marketing opportunities), as exhibited in Figure 4.29.

The growth in value of a company is often increased by improving its efficiency (e.g., setting up a leaner production, identifying gluts and releasing them, arbitraging between outsourcing or insourcing functions), as shown in Figure 4.30. Figure 4.31 illustrates the different tools used by LBO fund managers to create value, at the different stages of the operation.

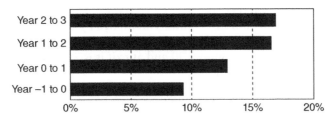

FIGURE 4.29 Evolution of annual sales (%, year 0 = year of LBO)
Source: CMBOR/EVCA 2001.

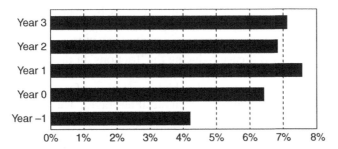

FIGURE 4.30 Increase of earnings before interest and taxes (% of sales, year 0 = year of LBO)
Source: CMBOR/EVCA 2001.

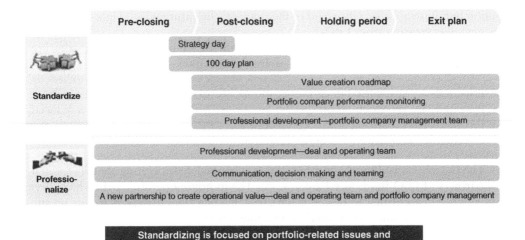

FIGURE 4.31 Tools in use by LBO fund managers to create value at the different stages of a deal
Source: BCG 2012.[37]

---

[37]Figures referenced as BCG 2012 are from the report of Brigl *et al.* (2012).

A summary of three different studies[38] by Quiry and Le Fur (2010) states that on average, the equity investment of LBO funds is multiplied by 2.72 over a holding period of 3.5 years (an IRR of 48%). Excluding outliers, the median IRR is 33%. At entry, the debt/EBITDA ratio is shown in Figure 4.30 and at exit it is 2.7. The 2.72 multiplier of value can be broken down as follows:

(i) A financial leverage (debt) explains 0.89 of the 2.72 (that is to say, a third of the performance).

(ii) An increase of the multiples (EV/EBITDA) explains 0.47 (that is to say, 17%).

(iii) The rest is from operational improvement – increase of the EBITDA (29%, of which 77% is due to an increase of the turn-over and 23% to an increase of margins) and increase of cash flows to reduce the debt of acquisition (15%). Figure 4.32 illustrates the effective use of the different tools by general partners. However, Mariathasan (2011) wonders where the growth is going to come from in the future, notably in Europe. Schwartz (2012) argues that it will be efficiency that will drive private equity's success (hence reducing the 'frictions' in the economy).

The period 1989–2000 witnessed a higher creation of operational value, while 2001–2006 has seen a higher impact of financial leverages. The best IRRs came from investments made in difficult times (1991–1993 and 2001–2003), while most of the operational improvements came from the growth of turn-over.

According to Quiry and Le Fur (2010), excluding financial leverage, LBOs outperform investments in listed companies by 600 basis points (LBO IRRs are 31%, while for listed companies they are 25%). The gross IRR of LBO fund managers is hence 31% and after carried interest (20%) and management fees (2%), the net IRR is 25% (that is to say, the same as investing in listed companies). These conclusions are subject to caution but illustrate a specific trend of the academic literature which vigorously denies any net value creation from LBOs.

Corporate governance and management incentives are major drivers of value creation. LBO fund managers are creating performance when:

- Principals are specialised in certain economic sectors that they know very well.
- Principals are very focused on specific questions, as their learning curve is reduced.
- Principals have a strong ability to identify early investment opportunities, as they can resume the process of acquisition faster.

The Boston Consulting Group has in fact identified six operating models for general partners of LBO funds (see Figure 4.33). The in-house operating teams have been gaining ground according to Bain Capital 2019, leading fund managers to line up successively deal teams and operational improvement teams.

Figure 4.34 demonstrates the role of the LBO in the private equity ecosystem, notably as a 'breathing factor' for the stock exchange. It also helps non-listed groups with the succession plans of their owners or with the restructuring of their shareholding structure. Some market observers have announced that for a certain time there will be an increasing volume of activities linked to a generational change at the helm of

---

[38] Achleitner (2009), Acharya, Hahn and Kehoe (2010), Brigl *et al.* (2008).

Initiatives

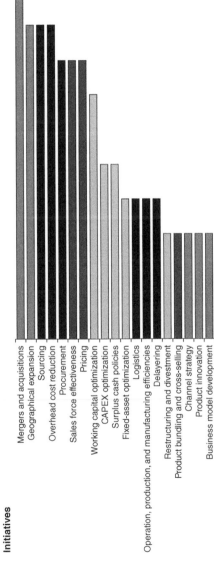

Financial

Bottom Line

Top Line (core)

Top Line (expansion)

Firms that systematically use this initiative (%)

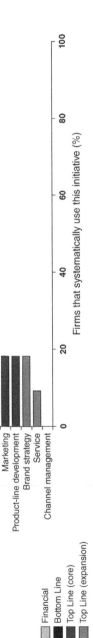

FIGURE 4.32 Effective use of the different tools available by LBO fund managers

Source: BCG 2012.

	No internal capability		Operating partners		In-house operating teams	
Model	None	Advisors	Generalist	Functional	Small	Large
Description	Neither internal operating capabilities nor external advisors	External network of senior advisors with equity stake in the portfolio company or fund	Single layer (sometimes two) of executives on private equity firm payroll with generalist expertise (for example, sector knowledge); do not necessarily have an equity stake	Single layer (sometimes two) of executives on private equity firm payroll with functional expertise; do not necessarily have an equity stake	Multi-level group of operating professionals on private equity firm payroll	Multi-level group of operating professionals on private equity firm payroll
Profile	Not applicable	Former CEOs and CFOs	Former senior executives; high level general managers	Former executives and consultants with expertise in a specific functional area (for example, procurement, sales, or IT)	Operating team significantly smaller then deal team with different terms of compensation terms	Operating team as large as deal team with comparable compensation
Activities	Deal teams interact with portfolio company through board; no project management role; no involvement day-to-day operations	Advisors serve on portfolio-company board, usually in role of chair; may assist in diligence phase to build value creation plans	Will work on more than one portfolio company at a time	Will work on more than one portfolio company at a time	Will work on one portfolio company at a time along entire investment process; will stay on site for up to 1 year	Will work on only one portfolio company at a time along entire investment process; will stay on site for up to 1 year

FIGURE 4.33 Operating models for general partners of LBO funds

Source: BCG 2012.

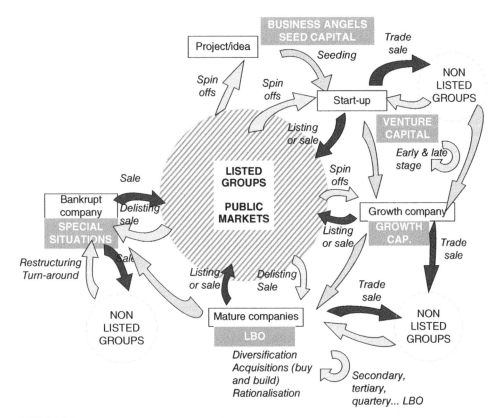

FIGURE 4.34 Lifecycle of a company and LBO
Source: Demaria (2006, 2008, 2010, 2012).

private groups. This does not necessarily imply a radical change of ownership, but can involve funds to help the current owner in the sale of his stake. LBO fund managers bring know-how, offer ways to reinforce the management structure and finances, and promote the development of these companies.

4.1.3.4 Challenges and Limits

There is a limit to what LBO funds can do. Not every company can be a target for LBO funds, as it needs to have stable and recurring cash flows. These cash flows will come under pressure in the event of an LBO operation.

The commoditisation of LBO techniques and its consequences

Still, the multiplication of LBOs in mid-sized companies, and the perspectives of consolidation, have a real impact on the American and European economic landscapes. The multiplication of LBO funds, the inflation of the capital to be deployed by fund managers, the professionalism of sellers and intermediaries, as well as the strong increase in the number of deals done have contributed to the inflation of company valuations.

In fact, by accelerating the transmission of companies and restructuring economic sectors rapidly, it is possible that the LBO will experience further changes. The technique of LBOs has become a commodity and the 'easy target' companies have already largely been targeted by an LBO. It seems quite improbable that LBO fund managers will be able to structure deals without any value creation (see above).

This excess of liquidity has granted LBO fund managers the cash to structure very large operations such as Kinder Morgan (USD 22.4 billion), HCA (USD 32.7 billion), Equity Office Properties (USD 38.9 billion) or even TXU (USD 43.8 billion). In 2006, 80 deals reached the billion threshold (as opposed to 12 in 2002). Some of these companies were in a difficult situation during the crisis, and LBO fund managers are supposed to help them weather the storm. This can prove difficult, as even industrials sometimes fail to succeed in this task. The acquisition and further sale to a private equity fund of Chrysler by Daimler-Benz is one of those examples. An acquisition without restructuring and dedicated and appropriate monitoring can simply lead the resulting group into more difficulties. LBO fund managers are not necessarily handling these troubled groups better, and the case of Chrysler is only one illustration. Table 4.5 provides some background on how the LBOs from the bubble years have fared.

Restructuring gives birth to new companies or new subsidiaries, which can be deal opportunities for growth capital or LBO funds. This was illustrated by Clear Channel selling its TV stations to Providence Equity Partners in 2007.

An increased connection between LBO deals activity and the debt markets

The availability of LBO debt has been reduced dramatically since 2007–2008 (see Figure 4.35), hence reducing the number of deals (see Figure 4.36). LBO activity has decreased significantly in 2008. In Europe, LBO loan volumes represented less than 25% of the total in 2007 (which reached USD 290 billion, according to Dealogic). With the time lag owing to the conclusion of transactions that were signed in 2007 but effectively realised in 2008, the 2008 volume has to be discounted by a further 30%. In the USA, volumes have decreased by 80%, from USD 379 billion to USD 77 billion. In Europe and the USA, these figures can be compared to the pre-bubble situation (i.e., the period 2004–2005).

This specific case illustrates how LBOs depend heavily on the state of the debt markets. These debt markets are composite: small and mid-sized LBOs rely on debt provided and held by banks, while large and mega LBOs rely on debt structured by investment banks and later sold to high-yield bond specialists. This means that small and mid-sized LBOs are more constrained in their leverage structures, but also more resilient to crises. Large and mega LBOs can be structured more creatively and aggressively, but suffer in a context of low appetite for risky debt instruments.

LBO segments post financial crisis: a moderate recovery ...

Figure 4.37 illustrates the resilience of the small LBO segment. The mid-market shrank significantly but remained active. This figure shows that indeed large and mega LBOs had almost disappeared in 2009, but recovered relatively well in 2010.

Figure 4.38 shows that the volume of activity recovered to a robust level, while the amounts considered remain rather low (half of the peak of 2007). Interestingly, the average equity contribution to the deal decreased as soon as the mega LBOs picked up, hence confirming that the debt-to-equity ratio for mega LBOs is higher than for other deals.

... in a split debt market, with low interest rates ...

In fact, there is a widening gap between LBO debt provided by banks (a shrinking pool, due to the Basel Agreements and the overall de-leveraging of banks' balance sheets) and debt provided by financial markets, which is expanding due to a certain thirst for returns from bond investors, in a context of low interest rates.

TABLE 4.5 What have they become? Winner, neutral and loser LBOs of the bubble years

Position on the largest deals list	Name of company	Year	Size (bn USD)	Sponsor(s)	Winner, neutral, loser?	What happened?
1	Energy Future Holdings (fka TXU)	2007	43.8	KKR/TPG	L	Zero value for equity, restructuring of debt (for USD 22.5 billion)
2	Equity Office Properties	2007	39	Blackstone	W	60% of portfolio quickly sold to other buyers (debt reduction)
3	Caesars Entertainment (fka Harrah's)	2008	31	Apollo/TPG	L	IPO cancelled in 2010, then succeeded in 2012. Heavy debt and falling revenues. Chapter 11 restructuring of debt
4	First Data	2007	27.7	KKR	L	Acquired for USD 29 billion, listed in 2015 at a USD 14 billion market cap. Fiserv bought First Data in 2019 for USD 22 billion in a stock deal
5	Alltel	2007	27.5	TPG/Goldman Sachs Cap.	W	Verizon bought it a few months later for USD 28.1 billion
6	Hilton Hotels	2007	25.8	Blackstone	W	Initially lost 70% of value. It had to be recapitalised and was relisted in 2013. Blackstone finished to divest in 2018 and multiplied its investment by more than three times
7	Kinder Morgan	2007	22	Goldman Sachs/ Riverstone Carlyle	W	IPO in 2011 (profit: USD 13.5 billion at time of IPO)
8	HCA Holdings	2006	21	Bain Capital/ KKR/Merrill Lynch PE	W	Equity injected: USD 4.9 billion. Owners did a dividend recapitalisation of USD 4.3 billion. IPO at USD 4.35 billion (largest for a PE-backed firm)

(*continued*)

TABLE 4.5 (*Continued*)

Position on the largest deals list	Name of company	Year	Size (bn USD)	Sponsor(s)	Winner, neutral, loser?	What happened?
9	iHeartMedia (fka Clear Channel)	2006–2008	17.9	Bain Capital/ Thomas H Lee Partners	L	Providence Equity Partners bought TV stations in 2007 for USD 1.2 billion. Rumours of bankruptcy in 2010. Debt refinanced (USD 20 billion). The company filed for bankruptcy in 2018
10	Freescale Semiconductors	2006	17.6	Blackstone/ Carlyle/ Permira/TPG	L	Equity lost 50% of its value at IPO time in 2011. NXP bought Freescale in 2015 for USD 11.8 billion in cash and stock. PE funds owned 66.24% of the firm at that time
11	Archstone Smith	2007	15.5.	Bank of America/ Barclays/ Lehman Brothers/ StrategicVentures/ Tishman Speyer	L	Debt restructuring in 2010: the lenders own the company. The bankruptcy estate of Lehman Brothers (owning 47%) bought out the stake of Bank of America and Barclays (53%) for USD 1.6 billion in 2012
12	NXP Semiconductors	2006	8.2	Bain Capital/KKR	W	4–5x on the 80% ownership after IPO in 2010
13	Chrysler	2007	7.4	Cerberus Capital Management	L	Bankruptcy in 2009
14	Dollar General	2007	6.9	KKR/Goldman Sachs	W	IPO in 2009 at USD 21 per share. Final exit after a series of block sales in 2013 at USD 61 per share

Source: Author.

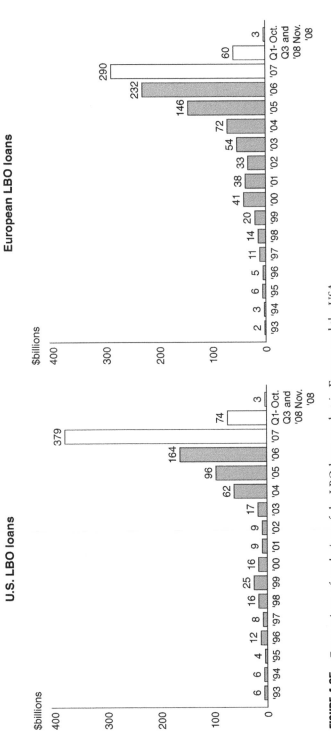

FIGURE 4.35 Comparison of evolution of the LBO loan market in Europe and the USA

Source: Dealogic 12/2008.

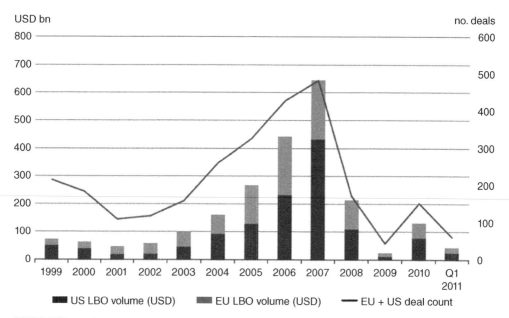

FIGURE 4.36 Value and volume of LBO in the USA and Europe
Source: Crédit Suisse, Bloomberg, S&P, IDC 2011.

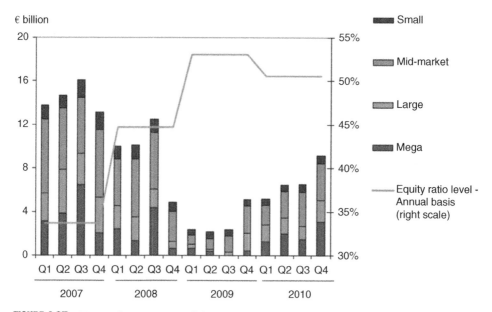

FIGURE 4.37 Types of LBO operated (by quarter) and average equity contribution in Europe
Source: EVCA, S&P LCD 2010.

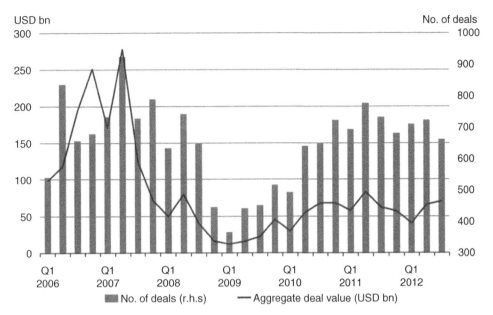

FIGURE 4.38 LBO deal activity worldwide
Source: Crédit Suisse, Preqin, IDC 2012.

... and thus high valuations, hence leading to a 'new normal'

The usual targets of small LBOs see their attractiveness increase sharply in the wake of the rise of company valuations, notably due to increased activity in buy-and-build. This is very visible when a market approaches its peak (Figure 4.39). Multiples are lower than for big companies and financial levers are more moderate, but the impact

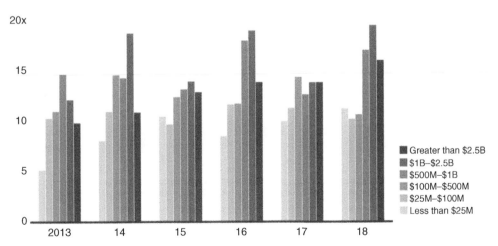

FIGURE 4.39 Median EBITDA purchase price multiple for global buy-out transactions, by deal size
Source: Bain, PitchBook 2019.

is materialising at the time of company sales. Notably, small LBOs can capitalise on an increase for the multiples of EBIT (or equivalently, to calculate the price of the company sold) as the company has reduced its intrinsic risk and acquired a certain size. The volume of add-on acquisitions has increased fairly regularly since 1996 (Figures 4.40 and 4.41).

As an alternative to build-up strategies, large LBO fund managers started to specialise more (building, for example, internal consulting practices, providing mutualised purchasing services for all their portfolio companies) or focus on finding new areas of intervention (e.g., in certain regulated jobs). They feel a significant pressure to do so, as

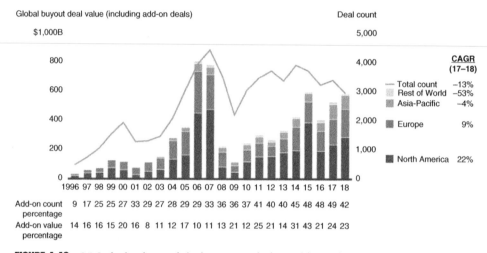

FIGURE 4.40 LBO deal value and deal count, including add-ons, by region
Source: Bain, Dealogic 2019.

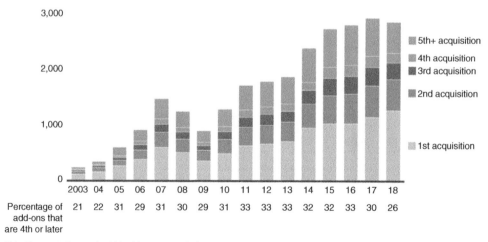

FIGURE 4.41 Total global add-on deals, by sequence for platform company
Source: Bain, PitchBook 2019.

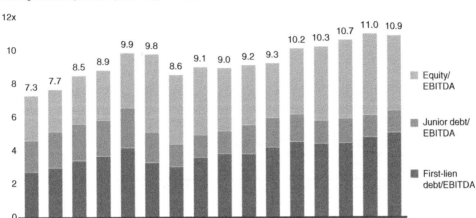

FIGURE 4.42 LBO valuations in multiples of EBITDA in the USA and breakdown between
debt and equity
Source: Bain, LPC 2019.

the price of investment opportunities has increased significantly over time. The average
purchase price multiple for US LBOs was 7.3× EBITDA (earnings before interest, taxes,
depreciation and amortisation) in 2004, reached 9.9× in 2007 and decreased to 8.6×
in 2009 (see Figure 4.42). These multiples remained stable from 2010 at 9.0–9.3× but
started to increase again in 2014 and reached 10.9–11.0× in 2017–2018 from 6.5–6.9×
in 2000–2003 to 8.4× in 2006. Overall, the multiple of debt proceeds followed the
increase of the multiple of purchase price, as shown in Figure 4.42. The increase in
prices was largely financed by an increase in debt, not by an increase in equity, despite
guidance from the US and European regulators to limit the debt leverage to 6× EBITDA.
How do fund managers reconcile an increase in debt levels and the regulatory informal
cap? By adding back to EBITDA calculations elements such as expected synergies or
non-recurring factors, so that the debt fits in the guidelines.

This is notably due to the fact that debt remains cheap (when available) and the
equity available for private equity funds (the 'dry powder') is of high quantity as well
(see Figure 4.43). According to Bain/Preqin, roughly USD 2 trillion was available for
private equity investments at the time of writing. Of this amount, 35% is for LBO
investments.

The emphasis on divestments is unabated …

Exits are more than ever an important topic. Some of the commitments of fund
investors rely on the assumed liquidity of the current portfolios to be recycled in new
funds. A lack of liquidity events can put fund investors in a liquidity squeeze, hence
forcing them to sell other assets or to divest from some of their private equity funds.
However, after the financial crisis, a new phenomenon appeared: net positive distributions (Figure 4.44). Fund investors have to maintain an exposure to private markets. If
fund managers dispose of assets too fast and return capital to fund investors, then the
latter record an effective under-allocation to private equity compared to their target.

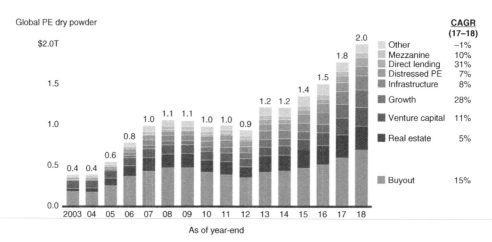

Buyout ($B) 184 176 256 374 438 478 479 424 392 357 424 441 475 516 602 695

FIGURE 4.43 Committed and uninvested capital ('dry powder') in private equity
Source: Bain, Preqin 2019.

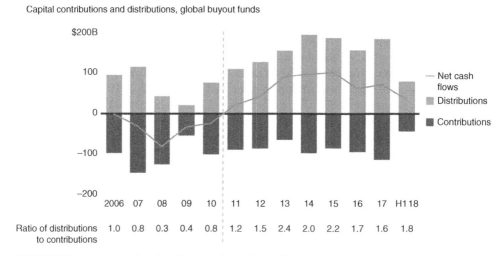

Ratio of distributions   1.0   0.8   0.3   0.4   0.8   1.2   1.5   2.4   2.0   2.2   1.7   1.6   1.8
to contributions

FIGURE 4.44 Aggregated cash inflows and outflows of LBO funds globally
Source: Bain, Cambridge Associates 2019.

To find a lucrative exit, the choices are:

- To resell the companies in question to strategic investors (trade sale) at a higher price (including the payment of a premium). Some groups are difficult to sell because the prices are too high for industrial groups, which cannot find synergies and industrial perspectives in order to get an acceptable return in acquiring these companies. This is the most frequent exit scenario (see Figure 4.45 for an illustration with LBO).
- To sell them to another financial investor (secondary sale, or 'sponsor-to-sponsor'). One of the consequences of a high level of 'dry powder' is the resilient activity of

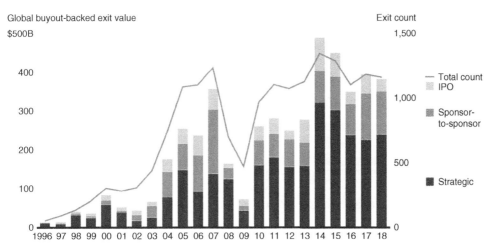

Notes: Bankruptcies excluded; IPO value represents offer amount and not market value of company

FIGURE 4.45 Exit from LBO globally
Source: Bain, Dealogic 2019.

secondary operations, as shown in Figure 4.45. This is true for secondary, tertiary, quaternary, etc. LBOs, but also increasingly in the case of VC investments sold to LBOs (Demos, 2012). This has become the second most frequent exit scenario.

- To list them on the stock exchange (IPO) at a high multiple (which is difficult to assume, as stock exchanges can be in a down cycle). This is the least frequent scenario.

In case of failure, the alternative is to restructure them. This can lead to cost cutting when the market does not show the expected growth, and eventually to asset sales in the case of declining cash flows. This is one of the reasons why LBO funds are sometimes identified as specialists in downsizing, with the social consequences attached to it. After focusing on the restructuring of some of their portfolio companies in 2009–2010, trade sales have recovered (though moderately) as well as the IPO market. If this does not work, then investments are written off. The ownership of companies is transferred to the creditors in case of LBOs, or at times directly liquidated. A failed VC investment generally leads to a direct liquidation (that is to say, the sale of the remaining assets and the termination of the company).

... leading potentially to excesses: dividend recaps are an illustration

Cheap debt has also helped fund managers do recapitalisations (or 'dividend recaps'), which are another (criticisable) way to provide liquidity to fund investors. The principle of dividend recaps is simple: a private equity fund acquires a healthy company through an LBO. Theoretically, this company should be sold after a few years, which was in fact not possible due to the past crisis. The leverage effect decreasing over time (the debt of acquisition being regularly repaid), there is still the option to re-leverage and distribute 'anticipated profits' to fund investors.

Theoretically, dividend recaps are putting everyone at ease. Fund managers can please fund investors with distributions, and hence prepare comfortably their next

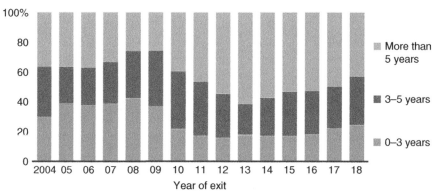

FIGURE 4.46 Distribution of LBO exits globally, by length of time held in fund portfolio
Source: Bain, Preqin 2019.

fundraising. The underlying company has no right to voice any concern, but its management is relatively pleased to avoid any additional pressure to find a trade buyer which does not exist at that time. Fund investors get cash in a period when liquidity and rates are low. Dividend recaps ease concerns when holding periods are creeping up, as was the case after the recession of 2007–2009 (Figure 4.46). In that respect, dividend recaps have contributed to the net distributions illustrated above in Figure 4.43, but the duration of ownership had remained substantially higher. In 2010, USD 234 billion was granted in leverage loans (vs USD 77 billion in 2009) according to S&P LCD. 84% of these loans were granted to distribute dividends to private equity funds. Clearwire Communications and HCA, among the largest LBOs of the 2006–2007 bubble, were the target of dividend recaps.

Dividend recaps have two main consequences. The first is to add risks in existing LBO deals. In a classical LBO structuring, the highest point of the risk is during the first months, when financial leverage is high. Theoretically, this risk is compensated by the added value which will be created by the investor. Re-leveraging is not compensated by an additional value creation – it is a 'wait and see' solution.

The second aspect is that these dividend recaps have the inconvenience that they 'break the return thermometer', that is to say, they may suddenly skew one of the private equity fund return measurements: the IRR. A small example (see Table 4.6) shows that an anticipated cash distribution by a dividend recap can simultaneously increase the IRR and impoverish the investor: the investor realises an IRR of 20% and multiplies his investment by 3, while the investor who realises an IRR of 26% multiplies his investment by 2.5.

The classical answer of fund managers is that fund investors will always prefer liquidity to increased performance. This remains to be proven. First, there is no guarantee that fund investors will find an investment opportunity performing at the same level as the original deal. Second, the transaction costs to find and invest in an LBO of the same quality will lower the overall performance of the fund investors' portfolio.

TABLE 4.6 Multiples and IRRs of an investment with and without dividend recap

	Without dividend recap	With dividend recap
Initial investment	−100	−100
Year 1	0	0
Year 2	0	0
Year 3	0	150
Year 4	0	0
Year 5	0	0
Year 6	300	100
Multiple of investment	3	2.5
IRR	20%	26%

Source: Author.

4.1.4 Special Situations: Turn-around Capital[39]

The inflation of company valuations was an incentive for some LBO fund managers to widen the spectrum of their interventions. Some teams have initially specialised in regulated sectors (e.g., Carlyle in the USA). Other fund managers, such as Butler Capital Partners in France, have targeted companies with specific problems (working capital shortage, imbalanced balance sheet or temporary insolvency), operating turn-around investments.

Turn-around capital (also known as rescue capital), which targets ailing businesses before their effective bankruptcy, is still a niche, overshadowed by distressed debt investments (see below). The two are often blended together, but differ. Turn-around capital is about new investors buying the equity of an ailing business for a symbolic amount. Sometimes the new owners are paid by the current ones (sellers) to restructure the business out of court, thus avoiding an expensive and sometimes unpredictable outcome in bankruptcy courts. The sellers avoid issues such as reputational damage (bankruptcy is a public legal process), but also operational difficulties. Clients and providers of an ailing business can continue to work with the company operating as a going concern, while its issues are sorted out. Indeed, suppliers and creditors could be reluctant to maintain business relationships with the company under administration.

In some pre-bankruptcy procedures (at times referred to as 'pre-packed bankruptcies'), the intervention of external administrators is supporting the restructuring. Sometimes, the arrangement between the company and its creditors is approved by a court. This is the case for example in the UK, with the scheme of arrangement (also known as 'scheme of reconstruction'). The arrangement altering the creditors and shareholders rights is therefore approved by a judicial authority.

One of the benefits for the buyer of an ailing business is that it usually has accumulated significant losses, which will become in effect a tax shield for the profits of the restructured business until these losses are fully compensated. Turn-around capital therefore benefits from a tax leverage close to the one described above for LBO.

---

[39]Special situations include various niche strategies beyond turn-around capital. Given the lack of data on turn-around capital itself, we will use data for special situation funds as a proxy for turn-around capital.

The appetite for this type of investment is very opportunistic. This activity is a niche that is not widely documented. Preqin estimated that as of 2016, 47 fund managers were active in this strategy. North America represents roughly 70% of the market, and Europe the rest. This investment strategy is very sensitive to the macro-economic conditions, but also somehow decorrelated from the rest of the private equity investment universe (see Table 4.7 – though this focuses on hedge funds dedicated to distressed situations, and Figure 4.47 showing the IRRs of special situations depending on the vintage years of the fund). Turn-around investments perform very well when acquisitions are made during or right after a recession (as in 2001), and then under-perform when investments are done in boom times (as in 1996–1999). They are therefore a useful strategy to build a balanced and diversified asset allocation.

This is reflected by the fundraising figures. Figure 4.48 illustrates that the amounts committed increased in 2007 and 2008, probably in expectation of a bubble burst.

TABLE 4.7   Distressed hedge funds correlation matrix

Correlations	Distressed	Hedge funds	S&P 500	Treasuries	Investment grade	High yield	HY spreads
Distressed	1						
Hedge funds	0.67	1					
S&P 500	0.60	0.55	1				
Treasuries	−0.30	−0.13	−0.29	1			
Investment grade	0.27	0.33	0.04	−0.18	1		
High yield	0.65	0.52	0.59	−0.26	0.54	1	
HY spread	−0.41	−0.26	−0.20	0.10	−0.14	−0.39	1

Source: EVCA, CMBOR, Barclays Private Equity, Ernst & Young 2010.

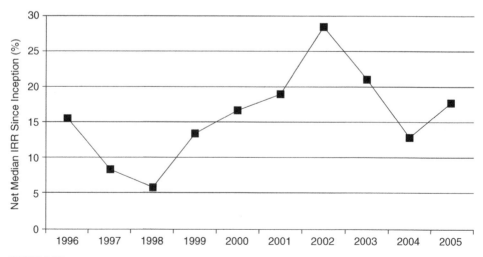

FIGURE 4.47   Median IRRs of special situation funds
Source: Preqin 2008.

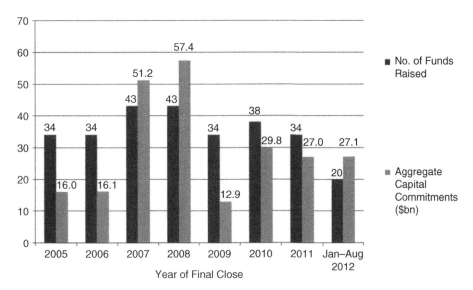

FIGURE 4.48   Fundraising in special situations (2005–08/2012)
Source: Preqin 2012.

Though 2009 was affected by the crisis as much as the rest of the private equity sector, there was vigorous activity in terms of fundraising in 2010–2012: fund investors expected a further downturn, probably when the quantitative easing waves would have stopped and the economy had restructured (either in the USA or Europe, with expectations as reflected in Figure 4.49). As a result, turn-around funds in Europe raised a record amount in 2011.

Opportunities in Europe could have been significant (see *Financial Times*, 2011a),[40] as European banks usually suffer for a long time from the aftermath of the crisis (notably in Spain after the crisis of 2007–2009; see White, 2012) and would require alternatives to dispose of non-performing loans. Opportunities have not materialised in a 'wave' (*The Economist*, 2012b)[41] due to the special programmes undertaken by central banks and governments after the crisis.

In any case, Europe has still to find its own model of turn-around capital, and is therefore following the USA on the path to offering full support to companies over the course of their lifetime (see Figure 4.50). Continental Europe does not have the equivalent of the American Chapter 11, which means that turn-around capital is the only option for companies in difficulty to restructure with the help of professional investors. Most of the time, when a company asks for bankruptcy protection, it is too late to find another solution (see Milne, 2012 explaining that the troubled airliner SAS would have benefitted from the equivalent of the US Chapter 11).

---

[40] As mentioned: Thomas Cook, Premier Foods, Seat Piagine Gialle, Eksportfinans, La Senza.
[41] 'So far, however, distressed-debt investors have been disappointed. "There's not been a deluge [in Europe], we had been hoping for a deluge", was the recent verdict of Howard Marks, Oaktree's chairman.'

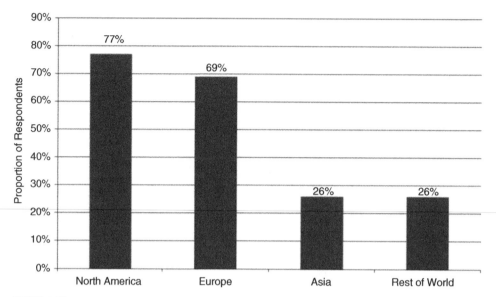

FIGURE 4.49   Geographic preferences for special situations funds
Source: Preqin 2012.

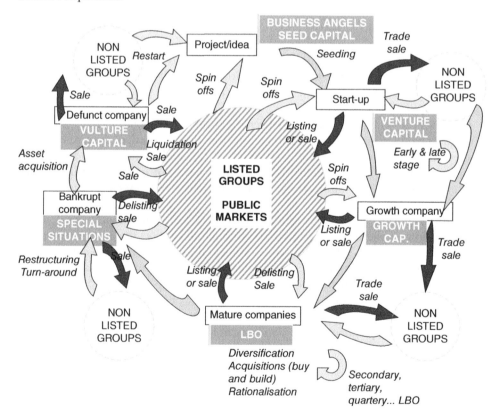

FIGURE 4.50   Lifecycle of a company and interventions in private equity (synthesis)
Source: Demaria (2006).

However, regulations are not the only obstacle to the emergence of this kind of business. Some successes in turn-around did not involve a financial backer, such as the lingerie company Aubade in France. An entrepreneur bought the ailing brand and redeveloped it with a specific positioning. It is the ability to take risks and adopt an entrepreneurial attitude, even in a difficult context, which will eventually change the course of the company.

The shame associated with the bankruptcy procedure is widely blamed, notably on the Continent. European cultures and regulations are still refraining CEOs of troubled businesses from asking for the protection of the courts and trying to find a solution. Moreover, turn-around capital does not necessarily fit with the private equity constraints in Europe. More specifically, most of the actors involved in these sorts of private equity activities in Europe are using holding companies – not private equity fund structures. The take-over, restructuring and exit process would take more time than is manageable in a 10-year structure. Another element is that turn-around investors have usually set up an industrial approach, which offers services to businesses to help them through restructuring.

4.1.5 Aiming at the Margins? Interacting with the Stock Exchange and its Ecosystem

Private equity is not limited to unlisted securities. This is the case with PIPEs and delistings (or 'public-to-private').

Private investments in public equities

The purpose of PIPEs is to take a mid- to long-term stake in a listed company which is struggling to raise capital on the stock exchange. A private equity (usually growth capital) fund invests in exchange of specific advantages, such as a lower price per share at acquisition than the market price, and the seats on the Board. The fund agrees to hold these shares ('lock up') for a predefined minimum time during which the company will make significant changes. Once the changes are made, and the lock-up period expires, the fund is free to sell its stake on the open market.

Public-to-privates

Private equity funds sometimes take control of listed companies in order to delist them. The purpose of this operation is to give back some flexibility to the company and restructure it more easily. Local laws often specify acquiring at least 90% or more of a listed company, to force minority shareholders to sell their shares ('squeeze out'). Hedge funds can find interest in acquiring a stealth blocking minority position and negotiating a premium to pave the way for a successful delisting by the private equity fund.

Public-to-private (such as HCA, Kinder Morgan, Univision or Petco) deals, though attractive in boom times, present some difficulties – such as regulatory costs, a high purchase price, closing risks, threats of stockholder litigation and reverse break-up fees (Weisser & Germano, 2006).

Large listed groups are no longer immune from take-overs by LBO funds. Vivendi, one of the largest European listed companies, was eventually named in 2006–2007 as a potential target at EUR 40 billion by KKR. Kraft Heinz – formed in 2015 by the merger of Kraft Foods and H.J. Heinz,[42] owned by the Brazilian PE firm 3G Capital and Berkshire Hathaway – approached Unilever for an attempted take-over of USD 143 billion in 2017. LBO funds routinely reach the multi-billion threshold: Blackstone, KKR, Goldman Sachs and Apollo raised funds of over USD 20 billion.

Hedge funds and private equity interactions

The increasing participation of private equity in other capital markets, including the stock exchange, confronts it with the strategy of other players, such as hedge funds. Hedge funds identify market opportunities such as listed undervalued companies, take positions and liquidate them when the markets have evolved as anticipated.

The confrontation with private equity is due to the fact that fund managers can target under-valued firms too, but for different reasons, such as a delisting. As the size of private equity deals has increased, very few companies are out of reach of a private equity take-over, offering multiple arbitrage opportunities to hedge funds.

Having saturated their home investment market, some hedge fund managers tried to diversify by combining their methods with those of private equity. This was the case for Kmart, the American supermarket chain, which was acquired by ESL, a hedge fund directed by Eddie Lampert, who merged it with Sears for USD 11.5 billion in 2004. As Mr Lampert discovered, it is not easy to morph oneself into a private equity investor.[43] Eddie Lampert was voted worst CEO of the year 2007 by MarketWatch (Greenburg, 2007).

4.2 PRIVATE DEBT: SENIOR/DIRECT LENDING, SUBORDINATED DEBT AND DISTRESSED DEBT

Private debt (PD) funds provide companies and asset financing when usual lenders do not and when the risk–return profile of the investment is not adapted to private equity. The implication of fund managers can vary from moderately hands-on, relying on strong due diligence and strict covenants (and the rule of law to enforce them) in the case of direct/senior lending funds, to very hands-on, in effect becoming the owners of the

---

[42]The public-to-private of H.J. Heinz was operated by 3G and Berkshire Hathaway in 2013 for USD 23.2 billion. The group merged with listed group Kraft in 2015. Rounds of layoffs and savage cost-cutting did not produce the expected results. In 2019, the merged entity announced a USD 15.4 billion write-down of the Kraft and Oscar Mayer brands it owned. The SEC launched an investigation of its accounting practices.

[43]In 2002, Kmart filed for bankruptcy after an accounting scandal. Its management was accused of misleading investors. ESL bought the debt of Kmart during the bankruptcy procedure and took over the firm in a distressed debt (debt-for-control) operation for less than USD 1 billion. The company went through successive rounds of store closures and layoffs before and during its bankruptcy. It emerged in 2003 and was listed on the NASDAQ. In 2004, Kmart essentially merged with Sears. Further store closures and layoffs were initiated. In 2017, Sears Holdings admitted the uncertainty of the survival of Kmart and Sears. In 2018, Sears Holdings filed for bankruptcy. After pondering a liquidation, the company reached an agreement with Eddie Lampert to prevent this and sold its assets to ESL Investments. A group of unsecured creditors claimed that Lampert had been 'engaged in serial asset stripping' of the companies. As of December 2019, 114 locations remain.

business and executing a turn-around with the help of the management in the case of distressed debt and non-performing loan investing. Preqin estimated that as of December 2017, PD funds managed USD 667 billion, of which more than USD 240 billion was 'dry powder'. The Alternative Credit Council estimates that it could reach USD 1 trillion by 2020.

4.2.1 Senior Lending: Direct Lending and Unitranche

Also called 'alternative credit', 'private credit' or 'senior debt', direct lending could be considered as equivalent to the senior lending activity operated by banks. The activity consists of providing usually small and mid-sized businesses with loans, but the difference with bank loans is that the purpose of the operation is specific. While banks provide loans to do more of the same, such as for example producing more or opening a new shop, direct lending usually finances unusual and often one-off operations.

Direct lending in effect finances the launch of a subsidiary abroad, or of a new product/service, or even an acquisition. This type of risk is difficult to assess for a bank, as it is very specific. Scoring is thus difficult or impossible. Direct lending fund managers apply techniques that are closer to the private equity toolbox. They undertake due diligence, which implies meeting with the management and going beyond a pure documentation analysis. The perimeter of this due diligence varies depending on the fund manager, but can extend to market and competition analysis.

Direct/senior/unitranche debt is provided by active fund managers carefully assessing risks thanks to a due diligence. Besides active risk assessment and mitigation by the fund manager, the downside risk protection of direct/senior and unitranche debt funds come from the fact that they have a first claim on assets and strong covenants (that is, clauses to monitor and enforce the loan terms). These covenants are crucial to manage risks and act in case the borrower experiences financial difficulties.

Not surprisingly, direct lending fund managers operate essentially in countries with stable and low inflation rates, with strong and predictable legal environments, and where courts can rule relatively fast and judgements can be enforced without major hurdles. Developed markets, namely the USA but also more recently Western Europe, are the main locations of this type of activity.

The USA has a rather long history of providing alternative forms of credit to companies, notably by using bonds, structured credit instruments and securitisation of loan portfolios. American direct lending fund managers also offered an alternative to banks, even before 2008. This activity has been developing fast, particularly since the financial crisis of 2008–2009. International regulatory frameworks such as the Basel III Agreements, as well as major overhauls of national banking legislation, have redefined the perimeter of the lending activity of banks. Notably, these regulations have reset risk thresholds for banks and adjusted solvency ratios to these new assumptions. As a consequence, banks have retreated from lending activities, and reduced significantly their lending activity to small and mid-sized businesses. Lending to these businesses was perceived as less profitable due to the increased costs of risk analysis and compliance, while risk assessments were less favourable to these businesses.

Unitranche financing

This type of debt combines in one single tranche (hence its name) features of senior, second lien and mezzanine debt. Unitranche financing is a more flexible version of the straightforward direct/senior debt, combining different tranches of debt such as junior, subordinated and second lien tranches, and even possibly mezzanine debt. Unitranche debt diverges significantly from mezzanine financing as it is repaid and collects interest progressively and regularly, and does not necessarily embed conversion rights. Therefore, we account for unitranche debt funds in the direct/senior lending category. The expected gross IRR is between 9% and 11%.

Before the financial crisis, the Western European legal bank monopoly on lending essentially prevented the emergence of direct lending funds. Subordinated debt, and notably mezzanine funds, were however present. As the rules on lending were relaxed, fund managers launched direct lending strategies. This coincided with the erosion of the market for mezzanine debt associated with the fall of interest rates. Mezzanine fund managers not only reinvented themselves as unitranche lenders, but also direct lenders.

In the absence of actual data, it is difficult to estimate the market for direct and unitranche lending. We estimate that direct/senior/unitranche debt funds currently represent roughly 57% of PD funds and 10% of PM funds. In 2017, USD 52.6 billion was raised by direct lending funds out of a total of USD 118.7 billion by private debt funds, according to Cox and Hanson (2018). As a matter of comparison, mezzanine funds raised USD 14.9 billion that same year.

4.2.2 Subordinated and Mezzanine Debt

Subordinated debt funds provide flexible financing to a borrower. The borrower is the owner of a business, who pledges this business as the collateral of the loan. The repayment of this loan is subject to the prior refund of more senior loans (which also have priority in terms of access to the collateral). The profits distributed by this business are used to pay the interest (and possibly some or all of the principal) to the lender. If the business fails to distribute these profits, the borrower can seize the business and auction it off. The proceeds are then used to compensate the lender.

Mezzanine debt

Mezzanine debt is the main subordinated debt instrument used in private debt, generally involved in medium to mega LBO structuring. The main principle is to offer mid- to long-term debt, which is repaid *in fine* (all at once at the term of the debt). Because the debt supports a higher risk than the usual plain vanilla debts, its provider charges higher interest rates. The fact that it is repaid *in fine* is another risk, which is compensated by an option to convert the debt into equity. The lender has the right to convert its debt at a predefined debt-to-equity ratio, and hence to participate in the upside. This right can be exercised upon materialisation of a liquidity event or bought back by the borrower (usually at pre-agreed terms). The lender, however, remains protected until the moment that it chooses to convert its debt.

Mezzanine debt generates a blend of yield and capital gains. Thus, the terms negotiated between the borrower and the lender are the interest rate, the conversion rights (sometimes referred to as 'equity kicker'), the duration of the loan and its repayment (usually in fine, that is at the term of the loan) and the covenants of the loan. Interest is usually defined as a margin over a base interest rate and can be paid as ongoing and/or capitalised (and therefore accruing) to the principal. The covenants are the clauses of the lending contracts that define the information rights of the lender and its recourse in case the loan does not develop according to plan.

Mezzanine debt is often compared to leveraged loans, as both are provided to companies with no rating – or rated below investment grade, such as the ones targeted by LBOs. However, leveraged loans are usually collateralised and thus senior, whereas mezzanine debt is not (as it is subordinated). Leveraged loans are usually provided by banks, which keep them to maturity or more frequently package and resell them (notably as collateralised loan obligations, see below). According to some estimates, the leveraged loans market in the USA reached USD 1 trillion in 2018 and is on the verge of catching up with high-yield bonds (USD 1.1 trillion).

Mezzanine debt can theoretically be provided by banks but is in practice provided by non-traditional lenders such as mezzanine funds. The mezzanine debt can be 'sponsored' if the equity provider is a financial institution such as an LBO fund. The fund acquires a company (via one or multiple holding companies, see above) and places the mezzanine debt in one/the holding company. However, the mezzanine debt can also be 'unsponsored' if there is no intervention of a financial institution as an equity provider. The owner can, for example, be the management of the business.

Mezzanine debt is provided by active fund managers, who carefully assess the risk associated with the borrower and its business. This is not a credit-scoring approach, but a full due diligence operated by the fund manager, in partnership with the equity provider in case of sponsored mezzanine. As a result, the loss ratio is supposed to be minimal or nil. Mezzanine debt provides an exposure to the upside of LBOs (in case of sponsored operations) while limiting the risks associated with this type of operation. This strategy provides investors with the opportunity to get an exposure to transfers of ownership of mid- to mega-size deals, including those that are not sponsored by LBO funds. The investment universe is therefore partially diverging from LBO funds.

Mezzanine debt is popular with lenders, because the interest rates are higher than for senior debt and there is potential for conversion. It is also popular for borrowers, because it means having debt without bearing repayment over the course of the holding period. Even if the interest rate is higher for mezzanine than for senior and junior debt, it is still perceived as 'cheap' because of the repayment *in fine*.

Mezzanine debt is relatively expensive when compared to senior debt. During the last credit cycle (until 2008), subordinated non-convertible debt emerged as an alternative: the second lien debt (sometimes referred to as 'junior debt'). Unlike mezzanine debt, which aims to generate a gross IRR of 15–18%, second lien aims for 10–12% gross IRR.

According to Partners Group, mezzanine debt has shown a certain stability during the financial crisis (the average volatility was 11%, against 50–60% for other asset classes, see Figure 4.51). In case of default, the debt is usually recovered at around 50%. Historically, the recovery rate is high, with a default rate of 2–4% (in 2008, it culminated at 12–13%).

Second lien debt

Other instruments – such as 'second lien' loans, which are the equivalent of mezzanine debt without conversion rights – are competing with mezzanine debt. Second lien debt rose on the premise that mezzanine debt was not deemed to be converted owing to shorter holding periods. It was thus better to opt simply for another layer of debt, which would come after the senior and junior debt. Senior debt has the highest priority regarding repayment and junior debt comes next, generally after a certain number of years and sometimes depending on certain criteria. Because of this mechanism, second

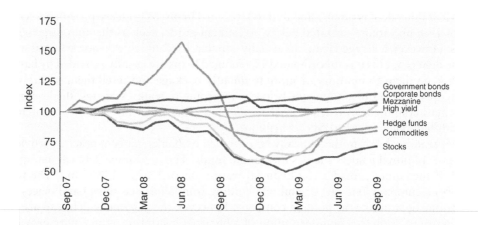

FIGURE 4.51   Compared risk of European mezzanine and other asset classes
Source: Partners Group 2010, from Bloomberg, Goldman Sachs Commodities Index,
Merrill Lynch EU Corporate Master Index, ML B-rated high-yield index, MSCI and
HRFI FOF.

lien was structured to be converted *in fine*. Figure 4.52 illustrates the fast growth of the
second lien loan market.

At the height of the last investment cycle, large/mega LBO investments were
increasingly structured to bear *in fine* debt repayments, thus increasing the need for
mezzanine and second lien debts. The second lien loan market presents many advantages for large/mega LBO fund managers. The repayment *in fine*, either by tranches or

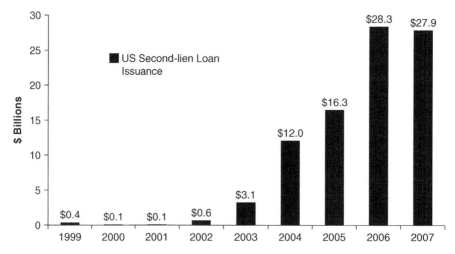

FIGURE 4.52   Evolution of the second lien loan market
Source: Credit Suisse, S&P LCD.

in total ('bullet'), even if it is a source of increasing valuation of the companies, is also a source of flexibility. The underlying portfolio company does not have to repay the debt before term. As the riskiest moment of an LBO is the first year, this means that repayment *in fine* happens when the company has more latitude to repay it.

Covenant strong or covenant light debt

The credit crisis has had many consequences, among them an economic downturn. This has obviously affected LBO funds' portfolio companies, which are supposed to reimburse the debt of acquisition through dividend payments. With sales and results under pressure, these portfolio companies struggle to make the dividend payments. As a result, defaults on payments have increased by a multiple of 3.6 between 2007 and 2008, with an estimated 5.8% default on European leveraged loans in the first semester of 2009.

A default in repayment usually triggers the potential transfer of ownership of the portfolio company from the fund to the bank(s). To avoid that, debts are usually restructured prior to that extreme. Debt restructuring is usually triggered by breach of covenants. Lenders and owners gather to review the reimbursement plan, according to a new development plan, which takes into account the new economic conditions.

For that reason, the volume of debt restructuring is probably as meaningful, in that respect, as the defaults on payments. A comparison of restructuring and defaults over the course of 2004–2009 shows that although defaults remain high for the first 2 months of 2009, the proportion of restructuring has increased significantly.

What makes debt restructuring successful is the assumption that the value of the company remains higher than the total of the debt of acquisition, and that the development plan will eventually bring significant income to pay the outstanding debt. It can involve a change in the loan mix, with a transfer of principal repayment *in fine*, for example.

Debt restructuring can also be the only way to face portfolio companies' difficulties, as the covenants of the debt may not trigger direct ownership by the lenders. As the difficulties appear earlier, hinting implicitly that the risk of structuring is far too high, the banks grant non-restructuring waivers more easily. The reason is that most of the banks do not want to book high losses, notably when there is a chance of recovery for the company. They also want to avoid becoming owners of ailing businesses.

Of the 64 companies which had covenant-related difficulties in 2008, 48% were breaches of covenant, 34% were redefinitions or waivers of covenant, 3% were an equity increase to prevent a breach of covenant and 14% restructured their debt owing to a breach of covenant. According to S&P, 2009–2012 was a period of acceleration of financial restructuring of leverage loans, and of increased breaches of covenant. The trend is particularly impressive, with a strong acceleration of amendments and waivers of covenant in 2009. As a consequence, 75% of American banks have increased their requirements as to covenants and have been more restrictive in the allocation of leveraged loans in 2008, according to the Federal Reserve (Bank for International Settlements, 2008). Logically, the allocation of covenant light loans dried up in 2009.

However, as soon as the effects of the crisis were gone, the covenant light loans came back (Primack, 2011; Burne, 2012). The low level of interest rates and investors' thirst for yield is driving this trend (Demos and Lauricella, 2012 illustrate this trend

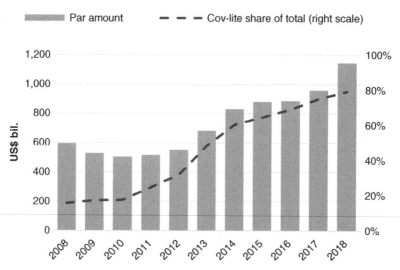

FIGURE 4.53 Evolution of the covenant light loan market
Source: S&P/LSTA Leveraged Loan Index.

with 'master limited partnerships' structured to own real assets such as coal mines and gas stations).[44]

Figure 4.53 depicts the evolution of the debt structure, with a decline of the fully secured debt from more than 80% to slightly more than 50% in 3 years. The rise of *covenant light* debt is impressive, given the short time over which it has developed. In that respect, the competitive pressure on banks has somehow promoted this segment of private equity loans to the rank of a bubble indicator (Tett, 2007).

The current credit cycle has seen the quasi-elimination of mezzanine and second lien debt as we know it in favour of so-called unitranche debt (see above). Mezzanine financing (as well as unitranche and senior debt) is essentially available in developed markets, with the USA and Europe representing the bulk. Mezzanine debt represents roughly 11% of PD funds and 2% of PM funds.

4.2.3 Distressed Debt

Distressed debt (DD) funds can be split into two categories: debt-for-trading and debt-for-control (also called 'loan-to-own'). Debt-for-trading is applied by hedge funds as they acquire the debt of an ailing business at a discount, expecting events to materialise for the business to recover and eventually selling the debt at a higher price. This is a hands-off strategy that requires liquid debt markets to operate.

DD investors dedicated to loan-to-own, such as in private debt funds, buy specific tranches of the debt of an ailing business at a discount with the target of eventually taking control of the business by converting some or all of this debt into equity. In the

---

[44] According to Barclays (quoted in Demos and Lauricella, 2012), the market for MLPs had grown from USD 65 billion to more than USD 350 billion in 2012.

process, equity investors will be washed out, DD investors will restructure the company to profitability and then sell it once its renewed viability is demonstrated. In private debt, DD refers to this hands-on loan-to-own strategy.

Restructuring a company is a high risk–return activity. Investors have tried to lower the risks associated with dealing with troubled companies, and also to enter the company earlier than its actual bankruptcy procedure (turn-around capital, see above). One of the ways to reconcile these two aims is to look at the liabilities of these ailing companies, and notably also their bank debts. Some companies have trouble repaying their debts, even if their fundamentals are sound and solid. US fund managers approach debt holders to acquire their debts at a discount. The seller of the debt could clear their books, register a loss and deploy their funding capacities elsewhere.

DD funds usually use the rights attached to holding the debt to negotiate with the management and the equity holders a sharp restructuring of the company. If successful, this operation would provide a significant benefit to the distressed debt holder, while protecting them from a full loss if the recovery does not happen. Oaktree Capital Management is one of the firms which have developed such strategies in the USA.

Whether with DD investing or turn-around capital, the new owner generally provides additional financial and specialist human resources, negotiates with the creditors and restructures the business according to a specific plan. However, to be viable, this activity has to be undertaken early on, soon after the business starts to experience difficulties. Often, business owners acknowledge these difficulties late, beyond the point at which DD or turn-around investing remains potentially successful.

The value creation attached to distressed debt is linked to the fact that banks are not usually able to handle an ailing business. Not only may the debt not give them a right to truly influence the management, but they are also usually not prepared for this eventuality. This is also why banks participating in LBO debts generally call for a renegotiation of the covenants of the debt rather than triggering the clauses which will entitle them to own the collateral (i.e., the business which was taken over thanks to the debt they provided). Here, the competition with hedge funds is clearly evident.

To operate, DD funds rely on appropriate bankruptcy procedures such as Chapter 11 of the US Bankruptcy Code, which is the most widely used in DD investing. It provides a list of the desirable criteria to see the emergence of such strategies in other jurisdictions. First, Chapter 11 freezes all debt repayment and interest due by the business placed in bankruptcy. This grants the business and its administrators a relief period during which it is possible to assess the options to restructure the business (or its liquidation, which falls under Chapter 7 of the US Bankruptcy Code).

Then, Chapter 11 places a judicial authority in charge of the process, notably to decide on specific issues related to the restructuring of the business. This authority can take specific actions such as approving a restructuring plan even if a minority of creditors do not. This authority can also reduce the capital of the company (thus washing out the former owners) and increase it by converting debt that was not originally designed to be converted.

Furthermore, Chapter 11 does not create any hierarchy between creditors besides the contractual seniority of the different tranches of debt. This provides potential buyers of the credit of the company a relatively clear picture of the tranches of debt to buy in order to have sufficient collateral in case of failure of the business, as well as to be able to force the restructuring of the business along a specific plan. For that matter, the buyer of the credit has to acquire a specific quantity of debt to reach a given majority.

Some jurisdictions, such as France, make a distinction by granting privileges to administrative bodies (tax and social administration), for example. In this case, these administrative bodies are not inclined to sell their debt at a discount. As a consequence, it is impossible for potential credit buyers to acquire the relevant tranches of debt and lead the restructuring.

Limits in Europe

Some jurisdictions, such as the UK, offer a similar bankruptcy regime and could emerge as a potential market for DD investors. More recently, India has reformed its bankruptcy regime to facilitate operations, shorten the process and possibly offer business under administration a way out of the process, notably thanks to the involvement of DD investors.

The UK is ranked as having the best legislation regarding creditor protection, ahead of Germany and France (Davydenko & Franks, 2006). It even allows the organisation of pre-packaged administration procedures (Scott, 2012), which make it easier to turn around a business (but in the process these pre-packaged processes leave the creditors in a difficult situation). In France, the priority given to the continuity of business and job protection reduces creditor protection. In the UK, first-ranking creditors have a right of veto on the decisions made by the directors upon default of payment from the company. They control the company from that moment on. In Germany, creditors are in the middle ground, in the sense that they retain a certain power in restructuring loans.

The consequence is that in the UK, the recovery rate is 92%, as opposed to 67% in Germany and 56% in France. All else being equal, the difference between the UK and France is that the recovery rate is 20% higher in the former. One interpretation is that the incentive for British banks to do their best to ensure that companies progress towards a positive outcome is higher, as they have a better prospect of recovering their debts.

Countries without an equivalent of Chapter 11 have limited activity in turn-around capital investing (see above). This type of operation is executed to avoid a formal bankruptcy procedure.

An alternative to distressed debt investing: non-performing loans

Banks structure their loans to maximise their risk–return profile in a given legal environment. In that respect, bankruptcy codes play a major role in the way creditors are reacting to default on debt, and also in how this debt is being handled afterwards. Banks have increasingly decided to keep the debt of defaulting companies, and thus become the new owners of these businesses (this was emblematic with Citi seizing a defaulting EMI from Terra Firma, and then auctioning it off to two trade buyers in 2012). These companies are sound, but they were acquired through an excess of leverage. As a result, European banks are injecting capital to help these companies with the double prospect of recovering their loans and eventually making a profit out of these defaulting companies (Cauchi, 2009).

An emerging segment in the distressed debt world has been non-performing loans (NPLs).[45] The 2007–2009 financial crisis led many banks, notably in Europe, to sell

---

[45]The Basel Agreements define a loan as non-performing when the borrower is 90 days or more behind the agreed payment schedule. The borrower is deemed unlikely to pay the credit in full without an action from the bank to seize the collateral of the loan.

these loans at a discount. The new creditor then engages in active recovery strategies, which could be classified in three categories:

- First, a pressure to recover the backlog of interest and principal repayments.
- Second, a restructuring of the debt to adjust payments to the capacity of the borrower.
- Third, an action towards seizing the assets pledged as collateral, later auctioned for repayment of the principal, interest and damages.

The first two strategies are at the core of active NPL investing (the third being the last-resort solution).

A significant number of LBO fund managers have diversified into distressed debt in the USA (the reasoning being that this is a synergetic way to increase their activities in a down cycle). LBO fund managers have launched distressed debt funds, sometimes with the obvious target of buying cheap the debt of their own portfolio companies (see Davidoff, 2012a for an example of this with Apollo's investments in Realogy). This would allow them to reduce the pressure on debt repayment, salvaging the investments made at the high point of the previous investment cycle. DD represents roughly 32% of the PD fund investment universe, and 6% of the PM investment universe. This does not include turn-around capital and NPL strategies.

4.2.4 Niche Private Debt Strategies

Venture debt is a niche private debt strategy which could be described as the equivalent of mezzanine debt for mature start-ups. Usually, interest is capitalised and funds get their capital, cumulated interest and possibly capital gain upon a liquidity event. Venture debt activity has been limited to a few select markets such as the USA and more recently Europe and Israel. Venture debt funds usually provide convertible debt to late-stage start-ups, often as a complement or an alternative to a new round of financing. According to Preqin, venture debt funds generated an average net IRR of 11.5% between 2007 and 2012. MOIC ranged from 0.83x to 1.43x and IRR from 1% to 60%. However, none of the funds observed were fully liquidated at the time of the report, so these figures have to be used with caution. Venture debt funds were willing to raise USD 4.4 billion in 2015. This has to be compared with a total of USD 214 billion for private debt funds.[46]

Litigation financing could also be seen as a form of private debt. The borrower can use it to finance pre-trial and trial proceedings (including lawyers' fees). In case of success, the fund gets a share of the financial compensation. In case of failure, the fund loses the investment. In certain instances, litigation financing can be used to finance the post-trial period, functioning as a receivable financing mechanism. The party that prevailed in a legal proceeding gets the financial compensation from the fund in exchange for a discount. The fund then takes over the process of recovering the amount due.

---

[46]Distressed debt funds (as defined in this book) were looking for USD 64 billion, mezzanine/subordinated debt USD 65 billion, direct/senior/unitranche funds USD 77 billion, royalty financing funds USD 2.5 billion, CLO funds USD 2.3 billion and funds of private debt funds USD 1.3 billion (Devine, 2015).

Royalty financing, aviation finance and even trade finance are also other forms of private debt financing which could potentially be seen as an overlap with private real asset debt. Each of these strategies uses either an asset (planes and parts) or claim on future cash-flow streams (royalties or payments) as collateral to provide capital upfront. The fund manager takes over the task of recovering the capital or selling the asset/claim. According to Devine (2015), royalty-financing funds were willing to raise USD 2.5 billion in 2015, representing 1.16% of the total sought by private debt funds.

Other private debt niche strategies, often gathered under the generic expression of 'specialty finance', include asset-backed financing. This could overlap with private real asset debt, as tangible or intangible assets are placed in a special purpose vehicle (SPV) structured with equity and debt. The benefit of the lender to the structure is that a specific asset is pledged as collateral for a loan. The owner of the SPV can use the proceeds of the loan for other purposes while avoiding complex negotiations on the loan.

4.3   PRIVATE REAL ASSETS: REAL ESTATE, INFRASTRUCTURE AND NATURAL RESOURCES

As illustrated at the beginning of this chapter, private real asset (PRA) funds provide financing at every stage of the development of intangible or tangible real assets (fixed or not). PRA funds offer some attractive features to their fund sponsors, notably recurring cash flows and reduced risks. The return perspectives, however, are lower than in private equity.

There is no entrepreneur at the core of the business in PRA investing, but an asset and potentially a project manager. PRA investing implies much more delimited actions by investors than in PE.

The equivalent of venture capital for PRA is called 'greenfield' investing. This often implies acquiring assets (such as land in the case of real estate, infrastructure, natural resources, timberland and farmland), securing the rights to build, managing the construction and delivering the final asset. This strategy bears significant execution risks, compounded by potential foreign exchange, regulatory and political risks associated with the geographical locations.

The equivalent of growth capital and LBO for PRA is most likely a combination of core, core-plus and value-added investing. Assets are developed, of medium to high quality, and with variable levels of change. Core assets require less debt and transformation, while value-added assets support more debt and require more transformation.

The equivalent of distressed debt and turn-around capital for PRA is opportunistic (or brownfield in private infrastructure), as well as distressed (including non-performing loans) investing.

Private real assets differ substantially from companies financed by private equity and private debt in the sense that they represent a clear and direct access to predictable future cash flows associated with the collateral represented by the asset itself. Therefore, while a hotel management company is a company, the hotel itself is the asset. Sometimes, the two are combined in one entity, and unless the management of the hotel is very lean and passive, it is considered as a company first, with significant assets on its balance sheet.

PRA funds have been growing, with an increased flow of investment opportunities. Multiple factors have contributed to this evolution. First, the trend towards a disengagement of states in the economy has led to the privatisation of public assets, as well as the emergence of public–private partnerships (to develop new infrastructures, for example). Second, public and private companies have been keen to focus their activities and reduce the size of their balance sheet. Their assets were immobilising financial resources that could be reallocated to compete more effectively. This led to the deconsolidation of assets from balance sheets, placed in SPVs in need of equity providers. Third, as financial institutions have seen their regulatory framework overhauled against the provision of such equity to SPVs, PRAs have seen an opportunity to jump in.

Private real asset funds finance assets through equity (PRA equity funds) or debt (PRA debt funds). Although PRA debt funds are emerging, most PRA funds finance assets through equity. Just as in the PD sector, PRA fund managers can be more or less hands-on depending on the sub-strategies. PRA can be broken down into multiples categories: private real estate, private infrastructure and investment niches.

PRA funds aim to generate a combination of income and capital gains, by acquiring, managing, transforming and selling assets over time. The mix of income and capital gains delivered to investors depends on the type of asset acquired and the transformation operated: the more transformation, the higher the potential capital gains.

4.3.1 Private Real Estate, Infrastructure and Exotic Assets

Private real estate (PRE) funds represent roughly 36% of the PRA market and roughly 10% of the PM universe. These funds acquire real estate such as office, commercial, industrial or residential units, as well as a combination thereof, or more specialised assets such as assisted living facilities or warehouses. Sub-strategies include core/core-plus, value-added and opportunistic, as well as distressed, debt and secondary.[47] For the latter three strategies, little information is available. They differ significantly in focus, strategy, character of underlying assets, level of manager involvement, leverage and other factors, all of which result in differing return and risk profiles.

Database provider Preqin estimated that as of June 2017, PRE funds managed USD 811 billion, of which USD 245 billion was 'dry powder'. North America represented 57.9%, Europe 25.9%, Asia 11.5% and the rest of the world 4.7%. Opportunistic PRE funds had USD 98 billion of dry powder, value-added PRE funds USD 61 billion, debt PRE funds USD 49 billion, core PRE funds USD 16 billion, core-plus PRE funds USD 11 billion and distressed PRE funds also USD 11 billion.

While listed real-estate funds provide investors with access to plain vanilla core real estate, PRE funds dedicated to core and core-plus differ. PRE implies a change of assets, leading to a capital gain. Core PRE funds invest at the lower end of the risk spectrum,

---

[47] According to database provider Preqin, debt PRE funds raised USD 27.9 billion in 2017 (25.3% of the total raised by PRE excluding funds of funds), distressed PRE funds USD 2.9 billion (2.6%) and secondary PRE funds USD 0.7 billion (0.6%). As a matter of comparison, PRE funds of funds raised USD 1.2 billion, core PRE funds USD 3.6 billion (3.3%), core-plus PRE funds USD 3.7 billion (3.4%), value-added PRE funds USD 34.9 billion (31.7%) and opportunistic PRE funds USD 36.5 billion (33.1%).

acquiring existing sound and stable assets (office, retail, industrial and/or multi-family residential) in prime metropolitan locations and established markets. The strategy might consist of upgrading the tenant base, or increasing the leasing rate further, or shifting the duration of contracts and/or operating mild improvements on the building. A pure buy-and-hold strategy is possible but limits the potential capital gains. Properties are already well maintained at acquisition time and require little or no capital injection. This strategy uses moderate leverage (15–30% of the value of the asset). Core PRE performance is primarily yield-driven (90–100%) with limited capital gain contribution (0–10%). Holding periods tend to be long (10 years or more).

Core-plus PRE funds invest in properties that are similar to the core sub-strategy, but require more work and/or are located in prime or confirmed upcoming areas. The quality of buildings might be lower and require enhancement. Some buildings might need to be repositioned and their tenant base to shift. This strategy uses leverage (30–50%) and usually requires a moderate capital injection. Core-plus PRE performance is also primarily yield-driven (80–90%) with limited capital gain contribution (10–20%). Holding periods also tend to be rather long (7 years or more).

Value-added (VA)[48] PRE funds focus on properties located at prime or secondary locations and that require more active involvement from the fund manager. The purpose of the intervention is to upgrade the building by redeveloping, refurbishing or repositioning it and/or change the tenant base (lease-up). Fund managers need to be able to identify and source appropriate target assets, implement relevant property and physical improvements and tenant-level strategy and provide ongoing asset management. Beyond the plain vanilla assets described above, value-added strategies can be applied to specialty types including notably hospitality, healthcare-related properties, student housing or self-storage. Performance is driven by a combination of income (30–50%) and capital gains (50–70%). Fund managers can use debt in the range of 40–70% of the value of the asset.

Opportunistic PRE funds are at the higher end of the risk spectrum. They target lower-quality buildings in prime, secondary or peripheral markets across the whole range of real-estate markets, including niches. Properties require significant overhaul to upgrade them to the higher level of quality, or even ground-up (re-)development. Fund managers are very hands-on in this type of situation, involving complex turn-around and redevelopment. Performance is driven by capital gains, with possibly some little income (0–10%). Fund managers can use debt in the range of 60–80% of the value of the asset.

4.3.2   Private Infrastructure

Infrastructure investing supports the construction, development, operation and overhaul of permanent structures facilitating economic activities. Among the sectors included are transportation (toll roads, ports, airports, bridges, tunnels and railroads), regulated utility and energy infrastructures (water, wastewater, electricity, gas and oil networks) and communications infrastructures (phone and fibre networks, transmission towers). Infrastructures benefit from a local (or national) monopoly in their activities, which makes them less sensitive to economic cycles than other investment

---

[48]Value-added is sometimes referred to as 'value add'. We will use both indistinctively.

strategies. They are usually regulated and rely on long-term contracts with their clients. Some authors include in infrastructures so-called 'social infrastructures' such as education, recreation, correctional, healthcare, fuel storage and warehouse facilities. These facilities are closer to private companies or real estate in their characteristics, so we exclude them from the definition.

In general, infrastructure funds provide investors with fairly stable and predictable income, a relative protection against inflation (as prices are indexed) and a low correlation with other investment strategies. Although the disengagement of states in the financing of infrastructure has paved the way for public–private partnerships and the opportunity for infrastructure investing, the financing gap of new infrastructures remains largely open. This is because infrastructure investing supports specific risks, such as regulatory and sovereign risk (even in developed countries such as Norway) and construction risk (for greenfield investments).

Although infrastructure is a recent sector of investment for institutional investors, private infrastructure funds invest in these tangible fixed assets in equity or debt. These funds can be classified in sub-strategies along the lines of real estate (see above) with core, value-added and opportunistic, which are sometimes blended and referred to as 'brownfield' when already built. 'Greenfield' finances the design and construction of infrastructure projects, and is an additional strategy. They represent roughly 41% of the PRA market and 11% of the PM universe. As in PRE, infrastructure debt funds have emerged as well. According to PitchBook, private debt infrastructure funds raised USD 7.2 billion in 2017. Database provider Preqin estimated that as of June 2017, private equity infrastructure funds managed USD 388 billion, of which USD 149 billion was 'dry powder'. The USA represents 38% of the total, Europe 30%, Asia 12% and the rest of the world 20%. The sector is quite concentrated, and the average fund size is USD 1.3 billion.

4.3.3 Natural Resources

PRA gathers a lot of investment niches, often under the expression of natural resources. This generic expression can be broken down into multiple investment areas, gathered around energy and commodities production. Another way to classify it is to differentiate between renewable and non-renewable production.

In the area of non-renewable energy, oil and gas have drawn recent interest for equity and debt (including convertible investments). Private energy funds can invest in the upstream (exploration and extraction), midstream (transport and pile-lines) and downstream (refineries, storage and distribution) segments. The focus of private energy funds is usually on midstream and downstream assets. The advantage of such funds is to provide investors with an exposure to the growing need of international energy while reducing the exposure to the volatility of oil and gas prices. Private energy funds focused on oil and gas represent roughly 22% of the PRA market and roughly 6% of the PM universe.

Private energy funds are likely to invest more and more in renewable energy, produced by solar farms, windmill farms, biomass plants, wave and tidal facilities, as well as hydroelectric dams. Unfortunately, there is limited data on this emerging field.

Renewable commodities production includes private farmland funds, for which there is limited data. Fortunately, their risk–return–liquidity profile can be compared to timberland. These two strategies are largely dominated by the USA, although more recently some funds have started to deploy capital in the rest of the world. They provide a combination of yield, as crops and trees are sold, and capital appreciation as the land gains in value. They also provide a certain hedge against inflation. In many respects, they could be compared with private real estate, except that the yield depends on market prices for the commodities they produce and not on regular rents (although for farmland, this could be an option as well).

US timberland funds represent roughly 0.7% of the PRA market and an estimated 0.2% of the PM universe. According to Preqin, farmland and timberland funds represented 5% of unlisted natural resources capital in 2016. According to Cambridge Associates, 24 timberland funds created between 2002 and 2008 and gathering USD 8 billion generated a pooled average of 4.2% and MOIC of 1.36x. The average time to liquidity is 7.49 years. Over 2004–2008, the PME based on the S&P Global Timber delivered 1.23x while timberland funds generated 1.30x.

Non-renewable commodities funds include private mining funds, for example. There is unfortunately limited information available about this investment strategy.

4.4 OTHER INTERVENTIONS IN PRIVATE MARKETS

As illustrated at the beginning of this chapter, there are multiple interventions that are at the border between private markets and asset management. To establish a border, the easiest path is to observe if there is a direct relationship between the entrepreneur (or project manager in the case of real assets) and the investor. If yes, the strategy might be a good candidate to be included in private markets. If not, then the strategy might not be a clear private markets strategy. Funds of funds are an example: they are an instrument to diversify and manage the exposure of fund investors to private markets. They are at the border of private markets and asset management. The secondary market is another one.

4.4.1 Funds of Funds

As mentioned over the course of the first part of this book, funds of funds have been a privileged tool to help fund investors diversify their private market investments, start a programme easily and at modest levels, and gain exposure and knowledge of the asset class.

The activity of private equity fund of funds activity is relatively recent. The oldest active fund of funds manager (Adams Street Partners) dates back to 1972, but only seven which have survived until now were created in the 1980s. This means that the emergence of the fund of funds industry is correlated with the financial liberalisation of the early 1980s – and the growth of the private equity asset class after.

The future of funds of funds

Funds of funds were the great losers of the crisis, notably as they bear their own management fees and carry interest.[49] Their number has shrunk as they struggled to

---

[49]To the point that some private equity gatekeepers even deny being involved in this market, see Caroll (2012).

attract larger institutions, the latter building their own fund selection and monitoring capacity. Their lack of legitimacy in systematically selecting the top performers was condemning them to be the first victims of the 'war on management fees' that fund investors had re-launched after the financial crisis (Meek, 2012).[50] Returns were declining[51] and one of the surest ways to preserve them was to bypass the funds of funds managers' fees (which are 0.8–1.0% of assets over 13 years at the moment, plus 5–10% carried interest for funds of funds).

The responses to these pressures are:

■ Consolidation. APG and PGGM sold AlpInvest (a private equity fund of funds manager managing USD 32 billion) to a joint venture between Carlyle and AlpInvest management in 2012.[52] Capital Dynamics bought HRJ Capital in 2009. BlackRock bought SwissRe Private Equity Partners in 2012. Gartmore Investment Management merged its private equity fund of funds activity with Hermes Fund Managers, later acquired by Henderson Group (for GBP 78.1 billion). Citigroup sold its private equity fund of funds business to Lexington Partners and Stepstone Group in 2010. Stepstone bought SilverBrook in 2010 and Parish Capital in 2011. Examples of such operations abound. The targets are not lacking, either because they do not have the critical mass, or because they have weathered difficult times, or both (Access Capital Partners was involved in the 'pay-to-play' scandal in the USA).
■ A race towards more assets under management. Partners Group targets organic growth (on average CHF 4 billion of new assets under management per year – though not broken down between its fund of funds activities and the rest of its divisions).
■ Some fund of funds managers offer segregated accounts (tailor-made products) to large institutional investors, where large institutions find a programme adequate for their needs. However, this opens up some difficult questions in terms of *conflict of interests*. Given the fact that the top-quality funds are usually attracting more capital than they really want to raise (over-subscription), investors are scaled down in order to serve at least partially the appetite of a select panel of investors. When a fund of funds manager has a regular programme and has to manage segregated accounts for some other clients, the attribution of the allocation granted by over-subscribed funds becomes tricky. The temptation could exist to serve the programmes where the manager receives the better incentive or derives most of its income, which thus would violate its fiduciary duties to serve the limited partners of the funds it is managing in their best interests.

According to Preqin, funds of funds accounted for USD 16 billion in 2011 (USD 10.7 billion in 2010 out of the USD 225 billion raised in private equity). The number

---

[50] http://realdeals.eu.com/article/28986, last accessed 16 May 2012.
[51] 11.6% as of 30 June 2010 (Preqin) and overall 19.2% according to State Street Private Equity Index (30/6/2010), in Jacobius (2011). Toll (2012) states that over 1985 to 2006 and based on 71 funds of funds, the average investment multiple is 1.3, the median multiple is 1.2. The median IRR (55 found in sample) is 5.84% (9.6% for top quartile, 1.5% for bottom quartile).
[52] This in turn helped to fuel the listing of Carlyle, which remains less diversified than its competitors KKR and Blackstone.

of private equity funds of funds and the capital raised by them had fallen since 2007 (USD 58.1 billion collected by 172 funds) to the lowest level since 2004 (Jacobius, 2011). Quite a few funds of fund managers have not raised capital for some time, which questions their added value. Moreover, they do not benefit from any special treatment (which they could have claimed due to their reduced risk profile) under Basel III, nor under Solvency II.

The retreat of funds of funds would have significant consequences for the private equity market. According to some estimates, they represented 15% of total private equity commitments worldwide (Jacobius, 2011). As stated by David Fann, President and CEO of PCG Asset Management: 'the attrition is particularly unwelcome for certain private equity funds, such as those offering niche investment strategies to raise capital' (quoted in Jacobius, 2011). The proportion seems to have stabilised in Europe to 11–12% according to Invest Europe's figures.

One aspect of the evolution of funds of funds would be a focus on advising fund investors and thus becoming pure gatekeepers, helping them to identify promising emerging managers and set up their investment policy and procedures according to their needs.[53] Another could be to create products with a specific focus:[54] certain emerging markets (Vietnam, Indonesia, Malaysia, African countries, Latin American countries); certain sectors (clean technologies, nanotechnologies, new materials); or strategies (small LBOs, distressed debt in Europe) which are difficult to assess (Mariathasan & Steward, 2011).

A third vector of evolution for funds of funds lies in their untapped capacity to create products which can either enhance the performance (through financial leverage, as applied by Ardian in certain fund of funds programmes), reduce the illiquidity period (either by structuring products, as Capital Dynamics did or by offering 'windows' of exit to fund investors), or provide a product with more regular cash flows (using a mix of debt and equity investments).

The real renewal of the fund of funds activity came with co-investments. As many fund investors are not equipped with the adequate resources to co-invest, they in effect delegate to fund of funds managers the task to evaluate, select and monitor co-investments. As a result, some managers have launched dedicated co-investments funds, while others have blended them into their funds of funds programmes, along with secondary investments (see next section). By co-investing, fund of funds managers offer a specific service to fund investors while reducing the overall load of their fees. Fund investors pay lower management fees and carried interest to managers on the funds of funds activity, which is comparatively more expensive than investing directly in funds. However, they pay reduced co-investment fees, which are less expensive than investing directly in funds. As a result, the blended product can deliver an attractive net performance for a low level of risk.

---

[53]'Investors not only require the services of a fund of funds – or a manager of managers, if you will – but they [also] want to be trained. A part of what we do is to train investors to evolve into being a direct investor ...', Kevin Albert, Global Head of Business Development at Pantheon, cited in Power (2012).

[54]'According to Albert, that means the old "one size fits all" approach is no longer sufficient' (Power, 2012).

4.4.2 The Secondary Market

As the private equity market was maturing slowly, a private equity secondary market emerged. The difference with listed markets is that the primary market in private equity represents most of the flows, whereas it is secondary transactions which compose most of the volume on the stock exchange. The secondary market is active at different levels:

- At the portfolio company level – fund managers usually take a stake in a private equity operation for a specific purpose. In various cases, the company cannot be listed or sold to a strategic investor (trade sale). In that case, other fund managers can take over the company in order to develop it further, thus making a secondary investment such as, for example, a secondary LBO.
- At the fund level – some fund investors, owing to cash requirements or the need to rebalance their portfolio, may need to sell their stakes in certain private equity funds before the term of these funds. They therefore sell these stakes to secondary buyers, who benefit not only from a shorter fund life span and a higher level of maturity of the portfolio company, but also a reduced expectation in terms of returns. These sales can be operated at a premium or a discount on the NAV of the fund, depending on the situation of the portfolio, the quality of the fund manager and the market situation, as well as the timeframe of the operation.
- As portfolio or single asset secondary sales ('direct secondaries') – some funds sometimes reach their term without having sold all of their assets. In that case, they put their remaining assets up for sale. Usually, this sale is operated at a discount and can be operated on the full portfolio or on a single portfolio company.

With the advent of the secondary market, a complete ecosystem is emerging. This is a rather recent market, which has been developing fast, essentially in the fund stake segment. *Liquidity being one of the key problems in finance*, the more the secondary market develops, the more private equity will mature and become an autonomous market with regard to other asset classes. Some fund investors are repeat sellers, hence using the secondary market for active fund portfolio management (Figure 4.54).

One of the factors which could thus emerge is that the value of portfolio companies could refer less and less to the listed market. As transactions operate on a specific secondary market, and become increasingly numerous, a specific pricing reference could emerge – as is the case for real estate, for example. The correlation with the stock exchange would vary with the maturity of the company and the holding period. This prospect would contribute to the reduction of the influence of the stock exchange as the main and quasi-unique reference for the pricing of assets.

According to the analysis of Bills (2010), the secondary market could be supported by a long-term trend, despite the fact that the crisis did not bring the wave of opportunities that secondary specialists were expecting. However, he quotes Charles Stetson (fund manager and co-founder of the secondary firm PEI Funds), saying that 'institutional investors, especially the pension funds of the world, are at a historic crossroads. In the United States, for instance, the baby boom generation – the largest population cohort in the nation's history – is beginning to retire, and other advanced economies, such as Japan's, are even further down that road. No longer will pension funds be raking in contributions from those workers; instead they will have to pay them out to

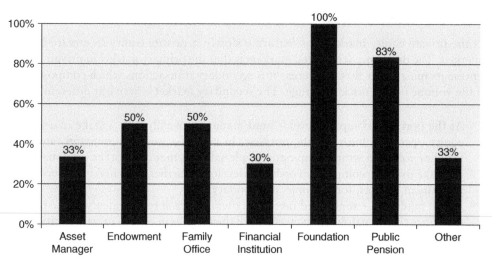

FIGURE 4.54   Repeat sellers of private equity fund stakes on the secondary market
Source: Cogent Partners, H1 2012.

retirees. This may dampen their enthusiasm for making decade-long commitments to illiquid investments with lumpy payout records [. . .]. And when the selling starts in secondaries, it is likely to trigger a rush for the exits, clobbering the values of asset sales and exacerbating the crisis.'

As private equity potentially offers a fully integrated financing chain, it could soon bypass the stock exchange. In certain countries or sectors, industrial companies are teaming up with private equity investors so as to benefit from their expertise. This was the case for mobile operators in Eastern and Central Europe, for example.

The professionalisation of private equity, thanks notably to the emergence of vendor due diligence, an increasing level of intermediation in the private equity operations, the specialisation of fund managers in certain private equity operations (regardless of their diversification out of private equity), the development of mezzanine and high-yield bonds, and the wider acceptance of private equity as a quasi-mainstream asset class will give credibility to a specific pricing reference from private equity.

This can only happen if these prices are communicated and accessible to the professionals who are not involved in the transactions. That remains to be seen and, so far, secondary operations, notably for distressed sales of fund stakes or portfolios/single assets, remain largely out of public sight. The future of private equity hence lies in a higher, tightly knit intermediation fed by a large ecosystem of specialised boutiques, not in disintermediation.

4.4.3   Collateralised Debt Obligations

With the growing size of LBOs, banks started not only to syndicate the loans, but eventually to package and sell them on the financial markets. Collateralised debt obligations (CDOs) or collateralised loan obligations (CLOs) are syndicated repackaged loans and debts combining features of funds of funds and secondaries. Hedge funds have been buying into the debt of large and very large buy-outs through these CDOs and CLOs, for many reasons. Not only do these debts offer a better return than some other assets, with lower risk, but they are also better able to handle cases of default. At a certain stage, the demand for high-yield bonds (e.g., non-rated debt) was so high that its cost fell close to investment-grade debt, despite the degradation of the financial health of companies. Hedge funds would have renegotiated tougher terms with LBO fund managers, but would not be afraid of the prospect of becoming owners of businesses.

LBO fund managers have sensed this change in the balance of power and to avoid a confrontation with hedge fund activists, they asked their lenders to include clauses in the contracts to prevent the selling of some debt tranches to hedge funds (see *The Economist*, 2012b for an illustration, in Australia, of the seizing of CVC's Nine).

These products were then rated and sold to institutional investors. When some of the debt packages defaulted (namely subprime mortgages in the USA), the risk–return profile of CDOs and CLOs tanked. The market was no longer liquid, as institutional investors flew from these packaged products. Large and mega LBOs have been virtually blocked for a while, as their debts were part of these CDOs and CLOs. One of the reasons is that financial leverage is now increasingly restricted, as banks had to rebuild their capital basis and review the risks associated with the credits they granted. New regulations might also force them to keep a higher proportion of capital in order to lend to businesses.

Prior to the crisis, the American National Association of Insurance Commissioners (NAIC) declared in 2006 that hybrid debts (ranking behind other debts as to priority of payment but benefitting from conversion options) must be accounted for as equity investments. Just as banks must keep a given amount in their balance sheets for every transaction that they make, insurers would have to save more capital in their balance sheets to cover the risk entailed by these instruments. The cover rate, that is the percentage of capital demanded for each investment, depends on the estimated risk of these investments. The greater the risk, the higher the cover rate will be, in order to offset possible problems arising from a given investment.

The NAIC decision has set an early example. Subordinated debts will be more expensive for insurers and therefore less attractive in relative terms. This means that return expectations for subordinated debts will probably be higher and therefore that the cost for borrowers (private equity funds) will increase. As a result, either mezzanine funds will demand higher returns through conversion rights, or the interest rates of mezzanine debt will rise. The balance of private equity deals will probably change because of this, once the effects of the crisis have been absorbed.

CDOs and CLOs are the second generation of the high-yield bonds (or 'junk bonds') which were *en vogue* in the 1980s to finance LBOs. The high-yield bond crashed along with the demise of the bank Drexel Burnham Lambert, which developed and was ruling more or less alone this market. Based on this experience, the professionals from Drexel went into other banks (and notably Lehman Brothers, which disappeared in 2008) to create these structured products. The need for high-yield debts, and their successors, by LBO operations, as well as investors (for the yields that they provide) means that this market will not disappear (Bullock, 2011). The products have re-emerged (*Financial Times*, 2012a,b) rather strongly.

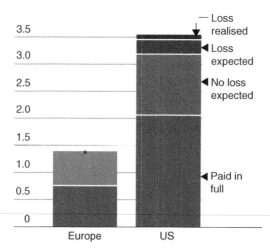

FIGURE 4.55   Losses on structured finance deals
in Europe and the USA (2007–2011)
Source: Financial Times, Fitch Ratings 2012.

The success of CLOs is related to their very low level of losses: only 1.9% over the
period 2007–2011 according to Fitch (see Figure 4.55). The heaviest losses came from
market prices and not defaults from underlying loans.

To re-emerge, CLOs and CDOs had to comply with very high capital requirements
from banks and insurance groups. That has changed the equilibrium of the products.
Transparency has improved, renewing the trust in these products. In particular, a higher
financial commitment is required from product makers (banks had to increase their
share of the products) and the rating agencies (which had to take into account the
jurisprudence and expectations from regulators and clients).

4.4.4   Exotic Assets

Some assets do not belong to the private equity asset class as they do not fit with the
definition outlined in the Introduction and are thus 'alternative alternatives' (Blessing,
2011). What about art and wine? Even though some funds have been launched in those
areas, the same criteria apply: follow the entrepreneur. A fund dedicated to invest in
fine art, even though structured as a private equity fund, does not belong to this area.
There is no entrepreneurial endeavour attached to this activity, as well as no separation
between the investor and the actor of the market. Here again, the art industry fund
differentiates itself in the sense that it focuses on companies belonging exclusively to
the fine art value chain, with entrepreneurs at the helm.

4.5   CONCLUSION

Private markets could be described as a financial ecosystem living in symbiosis with the
listed markets. While private markets are able to finance a company at any stage of its
development, it is however not a must-have for every company or asset.

4.5.1 Private Markets are a Financing Solution Designed for a Specific Need

Private markets are not necessary for any venture launched, developed or restructured. Most of the companies being created do not need the help of a venture capital fund. Professional capital infusions are made to support ambitious corporate projects which present (measurable) risks and returns, have specific needs and could not be financed otherwise.

4.5.2 Venture and Growth Capital

Thus, many start-ups financed during the venture capital boom of 1997–2000 did not really need a professional capital infusion, as was proven by the unusual rate of failures after this time and the number of companies remaining in fund portfolios. Private equity is useful when it is a matter of financing heavy investment; to save time in the development of a given product or service; to answer an urgent need from the market which is not addressed by incumbent players; or to capitalise on the successful proof of concept of a product or service.

4.5.3 Leveraged Buy-out

In the same respect, not all companies which are going through a transition of ownership need an LBO. This is quite obvious in the case of succession or retirement of an owner-manager. To be a target for this transition, the company must support the heavy burden of acquisition debt. LBO fulfils a need when there is no other possibility offered to the future buyer, where it does not have the equity or the expertise to do so. On many occasions, it is possible to think about a gradual payment of the acquisition, notably because the sale is usually accompanied by a disengagement of the current owner-manager. It is also possible to structure a sponsorless LBO transaction (i.e., without any involvement of an LBO fund).

Are there limits to the appetite of private equity investors? Is it a specific asset class? Will private equity, reputed to be 'hands on', evolve towards 'hands off', traditional investing in listed companies? To answer these questions, we will examine the dynamics of private equity, and notably the central place of the relationship between the entrepreneur and the investor in private equity (Chapter 5).

Private equity and employment

Though venture and growth capital are necessarily net creators of employment, LBO is sometimes accused of destroying employment (Applebaum & Batt, 2014). If the subject is still regularly debated,[55] a VP Bank analysis shows that this is not the case. According to Figure 4.56, switching the control from a family-owned to an institutionally owned company (through an LBO) is actually creating employment. The company has to create employment to be ready to be sold as an autonomous and self-reliant entity

---

[55] A study from the Private Equity Council in the USA states that between 2002 and 2005, the net job situation of companies under LBOs has shown an increase of 8.4%. In general, the companies which have been under LBOs have increased the number of jobs by 13.3% vs 5.5% for the American economy. For the manufacturing industry, the figures are respectively 1.4% vs −7.7%.

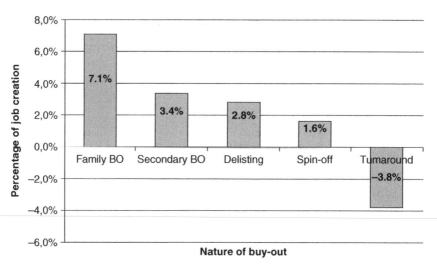

FIGURE 4.56   Evolution of the net job situation according to the type of private equity operation undertaken
Source: VP Bank, Thomson Datastream 2008.

to the next owner (an LBO fund is only a transitional owner). Secondary LBOs also create value, far from being pure financial investments and using only financial leverages. The reason is that as LBO funds are buying a company, they need to create value to sell it at a *higher price* to the next owner (unless one assumes that the next buyers are systematically over-paying to buy the portfolio companies of LBO funds, which is difficult to justify).

Interestingly, delisting does not translate into a reduction in jobs, but an increase in recruitment. The reasons for this increase could be variable, but it is probably related to the need to give a certain dynamism into the company which was delisted to accomplish a particular project (acquisition, launch of new product, internationalisation, etc.). The progression is more modest in the case of a spin-off, but still significant. This is due to the fact that the newly independent company has to recruit to support functions which were formerly shared with the parent company.

The case of turn-around capital could give rise to criticism. The regression of employment is potentially a big concern for this strategy and its impact on a given economy. However, there should be no concern, as the other alternative is more often than not the pure and simple liquidation of the company with full loss of jobs, as illustrated by the failed turn-around of Hostess Brands (Primack, 2012b),[56] which produces Twinkies and Wonder Bread (those brands will survive; Chernev, 2012).[57] The intervention of turn-around investors is helpful in restructuring the company, hence shedding some jobs in the process, but also preserving others – and later recruiting again, once the company has found its new path to growth. The net job situation might be negative, but this scenario is undoubtedly better than a full loss of jobs.

---

[56]http://finance.fortune.cnn.com/2012/11/16/dont-worry-twinkies-will-survive/.
[57]http://www.businessweek.com/articles/2012-12-06/how-much-is-a-twinkie-worth.

These figures have to be compared with the case of an acquisition by a strategic investor, as it is likely that the progression of recruitment would be more limited (notably due to the synergies between the parent and the subsidiary).

Understanding the market dynamics (and statistics)

As for the dynamic of the private equity market, France offers an interesting perspective (see Table 4.8). It is the second European private equity market in size, after the UK (which has de facto become the platform for pan-European investors and a net exporter of capital until now, although this could change as the UK leaves the EU). Its market is quite well structured and offers a clear picture of the dynamics of the private equity sector.

Table 4.8 shows the difference between funds raised, which will be invested over the 5 years following the raising of the fund; the amounts invested, illustrating the investments made in a given year; and the divestments which are the exits from investments made over the course of the years preceding the divestment. These three figures are related: a constant fall in fundraising dries up the financing of future years. On the contrary, low divestment levels on a recurring basis are in fact increasing the size of portfolios and do not return to investors to participate in the next private equity cycle.

As shown in Table 4.8, venture capital gathers each year approximately EUR 400–800 million, although 2017 and 2018 have been exceptional. These high figures echo those of the previous venture capital boom at the end of the 1990s. Growth capital shows a doubling of its volume over a period of 10 years. This is the result of strong public support for an investment strategy that is supportive of economic growth and employment. As the amounts started from a low level and seemed to catch up with the economic potential (supposedly higher than venture capital, as start-ups require on average less capital than growing established companies), this looks like a sustainable path of growth. The LBO sector is much more volatile, as it depends mostly on the opportunities and the availability of affordable debt for acquisition. As for the LBO figures in Table 4.8, they are accumulating the amounts invested in equity (i.e., they exclude debt).

It is thus important to consider private equity as a flow and not as an inventory of capital. If the total size of funds being raised is inferior to the total amount invested each

TABLE 4.8   Evolution of private equity investments in France

In million euros	2008	2009	2010	2011	2012	2013	2014	2015	2016	2017	2018
Investments	10 009	4 100	6 598	9 738	6 072	6 482	8 727	10 749	12 395	14 278	14 711
of which seed/ venture	758	587	605	597	443	642	626	758	874	1 224	1 619
of which growth	1 653	1 789	2 310	2 940	1 946	1 827	2 608	3 852	3 853	3 154	3 454
of which LBO	7 399	1 605	3 512	6 015	3 568	3 910	5 452	6 116	7 621	9 882	9 612
Divestments	3 164	2 782	3 967	6 288	3 454	5 681	9 348	6 518	8 961	9 628	9 822
Funds raised	12 730	3 672	5 043	6 456	5 008	8 152	10 117	9 712	14 691	16 538	18 693

Source: France Invest 2009–2019.

year, this can be interpreted either as a future lack of equity or a natural regulation of the sector after a brutal inflow of capital in the past. Figure 4.57 puts into perspective the figures given in Table 4.8, even though it leaves the question open for the consideration of the reader.

In the same way, significant volumes of investment can be related to inflated valuations of portfolio companies at the time of acquisition. This would then mean that these investments could be more difficult to manage in the future in order to create performance. It can also mean a change in the market, developing further operations under the influence of regulatory changes or corporate divestments.

Figure 4.57 shows a clear inflexion point in 2000, when EUR 5 billion was invested on an annual basis, hence signalling the end of the cycle of growth of investments. Sector stabilisation and consolidation appears between 2000 and 2004 ('Cycle 2'), before a clear increase of the amounts invested during the period 2004–2008 ('Cycle 3'). The peak of the cycle is in 2007, so the cycle could also be described as a 2004–2007 cycle. The reason why we include 2008 is that some of the deals negotiated in 2007 were effectively closed in 2008 and accounting during that year. A sharp decrease signals a drop in 2009 back to the levels observed in 2000–2004. The stabilisation and consolidation in 2008–2013 is visible ('Cycle 4') and sets a new floor for deals. A new cycle starts in 2013, after the European crisis triggered by the quasi-default of the Greek sovereign debt ('Cycle 5'), which could be projected to last until 2018 or 2019. Overall, the market appears to evolve between EUR 4 and 6 billion invested on a yearly basis, once operations above EUR 100 million are excluded.

This brief market analysis would not be complete without mentioning financing gaps. In fact, France has very few funds dedicated to company turn-around. Venture capital finances only a small portion of the companies in need of capital. In that respect, with the exclusion of the life science and IT sectors, very few companies can

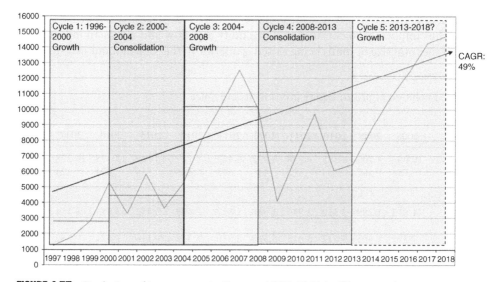

FIGURE 4.57   Evolution of investments in France, 1997–2018 (million euros)
Source: France Invest, PWC, Grant Thornton, author.

trace private equity funds to back their emergence and development. This could change going forward, owing to regulatory and tax incentives.

The evolution of private markets: neo merchant banking

The diversification of certain LBO fund managers can appear unusual. After all, funds have been focusing increasingly on specific private equity operations, as described earlier. The reason for moving away from the generalist fund model, which combined venture capital, growth and LBO investments in one product, was that fund managers did not have the relevant expertise to target these different operations properly.

Why are large buy-out operators diversifying into distressed debt, real estate, hedge funds, mergers and acquisitions, advisory and other sectors? One of the obvious answers is that investment banking skills and mega/large buy-out investment skills are basically the same. The profile and experience of the professionals in these firms confirm it. As big buy-out players were targeting larger and more complex businesses, they started to develop their own pool of in-house competence. They thus began to offer this competence on the market.

Another reason is that behind the scenes, fund managers have evolved considerably. From the little group of investment professionals supported by a chief financial officer and back-office staff, these companies have grown increasingly to integrate legal capabilities, a secretary general to coordinate the multiple funds and manage the fund manager structures, investor relations capabilities and other middle- and back-office functions. The most advanced ones provide services to their portfolio companies, ranging from recruitment and purchasing to operational advice.

These developments were driven by the increasing need for information from fund investors in terms of reporting and due diligence documentation. Fund managers also had to integrate some risk management functions into their practices, either under legal pressure or under pressure from their investors. France, for example, has ruled that every fund manager is comprised of a certain number of professionals, including one in charge of deontology, and disposes of a certain amount of capital as proof of financial solidity for the investors. Investors have increasingly requested detailed quarterly and annual reports in order to be able to evaluate the work of fund managers and the situation of the portfolio for themselves. This has subsequently generated an increased need for middle- and back-office professionals, which in return has necessitated a higher level of income.

The advent of the AIFMD in Europe and the FATCA in the USA brought significant changes. Fund managers have rightfully argued that multiple regulations (Basel III, Solvency II, AIFMD, Volcker rule, Dodd–Frank Act) have dried up some of the historical sources of private equity financing, and hence of private companies. The consequences of the AIFMD or the Dodd–Frank Act are not yet fully known, but they have resulted in a durable slowdown of the emergence of new fund managers and new strategies due to costs (see Table 4.9); and the temptation to get around the regulation either through innovation, or by exploiting loopholes. The latter might remind us of what happened in the past with junk bonds and securitisation: the misuse of interesting innovation to circumvent legislative excess, which led to another crisis.

As a consequence, the minimum threshold that has to be reached in order to create a fund management company and be able to manage third-party funds has increased. This could reduce the number of emerging managers arriving each year on the market, and thus the ability to finance under-served areas of the private equity sector. This can only provide an undue advantage to established teams which are not performing, but which

TABLE 4.9 Summary of added costs from new regulation (in basis points)

	LBO	Venture capital
Adaptation costs		
Delegation costs	8.25	8.25
Relocation	19.7	19.7
Legal structures	14.1	14.1
Total adaptation costs (basis points)	*33.8*	*23.2*
Total adaptation costs (million euro)	*45*	*451*
Annual costs		
Communication portfolio companies	2.9	3.7
Delegation	0.2	0.2
Evaluation	4.3	9.2
Capital	1.5	1.9
Custodian	5	10
Total annual costs (basis points)	*13.8*	*24.8*
Total annual costs (million euro)	*248*	*33*

Source: Charles Rivers Associates, October 2009.

were launched long ago. They can stay on the market simply because fund investors cannot fully allocate their capital to the asset class, and also because most of them do not have the skills to evaluate emerging managers.

REFERENCES

Books and Booklets

Applebaum, E. and Batt, R. (2014) *Private Equity at Work* (Russell Sage Foundation, New York), 381 pp.

Blessing, S. (2011) *Alternative Alternatives* (Wiley, Chichester), 242 pp.

Davydenko, S. and Franks, J. (2006) *Do Bankruptcy Codes Matter? A Study of Defaults in France, Germany and the UK* (University of Toronto/London Business School), 45 pp.

Demaria, C. (2006, 2008, 2010, 2012, 2015, 2018) *Introduction au Private Equity* (RB Editions, Paris), 1st, 2nd, 3rd, 4th, 5th, 6th edns, 128 pp.

Kocis, J., Bachman, J., Long, A. and Nickels, C. (2009) *Inside Private Equity, The Professional's Handbook* (Wiley, Hoboken, NJ), 262 pp.

Lerner, J. (2009) *Boulevard of Broken Dreams, Why Public Efforts to Boost Entrepreneurship and Venture Capital Have Failed and What to Do about It* (Princeton University Press, Princeton, NJ), 229 pp.

Newsletters and Newspapers

Arrington, M., 'The USD 4 million line', *TechCrunch*, 5 October 2010.

Bills, S., 'Do secondary sales signal a coming crisis?', *PEHub Wire*, 16 December 2010.

Bilton, N., 'Disruptions: with no revenue, an illusion of value', Bits, *New York Times*, 29 April 2012.

Bloch, M., Kolodny, J. and Maor, D., 'Israel, an innovation gem, in Europe's backyard', *Financial Times*, 13 September 2012.

Bradshaw, T., 'Entrepreneurs urged to shoot for the sky', *Financial Times*, 5 March 2012.

Braithwaite, T. and Demos, T., 'Geithner holds talks on dearth of small IPOs', *Financial Times*, 13 March 2011.

Bullock, N., 'Risky loans stage comeback', *Financial Times*, 13 March 2011.

Burne, K., '"Covenant-Lite" deals returning to U.S. loan market, data show', *The Wall Street Journal*, 23 April 2012.

Caroll, A., 'Faltering funds of funds', *RealDeals*, 2 May 2012.

Cauchi, M., 'Banks take more active role', *The Wall Street Journal*, 6 July 2009.

Chernev, A., 'How much is a Twinkie worth?', *Bloomberg Businessweek*, 6 December 2012.

Davidoff, S., 'The private equity wizardry behind Realogy's comeback', DealBook, *New York Times*, 9 October 2012a.

Davidoff, S., 'The risks of tapping your retirement fund for an alternative use', DealBook, *New York Times*, 30 October 2012b.

Demaria, C., 'Is the enemy, in fact, us?', *PEHub*, 7 December 2012.

Dembosky, A., 'Facebook to be keenly missed by private markets', *Financial Times*, 6 February 2012.

Demos, T., 'Dark pool launches private share market', *Financial Times*, 17 October 2011.

Demos, T., 'Venture capital – another breeding ground for private equity', Deal Journal, *The Wall Street Journal*, 18 October 2012.

Demos, T. and Lauricella, T., 'Yield-starved investors snap up riskier MLPs', *The Wall Street Journal*, 16 September 2012.

Financial Times, 'Distressed debt funds eye troubled groups', 15 December 2011a.

Financial Times, 'Lex: Social networks', 14 February 2011b.

Financial Times, 'Lex: Securitisation: second infancy', 2 January 2012a.

Financial Times, 'Lex: CLOs – the comeback year', 28 December 2012b.

Freeman J., 'Is Silicon Valley a systemic risk?', *The Wall Street Journal*, 8 April 2009.

Gage, D., 'The venture capital secret: 3 out of 4 start-ups fail', Small Business, *The Wall Street Journal*, 19 September 2012.

Gelles, D., 'Opening doors on private companies', *Financial Times*, 29 December 2010.

Gladwell, M., 'Creation myth', Annals of Business, *The New Yorker*, 16 May 2011.

Greenburg, H., 'Worst CEO award goes to Sears' Lampert', *MarketWatch*, 6 December 2007.

Haemmig, M. and Mawson, J., 'Corporations, the new conductors for entrepreneurs', *Global Corporate Venturing*, January 2012, 5 pp.

Jacobius, A., 'PE fund of funds fading due to changes in investor tastes', *Pensions & Investments*, 7 February 2011.

Jeffries, A., 'Jellyfish tanks, funded 54 times over Kickstarter, turn out to be jellyfish death traps', *Caveat Backer*, Betabeat.com, 15 March 2012.

Karbasfrooshan, A., 'Why bootstrapping is just as over-rated as raising venture capital', *TechCrunch*, 7 January 2012.

Knowledge@Wharton, 'Mid-life crisis? Venture capital acts its age', 21 July 2010.

Lattman, P., 'Private Goldman exchange officially closes for business', DealBook, *New York Times*, 12 April 2012.

Linley, M., 'SharesPost settles with SEC, gets a slap on the wrist', *Business Insider*, 14 March 2012.

Mariathasan, J., 'Private equity: keep a clear head', *Investments & Pensions Europe*, 1 May 2011.

Mariathasan, J. and Steward, M., 'Private equity: What are funds of funds for?', *Investment & Pensions Europe*, 1 May 2011.

Meek, V., 'Funds of funds on trial', *RealDeals*, 16 May 2012.

Milne, R., 'Chapter 11 might have lent wings to SAS', Inside Business, *Financial Times*, 22 November 2012.

Needleman, S., 'Rise in start-ups draws doubters', *The Wall Street Journal*, 15 February 2012.

Patricof, A., 'Another view: VC investing not dead, just different', DealBook, *New York Times*, 9 February 2009.

Pfanner, E., 'Europe aims to encourage young to be entrepreneurs', *New York Times*, 19 September 2012.

Power, H., 'Is bigger better?', *Private Equity International*, March 2012.

Primack, D., 'Random ramblings', The Term Sheet, *Fortune*, 2 March 2011.

Primack, D., 'Breaking down broken venture capital', The Term Sheet, *Fortune*, 11 May 2012a.

Primack, D., 'Don't worry, Twinkies will survive', The Term Sheet, *Fortune*, 16 November 2012b.

Rappaport, L. and Eaglesham, J., 'Private-share trade is probed', Technology, *The Wall Street Journal*, 23 February 2011.

Reuters, 'Internet boom 2.0 is here, starts to look bubbly', *New York Times*, 8 May 2011.

Schonfeld, E., 'The lean finance model of venture capital', *TechCrunch*, 4 December 2011.

Schonfeld, E., 'The SEC's crowdfunding conundrum', *TechCrunch*, 5 September 2012.

Schwartz, B., 'Economics made easy: think friction', *New York Times*, 16 February 2012.

Scott, B., 'Private equity defends pre-packs', *RealDeals*, 30 January 2012.

Surowiecki, J., 'Innovative consumption', The Financial Page, *The New Yorker*, 16 May 2011, p. 42.

Tett, G., 'Private equity raises "covenant-lite" loans', *Financial Times*, 20 March 2007.

The Economist, 'Special report on entrepreneurship', 14 March 2009.

The Economist, 'Another bubble?', 18 December 2010.

The Economist, 'Another digital gold rush', 14 May 2011.

The Economist, 'The lure of Chilecon Valley', 13 October 2012a.

The Economist, 'CVC's Australian loss – an isolated carcass', 20 October 2012b.

The Economist, 'Something in the air', 27 October 2012c.

The Founding Member, 'VC Open Letters: the year of the start-up default', TheFunded.com, 10 March 2011.

Toll, D., 'Returns Scorecard: 10 top funds of funds', *PE Hub*, 11 January 2012.

Wadhwa, V., 'When it comes to tech entrepreneurs and their successes, legends abound', Boston .com, 2 August 2011.

Waters, R., 'Dotcom boom's shower of gold passes Wall Street by', *Financial Times*, 1 December 2010.

White, S., 'Vulture funds smell blood from Spanish bank woes', *Business & Financial News*, Reuters, 5 June 2012.

Wilson, E., 'How to make a region innovative', *Strategy + Business*, Spring 2012, Issue **66**, 28 February 2012.

Papers and Studies

Acharya, V., Hahn, M. and Kehoe, C. (2010) 'Corporate governance and value creation: evidence from private equity', Working Paper, New York University, 2010.

Achleitner, A. K. (2009) 'Value creation in private equity', Centre for Entrepreneurial and Financial Studies – Capital Dynamics, 2009.

Bank for International Settlements (2008) Committee on the Global Financial System, 'Private equity and leveraged finance markets', CGFS Papers no. 30, 46 pp.

Bielesch, F., Brigl, M., Khanna, D. *et al.* (2012) 'Corporate venture capital – avoid the risk, miss the rewards', *BCG.Perspectives, The Boston Consulting Group*, 31 October 2012, 12 pp.

Brigl, M., Prats, J. M., Herrera, A. *et al.* (2008) 'The advantage of persistence – how the best private-equity firms "beat the fade"', The Boston Consulting Group and IESE Business School, 191 pp.

Brigl, M., Nowotnik, P., Pelisari, K. *et al.* (2012) 'The 2012 private equity report – engaging for growth', The Boston Consulting Group, January 2012, 26 pp.

CB Insights (2019) 'The 2018 Global CVC Report', 51 pp.

Cox, D. and Hanson, B. (2018) 'Welcome to the private debt show', Private Equity Analyst Note, PitchBook, Q1, p. 7.

Darcy, J., Kreamer-Eis, H., Debande, O. and Guellec, D. (2009) 'Financing technology transfer', Working Paper 2009/002, European Investment Fund, 32 pp.

Devine, A. (2015) 'He who dares', *Private Debt Investor*, June, pp. 16–20.

EVCA (2002) 'Survey of the economic and social impact of venture capital in Europe', Research Paper, 28 pp.

EVCA (2009) 'Annual survey of pan-European private equity and venture capital activity', in *EVCA Yearbook* (EVCA, Brussels), 624 pp.

EVCA (2010) 'Closing gaps and moving up a gear: The next stage of venture capital evolution in Europe', Venture Capital White Paper, 24 pp.

Guo, S., Hotchkiss, E. and Song, W. (2008) 'Do buyouts (still) create value?', Boston College, University of Cincinnati, 59 pp.

Kelly, R. (2011) 'The performance and prospects of European venture capital', Working Paper 2011/09, The European Investment Fund, 22 pp.

Kerr, W., Lerner, J. and Schoar, A. (2011) 'The consequences of entrepreneurial finance: evidence from angel financings', SSRN, NBER WP 15831, HBS WP 10-086, *Review of Financial Studies*, 27, pp. 20–55.

Monitor Group (2010) 'Paths to prosperity', 88 pp.

Mulcahy, D., Weeks, B. and Bradley, H. (2012) 'We have met the enemy . . . and he is us', Ewing Marion Kauffman Foundation, 52 pp.

PEI Media (2010) 'Inside the limited partner', 237 pp.

Quiry, P. and Le Fur, Y. (2010) 'Création et partage de valeurs dans les LBO', *La Lettre Vernimmen no. 84*, February 2010.

Weisser, M. and Germano, L. (2006) 'Going . . . going . . . going . . . gone private', Private Equity Alert, Weil, Gotshal & Manges, August 2006, 4 pp.

CHAPTER 5

The Process of Investment
A Matter of Trust and Mutual Interest

Whatever the type of private market operation envisioned, the analysis of investment opportunities follows a fairly standardised path: the progressive draft of a fair and complete portrait of the company (or asset), as well as its development perspectives. This long process (from 3 to 18 months, depending on the complexity of the project and its stakes) also participates in the establishment of a *mutual trust between investors and entrepreneurs* in the case of private equity and private debt investing.[1] This relationship is built slowly through the establishment of common work methods, a dialogue of good quality and mutual esteem. Not all investments reach this ideal state, but a great deal of success in private markets is the outcome of an active partnership between investors and entrepreneurs.

The primary analysis (see Section 5.1) is largely conditioned by the introduction of the investment to the fund manager. Depending on the scenario, and the degree of trust which is associated with the eventual intermediary who has introduced the investment opportunity, this preliminary analysis can be more or less thorough. Then, the detailed analysis, the valuation of the company and the evaluation of its development perspectives (see Section 5.2) will help to identify what would be the potential profit attached to this investment. At this stage, a preliminary risk and return assessment can be drawn, which filters out some opportunities. The negotiation (see Section 5.3) targets the establishment of a certain equilibrium between the seller, the buyer and the management of the business (the management can sometimes be the seller or the buyer). This is not only a matter of balance of power in reaching a price, but a set of elements which are relevant for the negotiation of such issues as the timing or the payment process, or the company's future in the hands of the new owner.

Once the valuation of the company is done and agreed on, the structuring of the deal (see Section 5.4) allows both the seller and the buyer to define precisely the terms of the deal and the operational process. Meanwhile, a systematic check (see Section 5.5) of all the company's documents is carried out, in order to make sure that the risks are fully

---

[1]As for private real assets investing, the relationship with the project manager or operator is also a matter of importance. At times, the investor and the asset operator are the same structure. In that case, the focus is thus on understanding precisely the situation and status of the asset.

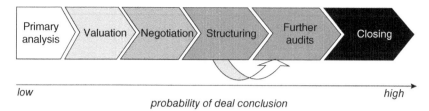

FIGURE 5.1 Steps from first contact to the conclusion of a private equity
investment
Source: Author.

assessed and that nothing has been left out. Some adjustments can be made, as these
audits deliver their results, and the transaction can finally be done (see Section 5.6).

This process (see Figure 5.1) is found mainly in the LBO sector, as venture and
growth capital investments are rather less technical in terms of financial engineering
(Kedrosky & Stangler, 2011). However, the preliminary analysis and valuation steps can
take more time in venture capital, as the technological choices and financial projections
are more difficult to assess. At the other end of the spectrum, legal and social impacts
have more weight in a company turn-around than in the case of a venture capital or
an LBO investment. It is hence necessary to adapt the following developments to the
operation's framework.

Private debt and private real asset strategies follow a similar process with some
tweaks. In the case of direct lending, the negotiation is not on the valuation of the
company and governance rights, but on the terms of the loan and its monitoring. As
for distressed debt investing, the process is driven by bankruptcy laws. Though the
potential buyer of the debt of the bankrupt company ultimately executes similar work
as in other private equity and private debt strategies, the operational process and the
order of the different steps are conditioned by legal proceedings. As for private real
assets, the assessment is often driven more by the operational assessment of the asset
by independent experts, and less by the establishment of a trust relationship with the
management. Nevertheless, the following steps are in general a good description of the
process of investing in private markets.

5.1   STEP 1: PRELIMINARY ANALYSIS

The success of an investor is largely conditioned by his aptitude to find the right
investment opportunities. The preliminary analysis aims to create a *trust relationship*
between the management team of the company and the investment team of the fund
manager. The nature of the information communicated at this stage varies a lot. The
level of information made public varies a lot depending on the jurisdictions in which
the company is registered. Moreover, some management teams will be more protective
of the information than others. For the investment team, this entails a certain number
of work meetings, presentations, information exchanges and analyses of the company
situation. Depending on the nature of the opportunity, one or more company visits can
be organised.

Investment teams are expected to follow deontology (or at least compliance) guidelines which are set by the professional associations to which they usually belong. In particular, confidentiality plays a significant role early on. A non-disclosure agreement can be signed early, as some sensitive information might be required by the investment team. Any information that is gathered by the investment team is supposed to be used only to support the analysis of investment opportunities.

These opportunities are usually referred by a network that the investor has built patiently, and which is composed not only of former entrepreneurs that he has already backed, but also other investors, accountants, lawyers, etc. These contacts help the fund manager source deals through his proprietary network. Depending on the source of the investment opportunity, the process can be accelerated or can take more time.

An alternative source of investment opportunities can be found through auctions organised by the sellers of companies (in the case of LBO) or assets (private real assets).[2] In that case, the seller mandates an intermediary, such as a corporate finance boutique or an investment bank, to run a competitive process. The potential buyers are contacted by this intermediary with a pre-packaged set of information (vendor due diligence) which is sent after the signature of a non-disclosure agreement (see above).

In the case of venture and growth capital, the competitive process is organised by the management of the company. Potential investors compete with each other on the terms but also on the nature of their value creation. The management of the company represents the existing investors and negotiates in their name with the prospective investors.

Overall, the investment team essentially checks the fundamentals of the investment opportunity. This is a filtering process, most of the investment opportunities being rejected and a few qualifying for further analysis. At this stage of the investment process, the costs for the fund are limited or negligible. Once the investment opportunity is qualified, significant resources will be consumed in a detailed analysis. For that reason, the filter is strict and systematic. Any opportunity which goes beyond this stage and does not lead to an actual investment will generate costs (aborted deal costs), which have to be recouped from the performance of other investments. The incentive for the fund manager is to avoid such scenarios as much as possible.

A first memorandum will be drafted by the investment team. This memorandum is the result of the evaluation of the investment team, and helps the different members of the fund managers to determine whether or not it makes sense to pursue the analysis further.

5.2 STEP 2: INITIAL VALUATION

The valuation process leads the team to determine a bracket of prices, with a lower and a higher bound for the acquisition of the company. This bracket is determined by investors when assessing the intrinsic value of the company, often by comparing it with other companies, notably those which are listed and disclose significant information. The valuation process is the application of a combination of methods defined by the

---

[2] As for distressed debt, the competitive process is effectively run by the bankruptcy court.

IPEV (see Chapter 4). One is using the listed comparables and most recent transactions in the sector thanks to an investment multiple analysis. This method uses the profit and loss statement and projections of the company. This is probably the method which is the most used in the private equity sector. Corporate finance manuals provide the basics, and one of the most comprehensive resources[3] is provided by Aswath Damodaran. In particular, this author provides up-to-date multiples per sector of activity, as well as indications for adjustments depending on the country considered and other factors.

Another method is to make projections of the company's cash flows and assess the value of the firm as the sum of its future cash flows (discounted cash flows). This method is based on the cash-flow statement and projections of a company. Using it determines the cash flows for the upcoming years, the discount rate and a realistic and satisfying growth rate for the company. This projection is thus somewhat difficult to model, as the discount rate and the infinite growth rate necessary to compute the formula have to be extracted from somewhere. If the analyses of listed comparables can be used again, the ratios have to be adjusted and this leaves room for a lot of interpretation – and potential haggling with the seller. However, this method provides a value *in fine*, which can be compared to the entry price. It can also help to model scenarios where the investment does not follow the expected path, and to design pre-emptive actions and be prepared for unfavourable scenarios.

A third approach consists of valuing the assets of the firm and determining the costs of their replacement. This approach uses the balance sheet of the company. It helps the investor to identify hidden sources of value (e.g., real estate which is fully amortised but has significant market value) or costs (e.g., a machine which is obsolete and not fully amortised and has to be replaced by a better one).

Valuing loss-making businesses such as start-ups and bankrupt companies can be difficult. In the first case, the company has no real operational performance, and projections are difficult to confirm. Transparency is paramount. Investors want to carefully assess the management's capacity to deliver, but also its knowledge of the market. Reference checking is crucial and helps to understand how the management will deliver. It still does not provide support for a valuation. Most investors will combine two approaches. First, they will look at the most probable exit scenario in 5 to 7 years. They will value the business at that date thanks to the multiple method described above, and apply a series of discounts to take into account the uncertainties and the time discount. This becomes the valuation at time of exit. They compare this valuation with the one requested by the current investors, and will take into account the future need for capital of the company (hence diluting their potential stake in the firm). The difference between the current expected valuation by the existing investors and the prospective valuation at exit (fully diluted) is the performance of the investor. This should match (at worst) or exceed the expected multiple of investment promised to fund investors.

The second approach, when assessing very early-stage start-ups, is to assign an arbitrary valuation to the firm providing the new investors with a significant stake (30% or above) and focus on governance rights to reduce the risks. The shareholders' agreement, as well as the rights embedded in the preferred shares issued by the start-up, become more important. Among the most important are the liquidation rights, which define

---

[3] http://pages.stern.nyu.edu/~adamodar/New_Home_Page/equity.html.

the timing and the priority of exit of shareholders and minimal guaranteed returns to specific categories of shareholders. Other rights might include a non-dilution clause, preventing current shareholders seeing their stake diluted by the emission of new shares in future rounds of financing, thus deflecting the burden on common shareholders.

These are fairly fragile risk reduction mechanisms, as the shareholders' agreement is only valid between current investors. Any new investor, in an upcoming financing round, might want to amend this document. Either current investors refuse, and will therefore have to support the start-up alone (or with the support of another investor yet to be found), or they will have to accept the new terms. The careful crafting of the shareholders' agreement, reflecting the balance of power at the investment date, will survive if the start-up is highly desirable by future prospective investors and therefore achieves or outperforms its target until the next fundraising stage.

In the case of bankrupt businesses, accumulated losses represent an asset which has to be valued as they are de facto a tax shield for future profits until these losses are fully compensated. The valuation requires extra steps to quantify the capital need of the business, the costs of restructuring, the time required for its recovery and ultimately its return to profits.

This initial bracket of valuations is useful to assess if, after the filtering (see previous section), the expectations of the investor and the seller are close enough. If the gap between these expectations is too large, it might be difficult to reconcile them through negotations. This bracket of valuations will also help the intermediary running an auction to decide who will be admitted in a restricted auction, or to give exclusivity to the leading contender for a specific period of time. During this exclusivity, the buyer and the seller hold talks directly and the other contenders are excluded.

The choice of the potential buyer is not only a matter of choosing the highest bid. The reputation matters too, when it comes to the ability to execute a professional due diligence on time, to execute the transaction (in particular when structuring debt is involved) and ultimately to execute a successful deal. The seller might be wary of selling a company or an asset and later seeing its reputation damaged from a botched acquisition. Beyond the reputation, the deal terms are also of importance, notably when it comes to the governance and the terms of the transaction (payment in multiple installments, combination of cash and shares, or other variations).

This first rough approach of valuations with brackets helps the potential buyer to determine what would be its profit at exit. In fact, the buyer will often recompute the projections of the firm according to specific scenarios. The buyer plans to execute a specific plan to create value in the firm. Assuming that this plan is successful, the value of the firm will increase. The buyer will value the firm at exit date and compare the current valuation at entry and the potential valuation at exit. The difference is the performance. Depending on the level of uncertainty, and therefore of risk, the performance might be rewarding or not. The younger the company, the more elements of uncertainty there are, and the more complex is the valuation exercise. At times, the buyer will assign probabilities to the multiple outcomes issuing from the scenarios. The result of this tree of options will help to determine the potential valuation.

The exit (or liquidity) scenario is crucial. Most of the successful exits are trade sales, then, in second place, come the sales to other investors and the smallest proportion is initial public offerings (see Chapter 4). Exit at a loss or liquidation are also a possibility that the potential buyer has to anticipate: this is the worst-case scenario analysis. It can be the result of adverse macro-economic or sector conditions, but also bad planning or unfit management. The buyer has to investigate these scenarios to avoid them.

Once the framework is established, the negotiation phase starts. To materialise a pre-agreement, a letter of intent (in the case of an LBO) or a preliminary term sheet (in the case of a venture or growth capital investment) is issued. It describes the purpose of the transaction, the object, the valuation and the most important governance terms. These are fairly general terms, subject to more thorough analysis and potential significant change as the due diligence proceeds forward.

5.3   STEP 3: DUE DILIGENCE AND NEGOTIATION

Once there is a basic agreement on the determining features of the company or asset, the price range and the main governance mechanisms, the full due diligence can start in earnest. At this stage, the relationship between the seller and the buyer is exclusive. The prospective buyer will systematically analyse and check every aspect of the business and the transaction. As this process progresses, the negotiation brings forward what this due diligence uncovers and the consequences on the terms of the deal (that is to say, the valuation and the governance). The purpose of the due diligence is to reduce the valuation bracket down to one figure, which reflects precisely the actual situation of the company or the asset.

The due diligence and negotiation are therefore the most resource-consuming and probably the most important step in the investment process. A due diligence usually takes multiple months to be executed. The management team, the investment team and the seller will be active in reducing the elements of uncertainty and reaching the best possible level of knowledge of the company. The final price is built as the due diligence confirms or uncovers information.

The management team plays an important role in the negotiation process, especially if it is not the main shareholder. In the case of venture and growth capital investments, it is common that the management team and the shareholders are at least partially the same group of people. In the case of an LBO, this can be different. In most cases, the management team must not only preserve the interests of the company as a moral entity, but also help the seller and the buyer to reach an agreement. The company management is also responsible for the transmission of the information given to the seller to help it observe its due diligence obligations. At this stage, the responsibilities of the company management are important, as any substantial mistake could have a significant impact on the sale price of the company.

Once a common vision between the seller and the buyer is established, thanks to an intense exchange of information, it is possible to list the complementary due diligence which must be performed, before determining the final price of the company and a first draft of the upcoming agreement. At this stage, the first banking agreements are negotiated for LBOs, as well as the shareholders' agreement, if necessary.

The debt of acquisition is thus defined by a double process: the structuring, which involves the bank negotiating the debt and organising the loan; and then the syndication, if there is one, where the banking agreements depend on the risk aversion of the banks.

Shareholders' agreements are quite standard, and specify a certain number of rules in terms of investment management. They can include a first right of refusal, if a shareholder wishes to sell his participation before the others. He must then offer his stake to the other investors and offer them this stake before going to market. The shareholders' agreement can also include liquidity conditions, which set the exit rules for the investors. The agreement can also contain a preferred right of liquidity, as a guarantee of having a priority return until the company reaches a certain valuation upon exit.

The end of the negotiation is triggered by multiple factors. Legally, offer and acceptance form a contract. However, this can be subject to further investigation, and subsequently to complementary audits (see below). In the case of restricted auctions without exclusivity, there can be a beauty contest between funds (or consortia of funds) willing to buy a stake in the company or acquire it.

Existing owners are free to accept or decline the offers to the best of their interests. As mentioned above, it is not necessarily the highest bid which will be accepted, as the quality of the investment team and what it can bring to the company are also highly regarded. The financial plan of the company and its success can depend on factors which are difficult to quantify. In that case, price adjustment and earn-out clauses are included in the sale agreement. These clauses are indexed on the performance of the company and the achievements that the shareholders and the management hope to realise after the actual transaction. Acquiring an existing company is usually associated with a certain number of precise risks related to the past management of the company. The acquiring fund can then request warranties and representations which will be waived (and compensated by the former owner) as the risks materialise, or not. Therefore, the transaction can happen while some of the characteristics, whether on the upside (with an earn-out for example) or the downside (with warranties), are still open.

The due diligence represents a significant effort. The purpose is not only to check the current status of the company or the asset, but also to design a plan so that it gains in value after the acquisition. By getting an intimate knowledge of the company or asset for sale, the buyer can indeed start to design an action plan even before finalising the transaction, define precisely the hypothesis, detail the immediate measures to implement (the 'first 100-days plan'), design monitoring indicators and prepare scenarios to run with the management. The reason for this early action is that the fund manager's performance uses some metrics which are time-sensitive, such as the IRR. Any delay in the launch and execution of the plan will postpone the advent of an exit, and therefore reduce the IRR. It is in the interests of the fund manager to plan ahead, and in particular to pre-plan answers to any deviation from the initial plan.

5.4   STEP 4: STRUCTURING

Depending on the nature of the operation, the financial structure can be more or less complex. A venture capital investment, taking a minority share in a start-up, can appear to be simple, but it necessarily entails a certain formal legal wording and probably the set-up of incentive tools (such as stock options) for the company staff. Given the high risks involved in the development of start-ups, the governance rights provided to investors will probably be comprehensive and detailed in the shareholders' agreement. Standard clauses include tag-along and drag-along rights to solve the question of joint exits from an investment; as well as veto rights on specific management decisions such as C-level recruitments, spending programmes and salary increases; or even exit clauses defining a contractual timeframe for an exit.

Whatever the type of structuring, it is in the best interests of investors that the staff reaches, and eventually goes beyond, the assigned targets of the company. Fund managers usually have a stock option plan. This lever can be very effective if the management team has a very small stake in the company. It is in the best interests of the investor to give a share of the profit to increase the likelihood of meeting the targets. It also aligns interests, as the management finds greater advantage in the sale of the company.

A stock option plan can also be set up to refund investors if the management fails to achieve its targets. In the case of a venture investment, the management is usually the founders who have a significant share of the start-up. If the start-up under-performs against the plan, the investors over-paid their shares and therefore can require to get new shares (hence diluting the founders) as compensation.

The structuring should also plan for the organisation of powers and communication between the investors and the managers. The more the fund managers are involved financially in the company, the more investors will control and monitor the activities of the management team. In the case of a majority LBO, it is not unusual for fund managers to have the majority of the seats on the Board. Venture capital fund managers generally require a monthly report to help them react more quickly to any discrepancy in the business plan, Board seats and significant shareholders' rights.

The covenants of the LBO debt are financial and non-financial. The volume of debt and the calculation of interest depend on the targets assigned to the company (EBITDA level, gearing, etc.). Moreover, other non-financial targets, such as monthly client acquisition, have an influence on the understanding of the operations and an impact on the eventual renegotiations with the banks.

In general, structuring is a reflection of the negotiations and targets the optimal exit of investments. Investors have therefore often identified the potential buyers for their portfolio companies at entry, in order to prepare and facilitate their investment exit. An LBO holding which will make complementary acquisitions in order to create a group (leveraged build-up) will integrate corporate governance and clauses which will assist in these acquisitions and govern the future entity.

Exit clauses for shareholders are also common, whatever the type of investment (venture capital, LBO, etc.). Funds taking minority stakes are especially attentive to the conditions under which they can sell their ownership. The shareholders' agreement can include a forced sale clause (drag along) according to financial, timing or other criteria, at the initiative of investment funds. This will guarantee the fund an effective exit path which the management of the company cannot refuse to comply with – even if it could buy out the fund at a determined price. In Central Europe, a certain number of deals, bringing together financial investors and strategic investors (in mobile telephony, for example), have used this kind of structuring. Investment funds took over a local company on behalf of an international group, restructured it and then sold it to this international group at a pre-defined price indexed on the performance of the local company.

5.5   STEP 5: COMPLEMENTARY DUE DILIGENCE

Complementary due diligence will assist in answering any remaining questions, in order to proceed to the conclusion of an effective transaction. In general, this due diligence is comprised of financial, environmental, social, tax and other audits. It is thus found mainly in growth capital, LBO and turn-around investments. Some of these audits require a certain amount of time, especially when the company has subsidiaries abroad, or large inventories to check.

Venture capital funds can also require complementary audits, notably in technology, regulation or contractual matters. Patenting innovation can take a certain time. The value of a company can ultimately depend greatly on the success of this process. However, it is important not to over-estimate the value of patents as such. Intrisically and isolated, they are not worth a lot. They are valuable as an array of claims on a stream of future cash flows. Investors will probably require some legal intellectual property expertise as well as industrial audits, in order to check the validity and originality of the concept to be covered by the patent request. The validity and the forced application of a contract with a major client can also be crucial for the evaluation of a young company. It is not uncommon for legal auditors to evaluate contracts, or for some further formalisation to be done before the investment.

5.6   STEP 6: TRANSACTION

The transaction is a process which involves the production of legal documents, such as a shareholders' agreement or an interim financial audit. In the case of an LBO, warranties and representations may be requested from the seller. The transaction is the result of a balance of powers and of a delicate equilibrium. It is not unusual that a transaction is cancelled because a new event with significant material consequences has happened prior to the signature.

An aborted transaction represents a significant cost for an investment fund. The due diligence represents expertise and other costs which cannot be compensated or refunded in the case of a disagreement over the transaction. In that respect, the multiplication of auctions in LBO offerings implies not only expertise in order to make an informed offer, but also a higher number of aborted transactions. Investors like to negotiate an exclusivity clause early enough so as to have a better chance of securing the deal.

Paradoxically, the failure of a transaction is not necessarily connected to the seller or the management of the company. Potential buyers can push the auctions higher, and eventually the pricing may become so aggressive that structuring is impossible to achieve. Banks and mezzanine investment funds may conclude that the deal is too risky and decide that they cannot participate in the operation. The auction has then failed and becomes a broken auction. The seller has to restart the sales process, with additional delays and the reputational damage associated with this broken auction.

A number of deals are negotiated and executed on the basis of a broken auction. This has an obvious impact on the seller, as the situation is less favourable. The seller not only has to decide which offer is the best financially, but must also name a reliable acquirer, who offers a genuine development plan and strategic perspective, and who is able to convince the banks to lend for the LBO.

Moreover, the creation of acquisition consortia is an answer to the auction and the competition of funds organised by the seller. The fund managers team up to make offers, each contributing financially and bringing their own expertise. This explains why very large buy-out deals are debated between three to four consortia of LBO funds. The leader of each consortium represents its group of auctioneers and manages the due diligence, the costs of which will be shared between the members of the consortium.

This practice is less common in venture or growth capital. Here, the current investors invite new investors to invest alongside them. This system, termed a 'cluster of investors', aims to create a group of shareholders which brings the assets that it needs in order to reach the next stage of development for the company. Some fund managers bring know-how in terms of commercial development, a network of partners, support for the internationalisation of the company, manager recruitment capacity or know-how in terms of initial public offering or trade sale.

5.7   STEP 7: MONITORING AND EXIT

Investment monitoring and exit are steps in the investment process in the sense that the exit conditions the performance. Negotiating an attractive price during an investment is an important step, but managing development and exiting at the most opportune time are as important as investment.

The most promising companies and assets are approached regularly by strategic acquirers or banks offering attractive exit paths. Anticipating the evolution of financial markets, valuation levels and industrial cycles is especially difficult. Some investment teams have recruited specialists to manage such monitoring, as well as the establishment of professional reporting on their portfolio companies. They have also recruited specialists in mergers and acquisitions or stock exchange listings, in order to 'industrialise' their divestment processes. In that respect, fund managers are increasingly being supported by consultants. The prediction of economic cycles and the management of investment timing so as to optimise the sale price are as much a matter of experience as self-control.

More generally, investment teams have the resources to cover not only most of the elements in the investment process, but also communication, advisory and strategic analysis. Slowly, they are becoming integrated and multi-functional investors. Some teams have even gone beyond this and established advisory practices which are active as independent advisors on the financial market. This is the case with The Blackstone Group, in the USA, which has evolved into an 'asset management house'. The status of this group, as well as the size of assets under its management, has transformed it into a merchant or an investment bank. The source of profits for the investment bank Goldman Sachs, for example, is mostly in hedge funds and private equity.

These two groups can go into partnership for a given operation (Blackstone providing the equity and Goldman Sachs the debt); or they can be clients and providers in another (Blackstone selling a company and Goldman Sachs listing it) and competitors in a third (Blackstone competing with Goldman Sachs for the acquisition of a business). The intricacy of these relationships can of course raise some concerns as to ethics and good business practice (see Chapter 6).

These developments may herald major changes, which are described in Chapters 6 and 7 and in the General Conclusion (Chapter 8).

5.8 CONCLUSION

Factors in the success of private equity funds are:

- Companies must have a strong potential for development, either nationally or internationally, or have a position with strong barriers to entry.
- Investments must be made at reasonable valuations and (if applicable) with solid and viable financial leverage.
- Managers of the company must be able to cope with the additional burden of reporting and managing the expectations of professional investors, who plan to exit at a given stage from company ownership.
- There must be a specific target for the operation, which is clear, achievable within a limited timeframe and a source of significant upside.
- Stakeholders – and not only the management – must have a competitive spirit, including the Board of the company and its investors.
- An exit path, which respects the ambitions of the investors and gives a prosperous future to the company.

The genuine resource of companies financed by private equity funds is and will remain the people in these companies, and their ability to seize opportunities, as well as manage risk and uncertainties (Chapter 6). Entrepreneurs may be the unique missing resource required to operate private equity investments in the future, and not capital – due notably to an increased risk aversion of the population in Europe and the USA.

In fact, entrepreneurs are the yardstick to measure the excess or lack of capital available. A social, economic and legal framework which encourages the adoption of measured risks is in fact facilitating entrepreneurship (see Figure 5.2). Taking risks does not mean importing practices from other countries, but adapting some of these practices to the local socio-economic framework. Facilitating entrepreneurship represents possibly the most important challenge for governments willing to have dynamic and healthy private equity activity. Training is crucial, as well as tax, legal and social support – so that a creator or a buy-out entrepreneur does not take unnecessary risks for himself and his family.

Figure 5.2 appears to show a recovery in the USA and globally in terms of entrepreneurial activity. However, the reality is much more mixed. A closer look at the USA, as the bellwether of entrepreneurship and the market which is best documented, shows that indeed the start-up activity index has recovered (Figure 5.3). However, the rate of new entrepreneurs has not increased significantly (confirming our developments on valuations of start-ups in previous chapters), as shown in Figure 5.4. The main reason is that some of the entrepreneurs captured in Figure 5.3 are launching a venture because they have no choice. This is a survival strategy, as it is confirmed that a significant proportion are immigrants (Figure 5.5), with a Latino ethnicity (Figure 5.6) and no formal education (Figure 5.7).

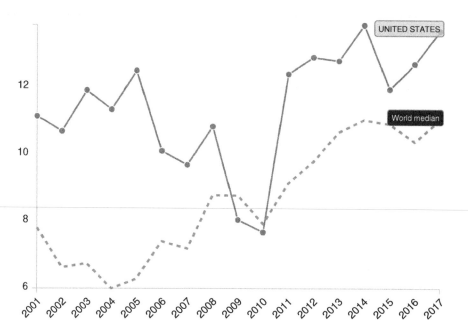

FIGURE 5.2   Total early-stage entrepreneurial activity in the USA and globally, as a percentage of the 18–64 population
Source: The World Bank, Global Entrepreneurship Monitor Adult Population Survey.

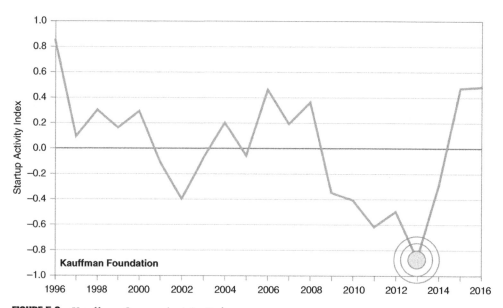

FIGURE 5.3   Kauffman Startup Activity Index
Source: Kauffman Foundation (Fairlie, Morelix & Tareque, 2017); index of start-up activity, based on CPS and BDS.

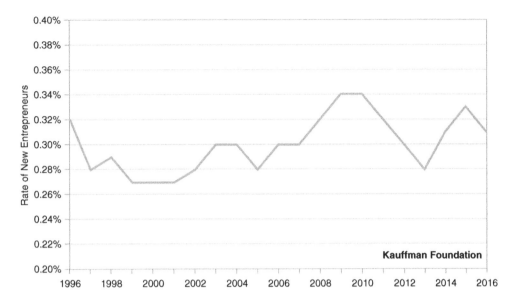

FIGURE 5.4 Rate of new entrepreneurs in the USA
Source: Kauffman Foundation (Fairlie, 2012), based on CPS.

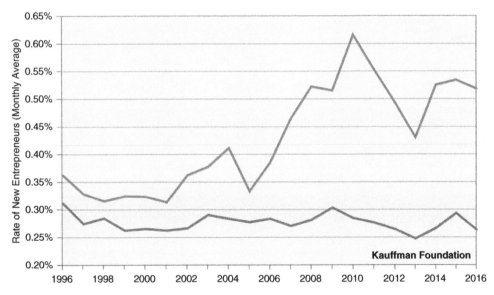

FIGURE 5.5 Rate of new entrepreneurs in the USA by nativity
Note: the upper lighter line is immigrant origin and the lower darker line is native-born
Source: Kauffman Foundation (Fairlie, 2012), based on CPS.

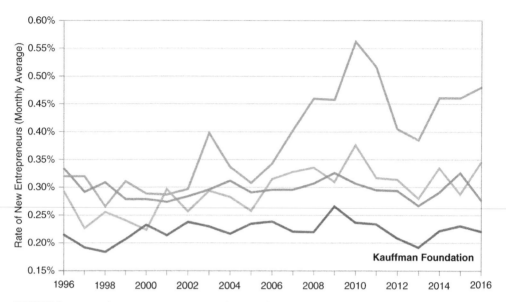

FIGURE 5.6 Rate of new entrepreneurs in the USA by ethnicity
Note: the upper lighter line is 'Latino', the second in order from the top and the lightest is 'Asian', then the third darker line is 'White' and the darkest and last is 'Black'
Source: Kauffman Foundation (Fairlie, 2012), based on CPS.

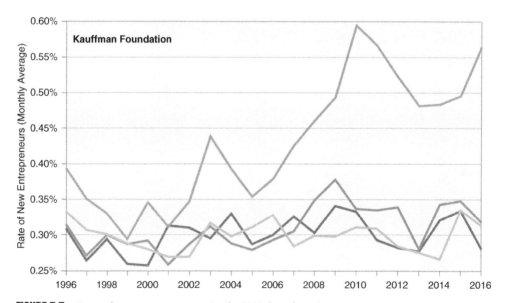

FIGURE 5.7 Rate of new entrepreneurs in the USA by education
Note: the upper lighter line is 'Less than high school', the second in order from the top and darker is 'High school graduate', then the third and lighest is 'Some college' and the last and darkest is 'College graduate'
Source: Kauffman Foundation (Fairlie, 2012), based on CPS.

In that context, not only are immigrants more prone to start a company, but the proportion has increased over time. In the case of native-born entrepreneurs, the proportion has been declining mildly except during the 2008–2009 recession, illustrating again that entrepreneurship can be a survival strategy. As the job situation in the USA has been improving, notably over the course of the last years tracked by Figure 5.5, native-born individuals have been drawn to traditional formal employment.

The proportion of entrepreneurs who voluntarily chose to become so, to create a viable venture and not just try to be self-employed, varies significantly over time (Figure 5.8). It fell significantly in 2001–2002, then further in 2009–2011. As the economic conditions improved, the proportion of voluntary entrepreneurs increased substantially, back to the level last seen in 1999–2000. Still, roughly 14% of the total did not choose to be independent and had to adopt a survival strategy. Entrepreneurs by choice are essentially in the same proportion whether they are immigrants or native-born (Figure 5.9). The proportion of immigrants who chose to be entrepreneurs varies much more significantly over time than the proportion of native-born. Foreign entrepreneurship is much more sensitive to macro-economic conditions in the USA than native-born.

The picture differs substantially when looking at the composition of the sample of entrepreneurs who choose to be so (See Figure 5.10). The highest proportion is Asian ethnicity, followed by White, Latino and Black. This confirms that the initial perspective provided by Figure 5.6 included a significant proportion of self-employed individuals without any other choice. Ethnicity produces different outcomes in chosen entrepreneurship. Asian entrepreneurs appear to be fairly resilient, except after 2001, but did not stop their entrepreneurial efforts in 2008–2009, while White entrepreneurs did not significantly resume after 2001 and reduced their initiatives even further after 2009. The recovery after is the most visible; they almost caught up with the level prior to the crisis of 2000–2001.

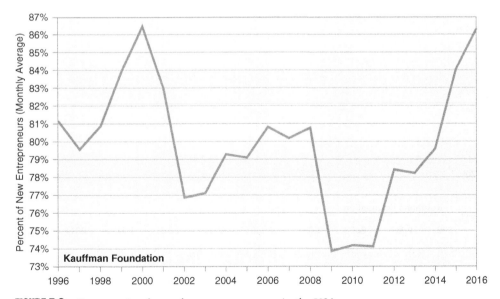

FIGURE 5.8 Opportunity share of new entrepreneurs in the USA
Source: Kauffman Foundation (Fairlie, 2012).

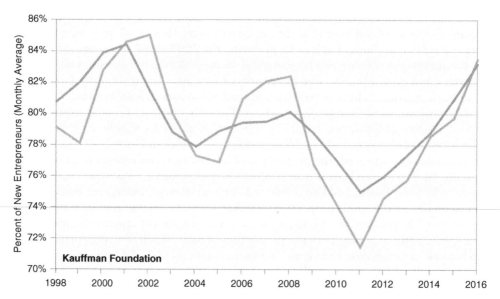

FIGURE 5.9 Rate of new entrepreneurs in the USA who choose to be so, by nativity (3-year moving average)
Note: the more volatile lighter line is immigrant origin, the more stable darker line is native-born
Source: Kauffman Foundation (Fairlie, 2012), based on CPS.

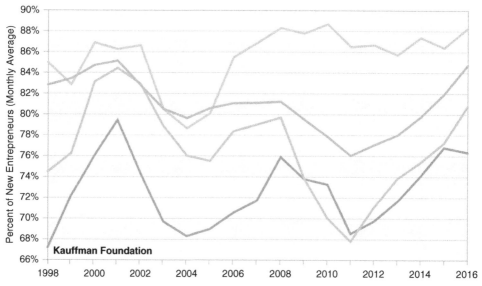

FIGURE 5.10 Rate of new entrepreneurs in the USA who choose to be so, by ethnicity (3-year moving average)
Note: the upper lightest line is 'Asian', the second in order from the top and third darker is 'White', then the third lighter is 'Latino' and the darkest and last is 'Black'
Source: Kauffman Foundation (Fairlie, 2012), based on CPS.

The starkest contrast lies in the educational background. Entrepreneurs by choice are the most educated, and the level of entrepreneurship declines with education (Figure 5.11). Thus, if the Latino immigrant with no formal education, forced to be self-employed, was an emblematic entrepreneur of the previous sample, this sample features a highly educated Asian native or immigrant who decides to start up. If the entrepreneur is a woman, she is highly likely to have chosen to be so (Figure 5.12), regardless of the macro-economic conditions, much more than her male counterpart. The logical conclusion is that, for all the talk about promoting female entrepreneurship, most women entrepreneurs choose to be so. The gender imbalance might not be as clear cut as usually discussed, especially as males are more often forced to work self-employed with no other choice than women.

Figure 5.13 provides further insights on the composition of the sample of entrepreneurs who choose to be so. First, the oldest cohort drives the pack, a fact which is a far cry from the myth of the young college dropout deciding to start up. However, the prevalence tends to decrease over time. Second, the 45–54 cohort appears to be relatively constant but is very sensitive to macro-economic conditions. It was recently overtaken by the 35–44 cohort, although this might be related to very favourable macro-economic conditions similar to those preceding 2000–2001, a period during which they were at par.

The most striking evolution is the decline of entrepreneurship among the youngest category of 20–34-year-olds. While it was fairly close to the 35–54 cohort combined

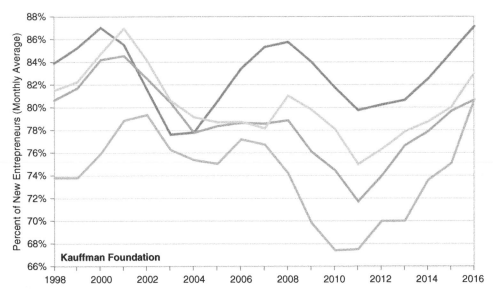

FIGURE 5.11 Rate of new entrepreneurs in the USA who choose to be so, by education (3-year moving average)
Note: the upper lighter line and the darkest is 'College graduate', the second in order from the top and lightest is 'Some college', then the third and the second darkest is 'High school graduate' and the last and second lightest is 'Less than high school'
Source: Kauffman Foundation (Fairlie, 2012), based on CPS.

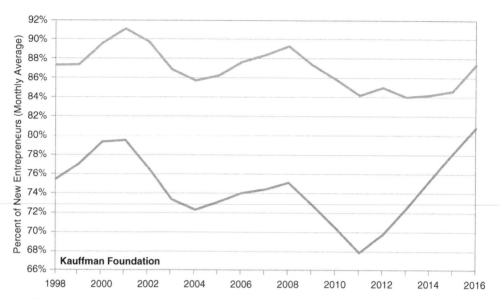

FIGURE 5.12   Rate of new entrepreneurs in the USA who choose to be so, by gender (3-year moving average)
Note: the upper lighter line is female, the lower darker line is male
Source: Kauffman Foundation (Fairlie, 2012), based on CPS.

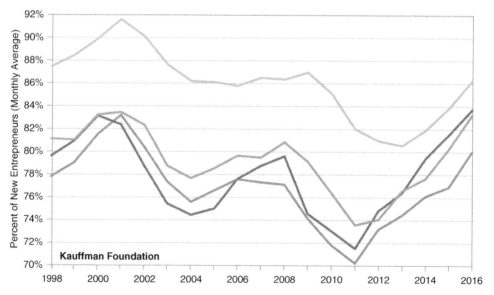

FIGURE 5.13   Rate of new entrepreneurs in the USA who choose to be so, by age (3-year moving average)
Note: the upper lighter line is 'Ages 55–64', the second darkest line is 'Ages 35–44', the third second lighest line is 'Ages 45–54' and the last second darkest line is 'Ages 20–34'
Source: Kauffman Foundation (Fairlie, 2012), based on CPS.

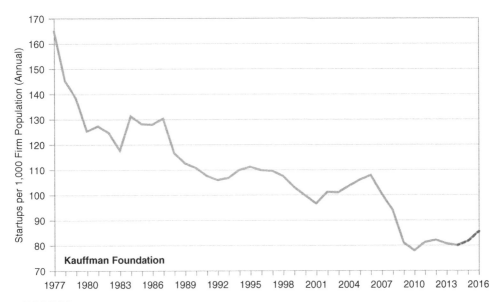

FIGURE 5.14 Start-up density
Source: Kauffman Foundation (Fairlie, 2012), based on BDS.

in 2001, it declined steadily and became the laggard in 2006. It only partially recovered recently and still lags the other generations significantly. This means that the entrepreneurial spirit of the younger population might not be as strong as it was two decades go. This would also result in a durably lower level of voluntary entrepreneurial effort, stabilising at roughly half what it was three decades ago (See Figure 5.14). As the US population has grown, the absolute number of ventures might not decrease, but the proportion has dropped significantly. With a lower proportion of older entrepreneurs, the chance of seeing a significant increase is limited. As the previous cohorts age, however, they might decide to take the leap.

REFERENCES

Papers and Studies

Fairlie, R.W., 'Kauffman Index of Entrepreneurial Activity (1966–2011)', Kauffman, 2012, 32 pp ((http://www.kauffman.org/uploadedFiles/KIEA_2012_report.pdf), last accessed 12 March 2013).

Fairlie, R., Morelix, A., Tareque, I., 'The 2017 Kauffman Startup Activity Index', Kauffmann, 2017, 52 pp.

Kedrosky, P. and Stangler, D., 'Financialization and Its Entrepreneurial Consequences' (2011) Kauffman Foundation Research Series: Firm Formation and Economic Growth, Kauffman, 20 pp.

PART III

Private Markets in Teenage Time

Trend Setting, Fads and Responsibilities

Private market operators strove to stay below the radar, but this no longer applies. As fund managers gain in importance and go public, are private markets going to stay private much longer?

As private market investing grows, it attracts more attention. It may move towards an organised market, which appears to contradict its nature. The increased participation of institutional investors in private market funds is driving the transformation of this market (Chapter 6). The financial power of multi-billion-dollar funds, in LBO but also increasingly in other private markets, raises some questions regarding the ethical rules applied by fund managers (Chapter 7).

Private Markets Evolution

Trends or Buzzes?

The growing interaction between listed and private markets has raised many questions, chiefly: is private equity going mainstream? (See Section 6.1.) As it evolves slowly into an institutionalised area for investments, this capital inflow may change the way private equity creates value (see Section 6.2). This could also raise the prospect of more bubbles (see Section 6.3). This section will focus specifically on private equity within private markets, as this is the most developed and advanced set of investment strategies within private markets. Private equity should therefore provide a fairly good perspective on what would happen to other private market strategies as they mature.

6.1   IS PRIVATE EQUITY GOING MAINSTREAM?

6.1.1   Large and Mega LBO Funds have Flexed their Muscles …

Large and mega[1] LBO funds have demonstrated their ever-increasing financial strength. They compete with corporate strategic buyers for acquisitions. Stock exchanges provide not only an exit path for their deals, but also a source of deal flow. Very few listed companies are now out of the reach of private equity firms. At the peak of the business cycle leading to the 2008–2009 crisis, Microsoft was even named in a paper from the *Financial Times* as being a possible target for a deal.[2] The roster of deals at that time is indeed impressive. In 2006, Equity Office Properties[3] delisted for USD 36 billion by Blackstone. HCA delisted for USD 33 billion by Bain Capital, KKR and Merrill Lynch. Harrah's[4] delisted for USD 27.8 billion by Apollo and TPG. Kinder Morgan delisted for USD 22 billion by Goldman Sachs Capital Partners, Carlyle, Riverstone and AIG. Clear

---

[1]The definition is shifting over time, but small LBO aims at companies with an enterprise value below USD 350 million, mid-sized LBO aims at companies with an enterprise value between USD 350 million and USD 1 billion, large LBO aims at companies with an enterprise value between USD 1 and 3.5 billion and mega LBO aims at companies with an enterprise value above USD 3.5 billion.
[2]18 August 2006.
[3]Later renamed as EQ Office.
[4]Later renamed as Caesar Entertainment.

Channel Communications delisted for USD 18.7 billion by Thomas H. Lee Partners and Bain Capital. Freescale Semiconductor[5] was bought for USD 17.6 billion by Blackstone, Permira, Carlyle and TPG.

In 2007 the list continues, with TXU[6] bought for USD 45 billion by Goldman Sachs Capital Partners, KKR and TPG Capital. Hilton delisted for USD 26 billion by Blackstone. First Data Corporation delisted for USD 29 billion by KKR. Alltel delisted for USD 27.5 billion by TPG Capital and Goldman Sachs Capital Partners. This trend was also visible in Europe. The French Group Vivendi was approached by KKR for a EUR 40 billion take-over in October 2006, which was subsequently declined. The same year, the Danish telecom group TDC was acquired for USD 15.3 billion by Apax Partners, Blackstone, KKR, Permira and Providence Equity Partners. In 2007, the British firm Alliance Boots was taken private for GBP 12.4 billion by KKR and its CEO Stefano Pessina.

6.1.2 ... at Times with Mixed Success, and Important Consequences ...

TXU became the largest LBO ever made, a title held for a long time by RJR Nabisco, which was acquired in 1988 by KKR for USD 25.1 billion. It also became, as RJR Nabisco, the beacon of the peak of the cycle. RJR Nabisco is assumed to have generated a loss of USD 730 million on a USD 3.5 billion investment.[7] TXU failed spectacularly, along with Harrah's. Freescale and First Data Corporation were close to following the same track and ultimately generated a loss for their investors. These high-profile failures triggered questions about LBO fund managers as being too greedy and careless. The SEC in the USA started to investigate the practice of club deals, seen as potentially anti-competitive.

The aftermath of 2008–2009 led to multiple and substantial changes in LBOs. First, the SEC and then its European counterpart ESMA issued recommendations for structuring financial leverages in LBOs. Fund managers are advised to limit their debt levels to six times EBITDA. Second, fund managers took the cue from the SEC investigation in club deals and decided to switch and structure their deals through co-investments with their fund investors, if the deals exceeded the target deal size for the fund. Third, fund managers saw increased competition from corporate buyers, who could access large pools of cheap debt without any cap on their leverage ratio. Fourth, some fund investors decided to do direct deals alone and acquire potential LBO targets.

6.1.3 ... But Large Deals are Here to Stay

LBO funds have seen their share of global mergers and acquisitions fluctuate between 14% and 19%. According to the White & Case Mergermarket M&A Explorer, LBO funds were buyers in 2753 out of 14 700 deals (18.7%) in 2006, and 2959 of 16 112

---

[5]Now part of NXP Semiconductors, which acquired it in 2015.
[6]Later renamed as Energy Future Holdings.
[7]Norris (2004) (www.nytimes.com/2004/07/09/business/worldbusiness/fund-books-loss-on-rjr-after-15-years-a-long-chapter.html).

deals (18.4%) in 2007. The proportion dropped to 1397 out of 9920 deals (14.1%) in 2009. It was only in 2016 and 2017 that the proportion recovered, with respectively 3015 out of 18 593 deals (16.2%) and 3530 out of 19 973 deals (17.7%).

However, very large operations decreased in number and size after 2009 but did not disappear. In 2013, 3G Capital and Berkshire Hathaway acquired HJ Heinz for USD 23.2 billion, merged in 2015 with Kraft for a combined value of USD 50 billion. Interestingly, the two companies were not taken private but remained listed, with the combined entity on NASDAQ. The same year, Dell was taken private by Michael Dell and Silver Lake for USD 24.4 billion, which acquired EMC for USD 67 billion in 2015. In 2014, PetSmart was bought in the UK for USD 8.7 billion by BC Partners. In 2015, Veritas was acquired from Symantec for USD 8 billion by Carlyle Group and GIC.

6.1.4 The Importance of Public-to-Private Deals

The above list illustrates the trend for listed companies to go private through an LBO. A growing number of listed firms leave the stock exchange so as to avoid the pressure of increased regulation (Sarbanes–Oxley has been blamed for costs and administrative burdens) and quarterly reporting. This was explicitly the motivation of Michael Dell to take the company that he founded and managed private. Listing the company again, as was announced in 2018, tends to contradict this motivation. The number of public-to-private deals reached 421 in 2006 and 395 in 2007, fell to 27 in 2009, and then recovered to 179 in 2017 and 227 in 2018 according to Bain and Company (2019).

The costs and benefits of a listing have changed. Companies which do not find relays of financing on the market, because of a stagnating share price and/or a lack of interest from analysts, view a delisting as a source of flexibility and a way to get the necessary capital injection in order to boost their growth. This phenomenon has mainly been observed in the USA thus far, but is spreading to other markets.

Private equity has grown symbiotically with the stock exchange, but is now organised as an ecosystem, which can finance companies at every stage of their development. Not only may a company grow theoretically through multiple rounds of financing by venture and growth capital, and then later on be taken over by an LBO fund, but it could also be refinanced by LBO funds regularly, through secondary, tertiary and quaternary operations (Frans Bonhomme, in France, has been the target of five successive LBOs between 1994 and 2006). Private equity is gaining its autonomy from traditional exit paths (trade sales and IPOs), even though secondary venture capital funds have yet to emerge formally.

This independence gives private equity the characteristics of an institutionalised and organised market. This is not only true for the exit side, but also the deal sourcing side, where auctions are more frequent in large and now mid-market buy-outs. LBO funds are now surrounded by service providers for their due diligence processes, such as lawyers, auditors, consultants, market analysts and bankers. Buyers' due diligence is common, but vendors' due diligence is also established increasingly in order to negotiate in good faith and have a common basis for discussion.

6.1.5 Private Equity Strives on Innovation

Given its private nature and lack of transparency, can private equity survive in an organised market? The answer lies probably in its flexibility and its ability to innovate. Private equity is constantly testing new techniques and the limits of its intervention. In that respect, the venture financing sector is now proposing debt-like tools such as venture lending (mainly in the USA, and developing in Israel), granting late-stage companies the equivalent of mezzanine financing. Some technology groups have even proposed venture leasing to start-ups which were strategically important in order to develop certain markets, but then retreated as a result of difficulties experienced in 1999–2003.

Growth capital and LBO funds have begun to make PIPEs, negotiating special rights with listed companies if they invest a certain amount and seal their commitment for a certain time. The idea is to apply private equity techniques to these companies, which are languishing on the stock exchange and have the potential for a substantial upside without the need to be taken over or delisted.

To fend off the competition and address high valuations as witnessed over the course of the years 2016 to 2019, LBO funds developed differentiated strategies. One is to carve out business units from groups, to later acquire them through an LBO. Another is to operate a buy-and-build strategy, which consists of acquiring smaller companies (the 'platform' deals) than the usual target size for a fund, and then acquiring complementary businesses (so-called 'add-ons') and integrating them in the platform. The purpose is to average down the price of the acquisitions (as smaller companies are comparatively less expensive, trading for example at four or five times EBITDA) and generate synergies when they will be integrated. The resulting entity should gain in value thanks to its increased combined efficiency and its increase in size, which in turn increase its value (trading for example at six or seven times EBITDA).

Players in the LBO market have also started to develop hybrid products, mixing debt and capital, such as mezzanine and unitranche financing (see Chapter 4). As this debt is substantially riskier than traditional debt, mezzanine funds usually negotiate a partial conversion of their debt (or options) so as to benefit from the upside created by this cash injection with no upfront costs.

Players in the turn-around/restructuring area have also taken the approach of colonising the debt side, acquiring the debt of distressed companies (distressed debt funds) at a discount. Once the debt has been acquired, they wash out the existing shareholders and turn around the company. This shows how far private equity techniques can be extended and applied to companies in very different situations.

6.1.6 A Matter of Syndication

The emergence of club deals between LBO funds and then co-investments between LBO funds and fund investors (see above) is another example of this adaptability, while recognising a rapid commoditisation of this financial technique.[8] LBO funds have begun to team up and target assets that they would otherwise not be able to reach, allowing them to target large listed companies, even in a hostile take-over.

Why do funds not want to invest alone? Venture capital has a long tradition of syndicating deals and attracting additional investors within subsequent rounds of financing. This is linked to the necessity of providing different assets, aside from capital, to the

---

[8] Hedge funds have begun to recruit some private equity professionals with regard to some of their holding companies.

portfolio company, as well as spreading the risk between multiple investors. For large buy-outs, the same reasoning may apply.

Blackstone, KKR, Apollo and other mega LBO fund managers regularly raise USD 20 billion funds[9] to invest in mega buy-outs. However, with deals above USD 30 billion, even after leverage, it is necessary to spread the risk among multiple investors. Moreover, in the HCA deal, the investors include a typical private equity house, with a fund associated with a consulting firm and an investment bank. These three players provide different skillsets for the portfolio company and thus have an interest in teaming up.

On a fund investor level, however, club deals or co-investments bring an overall reduction in the diversification of the portfolio. If a fund investor is in multiple funds co-investing in the same company, its portfolio may be over-exposed to a specific risk. The same applied for co-investments. The fund investor may also be investing in funds competing with each other for a certain company, and thus bidding against each other. The funds it has invested in will support this price increase (for the winning bidder) and also broken deal costs (for the defeated bidder).

6.1.7 The Temptation of Permanent Capital

Private equity fund managers have to regularly fundraise. This process is time and resource-consuming, and fairly expensive (even though the costs are effectively supported by fund investors through the fund's set-up costs). It is also one of the few instances during which fund investors have the choice to reinvest or not with the same fund manager. Fundraising forces the fund manager to go back to the drawing board and explain the strategy (and its adjustment), past investments, value creation, exits, performance, failures and successes, and ultimately convince the fund investors. This process is therefore demanding and forces fund managers to face tough questions. This is probably one of the few times that they have to exercise restraint and show some form of humility. Fund investors, the real owners of private equity funds, can exercise their right to operate a detailed due diligence and leave no stone unturned.

The temptation for fund managers is therefore to set up a pool of permanent capital, to avoid such a consuming process and also to increase their discretion and freedom. Two main conduits have been tested so far, with rather mixed results: listing vehicles on the stock exchange, and more recently setting up longer-denominated funds.

Multiple fund managers have tried to *list structures*. Three possibilities are offered to them: list a closed-end or an open-end investment vehicle, list the fund manager itself or list a combination of an open-end fund and a fund manager (listed holding). Listing closed-end investment companies (such as BDCs in the USA) funds does not solve the issue of fund managers willing to avoid the regular fundraising of new structures. These structures have to be raised in compliance with regulations applicable to listed markets, which are more demanding than the private placement of funds. They also have to be managed under the scrutiny of listed investors and analysts. In particular, fund managers have to provide a minimum of information about the underlying private companies (or assets), thus to the competitors of these private companies and the

---

[9]As a matter of illustration, Apollo raised a USD 25 billion fund in 2017.

potential buyers. A closed-end structure has a term, forcing the fund manager to sell the underlying companies (or assets) and potentially limiting its bargaining power.

Listing open-end investment vehicles is most likely one of the most appealing approaches for fund managers. The capital is raised and then used as needed to make investments in private companies or assets. In the USA, it is so far not allowed to list private market funds, although the SEC opened a consultation in 2019[10] to potentially change the status quo. The only approach is to set up a SPAC, which is initially structured as a trust in which investors pre-commit capital. Managers scout the market to find and negotiate the acquisition of a private firm within a specific time (usually 2 years). They then ask investors if they agree to the acquisition. If the answer is positive, then the capital is called and the SPAC is automatically listed. If the answer is negative, then investors incur some costs and the structure is dissolved. One of the drawbacks of this approach is that there is one asset per SPAC, which means that investors do not get the diversification associated with a fund.

Out of the USA, there were attempts to list closed-end and open-end funds. For example, Better Capital initially listed two on the London Stock Exchange in 2009 and 2012, which were later converted to open-end structures (Guernsey Protected Cell Companies). KKR listed an investment vehicle on Euronext Amsterdam in 2006: the KKR Private Equity Investors (KKR PEI) with an original target of EUR 1.5 billion, later expanded to USD 5 billion. This solution thus avoided for KKR not only the necessity of complying with regular fundraising, but also the pressure to sell investments too early. Dividend recapitalisations are a regular source of substantial profits for LBO investors, and it is possible to envisage a scenario where listed private equity vehicles will become an intermediary between the stock exchange and portfolio companies, thus providing liquidity, but preserving them from the burden of a listing. This would also mean the end of the secondary market at a fund investor level. The evolution of the share price (see Figure 6.1) of KKR PEI has cast a shadow on this scenario.

Listed private equity funds face multiple challenges. First, they suffer from a lack of transparency. The underlying assets are not documented enough for investors in the listed structure: most of the information is provided on a quarterly basis, at best, with

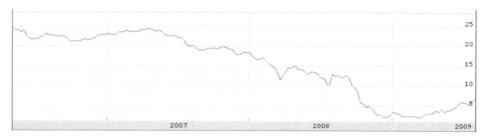

FIGURE 6.1 Evolution of the share price of KKR PEI (May 2006–July 2009)
Source: Google Finance.

---

[10]US Securities and Exchange Commission, 'SEC seeks public comment on ways to harmonize private securities offering exemption', Press release, June 18, 2019 (https://www.sec.gov/news/press-release/2019-97).

a significant lag. Moreover, the details on each underlying asset are scarce. As a result, the listed structure trades at an average 30% discount on the net asset value of the fund. Second, the listed structure suffers from a performance drag associated with the unused capital. When the structure is created, it still requires time to deploy its capital efficiently. The unused capital suffers from an opportunity cost. When the listed structure sells an asset, the capital and the undistributed proceeds will sit idle on the balance sheet until the manager finds another investment opportunity. Third, the alignment of interest between the investors in the listed fund and the managers is looser than with a standard private structure. Fund managers have no pressure to maximise the performance and return the capital to investors. Investors might suffer from implicit opportunity costs as the capital is used but maybe not to their best interest. This explains why listed ('evergreen') funds did not take off as an alternative to the standard private market fund structure. In the case of KKR PEI, it was used for a reverse take-over of KKR itself, the fund manager becoming public and having transferred it to the NYSE.

However, listed private market fund managers themselves did not fare particularly well, as illustrated by KKR (Figure 6.2). The listing of Blackstone in 2007 triggered a wave of listing, with Apollo, Oaktree and many other private market fund managers following through (Figure 6.3). All of them have under-performed the S&P 500. Fund managers provide investors with access to the stream of management fees that they collect as fund managers, as well as their performance fee. In effect, they are asset managers and considered as such by investors – not as a conduit to private market investments. Moreover, investors have only limited visibility on the upcoming performance fees, and no say in the pay and expenses of the employees of the fund managers. The attractiveness of these structures for fund investors is therefore limited.

From the above, it will come as no surprise that listed holding companies did not do better. They combine the drawback of listed fund managers and listed open-end funds, with the added complexity of understanding these two structures with one set of accounts. 3i, Eurazeo, GIMV and some other private equity houses have been offering such vehicles in Europe for a long time without generating a trend.

Another approach, more recent, has been to *set up longer-denominated funds*, created for 15 years or more. The idea of fund managers, such as BlackRock and Blackstone, has been to buy and hold assets, creating value over a longer period of time. This faces multiple obstacles. First, holding assets for a longer time requires a very patient investment team. The performance fee will necessarily come later, and this might not be a sufficient incentive to keep the staff motivated and happy. Second, the investment

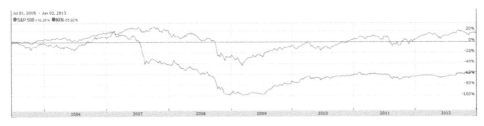

FIGURE 6.2 Comparison of evolution of the share price of KKR Financial Holdings and the S&P 500 (July 2005–December 2012)
Source: Google Finance.

FIGURE 6.3 Comparison of evolution of the share price of Blackstone (BX), KKR, Ares, Oaktree (OAK), Apollo (APO), Carlyle (CG) and the S&P 500 (July 2005–December 2012) *Source:* Yahoo Finance.

plan has to be different than for the traditional private equity operations, or should combine multiple successive plans with the same discipline as when they are executed one after another in successive LBOs. Fund managers have still to prove that they can execute these different strategies or that they can successfully implement very different strategies on one single asset. Third, fund investors have to be more patient than with existing fund structures already perceived as fairly long. So far, the experiment of longer-denominated funds has remained marginal and did not gather momentum.

6.2   IS PRIVATE EQUITY (STILL) CREATING VALUE?

The lack of transparency in private markets has often been associated with the source of their performance. Information asymmetries can play in favour of fund managers, used to execute detailed due diligence and handle a relative lack of information (at least compared to the level of information available on stock exchanges).

Among the reasons given as to why private markets deliver higher returns than other traditional asset classes, lack of liquidity is often cited. To be competitive, private markets would have to deliver an 'illiquidity premium'[11] above stock exchange returns, hence compensating a 'higher risk'. Unfortunately, this explanation does not really hold. First, the notion of 'illiquidity premium' only applies to fixed-income investments: the lender gets compensated for postponing the consumption of its capital, as well as for the risk of lending. This is not applicable to equity and active investments. Second, the notion of an 'illiquidity premium' is not compatible with the fact that to operate, private market fund managers require a minimum of 3 to 8 years, depending on the private markets investment strategy that they apply. The lower liquidity of their investments is not a risk but a dimension of investment.

The second reason that is often given is that private market fund managers create greater value than the typical selection of stocks or bonds, on the stock exchange. In private markets, value creation evolves around what the investor can bring to the investee company (or asset) beyond the capital provided. This can vary from one investor to another, depending on the nature of the investment (venture capital or LBO, for example), the needs of the company (staffing, advice, structuring, M&A, etc.), the specificities of the fund investing in the company (local/international, focused/diversified, etc.) and the personality of the executive representing the fund on the Board. This value creation is often described as a 'hands-on' approach in venture capital, where the executives of the venture capital fund are widely involved in the life and development of their portfolio companies. The limit of this intervention, however, is defined by a simple rule: the investor shall not 'cross the management line'. This is defined mainly by the laws and regulations of each country and may be enforced by local courts.

The distinction between advising and directing can be very narrow. Some venture capital funds in Silicon Valley often assign one of their executives to work within a definite timeframe as an executive in their portfolio companies in order to fill a gap or support a given effort. This is not possible in many European countries, as the sponsors of the funds would be considered 'de facto managers' and thus liable if the company went bankrupt – which is, however, less likely to happen than for other companies which are not backed by private equity players, as was explained in a paper in the *Harvard Business Review* (Salter, 2007).

The management is responsible for the direction of the company, but investors are nevertheless supposed to support, advise and control (if admitted to the controlling organs, such as the Board of Directors) portfolio companies. In that respect, Boards of professionally sponsored buy-outs appear as more informed, hands-on and interventionist than their equivalent in public companies. This is probably a determining factor in the value creation of private equity teams.

This effect is the result of a better alignment of interests between private equity Board members and shareholders, as they are significant shareholders. They not only have an incentive to identify key issues and ask the management to resolve them, but also to do this at an early stage and ask the management proactively for information. This is possible because private equity teams have a deep knowledge of the companies they have invested in, thanks to the initial due diligence they have done and the ongoing detailed monitoring they are exercising.

---

[11]This has been estimated at between 400 and 600 basis points above average returns on the stock exchange at a fund level.

Private equity Board members usually go beyond the walls of the boardroom, and do not hesitate to call the management and go on site in order to determine the best actions to be taken. The dialogue is much more intense and focused on key issues. In this respect, the expertise, experience and network of private equity Board members make a substantial difference because these are leverages servicing the investment that the fund has made.

Value creation varies according to the maturity of the company financed and the nature of its needs. Venture capital and growth capital investors define themselves as 'growth financing investors'. Early-stage investors help the company to set up its organisation, recruit, go through the R&D process and put the product on the market. Value creation from the investor is defined mainly as complementary to the entrepreneur's skills. It provides leverage for the new-born firm to find the resources it needs to reach a certain number of milestones. Late-stage venture capitalists often provide the company with an international network, additional recruitment and support in going global or preparing a listing or a trade sale.

Growth capital focuses on financing companies which need to develop their activity at a fast pace, identifying new markets and sometimes acquiring key positions on a given market through M&A. The risks associated with growth financing in development capital are more about streamlining operations, avoiding the extra costs of post-merger integration and identifying key assets at a reasonable price (thus looking at the market for alternatives to internal development).

With LBOs, and especially large buy-outs, the concept of value creation runs closer to a typical financial and advisory business. With large buy-outs, value creation by the investor comes more from a strategic and operational analysis than from finding new markets or introducing new clients. In this regard, Bain Capital, Blackstone, KKR and some other large buy-out players have developed an integrated and proactive approach to acquisitions. Blackstone has developed a quasi-industrial approach to financing, by developing business units focused on LBO, distressed debt, real estate and alternative sub-asset classes, which interact regularly to assess investment opportunities. KKR designs a 'first 100 days' plan for each of its acquisitions, which describes precisely what is to be expected from the company during this time in order to develop towards the projected plan.

Top line growth is one of the four areas on which an LBO investor is willing to focus, especially if it is possible to structure a buy-and-build strategy. This type of deal is structured in order to acquire a 'platform company' which will then position itself as an acquirer to consolidate a given market. The growth of its turnover is thus assured through the aggregation of other companies. It can also be a vertical integration, where the platform company will acquire providers and clients to create an integrated offer. In that respect, top line growth is often associated with economies of scale, as well as operational improvements.

Operational improvements are the second leverage of value creation for an LBO investor. This is due to a combination of restructuring of a company, staffing it differently, and sometimes outsourcing part of its processes, optimising its cash-flow management and even using advanced financial techniques such as sale lease-back. LBO investors can benchmark their new acquisitions and identify untapped sources of value. Successive LBOs can thus target multiple sources of value creation, thereby explaining the viability of secondary, tertiary and further LBO operations. LBOs can thus support the structuring and build-up of a company, manage a 'transforming acquisition' and prepare its listing.

LBO funds have, however, been criticised for their quick buy-and-sell strategy, raising some concerns about their value creation. In the USA, Hertz has been acquired from Ford by a consortium of LBO funds and was planned to be listed less than a year after its acquisition. In Europe, Legrand has been listed less than 2 years after its acquisition by KKR and Wendel. Despite the 'first 100 days' plan and operational improvements, the results of value creation by funds have to be shown in the financial statements of the companies. Selling acquisitions less than 2 years after their acquisition raises many questions concerning the efficiency of this strategy.

The increasing number of quick buy-and-sell operations during the last LBO boom was short-lived. Funds, and especially LBO specialists, may find an interest in shortening the holding period of portfolio companies as one of the ways to measure their performance. Funds can deliver very high IRR with relatively modest multiples, if they can manage to rotate their assets quickly. This could explain the focus on quick exits, and notably on PIPEs as the exit issue is partially solved in this latter case.

The rapid delivery of good IRRs through realised investments eases fundraising for subsequent funds. Fund managers may find an incentive to focus on this metric, despite the modest absolute returns generated. Studies have shown that patient investors deliver substantially higher absolute returns than those placing the emphasis on delivering returns quickly. LBO funds show a strong focus on recapitalisations and other financial operations, as they are a way to show partially realised performance and announce flattering IRRs quickly. It is thus in the best interests of the investor to understand how the performance was generated, and especially to factor in the rotation of assets, the leverage effect (and possible recapitalisations), as well as the difference from multiples of EBIT or EBITDA between entry and exit. Once these factors have been identified, it is possible to truly assess the value creation of a given investor by excluding them.

A Citigroup study, published in November 2006, has shown that pure financial operations, and especially leveraging, are not a value creation. According to Michael Gordon (*Financial Times*, 2007), who had access to this research, buy-out funds under-performed public equity in the 1980s and 1990s if the same level of leverage is applied to public equity ownership. The Citigroup team applied the leverage used by private equity firms to a basket of American mid-cap listed stocks and backtested the performance over a 10-year period. The declared annualised return from this portfolio was 38% (above the 36% reported for top-quartile buy-out funds and the 14% for the LBO average). This method remains open to criticism, as it applies a technique to a basket of values which are then backtested. This introduces a certain bias for a real comparison with top-quartile funds. However, the difference in performance between the 38% and the average of the LBO sector still shows that value creation is not systematic when it is a matter of LBO investments, and remains to be assessed carefully in order to further analyse the reproduction of the performance in the future.

Value creation, at every level of the private equity ecosystem, is a reality. Hedge funds have been chasing private equity talent in their quest to find new ways of generating performance. The emblematic operation of the hedge fund KSL, which acquired the bankrupt public retailer Kmart in order to restructure it and later merge it with Sears, has shown clearly that there could be an overlap between private equity investing and hedge fund financing. This overlap remains limited, given the scope of the intervention of these two alternative sub-asset classes. However, hedge funds have carried on chasing talent in private equity, and this trend proves that private equity is able to deliver a consistent and substantial performance through real value creation.

With the diffusion of private equity techniques to other asset classes, whether hedge funds, real estate or other sectors, are private equity techniques in the process of being commoditised? Or, in other words, is private equity going mainstream? These questions lead to the possibility that private equity could see its returns decrease over time. Leveraging an acquisition is a standard procedure which is well known on the market. However, value creation remains a key element of the performance of LBO funds. A study (Cao & Lerner, 2006) has shown that listed companies which were backed by LBO funds were outperforming the market and other IPOs between 1980 and 2002.

Analysing the value creation of private equity firms should go beyond pure IRR and multiple approaches, to go further into deal structuring, execution and exit. Reference calls with CEOs of companies are not only part of the due diligence process for an investor, but also with other parties involved in the investment process, including advisors and bankers. Moreover, the subsequent performance of portfolio companies once exited is important, as this determines whether the company was generating returns for the fund on the verge of a bubble high, or whether it has stood the test of time and could resist not only a listing, but also in the long term the pressure of the market. The crashed IPO of the IP telephony company Vonage (see Figure 6.4) provides an example of the market backlash when a company does not provide sufficient grounds for further development.

FIGURE 6.4 Comparison of evolution of the share price of Vonage and the S&P 500
Source: Yahoo Finance.

6.3 PRIVATE EQUITY: BETWEEN BUBBLES AND CRASHES

Private markets are affected by economic, financial and industry-specific cycles. They are influenced by *economic cycles*, as the underlying companies and assets which funds are investing in are affected by these cycles. The level of confidence of consumers, the current and projected demand, the adoption rates of technological innovation and other parameters influence sectors of investment and condition the performance of portfolio companies. Depending on this performance, exits will be more or less lucrative for funds, and thus their performance will be impacted.

Private markets are also affected by *financial cycles*, which are measured by the *percentage of capital allocated* to the asset class and by *interest rates*. *Capital inflow* in private markets is one of the ways to measure where we are in the cycle. However, more than the overall capital collected in a given year, it is the total amount collected per segment (such as venture capital, LBO or distressed debt) and sub-segment (hi-tech, biotech, small, mid or large caps, etc.) which is important, as well as the geographical allocation. It is also important to compare the amounts collected, invested and to be invested, as well as the divestments. For a given vintage, the investment period is usually 5 years (less for specific strategies). The holding period of a company varies greatly but is generally 3 to 5 years in private equity, and the divestment process can take some time. It is thus difficult to determine if there is an over-allocation to private markets in terms of capital allocation at a given time.

Capital inflow is dependent on the overall amount to be invested by:

- High net worth individuals, as determined by their liquid personal wealth and the allocation strategy advised by private banks, family offices and foundations.
- Insurers and banks, as determined by solvency and prudential ratios, the total assets under management and the allocation strategy of these institutions.
- Corporations, as determined by their net results, the total of their assets and their investment policy.
- Pension funds and plans, as determined by their total assets under management and their allocation strategy.

These criteria can create booms and busts in private markets. A change in the allocation strategy of pension plans can suddenly liberate a vast amount of capital to be invested in a relatively short period of time in private markets. This is what happened when CalPERS and CalSTRS and other pension funds in the USA decided to increase their exposure to this asset class in order to improve the performance of their investment portfolio. The sudden capital inflow could create conditions for a sub-optimal allocation, as it is difficult to evaluate what is the right size for private markets and the investment opportunities for a given year.

A change in the calculation of the prudential or solvency ratio can also have a dramatic impact as well. The Basel II and III Agreements have redefined the calculation methods for banks to evaluate their risk and to cover it. Suddenly, the private equity sector was weighted differently owing to the risk it was assigned, and financial institutions had to cover their commitments with more capital off their balance sheet. By increasing the cost of capital for banks to invest in private equity, the Basel II and III

Agreements dried up one of the main sources of private equity financing, notably in Europe.

The level of *interest rates* conditions the capacity for funds to structure attractive LBO deals. If debt is cheap, it is possible for funds to buy companies at a higher price and possibly to increase the debt-to-equity ratio of a deal[12] and thus the leverage effect. Interest rates also have an impact on exit paths for portfolio companies: the purchasing power of large companies depends partly on their ability to raise debt at a cheap price for the acquisition of private equity-backed companies.

If the level of financial leverage, and subsequently the potential default rate of the debt, is increasing, there is a probability that fund managers have structured their deals too aggressively (too much leverage). Portfolio companies may have trouble delivering the dividends to match the payment schedule. In the 1980s, the use of junk bonds was common in LBOs to finance the take-over movement. From 1983 to 1993, on average 14.3% of the proceeds from high-yield debt was used for financing LBOs. It was in 1986 to 1989 that LBO activity outpaced such refinancing, hinting at a bubble. By 1990, the default rates on high-yield debt had increased from 4% to 10%, revealing an overheating market (Scott, 2000).

2006 was cited as a high for LBO and VC, with a bubble being created. The difficulty of assessing the existence of a bubble in private equity lies in the fact that its natural cycles need to be appreciated in the context of a growth of assets under management. These cycles can be seen in the USA through the junk bond default rate for the 2002–2008 cycle (see Figure 6.5). The increase of capital managed by LBO fund managers is sustaining large take-overs which were never possible before the influx of capital. So, equity inflow may not be relevant to estimating the prospect of a bubble in a shifting market.

As for the debt side, even though the issuance of junk bonds has grown, default rates have remained under control and fell to record lows since 2010 as of the time of writing (August 2019). Anticipation from lenders reveals confidence that this will not change substantially as high-yield interest rates have not moved up significantly compared to investment grade debt. However, the debt market has its own dynamics which are driven by the prospect of default and reimbursement. The fact that covenants of debts are being relaxed (Tett, 2007) tends to prove that the default signal might have shifted. The debt market does not provide a long-term indication of the sustainability of the pace of investment by private equity.

Investors want to avoid investing during a financial bubble because this is synonymous with relative or absolute losses on investments. One of the ways to anticipate losses is to identify when asset prices are rising at a level which is deemed to be unsustainable, that is to say where the prospect of an ulterior sale will not generate returns.

This can be identified when the price paid for a company (in terms of multiple of EBIT or EBITDA for LBO and pre-money valuation for VC companies) is rising to a level which is also the level where the company will be acquired. However, in an efficient market, this phenomenon could be qualified as natural, especially as private

---

[12] Assuming that low interest rates increase the competition amongst banks to be involved in more lucrative deals and that regulators allow such practices.

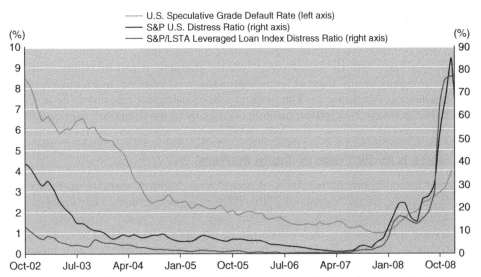

S&P distress ratio is defined as the number of speculative-grade issues with option-adjusted spreads above 1,000 bps divided by the total number of speculative-grade issues. Loan distressed ratio is defined as the percent of performing loans trading below 80 cents on the dollar. Data through Jan. 15. 2009.

FIGURE 6.5   Speculative grade default rate vs S&P distressed credit ratio
Source: S&P Global Fixed Income Research, S&P Credit Pro, S&P LCD, LSTA.

equity firms and strategic acquirers are competing for the same assets in LBOs. The diffusion of auctions for the sale of companies in LBOs is strengthening the idea that sooner or later, there will be a market price for any significant private asset. A discount on the market price granted to private equity firms for a specific asset would mean that this asset requires dedicated work. This is probably where private equity firms bring value.

The relative performance between asset classes, as well as the risk aversion of limited partners, determines the relative capital inflow in private equity. This can create shocks for the capital inflow, which is delayed compared to the true performance of each private equity segment. It is therefore difficult to determine whether there is a financial bubble at a given moment in a specific sector and segment of the private equity market without first assessing what is the market need for capital inflow and what is the reasonable level of valuation for a company at its current development stage.

The market need for capital inflow is difficult to determine, as this is conditioned partly by the number of company creations eligible to be venture capital-backed. These company creations are the result of the innovation potential of countries and the entrepreneurial spirit of their citizens. The need for capital inflow is also determined by the number of companies needing growth financing, which is formed by current economic and other business conditions, as to development capital. For LBO, it is a mix of development, acquisitions, internationalisation, reshaping and restructuring. These are determined by market conditions, macro-economic drivers (such as trade negotiations, for example), and also social and demographic factors (generational change, with baby boomers heading companies now preparing to retire; EVCA, 2005).

6.4   CONCLUSION

As a matter of synthesis, private markets could be described as a financial ecosystem living in symbiosis with the listed and non-listed markets. If private equity is able to finance a company at any stage of its development, it is, however, not a must-have for all companies (see Section 6.1). The optimal size of the sector remains to be assessed, due notably to the time-lag effect, but there is no capital overhang (see Section 6.2).

6.4.1   There is No Such Thing as 'Capital Overhang'

Each crisis affecting private equity is an occasion to doubt its viability, its future and even its role. The liquidity crisis of 2007–2009 was one of them. That crisis has led fund managers to lengthen the deployment time of their capital. Nevertheless, fund investors are still increasing their allocation to private markets. The apparent contradiction appears to drive observers to conclude too quickly that there is a mismatch between what is raised (Figure 6.6) and what can be deployed.

The question is: too much capital compared to what? Private equity represents roughly 4% of the market capitalisation of listed companies, which themselves represent 1% of the companies of the OECD. The potential pool of investment opportunities seems to be fairly large, even though no active company in the world is a potential target for a private equity investment. The underlying criticism of capital overhang is that some fund managers are accumulating capital, are unable to deploy it and will be unable to generate the expected returns. A small demonstration illustrates the difficulty of making such a statement confidently.

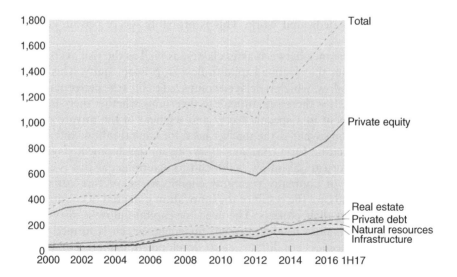

[1]Data not available for full 2017 year.

FIGURE 6.6   Capital committed and not deployed (USD billion)
Source: McKinsey 2018, based on Preqin.

6.4.2 Elements of Analysis

At first glance, year on year, the funds raised are overshadowing the amounts invested. This was the case, for example, in Europe over the period 1997–2011, with the exception of 1999, 2002–2004 and 2009–2011 (see Figure 6.7). Even worse, divestments are showing an increasing gap with investments. According to a year-on-year analysis, private equity would accumulate funds and be unable to liquidate its portfolio.

This is not the case. A first approach tends to prove that there is not too much capital (Figure 6.8). This illusion is attributed to the specificities of private equity, such as:

1. A capital deployment of funds raised over the course of the following 3 years. The correct assessment implies smoothing the funds raised according to a cash-flow pattern which is common to most private equity funds. To do so, the following simplified pattern of capital deployment has been used:

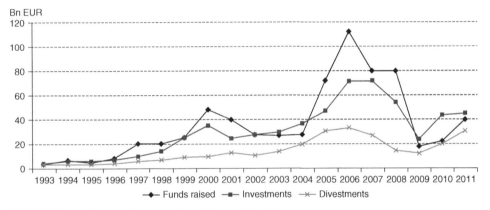

FIGURE 6.7 Funds raised, invested and divested in Europe
Source: Invest Europe (ex-EVCA, 1993–2011).

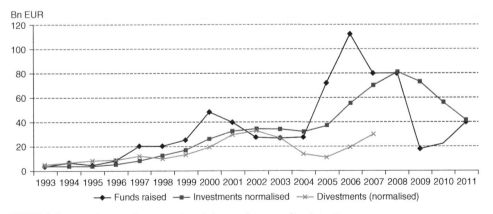

FIGURE 6.8 Funds raised, invested and divested (normalised) in Europe
Source: Author, from Invest Europe (ex-EVCA) figures (1993–2011).

	Year 1	Year 2	Year 3	Year 4	Year 5
Investment pattern	20%	25%	25%	20%	10%

A deployment of 100% of funds raised according to a classical investment curve explains the true investment curve and notably the smoothing effect of peaks and holes in fundraising efforts.

2. A holding period of 2 to 3 years on average (we assumed 2 years). To find the destiny of investments for a given year, it is necessary to look at the divestments 2 to 3 years after the investment (which is done, on average, 2 to 3 years after the fundraising – we assumed 2 years).

The result is not precise, nor perfect, as divestments appear to exceed investments in 1993–1997. This is due to the fact that holding periods vary over time, with fast exits for venture capital during the Internet bubble (prior to 2000) and then dividend recapitalisations when lending conditions are favourable in LBOs (hence returning capital fast, sometimes as early as after 12 to 18 months).

6.4.3 From 'Capital Overhang' to 'Dry Powder'

The picture is suddenly quite different: from the curves year-on-year which give an appearance of a growing gap, the normalised curves are showing curves which are converging towards the same trend. The two gaps which appear for the periods 1999–2002 and 2004–2008 (see Figure 6.9) between funds invested (normalised) and divestments (normalised) are the build-up of portfolios. As soon as this portfolio is built, and a threshold has been reached, further fundraisings are maintaining the activity. Figure 6.10 shows that LBO funds have on average around 1 year's worth of deals as a reserve of capital.

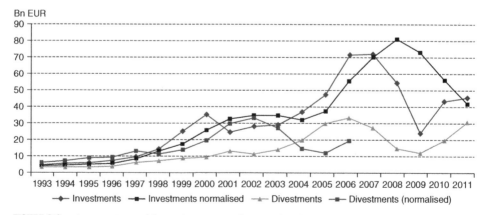

FIGURE 6.9 Comparison of factual curves and normalised curves
Source: Author, from Invest Europe (ex-EVCA) figures (1993–2011).

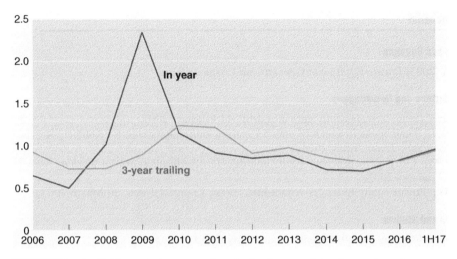

FIGURE 6.10 Available capital compared to deal volume activity, in number of years
Source: McKinsey 2018, based on PitchBook and Preqin.

As LBO secondaries are slowly developing as a major exit scenario for LBOs (or transfer from VC to LBO ownership, as IPOs are still at a very low level), the 'dry powder' is put to use and probably contributes to structuring a sector with its own dynamics.

It is not the volumes, but the acceleration and deceleration of capital deployment which are the most prejudicial to private equity. The core of the debate is thus the expected performance, which is conditioned by the amounts allocated to the sector and the timing of this allocation.

Obviously, the bubbles have been generated by an acceleration of the investments, as was the case in 1998–2000 and 2005–2006. On the contrary, the corrections of 2001 and 2008–2009 also appear clearly. The inversion of the curves in 2002 and 2009 have repercussions for the returns on investments: these are some of the vintage years generating the best returns on investment.

The collective responsibility of fund investors is in that respect very important in the determination of future rates of return (see in that regard Mulcahy, Weeks & Bradley, 2012). Paradoxically, it is the fund investors which are increasing brutally and massively their allocations to private equity (which is in fact ill-prepared for this massive and brutal capital inflow) that are contributing the most to the degradation of performance of the sector.

The question is therefore the following: are fund investors able to adopt a certain Malthusianism and master the deployment of their capital collectively? Or can they support a strong dynamic of financial innovation and place private equity in the ranks of asset classes to be backed as such? This would mean revising the number of fund managers applying the same investment strategy and bidding for the same assets, facilitating the concentration of these structures to lower the fees per euro invested. With regard to these questions, the maturity of fund investors as to these issues remains to be assessed.

REFERENCES

Books and Booklets

EVCA (2005) *Private Equity and Generational Change*, 48 pp.

Newsletters and Newspapers

Financial Times, 'Private equity goes into debt', 11 February 2007.

Norris, F., 'Fund books loss on RJR after 15 years: a long chapter ends for Kohlberg Kravis', *The New York Times*, 9 July 2004.

Salter, M., 'Learning from private equity boards', *Harvard Business School Working Knowledge*, 17 January 2007.

Tett, G., 'Private equity raises "covenant-lite" loans', *Financial Times*, 20 March 2007.

Papers and Studies

Bain and Company (2019) 'Global private equity report', 88 pp.

Cao, J. and Lerner, J. (2006) 'The performance of reverse leveraged buyouts', Boston College, Harvard University and National Bureau of Economic Research, 48 pp.

Mulcahy, D., Weeks, B. and Bradley, H. (2012) 'We have met the enemy ... and he is us', Ewing Marion Kauffman Foundation, 52 pp.

Scott, J. (2000) 'Drexel Burnham Lambert: a ten-year retrospective', Austrian Scholar's Conference, Auburn University, 41 pp.

CHAPTER 7

Private Equity and Ethics
A Culture Clash

It is no small claim to make that until the emergence of private markets as a modern financial sector (see Chapter 2), there would have been no reason to write this chapter at all. Prior to that the subject of ethics was either aligned with entrepreneurial spirit through what Adam Smith described as 'acting in one's and at the same time the general public's best interest'; or was associated with religious and political endeavours and had no chance to be assessed separately – and even less to be debated.

The emergence of the rule of law has separated practices which used to be connected, such as setting the rules and benefitting from them; or the roles of manager and controller being combined in one person. The professionalisation of private markets has also introduced separation between principal and agent (see Chapter 2), which has increased the potential for conflicts of interest.

The list of potential malpractices would be very long and it is not the purpose of this chapter to list them all, but to understand their dynamics, make an attempt at classification and derive some lessons from them. Private equity being a small and mainly local activity until 20 years ago, fund investors and managers would know each other well. The sanction of an ethical breach would be simply the exclusion of the sector, as word spread fast amongst the community of private equity stakeholders. With a massive influx of capital, private markets had to face a sudden change in the number of participants in the private markets value chain, and the volume of potential breaches involved. The sanction of ethical breach was far less easy to apply, and the law – the last resort – was used more often.

The more an economic sector develops, the more it tempts individuals willing to benefit from this growth at all costs. Legal sanctions are not enough to guarantee that private markets can be practised in safe conditions (see Section 7.1). As getting rich quick is considered to be socially abnormal, successful individuals decided to buy themselves some moral credentials through philanthropy (see Section 7.2). To limit inequalities and establish some boundaries for market or public intervention, the main rule which was applied was transparency (see Section 7.3). However, this solution has proven to be imperfect, and private markets have to work on deontology, self-regulation and ethical behaviour (see Section 7.4). It is only checks and balances that can reconcile the market's need for flexibility and the public's need for collective and individual protection from predatory practices.

7.1   GREED

The financial crisis has exposed some of the hidden practices of financial agents. Private markets have evolved within the space of approximately two generations from a traditional and informal practice to a separation between investors and investment managers. By comparison, the stock exchange has had a hundred years of evolution in which to cope with its increasing sophistication and transformation. In that sense, private markets provide a mixed picture, dominated by a certain *greed* on the part of fund managers. However, the main challenge, once this transition was made – along with the emergence of new ethical standards, was to manage the long-term and potentially disruptive and destructive impact of private equity.

Fraud: AA Capital Partners and John Orecchio (USA)

A few cases of *obvious fraud* emerged, such as that at AA Capital Partners, a Chicago-based private equity firm.[1] The firm managed USD 200 million for six unions and advised on pension funds from 2002 to 2006. One of the two founders, John Orecchio, had spent money on travel, entertainment and in a Detroit strip club where he had a mistress, according to the SEC (FinAlternatives, 2009). Orecchio bought some real estate in Michigan for his mistress and her mother, including a horse farm (also covering the costs of renovation), a boat, luxury automobiles and jewellery worth a total of USD 1.4 million.

In 2004, Orecchio asked AA Capital Partners' CFO to withdraw money from the client trust accounts, to put it into AA Capital's operating account, before wiring it into his personal account. At least 20 withdrawals were made for a total of USD 5.7 million.

The SEC also described how Orecchio lied to his partner Oliver about a real-estate development investment, stating that the costs amounted to USD 8.7 million when he had in fact invested only USD 1.3 million. The remaining USD 6.9 million was used to renovate the above-mentioned real estate belonging to his mistress (the horse farm and strip club) and for the acquisition of a condominium in Las Vegas.

Orecchio also claimed reimbursement for expenses that were not billable to AA Capital's clients: political contributions, visits to casinos and strip clubs, and tickets to concerts or events. To fulfil a need for income of USD 10 million, the CFO withdrew money from the client accounts. Orecchio benefitted from the help of his business partner and the CFO of the firm.

In this case, the violation of the law is clear: an investment advisor engaged in transactions, did business and employed practices at the expense of his investors. However, not all frauds are so obvious, and thus detectable by the SEC.

Fraud: Private Equity Management and Danny Pang (Asia)

In another case which was investigated (AltAssets, 2009), Danny Pang, founder and former chief executive of Private Equity Management, was accused of having used his

---

[1]Another case emerged in 2017, with Andrew Caspersen, a former principal at Coller Capital and executive at Park Hill, specialised in secondaries investing. He was convicted of securities and wires fraud and sentenced to 4 years in prison. He created a fake credit facility related to a staple secondary transaction, trying to defraud two institutional investors out of USD 95 million to feed his gambling habit. The lack of transparency which characterises private markets, and specifically the secondary sector, provided the 'perfect cover' for this fraud, according to Igor Rozenblitz, co-head of the private equity funds unit at the SEC.

family members as employees in order to cash cheques, the amount of which remained just below USD 10 000 (the minimum threshold for filing transaction reports). The total amount is assumed to have reached USD 83 million. In another case, Pang was accused of defrauding investors based in Asia for many million dollars (between USD 287 and 654 million). In both these cases, the alleged fraudster used geographical distance and a certain legal flexibility in order to misappropriate funds.

Geographical distance plays a role not only in variations between legal systems, but also in cultural differences. Many investors have invested in emerging markets on the assumption that the local fund managers – sometimes educated in Western universities – were conforming to Western business practices. However, the perception of conflicts of interest and good business practice in China and India may differ substantially from that which is perceived as such in the OECD. In particular, some countries may not have reached the degree of political, social and economic maturity which forms the background for modern private equity in Europe and the USA.

Interpretative and cultural differences are not merely anecdotal in private equity. As discussed in Chapter 5, human interactions are at the centre of the generation of deal flow, the investment process, investment management and divestment management. It is especially difficult to draw a clear line between what is an exchange of services and what is the misappropriation of interests. For example, doing business in China may imply spending money in order to gain access to certain attractive opportunities.

Fraud: Abraaj Group, Arif Naqvi and KPMG (Middle East)

In a similar fashion, the executives of Abraaj Group defrauded fund investors. Created in 2002, this fund manager quickly rose to be the largest in the Middle East, managing USD 14 billion, having launched 30 funds in private equity, private debt, private real estate and energy strategies, as well as an impact investing activity dedicated to Africa, Asia, Latin America and Turkey. In 2015 alone, the structure raised USD 1.4 billion to invest in Africa. The firm faced recurring issues of overspending, accumulating losses and debts.

In 2018, fund investors, among them the IFC and the Bill and Melinda Gates Foundation, accused the fund manager of mismanaging capital of USD 230 million from a USD 1 billion healthcare fund. USD 300 million appeared to be missing from its USD 1.6 billion Fund IV. KPMG was mandated to investigate the case and exonerated the firm. However, the auditing firm had very close ties to Abraaj. The CEO of KPMG in Dubai had a son who worked at Abraaj, notably; and was the auditor of portfolio companies of Abraaj. The case was further complicated by the fact that the funds raised before 2013 did not have any external administrator.

Abraaj applied for provisional liquidation in June 2018. In 2019, the Dubai Financial Services Authority fined the group USD 315 million for deceiving investors, misusing investor funds to cover operational expenses and carrying out unauthorised activities. In the USA, the same year, the founder of Abraaj Arif Naqvi and other senior executives were indicted for misappropriating funds to cover operational expenses. Naqvi himself is accused of personally misappropriating USD 250 million, and is under house arrest in London at the time of writing.

British fund manager Actis took over the management of Abraaj's fourth buyout fund, as well as one of its African funds. American fund managers TPG and Colony Capital have taken over its healthcare fund and Latin American fund.

Collusions and insider trading (France)

In 2007 in France, the Autorité des Marchés Financiers (AMF) investigated potential collusion between hedge funds and private equity funds (names were not disclosed) to force a listed company to accept a buy-out (Mackintosh & Arnold, 2007). There was a suspicion that activist funds pushed the management into selling the companies while having at the same time a pre-arranged sales agreement with some buy-out firms. The collusion of different actors is especially difficult to detect and can cause severe damage to the economy.

Collusion and insider trading: New Silk Route and Galleon (India)

Insider trading is difficult to prove, notably in the case of private equity. Nevertheless, connections are sometimes a hint that some fund managers are built on a fragile basis. This is the case of New Silk Route, an 'Asia-focused growth capital firm focused on the Indian subcontinent' (see Primack, 2011), which is connected to three persons convicted in the USA for insider trading:

- Rajat Gupta, who was charged in the Galleon Management case, is chairman and co-founder of the firm which manages USD 1.4 billion.
- Raj Rajaratnam, who was also convicted in the Galleon Management case, was listed in 2008 as a principal of the firm. New Silk Route (formerly known as Taj Capital) originally allocated USD 600 million to invest in the Galleon hedge funds, hence raising deep concerns in terms of management of conflicts of interest.
- Victor Menezes, who was investigated in 2006 by the SEC for insider trading of USD 30 million for selling Citigroup stocks just before the bank announced major losses related to the Argentinean debt crisis. He settled with the SEC without admitting or denying any wrongdoing for USD 2.7 million.

Such a network of dubious individuals raises concerns when fund investors have to select emerging fund managers on emerging markets. At the time of investment in New Silk Route, these facts were unknown (except maybe for Victor Menezes). However, this case illustrates the difficulty of analysing the quality of a fund manager and the need for thorough due diligence.[2]

Collusion and corruption: 'pay to play' (USA)

Another illustration of collusion (and corruption) is the so-called 'pay-to-play' scandal. Nineteen private equity firms[3] were awarded advisory mandates by pension funds and public investment vehicles as a reward for donations to the campaigns of elected officials (FinAlternatives, 2009). As a result, the SEC have barred investment firms whose executives and employees donate to the campaigns of elected officials from being awarded such mandates.

---

[2]This can go as far as recruiting private investigators such as Kroll to assess the background of individuals and their situation when the information is scarce – notably on emerging markets.

[3]Of which FS Equity Partners, Wetherly Capital Group, Ares Corporate Opportunities, Aldus Equity, Levine Leichtman Capital Partners, Odyssey Investment Partners, Carlyle Realty Partners, Carlyle Europe Real Estate Partners, Carlyle/Riverstone Global Energy & Power, Carlyle/Riverstone Renewable Energy Infrastructures, Quadrangle Capital, Paladin Homeland Security, Pequot Private Equity, GKM, Lion Capital, Sector Performance, Strategic Co-investment, Falconhead Capital Partners, Access Capital Partners – see Hausmann (2009).

This measure was the consequence of an investigation by Attorney-General Andrew Cuomo, who revealed that placement agents paid kickbacks to the New York Comptroller in exchange for mandates from the NY Common Retirement Fund. These placement agents (namely Aldus Equity) were acting in the name of private equity and hedge fund managers. The Attorney-General settled the case in exchange for fines (USD 20 million for Carlyle) and an agreement that these groups would stop using placement agents from that point on.

Whether these measures will help to prevent future scandals of this nature is difficult to assess. Placement agents have a genuine function in gaining access to capital providers, notably because they know the executives who make the decisions. This saves time and money in the fundraising process. Moreover, it is especially difficult to exclude some sort of bargaining in the award of such mandates, notably because of the human element in their devolution. If there were no financial rewards involved, there could be other forms of compensation that would be difficult to trace or even to criticise.

What if a politician is a direct, or even more difficult, indirect (through funds of funds, for example) fund investor in a fund; that this fund is awarded a mandate; and that this mandate has been distributed with the consent of this politician? Would it be bad? Yes, *if* the politician gives the mandate on the basis that he knows the fund manager. No, *because* the politician gives the mandate on the same grounds. In the first case, there is a violation of the rules of impartiality which regulate the administration of public money and the set-up of calls for tender offers. In the second case, there is compliance with the best practices of private equity which require an investor to know the fund manager with whom he is investing. He would not choose an incompetent fund manager because he has put his own money in the fund managed by this particular fund manager. He would hence align his interests and the public's interest. But he may be tempted to choose the fund manager because he has invested with it.

Should we 'ban the politicians' from such decisions, as was suggested (Private Equity Online, 2009)? The debate stands between people who are accountable for their decisions (politicians) and people who are not (administrative executives). Politicians need to be elected, which costs money, but can be ousted for bad management/results. Administrative executives have the security of the job, and thus are theoretically less prone to corruption, but also more difficult to fire for bad management/results.

Valuation manipulation and fundraising: Roc Resources (USA)

The SEC launched an investigation in 2012 on Roc Resources[4] (formerly Oppenheimer & Co's private equity firm, which spun off 2 weeks after the start of the investigation; see Zuckerman, 2012). The fund of funds invested in a Romanian holding, valued at USD 6 million as of 30 June 2009 (NAV). During a fundraising in November 2009,

---

[4]A more recent case of valuation manipulation involves Veronis Suhler Stevenson, this time in the case of a fund restructuring. The firm was charged, as well as its managing partner Jeffrey Stevenson, by the SEC that it failed to provide fund investors with material information on a change of value of a 1998-vintage fund. VSS and Stevenson had set in 2015 a tender offer process to buy fund investors' stakes (GP-led restructuring). They failed to disclose that the NAV of the fund had risen after the offer letter. They settled the charge for a USD 200 000 civil penalty without admitting or denying the charges.

the valuation was USD 9.2 million, still announced as of 30 June 2009 (NAV). Primack (2012a) states that 'the change increased the fund's overall net IRR from −6.3% to +38.3%'. The fund raised more than USD 55 million from individuals and institutions.

This valuation is contentious, because the underlying asset was listed on the OTC, so it had a public price (7 cents for the Romanian assets vs 20 cents reported by investors). The Romanian asset was worth USD 2 million based on trading, reported at USD 6 million by its holding (Cartesian Capital) and at USD 9.3 million by Oppenheimer.

Excessive fee collection: Lincolnshire Management (USA)

Acconci Trust has sued Lincolnshire Management for not distributing the proceeds from a court decision to award USD 99 million in a case involving Cendent Corp (Vardi, 2011). The Trust claims that Lincolnshire Equity Fund wrongfully deducted fees, expenses and interest and misappropriated an additional USD 7.6 million from the case. Lincolnshire Management denies any wrongdoing.

In 2004 Acconci Trust bought a stake in the Lincolnshire Equity Fund 1994 on the secondary market – it owns 51% of the fund managed by Lincolnshire Management. The management fee is capped at 2% of assets under management, and all fees above the cap have to be returned to the fund. After selling a portfolio company (Credentials Services International) in 1998 to Cendant for USD 125 million plus an earn-out, Cendant was sued for breaching the terms of the agreement. Out of the USD 99 million awarded in 2009 by the court, USD 74 million remained in 2009 after legal fees, but only USD 45 million was distributed to the limited partners. Lincolnshire was charging 'litigation expenses' of USD 4.1 million and interest on amounts advanced for expenses of USD 1 million. USD 5 million was charged for the time spent on the dispute, and USD 7.6 million deducted as a refund of an unrecorded loan.

In 2014, Lincolnshire Management paid USD 2.3 million to the SEC to settle other charges of improper expense allocations, involving two of its funds' investments in Peripheral Computer Support, which subsequently acquired Computer Technology Solutions. The SEC accused the fund manager of breaching its fiduciary duty to the two private equity funds when it misallocated costs related to its management to Computer Technology Solutions. In practice, it favoured one fund over the other.

Excessive fund extension: Behrman Capital (USA)

In 2000, Behrman Capital raised USD 1.2 billion for its third LBO fund (Primack, 2012b). In 2012, the fund raised USD 1 billion, because the fund manager refused to liquidate the fund's five remaining portfolio companies. Primack states that while 'some limited partners are pleased that they're getting bought out [. . .] others are livid [. . . as] all of them are practically powerless to do anything about it'. This is an example of secondary operation where the fund manager is the buyer and the seller of the assets, in a so-called GP-led restructuring.

Indeed, Behrman sold the portfolio for USD 750 million, plus an additional USD 250 million for new investments, to the Canada Pension Plan Investment Board and additional investors. Hence, Behrman gets the carried interest on the current exit and will get additional carried on the upcoming liquidations, as it remains the fund manager. Meanwhile, it will receive management fees.

Primack explains: 'Can't the LPs [limited partners] just refuse to let this happen? Technically yes. Pragmatically no. Imagine the LPs refused to accept this deal. What is their next move? Hire a new GP or consultant to manage out the remaining portfolio – one that is less familiar with the underlying companies? Simply refuse to keep paying fees to Behrman GPs – ok, but what incentive do Behrman GPs have to show up at work [...]?'

As a conclusion: 'Behrman also gets to raise new primary capital (which generates brand new fees) without formal fundraising process (like the one that largely failed in 2007). In short, it's just another example of how general partners hold almost all the cards, no matter how the original agreement is written.'

Since then, the practice of GP-led restructuring has developed and gained ground. The potential conflicts of interest are largely unresolved, but the practice is increasingly frequent.

Potential solutions and evolutions

The solution may lie in the separation of functions, between control and decision, with real sanctions when one fails. Another can be seen in the fact that everyone has to be on the control side of other actors in the private equity chain, while also taking their own decisions, which are controlled by the others. Even though this does not guarantee an absence of misbehaviour, it helps to prevent it. If control is assumed by more than one player, then it is difficult to fool the controllers substantially and on a recurring basis.

At the moment, these financial checks and balances do not exist. This is why the fund manager's personality, integrity and ethics need to be assessed carefully. This is becoming increasingly difficult.

The first difficulty stems from the lack of references and immersion in the fund manager's environment. Despite lists of references that a fund investor may call upon – usually friends and business partners of the former – it is difficult to learn about his reputation, actions and overall his philosophy of investing.

The second difficulty is related to the professionalisation of fund manager. Speeches and documents are polished until they almost reach perfection, and it is difficult to get behind this façade. The lack of time for both fund investors and managers reduces their interaction and their ability to gain mutual understanding of their respective approaches.

In the short term, regulators have ramped up their efforts. The SEC has 'launched a wide-ranging inquiry into the private equity industry, particularly with respect to insider trading and how firms address conflicts of interest' (Burwell, 2012). The SEC will notably control whether private equity fund managers (managing more than USD 150 million) comply with the Dodd–Frank Act, as 'investment advisers' and have effective policies and procedures to prevent insider trading.

As for conflicts of interest, Burwell mentions that the SEC focused on the following questions:

- The use of consistent and documented valuation methods.
- The use of side letters to give certain fund investors preferential treatment.
- Fundraising beyond the operational means to deploy the capital raised, to maximise the fees.
- The allocation of opportunities between multiple funds managed by a single fund manager.
- The accuracy of the reporting to fund investors in terms of fund performance.
- The determination and disclosure of fees charged to portfolio companies.
- The management of 'zombie' companies, notably in case of extension of the lives of mature funds.

Whether the SEC will be able to cope with the amount of work that this represents remains to be seen. According to Private Equity Online (2011): 'about 800 SEC employees monitor the existing 11 000 registered investment advisors, and insiders say the SEC's plan to hire 400 more people likely won't be enough. [. . .] That's a worrying prospect for an industry that needs regulators to fully appreciate and understand their various strategies, or risk becoming targets of time-consuming (and expensive) audits or other compliance inquiries.'

However, this effort might actually lead to better disclosures, a higher level of transparency and also clarify performance (Sutton, 2012). This is notably related to the LBO payout investigation from the SEC, related to the distribution of proceeds, as well as 'broken deal' fees.

7.2 DESTRUCTION

In many countries, private markets still have room to grow. When assessing the development of private markets, we rely mainly on national statistics gathered by national or regional associations. These statistics are assembled by means of declarations by local fund managers and present a bias: they do not account for the activity of private market investors who do not belong to these associations (such as corporations, sovereign wealth funds, family offices and independent funds). Moreover, there can be a significant difference between the money managed in a given country and the money invested in that country. Some countries are net exporters of capital, others are net importers. This has significant consequences for local economies which cannot rely on permanent resources.

In its World Investment Report, the United Nations Conference on Trade and Development (UNCTAD, 2006) stated that more than half the capital of private equity funds was being used for foreign direct investment (FDI). In 2005, more than USD 100 billion (out of a total of USD 904 billion) was invested outside the country where the fund's manager was based. The concern of the United Nations is that *with this capital outflow, there is no associated transfer of technology* and the investments are made on a comparatively shorter term than the usual FDIs (the consequences of this were seen in Section 4.1, as emerging markets have seen some of their sources of financing dry up). We would add that some of these flows are very volatile and can dry up quickly.

Employment and private equity

Furthermore, UNCTAD raises some concerns about the employment balance of these investments. Private equity is a net creator of employment in Europe and the USA. This appears to be obvious for venture capital and growth capital, which create employment at their genesis and with the ramp-up of revenues. Chapter 4 also develops the question of employment creation in LBO and turn-around investing. However, the question of job creation merits two specific developments: the need to approach job creation from a top-down perspective, and the timeframe involved.

Venture capital finances start-ups, which are by construction creating new positions from scratch. However, the reasoning does not stop there. These positions might be created for a limited amount of time if the start-up does not succeed, which then reduces the track record of venture capital in terms of employment. One might even argue that these short-lived positions might generate negative externalities for the wider economy and society. More importantly, the positions created in a start-up might have eliminated one or more in the larger economy. The positions eliminated in the larger economy have to be taken into account. An illustration would be the replacement of employed taxi drivers with a stable position by precarious freelancers in the so-called gig economy.

As for net job creation in the case of LBO, the case rests on observing the evolution of companies on an aggregate basis over the mid term. However, in the short term, an acquisition might lead to the suppression of positions. This stresses the economic and social system until the company creates new positions, which might be filled by different profiles. The result might be unemployed workers with skills difficult to reuse or change, the cost of which is supported collectively – instead of having the company taking over this task through training and reconversion of its workforce.

Growing responsibilities

Is economic growth fuelled by private market investments? Venture and growth capital participate in the emergence of companies and new activities. LBO could have an impact on long-term productivity gains, even though the scale of its contribution to long-term GDP growth has yet to be demonstrated. As private equity's influence grows along with the amount of capital it manages, its responsibilities increase correspondingly.

Adopting the vision of private equity as part of the financial and economic ecosystem means that private equity must assume the burden which comes with its new position – and generate positive externalities. Private equity not only plays a crucial role in the development of the countries in which it invests, but also influences how the companies in which it invests will behave with regard to their social, economic and general environment.

Private equity creates value through better governance (Guo, Hotchkiss & Song, 2008 for LBOs; Gompers & Xuan, 2008 for venture capital) and tighter monitoring (Katz, 2008 – this applies to LBOs but is true for venture capital too). Thus, fund managers have the tools to exert a critical influence on the behaviour of the management of their portfolio companies. They are able to dictate the requirements of respecting the ethical, social and environmental criteria which are demanded by sustainable development at an early stage.

This goes beyond the typical pledges made by large firms about their commitment to act in favour of protecting the environment or against climate change. These are merely cosmetic measures and a matter of fashionable corporate image ('green washing'). Private equity fund managers' concentration of ownership gives them the power and the responsibility to act in support of these principles. They have the financial resources to apply – and even to develop – state-of-the-art measuring tools and to contribute actively to the establishment of triple bottom line evaluation (economic, social and environmental). In this respect, they have no excuse for lagging behind the meagre efforts of listed companies.

Towards the internalisation of externalities: the triple bottom line

What could push fund managers to act in favour of the development of this triple bottom line is the importance of their *reputation*. As we have seen earlier in this chapter, fund investors are extremely sensitive to the reputation of fund managers, and even more so since the sector has expanded rapidly and widely. Many academic papers show that the reputation of fund managers, whether in venture capital (Gompers & Xuan, 2008; Hsu, 2004) or in LBOs (Guo, Hotschkiss & Song, 2008; Katz, 2008), is their main asset. This reputation allows them to attract the best investment opportunities, to negotiate favourable terms with entrepreneurs (this can reach a 30% discount on the company valuation; Hsu, 2004) and to exit under favourable terms (Gompers & Xuan, 2008).

Fund managers can reduce the destructive impact of their activities and optimise the triple bottom line by:

- Exercising social and environmental due diligence aside from their other audits when they evaluate an investment opportunity (buyer due diligence).
- Setting measurement criteria to monitor these elements, as well as assessing the corporate culture of the company on a regular basis.
- Exercising exactly the same due diligence as at entry, when selling the company (vendor due diligence).

Beyond words: the EDF private equity management tool

The Environmental Defense Fund (EDF) has set up and provided to the public[5] an environmental, social and governance (ESG) management tool for private equity. Figure 7.1 provides the general framework, which is then broken down into 22 criteria. These criteria, once documented, allow fund managers to position the investment according to best practice and to follow the progression over time.

Figures 7.2 and 7.3 then sum up the input and the results, which are used as a support for further action. This evaluation is a support to action and improvement for fund managers. Given their ability to develop new methods and monitoring tools, there is no reason why they cannot carry out this three-step procedure in record time.

It is up to the fund investors to impose these requirements when they commit to a fund. If a fund investor is excluded because it wants to integrate the triple bottom line with the evaluation of the fund's performance, it can leverage the reputation effect and weigh in to change this attitude (see Section 7.3). Foundations and insurance groups should logically be the first in line to put pressure on fund managers.

Do fund managers have the means to work on these issues? As they have a significant control on their portfolio companies (Kelleher, 2011), and as these companies are more flexible and adaptable than most of the large listed group, the answer is yes. Moreover, often enough, the dimensions which are highlighted in the EDF document are actually part of the value creation assessment which is done by fund managers at the time of investment (see Chapter 4).

The only obstacles which could prevent implementation are:

(i) The costs involved – setting up this monitoring, on top of the others, requires time, effort and money. Whether the investment will be recouped is a matter of documenting and communicating the results. Indeed, as a significant proportion of the value of portfolio companies is immaterial, documenting the human capital, the know-how, the expertise, the processes and other areas of the activity of the company can only help at exit time to optimise the value.

---

[5] www.edf.org/greenreturns.

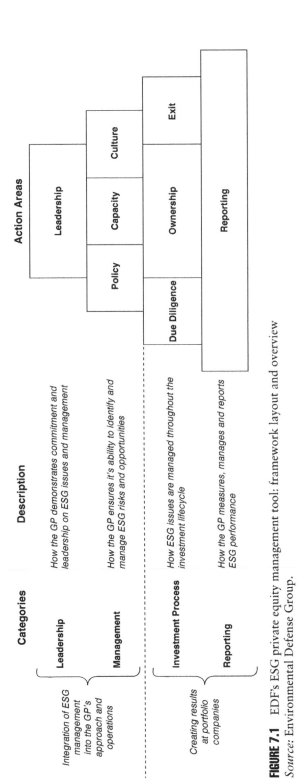

FIGURE 7.1 EDF's ESG private equity management tool: framework layout and overview
Source: Environmental Defense Group.

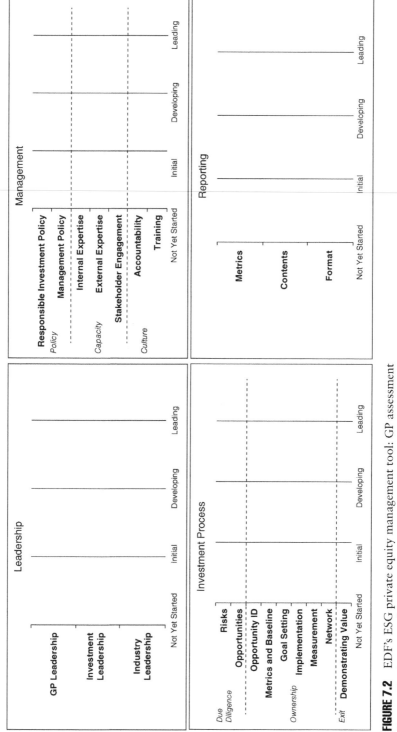

FIGURE 7.2 EDF's ESG private equity management tool: GP assessment

Source: Environmental Defense Group.

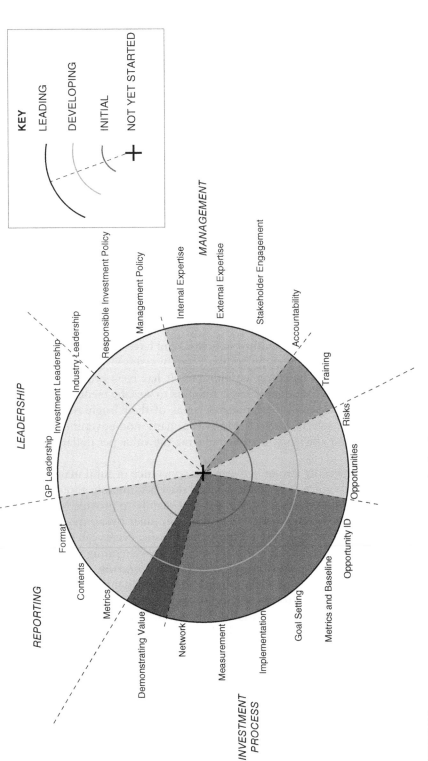

FIGURE 7.3 EDF's ESG private equity management tool: visual assessment
Source: Environmental Defense Group.

(ii) The conflicting outcomes of a financial analysis (cost cutting, for example) and of the EDF assessment. The temptation would be to bypass the second element to give way to cost cutting. However, as the second assessment is also a long-term commitment, it might be that this conflict reveals a deeper concern about the strategy, the positioning and the overall assumptions on which the business is made. If reducing the number of employees conflicts with the EDF assessment in human management, it might be time to review the training policies, the insourcing/outsourcing approach of the company and other elements which actually influence the conflicting diagnostics.

7.3 PHILANTHROPY

The fig leaf of philanthropy

Philanthropy has been promoted to the rank of ethical proof of good behaviour. Many hedge and private market fund managers have been actively involved in the charity business, thus promoting their names and giving an appearance of morality to their activities. Not only are these actions done mainly in order to achieve self-promotion, sometimes aiming at the survival of a reputation beyond one's lifetime, but their impact is also far from being optimal.

Private and uncoordinated philanthropic actions can have disastrous consequences, notably because the needs of the population are rarely assessed locally but according to a grand scheme which is based on assumptions. It has been proven, for example, that private foundations which donate large amounts to specific medical research programmes are depriving other medical research areas of their brightest professionals, thus having an adverse selection effect. Moreover, many non-governmental agencies lack professionalism and efficiency, thereby reducing the value per dollar collected for or granted to them.

The contrast is especially strong between the reluctance of fund managers to pay taxes (a lingering debate since 2007 in the UK and the USA, notably about treating the carried interest as income tax-wise), which are used mainly to provide public services and support the more deprived population groups, and their over-exposed role in the philanthropic area. The cost of galas and charity fundraising events often looks obscene when compared to the practical result that these sums are generating.

Venture philanthropy, social venturing, community venturing …

'Social' or 'community' venture capital and 'venture philanthropy' (see Balsham, Brown, Lee & Rubalevskaya, 2011) embrace an impressive set of initiatives. It is not the purpose here to criticise these efforts or their goals. However, it has to be noted very precisely that the borderline between high-risk/high-return for-profit activities on the one hand and low- or no-return activities on the other may not exist.

Private equity has built a powerful model (as seen in the previous six chapters) to generate profits and distribute them. This model is built on a strong alignment of interests between providers of capital (fund investors) and their agents (fund managers). To do so, corporate governance has been pushed forward, and incentives are used to motivate the staff (stock options) and to put pressure on them to succeed (financial leverage in the case of an LBO, remaining cash until the next milestone – and subsequent fundraising for ventures).

Would this model be used for non-profit? First, alignments of interest are difficult to structure, because the providers of capital may have very different motivations for being involved in such social endeavour (recognition, reputation, involvement, religion, etc.). It is hence difficult to align them with the social venture which is financed as these goals are heterogeneous – and also difficult to measure.

Profit is rather easy to measure as there is a common standard for it. Measuring the impact of a social endeavour is much more difficult. How can one measure the reputation improvement associated with a social venture?

Incentives are even more difficult to put in place. First, because beyond the satisfaction of working on such a project, the outcome will be mostly immaterial and often not even distributable. Hence, the activity itself is the reward for the staff involved – but that does not guarantee efficiency and the best use of the resources provided.

Name, shame and remember: the powerful leverage of reputation

In other words, it is the responsibility of each fund manager to do what social or community investors do, without any doubt or exception. However, this should be the case for every single fund manager – social, philanthropic, community or any other 'classic' one.

Rejecting this statement is proof that the fund manager is itself a source of risk which is not mitigated – and cannot be by the fund investor itself in any way. As a matter of fact, negative externalities, whether environmental, social, reputational or any other, eventually form a backlash which is increasingly hitting the fund manager, but also its fund investors as well.

Pension funds as fund investors are very sensitive to these issues. For example, Cerberus Capital Management divested from Freedom Group after the Newton school shooting in 2012 under the pressure of its limited partners (among them CalSTRS). Freedom Group manufactured the weapon used to kill 28 people in an elementary school. The indirect share of CalSTRS in Freedom Grop amounted to 2.4%. Although Cerberus put Freedom Group for sale 4 days after the shooting, there were no takers. CalSTRS voted to divest from firearms holdings in January 2013, but it was only in June 2015 that it could effectively divest from Freedom Group as Cerberus effectively created a twin fund to the existing one without the ownership of Freedom Group. The company ultimately went bankrupt in 2018.

As much as non-financial issues are concerned, it is hence reputations which are at the core of private markets. They are the leverage through which fund managers are motivated to act and take into account the context of their activity – much more than giving, pledging and rubbing shoulders with other socialites in evening gowns and black ties.

7.4 TRANSPARENCY

The long march to greater transparency started in San Francisco

In December 2002, the San Francisco Superior Court ruled (*Mercury News v CalPERS*) in favour of the application of the Freedom of Information Act (FOIA) to the private equity portfolio of CalPERS. The pension fund, followed by others in several American states, complied and published the individual performance of the private equity funds it invested in on a regular basis. This pressure in favour of transparency followed the initial disclosure of the private equity investments of Ross Perot in 1992 during the US Presidential election and later the Enron scandal (Chaplinsky, 2004).

The decision of the Court shed light on a very opaque sector: suddenly, the industry was no longer protected by a veil of confidentiality. One of the official concerns of the fund managers was the lack of general understanding about the performance, the J-curve phenomenon and the lack of liquidity of the asset class. This objection was quickly dismissed, as the press, which initiated the lawsuit, as well as the pension fund, are supposed to provide explanations about this performance.

Track records and fees once the wave recedes: who bathed naked?

Another issue was that any written communication between CalPERS and the fund managers should be disclosed – which could harm the portfolio companies of the funds issuing quarterly reports. However, some limits could be set for the disclosure in order to protect business secrets. In fact, CalPERS had only to disclose the performance of funds and possibly the fees collected by fund managers. The fact that CalPERS did not know until recently how much in fees was being collected by its fund managers generated some concern, highlighting knowledge gaps in such a large institution.

Fund investors reacted positively to this decision, which rebalanced the power between them and the fund managers by making the information more accessible. The industry suddenly realised that when it became an asset class, it was no longer able to keep parts of the most sensitive data secret from investors: fees and performance. Hence, it was possible not only to compare the performance of fund managers, but also to compare their valuation methods and to understand how they structured their fees.

What fund managers disliked was that it was now possible to further analyse their performance and compare their marketing pitch with the reality of the market. In particular, it was possible to ascertain the true contribution of funds to the success of their portfolio companies by benchmarking them with other funds of the same vintage.

As already discussed, reputation is important for fund managers. It is reputation which attracts the best opportunities, which enables fund managers to negotiate the terms of their investment and possibly get concessions from the other side and to obtain better exit conditions for their investments (Nahata, 2007). Reputation also supports their claims for management fees and carried interest. If the market becomes more transparent, investors will rely less on reputation and more on the facts. This also applies to entrepreneurs and managers.

Consequences

The consequences of disclosure were mixed. As there were more fund investors willing to enter the asset class than funds offered, existing fund investors had limited room left to negotiate a reduction of the fees and the carried interest. However, performance could be better analysed and the debate about the application of fair market value to the portfolios increased the analysis of unrealised performance.

Surprisingly, entrepreneurs were also better informed. It appeared that serial entrepreneurs were increasingly not so keen to work again with the same investors they had been working with before (Bengtsson, 2008). Entrepreneurs even started to share actively their knowledge about potential investors through initiatives such as TheFunded.com.

Transparency was therefore not a risk for their portfolio companies, but for the fund managers' own interests as agents. Even worse, the barriers to entry that they had built patiently through an existing track record (as opposed to a limited or no track record for new entrants) could suddenly be lowered dramatically by the fund investors' ability to obtain detailed means of comparison.

The movement towards transparency is still very much in development. Confidentiality will remain a necessary feature of private markets. Preserving business secrets, protecting innovation, maintaining some stability surrounding the investments: these factors are deemed to be preserved. Not only will transparency never be as complete as it could be for other asset classes, due notably to a necessary time lag and protection of underlying portfolio companies' business secrets; but also data itself does not replace the ability to interpret, confront and investigate this data so as to understand the true performance of fund managers. The goal of investors should be to reduce the asymmetry of information instead of targeting a higher quantity of data (*The Economist*, 2009).

7.5 SELF-REGULATION OR IMPOSED REGULATION?

The case for active self-regulation

On a broad scale, international self-regulation has to be at the core of fund managers' future action, even if that sounds rather optimistic. Not only because *national* self-regulation no longer makes sense, given the international reach of venture capital and LBO fund managers; but also because they are diversifying their interventions. The fact that LBO fund managers are now setting up hedge funds, distressed debt funds, real-estate funds, advisory services, M&As and fund placement activities has created some conflicts of interest, notably in the way they handle the information they collect and how they exercise the rights attached to these activities.

Even if they were and still are far from being effective in investment banking, private equity groups need to set up very strong Chinese walls. If they are set up, there is very little chance of generating and exploiting synergies between the LBO and distressed debt businesses (*Financial Times*, 2007b), for example. The same applies to private equity houses which have developed real-estate practices alongside their LBO activity: information gathered could be used by different internal practices for purposes other than those for which it was gathered. The incentive for setting up rules is therefore very limited.

Re-aligning interests: compensations, communication and valuation

The second element is to take the initiative to set fairer terms and conditions as to the management of the funds. This means that the industry should publish standard management fees and carried interest terms. Management fees should be defined according to the real needs of the fund managers, and also to avoid any competition to increase the fund's size just to collect more fees. If not mandatory, these terms should at least be an indication of the market standard and define the reasoning behind it.

Then, the industry should settle for a specific fair but prudent accounting and valuation standard and stick to it. Not only is there no reason why this should not be accepted by the rest of the financial industry, but it could also replace the race towards mark-to-market valuations. As this asset class is successful and generating substantial returns, the refusal of the fair market value will not harm its success – notably because capital inflow is still high.

In that respect, the valuation standards have to be framed precisely by the industry. Unrealised profits should not be booked, despite SFAS 159, until realisation. In private equity, options are worth nothing until they are triggered, as investments are deemed to be made over the mid to long term and the value of these options remains subject to high uncertainty. This uncertainty introduces volatility in returns, and thus a risk, which is not compensated by potential returns for fund investors. The only benefit is for the agent (the fund manager), for fundraising purposes (flattering performance) and incentive calculation. That should be discarded as a reason to apply SFAS 159 (*Financial Times*, 2007a).

The guiding principle of decisions should always be to act in the best interest of the fund investors. The agent's mission is to manage the funds for them. The collective interest of the fund managers is therefore to be the protectors of the fund investors' interest. This guiding principle should be enforced by professional sanctions, such as a ban on private equity activity, with a published list of the subjects of these sanctions.

Playing with the (stock exchange) fire: MBO on listed companies

Even though the 'eclipse of the public corporation' has been announced (Jensen, 1989), private equity professionals should pay particular attention to the way they deal with stock exchange investors. First, because these shareholders are the potential buyers of their portfolio companies (either directly at IPO time, or indirectly through another listed company). Second, because regulations have focused increasingly on the protection of stock exchange investors. And finally, because an increasing proportion of these investors are also their limited partners.

When a public-to-private transaction occurs, it is in the interest of the LBO fund managers to make sure that they pay a fair price for the company they acquire. The logic behind this is that they not only have to take the opportunity into account, but also the long-term prospects of the company. When a company is delisted, operational improvements are difficult to generate. There is a high risk that the LBO manager will be accused of using only financial leverage and traditional financial engineering methods (associated with lay-offs).

The delisting of Kinder Morgan (USD 15.2 billion) is one example where the CEO of the company led the LBO of his own firm (Lashinsky, 2007), resulting in conflicts of interest despite the presence of the Board in the company. This was firstly because the initial offer was announced at USD 84.41 per share and then increased to USD 107.5. Rich Kinder stated in front of his Board that, after restructuring, the stock could reach USD 163 per share by 2010 (this was before the 2007 crisis).

With the LBO, the share of the CEO in the company jumped from 18% to 31% without any capital injection from his side. The fact that this offer went out without further announcement was a shock, and the CEO was criticised for his lack of transparency. Shareholders demanded that they benefit from the same conditions as the CEO in the planned LBO ('staple LBO'), without any success.

In this case, it is obvious that the managers were looking at their interests first, and the company advisors at theirs – and not at all at the interests of the shareholders. Interestingly, Kinder was trained in the corporate world at Enron, where shareholders' interests and management's interests did not converge. Kinder and his partners had all the information, whereas the independent Board had to rely on what was provided to them by the management (who were part of the offer). Because Kinder and his partners planned the operation and structured an investment syndicate 2 months before informing the Board, there was little chance that a competitive bid would succeed – especially when the management was part of the current public offer.

Even worse, 20% of the profits from selling the group or listing it again went to the management (and 40% of that 20% to Rich Kinder himself). The debt of the LBO would have been paid with asset disposals, and the final reward would have come to a further IPO . . . at a much higher price.

Public anger is mounting against such practices (Stein, 2006). There is little that minority individual shareholders can do against a take-private LBO. The power of these shareholders is especially limited, as the managers of the companies are in full control of these operations. One of the conclusions is that the managers of a listed company should be excluded legally from any operation involving a take-private with a 5 to 10-year period of exclusion, so as to avoid such blatant conflicts of interest and misappropriation of latent profits. According to Stein, this is a major source of insider trading in the sense that the management uses the information for its own benefit at the expense of the stockholders.

7.6   CONCLUSION

Whether fund investors like it or not, private equity will remain a sector with small areas of transparency and large parts of the business obscured by confidentiality. Paradoxically, this is actually very good news. Transparency will force fund managers to constantly prove their value and continue to innovate in order to support their portfolio companies. Innovation in financial services is a way to distinguish and thus avoid the systematic application of a benchmark.

Confidentiality will keep fund investors on their toes and applying their judgement constantly, exercising their responsibilities and avoiding the outsourcing of their risk management – which was a major source of problems in the recent crisis (Blankfein, 2009). In that respect, rating agencies' reports on leveraged loans are only a small element in evaluating the health of LBO deals.

The alignment of interests is not only a matter of working in favour of the investors without favouring the agent's interest, but also working actively to achieve the best result possible for the ultimate beneficiaries – that is to say, the public who will eventually retire, need insurance cover, who own shares in listed companies, etc. Fund investors also have to align their interests with their own investors. This means that they have to assess precisely their risk–return profile for their private equity investments; they have to obtain the best insider knowledge in private equity; they have to negotiate the terms and conditions systematically to get the best terms possible and they have to act immediately once they have invested.

Surprisingly, the rewards for being a good fund investor are meagre. Compared to the lavish fees and carried interest, an endowment manager, an insurance executive or a pension fund representative has low incentives to maximise the use of its risk margins, to maximise their net returns by negotiating the terms and to proactively manage their portfolio of funds. Even very successful endowment managers, such as a former Harvard endowment head of investment, raise a public outcry when they are fairly compensated for their value creation.

It is no wonder that trustees or asset managers are tempted to collude with fund managers. It is difficult to justify such a discrepancy in compensation for jobs which are closely related, and for expertise which is rare and valuable on the market.

The result is that some fund investors' representatives are not qualified to invest and monitor private equity fund investments; or prepare their next move to either join one of the fund managers or to join/create a gatekeeper/fund of funds; or collude with the fund managers they are supposed to control.

In a complex market, when transparency and confidentiality are being combined, there should be a constant preoccupation to involve every actor in the market in a controlling role over other players, without any direct negative or positive individual impact if they have to punish bad behaviour. Everyone should therefore be a potential whistleblower. Setting up a system of checks and balances in the market, with the agreement of the main actors, is what fund investors and managers should be aiming to achieve.

REFERENCES

Newsletters and Newspapers

AltAssets, 'US private equity chief pleads not guilty', 28 July 2009.

Balsham, R., Brown, M., Lee, M. and Rubalevskaya, J., 'Private social investment in France: meeting two goals', Knowledge@Wharton, 26 January 2011.

Blankfein, L., 'Do not destroy the essential catalyst of risk', *Financial Times*, 8 February 2009.

Burwell, R., 'SEC Enforcement Division focuses on insider trading and conflicts of interest in private equity', Dealmakers, *Pitchbook*, 16 March 2012.

FinAlternatives, 'SEC moves to end "pay-to-play" at pensions', 27 July 2009.

Financial Times, 'Private equity goes into debt', 11 February 2007a.

Financial Times, 'The limits of fair value', 27 July 2007b.

Hausmann, D., 'Kickback scheme promises pain for private equity', *Dow Jones Private Equity Analyst*, April 2009.

Kelleher, E., 'Private equity chooses the responsible route', *Financial Times*, 27 February 2011.

Lashinsky, A., 'Rich Kinder's bigger slice', *Fortune*, 16 May 2007.

Mackintosh, J. and Arnold, M., 'French probe buy-out collusion', *Financial Times*, 6 July 2007.

Primack, D., 'Random ramblings', The Term Sheet, *Fortune*, 2 March 2011.

Primack, D., 'Drilling into Oppenheimer', The Term Sheet, *Fortune*, 20 March 2012a.

Primack, D., 'Private equity recaps (no, not that kind)', The Term Sheet, *Fortune*, 13 August 2012b.

Private Equity Online, 'Ban the politicians', 24 April 2009.

Private Equity Online, 'Why the SEC's good intentions may harm investors', 21 January 2011.

Stein, B., 'On buyouts, there ought to be a law', *New York Times*, 3 September 2006.

Sutton, S., 'Panel: regulation could clarify performance', *Private Equity International*, 8 February 2012.

The Economist, 'Economics focus: Full disclosure', 21 February 2009.

Vardi, N., 'Investor sues T.J. Maloney and his USD 1.8 billion private equity firm alleging bogus fees', The Jungle, *Forbes*, 26 April 2011.

Zuckerman, G., 'Private equity fund in valuation inquiry', *The Wall Street Journal*, 24 February 2012.

Papers and Studies

Bengtsson, O. (2008) 'Relational venture capital financing of serial founders', University of Illinois at Urbana-Champaign, 45 pp.

Chaplinsky, S. (2004) 'CalPERS vs. Mercury News – disclosure comes to private equity', Darden Business Publishing/University of Virginia, 22 pp.

Gompers, P. and Xuan, Y. (2008) 'Bridge building in venture capital-backed acquisitions', Harvard Business School Working Paper 08-084, 46 pp.

Guo, S., Hotchkiss, E. and Song, W. (2008) 'Do buyouts (still) create value?', Boston College, University of Cincinnati, 59 pp.

Hsu, D. (2004) 'What do entrepreneurs pay for venture capital affiliation?', *The Journal of Finance*, 59(4), pp. 1805–1844.

Jensen, M. (1989) 'Eclipse of the public corporation', Harvard Business School (rev. 1997), 31 pp.

Katz, S. (2008) 'Earnings quality and ownership structure: The role of private equity sponsors', NBER Working Paper No. 14085, 53 pp.

Nahata, R. (2007) 'Venture capital reputation and investment performance', Baruch College, 64 pp.

UNCTAD (2006) *World Investment Report*, United Nations Conference on Trade and Development, New York, 372 pp.

CHAPTER 8

General Conclusion: Private Markets Today and Tomorrow

Private markets have been expanding in terms of capital raised, number of fund managers and active fund investors. It has also generated some envy, attracting the attention of hedge fund managers in need of new sources of performance, but also pushing some fund investors to bypass funds altogether to do LBOs, venture investments and real-estate investments themselves or through co-investment. Does it mean that the job of fund managers will be commoditised?

8.1 A PREMIUM TO ESTABLISHED PLAYERS

The aftermath of the 2007–2009 crisis led BCG and IESE to announce the disappearance of 20–40% of fund managers within 2–3 years after the publication of their report (see Meerkatt and Liechtenstein, 2008). M&As are regularly announced in the fund of funds industry and in the funds industry.

Some form of concentration of the sector has started (see below), but it is more quietly – and at a very slow rate – diverging from the forecast. According to Preqin, 90 private equity fund managers disappeared in 2009 (only 14 disappeared in the aftermath of the Internet bubble burst), 183 were in run-off mode in 2011 (with 130 new managers appearing), with 4146 remaining in activity. This is a far cry from the estimates of BCG and IESE. There was no contraction of the sector.

The reason is that fund managers can count on management fee streams for a certain time before they run out of activity. The British LBO fund manager Candover went into liquidation in 2010, after 30 years of activity. The mid-market LBO firm Duke Street was one of the firms which could not raise money and will operate on a deal-by-deal basis. The prediction of BCG and IESE never materialised and the number of active fund managers has not decreased according to Preqin (Figure 8.1).

However, there are some signs that the sector is concentrating and there is a clear premium to established players. Three converging phenomena are supporting the concentration trend.

First, compliance with regulations generates costs, which can better be split if one fund manager gathers complementary strategies under one umbrella. Regulations create de facto barriers to entry. Compliance costs and branding are adverse conditions

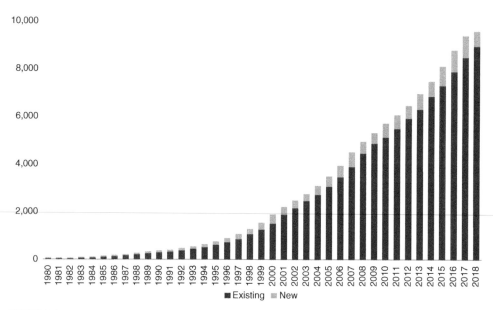

FIGURE 8.1 Number of active private market fund managers worldwide (1980–10/2018)
Source: Preqin 2019.

for emerging managers. These two factors reduce the incentive to innovate in terms of investment strategies. As there are usually 'grandfather rights' for installed fund managers, they benefit from an advantage – even if they are not necessarily the most efficient investors. Notably, some fund managers that have built a brand thanks to attractive past track records, but which are not necessarily relevant, could still gather the interest of fund investors who are not necessarily aware of these elements and base their analysis on quantitative elements.

Second, fund managers can leverage their brand to launch these new strategies, and fund investors have a financial and reputational incentive to invest with these large, established and known fund managers.

Third, the founders of fund managers have to manage their succession, having created their structures in the 1970s and 1980s. Though they could pass them on to the new generation, the temptation is to realise the wealth created by simply selling the structure.

The main challenge that private markets have to face in the short term is to offer better risk management instruments (see Section 8.2) to fund investors. Even though there is no indicator offering a single and direct reading risk measurement, assessing the fund managers' aptitude to think over the long term is crucial (see Section 8.3). Risk management can ignite a flow of initiatives towards financial innovation, but also bring some changes in the presentation of results (see Section 8.4), which could have a considerable negative impact on private markets (see Section 8.5). In that respect, private markets are at a crossroads: increased knowledge of the asset class can provide fund investors with more options (see Section 8.6), but could also transform the asset class into an overly regulated sector – which is a lose–lose scenario.

8.2 PROVIDE BETTER INSTRUMENTS FOR RISK MEASUREMENT

The limited tradability of private assets is an intrinsic component of private markets investing. Investors have to define a time horizon for their investments. If they cannot stay invested 3 to 8 years on average, depending on the strategy, then there is no point in investing in private markets. In that respect, the time to liquidity (or duration for direct lending strategies) is a dimension of investing, not a risk.

Risks in private markets are difficult to manage, as they cannot be reduced to one figure. At least five measures of risk have been identified by Demaria and He (2019). The investment strategy risk measures the variation of the aggregate performance of private market funds, by vintage year, over time. This top-down perspective is useful for portfolio construction and to assess the probability of a loss, and the amounts lost in case of a loss. The fund investment risk provides the frequency at which funds of a given private market strategy lose or make money, and the amount lost or gained. This top-down approach is also close in philosophy to the value-at-risk, and works well with fully liquidated funds.

Active funds risk measurement compares the quarter-on-quarter evolution of the performance of active funds of a given private markets strategy with the average performance of fully realised funds. The fund selection risk is a bottom-up approach, which measures the ability of the fund investor to select good funds. Finally, it is possible to quantify the variation around the average time to liquidity of a given private markets strategy, which effectively would be some form of 'liquidity risk' measurement.

These instruments are new and have the advantage of being replicable with listed assets. They might provide a convergence point when building portfolios mixing different assets.

Nevertheless, measuring risk remains difficult as these risks are at the same time endogenous and exogenous to private markets. Exogenous because for example private equity performance is correlated – up to a certain level – with the performance of the listed markets. Financial markets condition portfolio companies' exits, either through sale on a stock exchange, or a trade sale to a strategic acquirer. This acquirer can be listed. In that case, its price per share and the value of its bonds (and hence the interest rates) will determine its aptitude to make acquisitions. If the acquirer is not listed, it is the interest rates (and hence the overall economic climate) which will determine the aptitude of a non-listed group to make acquisitions. These two exit cases voluntarily ignore an acquisition strategy fully financed by the cash reserves of the strategic acquirer. This could indicate that the debt is too expensive (and that interest rates are too high, as the economic context is not favourable to acquisitions). The valuation of a portfolio company will thus be realised thanks to the listed comparable method and will be *in fine* linked to market conditions.

Endogenous because multiple factors are specific to private markets:

- *The difficulty for fund managers to reproduce the performance from one fund to another.*

  The performance of a fund is related to its investments, which are decisions taken according to the circumstances as much as a rational and rigorous process. Personal chemistry is a key component, which is neither quantifiable nor can be reduced to a technical process. Success calls for greater progress in that respect (reputation effect, see Chapter 7).

However, *past performance does not give any indication of future performance* in most cases (Gottschalg & Kreuter, 2007). Funds of funds illustrate this statement abundantly, despite the consistency of performance of private equity funds (Kaplan & Schoar, 2003). Funds of funds have an investment policy which backs the established names of private equity, despite mediocre performance. They perceive it as less risky than backing emerging and innovating teams. *Funds of funds are thus partially contributing to market inertia instead of correcting it*, and create a lagging effect which is prejudicial to private markets. The Yale endowment provides a different example, having established best practice in terms of portfolio performance and selection of emerging teams (Lerner, Schoar & Wang, 2008).

■ *The rapid evolution of private markets.*

Notably, the strong democratisation of technologies in the venture capital area and the increasing competition between the different funds over investing in the companies which fit their investment model best. This generates uncertainty about the performance of teams which have set up their strategy at a given time and are prepared to deploy the capital in a market evolving quickly over the course of the next 5 years (the length of a fund investment period).

This is why selection is made primarily on the fund offering, but through an *evaluation of the fund managers*. They have built a reputation over time, and have the capacity to identify attractive opportunities, negotiate investments, manage portfolio companies and prepare investment exits.

Top private equity fund managers work for the long term. Not only do they nurture portfolio companies, but they also *nurture future opportunities*. LBO fund managers approach potential sellers sometimes 18 to 30 months before effectively acquiring a company. They also develop a *network* patiently in order to attract opportunities that could fit their investment strategy. This is the case with venture capital, for example, where fund managers maintain contact with CEOs of their former portfolio companies. These CEOs not only recommend other opportunities, but can also launch new ventures themselves which might be of interest to venture capital investors.

One of the ways to reduce the volatility of performance lies in the capacity of the fund managers to build a network and to 'industrialise' their know-how, notably by waiting patiently for the right opportunity. Evaluating this wealth of future opportunities, for a fund investor, is paramount. To do so, fund investors need to immerse themselves in the environment of the fund managers. They have to get feedback from intermediaries, former CEOs of companies, former employees and any stakeholder that the fund manager had to interact with. *Frank and honest feedback* on the capacities and personalities of the fund managers is worth a lot of data crunching.

Another approach is to look at the *performance of the portfolio companies once they have been listed or sold to strategic acquirers* (Cao & Lerner, 2009). Have they survived this event? How did they perform? Were they gifted with the capacity to develop harmoniously? This also reveals the capacity of general partners to really create value, but even more importantly, it proves that they are able to *think over the long term*.

8.3   THE ONLY VALID LEITMOTIV: LONG-TERM THINKING

The fact that *an entire generation of fund managers is going to retire* in the upcoming years highlights the importance of this *long-term thinking process*: how will they handle this generational shift? Did they nurture talents that are able to take over the management of the fund manager? Did they train them adequately to face the upcoming challenges, including handling future performance?

In the future, performance figures will probably evolve downwards – as well as the risk associated with investing. If valuations can suffer from a drop in the near or mid term, over the long term, the trend could evolve differently, and notably towards increasing values. This is due to a capital inflow, as private markets become increasingly popular (see Section 8.4), which will drive down the marginal returns of investments. A downward performance trend has already been witnessed in the venture capital industry in the USA, which is the sign of a maturing sector. Large and mega LBOs in the USA are also following the same path. This trend will probably develop and apply gradually to each segment of private markets.

Fund investors, aware of this challenge, are overly conscious of the difficulty of selecting the fund managers they want to work with. At the same time, they want to limit the costs involved in investing in this asset class. This exercise is difficult, as fees and costs remain relatively stable over time.

8.4   THE IMPACT OF FAIR MARKET VALUE

In accounting, under the pressure of the new solvency and prudential ratios to be applied by institutional investors, fair market value has been promoted as a way of better pricing assets. These norms rely on reasoning methods which merely use analogies and market data, if it is available. Not only does this increase the volatility of performance, it also reinforces the habit of comparing listed stock prices with private share values – which is a wrong assessment, as explained in Chapter 4.

However, these norms (the FAS 157 accounting rules) appear to have encouraged financial volatility and have not, so far, brought the expected results as to the valuation of private equity portfolios. According to FAS 157, the value of portfolio companies must be reflected in a calculated equivalent of a market price. This *evaluation* is related not only to their *intrinsic performance compared to budget*, but also to their *comparables listed on the stock exchange*. This could contribute to changing substantially the value of private market portfolios and generating arbitrages from fund investors who have to manage their portfolio with regard to their balance sheet and their net result. This *negates the specificity of private equity*, that is to say the long-term commitment of fund investors and managers.

The volatility of private equity performance increases the costs of capital for fund investors. In finance, volatility equates to risks, and risks have to be covered partially or totally with cash or cash equivalents. By introducing volatility in private equity evaluations, the *FAS 157 accounting standards have increased the cost of investing in small and medium-sized businesses*. As fund investors are involved for the long term, and as the volatility of private equity performance will remain high with FAS 157 (at least more than with the historical costs method, which was prevailing until then), the impact will be durably high.

As mentioned throughout this book, private markets do not obey the same laws as listed markets. Furthermore, the sector is emerging slowly as an asset class, with some identified patterns and historical data which – even though imperfect – can be exploited statistically. The imperfections of private market statistics in that respect are far less damaging for the economy as a whole than FAS 157 as such. Not only does most private markets activity struggle to find acceptable listed comparables, but it is also against all sound reasoning to apply this method continuously – that is to say, when companies are not actively being put up for sale. Even worse, *FAS 157 represents a reverse of the history of private equity and the eclipse of public corporations* (Jensen, 1989).

Fund of funds managers have been deafeningly silent in the debate, even though statistically it appears to decrease the risk associated with private markets investing (Weidig & Mathonet, 2004). This once again *raises concerns as to their utility in the industry if they do not build their case.* They currently seem to focus more on reducing fees by bundling fund and co-investment, and selling the package to fund investors.

Interestingly, large and mega buy-out fund managers were voicing their support for fair market value in December 2003 through the Private Equity Industry Guidance Group (PEIGG). This was before the crisis; the PEIGG pressed the National Venture Capital Association (NVCA) to use it – and the NVCA finally endorsed it. Since 2008, fund managers such as Blackstone, who were initially promoting the rules, are complaining about their application – after the impact of the financial crisis had depressed the valuation of listed companies. This sheds an interesting light on the endorsement by those same groups, this time through the Private Equity Council,[1] created in 2006, of 'guidelines for responsible investments'.

There is no obvious solution to the problem that is raised by fair market value, except asking for an exemption from FAS 157 for private markets – with the exception of large and mega buy-outs. KPMG (2009) states that 'the fair [value] accounting rules should also be reassessed to distinguish between those that accurately reflect economic value destruction and those that unnecessarily precipitate actions that serve to exaggerate economic loss'.

Fund investors could thus use this partial application of fair market value to large and mega buy-out funds in order to set up their own valuation framework so as to determine the value of the funds in which they have invested. This could be slowed down by the difficulties of obtaining access to the underlying data and the details of portfolio companies with certain fund managers.

8.5   A LONG-TERM TREND: THE ATTRACTIVENESS OF PRIVATE MARKETS

The risk–return profile of private markets will remain attractive, which means that capital inflow should last (see Figure 8.2). Preqin estimates that assets under management in private equity have reached USD 3.4 trillion as of 2018 (USD 5.9 trillion for private

---

[1] Renamed the Private Equity Growth Capital Council in 2010, even though it essentially represented LBO funds, and after that the American Investment Council in 2016.

markets) and should reach USD 4.9 trillion in 2023 (USD 9.3 trillion for private markets). This has to be put in perspective: alternative investments should reach USD 14 trillion, a 59% increase compared to 2017 (USD 8.8 trillion). Investors are expected to come more from Asia-Pacific. Public and private pension funds are expected to be more active in private markets, as well as endowments and foundations, sovereign wealth funds and family offices (Preqin, 2018). According to Ford (2019), quoting Willis Towers Watson, institutional investors have allocated 14% of their assets to private markets and this is expected to reach 20% over the next 10 years.

However, that would mean overcoming the main hurdles that fund investors mention with regard to their commitment to alternative assets (see Table 8.1). In any case, the transition from a traditional asset allocation to a more diversified and return-oriented allocation, integrating private equity, should be very progressive as illustrated in Figure 8.2, except in the case of sovereign wealth funds. The latter are unconstrained investors, in the sense that they are free to allocate their assets without any regulation to comply with. According to JP Morgan, the asset allocation shifts are planned to be realised over an average period of 3.4 years.

Progressive deployment of capital in private markets is a blessing. Economies can only absorb so much of the capital available and transform it into profitable investments. If there is an excess over this capacity of absorption, then valuations increase and returns are affected. As private equity is first and foremost an activity based on human interactions, networks and activity tend to be local (except in large and mega LBOs). It takes time and effort to deploy the capital efficiently in a market dominated

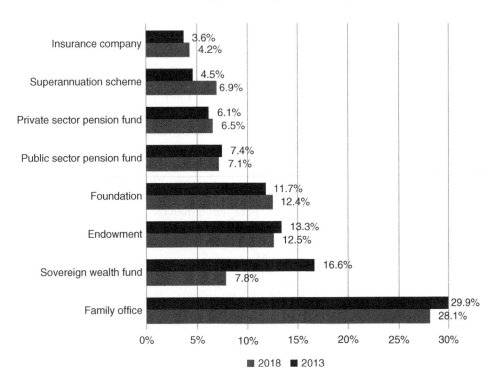

FIGURE 8.2 Allocation to private equity, by investor type (excluding funds of funds)
Source: Preqin 2018.

TABLE 8.1   Main advantages, drawbacks and hurdles of alternative investments

	Main advantages (% of answers)	Main drawbacks (% of answers)	Main hurdles (% of answers)
Hedge funds	▪ Diversification (73%) ▪ Returns (63%) ▪ Volatility of returns (51%)	▪ Fees (70%) ▪ Transparency (68%) ▪ Liquidity (67%)	▪ Transparency (59%) ▪ Fees (44%) ▪ Volatility of returns (28%)
Private equity	▪ Returns (94%) ▪ Diversification (68%) ▪ Access to managers (42%)	▪ Liquidity (85%) ▪ Fees (68%) ▪ Transparency (27%)	▪ Liquidity (62%) ▪ Transparency (43%) ▪ Fees (30%)
Real estate	▪ Diversification (81%) ▪ Protection against inflation (65%) ▪ Returns (63%)	▪ Liquidity (79%) ▪ Fees (48%) ▪ Leverage (34%)	▪ Liquidity (66%) ▪ Returns (29%) ▪ Internal resources (25%)

Source: JP Morgan Asset Management 2010.

by inefficiencies and asymmetry of information. The overall performance of the sector is hence dependent on the quality of the investment teams.

The relative immaturity of private markets in emerging markets should raise caution when they become unduly fashionable, or not. The notion of moderate and managed growth of private markets appears as a clear determinant of the future of this asset class: the economy can only absorb a certain volume of capital. Excesses are clearly visible, in venture capital (1999–2001, see Figure 8.3) and in LBOs (2007–2010).

According to Figure 8.3, the venture capital sector has attracted less capital since the bubble burst of 2001–2003, and the levels of fundraising have been significantly lower than the previous cycle. Fund investors have moreover focused their commitments on fewer teams, raising more money (with the consequences explored in Section 4.1: funding gaps in seed and early-stage rounds, higher valuations as fund managers chase the same deals and want to deploy a larger amount of money per company). According to Partners Group, LBOs followed the same path. Fund managers will raise more capital, and valuations shifted depending on the type of deals and the number of bidders. Large and mega LBOs in the USA were the most affected.

Cultural, economic, social and legal factors

Fund investors are the ones making the market, collectively. Their motivations to invest in private markets vary depending on which country is considered, but also their characteristics. As explained by Demaria (2015), fund investors are 'irrational investors subject to biases' such as fashion, fads, representativeness bias, aversion to ambiguity, under-reaction to information, sensitiveness to noise and reputation, home investing bias, over-confidence and fit into prospect theory. The determinants of fund investors' behaviour are asset allocation policies, investment decision guidelines and processes, recruitment and incentive policies, profiles and tenure of staff, network and integration

New commitments to US venture captial funds

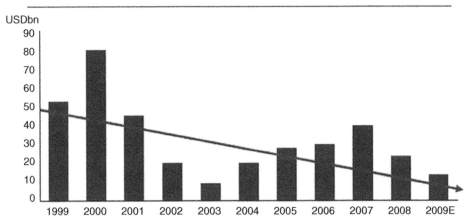

Median venture captial fund size (funds greater than USD 20m)

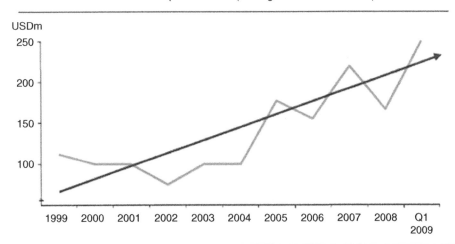

FIGURE 8.3 Evolution of commitments to US venture capital funds and median size of the new funds
Source: Partners Group 2009, Dow Jones VentureSource.

in the fund investors' community, as well as reputation as a fund investor. However, these elements depend first and foremost on the size of the investor, which determines the total capital currently deployed in private markets. This in turn conditions know-how and experience, which is a function of the time spent in the asset class and the network built by the fund investor.

Depending on the commitment, the investment activity will evolve significantly and hence dramatically affect the private markets and economic landscape. Cultural, economic, social and legal factors are also involved in the development of private markets. A long-term convergence of the US and European private markets is expected (and later of emerging markets). The whole economy favours this convergence, notably to manage the generational change at the helm of companies in developed economies. The opportunities are numerous, due mainly to market imperfections.

8.6 PRIVATE EQUITY: FUTURE VICTIM OF ITS OWN SUCCESS?

Beyond the risk of bubbles, is the main risk facing the private equity sector its *commoditisation* (Lewis, 2006) in the short or medium term?

In 2005, Morgan Stanley stated that one-third of the initial public offerings over the course of 2003–2005 were of companies backed by private equity funds (half of them in 2005). Private equity funds were involved in one-quarter of M&As, and issued half of leveraged debt. This proportion increased to 30% of M&As in 2011. As of 31 December 2011, the amounts under management allocated to private equity represented EUR 1700 billion, that is to say 100 times more than 15 years ago. As of 2018, it doubled and reached EUR 3.4 trillion (see above). This represents 4.7% of the calculated total market capitalisation of listed companies worldwide. In 2017, USD 2.4 trillion was raised privately in the USA, to be compared with USD 2.1 trillion on listed markets, according to the *Wall Street Journal*.[2] Private markets financing took over from public markets in 2011.

However, *the impact of private equity may be under-estimated*. As a matter of fact, the total market for capitalisation of listed companies worldwide is an extrapolation of the price of their shares traded on the market. This means that if the total of the capital of a given company had to be sold on a specific day, the price of its shares would be dramatically different from its marginal price on a given day. In other words, the total to be allocated to private equity is a firm commitment, whereas the total value of all listed companies worldwide is just an extrapolation which would differ substantially as it has to be totally liquid from one day to the next.

This conclusion provides an interesting perspective on the application of fair market value. As illustrated over the course of this book, private equity fund managers have to produce reports valuing their assets as if they were to be sold the very next day. To do so, the recommendation is to use the value of comparable listed companies. However, these listed companies, if they had to be totally liquid the next day, would probably see their value drop dramatically (as happens in the case of market crashes).

In that respect, *the fair market value rule is just a complete nonsense*. Instead of taking the impact of time and the horizon of placement of each financial instrument into account, its promoters decided to adopt a rule which would free them from very difficult issues, despite the fact that it does not make any economic or financial sense. They became dazzled by the public market illusion: permanent and efficient pricing. This is a myth, but nevertheless, the rules of accounting are based on it. Sensible accounting rules would favour long-term investments, which are correlative to value creation. This is what accounting rules are supposed to measure and capture.

---

[2]Eaglesham, J. and Coulter, J., 'The fuel powering corporate America: USD 2.4 trillion private fundraising', *The Wall Street Journal*, 2 April 2018.

One of the most visible proofs of the fact that private markets should be considered as a specific asset class, with its own rules, is the emergence of a specific ecosystem. The development of secondary LBOs shows that private equity can acquire the logic of industrial growth. Theoretically, each fund brings its contribution to the growth of a company. For example, the French company Frans Bonhomme has been the target of four successive LBOs: in 1993, when it was bought by PPM Ventures from Bolloré for EUR 150 million; then, it was acquired by Apax in 2000, for EUR 400 million; by Cinven for EUR 520 million in 2003; before being sold in 2005 to Apax for EUR 900 million. EBITDA was respectively EUR 25, 43, 65 and 90 million (L'Agefi, 2005). Secondary LBOs are now the second exit path for LBO funds, and represent 30–40% of the total of LBOs.

Capital inflow in private markets will have positive consequences if this means that all the segments of financing receive money, and this money is invested regularly (which lowers the cyclicity of the sector). The market imperfections and lack of transparency will probably allow some actors to stay in traditional private equity markets, such as technological venture capital. However, the inflow of capital raises some concerns as to the consistency of performance over the long term, if all else remains equal.

Many funds will see their performance change, and the next crisis will act as a reality check in that respect. In the future, investors' allocation to private markets should include – for diversification and return enhancement purposes – segments such as non-IT venture capital, growth capital and turn-around capital, which are still under-developed. This opens up investment perspectives, but requires the appropriate environment and risk appetite. Will private market funds duplicate listed markets, but without the regulatory burden associated with the latter category, to execute the transformation which is necessary for certain companies? This would create a 'breathing space' for stock exchanges by creating a second 'economic and financial lung' for the economy, but would also raise many questions in terms of economic and financial governance. Many 'activist investors' in listed companies would like to introduce the methods which have been successful in portfolio companies of LBO funds (see Figure 8.4). However, the result of this action is visible only after a certain number of years, which makes it difficult to apply as such on listed markets.

This would require a certain evolution in the management of listed companies. These managers are not necessarily favouring these LBO methods, which involve a great deal of pressure and stress in their operation. It would not only be the responsibility of institutional investors to act in favour of an application of private equity methods (*Financial Times*, 2005), but also be in their interest (see Section 8.7).

The commoditisation of private equity would probably open the way to a new wave of innovation, but also a higher risk associated with it – if applying LBO techniques for example to different companies (riskier or more regulated). There is a limit to what private equity can do, given the constraints applied to funds. Moreover, the diffusion of private equity practices could lead to bad behaviour, most notably in the management of conflicts of interest, but also more failed high-profile operations such as Toys 'R Us which led a profitable company intro bankruptcy and massive layoffs.

The brief emergence of funds without management fees after the crisis of 2007–2009 reignited a long-standing debate: the reduction of the fees associated with private markets fund management. If high management fees have a meaning when it is necessary to set up a team and processes, and to comply with increased regulations,

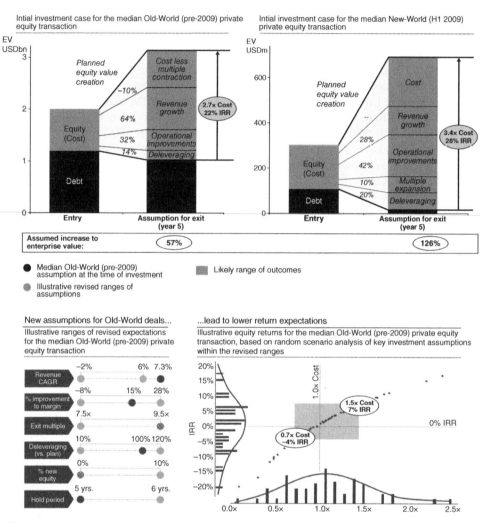

FIGURE 8.4 Consequences of the crisis on the improvement of the performance and sales of portfolio companies under LBOs
Source: Partners Group 2010.

it is in the same way logical that fund investors are rewarded for the risk taken when backing these teams. It would also be logical that fund investors of a given fund have a priority investment right for the subsequent funds raised by a fund manager that they backed when the latter started its business.

These issues, as well as the governance of private market funds, will nurture numerous debates over the coming years. This is the consequence of the success of private equity as an asset class, as well as its internationalisation. Generally, this internationalisation is good for each local economy. For a start, it brings capital and talent to local markets, creating the basis for the development of local private market managers. Then, fund investors will be able to identify highly promising investments in under-funded markets. In the long term, the capital inflow benefits to the source of capital will not only be in the form of profits, but also through the development of the global economy.

8.7 THE IMPACT OF A BETTER KNOWLEDGE OF PRIVATE MARKETS

Private markets can be a source of profits, advice and support to companies, but for that companies and assets have to remain less tradable. Private market funds provide 'patient capital' and they have to be perceived as such. The question of tradability can be solved at the fund manager level in many respects (see Sections 8.7.1 and 8.7.2), but should not hamper the development of underlying companies. In that respect, the temptation of co-investments has to be balanced carefully by fund investors (see Section 8.7.3). They should avoid the temptation of greed themselves (see Section 8.7.4), a temptation that fund managers have at times found hard to fight off (see Chapter 7); or there is a good chance that private markets will suffer from regulation which is generally not appropriate to the purposes of the business (see Section 8.7.5).

8.7.1 Understanding the Risk and Managing the J-curve

The more private market fund managers are active, and go through investment cycles, the more the knowledge of this asset class will increase. As a result, the profile of J-curves is better understood. According to the sector and the maturity of the investment targets, the profile of this curve can evolve substantially.

One of the lessons is that *a fund rarely invests 100% of its commitment at any given point in time*. The distributions from early divestments are usually recycled to face subsequent capital calls. This has convinced some fund investors to *over-commit to funds*. In order to deploy effectively 100% of their committed capital at some point, investors have decided to commit up to 130–140% of their planned allocation. This is based on the statistics according to which a fund, under normal conditions, only deploys 60–80% of its size at most. However, *this practice has backfired*, as there were no divestments during the crisis period and funds were continuing to call capital (notably to pay the management fees), and some fund investors have seen their real commitment outsize their strategic allocation. Fund investors are advised to model carefully their effective capital deployment and stress test it assuming a 6 to 18 months crisis during which there is no distribution and continuing capital calls.

Another lesson is that depending on the strategy (venture capital, LBO, growth capital, funds of funds, secondary funds or others), it is possible to determine the average profile of the expected J-curve. In fact, the nature of the risk changes radically as time goes by, and three periods can be distinguished (see Figure 8.5):

(i) The first period, which is the time from the fund's inception to the bottom of the J-curve.

Depending on the time it takes to reach the bottom and the depth of it, it is possible to infer (up to a certain degree of certainty) the time of the second period and the height of the third period (Demaria, 2015). The bottom of the J-curve

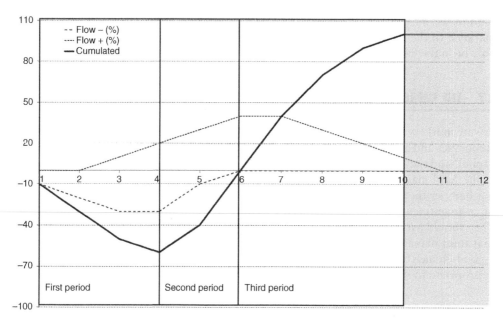

FIGURE 8.5   Staging the profile of the J-curve
Source: Demaria (2006, 2008, 2010, 2012).

coincides with a certain level of maturity of the portfolio. It provides an indication of which portfolio companies will survive or not, and their performance
against budget in particular. This period corresponds to the real risk taken by private market fund investors. This is where the risk is the highest, as well as the return
potential.

(ii) The second period, which is the time from the bottom of the J-curve to the
break-even point of the fund. The risk associated with this period is the time
to break even and the return potential. However, theoretically there is a good
picture of the portfolio structure, the generation of performance through early
exits and the expectations of the general partner. Here, the fund investor can
expect a premium if it has to sell its stake in funds, owing to cash constraints or
rebalancing. Even though it is not advisable as this would sever the relationship
with the fund manager, some fund investors could exit from funds because of
strategic allocation constraints.

(iii) The third period, which is the time from break-even to the total exit from the
fund (e.g., full liquidity) is actually a matter of cash flow management and exit
management. The risk is somewhat limited. The question is the time required to
reach liquidity rather than the level of return, which can usually be assessed more
or less precisely.

Through this analysis, combined with private equity statistics and macro-economic
assessments, it is possible to oversee increasing sources of liquidity at the fund investor
level. These sources do not necessarily imply cutting the relationships with the fund
manager, but structuring products with specialised intermediaries as seen below.

8.7.2 Innovating through Structuring

Finance and private equity are very innovative sectors. As innovation in the financial sector cannot be patented, there is a strong incentive to stay ahead of the competition by continuously finding new products and services to sell. Once the innovation is introduced on the market, the innovator's brand can maintain a relative advantage before the competition replicates the innovation. As the innovation is duplicated, it becomes mainstream and competition is increasingly placed on pricing. The product or service becomes a low-margin offer, which stimulates further innovation.

One of the elements that characterises *private equity* is that its *'frontiers' are known.* *Tradability* is one of them. It is not a problem at the fund level, but at the fund investor level, and can produce some *cash management difficulties*. Fund investors have to keep cash at hand to face upcoming capital calls. At the same time, they can receive distributions from divestments at any time. Cash usually should not stay idle at the fund investor level, as it is used to generate interest or profit.

It is possible that the fund investor cannot face some capital calls owing to a short-term cash need. In that case, the fund investor may be tempted to either sell its stake on the *secondary market*, with the consequence that it may lose part of the value of the asset (secondary discount) and probably also lose its relationship with the fund manager. To avoid these consequences, it is possible to *structure financial products*.

One way is to evaluate the potential of a given portfolio in terms of future liquidity and profit potential, and then *securitise* the portfolio according to certain criteria. The structured product will combine multiple tranches of debt (as is done in an LBO deal) and an equity part which will remain on the books of the fund investors. These securities will then be sold to other investors according to the risk associated with them. This solution, despite its cost, presents the advantage of generating immediate liquidity without severing the relationship with the fund manager.

Even though the 2007–2009 financial crisis has slowed down the growth of such structured products, they are still in *great demand*. Once *transparency* has increased as for *underlying portfolios*, these products will be easier to structure and the costs of structuring will decrease. The frontiers of liquidity will be expanded for fund investors.

Another *frontier* is the declared *decline of private equity returns* in the mid to long term. Here again, structuring can help. Statistically, the risk of the default of a portfolio of private equity funds created according to the industry standards is 1% (Weidig & Mathonet, 2004). This means that fund investors can *leverage their portfolios*. So far, the guarantee for the debt is still difficult to evaluate, but as the asset class is increasingly known, lenders will be more willing to consider private market funds as an acceptable collateral to the debt. Fund investors can use this debt to further commit to funds and hence get the spread between the interest paid to the bank and the returns generated by the underlying funds (assuming there is one). The risk for the fund investors would thus increase in case of under-performance of private market funds.

8.7.3 The Temptation of Co-investments

Among the emerging trends in private equity, co-investing has gained significant momentum (Stewart, 2012). According to Preqin (2012), 43% of fund investors actively sought co-investment rights when committing to funds (and a further 11%

considered such opportunities). As a result, the amounts invested through co-investment jumped from USD 40–50 billion in 2012–2013 to USD 100–110 billion in 2016–2017 according to McKinsey. As a matter of comparison, direct investments remained constant at USD 10–20 billion over the period 2012–2017.

Fund of funds managers account for the largest proportion of the co-investor universe (23%), not surprisingly, as this enables them to reduce the impact of their own fees on the returns provided to their own investors (they reserve on average 14% of their funds of funds for direct deals, and 9% for secondaries). Family offices come next (Collins, 2012), having increased their direct allocations to private equity and real estate.

Originally, co-investments were offered to fund investors because the size of certain operations prevented some funds from acquiring the company while maintaining their optimal level of diversification (Meads & Davies, 2011). Preqin (2012) observed that 66% of LPs with co-investment interest have over USD 250 million allocated to the asset class, and a significant 13% had a private allocation in excess of USD 5 billion. Therefore, opportunities were first proposed to the largest fund investors and then to investors negotiating with sufficiently strong arguments. They are now institutionalised and open to fund investors committing a defined minimum amount to the fund, who can co-invest up to their allocation and usually for a fee and carried interest. 61% of fund investors explain that co-investments are done at the expense of their fund allocation (39% have a separate allocation) and 63% co-invest alongside fund managers on an opportunistic basis.

The motivations to co-invest include better returns (51% of respondents) and lower fees (35%). Other reasons include further diversification of their portfolio, better transparency, better alignment of interests with fund managers and attractive opportunities. For family offices, it is privacy, control and customisation.

However, this strategy implies risk. For fund managers, it creates a certain level of uncertainty. First, when the deals are negotiated, fund investors might lack resources and time to do their due diligence and approve the investment in time. Then, fund investors are not necessarily able to actively participate in the investment, create value and provide the know-how that a fund manager does. Nevertheless, fund managers have to accommodate their fund investors as co-investors, and they might diverge on the options to adopt for the portfolio company.

Then, as the deals offered to co-investments are larger, they also present specific risks: more competition (hence higher valuation, hence potentially lower profits), and maybe less value creation potential. The other risk is the 'adverse selection' (Murray, 2012) associated with this strategy: a fund manager will offer as co-investment the operations that it will not be able to finance alone or that it wants to syndicate – and they might be the ones which are not going to be the 'homeruns'.

Moseley (2011) has listed the main risks that fund investors take while investing directly in companies alongside fund managers:

- Co-investing and fund investing require different sets of skills. Due diligence is compressed into a few weeks for direct investments, and can span several months for fund due diligence. The competences at stake once invested are also very different.
- Fund managers invest with a specific framework, differing from that of fund investors. The nature of the investor dictates its due diligence and the responsibilities that it will take after investing.

- Fund investors are directly exposed in co-investing. No specific treatment is undertaken (timing, pricing, etc.) and the minority shareholders' rights have to be negotiated carefully.
- Co-investing cannot replace a private markets programme, unless the fund investor wants to become the equivalent of a captive fund manager.
- There is no perfect deal, and losses are part of the risks associated with direct investing.
- Diversification rules apply in co-investing. This means that it should be a regular activity, with a reasoned programme to deploy a certain pool of capital.

To illustrate the extent of what co-investment means, one has to consider what happened to SPACs or to pledge funds (or deal-by-deal funds). Funds structured around a specific deal run the risk of pushing fund managers to do a deal not because of the potential, but because of the compensation attached to it (hence multiplying the adverse selection associated with it). Then, once the deals are done, there is no mutualisation of profits or losses. If it is a loss, the fund investor receives all of it. If it is a gain, it receives the profit minus the success fee of the fund manager.

If the fund investor is not the sole investor in a given pledge fund, it means that delays in reaching a decision by other fund investors are also creating additional risks – as well as a disagreement on investment and hence a failed operation due to a total capital below the amount necessary to do the deal.

8.7.4 Change or Die: The Pressure on Fund Managers

If private markets are an innovative financial sector, there is an area where changes have barely been made: the structure and level of fees. One of the reasons for this is related to the bargaining power of a fund manager, which writes the regulation of the fund, and negotiates it with each fund investor on a one-to-one basis. It is difficult for a fund investor to evaluate its capacity to negotiate lower fees, as it takes the risk of seeing the fund manager exclude it from the fundraising. However, the level of fees lowers the net results of the fund investors substantially, down to the point that at portfolio level, the risk–return profile of private market investments remains difficult to defend. The controversy has yet to be resolved over the ability of private markets to deliver substantial and consistent outperformance compared to traditional listed markets. However, there is a need to change the incentive structure of the private equity agent: the fund manager.

So far, some investors have adopted a very specific approach, by acquiring stakes in the fund manager itself. Thanks to this acquisition, they gain access to the finances of the fund manager and theoretically get back a portion of the fees that they pay to it, without introducing any damaging change into the traditional fee structure. These changes would apply to the entire fund investors' universe, as the 'most favoured nation clause' usually included in a fund's regulation is inapplicable. This clause states that fund investors get the best treatment granted to any investor in the fund automatically (this includes any side agreement). As the fund manager is concerned specifically, stake sales are out of scope.

By taking a stake in the fund managers, both investors and fund managers have defused immediate criticism about the cost to the final beneficiaries of the assets managed by investors. However, this attitude can only be a short-term approach. It is in the best interest of investors to generalise a significant decrease in fees collected by private market fund managers, notably those which are above EUR 250 million (the management fees of which are usually sufficient to cover the fixed costs of the fund manager). Not only are investors not systematically shareholders of the managers of the funds they invest in, but also overall, these fees are rippling through the entire financial market to the benefit of the fund manager. They set an example where other asset classes try to replicate their fee structure, and also create 'free options' for fund managers when markets are just going up.

Many suggestions have been made for decreasing the level of fees paid to the fund manager, notably by setting up a full (or more interestingly partial) fee offset mechanism where any income generated by the fund manager – aside from its management fee – would be repaid to the fund and compensate the other expenses it bears. The incentive for the fund manager to generate this side income would thus be limited in the case of a full fee offset mechanism. Neverthless, according to MJ Hudson, fee offset mechanisms are now almost systematically implemented in fund regulations.

Once the management fees are adjusted to pay only the fixed costs, the carried interest mechanism has to be reviewed. Whether we like it or not, fair market value has introduced listed markets as a competitor for asset allocation. It is thus necessary to set a benchmark deal by deal, which evolves according to the behaviour of the market – and gives the fund manager an incentive to generate systematically the return expected by the fund investors.

This debate examines the true perspectives of investing in small and medium-sized companies from afar, but it is revealing of the incentives, the motivation and the ethics of private market investors. It is difficult to convince the public and the regulators that fund managers pursue capital gains through value creation when, like Steven Schwarzman, they are paid more than USD 2.3 million in salary, but overall USD 700 million in stocks received through the vesting of 25% of the equity granted from the listing of The Blackstone Group. That made him the best-paid CEO of 2008 (Lattman, 2009), despite the crash in the value of the company which was only listed in 2007 (see Figure 8.6).

Given the media and public attention focused on hedge funds and private equity remuneration, it is only a matter of time before the profession will have to change. The question is mainly: will it do so voluntarily and sufficiently so as to appease the public, or will it be under regulatory pressure? The fact that pension funds have to disclose their private equity portfolio will act as a monitoring window for public scrutiny.

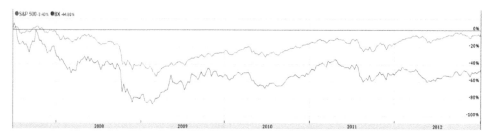

FIGURE 8.6   Evolution of The Blackstone Group stock price since its IPO (USD) compared to the S&P 500
Source: Google Finance.

8.7.5　Regulation: Damocles' Sword Looming over Private Markets

Private markets remain vulnerable to rapid and strong changes. The application of the Basel III Agreements and the 'Volcker rule' by banks have led to a significant decrease in their exposure to the private equity asset class. Banks were not ready to face the strong increase in capital costs that represents their direct involvement in the asset class. Because of the banks' prudential ratios, lending and investment conditions have recently been made more stringent for small and medium-sized businesses. This could be reversed in case of amendment of the Dodd–Frank Act, as pondered in the USA at the time of writing.

Regulatory evolution is not limited to banks: insurance companies have also been affected in their ability to finance small businesses through capital injection by the application of the European Directive 'Solvency II'. The retreat of banks will be difficult to compensate. If confirmed, the insurers' relative disaffection would be even more difficult to absorb in Europe, as they account for a fair share of sources of capital for private market funds in Europe.

Even though regulation has been favourable to private equity in the past, given its positive impact on emerging, small and medium-sized businesses, its reputation has changed notably because of large and mega LBO operations and the levels of remuneration of the fund managers doing these deals.

The first warning came with the 'asset stripping' strategy at the end of the 1980s in the USA. LBO fund managers were acquiring companies in order to reduce their overheads and restructured them heavily. The social consequences of these practices were important, because their social fluidity is meagre compared to their financial fluidity. The reputation of the general partners, described as 'Barbarians', suffered and they had to build a different image in order to avoid the intervention of the regulator.

This time, pressure has increased in the USA and also in Europe, and especially in the UK and Germany. These countries have reacted strongly against the remuneration levels of large/mega LBO fund managers and the tax treatment of these remunerations (which are low as to capital gains). Multiple projects for regulation have emerged, notably in the USA and the UK, to change the tax treatment of carried interest. The USA has introduced a mandatory registration of fund managers with the regulator, if the funds they manage are larger than USD 250 million for example. This was already the case in certain countries, for example in France, where fund managers have to be approved by the regulator in order to create FPCIs (the equivalent of a tax-efficient limited partnership).

However, what makes sense for the large and mega LBO fund managers may not be efficient for other private market fund managers. The cost of this regulatory burden can be high for small fund managers, thus creating barriers to entry if the regulation goes beyond a simple declaration and reporting of activity. Management fees are here to cover costs. Carried interest remains the true incentive for small fund managers, and their compensation is derived mainly from it.

In that sense, *large/mega LBO funds have to assess their position and take responsibility for their collective action*. Historically, they have benefitted from the lobbying of their venture capital peers, which were defending the industry's interests under the cover of general social and economic benefit. Today, their action is perceived as detrimental to the economy and puts the industry in a difficult position. Without any major change of behaviour and ethical amendment of their practices, the industry could face a split between large/mega LBO fund managers (who often describe themselves as a 'private equity house') and the rest of the industry which wants to stay within a low-regulation environment. Should this happen, the 'private equity houses' would become the new versions of merchant and investment banks, and the private equity sector would focus on entrepreneurship and value creation as understood in this sector.

To avoid ill-adapted regulations, perhaps this split is advisable.

REFERENCES

Books and Booklets

Demaria, C. (2015) *Private Equity Fund Investments*, (Palgrave Macmillan), 276 pp.
Demaria, C. (2006, 2008, 2010, 2012, 2015, 2018) *Introduction au Private Equity* (RB Editions, Paris), 1st, 2nd, 3rd, 4th, 5th, 6th edns, 128 pp.

Newsletters and Newspapers

Collins, M., 'Rich families cut back on buyout firms for direct deals', Bloomberg, 18 October 2012.
Financial Times, 'Lex: private equity', 24 October 2005.
Ford, J., 'The exorbitant privilege enjoyed by private equity firms', *The Wall Street Journal*, 8 September 2019.
L'Agefi, 'Ces sociétés qui supportent plusieurs LBO', 10–17 November 2005.
Lattman, P., 'Schwarzman tops best-paid CEO list for '08 at $702 million', *The Wall Street Journal*, 14 August 2009.
Lewis, J., 'Ka-ching', *Investment Dealers Digest*, 20 February 2006.
Meads, S. and Davies, M., 'Private equity calls big investors in for deals', Reuters, 2011.
Moseley, S., 'The seven sins of private equity co-investing', PEI Media, 18 November 2011.
Murray, A., 'LPs concerned about co-investment selection', RealDeals, 11 October 2012.
Stewart, M., 'Private equity: let's work together', Investment & Pensions Europe, 1 May 2012.

Papers and Studies

Cao, J. and Lerner, J. (2009) 'The performance of reverse leveraged buyouts', *Journal of Financial Economics*, 91(2), pp. 139–157.
Demaria, C. and He, R. (2019) 'Beyond volatility: five practical ways to measure private markets risks', *Critical Perspectives*, no. 71, Wellershoff & Partners, 25 pp.
Gottschalg, O. and Kreuter, B. (2007) 'Quantitative private equity due diligence: possible selection criteria and their efficiency', HEC Paris, 13 pp.
Jensen, M. (1989, rev. 1997) 'Eclipse of the public corporation', Harvard Business School, 31 pp.
Kaplan, S. and Schoar, A. (2003) 'Private equity performance: returns, persistence and capital flows', *Journal of Finance*, 60(4), pp. 1791–1823.
KPMG (2009) 'Turbulent times', *Frontiers in Finance, p.* 30.
Lerner, J., Schoar, A. and Wang, J. (2008) 'Secrets of the academy: The drivers of university endowment success', *Journal of Economic Perspectives*, 22(3), pp. 207–222.
Meerkatt, H. and Liechtenstein, H. (2008) 'Get ready for the private-equity shakeout: Will this be the next shock to the global economy', The Boston Consulting Group and IESE Business School, December 2008.
Preqin (2012) 'Special report: LP appetite for private equity co-investments', 9 pp.
Preqin (2018) 'The future of alternatives', October, 80 pp.
Weidig, T. and Mathonet, P.-Y. (2004) 'The risk profile of private equity', QuantExperts/European Investment Fund, 33 pp.

Template 1 (Fund): Architecture of the Private Placement Memorandum of a Private Equity Fund

*N*ote: *this template is for illustration only and does not replace professional advice in the conception of such documents.*

Submitted to: _____
Copy no.: _____
Date: _____

Confidential Private Placement Memorandum Of

[Fund Name, L.P.]
[Size]
[Date]
[Confidentiality and disclosure provisions – Legal disclaimer]

Table of contents

    h. Fund administrator

    i. Advisory Board

    j. Subscription period and process (closings, equal rights, capital calls)

    k. Distributions and distributions policy (reinvestment if applicable)

    l. Management fees, hurdle rate, catch-up (if any), carried interest structure, transaction fees, set-up fees, custodian and other fees, fee offset mechanism

    m. Commitment of the fund manager and co-investment opportunities

    n. Reporting and valuation

    o. Auditors and advisors

5. Risk factors

6. Regulatory aspects (including anti-money laundering, ERISA, VCOC if applicable)

7. Tax and other related considerations. Exhibit:

    i. Résumé of fund managers

    ii. Detailed track record

Template 2 (Fund): Structure of a Limited Partnership Agreement

*N*ote: *this template is for illustration only and does not replace professional advice in the conception of such documents.*

Copy no.: _____

Issued to: _____

Date: _____

Limited Partnership Agreement

[Fund Name, L.P.]

[Date]

[Amended and Restated as of _____ (if applicable)]

Table of contents

4. Accounting, records and reporting
   a. Capital accounts and records, accounting method
   b. Financial reporting
   c. Valuation of assets owned by partnership
   d. Annual reports
   e. Quarterly reports
   f. Tax information and returns
5. Allocation of profits and losses, distributions
   a. Sharing percentages
   b. Allocation of profits and losses
   c. Priority of distributions
   d. Form of distributions (incl. in kind if applicable), accounting of distributions
   e. Restriction on distributions (lock-up)
   f. Return of distributions by the general partner
   g. Withholding and clawback (if applicable)
   h. Tax matters
6. Duties and powers of and restrictions upon the general partner and the limited partners
   a. Investment policy
   b. Powers of the general partner
   c. Allocation of investments
   d. Other business relationships, parallel funds
   e. Powers of the limited partners
7. Liability of partners
   a. Liability of the general partner
   b. Liability of the limited partners
   c. No obligation to replenish negative capital account
8. Indemnification of general partner and management fees
   a. In general
   b. Management fees
   c. Expenses and others
   d. Other fees
9. Representations
   a. Investment representations
   b. General partner representations
   c. Additional representations
10. Transfers, removal and dissolution
   a. Capital contributions of the general partner
   b. Transfer of the general partner's interest
   c. Removal or withdrawal of the general partner (incl. bankruptcy, death)
   d. Transfer of the limited partners' interest
   e. Restrictions on transfers, transfers void
   f. No-fault removal of the general partner
   g. Continuity of partnership
   h. Term and dissolution procedures

11. Advisory Board
12. Miscellaneous
    a. Amendments
    b. Powers of attorney
    c. Successors in interest
    d. Certificate of limited partnership
    e. Applicable law and conflict resolution
    f. Side letters

Exhibits

i. Capital commitments
ii. List of limited partners
iii. Management agreement

*N*ote: *this template is for illustration only and does not replace professional advice in the conception of such documents.*

Each limited partner has its own motivations, targets and investment strategy, as well as tax, regulatory and statutory constraints. Due diligence is thus partly common to all limited partners, and also tailored to their specific needs.

Often, for public pension funds and large institutions, this due diligence is formalised into a request for proposal (RFP) or request for expression of interest (RFI). Some general partners exhibit specific features (first-time fund manager, emerging fund manager, specific investment strategy according to SRI[1] guidelines, etc.) which require complementary questions.

The PPM (see below) provided by the general partner will answer some of the questions. Other questions will be answered by ad hoc requests or interviews. Answers have to be as factual as possible.

Limited partners' due diligence on private equity fund offerings is organised around four topics:

1. The investment strategy of the general partner
   a. Investment strategy, market(s) targeted and competition
      i. Market opportunity, recent evolution
      ii. Strategy, differentiating factors
      iii. Competitive advantage of the fund and fund manager
      iv. Competition intensity
         1. Closest competitors, recent evolution
         2. Valuation: evolution and relation to competition
      v. Risks
         1. Risks involved by the strategy
         2. Risk management
   b. Execution of the strategy
      i. Deal sourcing
         1. Past – statistics
         2. Key differentiators in current and future sourcing
         3. Deals won/lost/rejected after due diligences (and reasons)
      ii. Deal structuring
         1. Lead investor/follower
         2. Board seats/observer

---

[1] Sustainable and responsible investments.

2. The general partner track record and performance
   i. Return generation
      1. Factors emphasised (top-line growth, operational improvements, turn-around, buy-and-build, etc.)
      2. Value-add generation (strategic, financial, operations, etc.)
      3. Copy of detailed investment profiles
      4. Copy of detailed investment returns (IRR, multiples, etc.)
      5. Copy of all quarterly and annual returns
   ii. Holding period
      1. Average past holding period
      2. Expected future holding period
   iii. Reproduction of performance
      1. Which factors remain valid? Why?
      2. How did the others evolve? Why? What are the consequences?
   iv. Investment guidelines
      1. Limits on a company investment (ratios)
      2. Limits on sectors (ratios)
      3. Leverage guidelines (if any)
      4. Limits on investment instruments
      5. Use of covenants (if any)
3. The alignment of interests between limited and general partners
   a. Terms and conditions
      i. Maximum and minimum levels of commitment allowed
      ii. Closing dates (first, final)
      iii. Legal structures (limited partnership, GP, feeder funds, 'blockers')
      iv. GP commitment (total, form, breakdown, % of personal wealth)
      v. Management fees and other GP compensation
      vi. Other fees and expenses born by the GP (detail set-up, fund administrator/custodian, etc.)
      vii. Preferred return (if any, compounded, flat, etc.)
      viii. Carried interest (proportion, calculation, distribution), catch-up (if any), clawback (if any)
      ix. Treatment of fees and other distributions (fee offset, split, attribution to GP)
      x. Allocation and distribution for income, gains and losses
   b. LPA and governance issues
      i. Termination and dissolution (no-fault, for cause, etc.)
      ii. LP opt-out, suspension
      iii. Limitation on transfers (LP, GP)
      iv. Key man clauses
      v. Advisory Board (composition, participants, role, etc.)
      vi. Investment limitations and restrictions
      vii. Indemnification (LP, GP, Advisory Board)
      viii. Co-investment rights (LP, GP, others)
      ix. Parallel funds
      x. Reporting, meeting rights, records and accounting, inspection, fairness opinions, etc.

      xi. Amendments

      xii. Tax issues

      xiii. Capital call procedures

4. The general partner's background and reputation
   a. Résumé of current principals and key professionals employed by the GP
      i. Provide a list of professionals having left the GP (incl. reasons and contact details)
      ii. Provide turnover rate of the professionals by hierarchical level, as well as hiring plans (professionals and principals), organisational growth management and succession plans in the GP
      iii. Provide a list of portfolio companies which had interacted with past employees (and their participation in the companies)
      iv. Provide a list of all agents, co-investors, lenders, intermediaries and service providers used in the last two funds
   b. Reference list for each principal of the GP
   c. Describe and discuss the role of each of the principals of the GP (incl. time allocation)
   d. Internal decision-making processes: description
      i. Provide a copy of the internal investment policies
      ii. Provide a copy of the internal investment approval reports
   e. Summary of all prior partnerships managed by the GP and each principal
   f. Details and structure of the general partner (including all affiliated companies)
      i. Ownership position of each principal of the GP and affiliated companies
      ii. Affiliations of each principal of the GP and the GP as an organisation (incl. voting rights, representation)
      iii. Side and other activities of the principals (political, philanthropic, for-profit)
   g. Discuss how interests of the limited and general partner are aligned
   h. Pro forma annual budgets for the general partner, funds (current and prospective)
   i. Provide the full compensation details of each principal (past, present and future) of the general partner
   j. Provide a comprehensive carried interest schedule for each principal (incl. all partnerships – past, present and prospective)
   k. Provide a management fee plan
   l. Provide a distribution waterfall
   m. Provide a summary of all board responsibilities of each principal of the GP
   n. Provide a copy of all side letter agreements with any investors (LP, GP and others)
5. Other topics of importance
   a. Liabilities of the limited partnership: management (notably post-term)
   b. Conflicts of interest: identify and discuss potential issues with the professionals involved in past, current or prospective funds
   c. Litigation: have the GP, its principals (past or present) or affiliates been subject to any litigation? (If so, provide details)

Template 4 (Fund): Quarterly Report Template

Note: this template is for illustration only and does not replace professional advice in the conception of such documents. The Institutional Limited Partners Association provide further documentation (http://ilpa.org/quarterly-reporting-standards/ and http://ilpa.org/standardized-reporting-resources/).

[Fund Name, L.P.]
Quarterly Report
[Date]
[Contact Details]

Table of contents

1. Letter of the general partner to the limited partners
    a. Market update
    b. Deal flow
    c. Portfolio update
        i. New investments
        ii. Current portfolio news
        iii. Divestments
    d. Capital calls and distributions
        i. Capital calls
        ii. Distributions
    e. Summary and conclusion
2. Portfolio summary as of [Date], [Unaudited/Audited]
    a. List of investments
    b. Breakdowns by sector, status, development stage, geography, cash needs in certain time horizon (if applicable), etc.
3. Portfolio companies
    a. Company A
        i. Business/activity/products/services
        ii. Market addressed
        iii. Financial and operational summary of the company (past, present, budget)
        iv. Short biographies of management
        v. Co-investors (if any)
        vi. Recent developments and current status
        vii. Action of the investor

        viii. Representation of the investor (board seat, observer seat, etc.)
         ix. Investment history (detailed)
    b. Company B
    c. Company ...
 4. Media and other portfolio company elements
 5. Financial statements of the fund [Audited/Unaudited]
 6. Capital accounts of the limited partners

Companies	Cost	Realised (distributed)	Unrealised (residual value)	Total value	Multiple of investment	IRR
Active						
A	1 000 000	—	200 000	200 000	0.2×	—
B	5 000 000	—	1 000 000	1 000 000	0.2×	—
C	6 000 000	—	6 000 000	6 000 000	1.0×	—
D	500 000	—	7 200 000	7 200 000	14.4×	—
Sub-total	12 500 000	—	14 400 000	14 400 000	1.15×	—
Public holdings						
E	11 000 000	19 000 000	—	19 000 000	1.7×	19%
F	1 000 000	100 000	546 120	646 120	0.6×	—
Sub-total	12 000 000	19 100 000	546 120	19 646 120	1.64×	—
Sold						
G	2 000 000	15 789	—	15 789	0.0×	—
H	3 500 000	6 549 000	—	6 549 000	1.9×	24%
I	800 000	1 081 267	—	1 081 267	1.4×	
Sub-total	6 300 000	7 646 056	—	7 646 056	1.21×	12%
Written off (not yet realised)						
J	1 000 000	—	—	—	0.0×	—
K	4 000 000	—	—	—	0.0×	—
Sub-total	5 000 000	—	—	—	0.0×	—
Written off						
L	500 000	—	—	—	0.0×	—
M	2 500 000	—	—	—	0.0×	—
Sub-total	3 000 000	—	—	—	0.0×	—
Total	38 800 000	26 746 056	14 946 120	41 692 176	1.07	—

	Year X	Diff.	Year X + 1	Diff.	Quarter xyz	Diff.	Quarter xyz + 1	Diff.	Year-to-do	Diff.
	Audited	%	*Audited*	%	*Current*	%	*Budget*	%	*Budget*	%
Sales (budget)	000		000		000		000		000	
Sales (realised)		x%		y%		z%				
EBIT ... (budget)	000		000		000		000		000	
EBIT ... (realised)		x%		y%		z%				
Income (budget)	000		000		000		000		000	
Income (realised)		x%		y%		z%				
Cash avail. (budget)	000		000		000		000		000	
Cash avail. (effective)		x%		y%		z%				
Eq. full-time employees (planned)	000		000		000		000		000	
Eq. full-time employees (real)		x%		y%		z%				

Date	Security	Invested (cost)	Raised	Post-money valuation	Price/ share	Current value/ share	Investment (current value)
MM/YY	Common A	EUR 0.1 m	EUR 0.4 m	EUR 2.0 m	EUR 22.8	EUR 36.3	EUR 0.1 m
MM/YY	Pfd B	EUR 0.2 m	EUR 0.5 m	EUR 6.2 m	EUR 47.8	EUR 36.3	EUR 0.6 m
MM/YY	Pfd C	EUR 0.2 m	EUR 0.3 m	EUR 1.5 m	EUR 6.6	EUR 36.3	EUR 6.5 m
Total		**EUR 0.5 m**	**EUR 1.2 m**				**EUR 7.2 m**

Note: this fund applies the historical cost method (as opposed to fair market value) to value its portfolio.

Template 5 (Company): Non-Disclosure Agreement

*N*ote: *this template is for illustration only and does not replace professional advice in the conception of such documents.*

Attention to _____

[Company]

COMMUNICATION OF CONFIDENTIAL INFORMATION AND NON-DISCLOSURE AGREEMENT

Dear [Mr/Mrs_____],

In connection with the potential interest of [Company] ("The Company") for the businesses and the projects of our company, [The Business] has agreed to provide you with a confidential information package concerning [The Business], its businesses and projects (the "Information Package"), upon the terms and conditions hereinafter set forth in this letter (the "Agreement").

The making of an investment by The Company as well as all acts preceding or succeeding such investment, whether committed by The Company or The Business, which are directed towards or related to a potential investment by The Company shall hereinafter jointly be referred to as the "Investment Process".

In this Agreement, unless the context otherwise requires, the term "The Company" shall include also The Company's affiliates and The Company's and its affiliates' respective directors and employees ("Representatives").

In case The Company wishes to involve any external party (including *inter alia*, financial, legal, technical, commercial advisors, financing banks, auditors, etc.) in the Investment Process and/or to give any external party access to the Information Package, The Company shall require the prior written consent of The Business, which consent may be withheld for any reason and/or may be rendered contingent upon the receiving party entering into a confidentiality undertaking with The Business. The Company's access to any information regarding The Business and/or the Investment Process shall remain contingent upon The Company's compliance with such consent requirements.

1. Without the prior written consent of The Business, The Company shall refrain from initiating, accepting or engaging in any contact concerning the Investment Process with any persons other than those specifically designated for such purposes in writing by The Business; in particular The Company shall refrain from, directly or indirectly, contacting or entertaining any person connected with The Business or

343

any of its managers, directors or employees in relation to any aspect concerning the Investment Process.

2. All business, financial, operational and marketing information, or other information or documentation, relating to The Business and its businesses and projects, which may be disclosed to The Company preceding or during the Investment Process orally or in writing, including but not limited to the Information Package, as well as, but not limited to, analyses, compilations, forecasts, studies or other documents prepared by The Company containing or otherwise reflecting such information or The Company's review of The Business and its businesses and projects (hereinafter collectively referred to as the "Confidential Information") shall be kept strictly confidential, shall be treated with the same degree of precaution and safeguards as The Company uses to protect its own confidential information of like importance, and shall be used solely for the purpose of evaluating an investment in connection with the Investment Process and shall not be used in any other way.

3. The term Confidential Information does not include any information which,
   (a) at the time of its disclosure to The Company or thereafter, is generally known by the public, provided that such disclosure is not the result of any violation by The Company of any of the terms and conditions set forth in this Agreement; or
   (b) has been independently acquired or developed by The Company without violating any of the obligations pursuant to this Agreement and without using any of the Confidential Information.

4. The Company shall not disclose the Confidential Information in whole or in part to any person or entity except those Representatives that are directly involved in the Investment Process and who need to know such information for that purpose. The Company shall procure that, except for the Representatives referred to in the previous sentence, no other persons or entities shall become acquainted with the Confidential Information. The Company shall procure in any event that any person to which Confidential Information shall be disclosed, prior to such disclosure, shall have acknowledged the contents of this Agreement and shall have committed to unconditional and strict compliance with the terms and conditions set forth herein, as if such person were a party hereto.

5. The terms and conditions set forth under 4 herein do not apply with respect to Confidential Information or any part thereof that must be disclosed by The Company pursuant to applicable law; provided, however, that The Company in such event shall have given timely advance written notice of such obligation to The Business insofar as permitted by the applicable law, in order to provide The Business with the opportunity to consult The Company regarding (a) the contents of Confidential Information intended to be disclosed thereby, (b) the timing, manner and form of such disclosure, and/or (c) the desirability of submitting the scope of such disclosure obligation to a competent court. The Company shall in any event exercise its best efforts to ensure that any such disclosures result in the maximum possible level confidential treatment accorded to the Confidential Information thus disclosed.

6. Without the written prior consent of The Business, and except as set forth under 5 above, The Company shall neither directly nor indirectly make any oral or written disclosure to any person or entity concerning facts or acts which relate to the Investment Process or otherwise set forth in this Confidentiality Agreement; the scope of the foregoing includes but is not limited to disclosures relating to the fact that The

Company has been invited to consider an investment in The Business, has received information regarding The Business, its businesses and projects, that The Company is involved or has been involved in the Investment Process, or more generally that an investment in The Business is being contemplated.

7. The Confidential Information does not entitle The Company to exercise any right, except as expressly set forth in this Agreement. The Company expressly acknowledges that Confidential Information which is disclosed to it prior to, during or in connection with the Investment Process as well as any other documents, correspondence and/or oral information made available to or directed to The Company shall not constitute any offer with regard to The Business, and The Company furthermore acknowledges that such Confidential Information shall not form the basis of any investment decision or contract, unless explicitly otherwise agreed with The Business in writing.

8. This Agreement does not constitute any offer, invitation, agreement or obligation to negotiate an investment in The Business. The Business reserves the right at any time, in its absolute discretion and without advance notice, to terminate discussions or negotiations with The Company regarding a transaction involving an investment in The Business its businesses and projects. The Company explicitly acknowledges that neither The Business, nor the direct or indirect shareholders of The Business, shall have any obligation to accept or otherwise respond to any offer or proposal made during the Investment Process by The Company, without regard to the contents of such offer or proposal. The Company shall furthermore not be entitled to claim any form of exclusivity with respect to the Investment Process. The Business shall not be bound towards The Company with respect to the possible investment in The Business, nor shall The Business have any obligation towards The Company to enter into any (exclusive) negotiations, unless and until such may have been explicitly and expressly agreed upon by means of a written agreement duly signed by or on behalf of The Business and The Company.

9. The Company shall hold none of The Business, its shareholders, or any of its directors, employees, representatives or external advisors (the "Indemnified Persons") liable in any respect regarding the completeness or accuracy of any information contained in the Confidential Information and/or any other oral or written representation made by or on behalf of any Indemnified Person.

10. In the event that the Investment Process shall not result in a definitive investment or agreement, The Company shall hold none of the Indemnified Persons liable for any consequences therefrom, including without limitation any damages suffered or costs incurred, irrespective of the reasons for the investment or agreement not being concluded.

11. All materials embodying, or copies of, Confidential Information, in whatever form, shall be returned to The Business immediately upon the first request by The Business, and no copy of such documents shall be retained by The Company. The analyses, compilations, forecasts, studies or other documents prepared by The Company with respect to the Confidential Information shall be destroyed upon the expiration of this Agreement, or if sooner, upon the first request by The Business, and The Company shall in any such event confirm to The Business in writing that such destruction has indeed taken place.

12. The Company shall indemnify and hold harmless the Indemnified Persons against any losses, claims, demands, liabilities, charges and expenses of whatever nature arising out of a breach by The Company of any of its obligations hereunder.

Under no condition shall The Business be held to have waived any of its rights or defences pursuant to this Agreement unless such has been stated to The Company explicitly and in writing by The Business.

The Company hereby waives any rights to rescind or nullify the agreement set out in this Agreement.

The Company acknowledges and agrees that The Business is a newly created company and that any breach by The Company of any of its obligations hereunder will constitute a strong and heavy loss to The Business or any other Indemnified Person in the carrying out and development of its activities.

This Agreement shall remain valid for a period of three years. For the avoidance of doubt, upon the termination of the Investment Process, the terms and conditions set forth in this Agreement shall remain in full force and effect until the expiration of such [number] year term.

The provisions set out in this Agreement shall be severable in the event that any of the provisions hereof are held by a court or arbitral tribunal of competent jurisdiction to be invalid, void or otherwise unenforceable, and the remaining provisions shall remain enforceable to the fullest extent permitted by law.

This Agreement shall be governed by and construed in accordance with the laws of [Country/Jurisdiction]. Any dispute arising out of or in connection with this letter and any letter and/or agreement resulting herefrom shall be finally settled by the Court of [City/Jurisdiction].

If you are in agreement with the foregoing, please sign (including by initialling each page) and return the enclosed copy of this Agreement which shall constitute our agreement with respect to the subject matter of this letter.

Yours faithfully,
The Business
[Signatories]

FOR ACKNOWLEDGEMENT AND APPROVAL:

The Company

_____

(Name)

_____

(Function title)

_____

(Place and date)

*N*ote: *this template is for illustration only and does not replace professional advice in the conception of such documents. This document is adapted from a template of the Australian Private Equity & Venture Capital Association (www.avcal.com.au/looking-for-capital/preparing-a-business-plan). The page also provides advice to structure an elevator pitch.*[1]

The business plan is the defining document to convince investors (who view hundreds of these documents per year) that the company and its management team have the ability to achieve their goals within a specified timeframe matching the investors'. This document should explain:

- The nature of the business.
- What the management wants to achieve.
- How the company is going to reach this goal.

The management of the company prepares the business plan, which should set ambitious but achievable targets.

Business plans range from 30 to more than 100 pages. They should address a rather broad public of investors, executives (current or would-be), stakeholders (including potentially banks, leasing companies, etc.), and thus be understandable by an educated but non-specialised public. They should hence avoid jargon and also baseless statements (i.e., all affirmations should be based on facts and figures).

The document should be revised regularly to reflect the progresses, obstacles encountered and new targets of the company. These update cycles are the occasion to reflect on past projections and targets, learn from the gaps between targets and achievements to set forth more accurate targets and achieve them with a higher degree of confidence.

The business plan should at least include the following elements:

Executive Summary

This section is probably the most important. It sums up the content of the business plan, placed at the beginning to highlight the most important points, hence delivering

---

[1] The elevator pitch is a 1–3-minute introductory speech designed to provide the auditor with the substance of a project and lead to further detailed discussions.

the core messages of the business plan and guiding the reader. Hence, it is best written last, with significant effort, thought and time. In effect, investors will filter most of the opportunities in a first approach based on this section of the business plan.

The executive summary is not only factual, but also very clearly written, to the point and persuasive. It is an example of balance between a sales pitch (which refers to the offering and the market need) and a grounded argumentation (which refers to the operations, the processes and the company building).

The executive summary is usually developed over two to three pages (almost exclusively text).

Background on the Company

Every company has a start – even if yet to be created. This section should provide the origins of the company and its history, its current situation, its activity (including past, present and projected), and what the management expects to achieve with the company in the future.

Product(s) and/or Service(s)

What does the company do? It is important to describe its product(s) and/or service(s) not only in detail, but also in English understandable by an educated (but non-specialist) reader. Regardless of the level of technical sophistication of products or services, this section has to be written without jargon or technical language.

Beyond descriptions, this section should emphasise what is (are) the competitive advantage(s) of the product(s) and/or service(s) (against current or prospective competition), and what actual/prospective need this product/service fits (hence linking it with a solvent demand).

This section should also state precisely the current stage of development of each product and/or service, without anticipating this development stage (for example, idea, prototyping, beta-testing/pilot, go-to-market, industrialisation, export for consumer electronic products). As a matter of fact, the type of financing is related to the stage of development of the company and its products, as it requires different expertise, know-how, contacts and level of financing from the investors. Stating factually where the company stands on each product line and/or service.

It is also important to emphasise not only what will be done, or is currently done, but what has been done so far (including trials/errors, changes of course, past products and services) and it helps the investor to determine the strength of the current argumentation and to assess the product(s) and/or service(s) dynamics, vulnerability, pace of obsolescence and place in a given value chain.

Intellectual property and the protection thereof is hence part of this section, notably the patents (and current status), know-how, brands and other elements of protection.

Exhibits:

- A Gantt diagram.
- A schedule.

These are advised as they help to figure out the degree of professionalism of the management, as well as its ability to cope with deadlines and milestones.

In venture capital, this is crucial as each capital injection is realised to reach the next milestone. Delays might imperil the company and/or the investments done so far (notably if fundraising happens as an emergency solution as a 'down round', which is highly dilutive for the current investors as the valuation of the company is drastically revised downwards). Investors have hence to assess how realistic the schedule is.

Customer Needs, Market Size and Solvency of Customers

A product/service without a significant and solvent market is useless. This section should combine descriptions and analysis, based on facts, to identify:

- What need the product/service answers. This should lead to the description of the industry and sectors where the company is positioned and later pave the way for a competitive assessment. The market(s) size(s) should be estimated here with factual data, as well as its/their past, current and future dynamics. The degree of maturity of the market has also to be assessed and connected to the section below (and notably which segment of the market is then addressed and how).
- Who are the customers? This should lead to a clear and grounded market segmentation. This should include distribution channels, purchase behaviours, description of purchase cycles, identification of the buyers, the payers and the users (who might be different groups of individuals); details about the solvency of the buyer (including how high/critical the purchase is on its list of purchases, as well as the rapidity of adoption of the product/service, and also price sensitivity); the delays in payments (including statistics about delinquencies) and other factual data to assess clearly the marketing strategy in the next section.
- How does the competition answer (at least partially) the need identified? This should encompass any alternative, including free/self-made products/services. Competitors can be current or prospective (note that some of the prospective competitors might be buyers of the company that the investor would finance). What are the strengths and weaknesses of the competitors? What are the barriers to entry/exit of this market? What is the market share of the main competitors? Who sets the pricing structure of the market (the market leader(s) usually do)?
- What were the main hurdles faced by existing actors in the past to answer the customer's needs? How were these problems overcome by the market (if they were)?
- What are the current risks, issues and concerns affecting your business and the industry?

Exhibits:

- A typical Porter's 'SWOT' (strengths, weaknesses, opportunities and threats) analysis would help.
- A positioning on the marketing 'S-curve' of any given service/product might prove very helpful to discuss with and convince investors.
- Market studies, panel of prospects, sales figures, etc.
- Projections for the company and the market.

Marketing

How will the business address the prospective customers and exploit opportunities?

- What is the sales and distribution strategy? How does the competition sell and distribute? How will the direct/indirect sales forces be built? What is their training period? Their expected success rate? What is the level of renewal of unsuccessful sales forces? What is a typical sales cycle (including pre-sales and post-sales management)?
- How does the company address its different market segments? What is the branding and communication strategy? Who are the main market prescriptors and how does the company plan to engage with them?
- How do foreign markets compare to yours? How do you plan to address them?
- What is the pricing strategy? How was it defined? How does it position the product/service compared to the competition? What are the margins on the products?
- What are the communication, advertising, public relations and promotion plans?

Operations

How will the business be structured, operated and make the products or provide the services?

- What is the production cycle? How does it position the company in the industry value chain? What are the relative powers of the suppliers? The customers? How does the company organise its relations with them? Its competitors? Its stakeholders (corporate unions, labour unions, lobbies, regulators)?
- What are the physical, financial and labour resources needed by the company to operate? What are the costs associated with these resources? What are the alternatives (out-sourcing, leasing, etc.) and the costs and rigidities associated with them? What are the switching points (where reallocating resources or switching production modes make sense) to monitor?
- How is the company's R&D organised? What are the expected deliverables and what is the timeframe?

Management Team

This section should prove that the management will be able to turn the business plan into reality. Additional experience is necessary (strategy, finance, marketing, operations, etc.), as well as different types of experience (large corporations, labs, ventures).

- The responsibilities of each team member should be highlighted, as well as what each person brings to the venture.
- Current and potential skills gaps: What are they, and how does the management plan to fill them? Investors sometimes help to fill these gaps.

- What are the management and staff performance measures, compensation mechanisms (including stock options), controls and other mechanisms in place or to be put in place?
- What are the service providers to the company (outsourced functions, etc.)?

Exhibits:

- Concise résumés for each team member (including achievements).
- Reference lists for each team member.
- Current and future organisation chart.

Financial Projections

These projections should be in line with the above-mentioned sections, notably in the revenue and income projections, as well as recruitment. They should be ambitious, but realistic and grounded in fact. Realism should always take precedence over optimism or ambition.

What are the hypotheses supporting sales, costs (fixed and variable) and other elements of the profit and loss statements? How is the working capital built? What are its constraints? How can it be optimised going forward?

- What are the fundamental trends and elements affecting cash flows? What is the worst-case scenario? What are the triggers to correct the course of the cash flows in case of problems? Solutions?
- What are the past, present and budgeted pro forma profit and loss and cash flow statements? Provide past and current balance sheets.
- Explain the margins, how they are built, how sensitive they are to pricing, to competition and other input fluctuations (raw materials).
- What are the current tangible and intangible assets of the company? Do they have an actual market value (liquidation value assessment)?
- Are there debts? If so, how are they structured and what are their durations and rates? What is the collateral? What is their seniority level?
- Details of costs should be provided, as well as their evolution and importance to the business.
- What are the sales prices (or fees charged)? Are there rebates involved? If so to whom, for which reason and at which level?
- Provide key ratios for further analysis and discussion with the investor.
- Provide best, base and worst-case scenarios, the triggers, the plan to address the worst-case scenario, the delays associated with it and the metrics to observe.
- What were the past capital increases (date, amounts, valuations, special rights such as options)? What are the current amounts required (if any) and under which conditions? What are the future amounts required (if any)? The same question applies to debt.
- What is the capital structure (capitalisation table) before and after financing, including options and dilution triggers?

Exhibits:

- Capitalisation table (current and future).
- Financial statements (past, present and future).

Exit

What are the different exit scenarios (type, horizon) for the investors and for what kind of expected returns? Provide the current valuation method and result, and explain how the future return could be made.

Exhibits:

- Valuation table for the company.

*N*ote: this template is for illustration only and does not replace professional advice in the conception of such documents. This document is adapted from a template of the Swiss Private Equity and Corporate Finance Association (www.seca.ch/sec/files/legal_and_tax/modal_documents/SECA_Term_Sheet_2011223.doc).

Term Sheet

PROPOSED INVESTMENT IN

[*Name of the company*] (the "**Company**")

This Term Sheet summarises the principal terms of a potential investment (the "**Series Capital Round**") in the Company, a stock corporation having its registered office at [*address*], [*country*]. It is for discussion purposes only, and except as specifically set forth below there is no legally binding obligation on the part of any negotiating party until definitive agreements are signed and delivered by all parties. This Term Sheet does not constitute an offer to sell nor an offer to purchase securities in the Company.

Company/Issuer	[*Name of the company*]
Investment Amount	[*amount*]
Investors	[*Investor 1*] [*currency*] [*amount*]
	[*Investor 2*] [*currency*] [*amount*]
	[*Investor 3*] [*currency*] [*amount*]
	Total [*currency*] [*amount*]
Type of Security	[*number*] of newly issued [preferred/common] ----- shares with a nominal value of [currency] [*amount*] each ("[preferred/common] ----- **Shares**")

Company/Issuer	*[Name of the company]*
Issue Price per [preferred/ common] ----- Shares	[currency] [amount]
Pre-Money Valuation	[currency] [amount] fully diluted pre-money valuation (including the effects of shares issuable to holders of options, warrants and other convertible securities of the Company, if any)
Pre-Closing Shareholder Structure	*[Founders]* [number] shares [%]% of issued share capital *[Other Shareholders]* [number] shares [%]% of issued share capital *[Management]* [number] shares [%]% of issued share capital

Total [currency] [**amount**]

Employee Participation/ Option Pool	*[Information about existing employee participation/option pool, if any, as well as information about employee participation/option pool to be implemented together with Series ------- Capital Round]*
Shareholder Structure after Series ------ Capital Round	As of completion of the Series ------- Capital Round the Company shall have an issued share capital of [currency] [amount] divided into [number] common shares and [number] [preferred/common] ------ Shares with a nominal value of [currency] [amount] each and the ownership structure of the Company [on a fully diluted basis] and the holdings of each shareholder in the respective class of shares shall be as set forth in Appendix 1.
Use of Proceeds	[All corporate purposes/activities consistent with the business plan]
Ranking	Up to the [preferred/common] ----- Amount the [preferred/common] ----- Shares will rank [senior to the -------- shares, and/or junior to the ------- shares] of the Company with respect to liquidation and dividends.
[Preference] ----- Amount	[Preference] ------- Amount shall mean the sum of (i) the aggregate Issue Price paid by the respective holder of [Preferred] ------ Shares and (ii) interest of [%]% per year on the Issue Price (to be calculated on the basis of the Issue Price paid and not yet compensated by a preferred repayment) since payment of the Issue Price until payment of the [Preference] ------- Amount in full.

Company/Issuer	*[Name of the company]*
Dividends	Dividends which will be payable when, as and if declared by the shareholders upon proposal by the Board of Directors, shall be paid in first priority to the holders of [Preferred] ---- Shares pro rata to their holdings in the [Preferred] ---- Shares. The maximal amount of preferred dividends shall not exceed the [Preference] ------ Amount less any proceeds received by a holder of [Preferred] ----- Shares resulting from a liquidation or Sale of the Company. Further dividends to be paid to all holders of [Preferred] ----- Shares and common shares pro rata to their respective aggregate holdings of shares in the then issued share capital of the Company will be paid only provided the [Preference] ---- Amount has been fully paid.
Liquidation Preference	In the event a voluntary or non-voluntary liquidation, a dissolution or winding up or a Sale of the Company occurs, the proceeds resulting from these operations shall be allocated as follows: In first priority and up to the [Preference] ----- Amount to the holders of [Preferred] Shares pro rata to their holdings in the [Preferred] ----- Shares. The maximal amount payable to holders of [Preferred] ----- Shares shall not exceed the [Preference] ----- Amount less any proceeds received by a holder of [Preferred] ----- Shares resulting from a previous Sale or preferred dividends. In second priority, if and to the extent the [Preference] ----- Amount has been fully paid, to all holders of [Preferred] ----- Shares and common shares pro rata to their respective aggregate holdings of shares. A "Sale" shall mean the sale, transfer or other disposal (whether through a single transaction or a series of related transactions) of shares in the Company that result in a change of control or the sale of all or [substantially all] [a major part] of the Company's assets.
Conversion	Voluntary Conversion: Holders of [Preferred] ----- Shares may convert their [Preferred] ----- Shares at any time into common shares at the conversion rate of *[rate]*.

Company/Issuer	*[Name of the company]*

Mandatory Conversion:

Each [Preferred] ----- Share will be automatically converted into common shares of the Company [at the then applicable conversion rate] upon (i) an IPO with a firm underwriting commitment of the underwriter(s)/global co-ordinator(s) in respect of newly issued Shares representing an aggregate issue price in excess of [currency] [*amount*], or (ii) a Sale that values the Company in excess of [currency] [*amount*], or (iii) the consent of [each of the Investor Directors]/[the majority of the Investor Directors]/ [the affirmative vote of the Investors holdings more than [·]% of the then outstanding [Preferred] ----- Shares].

Anti-Dilution	[Weighted average/Full ratchet.] [By transfer of shares for no consideration.] [By issuance of shares at nominal value.]
Voting Rights	Each [Preferred] ----- Share carries one vote; i.e., the same vote as each common share.
Qualified Majorities	Important Shareholders Matters as listed in Appendix 2 shall be subject to the following approval requirements:

[(i) two thirds (66 2/3% of shareholder votes [and the absolute majority of the then issued nominal share capital] of the Company and (ii) two thirds (66 2/3%) of shareholder votes of the holders of Preferred A shares]

Important Board Matters as listed in Appendix 2 shall be subject to the following approval requirements:

Besides the consent of the majority of the board members present at the meeting [consent of [each]/[at least [number]] of the directors nominated by the Investors.

Board Composition	The Board shall comprise a maximum of [*number*] Directors. Each Investor shall have the right to be represented on the Board by [*number*] Director[s] nominated by [each of]/[the absolute majority of the voting rights represented by the] Investors[, if and as long as the aggregate shareholdings of [such Investor]/[all Investors] reach or exceed [number] percent of the Company's then issued and outstanding share capital] (each an **"Investor Director"**).

Company/Issuer	*[Name of the company]*
	The [Founders]/[Other Shareholders] shall have the right to be represented on the Board by [*number*] Director[s] nominated by [the absolute majority of the voting rights represented by] the holders of Common Shares[, if and as long as the aggregate shareholdings of all Common Shareholders reach or exceed [number] percent of the Company's then issued and outstanding share capital] (each a **"Common Shareholder Director"**).
	The [Board]/[Shareholders collectively by [the majority] of voting rights represented by the Shareholders] shall from time to time nominate [*number*] independent Director[s] (each an **"Independent Director"**).
Information Requirements	Each [Investor]/[shareholder holding at least [*number*]% of [Preferred] ----- Shares] will receive the information listed below and will have the right (i) to discuss any issues relating to its investment and the Company with the Company and (ii) to periodically inspect the books, records and facilities of the Company.
	within [90 days] of the end of each financial year, audited financial statements;
	within [30 days] of the end of each fiscal quarter, unaudited quarterly financial statements [and a 12 month rolling forecast];
	within [20 days] of the end of each month, monthly management accounts (i.e., balance sheet, profit and loss statement, cash flow statement); and
	no later than [60 days] prior to the end of each financial year, the proposed budget for the next following financial year.]
	[Alternative: The Investor[s] will have customary financial and other information rights.]
Subscription Preference	Except for shares to be delivered under Employee Participations each holder of [Preferred] ----- Shares shall have a [preferential] right to subscribe for any new equity or equity related securities offered by the Company at the same terms and conditions as specified in such offer, i.e., that new equity or equity related securities offered shall be available to holders of [Preferred] ----- Shares in their entirety [if and to the extent necessary to effect the anti-dilution protection of each holder of [Preferred] ----- Shares].

Company/Issuer	*[Name of the company]*
General Transfer Restrictions	No transfer other than transfers in accordance with the transfer restrictions foreseen in the Series ----- Shareholders Agreement.
Right of First Refusal	In first priority the Investors, in second priority the Company and in third priority all other shareholders will have the right of first refusal to purchase any shares any shareholder wishes to transfer to another shareholder or a third party in any transaction other than a transfer of an Investor to an affiliate of such Investor.
Tag-Along Right	Each of the shareholders shall have the right to participate, on a pro rata basis on identical terms, in any transfer or sale of shares by other shareholders provided such transfer or sale of shares would relate to [[%]% of all shares]/ [[%]% of all [Preferred] Shares]/[result in a Change of Control]
Drag-Along Right	In the event [a holder of [Preferred] ----- Shares]/[a group of holders of more than [50]% of [Preferred] ----- Shares]/[all holders of [Preferred] ----- Shares] wish[es] to transfer 100% of [its]/[their] aggregate shareholdings in the Company in one or a series of related transactions to a proposed acquirer (including another Shareholder) who wishes to acquire all (but not less than all) Shares in the Company pursuant to a bona fide purchase offer, [that holder]/[that group of holders]/[all holders] of [Preferred] ----- Shares (the **"Relevant Selling Shareholder[s]"**) shall, [subject to customary exclusions] have the right (but not the obligation) to require all other shareholders to sell, and the other shareholders hereby irrevocably agree to sell, all of their Shares then held to the proposed acquirer for the same consideration per Share and otherwise at the same terms and conditions as applicable to the Relevant Selling Shareholder[s].
Purchase Option	Each [shareholder]/[holder of [Preferred] ----- Shares] shall have an option to purchase the shares of another shareholder [in proportion to the nominal value of such shareholder's shareholdings in the Company][pro rata to such shareholder's holding of [Preferred] ----- Shares] upon the occurrence of [certain events to be defined in the Series ----- Shareholders Agreement and subject to the terms and conditions agreed in the Series Shareholders Agreement]/ [the following events:

Company/Issuer	*[Name of the company]*

   i. such shareholder dies, becomes incapable of acting or otherwise loses its capacity to exercise its rights and obligations under the Series Shareholder Agreement;
   ii. such shareholder becomes insolvent, bankrupt or petitions or applies to any court, tribunal or other authority for creditor protection or for the appointment of, or there shall otherwise be appointed a liquidator, trustee or other similar officer;
   iii. such shareholder commits a criminal act against the interests of another shareholder, of the Company or of any of its subsidiaries;
   iv. such shareholder materially breaches a provision of the Series Shareholders Agreement (unless such breach and its effects are fully cured within an agreed period of days); or
   v. any board membership, employment or consultancy agreement, as the case may be, between such shareholder and the Company is terminated.

Other than in (i) and a good leaver situation in (v) above, the purchase price shall be the lower of the fair market value and the nominal value of the Shares.]

Related Party Transactions	All transactions and dealings between the Company and its shareholders and/or members of senior management will reflect market conditions and be made on arm's length terms.
Confidentiality	The terms and existence of this Term Sheet are confidential and will not be disclosed by the undersigned except as otherwise agreed in advance by each of the parties hereto.
Exclusivity	From the date hereof until [date], or such earlier date upon which the Investor[s] and the Company agree in writing to terminate discussions contemplated by this Term Sheet, the Company [and the members of the senior management]/[and Founders] will not, directly or indirectly, solicit or participate in any way in negotiations with, or knowingly provide any information to, any person (other than the Investor[s] or any representative of the Investor) concerning any potential investment in the debt or equity securities of the Company (an **"Alternative Proposal"**) or otherwise facilitate any effort or attempt to make or consummate an Alternative Proposal.

Company/Issuer	*[Name of the company]*
Documentation	The investment into the Company shall be made pursuant to the agreements and documents listed below drafted by the counsel to [Investor[s]/[Company]: – Series ----- Investment and Subscription Agreement (such agreement to contain, among other things, customary representations and warranties for a transaction of this nature, indemnification provisions, and such other matters as the Investor[s] shall reasonably determine); – Series-----Shareholders Agreement; – Series -----Articles; and – Board Regulations.
Conditions to Closing	The consummation of the Series ----- Capital Round contemplated by this Term Sheet shall be subject to satisfactory due diligence and the approval and signing of the Documentation by the Investor[s].
Legal Fees and Expenses	The Company will reimburse the Investor[s], or pay at the direction of the Investor[s], for the reasonable legal fees and expenses incurred by counsel to the Investor[s], payable at Closing such fees and expenses not to exceed [currency] *[amount]*. Should the investment not complete each side shall pay their own costs. [The Investors agree amongst themselves to share the costs of legal counsel and other due diligence expenses and costs.]
Non-Compete	*[wording regarding any non-compete undertakings by the founders and/or the managers to be added if appropriate]*
Timing	Due Diligence: [date] Negotiations: [date] Signing: [date] Closing: [date] End of Exclusivity: [date]
Effect of Term Sheet	The parties expressly agree that, with the exception of the obligations as set out under the headings ["Confidentiality", "Exclusivity", "Timing", "Legal Fees and Expenses", "Effect of Term Sheet" and "Governing Law"] which are intended to be and shall be legally binding, no binding obligations shall be created by this Term Sheet until definitive, legally binding agreements are executed and delivered by the parties.

Company/Issuer	*[Name of the company]*
Governing Law	This Term Sheet as well as the Series ----- Investment and Subscription Agreement and Series A Shareholders Agreement shall be governed by *[nationality]* law and shall provide for either the jurisdiction of the ordinary courts of *[place]* or binding arbitration in *[place]* in accordance with the *[nationality]* Rules of International Arbitration Rules of the *[nationality]* Chambers of Commerce.

[Signatories]
BY: _____
NAME: _____
TITLE: _____

*B*usiness case prepared by Cyril Demaria & Rafael Sasso, January 2013.[1]
It is a busy morning in São Paulo, this 24th June 2009. Advent International has just announced its investment in one of the major listed educational companies: Kroton Educacional SA. The press headlines reflect the stock exchange's reaction: a bold move, which can pay off tremendously but has high stakes.

The market sentiment is that the Brazilian education market is on the verge of major shifts. It has been growing at a fast pace, propelled by the economic growth and the need for highly skilled workers. Private companies have thrived in this context. Some of them are now listed and the market is evolving fast, notably towards distance/e-learning. At the same time, competition is intensifying.

While Kroton Educacional SA is a very promising investment, stock prices of listed educational companies are languishing against the main index of the Brazilian stock exchange (BM&F Bovespa). Advent has now to prompt change in its new portfolio company, and there is more than one investment thesis at stake in private equity investing. Which of his options would be the best to transform Kroton into the Brazilian market leader?

THE BRAZILIAN EDUCATION MARKET

The Brazilian private education market really took off in 1997–1999. A regulation change paved the way for the development of private for-profit educational institutions. Following this change, the market grew for 25 years at double-digit rates, however at a rather low margin, as a price war erupted between the different providers. Moreover, a certain lack of professionalism and ability to scale up their offer markedly affected certain companies.

---

[1]The case has been developed solely for class discussion purposes. It should not be used, and has not been written to illustrate, endorse, judge or criticise management; and is not intended to be a source of primary data.

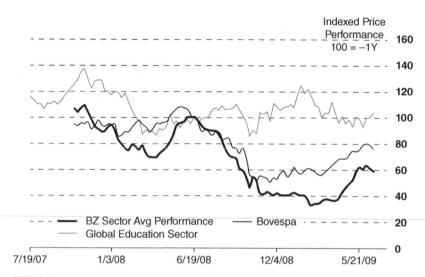

FIGURE BC.1 The Brazilian education sector has under-performed the Bovespa
Source: Morgan Stanley 2009.

Due to the combination of the price war, low margins and strong competition, the education sector has under-performed the Brazilian stock exchange evolution by 35% (see Figure BC.1).

The Brazilian education industry is highly fragmented. The private education market numbers 2472 schools, of which only 58 count more than 10 000 students, and 711 more than 1000 students. The top 20 schools account for only 20% of enrolments. In that respect, 2009 may be a catalyst for change: it has been a bad year for the sector, notably in terms of earnings degradation due to poor employment figures and the impact of delinquency on tuition payments (which can only be accounted for after 6 months).

The private education market in Brazil is composed of two segments: K-12 and the postgraduate segment.

K-12 Market

The Brazilian government has strongly supported primary and secondary education over the last few years, which has led to a surge in national literacy rates (higher among 15–24-year-olds than in the general population). This in return has increased the percentage of the population which could potentially attend post-secondary schools. Education facilities are used in a dual way: during the day, they are schools for K-12 students. In the evening and at night, they support distance learning.

Kroton Educacional has a large national coverage through its offering in basic and secondary schools. Kroton's network counts roughly 600 schools (and 200 000 students) operated under the Pitagoras brand (see Exhibit 9).

Post-Secondary Market

Accelerated growth in the private sector appeared after the approval of the LDB[2] in 1996 (see Figure BC.2). From 1980 to 2000, the number of enrolled students doubled, and from 2000 to 2008 it doubled again.

As of 2009, there are 2250 public and 244 private higher education institutions, but the private sector accounts for around 75% of undergraduate enrolments as the public system is unable to meet demand. The public system has a very elitist approach to higher education and covers only 12% of offers. 1 770 000 students are excluded yearly from the public system. The private sector can absorb every year roughly 825 000 who can afford the tuition fees, leaving 945 000 students outside the system. This adds up to 7 000 000 people excluded from higher education: hence less than 14% of 18–24-year-olds undertake higher education studies, making Brazil one of the worst performers among OCDE countries in terms of access to education.

The private schools' monthly standard tuition fee is around R$457. Students in a public university cost the Brazilian state nearly R$27 400 a year (in line with the cost in developed countries). From 2003 to 2008, the number of public university students jumped from 281 000 to 330 000. During the same period, the private sector expanded its enrolments from nearly 1 700 000 to more than 2 500 000.

From 1997 to 2003, the private sector grew fast (16.8% on a yearly average, or 154% over the period). But in 2003 and 2004, the growth slowed respectively to

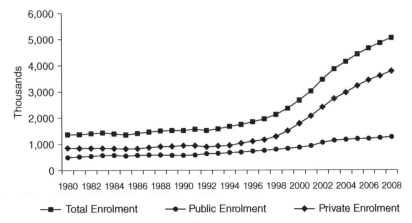

FIGURE BC.2   Rate of enrolments in public and private post-secondary education in Brazil
Source: Strauss and Borenstein – Analyzing the Brazilian Higher Education System using System Dynamics (2010).

---

[2]The Law 9.394/1996 (Directives and Bases of Education in Brazil) adopted in 1995 facilitated access to higher education, notably by changing the rules to launch courses and structure educational institutions. A rapid growth in higher education ensued, driven primarily by the private sector.

7.7% and 2%. The Brazilian government subsequently launched the ProUni programme (see below), and the growth rate recovered to 9.1% in 2005 (with 80 000 students benefitting from ProUni). Despite this programme, 2006 and 2007 saw the growth rates of the education market stall (3.8% and 2.8%, respectively).

Still, contradicting this trend, most of the analysts expect organic post-secondary growth to be the main driver of for-profit education companies in the following years, driven by a demand for skilled employees in industry. Morgan Stanley, for example, expected in June 2007 that the number of enrolments in post-secondary education would grow between 2007 and 2010 at an annual compound rate of 9.1% (see Figure BC.3).

According to the National Educational Plan (PNE), the Brazilian government is targeting a 50% gross enrolment rate in tertiary education by 2020 (vs roughly 30% in 2009, see Figure BC.4). The reward for post-secondary graduates is an increase in wages: on average they grow by 171% in Brazil (vs 62% in the USA), according to Hoper Educacional.

As of 2009, most post-secondary students in Brazil did not have access to public or private loans (unlike students of for-profit organisations in the USA). Brazilian students hence have to self-finance their post-secondary education, usually on a monthly basis, over the duration of the programme. The postgraduate segment is hence sensitive to macro-economic data, such as unemployment levels, working adults' sentiments about the future and their economic prospects, and access to credit to finance studies. Brazil has a low gross enrolment ratio compared to more developed countries (24% vs 70%), essentially because many families cannot afford to pay for private education. Credit is hence a key factor. Kroton used to offer a financing programme (INED[3] programme) through which students could pay for their 24–30-month programme in a maximum of 36 instalments.

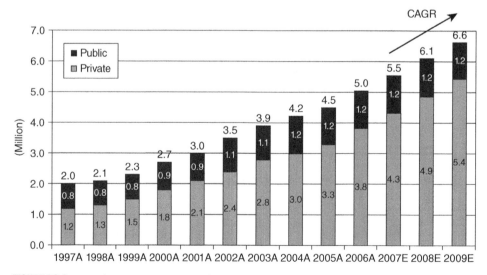

FIGURE BC.3   Enrolments in post-secondary education in Brazil
Source: Company data & Morgan Stanley 2007.

---

[3]See Exhibit 9 for the brand segmentation of Kroton.

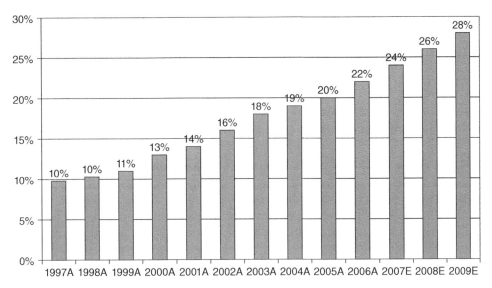

FIGURE BC.4 Rates of enrolment in post-secondary education in Brazil
Source: Company data & Morgan Stanley 2007.

Tuition Financing Mechanisms

Alternative financings to fund higher education studies exist:

- Since 2006, Ideal Invest SA has managed funds dedicated to education, and has provided students with loans to finance college tuition (funding it on the capital markets through securitisation).
- PRAVALER is the main private programme to fund university studies in Brazil. Developed as an alternative to public schemes, it counts more than 260 education institutions as partners. Its shareholders count, among others, a fund managed by Victoria Capital Partners, the International Finance Corporation (IFC, the World Bank's financial arm), a fund managed by EOS Investments and Itaú Bank. 12 500 courses are financed in the programme. Monthly interest rates vary from 0% to 1.99%.

To give access to post-secondary education to students (who are working adults) from middle- and low-income families, the government created programmes that have largely driven the increase in student enrolment numbers, mainly young working adults seeking better salaries and employment opportunities. The main programmes are ProUni (Programa Universidade Para Todos) and FIES (Financing for Higher Education Students).

(a) ProUni – Programa Universidade Para Todos

This programme, established in 2005 (see Table BC.1), exempts education institutions granting scholarships to low-income undergraduate students from certain federal taxes. To join the programme, institutions must:

TABLE BC.1 Grants provided under the ProUni programme

Year	Partial grants	Total grants	Total
2005	40 370	71 905	112 275
2006	39 970	98 698	138 668
2007	97 631	66 223	163 854
2008	99 495	125 510	225 005

Source: Sesu/MEC, Financiamento estudiantil no ensino superior, Andrés 2011.

- Sign a contract for 10 years (renewable for a further 10 years), setting forth the number of scholarships to be offered in each programme, campus and course.
- Be up to date with their tax obligations.
- Offer scholarships to low-income students (at least one full scholarship for every 10.7 regular fee-paying students enrolled at the end of the previous academic year; or 8.5% of total revenue; or a full scholarship for every 22 regular fee-paying students in undergraduate and associate programmes, as long as they also offer 50% or 25% scholarships that add up to a total figure equal to 8.5% of the institution's annual revenue).

(b) FIES – Fundo de Financiamento ao Estudante do Ensino Superior

In 1999 the Brazilian Ministry of Education launched Financing for Higher Education Students (FIES) to finance the post-secondary education of students enrolled at private institutions (higher education institutions). FIES finances up to 100% of the post-secondary tuition fees owed to the institutions enrolled in the programme. More than 500 000 students have already benefitted from it, and the number of institutions belonging to the programme increases constantly. Since 2005, FIES has begun to support students also in the ProUni programme, hence financing the remaining 50% of their post-secondary education costs with a loan. Many students have begun to use both programmes jointly.

Many discussions are currently taking place to change FIES and the ProUni programme. The MEC (Ministry of Education) is evaluating the possibility of students applying for FIES before getting into university, at any time during the year, with more time to repay and without a guarantor. Another possibility is the inclusion of banks in the process.

CURRENT SITUATION IN BRAZIL

Employment

From 7.5% in August 2008, the unemployment rate reached 9% at the beginning of 2009. Signs of recovery appeared, and the unemployment rate seems to have stabilised.

Higher Education Market

The discussions in the industry are, in the short term, about margin normalisation driven by maturing capacities. Cost management emerges as a priority. In the long term, credit availability, economies of scale, branding and pricing power are identified as core topics. Distance learning is on everyone's lips and appears as a major relay of growth.

Private Equity Investments

The fragmented Brazilian post-secondary education market has attracted the attention of private equity funds. Education institutions appeared as an investment opportunity, notably because of their growth prospects and as a market with a rising solvent demand. Patria Investimentos listed Anhanguera in 2007, thus making a good case for other institutions to follow suit. In May 2008, GP Investments acquired a 20% stake in Estácio, a major listed educational player. The firms are following an aggressive growth strategy through acquisitions and operational improvements.

COMPETITION OF KROTON EDUCACIONAL SA

At the beginning of 2009, four main contenders (including Kroton) were shaping the Brazilian educational market (see Exhibit 5). All of them are publicly listed on the Brazilian stock exchange (BM&F Bovespa). They are among the largest companies in this fragmented market.

Anhanguera Educacional – AESA

AESA was created in 2003 by four institutions, with at that time approximately 8848 students enrolled in seven campuses, in six cities in the state of São Paulo. Instituto Superior de Comunicação Publicitária (ISCP) and the holding company of Universidade Anhembi Morumbi are notable shareholders, which contributed financially to launch campuses (10 were open by the end of 2005) and brought to AESA their expertise and knowledge of the market. In 2005, the private equity house Pátria Investments invested in AESA. Meanwhile, ISCP sold equity in AESA to the Fundo de Educação para o Brasil (FEBR), which injected new funds in AESA. FEBR obtained a credit facility from the International Finance Corporation (IFC) of USD 12 million for AESA. As a result, FEBR became AESA's controlling shareholder. As of 2009, AESA was the largest Brazilian for-profit educational organisation with 54 campuses, 450 e-learning centres and 650 teaching centres (according to the company).

The Anhanguera strategy is based on a unified pedagogical platform and a multi-operational model (providing AESA with scalability and economies of scale). In most cases, Anhanguera offers the lowest prices on the market. The teaching units are, in general, small to medium (with a capacity of 2000 to 7000 students). They are located in convenient places with easy access to public transport. The students are essentially young workers from D and C classes[4] looking for career development.

---

[4]See a description of Classes A, B, C and D in Exhibit 10.

Estacio

Created in 1970, the Estácio de Sá Law School is at the origin of the Estacio group. In 1972, with more undergraduate courses, it became Faculdades Integradas Estácio de Sá and in 1988 it reached the status of university. In 1992, expansion began in the city of Rio de Janeiro and in 1996 in the state of Rio de Janeiro. In 1998, the national expansion began with the creation of new campuses and teaching centres in the states of São Paulo, Minas Gerais, Espírito Santo, Santa Catarina, Mato Grosso do Sul, Bahia, Pernambuco, Pará and Ceará (with the first private medical school in the country), and Goiás in 2004. In 2000, the university was allowed to provide postgraduate courses (Masters and Doctorate).

In 2006, international academic programmes were developed (in partnership with the École Hotelière de Lausanne and Alain Ducasse Formation), as well as an academic partnership with Microsoft. In 2007, the process to turn the group into a for-profit institution was launched. In 2008, Moena Participações S.A. and the private equity fund manager GP Investments (through GP Capital Partners IV, L.P.), acquired 20% of Estacio, while gaining control of the company. In 2009, the group started an e-learning programme and launched a shared services centre (CSC), which executes the administrative, financial, accounting and IT functions of a university.

Estácio numbers more than 241 000 enrolled students in face-to-face or distance undergraduate and postgraduate courses, 29 campuses and 51 e-learning centres. Estácio's strategy is now focused on management professionalisation, the centralisation of back-office activities, distance learning expansion and acquisitions.

SEB

SEB (Brazilian Educational System) was founded in 1963 in the region of Ribeirão Preto[5] as a school and an actor in the educational sector. Through its C.O.C. brand, the company developed its reputation as a producer of education materials. Between 1990 and 2000, the company focused on building its facilities in Ribeirão Preto, developing a complete teaching methodology and introducing pre-primary education. In 1999, SEB began operating its post-secondary education line, UNICOC, and in 2001 created 'C.O.C. at Home', an educational Internet portal for primary, secondary and post-secondary offering content and communication tools. In 2006, the company launched Tele Sala and Future Class to expand its post-secondary segment through distance education (see Table BC.2).

Through its 46 years of operation, SEB has expanded its network through partnerships (both private and public), and developed tools and mechanisms to monitor its schools and campuses throughout Brazil and even abroad, ensuring a certain level of efficiency and quality. Today, SEB operates on the principal segments of the Brazilian education sector in a vertically integrated and systematic manner and offers:

- Primary and secondary education in its own schools.
- Primary and secondary learning systems (education methodology, content, training for teachers and educational services for associated private schools and associated municipalities).

---

[5] A rich region in the state of São Paulo known for its sugar cane production.

TABLE BC.2   Distance learning education (undergraduate programmes) at SEB

		Revenue breakdown (%)				
		2006	2007	2008	1Q08	1Q09
K-12	Own schools	47	46	42	38	40
	Learning system	35	34	31	37	30
Post-secondary	Own schools	17	16	18	18	17
	Learning system	1	4	9	7	13

Source: SEB Report – 1Q 2009.

- Post-secondary education on its own campuses for undergraduate and graduate programmes.

SEB's current strategy is focused on the expansion of its distance learning offer; implantation and expansion of post-secondary courses in the regional centres; continued investment in technology for education purposes; scalability and replication of offers; and continuing public sector partnerships.

KROTON EDUCACIONAL SA

Kroton Educacional SA is a Brazilian for-profit organisation dedicated to private education, namely the K-12 and the post-secondary segments.

Kroton is listed on the Bovespa under 'level 2',[6] which means that preferred shareholders have special rights under certain circumstances. This includes full tag-along rights in the case of a change in control; voting rights in the event of a merger, acquisition or spin-off; and approval of agreements between related-party transactions.

Since its IPO on the Bovespa (ticker: KROT11) at the end of 2007, the stock price of the company has been languishing (see Exhibit 2), despite significant financial results (see Exhibit 1) and growth in student enrolments (see Exhibit 7). The market capitalisation as of June 2009 was R$502 million (USD 255.7 million), for 31.5 million shares outstanding. The free float is 39%.

Kroton's Business Model

Kroton Educacional's business can be broken down into different activities:

- The management of pre-school, elementary, secondary and college preparatory schools ('K-12').
- Delivery of higher, professional and post-graduate education.
- Delivery of free courses, and other related educational activities.
- Wholesale, retail, distribution, import and export of textbooks, course books, magazines and other publications related to education.

---

[6] Kroton moved to Novo Mercado on 5 December 2012 and is now listed under KROT3.

The original business model of Kroton was developed and refined for the K-12 segment in the 1980s. Its offer was developed to be flexible and adapted to different local needs, while at the same time ensuring the delivery of contents subscribing to a constant level of quality. This approach is the key to Kroton's success and has been the source of its penetration into the post-secondary market. Thanks to this approach, Kroton benefits from a competitive advantage: its development is smoother and quicker.

This standardised platform provides Kroton with economies of scale, as well as ensuring at the same time a constant level of quality for every new school or campus added (whether an existing one or a new one). To deliver this high level of quality, Kroton closely tracks and oversees each partner or campus and provides high-quality training to professors and staff. Economies of scale are generated through the addition of new schools and campuses, as this requires very little or no adaptation of this plat-form. As the academic plan is standardised, this helps local staff to save time in planning and coordinating as well. Hence the network developed by Kroton is able to deliver the level of quality with no additional marginal cost.

So far, Kroton has been able to replicate this model and successfully implement it on 25 campuses. The company is hence perceived as a high-quality provider of basic and secondary education. It has successfully marketed its learning system to many private schools, based on a sales pitch of efficiency and cost-effectiveness towards quality. As a consequence, the Pitagoras[7] offer has reached a 98% renewal rate for its learning system products and services. This has positioned Kroton as a leading company, ranked by number of students (see Figure BC.5). However, the number net of acquisitions actually decreased in Q1 2009, compared to Q2 2008 (see Exhibit 7).

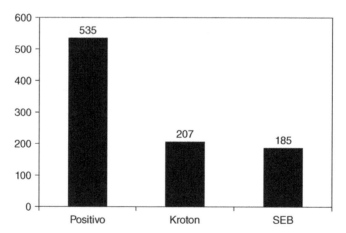

FIGURE BC.5 Positioning of Kroton Educacional SA as a provider of learning systems to the private sector (thousand students)
Source: Morgan Stanley 2009.

---

[7]See Exhibit 9 for the brand segmentation of Kroton.

The Strategy of Kroton Educacional SA

So far, Kroton Educacional SA has essentially been propelled by organic growth (by opening new campuses or purchasing licences to start them). This has allowed the company to keep its costs rather low compared to the competition (see Figure BC.6), which focuses on buying existing campuses and then streamlining them.

Challenges

One of the questions faced by Kroton is whether it will be able to implement its platform in other segments of the education industry, such as public schools, post-secondary education and distance learning. Distance learning in particular has been a difficult area, where the competition has struggled to develop so far.

Public schools (52% of which are municipal schools) have witnessed an increase in their budgets and correlatively higher levels of expected quality, set by the national Education Development Plan (PDE). Private learning systems would help them to meet these academic goals. SEB, which declares 145 000 learning students on its system, has already started to actively market to this category of customers as the content for public schools is the same as for private schools. If that market segment were to help amortise the costs of Kroton over a broader base, that would also mean a more aggressive pricing strategy in this segment to gain market share.

Expectations

Kroton has one of the highest growth rates amongst education companies in Brazil. Its growth so far has essentially been organic, through the (re-)development of schools and campuses. This approach represents a cost advantage, compared to strategies based on mergers and acquisitions. According to Morgan Stanley, Kroton should reach 137 000 post-secondary enrolments by the end of 2012, representing growth of over 400% in the period, equivalent to a 39% CAGR. At the same time, Kroton should deliver a 5-year EBITDA CAGR of 57% (2007–12E).

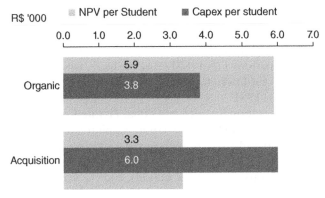

FIGURE BC.6 Compared economics between organic and external growth
Source: Morgan Stanley estimate 2009.

The Assets of Kroton Educacional SA According to Financial Analysts

Financial analysts highlight the fact that Kroton has a strong balance sheet to support its growth. Moreover, its platform is becoming more diversified as it combines its post-secondary business with its K-12 segment (mainly via its learning system). An upside compared to the analyst's base case could arise from the implementation of learning systems in public schools and distance learning.

The Risks of Kroton Educacional SA Listed by Financial Analysts

Financial analysts list the following risks:

- Increased competition.
- Failures in integrating the acquired companies.
- Stricter regulations (mainly on distance learning).
- Poor macro-environment leading to a slowdown in demand and higher drop-out rates.
- Possible funding gap to execute the business plan.
- Acquisitions made under the pressure of a large cash position.
- The employment recovery in Brazil could take longer than expected.

Kroton's growth profile is exposed to regulatory uncertainties (the Ministry of Education can take up to 3 years to approve a new campus) and uncertainties on attracting new students into a new city.

ADVENT INTERNATIONAL: A PRIVATE EQUITY PIONEER

History of Advent International

Created in Boston in 1984 by Peter Brooke, Advent International is a private equity firm which originally spun off from TA Associates. From the start, the firm had a 'specific brief of investing internationally', which contrasted with the US-centric approach of most private equity firms. For example, the same year it was created, Advent co-founded SEAVI, the first venture capital firm focused on Southeast Asia.

In 1987, Advent raised USD 225 million for its first institutional fund: the International Network Fund (the 'private equity industry's first global fund'). In 1989, it raised the European Special Situations Fund (USD 231 million), which is the 'first integrated pan-European fund'. Advent International opened an office in London in 1989, then in Frankfurt and in Milan in 1991.

In 1994, Advent International raised its Global Private Equity (GPE) II fund (USD 415 million). The firm absorbed UK-based Trinity Capital Partners. The same year, the firm raised its first Central and Eastern European private equity (ACEE) fund (USD 58 million).

In 1996, GPE III was raised (USD 1.2 billion), and the same year saw the opening of the Paris office. ACEE II was raised in 1998 (USD 182 million) and the Warsaw office was opened, followed by Bucharest in 2000. GPE IV (USD 1.9 billion) was raised in 2001, and the Madrid office opened in 2002. ACEE III (EUR 330 million) and GPE V (EUR 2.5 billion) in 2005.

In 2007, the Prague and Kiev offices were opened. Only a year later GPE VI (the largest mid-market buy-out fund, with EUR 6.6 billion) and ACEE IV (EUR 1 billion) were launched. The Mumbai office was then opened in 2009.

As of 2011, Advent International focused on 'mid- and upper-mid-market buyouts', with roughly 170 investment professionals of 29 nationalities. It declares that it has invested in more than 600 companies in 41 countries, which has led to 140 IPOs.

The LAPEF Programme

It was in 1996 that Advent International opened its Buenos Aires and Mexico City offices, and the Latin American private equity fund (LAPEF) (USD 230 million) was launched. The São Paulo office opened in 1997. LAPEF II was raised in 2002 (USD 265 million). LAPEF III was raised in 2005 (USD 375 million). LAPEF IV was the largest-ever private equity fund focused on Latin America with USD 1.3 billion, and was raised in 2007. LAPEF V was launched in 2010, with USD 1.65 billion, which also marked the opening of the New York and Istanbul offices. The following year, the Bogotá office was opened.

The LAPEF programme is focused on growth buy-outs of cash generative service businesses, with a primary geographic focus on Brazil, Mexico, Argentina and other selected Latin American countries. The typical equity investment realised is USD 50–200 million, in companies with a typical enterprise value of USD 50–750 million (or sometimes larger).

The industries targeted by the LAPEF programme are business services (including airport services and outsourcing), financial services, retail, consumer and leisure. Other sectors of investment include healthcare, industrial sectors, technology, media and telecommunications.

Its methods of investment are overall through control positions, but Advent International also considers minority investments if the proper governance is in place. Buy-outs are hence the main strategy of investment (acquisition of a business from its current owner, being a corporation, a family, a founder or through a de-listing). Expansion funding is another way of investing, to fund organic growth or market consolidation.

Values and Investment Philosophy

Advent International prides itself on working as a single and integrated team. All decisions are based on 'analytical study, open debate and consensus conclusions'. Advent's declared investment philosophy is 'centered on value creation driven through an active ownership approach'. One of the main differentiating factors, beyond the international approach which has characterised it since its inception, is a focus on growth (organic, external) and operational improvement, 'not on financial engineering'. It highlights the operational and consulting background of its professionals, as well as 60 'industry-specific operating partners'.

Acting as independent advisors, operating partners are former C-level executives who work alongside Advent's investment team to help portfolio companies in their development. These operating partners offer a strong industry knowledge, operational know-how, management experience and contacts. They can hold positions such as chairman or Board member in the portfolio companies, or may even be interim managers.

Investment decisions are taken by regional investment advisory committees, 'which review potential investment opportunities and oversee existing portfolio companies'.

These committees are made up of professionals from a specific region and a partner from another region 'to provide continuity and consistency across the process globally'.

The São Paulo Office

Headed by Juan Pablo Zucchini, Managing Director and Patrice Etlin, Managing Partner, the Brazilian office of Advent International numbers 19 employees (of which 13 are investment professionals). By comparison, the Mexico office numbers 19 employees (14 investment professionals), the Bogotá office 11 employees (8 investment professionals) and the Buenos Aires office 6 employees (4 investment professionals). Advent International won the 'Latin American Private Equity Firm of the Year' poll from the *Private Equity International* review in 2005, 2006, 2007, 2008, 2009 and 2011. Table BC.3 provides examples of investments realised by the São Paulo office.

TABLE BC.3   Investments of Advent International in Brazil

Name of company	Description	Sector
Terminal de Contêineres de Paranagua	Third largest container port terminal in Brazil	Business services
CETIP	Largest central depository and trading platform (OTC and private fixed-income securities)	Financial services
Kroton Educacional	Private education	Business services technology
Frango Assado	Highway restaurants	Consumer and leisure
Quero-Quero	Home-improvement retailer, credit card issuer and consumer finance	Retail financial services
Viena	Leading casual dining restaurant chain	Consumer & leisure
Grupo RA	Largest operator of restaurant concessions in airports	Consumer & leisure
Parana Banco	Consumer credit bank	Financial services
International Meat Company	Leading multi-brand, quick casual restaurant chain in Latin America	Consumer & leisure
Brasif Duty Free	Leading travel operator	Retail
Proservvi	Leading provider of back-office processing services for financial institutions	Business services Financial services
J. Malucelli Seguradora	Largest surety bond provider	Financial services
Atmosfera	Largest provider of textile services in Latin America	Business services
Atrium Telecomunicações	Building-centric local exchange carrier	Telecommunications
Microsiga	Largest provider of ERP software	Technology
Asta Medica	Business development, licensing and distribution of drugs	Healthcare pharmaceutical producer
CSU	Largest independent credit card administrator	Financial services Business services

Source: Advent International (as of 2011).

THE TRANSACTION

On 24th June 2009 (see Exhibit 6), Kroton Educacional SA and Advent International announced that the latter would invest R$280 million (at R$16.2 per share, a 1.3% premium on the previous day's price and a 19% premium on the average price of the last 60 trading days) for a 50% stake in PAP (Pitagoras Adm. e Part.). PAP is the controlling entity of Kroton (see Exhibit 4), with a 55% stake. The private placement will lead to a subscription of Advent of 101.98 million common shares and 20.93 million preferred shares.

Following this investment, PAP would increase Kroton's capital by R$220 million at a price of R$12.53 (the subscription ratio is 1.016:1 at R$12.53/unit, a 7.7% discount to the stock's average price on the prior 60 days, and a 22% discount on the previous day of closing). Minority shareholders benefit from subscription rights, which could lead to an equity increase of R$387 million. If they do not participate, that would imply a dilution of 36% in terms of number of shares. The free float would drop from 39% to 25%. The final amount of the capital increase was R$387 million (100% subscription).

As a result, Advent International will have three seats on the Board (out of a total of nine, see Exhibit 8) and will chair the human resources and financial/M&A committees. The academic and audit committees will be presided by other experts.

QUESTIONS SUPPORTING THE CASE RESOLUTION

(i) How would you describe Advent International's investment in Kroton? To what extent is it a typical private equity investment? How much does it differ from a typical private equity investment?

(ii) What is the rationale of Advent International's investment in Kroton? What is the current strategy of Kroton? How would Advent International's investment modify this strategy?

(iii) What are the main challenges that Kroton faces? What are its assets to answer these challenges? (To answer this question, a SWOT analysis may be required.)

(iv) How would you explain the premium and discounts that Advent International pays/benefits from at the time of investment? What could justify both of them?

(v) Value Kroton with the DCF and multiple methods and compare the result with the current share price of Kroton (R$16.00/share) and the price paid by Advent International (see Exhibit 3 to support your reasoning). What are your conclusions?

EXHIBIT 1 Financial statements of Kroton Educacional SA

Balance sheet (million BRL)	31/12/2009	31/12/2008	31/12/2007
Assets			
Cash and ST investments	410.38	124.22	325.28
Receivables (net)	75.62	72.04	40.49
Total inventories	17.86	25.18	12.87
Prepaid expenses	0.37	0.45	0.29
Other current assets	3.00	2.49	1.89
Current assets – total	507.24	224.37	380.82
Long-term receivables	0.25	1.01	0.21
Property, plant & equipment – net	167.65	133.74	38.93
Property plant & equipment – gross	203.70	159.17	53.56
Land	14.15	14.15	N/A
Buildings	41.63	26.55	0.55
Property, plant & equipment – other	110.39	79.82	39.27
Accumulated depreciation	36.04	25.44	14.64
Other assets	189.17	168.29	70.37
Total assets	864.31	527.41	490.32
Liabilities & shareholders' equity			
Accounts payable	9.90	22.53	7.72
ST debt & current portion of LT debt	5.17	5.45	1.43
Accrued payroll	16.36	16.31	9.88
Income taxes payable	1.78	1.89	5.78
Dividends payable	0.00	12.95	0.00
Other current liabilities	16.17	19.05	16.86
Current liabilities – total	49.37	78.18	41.67
Long-term debt	9.70	12.00	15.63
Provision for risks and charges	5.27	0.99	0.02
Deferred taxes	−5.91	−9.25	−13.08
Other liabilities	10.78	11.52	8.62
Total liabilities	69.21	93.44	52.85

EXHIBIT 1 (*Continued*)

Balance sheet (million BRL)	31/12/2009	31/12/2008	31/12/2007
Shareholders' equity			
Minority interest	0.02	−0.04	0.01
Preferred stock	0.00	0.00	0.00
Common equity	795.07	434.01	437.47
Common stock	821.02	454.40	454.40
Other appropriated reserves	14.96	0.68	N/A
Retained earnings	−19.47	N/A	−16.93
Treasury stock	21.44	21.07	0.00
Total liabilities & shareholders' equity	**864.31**	**527.41**	**490.32**

Profit & losses (million BRL)	31/12/09	31/12/08	31/12/07
Net sales or revenues	352.94	279.56	87.54
Cost of goods sold	215.02	170.58	52.47
Depreciation, depletion & amortisation	16.45	19.54	4.47
Gross income	**121.47**	**89.44**	**30.60**
Operating expenses – total	359.12	252.90	113.71
Operating income	**−6.18**	**26.66**	**−26.17**
Extraordinary credit – pre-tax	0.00	0.00	0.00
Extraordinary charge – pre-tax	1.43	0.00	0.00
Non-operating interest income	23.67	26.64	17.73
Other income/expenses – net	−14.65	−2.05	−3.74
Earnings before interest and taxes (EBIT)	**1.41**	**51.24**	**−12.18**
Interest expense on debt	2.80	10.66	3.84
Pre-tax income	−1.40	40.58	−16.03
Income taxes	6.65	10.08	0.56
Current domestic income taxes	4.37	6.84	−0.33
Current foreign income taxes	0.00	0.00	0.00
Deferred domestic income taxes	2.28	3.24	0.89
Net income before extra Items/Preferred Div	−8.10	30.56	−16.58
Net income before preferred dividends	−8.10	30.56	−16.58
Preferred dividend requirements	0.00	0.00	0.00
Net income available to common financial ratios	**−8.10**	**30.56**	**−16.58**

Profitability	31/12/09	31/12/08	31/12/07
Return on total equity	−1.32	7.01	−7.06
Reinvestment rate	−3.28	7.01	N/A
Return on assets	−0.76	7.58	−4.56
Return on invested capital	−0.84	8.52	−4.90

EXHIBIT 1 (*Continued*)

Balance sheet (million BRL)	31/12/2009	31/12/2008	31/12/2007
Cash earnings return on equity	2.79	13.84	1.84
Cash flow to sales	4.85	21.57	4.95
Cost of goods sold to sales	60.92	61.02	59.94
Gross profit margin	34.42	31.99	34.95
Operating profit margin	−1.75	9.54	−29.90
Pre-tax margin	−0.40	14.52	−18.31
Net margin	−2.30	10.93	−18.94

Asset utilisation	31/12/09	31/12/08	31/12/07
Assets turnover	0.41	0.53	0.18
Inventory turnover	9.99	8.97	4.94
Net sales to gross fixed assets	1.73	1.76	1.63
Net sales pct working capital	0.77	1.91	0.26
Capital expend. pct fixed assets	23.77	146.16	43.63
Capital expend. pct total assets	7.17	15.97	16.45
Capital expend. pct sales	10.72	28.00	12.89

Leverage	31/12/09	31/12/08	31/12/07
Total debt pct common equity	1.87	4.02	3.90
LT debt pct common equity	1.22	2.76	3.57
Minority interest pct total capital	0.00	−0.01	0.00
Total debt pct total capital and ST debt	1.84	3.87	3.75
LT debt pct total capital	1.21	2.69	3.45
Equity pct total capital	98.79	97.32	96.55
Preferred stock pct total capital	0.00	0.00	0.00
Total debt pct total assets	1.72	3.31	3.48
Common equity pct total assets	91.99	82.29	89.22
Total capital pct total assets	93.12	84.56	92.41
Fixed charge coverage ratio	0.50	4.81	−3.17
Fixed assets pct common equity	21.09	30.81	8.90
Working cap pct total capital	56.89	32.78	74.85

Liquidity	31/12/09	31/12/08	31/12/07
Quick ratio	9.84	2.51	8.78
Current ratio	10.27	2.87	9.14
Cash ratio	80.91	55.36	85.42
Receivables pct current assets	14.91	32.11	10.63
Inventories pct current assets	3.52	11.22	3.38
Accounts receivable days	76.35	73.46	115.45
Inventories days held	36.53	40.70	73.93

Source: Worldscope & ThomsonOne Banker.

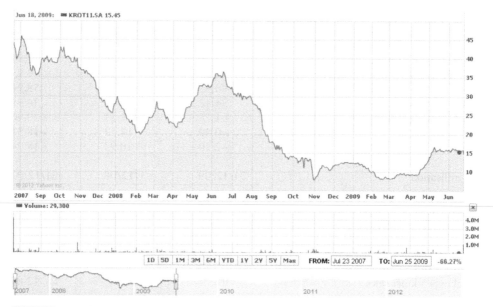

EXHIBIT 2   Stock price evolution of Kroton Educacional SA (BOVESPA: KROT11) – 23 July 2007–25 June 2009
Source: Yahoo Finance.

EXHIBIT 3   Peer group of Kroton Educacional SA

Company	Market capitalisation (USD m)	PER			EV/EBITDA			PBV		
		2008	2009 (e)	2010 (e)	2008	2009 (e)	2010 (e)	2008	2009 (e)	2010 (e)
Kroton Educacional	256	22.3	12.7	10.1	18.7	6.6	6.6	2.1	1.0	1.0
Anhanguera	1210	27.4	15.3	12.1	17.6	10.8	9.0	2.2	2.0	1.8
Estacio	845	21.8	14.2	10.1	12.4	9.0	6.7	3.4	2.8	2.3
SEB	316	14.0	12.3	12.1	9.0	9.3	8.0	2.2	1.9	1.7
Sector average (Brazil)	656	21.4	13.6	11.1	14.4	8.9	7.6	2.5	1.9	1.7
US average	1919	29.7	27.7	22.5	18.4	10.2	7.9	10.9	8.0	5.7
Chinese average	1229	35.1	50.6	42.7	25.5	27.8	13.8	4.4	3.7	3.7
Other countries average	2038	23.7	21.9	25.0	10.5	9.7	7.3	3.6	3.2	2.6

Source: FactSet, company data, Morgan Stanley Research (June 2009).

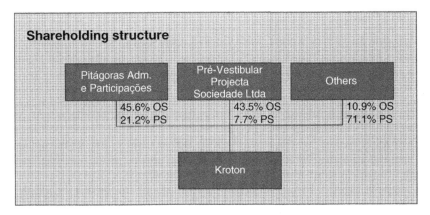

EXHIBIT 4   Ownership structure of Kroton
Note: OS refers to voting shares; PS refers to non-voting shares
Source: company data.

EXHIBIT 5   History of the Brazilian education sector

Kroton Educacional SA
1966: Creation of Pitágoras courses in the state of Minas Gerais
1971: Creation of Colegios Pitagoras (primary/secondary)
1980: Starts its replicable business model, develops it in other Brazilian states and abroad
1997: Launch of its educational and management technology which it commercialises to private schools
2001: Apollo International (a US-based private equity firm) invests in Kroton. Kroton enters the post-secondary market
2005: The brand INED is used to offer post-secondary education
2006: Apollo's stake in Kroton is bought back by Pitagoras Founders
2007: IPO of Kroton on the Brazilian market. Acquisition of Divinopolis (3100 students), Vitoria (550 students), Londrina (3 080 students), Jundiai (945 students)
2008: Acquisition of Guarapari (1200 students)
2008: Acquisition of NABEC – Nova Associação Brasileira de Educação e Cultura Ltda
2008: Acquisition of Faculdade Uniminas (3632 students)
2008: Acquisition of SUESC (3500 students)
2008: Acquisition of Faculdade Unilinhares (2547 students)
2008: Acquisition of Faculdade CBTA (802 students)
2008: Acquisition of FATEC-Londrina-CEPEO (Centro de Ensino e Pesquisa Odonto-logica)
2008: Acquisition of FACTEF – Teixeira de Freitas (1600 students)

Anhanguera Educational
2006: Acquired two campuses in the states of Goiás and São Paulo and developed a third through organic growth in the state of São Paulo

EXHIBIT 5 (*Continued*)

2006: Preparation for an IPO in 2007, AESA's shareholders used an SPC to acquire 100% of Anhanguera Educacional Participações S.A. Aesa Participações, formerly Mehir Holdings S.A. – a public company registered with CVM (Brazilian SEC, the market authority)

2006: FEBR participated in a capital increase in Aesa Participações and exchanged its Aesa Participações shares for 100% of the AESA shares held by individual shareholders. FEBR initiated a second capital increase in AESA Participações, combined with its recently acquired AESA shares, hence holding all AESA shares

2007: IPO of AESA, issuing 20 million units at R$18.00 per share, raising R$360 million

2007: 13 acquisitions adding 18 new campuses, extending presence in the mid-west, south and southeast of Brazil. Another five campuses added organically

2008: 15 campuses acquired from other educational institutions and another six added organically

2008: A follow-on offering on the stock exchange raises R$508 million

2008: Two important acquisitions to expand distribution channels and courses: 30% in Editora Microlins Brasil S.A. (which subsequently changed its name to Escola de Profissões S.A.) and LFG (the holding of Rede LFG), including the brands LFG, Prima, Rede Pró and Premier. This represents 70 000 students enrolled in 62 courses and 322 learning centres

Estacio

2007: IPO of Estacio (19 864 000 shares sold at R$22.50 per share)

2007: Acquisition of IREP, Sociedad de Ensino Superior, Medio et Fundamental Ltda and Faculdade Radial De Curitiba Sociedade Ltda representing a total of 19 100 students to expand to São Paulo and Paraná, for R$5152 million

2008: Acquisition of Faculdade de Brasília de São Paulo for R$2234 million; Sociedade Interlagos de Educação e Cultura for R$6296 million; and Sociedade Abaeté de Educação e Cultura for R$8352 million

2008: Acquisition of União Cultural e Educacional Magister Ltda for R$4343 million

2008: Acquisition of Sociedad de Enseñanza Superior S.A. (SESSA), from Assumssion Paraguay, Universidad de La Integración de Las Americas (UNIDA), with 2100 students for R$2337 million

2008: Acquisition of the control block through a capital increase of R$15 466 million, of SESSE, SESAL, UNEC e SESAP in the states of Alagoas, Sergipe and Amapá, with respectively 2900, 4000, 1600 and 1500 students

2008: Acquisition of Montessori, Cotia e Unissori, with campuses in São Paulo, Cotia and Ibiúna, for R$10 288 million

SEB

2005: Acquisition of the 'Colégio Sartre' school in Salvador de Bahia, with approximately 1800 students enrolled, the first move on expansion outside the state of São Paulo. SEB launches a shared administrative centre (in Ribeirão Preto) to centralise all operational support activities such as IT, HR, accounting, controllership and others

2006: Launch of the primary and secondary education units in Espírito Santo state

EXHIBIT 5 *(Continued)*

2007: Preparation of its IPO; the group starts a restructuring process. On 18 October, the IPO takes place on the São Paulo stock exchange (Bovespa) with pricing of R$33.00 per share under the ticker SEBB11

2007: Acquisition of the primary and secondary education group Nobel de Educação Básica, in Salvador de Bahia (794 students). Acquisition of a 95% interest in a post-secondary educational institution (350 students), the 'Instituto de Ensino Superior de Salvador Ltda' (ESAMC), for R$4.8 million

2007: Acquisition of Faculdade Metropolitana in Belo Horizonte (Minas Gerais), a post-secondary with 2700 students enrolled, for R$10 million

2008: Acquisition of Grupo Dom Bosco (Curitiba, State of Paraná), one of the largest and most recognised education groups in Brazil, with a strong presence in the south. With approximately 8000 students per year in the primary and secondary education segments and also a teaching system that served 105 000 students in roughly 500 associate institutions. In the post-secondary segment, the Group operates Faculdades Dom Bosco, which at the time of the acquisition had approximately 3000 students. The acquisition was for R$94.5 million

2008: Acquisition of Associação Brasiliense de Educação Integral (ABEDI) with approximately 600 students in Brasília (Federal District), for R$2.3 million

2008: Acquisition of Associação Alagoana de Educação Integral (ALEDI) with 1850 students in Maceió (Alagoas), for R$4.7 million

2008: Acquisition of Instituto Dínatos Ltda, an operator of preparatory courses for college admission exams in Brasília with 550 students, for R$2.5 million

2008: Acquisition of Praetorium – Instituto de Ensino, Pesquisa e Atividades de Extensão em Direito Ltda, located in Belo Horizonte, which provides leading preparatory courses for the bar exam, civil service exams in the judicial branch and graduate programmes in law (1900 on-site students and a franchise network with 117 franchisees, providing distance learning programmes to another 3000 students) for R$11.2 million

2009: Acquisition of Grupo Educacional Efigênia Vidigal, a primary and secondary education institution in Belo Horizonte with 1100 students for R$3.9 million

2009: Acquisition of Empresa de Comunicação Multimídia S.A. ('Unyca'), specialised in distance education though courses and training programmes. The company also develops planning, management and production tools for corporate TV. The acquisition was for R$1.96 million

2009: Acquisition of Klick Net, which provides content for primary, secondary and pre-school education with approximately 241 230 users for R$3.3 million

2009: Acquisition of Pueri Domus Group, a 40-year-old institution in the São Paulo metropolitan area, with diversified operations in various segments of the K-12 market, with more than 48 000 students (direct enrolments or through partner schools) for R$41.5 million

2009: Acquisition of Colégios Monet in the metropolitan region of Salvador de Bahia with 416 students for R$1.24 million

Source: Authors, companies' websites.

EXHIBIT 6   Press release of the investment of Advent International in Kroton Educacional SA

Kroton Educacional to receive investment from Advent International
With funding from Advent International, controlling holding company of Kroton will inject
  R$220 million for a capital increase in the company to support its expansion plans.
Kroton Educacional S.A. (Bovespa: KROT11) – 'Kroton' or 'the Company', one of the largest
  private education companies in Brazil, and Advent International, a global private equity firm,
  today announced an agreement in which PAP (Pitágoras Administração e Participação S.A.),
  the holding company that controls Kroton with 55% of its capital, will receive a capital
  injection of R$280 million from Advent International, R$220 million of which will be used
  to fund a capital increase in Kroton through a private subscription of additional shares in a
  total amount of up to R$387.9 million. After the deal, Advent will have 50% of PAP and
  indirectly approximately 28% of Kroton.
Kroton is Advent's 15th investment in Brazil since 1997, when it started its activities in the
  country. Funding for this deal will come from LAPEF IV (Latin American Private Equity Fund
  IV) raised in 2007 and capitalised at US$1.3 billion. Since the raising of LAPEF IV, Advent
  has already invested in four companies in Brazil: Viena, Brazil's leading casual dining
  restaurant chain; Frango Assado, Brazil's leading highway restaurant chain; Quero-Quero, a
  home-improvement retailer in southern Brazil; and CETIP, the largest central depository for
  private fixed-income securities and over-the-counter derivatives in Latin America. Founded in
  1966, Kroton offers primary, secondary and post-secondary education programmes
  throughout Brazil. In the K-12 segment (kindergarten to high school), the company has 654
  associate schools in Brazil that make use of its Pitagoras learning system. In the
  post-secondary segment, it has 28 campuses (17 Pitagoras units which offer 4- to 5-year
  undergraduate and 1-year graduate programmes and 11 INED units which offer 2.5- to
  3-year associate programmes). Kroton has more than 43,000 post-secondary students and
  226,000 K-12 students.
Since July 2007, when Kroton raised R$455.8 million (US$245 million) with its initial public
  offering on Bovespa, the Company has embarked on an aggressive expansion plan, which has
  included the acquisition of 12 colleges and the opening of new campuses. Today, Kroton has
  the highest growth rate of any education company in Brazil, with net revenues of R$279.6
  million and EBITDA of R$51.5 million in 2008. In the first quarter of 2009, the company
  posted net revenues of R$107.5 million and an EBITDA of R$35.7 million, rising 51.4% and
  37.6% respectively over the year-earlier figures.
'Kroton combines high-quality education services, a proven track record of organic and
  acquisition-led growth and a highly-skilled management. We believe the company provides a
  strong platform from which to consolidate the education sector in Brazil and we look
  forward to working with the management team to accelerate the expansion of the business,'
  said Juan Pablo Zucchini, a Managing Director in Advent International's São Paulo office.
  Mr. Zucchini led the investment in Kroton.
'It's a very fragmented market, with many opportunities ahead', Mr. Zucchini added. 'The
  Brazilian education sector has been growing at a compound annual rate of 10% over the past
  decade and is still characterized by a low number of students with post-secondary degrees,
  even relative to other countries in Latin America.'

Source: Advent International SA, 25 June 2009 (website – last accessed: November 2012).

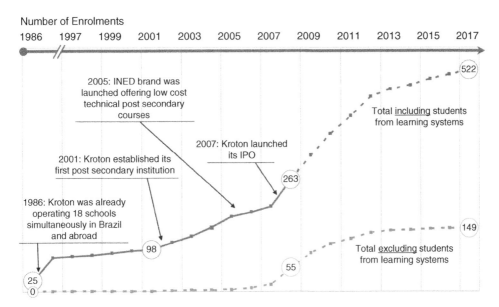

Number of Enrolments

EXHIBIT 7   Evolution of the number of students of Kroton Educacional SA
Source: Morgan Stanley 2008.

EXHIBIT 8   Management and board short biographies of Kroton Educacional SA (as of 24 June 2009)

Walfrido Silvino dos Mares Guia Neto, 68, Member of the Board of Directors. He holds bachelor's degrees in Chemical Engineering from the Engineering School of the Federal University of Minas Gerais – UFMG (1966) and in Business Administration from the School of Economic, Administrative and Accounting Sciences of Belo Horizonte – FUMEC (1973). He joined the Company in 1966 as one of its founding partners. He has held various public offices, most recently during the Lula Administration as Tourism Minister (2003–07) and as Head of the Institutional Relations in the Secretariat of the President's Office (2007).

Luiz Aníbal de Lima Fernandes, 67, independent Member of the Board of Directors. He was awarded a bachelor's degree in Mechanical and Electrical Engineering from the Engineering School of the Federal University of Minas Gerais (UFMG) in 1965. He has sat on the Board of Directors, Advisory Board and Fiscal Council of various companies, such as Acesita S.A., Cemig and Light S.A. In 1982, he received the prestigious 'Incofidência' Medal of Honor of the state of Minas Gerais. From 1979 to 1983, he served as President of the Minas Gerais State Development Bank (BDMG), and from 1995 and 2005 he served as CEO of Acesita S.A. (Arcelor Group).

Evando José Neiva, 63, Chairman of the Board of Directors. Holds a bachelor's degree in Electrical Engineering from the Federal University of Minas Gerais (UFMG), graduating with the institution's silver medal for academic merit. He also holds a master's degree in Educational Leadership and School Supervision from the University of San Francisco in California. He was a professor of physics at UFMG and President of the Education Council of the Minas Gerais State Manufacturers' Federation (FIEMG). He joined the Company in 1966 as one of its founding partners and served as the group's chief executive officer from 1994 to 1999. He currently serves as president of the Pitágoras Foundation and the Education Councils of the Minas Gerais Commercial Association Gerais (ACMinas) and the Minas Gerais Federation of Foundations (Fundamig).

EXHIBIT 8 (*Continued*)

Júlio Fernando Cabizuca, 68, Member of the Board of Directors. He holds a bachelor's degree in Mechanical and Electrical Engineering from the Engineering School of the Federal University of Minas Gerais (UFMG). He joined the Company in 1966 as one of its founding partners. He was a professor of mathematics and a director of some of Kroton's campuses in Belo Horizonte and director of the Pitágoras campus located in Iraq. Previously he has served as Kroton's operations superintendent, vice-CEO and CEO.

Leonardo Emrich dos Mares Guia, 32, Member of the Board of Directors. Holds a bachelor's degree in business administration from the Instituto Izabela Hendrix, in Belo Horizonte – Brazil, and studied for the International Baccalaureate at St Clare's College, Oxford, England. He joined the company in 2007 as a member of the Board of Directors.

Alicia Maria Gross Figueiró Pinheiro, 44, Executive Vice-President and Investor Relations Director. Holds a bachelor's degree in business administration and in accountancy from Pontifícia Universidade Católica de Minas Gerais – PUC-MG and a post-graduate degree in Financial Management by Fundação Dom Cabral – Minas Gerais – Brazil. She started her career at Arthur Andersen Consulting and joined the company in 1988.

Walter Luiz Diniz Braga, 53, Chief Executive Officer since June 2007. He joined Kroton in 1980, as a lecturer in mathematics and manager of various campuses throughout Brazil, as well as Superintendent of School Operations. He served as a mathematics teacher, executive officer of education institutions and consultant on education projects in and outside Brazil. He has served as a Director of Kroton Educacional S.A. since May 2007. Mr Braga holds a bachelor's degree in Mathematics from the Newton Paiva Ferreira Cultural Institute, or ICNP, a graduate degree in Marketing from ICNP, and a specialisation degree in Quality Systems from Pennsylvania State University, USA.

EXHIBIT 9 Kroton's brand segmentation

Education	Brand	Programmes	Prospects
K-12	Pitagoras	Primary (pre-school, elementary, middle school), secondary and high school	Middle class
Post-secondary	Pitagoras	Undergraduate (4 to 5 years)	Upper middle class Middle class
Post-secondary	INED	Associate degree (2 to 2.5 years)	Middle class Working class

Source: Kroton Educacional SA.

EXHIBIT 10 Brazilian social class brackets, defined by total household income (R$/month)

	Inferior	Superior
Class A	9050.00	—
Class B	6941.00	9050.00
Class C	1610.00	6941.00
Class D	1008.00	1610.00
Class E	—	1008.00

Source: PNAD

100-Day plan Series of measures and dispositions that a company acquired through an LBO (*see this expression*) is expected to execute after its acquisition. This series includes back-up measures in case the original plan fails to deliver the expected results.

A

Aborted deal costs *See* 'Broken deal costs'.

Accelerated monitoring fees At the time of investment, the LBO fund manager determines an annual monitoring and control fee charged to a portfolio company along an expected holding period. If the portfolio company is sold or listed ahead of the planned schedule, the remaining amount due is then charged all at once by the LBO manager before the exit: it is the accelerated monitoring fee.

Accelerator Also referred to as 'start-up accelerator'. This is a 6- to 18-month programme dedicated to supporting entrepreneurs at the inception of their company. Accelerators usually provide a mix of lectures, workshops, mentorship and events with the aim of supporting the start-up in its fundraising. Most programmes culminate in a final event where start-ups can pitch (*see this expression*) themselves to potential investors.

Accredited investor An investor deemed sufficiently informed and sophisticated, who benefits from a satisfactory knowledge of investments and is thus able to handle private market investments, which do not benefit from the protection offered by stock exchange regulations. In the USA, this status is defined by the Investment Company Act of 1940.

Acquiror due diligence Also known as 'buy-side due diligence'. *See* 'Due diligence'.

Acquisition The take-over of a portfolio company by another industrial or financial company.

Active ownership For a shareholder, consists of exercising dutifully his/her rights and fulfilling all associated duties, and actively advising the management of a firm. If the shareholder is a Board member of a company, this includes exercising the rights and duties of a Board member.

Activism In finance, consists of a series of actions supporting a campaign to bring significant change in the management and governance of a company. An activist investor usually acquires a minority stake in a listed company, launching a communication campaign to get support for a bid for one or multiple Board seats. The purpose is to act decisively to change the strategy of the company by convincing or changing the management of a firm. Activist investors are compensated by the resulting increase in price of the shares they own and/or distribution of dividends.

Add-on transaction Direct or indirect acquisition of a firm by a private equity fund, to be further merged or associated with a company already in the portfolio of the fund: the platform (*see* 'Platform deal').

Adverse selection Any situation when an investor systematically gets investment opportunities of lower quality or return potential due to a disadvantage when interacting with a better-informed party.

Advisory Board Group of fund investors or third parties advising a fund manager on a specific fund. The powers of this Board are limited to simple advice on topics ranging notably from valuation of assets to solving conflicts of interest.

Advisory Committee Informal group of individuals advising a fund manager on specific questions.

Agency theory A branch of economic theory that deals with the question of asset owners and their agents. An agency relationship exists when the owner pays the agent to take decisions in his place. The contract plays an important role in ensuring that the agent acts in the best interests of the owner. Agency costs are evidenced by the fact that contracts are costly and difficult to enforce. They include structuring costs, management costs and the application of multiple contracts between agents with different interests.

AIFMD *See* 'Alternative Investment Fund Manager Directive'.

Alignment of interests Usually refers to an arrangement between an agent and a principal in which the agent stands to benefit more from a cooperation with the principal than if the agent tries to maximise his own single outcome.

Alternative assets If traditional investments refer to listed stocks, listed bonds and cash, alternative assets refer to non-traditional investments. This category includes notably private market investments, hedge funds, commodities and derivatives.

Alternative Investment Fund Managers Directive EU-wide regulation introduced in 2011 to provide a common regime for managers of funds dedicated to non-traditional assets, namely hedge funds and private market funds. To market their funds within the EU, alternative investment fund managers have to obtain authorisation from at least one national EU regulator. This authorisation is delivered upon compliance with transparency and investor protection provisions.

American waterfall Variant of the schedule of distribution of the performance fee ('carried interest', *see this expression*) of a fund manager. According to this, the carried interest (if any) is distributed to the fund manager each time an investment has been sold profitably by the fund and the 'hurdle rate' (*see this expression*) has been paid. If the fund sold investments at a loss, some or all the carried interest distributed to the fund manager has to be recalled according to a 'clawback clause' (*see this expression*) to compensate the investors for their loss.

Anchor investor *See* 'Cornerstone investor'.

Angel investor A high net worth individual who invests in venture capital to help companies and let them benefit from his experience, his network and his know-how. Also called 'business angel'.

Anti-dilution clause Clause in a shareholders' agreement (usually of a start-up) that entitles some investors to maintain their ownership percentage in a company by buying additional shares of a company in subsequent financing rounds. If the subsequent round of fundraising is done at a lower valuation than the current one (a 'down round', *see this expression*), the option will compensate beneficiary investors with additional shares to maintain their ownership percentage.

Asset allocation Breakdown of a portfolio between different categories of assets. For an institutional investor, this usually involves listed stocks, listed bonds, local and foreign currencies, hedge funds, commodities, gold and private market investments. For a fund manager, this usually involves companies of different sectors and possibly geographical regions.

Asset stripping Process of selling off part of a company with the hope that the proceeds from this sale will be higher than if the company was sold as a whole.

Assets under management The sum of all the assets managed (that is to say, those available for investment and those already invested) by an investment team in private market deals.

Asymmetry of information Situation in which one economic agent has better information than another, placing the second at a disadvantage compared to the first when choosing an investment. For example, an entrepreneur can benefit from a higher level of information than an investor in a company. The entrepreneur extracts this information from his day-to-day activity while the investor relies on the summary provided by the entrepreneur for his information. Current investors in a company also benefit from higher information than prospective ones, which is why the latter undertake due diligence (*see this expression*) to reduce or eliminate the asymmetry of information.

Auction Process of selling a company potentially involving multiple competing buyers. The purpose of this process is usually to maximise the proceeds for the seller.

AUM *See* 'Assets under management'.

B

Balance sheet The picture of the financial situation of a company at a given time. The balance sheet is the synthesis of the value of assets, debts and capital of the company.

Balanced fund An investment strategy in private equity designed to build a portfolio of companies at different stages of development (venture capital, growth capital, and/or leveraged buy-out).

Bankruptcy Legal status declared by a special court under which a company which is either insolvent (*see this expression*) or has sustained cumulated losses superior to its total capital for a prolonged period of time (usually 2 years) is placed under administration and supervised by an independent third party. The debt (interest and principal) repayment of the company is suspended for the length of the bankruptcy procedure (usually 6 to 18 months), which usually ends with the restructuring of the company or its liquidation.

BDC *See* 'Business Development Company'.

Beauty contest Competitive process in which each potential buyer of a business/asset tries to convince a seller (and his agents) and win over other potential buyers. This process can be compared to an auction, except that the decision factors are not only the price offered but other elements such as reputation, credentials or track record.

Benchmark Metrics of performance, risk and liquidity of a fund or a company, to support a comparison with a peer group (*see this expression*).

Blind pool Feature of a fund according to which investors do not know at the time of investment which assets will be acquired and have no influence on the choice of these assets. Investors usually know at least the detailed investment strategy applied by the fund, that is criteria such as geographical area, type of investment strategy applied, size and type of asset and time at which industrial sectors targeted.

Blocker Structure set up in a specific country to gather commitments in a fund located in another country. *See* 'Feeder fund'.

Bolt-on transaction *See* 'Add-on transaction'.

Book value Using the balance sheet of a company, it is computed as the total value of the assets (after depreciation) minus the outstanding liabilities.

Bottom quartile 25% of a sample ranking lowest according to specific criteria, such as a performance metric.

Bottom-up Progressing from the lowest (or most granular) to the highest (or least granular) level of an analytical process. In the context of asset allocation, this consists of analysing the micro-economic factors of an asset to draw specific conclusions and build a portfolio from this analysis. The positive side of this approach is that it is empirically verifiable and can be concretely applied. The negative side of this approach is that it depends on observable samples and therefore might lack systematism. A complementary approach is 'top-down' (*see this expression*).

Break-up fee Financial sanction that the seller of a company in an LBO transaction has to pay when walking away from the transaction. If it is the prospective buyer who walks away, then the fee is called a 'reverse break-up fee'.

Bridge financing Short-term financing generally provided as a credit to a company expecting a financing event (IPO or further round of financing) in the coming 6 to 12 months. The bridge financing can combine debt and equity features. If so, this debt instrument is then generally converted into shares at the time of the liquidity event.

Bridge loan *See* 'Bridge financing'.

Broken auction Competitive sale process of a company which failed to effectively translate into an effective acquisition.

Broken deal costs *See* 'Broken deal fees'.

Broken deal fees Buy-side expenses associated with the analysis of an investment opportunity that did not materialise into an effective investment. These expenses are supported by the potential buyer with no associated investment to recoup them.

Brownfield Refers to real assets, such as real estate or infrastructure, which have already been developed and are not currently in use. The underlying land can be contaminated, notably by pollution.

Bullet payment Feature of a loan according to which the principal and the cumulated interest is paid all at once, usually at the end of the duration of the loan.

Burn rate Measure of the net cash spent by a start-up at a given time occurrence (usually monthly). It is notably used to assess how many months the start-up can operate before it runs out of funds (and therefore plan for a new round of financing).

Business angel *See* 'Angel investor'.

Business Development Company Listed US closed-end investment vehicle created in 1980 through an amendment of the Investment Company Act of 1940. If a company elects to be a BDC, and matches the criteria, it pays little or no corporate income tax as it is a pass-through tax structure.

Business plan Document prepared by the management of a company, often with the help of advisors, detailing its past, present and expected performance and activities. This document contains not only a detailed analysis of the human, financial and physical resources of the company, but also its history, competitive position, pricing scheme, as well as financial projections for the next 3 to 5 years following its last exercise. It details the strategy, defines the targets and is used to monitor future performance.

Buy-and-build LBO strategy in which a fund buys companies from a given sector with the aim of combining them and capitalising on their synergies. The initial transaction is called the 'platform transaction' (*see this expression*) and the subsequent acquisition the 'add-on transaction' (*see this expression*).

Buy-in *See* 'Leveraged buy-in'.

Buy-in management buy-out (BIMBO) A leveraged buy-out that involves current managers (management buy-out) and incoming managers (management buy-in).

Buy-out *See* 'Leveraged buy-out'.

Buy-side due diligence *See* 'Due diligence'.

C

Capital account Report on the position held by an investor in a private market fund, including capital committed, capital paid in, investments, valuations and realisations.

Capital call Operation through which the fund collects a portion of the commitments of its fund investors to invest in portfolio companies and pay for its expenses (and notably the management fees).

Capital increase Operation in which investors provide additional resources, in cash or in kind, to a company in exchange for shares. As a result, the equity of the company increases.

Capitalisation table List of shareholders of current and future company, usually detailing the percentage of ownership, number of shares and stock options owned by each of them.

Captive manager A private market fund manager that is totally (captive) or partially (semi-captive) owned by a large group or a financial institution.

Carried interest The share of the profit generated by a fund manager that is dedicated to the investment team (fund manager) without any initial financial contribution to the fund. It is generally 20% of the profits generated by the fund ('whole fund carried interest', also called European waterfall), or sometimes by each of the investments of a fund ('deal-by-deal carried interest', also called American waterfall).

Carve-out Conversion of an activity, a business unit or a division of a company into an independent company, which can subsequently be sold by the corporation it originates from.

Catch-up Mechanism entitling the fund manager to collect the pro rata of the 'hurdle rate' (*see this expression*) collected by fund investors.

Cherry picking Choosing only the best opportunity from what is available.

Chief investment officer Board-level executive of an institutional investor (or a family office) in charge of overseeing the asset allocation (*see this expression*), the investment selection, monitoring and reporting.

CIO *See* 'Chief investment officer'.

Clawback clause Requires the fund manager to return distributions to fund investors. This provision is associated with the early distribution of carried interest (*see this expression*) to the fund manager under an American waterfall (*see this expression*). The carried interest distributed with the successful realisation of early investments could be clawed back if successor deals fail to generate sufficient performance to return the capital to fund investors (and the associated potential hurdle rate). If a fund distributes carried interest deal by deal and registers highly successful exits initially and weaker ones later on, this provision ensures that fund investors will ultimately get back was is owed to them according to fund regulations.

CLO *See* 'Collateralised loan obligation'.

Closed-end Feature of a fund according to which it is created and dissolved at a pre-determined specific date. The lifespan of the fund is thus set at the start. It is not opened to new investors after the end of its fundraising period and investors have no redemption right before the dissolution.

Closed-end fund *See* 'Closed-end'.

Closed-ended *See* 'Closed-end'.

Closing During the creation of a fund, the fund manager accumulates the commitments of the investors who are interested. The closing is the effective gathering of a critical volume of commitments and the signature of subscription agreements to the limited partnership agreement (*see this expression*). The fundraising can last a year or more, and the fund manager can make multiple closings (initial, intermediate and final) to indicate the progress of the process, set up its operations and begin to invest rapidly.

The term also applies to the materialisation of an investment in a portfolio company. The closing is the signature of the transfer of ownership (LBO) or of the capital increase (venture capital and growth capital).

Club deal Leveraged buy-out operated by a group of private equity funds.

Cluster of financing Geographical aggregation of venture capital investors that have reached a critical mass to attract companies and entrepreneurs and have developed sector expertise. The most emblematic cluster is the American Silicon Valley in information technologies.

Co-investment Option or right offered to invest alongside a private market fund directly in a portfolio company or asset. The investor is usually also investing in the private market fund itself, but can hence choose to increase his exposure in select companies or assets.

Co-investment fund Private market fund investing in portfolio companies or assets jointly with other vehicles managed by a fund manager. This fund is usually offered to specific investors only, and supports lower fees and carried interest than usual.

Co-lead investor Prospective investor (usually in a start-up) who negotiates jointly with another one (the lead investor) the terms of a capital increase in a start-up with usually the management of the firm (representing existing investors).

Collateral An asset from a borrower pledged so that a debt or a security will be repaid or refunded. This can be linked to a specific debt or a series of transactions. For example, entrepreneurs must sometimes provide personal collateral for the loans provided to their company.

Collateralised loan obligation Securitisation vehicle often rated by an independent agency, in which a large number of loans are pooled together and then sliced in tranches with various levels of seniority (and therefore risk). These tranches are then sold to investors, who are entitled to the payment of interest and the repayment of the principal. The interest rate varies according to the risk supported by the investor in a given tranche.

Commingled fund Investment vehicle that gathers capital from different sources and blends them together. Private market funds of funds (*see this expression*) are commingled funds as opposed as mandates (*see this expression*).

Committed capital *See* 'Fund size'.

Commitment The obligation for an investor to provide a certain amount of capital to a fund. By extension, it is the amount committed by an investor in a fund or fund of funds, including those that are agreed on but not yet called. The sum of the commitments of all investors equals the fund size.

Common equity *See* 'Common shares'.

Common shares Group of securities representing the ownership of a company that embeds one voting right and one dividend right per share. Any divergence from this rule qualifies these securities as 'preferred shares' (*see this expression*) if they have more rights. Common shares are usually held by entrepreneurs and employees of a company.

Companion fund *See* 'Parallel fund'.

Concerted action Shareholders acting in concert according to a (formal or informal) agreement for the acquisition of the shares of a company, to achieve, maintain or increase their control over this company.

Conflict of interests Position in which an economic agent has competing professional or personal motivations, leading to a risk of unethical or improper actions.

Consulting fees Compensation paid to the provider of services to a portfolio company.

Conversion rights An option or financial right attached to a debt financing instrument, notably mezzanine debt. Under specific pre-negotiated conditions, it guarantees that the owner of this financing instrument will get access to an equity stake in the company and hence a share of the profits. In that respect, subordinated debt providers can be paid for the higher risk that they take, compared to other debt providers.

Convertible debt Often subordinated, this tranche of debt can be converted (optional conversion) or has to be converted (mandatory conversion) into a given company's equity by the creditor upon the materialisation of certain events (and/or the wish of the creditor).

Cornerstone investor Financial institution (or sometimes family office) supporting the fundraising effort of a fund manager by committing a significant percentage of a private market fund. This investor often supports the fund manager, notably with branding, introduction to other investors and even operational support. Cornerstone investors receive in exchange Advisory Board seats and possibly additional rights such as co-investment rights.

Consultant Agent operating for institutional investors, providing asset allocation and fund selection services. If the consultant is specialised in fund selection and has a discretionary mandate, it is a 'gatekeeper' (*see this expression*).

Core Conservative investment strategy applied in private real estate and private infrastructure, essentially aiming to deliver income to investors, and possibly a capital gain. This strategy is characterised by a rather low risk–return profile. Assets are stable, in top location, fully leased and held for a rather long period, requiring low or no management from investors and are often characterised as high quality. Tenants rent these assets on long-term leases and are usually of high quality. The debt used to acquire these assets is 30–40%.

Core-plus Investment strategy with a low to moderate risk applied in private real estate and private infrastructure. It aims to deliver a mix of income and capital gains to investors. Assets are held for a rather long period, and are of high quality but require light improvements, and/or an increase in management efficiency, and/or an increase in the quality of tenants. Similar to the core strategy, tenants rent these assets on long-term leases and are usually of high quality. The debt used to acquire these assets is 40–60%.

Cornerstone investor Financial institution or family office that acquires a significant stake (between 15% and 30%) in a private market fund. This institution usually supports the fundraising effort of the fund manager in various ways, such as branding, serving as a reference and actively marketing the fund.

The expression is sometimes used in venture capital when an investor acquires a large stake in a start-up and serves as a due diligence reference.

Corporate governance Principles, mechanisms and processes of direction and management control of corporations by their owners. The rights and responsibilities of the owners are usually defined legally and contractually, in the latter case in the shareholders' agreement (*see this expression*). The aim of corporate governance is to reduce and eliminate conflicts of interest among corporate owners, as well as between corporate owners and managers. In private markets, corporate governance plays a central role in the value creation of investors in the assets they control.

Corporate venture capital *See* 'Corporate venturing'.

Corporate venturing Large companies can buy a stake in, or establish a joint venture with, a smaller company in order to help it develop new products, services or technologies and benefit from certain synergies. The large company can thus not only provide capital, but also managers or marketing resources. Corporate venturing can also support spin-off (*see this expression*) processes.

Cost of capital Rate of return expected by the shareholders of a company. It is usually measured by the CAPM model, which states that the capital cost equals the risk-free rate plus a premium which varies according to the systemic risk (which cannot be diversified by the portfolio construction) and the market price of risk (around 6.5% by unit of beta).

Cost of debt Interest rate requested by the banks from a company.

Cost of liabilities Rate of return expected for the different means of financing. The total cost of liabilities is the compounded average rate of return of all the sources of financing used by the company.

Covenant-light Qualification applied to a loan whose contract includes a lower number of clauses protecting the lender than in a usual contract. The borrower thus benefits from a higher flexibility, often without incurring a higher interest rate. The flexibility can be related to the repayment schedule, the ability to contract additional debt, make investments, pay dividends, forgo and accumulate the payment of interests for a certain period of time or any other form of flexibility that would usually be limited or prohibited.

Covenant-lite *See* 'Covenant-light'.

Covenant-loose Qualification applied to a loan whose contract includes a very low number (usually one or two) of clauses protecting the lender, providing the borrower with high flexibility.

Covenants Restrictions imposed by a lender on a borrower. Generally associated with the necessity of maintaining a certain level of cash, or certain ratios, or certain levels of investment in an LBO.

Credit line *See* 'Equity bridge financing'.

Cross investment Process in which two funds managed by the same fund manager invest in the same underlying asset. Cross investments can create a conflict of interest for the fund manager if the two funds have different time horizons (one might have to sell its assets earlier than the other, for example).

Crowdfunding Mechanism matching a company in fundraising mode with a multitude of potential investors (often retail or business angels), notably over the Internet, hence disintermediating the process of private market investing. The company can raise capital (equity crowdfunding), debt (crowdlending), or collect money as a donation or against a product or service.

Crowdlending *See* 'Crowdfunding'.

Custodian Specialist institution dedicated to the certification of cash flow movements of funds. It acts as a trusted third party to guarantee that the fund manager handles the cash of a private market fund in a specific way.

D

Data room Large series of detailed documents gathered by the seller of a company to prepare the due diligence of (a) prospective buyer(s).

Deal-by-deal carried interest *See* 'American waterfall'.

Deal flow Investment opportunities presented to a financial institution.

Debt-for-trading Distressed debt investment strategy usually applied by hedge funds and consisting of acquiring at a discount listed bonds or loans of a distressed company. Once the company has solved its issues, bonds or loans recover their value and investors can then sell and book a profit. *See* 'Distressed debt investing'.

Decile The segment of a sample representing a sequential 10%. Thus, the first 10 of 100 funds are the first (or top) decile and the last 10 are the last (or bottom) decile.

Default Event in which a promise to pay out a financial obligation (such as repaying a loan or answering a capital call) has been breached.

Defaulting investor Fund investor who does not answer a capital call.

Delisting A private equity transaction implying an offering on the total of the capital of a listed company to take it private.

Development fund Venture capital fund dedicated to later-stage start-ups. *See also* 'Expansion capital'.

Dilution A process through which the percentage of participation of an investor in a company is reduced by the issue of new shares.

Direct alpha *See* 'Public market equivalent'.

Direct investment Capital increase in or acquisition of a company with no intermediate investment vehicle. A direct investment can be a 'co-investment' (*see this expression*) or a 'solo investment' (*see this expression*).

Direct lending Private debt strategy similar to traditional bank lending. A lender provides a borrower with an amount of debt that is progressively repaid along with the interest computed on the outstanding amount still due. Also known as senior lending.

Direct secondaries *See* 'Secondary investing'.

Discount rate Price value of time. It is notably used to determine the present value of future cash flows in the formula $VA = FV_t/(1 + K)^t$, where VA is the present value, FV_t is the future value at end of year t, and K is the cost of capital.

Discounted cash flows (DCF) A method of evaluating investments by compounding the value of the future cash flows of a company by the actual value of these flows. When it is necessary to decide whether to invest or not in a given project, the future cash flows of an investment are discounted to get a value at the time the project would be initiated. The discount rate is the expected rate of return from the investors. In theory, if the actual value of future cash flows is higher than the invested amount, the investment should be made.

Dissolution of a fund Point of the lifespan of a fund at which its assets have all been sold, it is free from any warranty or obligation and can be effectively wound up.

Distressed debt investing Acquisition at a discount of some of the debt of a company in financial trouble. This strategy is a case where hedge funds and private debt funds can overlap in their activities. Distressed debt hedge funds acquire the debt and hold it until the value increases ('debt-for-trading'). Private debt funds focusing on distressed debt acquire the debt and convert some or all of it to shares. They restructure the company and sell it once the company is back on track ('loan-to-own').

Distribution Payment made by a fund to its fund investors, usually in cash. If not, it is a distribution in kind (*see this expression*).

Distribution in kind Although very restricted, or outright forbidden, some fund regulations allow the distribution of securities to fund investors, instead of cash. These securities are usually traded on an organised and regulated financial market with a minimum threshold of liquidity. These securities can be subject to a 'lock-up period' (*see this expression*) if they are distributed after an 'initial public offering' (*see this expression*).

Distribution to paid-in (DPI) Ratio between the amount distributed by the fund (from the proceeds of its divestments) and the total of capital calls (paid-in).

Distribution waterfall Schedule of distribution of the performance fee (carried interest) of a fund manager. Two variants are usually differentiated: the American waterfall (*see this expression*) and the European waterfall (*see this expression*). Each variant can involve different features such as a clawback clause (*see this expression*) for the American variant, or a catch-up clause (*see this expression*) in the European variant.

Divestment The sale of a part or all of an investment through a trade sale or an initial public offering. *See* 'Exit (of an investment)'.

Divestment period Subsequent to the investment period, the divestment period represents a 5- to 12-year timeframe during which a fund develops and sells or lists its investments. If necessary, this period can be extended by 1 to 3 years, if the fund regulations allow it. At the end of the divestment period, the fund is supposed to have sold all its holdings and be free of any warranties. If not, the fund manager has the choice to sell the assets on the secondary market ('direct secondaries', *see this expression*) or to other investors, transfer these assets in a new fund ('GP-led restructuring', *see this expression*) or extend the lifespan of the fund beyond the initial plan.

Dividend recapitalisation Partial or full refund of the capital injected in an LBO thanks to the payment of a special dividend by the holding. This dividend is usually the proceeds of an increase in debt, or, more rarely, the disposal of an asset of the underlying portfolio company.

Down round Venture capital investment round where the valuation of the company is inferior to the previous one.

Downstream Generally refers, in the oil and gas industry, to the refining of crude oil and the processing and purifying of natural gas, as well as the distribution of derived products.

DPI *See* 'Distribution to paid-in'.

Drag along clause Disposition of a shareholders' agreement according to which the majority shareholder can force minority shareholders to sell their shares at the same price as his/hers to a third party, unless minority shareholders buy his/her shares at the price offered by this third party.

Drawdown *See* 'Capital call'.

Dry powder At a fund level, the portion of the fund size that has not yet been called. At the private market industry level, the sum of all the capital committed but not yet deployed.

Due diligence Investigation resulting in independent and detailed analysis process preceding an investment. It is realised by or for investors of a given target company or a fund. In the case of a company, this includes a detailed analysis of the hypothesis of a business plan, as well as checking material facts (client accounts, contracts, bills, etc.)

and opinions. Applied to a fund, this consists of determining the attractiveness, risks and issues of an investment strategy, a track record and the set-up of the fund and its manager.

Duration of a fund *See* 'Lifespan of a fund'.

Duration of an investment *See* 'Holding period'.

E

Early-stage financing This includes seed investments and the first rounds of financing of a company.

Earnings before interest and taxes (EBIT) This measure is calculated in the profit and loss statement of a company. Depending on the accounting methods, it can be calculated from the turnover of which inputs such as costs of goods and services sold are deducted: wages; marketing, general and administrative expenses; depreciations and amortisations. *See* 'EBITDA'.

Earnings before interest, taxes, depreciation and amortisation (EBITDA) This measure is calculated in the profit and loss statement of a company. Depending on the accounting methods, it can be calculated from the turnover of which the inputs such as costs of goods and services sold are deducted: wages; marketing, general and administrative expenses. Depending on the financial structure and the activity of the company, it can be relevant to use a multiple of EBIT (or EBITA for telecom companies) or EBITDA, or any other financial instrument of measurement (EBITDAR – with R standing for rental of aircraft – for airlines, for example).

Earn-out clause The final price to be paid to the vendor by an acquirer depends on the realisation of results announced in the business plan. To ease negotiations, the vendor and the buyer can settle on a temporary price and simultaneously negotiate a future potential complementary payment (the earn-out) to the vendor. This complementary payment to the vendor is triggered by the realisation of certain results by the company. These results are the fruits of efforts initiated before the transaction by the vendor, but which will be materialised after the acquisition and hence attributed to the buyer. Thanks to this mechanism, the vendor can retain an interest in the company for the compensation of efforts he has undertaken and results that he has contributed to, but the proceeds of which are difficult to evaluate at the time of the sale.

Employee buy-out (EBO) An LBO in which the employees have the opportunity to acquire a significant amount of shares in the company.

Employee stock-option plan (ESOP) Programme enabling a firm's employees to become owners, as compensation for work done.

Endowment Process of transferring the ownership of assets to a non-profit structure. By extension, it designates the tax-efficient structure in which assets are transferred to a beneficiary owner, which can be an institution (such as a university, for example). Assets can be in cash or in kind. The endowment is managed independently and invests these assets whenever possible. The endowment can then spend the proceeds of these investments, and only these. The assets bequeathed to the endowment cannot be spent. To keep their tax-exempt status, endowments have to respect specific rules.

Enterprise value (EV) Sum of the equity value and the net debt of a firm.

Entry multiple Valuation ratio set when an investor acquires or invests in a company or an asset (the 'entry'). It is usually computed by dividing the enterprise value of the company or asset at entry by a subtotal from its profit and loss statement (such as the EBIT, *see this expression*) or cash flow statement.

Environmental, social and governance (ESG) criteria Set of informal standards used by investors to screen opportunities to invest in projects and companies. Environmental criteria support the analysis of a company's or an asset's stewardship of nature. Social criteria support the analysis of a company's or an asset's relationship with the community in which they operate, such as employees, suppliers, clients, partners and stakeholders. Governance criteria support the analysis of a company's or an asset's ownership framework, including management control and sanction, and owners' rights and duties.

Equalisation mechanism Process consisting of establishing a strict equality between investors joining the roster of a fund at different closing dates. Investors joining after the first closing have to compensate initial investors, usually by paying initial investors interest. Interest is in effect collected by the fund manager and paid pro-rata to investors in the first closing.

Equity Sum of capital provided by shareholders plus the sum of undistributed profits or losses.

Equity bridge financing Also known as 'credit line', 'subscription line facilities' or 'capital call facilities', these financing instruments are short-term (less than 365 days) loans provided to private market funds backed by the commitments of fund investors. Capital calls can then be delayed, along with the start of the computation of the IRR associated with them. Distributions can also be anticipated, thus affecting the computation of the IRR.

Equity crowdfunding *See* 'Crowdfunding'.

Equity kicker *See* 'Conversion right'.

End of life Point at which a closed-end fund reaches its maximum contractual lifespan.

ESG *See* 'Environmental, social and governance criteria'.

ESOP *See* 'Employee stock-option plan'.

European waterfall Variant of the schedule of distribution of the performance fee ('carried interest', *see this expression*) of a fund manager. According to this, the carried interest (if any) is distributed to the fund manager only once the capital of the fund has been returned to investors and the 'hurdle rate' (*see this expression*) and 'catch-up' (*see this expression*) have been paid.

EV *See* 'Enterprise value'.

Evergreen vehicle An open-ended private market investment vehicle (often a holding company), usually listed on the stock exchange. An evergreen vehicle can be a fund, a fund management company or a combination of the two.

Exit (of an investment) A means by which investors in a portfolio company sell part or all of their stakes. Common means of exit are initial public offerings or trade sale to an industrial group. Other options such as secondary LBOs are becoming increasingly frequent. *See* 'Divestment'.

Exit multiple Valuation ratio set when an investor sells or divests a company or an asset (the 'exit'). It is usually computed by dividing the enterprise value of the company or asset at exit by a subtotal from its profits and losses statement (such as the EBIT, *see this expression*) or cash flow statement.

Exit process Series of steps leading to the initial public offering, trade sale to a company, financial secondary sale to an investment group, sale to the management or liquidation (write-off) of a stake in a company. This therefore excludes dividend recapitalisations.

Expansion capital Financing provided to a start-up company at a later stage of its development.

F

Fair market value Estimate of the net asset value of a fund using the assumption of what a buyer would pay in an open market operation for an asset (or a group of assets such as portfolio companies of a private market fund).

Fair value Company or asset price agreed upon by willing market participants in an orderly transaction at the transaction date.

Fairness opinion Evaluation given by a trusted third party on the situation and value of a portfolio or a portfolio company. This service is often used when a potential conflict of interest is perceived by a fund investor in the valuation of a portfolio or a company by a fund manager.

Family office Independent and professionally managed private structure dedicated to the management of the wealth of very or ultra 'high net worth individuals' (*see this expression*) or families.

Farmland Sub-category of private real-asset investing, referring to agricultural space use for raising crops or livestock.

Fee offset mechanism Distributions from portfolio companies (e.g., dividends, service fees, Board attendance fees) are often not tax efficient if made to the fund. However, they are not theoretically payable to the fund manager as the latter is paid (thanks to the management fees) to manage the fund and its portfolio. The mechanism is hence set up to direct the distributions to the fund manager, and these distributions will be compensated to the fund by reduced management fees.

Feeder fund Local legal structure used by investors to invest in a fund, often used for tax and regulatory purposes.

Finder's fund Small fund used to source investment opportunities for the account of the investors who then usually finance the investment or the acquisition themselves directly.

First closing Operation handled by a fund manager, materialising the creation of the fund and the beginning of its investment period. A fund can hold a single closing (first and final) or multiple subsequent ones, usually over a period of 12 to 18 months since the beginning of the fundraising period.

First lien Highest legally enforceable claim on the collateral of a loan in case a borrower defaults.

First round of financing The first investment made by external professional investors.

First-time fund Initial investment vehicle of a series launched by an established or emerging fund manager. The fund manager usually capitalises on a pre-existing track record, for example built in a previous institution.

Follow-on investment Re-investment by a venture capitalist in an existing portfolio company.

Fonds Commun de Placement à Risque (FCPR) Predecessor in French Law of the Fonds Professionnel de Capital Investissement. The FCPR can be 'authorised' by the French Autorité des Marchés Financiers (AMF, the regulator of French financial markets), 'declared' to the AMF or simply contractual. The FCPR's management company has to be duly authorised by the AMF to create such funds.

Fonds Commun de Placement dans l'Innovation (FCPI) French FCPR (*see this expression*) dedicated to venture capital investment and retail investors. An FCPI is created for 8 years and its fund investors are entitled to a tax break on the amount committed to the FCPI (up to a certain amount).

Fonds d'Investissement de Proximité (FIP) French FCPR (*see this expression*) dedicated to regional private equity investment and retail investors. A FIP is created for 8 years and its fund investors are entitled to a tax break on the amount committed to the FIP (up to a certain amount).

Fonds Professionnel de Capital Investissement (FPCI) Equivalent of the limited partnership in French law. The FPCI is managed by a 'management company' (equivalent of the fund manager). The FPCI is contractual and does not have to be authorised by the French regulator (AMF). However, its management company has to be duly authorised by the AMF to create such funds.

For cause Pre-established conditions for the termination of the fund manager's mandate. These conditions usually refer to an agreed-upon level of negligence or key man clauses (*see this expression*).

Foundation Refers to a non-profit organisation usually created to support a specific cause. Foundations can collect capital or invest capital. In the latter case, some or all of the proceeds are then used for charitable purposes. Foundations can use their financial resources to support other organisations through donations or for their own charitable purposes. They are a legal category that notably benefits from tax incentives.

Fund A private market fund is an investment vehicle created to pool capital from investors and invest it in equity or debt in different companies or assets. The fund can be a registered vehicle (most of the time for tax reasons), such as a French FCPR, or a non-registered vehicle, such as a limited partnership.

Fund administrator Service provider in charge of the operational aspects of the management of a fund, such as handling cash inflows and outflows, calculation of fees and carried interest, and reporting.

Fund investor Investor in a private market fund. A fund investor is responsible for an investment in a private market fund only up to its initial commitment, not more. An investor in a limited partnership is called a 'limited partner' (LP).

Fund management company *See* 'Fund manager'.

Fund manager A group of principals (*see this expression*) managing a fund or a fund of funds, and by extension the staff working for these principals. If the fund is a limited partnership, the fund manager is called a 'general partner' (GP). The fund manager sources, structures, executes and monitors investments. Additional responsibilities include operational fund management, as well as reporting to and communication with fund investors.

Fund of funds A financial instrument of which the purpose is to acquire stakes in private market funds. Funds of funds investing mainly in new funds are primary funds of funds. Funds of funds acquiring mainly stakes in existing funds are secondary funds of funds. Funds of funds combining primary and secondary investments are balanced funds of funds.

Fund regulation Contractual agreement between investors and the fund manager of a private market fund. This agreement defines the rules governing the management of the fund, the relations between the fund and its investors and the rights and duties of the fund manager. Fund regulations are a manual of the activity of the fund in the sense that they describe all the legal elements, fees, structure and other elements agreed on by the investors and the fund manager. They can at times be amended and completed by side letters (*see this expression*). An example of fund regulation is the limited partnership agreement (*see this expression*).

Fund secondary *See* 'Secondary investing'.

Fund size The sum of the commitments of all investors in a given fund.

Fund sponsor *See* 'Sponsor'.

Fundraising A process during which the fund manager accumulates the commitment of fund investors to create a private market fund. These funds are raised from private investors, institutions and companies, which become fund investors of the fund that will be invested in by the fund manager.

Fundraising period Refers to the time between the beginning of the marketing of a private market fund and its final closing. It can be as short as a few weeks and as long as 12 to 18 months.

G

Gatekeeper Advisor to fund investors dedicated to the selection of private market funds. A gatekeeper usually has a discretionary mandate (*see this expression*).

General partner *See* 'Fund manager'.

Goodwill The difference between the price of acquisition of an asset and its net market value at a given time.

Government agencies Permanent or semi-permanent public organisation in charge of specific functions, established by legislation or executive powers. Their autonomy, independence and accountability can vary significantly. Their functions are normally executive and encompass financing of outside bodies or organisations supporting their goals, if necessary.

GP-led restructuring Proactive liquidation of a private market fund heading towards the end of its lifespan by its manager. This involves the transfer of the remaining assets of the fund to be liquidated to a new fund managed by the same manager. This new fund is not allowed to make new investments and is purely dedicated to the management of the existing assets.

Greenfield Refers to the construction of a new real asset, such as an infrastructure or a piece of real estate, on virgin land.

Growth capital Financing provided by funds that are targeting companies already established on the market and which need additional financing in order to exploit growth opportunities.

H

Hands on/hands off Depending on the degree of involvement of investors in private markets in the management of their portfolio company/assets, they can be qualified as 'hands-on' or 'hands-off' investors. A hands-on investor is generally a non-executive director on the Board of portfolio companies. A hands-off investor will have only a low degree of involvement in the management of a portfolio company. European continental laws limit the degree of involvement of a private equity investor in a portfolio company (not crossing the management line is interpreted strictly).

Harvesting period *See* 'Divestment period'.

Hedge fund Alternative investment vehicle employing strategies and instruments to provide specific exposure to their investors. Managers often use derivatives to actively seek high absolute or relative returns. Hedge funds are accessible to accredited investors, are less regulated than mutual funds and are often leveraged.

High net worth individual (HNWI) Natural person with a net wealth evaluated at more than USD 1 million (excluding the value of their primary residence). An alternative definition includes natural persons with a lower net wealth but earning at least USD 200,000 per year. Very high net worth individual (VHNWI) often refers to a subset of this category with a net wealth of at least USD 5 million. Ultra high net worth individual (UHNWI) refers to another subset with a net wealth of at least USD 30 million. HNWIs are deemed to be accredited investors, able to invest in private market funds.

Historical cost The value of assets as shown by the financial statements of the company, but not necessarily reflecting the market value of these assets.

HNWI *See* 'High net worth individual'.

Holding period Amount of time during which a portfolio company remains in the ownership of a private market fund.

Hurdle rate *See* 'Preferred rate of return'.

I

ICM *See* 'Index comparison method'.

Impact investing Investment philosophy combining financial performance with other targets, such as social, environmental or other aims. The financial performance of impact investing is therefore usually lower than the performance of traditional investments.

Incubators Structures supporting entrepreneurs or start-ups in their effort to launch their operations. They usually provide the fledgling ventures with access to operational resources, such as facilities, at low or no cost. They also foster networking opportunities, experience sharing and at times access to sources of capital. Some of them require payment for these services, in cash and/or stocks.

Indemnification Agreement between fund investors and the fund manager to provide security, protection and/or compensation for unplanned circumstances that might arise over the course of the partnership's duration.

Index comparison method Proposed in 1996 by Austin M. Long and Craig J. Nickels, this performance benchmarking approach consists of comparing private market investments or funds with an index. *Also see* 'Public market equivalent'.

Infrastructure Fixed tangible assets supporting productive activities, such as roads, highways, bridges, airports, ports or networks (telecom, water, sewer systems). At times, this definition is stretched to so-called 'social infrastructure' such as prison and school systems.

Initial public offering (IPO) First listing on a stock exchange of existing or new shares of a private company.

Institutional buy-out (IBO) A leveraged buy-out in which an institution is involved.

Institutional investor An investor, such as an investment company, insurance group, bank, pension fund, endowment or foundation, which generally manages substantial assets and benefits from a significant investment experience. In many countries, institutional investors are not protected by stock exchange regulations, as small investors are, because they are supposed to have a deep knowledge of finance and are better able to protect their own interests.

Internal rate of return (IRR) The discount rate which equals the future cash flows with initial investments of a project, that is to say the discount rate at which the net asset value of a project is equal to zero. This is the way to express in percentage terms the (annual) rate of return of an investment project. The calculation takes into account the amounts invested, the amounts earned and the impact of time on these operations. This measure can be net or gross of fees.

International Private Equity and Venture Capital Valuation Guidelines Set of recommendations issued by a large group of international, regional, national and local private equity associations, designed to support their members in the task of valuing private market investments.

Investee company *See* 'Portfolio company'.

Investment committee When applied to a fund manager, a group of executives deciding on behalf of a private market fund to invest in private companies or assets. When applied to an institutional investor, a group of executives deciding to invest in private market funds.

Investment period Initial 3- to 5-year timeframe during which a fund is allowed to make new investments. If necessary, this period can be extended, usually by 1 year, if the fund regulations allow it. After the end of the investment period, the fund is not allowed to make new investments, but can reinvest in existing portfolio companies if needed, and if the fund regulations allow it.

Investment strategy Rules and processes designed to support the choice of assets by an investor, usually along the lines of potential returns, risk and liquidity (or duration) dimensions. By extension, refers to unique sets of rules and processes clearly differentiated from others, such as venture capital (*see this expression*) and leveraged buy-outs (*see this expression*). An investment strategy is usually refined thanks to additional dimensions such as the maturity of the underlying asset, its industrial sector, its geographical location and the type of expected plan to be applied to it to create value and generate profit.

Investor protection Rules and processes designed to prevent capital providers being misled in the process of selecting assets, and therefore supporting them in preventing financial losses. This ranges from fraud prevention to the provision of certified information, and can include guarantees, warranties or insurance schemes.

Investor(s) *See* 'Limited partner'.

IPEV *See* 'International Private Equity and Venture Capital Valuation Guidelines'.

IPO *See* 'Initial public offering'.

IRR *See* 'Internal rate of return'.

J

J-curve The curve generated when tracing the cash flows of a private market fund as time goes by from its inception to its liquidation has the form of a 'J'. The reason for the initial downward evolution is that the management fees and set-up costs are paid from the initial capital call, and are followed by further capital calls for management fees and investments. This means that the fund will first show negative cumulated cash flows. When the first distributions are made, the curve will change direction. After 4 to 7 years, the fund will usually break even and start to record net positive cumulated cash flows.

Junior debt Form of subordinated debt. The payment of its principal and interest is second to senior debt. It can be secured or not. Has priority over more subordinated forms of debt such as mezzanine debt. Usually not convertible to equity.

K

Key man clause Clause of a fund regulation stating that (a) fund manager(s) specifically named has/have to participate in the fund management. Should this/these manager(s) be impeached, the fund is prohibited from making new investments and is pursuing its activity only towards winding down.

Key person clause *See* 'Key man clause'.

L

Later-stage investing Venture capital financing dedicated to the development of a start-up once it has reached a certain number of milestones, and notably to help it grow abroad, and/or by launching new products/services and/or to acquire competitors.

LBI *See* 'Leveraged buy-in'.

LBO *See* 'Leveraged buy-out'.

LBU *See* 'Leveraged build-up'.

Lead investor In syndicated investments, this is the investor who identifies, structures and plays the main role in negotiating the terms of an investment. Large buy-outs can involve a lead equity investor and a lead debt investor.

Letter of confidentiality *See* 'Non-disclosure agreement'.

Letter of intent (LOI) The letter from an investor expressing an interest, the will or the intention to go into a form of transaction. It usually precedes the negotiation of a full agreement and is generally structured so as not to be legally binding.

Leveraged build-up (LBU) An operation in which capital is provided to a holding company in order to finance the acquisition of initially one ('platform deal') and then other companies ('add-ons'). This is a source of consolidation in certain industries.

Leveraged buy-in (LBI) Operation of a company by an investor, or a group of investors, through an LBO (*see this expression*) in which the investor(s) bring in new management.

Leveraged buy-out (LBO) The acquisition of a company by an investor, or a group of investors, owing to a dedicated structure (holding company) and to a significant borrowed amount (generally 60–70% of the total). The debt of acquisition is then repaid from the cash flows generated by the company or the help of an asset sale. LBOs are generally financed by means of so-called 'junk bonds'. Generally, the assets of the target company are used as collateral for the debt structured by the acquirer. This structuring can also be used by the management team to take control of the company it operates (management buy-out, *see this expression*).

Leveraged loan Type of loan used in an LBO for highly leveraged take-overs. Considered riskier than most credit instruments. Leveraged loans are usually split and held (thus syndicated) between multiple lenders.

Leveraged recapitalisation *See* 'Dividend recapitalisation'.

Leveraging Practice consisting of borrowing debt to acquire a company or an asset, in order to increase the performance of the capital also used for this acquisition. Results in increasing the risk of the capital investment.

Lifespan of a fund For a closed-end (*see this expression*) fund, the start of the lifespan of a private market fund is determined by either its first or its last closing, depending on the fund regulations. The end is usually determined by the fund regulations as well, including extensions. At times, the lifespan of a closed-end private market fund can extend beyond what was planned by the fund regulations. For an evergreen (*see this expression*) fund, the lifespan starts at the creation of the structure and is indefinite.

Limited partner *See* 'Fund investor'.

Limited partnership A legal structure used by most of the private market investment vehicles. A limited partnership is created for a given time. It is advised by a general partner (the fund manager that bears unlimited liabilities). The general partner manages the limited partnership according to the policy that is described in the limited partnership agreement (LPA). The limited partners are investors who have a limited responsibility and are not involved in the day-to-day activity of the limited partnership.

Limited partnership agreement (LPA) Form of fund regulation (*see this expression*). The limited partnership agreement defines the relationships between the fund investors and between the general partner and the fund investors.

Liquidation preferences Organisation of the priority claims that shareholders might have upon exit from a private market investment. A category of shareholders might have a priority claim on getting its capital back before any other category, and at times this claim extends to a minimal return on capital as well.

Liquidity Degree of quickness with which a private market asset can be sold to a third party without affecting negatively the asset price.

Listed private market fund Investment structure listed on the stock exchange, which is most of the time evergreen (*see this expression*). This structure is dedicated to private markets (*see this expression*) investments and usually has limited or no organisational expenses. Investors in these structures theoretically have access to the proceeds (capital gains or dividends) generated by these investments. An example of a listed private market fund is the master limited partnership (*see this expression*).

Listed private market fund managers Private market fund managers listed on the stock exchange, theoretically providing their investors with access to the cash flow streams generated by management and other fees, as well as the carried interest of the team. Most listed private market fund managers do not hold private market assets, and therefore do not provide access to capital gains (only funds, listed or not, do).

Living dead company *See* 'Zombie company'.

Loan-to-own *See* 'Distressed debt investing'.

Loan-to-value Measure of risk that provides a lender with a ratio of the total lent divided by the value of the collateral pledged for the loan.

Lock-up period The time during which the shareholders of a company have agreed not to use their right to sell the shares they own in a listed company after an IPO (*see this expression*). Investment banks in charge of managing the initial public offering generally insist that the lock-up period lasts at least 180 days for the main shareholders (who own at least 1% of the capital) in order to let the floating part of the shares acquire the characteristics of a normal flotation, and notably find an equilibrium price.

LOI *See* 'Letter of intent'.

LP secondaries *See* 'Secondary investing'.

LPA *See* 'Limited partnership agreement'.

LPX Sponsor of a series of indexes of listed alternative investment vehicles. By extension refers to the indexes produced, such as the LPX 50. It is in substance an index of listed financial institutions, highly correlated with the usual indexes of listed stocks.

M

Majority ownership In the case of majority control ownership, an investor or a group of investors collectively own half plus one of the political (voting) rights in a company. In the case of a simple or qualified majority, an investor or a group of investors collectively reach a pre-set threshold of political rights in a company. Thresholds are often set by the shareholders' agreement to take specific decisions.

Management buy-in (MBI) The transfer of a company where the new management team, which has control, did not work for the company before and where the current management does not necessarily have a common previous experience. The transaction generally implies the acquisition of a part of the company by the new management and the financial backers.

Management buy-out (MBO) The transfer of a company from its current owner to a new group of owners where the existing management and staff play an active part. In large buy-outs, managers have little chance to have a minor part of the company owing to the size of the operation. If the operation is open to all employees, it is then an employee buy-out.

Management company *See* 'Fund manager'.

Management fees Financial remuneration for the service provided by a fund manager, usually paid quarterly by the fund to the fund manager. The fund manager uses management fees to cover its operational costs such as wages, office rent and other costs. Management fees usually range from 0.5% to 1% for a fund-of-funds manager, 1.25% to 2.5% for a private equity fund manager, 0.4% to 2% for a private debt fund manager, and 0.8% to 2% for a private real-asset fund manager. Management fees are determined notably by the size of the fund raised, the size of the fund manager, the type of strategy and the region where the manager is based. Macro-economic conditions and the relative bargaining power of the fund manager and fund investors during the fundraising also influence the level of fees. Management fees can be reduced by a 'fee offset mechanism' (*see this expression*).

Management team A group of managers in charge of a company, for example a start-up, who can initiate the contact with one or multiple fund managers that then leads to an operation of private equity.

Mandate Investment delegation to a gatekeeper by an investor to define and invest a certain amount in private market funds according to the preferences and objectives of the investor.

Market value The value of an asset once it has been re-evaluated at a current price.

Marketing of a fund *See* 'Fundraising'.

Master limited partnership (MLP) Private market investment structure listed on a stock exchange. It combines the benefits of the tax transparency of a private market fund with the liquidity associated with a listing. MLPs are most frequently used in the energy sector, for example to invest in oil and gas pipeline operators. They could also be used in the real-estate sector.

MBI *See* 'Management buy-in'.

MBO *See* 'Management buy-out'.

Mezzanine debt The most subordinated (*see this expression*) form of debt, convertible to equity. It is ranked above equity but after every other form of debt as to its repayment. Its interest can be capitalised and repaid as a bullet payment (*see this expression*), or distributed regularly. The forms of mezzanine debt vary from senior mezzanine debt, which is less flexible and therefore cheaper, to junior mezzanine debt, which is more flexible and for example bears no regular interest payments.

MFN *See* 'Most favoured nation clause'.

Midstream Refers to, in the oil and gas industry, the transportation (by any means) to refineries, storage and handling of crude oil and unrefined natural gas.

Milestone Pre-set target for a company to reach to raise a new round of financing or release a tranche of an existing financing facility.

Minimum commitment Lowest threshold to reach for an investor to be accepted in a private market fund.

Minority ownership Literally any investor who does not reach an ownership threshold of half plus one shares. Different levels of minority ownership can be differentiated, such as a significant minority ownership or a blocking minority ownership, which entitles the owner(s) to have special rights in the shareholders' agreement.

Minority protection rights Set of legal and contractual provisions protecting the minority shareholders (*see this expression*). Contractual provisions are essentially set in the shareholders' agreement, which notably defines information, monitoring, control and action rights for minority shareholders. These rights are targeted to handle relationships with other shareholders, whether minority or majority owners, as well as with the management of their investment.

MLP *See* 'Master limited partnership'.

MOIC *See* 'Multiple of invested capital'.

Monitoring A process by which investors follow the actions of the portfolio company's management directed at the realisation of pre-set targets, such as sales, cash situation and (if applicable) debt service and repayment. Methods of monitoring include presence on the Board, regular reports and meetings. These methods should provide investors with a way of identifying any problems early and taking corrective action rapidly. This provides management with access to new ideas, contracts and a certain amount of help from investors.

Monitoring fees To monitor and control a portfolio company, LBO fund managers can decide to charge to the company an annual fee. This fee can be attributed to the fund manager, the fund investors or shared between the fund manager and the fund investors.

Most favoured nation clause Provision of a fund regulation in which the fund managers agree to automatically provide each fund investor with the best terms negotiated by any other investor in the fund, including by way of direct negotiation with the fund manager in a side letter (*see this expression*), for example.

Multiple expansion One of the sources of performance generation for a private market fund. It is the difference between the entry multiple (*see this expression*) and the exit multiple (*see this expression*), and therefore can be positive or negative.

Multiple of invested capital (MOIC) The ratio between the proceeds from the realisation of an investment and the amount invested.

N

Natural resources Materials or substances readily available as raw input that are extracted and exploited for profit.

NAV *See* 'Net asset value'.

NDA *See* 'Non-disclosure agreement'.

Net asset value (NAV) Estimate as of date of the value of the companies or assets held by a private market fund.

Net cash flows The difference between the incoming and the outgoing cash flows of a company over a certain period of time. In a leveraged buy-out operation, the cash flows are a better indication than the net result of a company for an assessment of its capacity to repay its obligations towards its debtors.

Net debt Total value of the liabilities of a company minus the available cash and cash equivalent.

Net present value The actual value of future cash flows of an investment, less the initial investment. In theory, if the net asset value is above zero, the investment should be made.

No fault divorce clause Provision of a fund regulation such as a limited partnership agreement (*see this expression*) allowing the fund investors to change the fund manager, even if the latter did not mismanage the fund.

Non-disclosure agreement Legally binding document between two economic agents, which agree to actively not disclose and prevent the disclosure of information described and proven confidential. This document is often signed between a prospective portfolio company (represented by its management) and a VC/growth fund manager, or between a business owner and an LBO fund manager.

Non-performing loan Amount due by a borrower which is not repaid and/or whose interest is not paid. The debt is in default or close to it.

NPL *See* 'Non-performing loan'.

O

Open-end *See* 'Evergreen'.

Open-ended *See* 'Evergreen'.

Open-end fund *See* 'Evergreen'.

Operating partner Executive paid by a fund manager whose role is to work with the portfolio companies to increase their value.

Operational costs Costs associated with the operation of a private market fund, such as audit, accounting, fairness opinions and other expenses that are not covered by the management fees. This encompasses notably the custodian fees and the broken deals expenses.

Operational improvements Effort of a portfolio company to increase its efficiency in sales and/or profitability.

Opportunistic Theoretically, the riskiest investment strategy applied in private real estate and private infrastructure, essentially aiming to deliver capital gains to investors. Assets require significant improvements, sometimes being entirely redeveloped or repositioned. The debt used to acquire these assets is 70% or more.

Over-commitment Operation leading a fund investor to promise to contribute to a private market fund a higher amount than effectively planned. The expected result is to help the fund investor deploy on a net basis more capital, if possible close to the planned target. Thus, the purpose of over-committing is to compensate the early distributions of a fund to reach a higher level of net exposure.

Over-subscription Situation in which demand from investors exceeds significantly the supply of a financial instrument, such as a private market fund.

Owner buy-out (OBO) Leveraged buy-out operated on a company by its current owner, either to get full control (exit of a co-owner), or to prepare the transition of ownership to an heir.

P

P2P *See* 'Public-to-private transaction'.

Paid-in Sum of the capital called by a private market fund.

Parallel funds Investment vehicles set up to accommodate investors with specific legal and/or tax needs. They usually operate on a *pari passu* (*see this expression*) basis with the main fund that they are mimicking. Some parallel funds are set up for employees or close business relations of fund managers, usually with more favourable terms than the main fund.

Pari passu Latin expression referring to the equality between parties. In the context of credit, lenders whose loans have a *pari passu* status should collect any amount on an equal footing, including in a case of insolvency.

Partial exit An investor receives proceeds from the exit of an investment but still remains partially invested. This happens for example during a dividend recapitalisation (*see this expression*), or when an investor sells part of its stake in a portfolio company but also keeps some of it.

Partner *See* 'Partners'.

Partners The owners of the fund management company (*see this expression*) or fund manager (*see this expression*).

Payment in kind Feature of a loan according to which interest is capitalised and paid, usually along with the principal, not in cash but with securities.

Peer group Sample of funds that are similar in their investment strategy (including target maturity and size), geographical reach, industrial specialisation (if any) and vintage year.

Pension fund/plan Organisation collecting employer and/or employee contributions to invest them and later distribute these contributions and the eventual investment proceeds to the employees upon and/or during retirement.

Performance fee *See* 'Carried interest'.

Persistence of performance Refers to the ability of a private market fund manager to either perform within a specific subset of a peer group or to perform consistently above or below a specific threshold.

Pitch Refers to the rather short and condensed form of commercialisation of an investment.

Placement agent Intermediary specialised in the support and services to fund managers willing to raise a private market fund. Its services can be regulated (or even banned) in some jurisdictions.

Platform transaction In the context of a buy-and-build (*see this expression*) strategy, refers to the first and/or largest of a series of investments leading to create a larger company thanks to add-on transactions (*see this expression*).

Pledge fund Investment vehicle designed so that investors can finance specific deals along the lines pre-agreed with the fund manager. Investors have to approve the transaction.

PME *See* 'Public market equivalent'.

PME+ *See* 'Public market equivalent'.

Portfolio company (also known as investee company) A company or entity in which a fund invests directly.

Post-money value The valuation of a company after the most recent round of financing. The value is calculated by the multiplication of the total number of shares by the price of a share applied at the most recent round of financing.

PPM *See* 'Private placement memorandum'.

PPP *See* 'Public–private partnership'.

Pre-emption right Shareholders have the right to maintain a certain percentage of ownership in a company by buying the pro rata of shares in the case of the issue of new shares. This can also be exercised in the case of the sale of shares to an existing shareholder, before opening the sale to third parties.

Pre-marketing Series of actions undertaken by a fund manager with no actual or immediate fund to sell, aimed at testing and assessing the idea of raising a new fund with investors. This usually implies describing in broad terms the strategy, aim and operations of this new fund. This activity can be regulated in specific jurisdictions.

Pre-money value The value of a company before a planned injection of capital.

Preferred equity In the secondary (*see this expression*) market, tranche of financing sitting between debt and equity. This instrument is provided by a third party to an existing fund investor unable or not willing to answer current and upcoming capital calls. The third-party specialist provides the capital to answer the calls and gets some of the returns provided to the fund investor. The benefit for the fund investor is to stay invested and possibly keep the opportunity to reinvest in successor funds from the same manager. For disambiguation, *see also* 'Preferred shares'.

Preferred rate of return The minimal yearly rate of return acceptable for the investors in a private market fund, which is often set at 8% on capital invested. It is therefore calculated as an internal rate of return (*see this expression*). This rate has to be paid to investors before the 'carried interest' (*see this expression*) is paid to the fund manager.

Preferred shares The class of shares which includes specific rights, not attributed to common shares, such as, for example, a preferred redemption with a guaranteed minimal multiple of investment.

Principal Key executives working for the fund manager and putting in place the strategy and who can claim a portion of the carried interest.

Private debt investing Institutional lending to businesses that is not done by banks. The purpose of this investment strategy is to lend, recover or restructure the debt of a company to generate interest and/or capital gains. This investment strategy includes direct lending (also known as senior lending), venture debt, unitranche, mezzanine financing, distressed debt, non-performing loans investing and other niches such as litigation financing and trade finance, for example.

Private equity investing Capital infusion in a company or its transfer of ownership, with the intention to implement a plan in this company to increase its value and eventually sell it, usually after 3 to 7 years at a significant profit. This plan is set up with the full support of the entrepreneurs/management of the firm. This investment strategy includes venture capital, growth capital, leveraged buy-out, turn-around capital and other niches such as private investment in public equities, for example.

Private investment in public equities (PIPE) A significant stake in a listed company is sold through a private placement (*see this expression*). This is in general linked to a capital infusion in the listed firm. This operation leads to the sale by the company of shares at a discount compared to the public price of the shares. This discount is justified by the commitment of the owner of this stake to hold the shares for a minimum amount of time, usually at least 24 to 36 months.

Private placement Sale of securities at arm's length, that is to say out of the stock exchange.

Private placement memorandum Prospectus summing up the features of a private market fund to be created. This sales document notably includes an executive summary, a detailed investment strategy, a description of the operational capacity of the fund manager, its track record (if any), it differentiating factors, as well as the key terms of the fund.

Private real-assets investing Equity or debt investment in private assets, whether tangible or not, fixed or not, thus ranging from royalties to airports. The purpose of this investment strategy is to develop, structure or restructure the asset to generate a mix of dividends and capital gains. The holding period is usually 3 to 12 or even 15 years. This investment strategy includes private real estate, private infrastructure, the oil and gas value chain, timberland and farmland, and other niches such as intellectual property and royalty financing, mining or leasing.

Privatisation Acquisition of a state-owned company or asset by a private owner (or a group of private owners).

Proceeds Cash generated and collected from an investment activity.

Proprietary deal flow Sourcing technique in which the potential buyer is the first and only one looking at an investment opportunity.

Prudent man rule American legal principle according to which an agent managing the asset of a client should apply the philosophy of an individual seeking reasonable income and the preservation of capital.

Prudent person principle *See* 'Prudent man rule'.

Prudential ratio A regulatory ratio that defines the quantity of capital that a bank must keep in-house in order to cover the risk of its commitments.

Public market equivalent Performance benchmarking method to compare the performance of a private market investment or fund with an index. Different variations exist, such as the ICM (also referred to as 'PME' or 'LN-PME') which essentially mimics the cash-flow pattern of a private market fund with an index. This method supports the comparison of the performance of a fund with equivalent investments in the index. The method has a shortcoming: if the cash distributions are significant, the index performance could be negative. The PME+ of Christophe Rouvinez and the mPME of

Cambridge Associates regulate the distribution by computing either a factor adjusting the NAV of the fund (PME+) or the weight of the distribution in the fund (mPME). Additional variations around these three methods, such as the KS-PME by Steve Kaplan and Antoinette Schoar, aim at determining a direct indication of performance in a single figure. The Direct Alpha by Oleg Gredil, Barry E. Griffiths and Rüdiger Stucke is another variation on this approach.

Public–private partnership Agreement between one or multiple governmental agencies and private sector companies, leading to the creation, improvement or regeneration of a company or an asset.

Public-to-private transaction Acquisition of a listed company or asset by a private owner (or a group of private owners), and its subsequent delisting.

Q

Qualified investor Entity or person that invests large volumes in the securities market, which allows for better negotiation conditions, lower commissions, etc. The regulations generally provide them with lower levels of protection than small investors, given that, due to their institutional or professional nature, they have sufficient knowledge and experience to assess the risks they assume and make their own investment decisions. Qualified investors are considered to be institutional investors (banks and savings banks, insurance companies, investment fund management companies, pension fund management entities, funds and investment companies, etc.), small businesses and individuals who, in compliance with certain criteria, request to be considered qualified investors. They are allowed to invest in private market funds.

Quartile The segment of a sample representing a sequential quarter (25%). Thus, the first 10 of 40 funds are the first (or top) quartile and the last 10 are the last (or bottom) quartile.

Quasi-equity Instruments such as shareholders' loans, preferred shares, etc. These instruments are not guaranteed by collateral and are convertible at exit.

R

RAIF The reserved alternative investment fund is a legal form available in Luxemburg to create rapidly and flexibly private market funds to be marketed in the EU. The fund manager is regulated under the AIFMD (*see this expression*) that dispenses the fund to be.

RCF *See* 'Revolving credit facility'.

Real assets Tangible (and by extension intangible claims on tangible) properties that have value on a stand-alone basis due to their substance or features. This category notably includes real estate, infrastructure and natural resources.

Recapitalisation A change in the initial financing structure of a buy-out to reschedule the debt payments or capitalise the structure further, because of insufficient results to pay the debt of acquisition or because of a capital need linked to further investments. Alternatively, a recapitalisation could lead the initial investors to exit from a successful LBO, so as to enable the management team to continue without any IPO or trade sale.

Recycling of distributions *See* 'Reinvestment of distributions'.

Redemption Withdrawal of an investor from a fund. The fund pays back the capital (and distributes the eventual losses or profit associated with it) to the investor.

Reinvestment of distributions Provision of fund regulations allowing the fund manager to reinvest early distributions, as long as the fund is in its investment period. The aim is to allow the fund manager to effectively invest up to 100% of the fund size, therefore compensating for the fees paid by the fund.

Removal of fund manager Clause in a fund regulation leading to the replacement of the manager for cause and/or without cause.

Replacement capital Financing provided by funds to buy out one or multiple shareholders. This can be the way for shareholders of a family business to sell their shares without necessarily obliging the family to lose control.

Reporting Process supporting the regular and recurring information of investors by their agent. In the case of a private markets fund, the reporting is often quarterly and is a written report from the fund manager to the fund investors. In the case of a private company or asset, the reporting is from the management to the investors and can be monthly, quarterly or less frequent.

Representations Series of contractual clauses usually used when a transfer of ownership of a given company or asset occurs (for example in a leveraged buy-out operation in private equity). It allows the buyer of a company to make sure that the means necessary for the company to operate belong to the latter. However, it does not cover an over- or under-valuation of the company. It is often combined with warranties.

Residual value Sum of the net asset value of all the assets held by a private market fund as of date.

Residual value to paid-in (RVPI) Ratio between the net asset value of a fund (its residual value) and the total capital called by this fund (paid-in).

Responsible investing *See* 'Environmental, social and governance (ESG) criteria'.

Restart Process of launching a new company out of the ashes of a failed one.

Restructuring Process consisting of a series of actions undertaken by the management of a company to significantly or radically improve its financial and/or operational situation.

Retail investor Non-professional, qualified or accredited individual purchasing financial instruments for his/her own personal account.

Re-up Process in which an investor in a fund decides to invest in the next fund from the same fund manager, with the same specific investment strategy.

Reverse break-up fee *See* 'Break-up fee'.

Revolving credit facility Permanent credit line from a bank.

Round of financing Designation of a capital increase operation in a given venture capital-backed (or business angel-backed) company, which is usually supporting it to its next stage of development. Usually referred to as 'Series A', 'Series B', 'Series C', etc. until the company reaches profitability. As growth capital is not operated in stages, there is no round of financing.

RVPI *See* 'Residual value to paid-in'.

S

Sale-and-leaseback Financial transaction in which an asset, such as a machine or a building, is sold and immediately leased back for the long term. The seller is no longer the owner but continues to use it.

Scale up Refers to the growth phase of a start-up, after the launch of its product or service (also known as 'go to market' milestone). This includes the mass commercialisation, internationalisation, acquisition of competitors and even the launch of additional products or services.

Scheme of arrangement Agreement between a company and its creditors that is approved by a bankruptcy court. This type of arrangement is usually undertaken to significantly alter the structure of a company and the rights of its creditors. It can be used to reschedule its debt, amend priorities of creditors or their claims on the assets of a company, for example.

Search fund *See* 'Finder's fund'.

Second lien Debt subordinated to the repayment of the senior debt (first lien), but exempt of conversion rights. It is usually secured against the same collateral as the senior debt, but this collateral can only be claimed if the first lien rights are extinct.

Secondary buy-out/buy-in The exit path from an investment where the initial professional investors can realise all or part of their investment through the sale to another professional investor.

Secondary investing Investment in a pre-existing asset. This can lead to the acquisition of an existing stake in a portfolio company by a fund ('direct secondary') or of an existing stake in a private market fund by a fund investor ('fund secondary'). Direct secondary investments differentiate themselves from direct primary investments in the sense that there is no new instrument created in the operation (no new shares in case of direct VC secondary).

Securitisation Bundling of assets into a fund vehicle further offered to investors under the form of notes or bonds that are often rated by independent credit rating agencies.

Seed investing Initial funding used for the proof of a concept, and eventually to develop the prototype of the product or service and initiate a formal or informal market study.

Segregated accounts Investment conduit held by a single investor. The account can be managed discretionarily by a third party through a mandate, or non-discretionarily.

Semi-captive *See* 'Captive manager'.

Senior debt A loan used to finance the leveraged buy-out of a company, which benefits from priority in the case of default of payment by the company or in the case of failure of the structuring. It is usually secured against the company as collateral.

Set-up costs Costs borne by a private market fund for its set-up. They usually include lawyers' fees, placement agents' fees and additional costs related to this initial operation, and range from 0.5% to 3% of the fund size.

Shareholders' agreement A contract between the shareholders of a company to establish their common and respective rights and duties. In particular, the agreement must determine the protection of minority holders against actions taken by the majority and which would be unfavourable to minority interests. This document is contractual and evolves with the ownership structure of the company.

SICAR (Société d'Investissement en Capital Risque) Luxembourg investment vehicle dedicated to private equity investments, combining a fund and a fund management company in a single entity. A SICAR distributes dividends.

Side letter Agreement signed between the fund manager and (a) fund investor(s) outside the fund regulations. This usually does not involve any significant change of the fund regulations, but adds precision, for example to ensure compliance with specific tax regulations. Side letters are often generalised to all the investors in a given fund due to the 'most favoured nation' clause (*see this expression*).

Sidecar fund Investment vehicle operated alongside a main fund but under different terms. This type of investment vehicle is usually reserved to the employees and specific partners of a fund manager, and can operate without supporting any management fee or carried interest.

SIF (specialised investment fund) Luxembourg investment fund dedicated to private equity investments. A SIF distributes capital gains.

SLP *See* 'Société de Libre Partenariat'.

Société de Libre Partenariat French equivalent of the limited partnership structure.

Solo investment Form of direct investment in which the investor acts alone.

Solvency ratio A regulatory ratio that defines the quantity of capital that an insurer must keep in-house to cover the risk of its commitments.

Sovereign wealth fund Investment vehicle owned and operated by a state or government agency. The source of capital is often related to the exploitation of natural resources, the constitution of large foreign exchange reserves or public savings.

SPAC *See* 'Special Purpose Acquisition Company'.

Special Purpose Acquisition Company Investment trust created by a manager with the purpose of investing in a private company. The manager identifies a target, trust unit holders vote on the project and if the vote is positive, the trust makes the acquisition and is converted into a listed special purpose acquisition company.

Special purpose vehicle Legal entity set up for a particular function, such as owning an asset as collateral for a loan.

Specialised fund An investment strategy in private equity designed to build a portfolio of companies that are specialised in some industrial sectors and possibly located in certain geographical areas.

Spin-off A group separates itself from a business unit but can maintain significant ownership in the resulting company. This can happen when strong commercial relationships are maintained and/or the ex business unit develops a new product which could be of interest to the group.

Sponsor In the context of raising a private market fund, refers to the institution that owns a significant part or the entire fund manager. The sponsor also acts as a cornerstone investor (*see this expression*).

Sponsored LBO Transfer of ownership of a private company in which a fund or a financial institution is involved. An unsponsored LBO is a transfer of ownership of a private company without the involvement of a fund or a financial institution, such as a pure management buy-out, for example.

SPV *See* 'Special purpose vehicle'.

Staple financing Form of secondary investing (*see this expression*) in which the acquisition of a stake in a fund is combined with the commitment of the next generation of fund (successor fund, *see this expression*) from the same fund manager.

Start-up The stage of development of a company where it develops its product or service, reaches the prototype stage and eventually starts to market the product or service. This company is usually structured or is only active for a short period of time (a year or less). Generally, this company has recruited key managers, designed a business plan and attracted some seed financing. A start-up is generally considered to be 5 years old or less.

Structuring Process of setting up a financial transaction, instrument or investment vehicle.

Subordinated debt Corporate credit whose repayment and interest payments are subject to the prior repayment of more senior credit. The claims of subordinated debt holders on the collateral of the debt are also subject to priority from those of senior debt holders. The concept of subordinated debt varies according to the legal regimes of different countries.

Subscription agreement Legal document signed by an investor to commit to a fund.

Subsequent closing Interim steps in the process of fundraising, materialising the commitment of fund investors who were not part of the initial closing (*see this expression*).

Successor fund Next generation of a series of funds dedicated to a specific investment strategy raised by a fund manager. The right to raise a successor fund can be limited by the fund regulations of the current active generation of the fund. For example, the fund regulations can state that a successor fund cannot be raised if the current one is not invested at least at 70% of its fund size.

Sweat equity Shares given to the management and/or employees of a company in exchange for their work and/or their intellectual property.

Syndicate/syndication A means of financing a company by splitting the risk between multiple investors. In the case of large buy-outs, there can be multiple syndicates for different forms of financial instruments (equity or debt).

T

Tag along Clause of a shareholders' agreement that protects the minority shareholder, in case of a sale by the controlling shareholder of their stake in a company. Minority shareholders have the right to sell their stake at the same conditions as the majority shareholders.

Take down *See* 'Capital call'.

Take private *See* 'Public-to-private'.

Target company Company which is to be acquired directly or indirectly by a private equity fund.

Term of a fund End date of a private market fund. For closed-end funds, this ranges from 8 to 15 years. There is no term for open-end funds.

Term sheet The synthesis of the main conditions proposed by the investor for a stake in a company.

Terms and conditions Statements of the rights of the fund investors and duties of the fund manager.

Theory of agency See 'Agency theory'.

Timberland Geographical area covered with marketable wood.

Top-down Progressing from the highest (or least granular) to the lowest (or most granular) level of an analytical process. In the context of asset allocation, this consists of analysing macro-economic factors to draw general conclusions and build a portfolio from this analysis. The positive side of this approach is that it is systematic and theoretically sound. The negative side of this approach is that it might not be applicable for the lack of actual assets in specific investment categories. A complementary approach is 'bottom-up' (*see this expression*).

Top-line growth Growth of the revenues of a given company.

Top quartile 25% of a sample which ranks highest according to a specific criterion, such as for example a performance metric.

Total value to paid-in *See* 'TVPI'.

Track record Historical performance of a private market fund manager, which includes notably multiples of investment (TVPI) and internal rates of return (IRR), and at times its public market equivalent (PME).

Tranche of equity or debt Defines the priority of payment of the holder of a security. The capital structure of a company may contain several tranches of both debt securities and equity securities.

Transaction fees Expenses born by a private market fund associated with investments or divestments.

Turn-around capital Acquisition of ailing businesses by specialised funds, with the aim of turning around these businesses thanks to a change in their business model, financial structure, capital, management and/or product or services. This type of investment is executed before the company goes bankrupt.

TVPI (total value to paid-in) Ratio between the total value of the portfolio of a given private market fund (hence the sum of its distribution and the net asset value of the portfolio) and the total of the capital called ('paid-in').

U

Undrawn capital Capital not yet called by a private market fund. Also referred to as 'dry powder'.

Unitranche debt Single loan structure combining multiple layers of debt ranging from senior to subordinated ranks.

Unrealised value *See* 'Residual value'.

Unsponsored LBO *See* 'Sponsored LBO'.

Upstream Also referred to as 'exploration and production', this refers to searching for crude oil and natural gas fields, drilling and operating wells.

V

Valuation Analytical process leading to the current or projected estimation of the worth of a company or an asset.

Valuation date Date on which a valuation is applied to a given investment.

Value add Moderate- to high-risk investment strategy applied in private real estate and private infrastructure, essentially aiming to deliver capital gains to investors, and possibly income. Assets require significant management from investors, solving vacancy issues, maintenance or operational issues, significant upgrading or renovation, and/or quality of tenants' issues. The debt used to acquire these assets is 60–75% maximum.

Value-at-risk Method to measure the probability of an investment loss and its extent during a set time period.

Value creation Result of a set of actions undertaken to increase the worth of a company or an asset.

VCT See 'Venture Capital Trust'.

Vendor due diligence Detailed report on a company or an asset provided by the seller to potential buyers.

Vendor financing Financing in which the seller of a company accepts a deferred payment from the buyer.

Venture capital Financing provided by funds targeting emerging businesses, notably start-ups with strong growth prospects. The venture capital investor provides at the same time capital, a network of contacts, know-how and additional experience.

Venture Capital Trust British investment vehicle allowing retail investors to gain exposure to venture capital investments. A tax incentive is associated with a commitment in this vehicle that is listed after its inception.

Venture debt Financing provided to mid- to late-stage under the form of convertible debt and complementary to equity financing. As most start-ups are usually free of debt, this type of loan is in practice senior and collateralised.

Venture leasing Investments in venture capital that are linked to the leasing of equipment or other fixed assets in a technology start-up. Compared to traditional leasing contracts (generally not available for start-ups), venture leasing implies some equity kickers to compensate for the risk borne by the leaser.

Venture philanthropy Subset of impact or ESG investments aimed at investing in emerging projects or companies with the purpose of achieving charitable targets, often leading to lower or no returns on investment. This approach applies venture capital techniques and criteria to select and invest in these projects and companies.

Vesting (carried interest) Procedure of attribution to each of the principals of the carried interest allocated to the fund manager. It can be immediate or progressive (over time).

Vintage year Year of creation of a private market fund and usually of its first capital call (or in specific cases, its final closing) or its first investment. This is also a reference point for the funds created the same year for comparison purposes.

Vulture investing Often confused with distressed debt or turn-around investing, this approach consists of taking control of ailing businesses with the clear target of shutting them down and selling their assets. Vulture investing thus differs from other strategies aimed at distressed businesses, as its only purpose is the liquidation of activities.

W

Warranties Series of contractual clauses usually used when a transfer of ownership of a given company or asset occurs (e.g., in a leveraged buy-out operation in private equity). It allows the buyer of a company to make sure that there are no hidden liabilities (or at least that the buyer will not support the financial consequences of past liabilities). However, it does not cover an over- or under-valuation of the company. It can be combined with representations.

Wash-out In the context of a distressed debt investment, a wash-out is the complete elimination of the current shareholders from the capitalisation table. In a more general context of capital increase, a wash-out round is when the entrepreneurs and managers of a company lose control of the firm.

Waterfall distribution Mechanism attributing the cash generated by a given private market fund to its stakeholders according to priorities (e.g., refund to the fund investors and the fund manager of their initial commitments, then distribution of the hurdle rate, then distribution of the catch-up, then distribution of the profits and carried interest).

Winding down of a fund Process of completely terminating the operations of a private market investment vehicle. This includes liquidating any remaining assets, liquidating escrow accounts and handling any outstanding right or duty, such as a warranty for example.

Write down Accounting and reporting operation reflecting the impairment losses of a portfolio company.

Write-off An action that changes the value of an asset/portfolio company to zero.

Z

Zombie company In the context of venture and growth capital investments, these are portfolio companies which are break-even but do not provide attractive prospects for a potential buyer or listing. In the context of LBO and private debt, these are portfolio companies that generate sufficient cash flows to service their debt and operate their daily activity, but cannot repay their debt.

Bibliography

Books and Booklets

Ante, S. (2008) *Creative Capital* (Harvard Business School Publishing, Boston, MA), 299 pp.

Appelbaum, E. and Batt, R. (2014) *Private Equity at Work* (Russell Sage Foundation, New York), 381 pp.

Blessing, S. (2011) *Alternative Alternatives* (Wiley, Chichester), 242 pp.

Brooke, P. and Penrice, D. (2009) *A Vision for Venture Capital* (New Venture Press, Lebanon, PA), 275 pp.

Brown, D. (1995) *Mesopotamia: The Mighty Kings (Lost Civilizations)* (Time-Life Books, New York), 168 pp.

Bunch, B. and Hellemans, A. (2004) 'Thomas Edison', in *History of Science and Technology* (Houghton Mifflin Harcourt, Boston, MA), 784 pp.

Burstall, A. (1965) *A History of Mechanical Engineering* (MIT Press, Cambridge, MA), 456 pp.

Bygrave, W., Hay, M. and Peeters, J. (1999) *The Venture Capital Handbook* (Pearson Education, Harlow), 362 pp.

Cendrowski, H., Martin, J., Petro, L. and Wadecki, A. (2008) *Private Equity: History, Governance and Operations* (Wiley, Chichester), 480 pp.

Cornelius, P. (2011) *International Investments in Private Equity* (Academic Press, Burlington, VA), 305 pp.

Cornelius, P., Diller, C., Guennoc, D. and Meyer, T. (2013) *Mastering Illiquidity* (Wiley, Chichester), 288 pp.

Cummine, A. (2016) *Citizens' Wealth* (Yale University Press, New Haven, CT), 280 pp.

Davydenko, S. and Franks, J. (2006) *Do Bankruptcy Codes Matter? A Study of Defaults in France, Germany and the UK* (University of Toronto/London Business School), 45 pp.

Demaria, C. (2006, 2008, 2010, 2012, 2015, 2018) *Introduction au Private Equity* (RB Editions, Paris), 1st, 2nd, 3rd, 4th, 5th, 6th edns, 128 pp.

Demaria, C. (2015) *Private Equity Fund Investments* (Palgrave Macmillan, Basingstoke), 276 pp.

Demaria, C. and Pedergnana, M. (2009) *Le marché, les acteurs et la performance du private equity suisse* (SECA Editions, Zug), 130 pp.

Demaria, C. and Pedergnana, M. (2012) *Le marché, les acteurs et la performance du private equity suisse* (SECA Editions, Zug), 2nd edn, 199 pp.

Demaria, C., Debrand, S., He, R., Pedergnana, M. and Rissi, R., *Asset Allocation and Private Markets* (Wiley, Chichester), forthcoming.

Draper, W. (2011) *The Startup Game* (Palgrave Macmillan, New York), 261 pp.

Durant, W. (1954) *The Story of Civilization, Vol. 1 – Our Oriental Heritage* (Simon & Schuster, New York), 1049 pp.

Fraser-Sampson, G. (2007) *Private Equity as an Asset Class* (Wiley, Chichester), 284 pp.

Frederick Lewis, A. (1949) *The Great Pierpont Morgan* (Harper & Row, New York), 306 pp.

Frei, P. (2006) *Assessments and Valuation of High Growth Companies* (SECA Editions, Zug), 291 pp.

Gompers, P. and Lerner, J. (2006) *The Venture Capital Cycle* (MIT Press, Cambridge, MA), 2nd edn, 581 pp.

Gupta, U. (2004) *The First Venture Capitalist* (Gondolier, Calgary), 240 pp.

Hobohm, D. (2010) *Investors in Private Equity, Theory, Preferences, Performances* (Springer-Gabler, Wiesbaden), 199 pp.

Johnson, S. (2010) *Where Good Ideas Come From, The Natural History of Innovation* (Riverhead Books, New York), 326 pp.

Kocis, J., Bachman, J., Long, A. and Nickels, C. (2009) *Inside Private Equity, The Professional's Handbook* (Wiley, Hoboken, NJ), 262 pp.

Kusukawa, S. and MacLean, I. (2006) *Transmitting Knowledge: Words, Images, and Instruments in Early Modern Europe* (Oxford University Press, Oxford), 274 pp.

Leleux, B., Van Swaay, H. and Megally, E. (2015) *Private Equity 4.0* (Wiley, Chichester), 258 pp.

Lerner, J. (2009) *Boulevard of Broken Dreams, Why Public Efforts to Boost Entrepreneurship and Venture Capital Have Failed – and What to Do about It* (Princeton University Press, Princeton, NJ), 229 pp.

Lerner, J. (2012) *The Architecture of Innovation* (Oxford University Press, Oxford), 224 pp.

Lerner, J., Leamon, A. and Hardymon, F. (2012) *Venture Capital, Private Equity, and the Financing of Entrepreneurship* (Wiley, New York), 464 pp.

Mathonet, P.-Y. and Meyer, T. (2007) *J-Curve Exposure: Managing a Portfolio of Venture Capital and Private Equity Funds* (Wiley, Chichester), 384 pp.

Mazzucato, M. (2015) *The Entrepreneurial State* (PublicAffairs, Philadelphia, PA), 260 pp.

Meyer, T. (2014) *Private Equity Unchained* (Palgrave Macmillan, Basingstoke), 320 pp.

Meyer, T. and Mathonet, P.-Y. (2005) *Beyond the J-curve* (Wiley, Chichester), 366 pp.

O'Brien, J. (2007) *Private Equity, Corporate Governance and the Dynamics of Capital Markets Regulation* (Imperial College Press, London), 484 pp.

Perkins, T. (2008) *Valley Boy* (Gotham Books, New York), 289 pp.

Phalippou, L. (2017) *Private Equity Laid Bare* (CreateSpace Independent Publishing Platform), 205 pp.

Ries, E. (2011) *The Lean Startup: How Today's Entrepreneurs Use Continuous Innovation to Create Radically Successful Businesses* (Penguin Books, London), 336 pp.

Senor, D. and Singer, P. (2010) *Start-Up Nation: The Story of Israel's Economic Miracle* (Little, Brown & Co., New York), 320 pp.

Swensen, D. (2009) *Pioneering Portfolio Management* (Free Press, New York), 408 pp.

Talmor, E. and Vasvari, F. (2011) *International Private Equity* (Wiley, Chichester), 747 pp.

Tirole, J. (2005) *The Theory of Corporate Finance* (Princeton University Press, Princeton, NJ), 640 pp.

Vijg, J. (2011) *The American Technological Challenge* (Algora Publishing, New York), 248 pp.

Zeisberger, C., Prahl, M. and White, B. (2017) *Mastering Private Equity* (Wiley, Chichester), 349 pp.

Newsletters and Newspapers

Alspach, K., 'Angel investing up in 2011, narrowing start-ups' financing gap', *Boston Business Journal*, 11 October 2011.

AltAssets, 'Survey reveals that 43 per cent of LPs denied access to all the funds they wanted over the last 12 months', 29 June 2005.

AltAssets, 'US private equity chief pleads not guilty', 28 July 2009.

AlwaysOn, 'Build rather than buy – competitive advantage', 12 January 2005.

Anselmi, F., 'L'échange de dette, base de la restructuration des LBO', *L'Agefi*, 19 March 2009.

Arnold, M., 'Private equity faces investor exodus', *Financial Times*, 13 May 2009a.

Arnold, M., 'State-led venture capital lags behind rivals', *Financial Times*, 5 August 2009b.

Arrington, M., 'The USD 4 million line', *TechCrunch*, 5 October 2010.

Balsham, R., Brown, M., Lee, M. and Rubalevskaya, J., 'Private social investment in France: meeting two goals', Knowledge@Wharton, 26 January 2011.

Bills, S., 'Do secondary sales signal a coming crisis?', PEHub Wire, 16 December 2010.

Bilton, N., 'Disruptions: with no revenue, an illusion of value', Bits, *New York Times*, 29 April 2012.

Blankfein, L., 'Do not destroy the essential catalyst of risk', *Financial Times*, 8 February 2009.

Bloch, M., Kolodny, J. and Maor, D., 'Israel, an innovation gem, in Europe's backyard', *Financial Times*, 13 September 2012.

Blohm, M., Fernandes, A. and Khalitov, B., 'Entrepreneurship in Colombia: "Try fast, learn fast, fail cheap"', Knowledge@Wharton, 2 January 2013.

Boscolo, R., Shephard, B. and Williams, W., 'The private equity landscape in Colombia', Knowledge@Wharton, 2 January 2013.

Bradshaw, T., 'Entrepreneurs urged to shoot for the sky', *Financial Times*, 5 March 2012.

Braithwaite, T. and Demos, T., 'Geithner holds talks on dearth of small IPOs', *Financial Times*, 13 March 2011.

Brockett, M., 'Home run', Bloomberg Markets, March 2006.

Bullock, N., 'Risky loans stage comeback', *Financial Times*, 13 March 2011.

Burne, K., '"Covenant-lite" deals returning to U.S. loan market, data show', *The Wall Street Journal*, 23 April 2012.

Burwell, R., 'SEC Enforcement Division focuses on insider trading and conflicts of interest in private equity', Dealmakers, PitchBook, 16 March 2012.

Caroll, A., 'Faltering funds of funds', RealDeals, 2 May 2012.

Cauchi, M., 'Banks take more active role', *The Wall Street Journal*, 6 July 2009.

Chasan, E., 'Crowdfunding industry braces for regulation', *The Wall Street Journal*, 5 April 2012.

Chernev, A., 'How much is a Twinkie worth?', *Bloomberg Businessweek*, 6 December 2012.

Collins, M., 'Rich families cut back on buyout firms for direct deals', Bloomberg, 18 December 2012.

Cox, D. and Hanson, B., 'Welcome to the private debt show', Private Equity Analyst Note, PitchBook, Q1/2018, p. 7.

Dasgupta, P., 'Dealing with "broken-deal" expenses: SEC recent action shows its continued focus on fee and expense practices of fund managers', Reed Smith, Client Alert, 5 October 2017.

Davidoff, S., 'Private equity looks abroad, but may be blind to the risks', DealBook, *New York Times*, 21 December 2010.

Davidoff, S., 'The private equity wizardry behind Realogy's comeback', DealBook, *New York Times*, 9 October 2012a.

Davidoff, S., 'The risks of tapping your retirement fund for an alternative use', DealBook, *New York Times*, 30 October 2012b.

Demaria, C., 'Is the enemy, in fact, us?', PEHub, 7 December 2012.

Dembosky, A., 'Facebook to be keenly missed by private markets', *Financial Times*, 6 February 2012.

Demos, T. 'Dark pool launches private share market', *Financial Times*, 17 October 2011.

Demos, T. and Lauricella, T., 'Yield-starved investors snap up riskier MLPs', *The Wall Street Journal*, 16 September 2012.

Deng, C., 'Finding an exit from China gets harder', *The Wall Street Journal*, 24 July 2012.

Elliott, S., 'Norway's Supreme Court rejects appeal over Gassled natural gas transportation tariff reduction', S&P Global Platts, 28 June 2018.

Favaro, K. and Neely, J., 'The next winning move in private equity', Strategy + Business, Summer 2011, Issue **63**, 24 May 2011, p. 10.

FinAlternatives, 'SEC moves to end 'pay-to-play' at pensions', 27 July 2009.

FinAlternatives, 'SEC: P.E. manager helped partner loot firm coffers', 28 July 2009.

Financial Times, 'Lex: Internal rate of return', 1 June 2005a.

Financial Times, 'Lex: Private equity', 24 October 2005b.

Financial Times, 'Lex: Private equity above its rank', 23 December 2005c.

Financial Times, 'Lex: Mezzanine finance', 14 February 2006a.

Financial Times, 'Lex: Hybrids', 26 March 2006b.

Financial Times, 'Private equity goes into debt', 11 February 2007a.

Financial Times, 'Private equity accounting', 29 March 2007b.

Financial Times, 'The limits of fair value', 27 July 2007c.

Financial Times, 'Private equity groups diversify', 20 December 2010.

Financial Times, 'Lex: High yield bonds', 10 February 2011a.

Financial Times, 'Distressed debt funds eye troubled groups', 15 December 2011b.

Financial Times, 'Lex: Social networks of guessworks?', 13 February 2011c.

Financial Times, 'Lex: Securitisation: second infancy', 2 January 2012a.

Financial Times, 'Lex: CLOs – the comeback year', 28 December 2012b.

Florman, M., 'Why private equity is needed now more than ever', *Financial Times*, 28 September 2011.

Foley, S. and Sender, H., 'Private equity firms fuel demand for CLOs', *Financial Times*, 20 December 2012.

Ford, J., 'The exorbitant privilege enjoyed by private equity firms', *The Wall Street Journal*, 8 September 2019.

Freeman, J., 'Is Silicon Valley a systemic risk?', *The Wall Street Journal*, 8 April 2009.

Gage, D., 'The venture capital secret: 3 out of 4 start-ups fail', Small Business, *The Wall Street Journal*, 19 September 2012.

Gelles, D., 'Opening doors on private companies', *Financial Times*, 29 December 2010.

Gladwell, M., 'Creation myth', Annals of Business, *The New Yorker*, 16 May 2011, pp. 44–53.

Gordon, M., 'Do we condemn or cheer the flight to private equity? – NO: Returns can be higher in public markets', *Financial Times*, 15 February 2007.

Gottfried, M., 'Private equity can't keep its powder dry', Heard on the Street, *The Wall Street Journal*, 25 September 2012.

Greenburg, H., 'Worst CEO award goes to Sears' Lampert', MarketWatch, 6 December 2007.

Gregson, J., 'Hitting a wall of debt', *Global Finance Magazine*, May 2010, p. 7.

Guerrera, F. and Politi, J., 'Flipping is a flop for investors', *Financial Times*, 19 September 2006.

Haemmig, M. and Mawson, J., 'Corporations, the new conductors for entrepreneurs', *Global Corporate Venturing*, January 2012, p. 5.

Hausmann, D., 'Kickback scheme promises pain for private equity', Dow Jones Private Equity Analyst, April 2009.

Henry, D. and Thornton, E., 'Buy it, strip it, then flip it', *BusinessWeek*, 7 August 2006.

Iver, S., 'Why the use of covenant-lite loans is growing in Europe', *Investment Dealers' Digests in CapitalEyes, Bank of America Business Capital*, July/August, 2007, p. 2.

Jacobius, A., 'PE fund of funds fading due to changes in investor tastes', *Pensions & Investments*, 7 February 2011.

Jeffries, A., 'Jellyfish tanks, funded 54 times over Kickstarter, turn out to be jellyfish death traps', Caveat Backer, Betabeat.com, 15 March 2012.

Kaczor, P., 'Les indices n'ont pas été décevants', *L'Agefi*, 16 November 2012.

Kahn, R., 'Please don't freeze in August', PEHub Wire, 19 August 2011.

Karbasfrooshan, A., 'Why bootstrapping is just as over-rated as raising venture capital', *TechCrunch*, 7 January 2012.

Karlin, A., 'The entrepreneurship vacuum in Japan: why it matters and how to address it', Knowledge@Wharton, 2 January 2013.

Kelleher, E., 'Private equity chooses the responsible route', *Financial Times*, 27 February 2011.

Knowledge@Wharton, 'Mid-life crisis? Venture capital acts its age', 21 July 2010.

Knowledge@Wharton, 'Risky business: private equity in China', 26 January 2011a.

Knowledge@Wharton, 'Private equity in Brazil: entering a new era', 26 January 2011b.

Kurian, B. and Zachariah, R., 'Global investors put Indian private equity story on hold', *The Times of India*, 26 July 2012.

L'Agefi, 'Ces sociétés qui supportent plusieurs LBO', 10–17 November 2005.

La lettre Vernimmen, January 2006.

Lashinsky, A., 'Rich Kinder's bigger slice', *Fortune*, 16 May 2007.

Lattman, P., 'Schwarzman tops best-paid CEO list for '08 at $702 million', *The Wall Street Journal*, 14 August 2009.

Lattman, P., 'Judge widens antitrust suit against private equity firms', *New York Times*, 8 September 2011.

Lattman, P., 'Private equity industry attracts S.E.C. scrutiny', *New York Times*, 12 February 2012a.

Lattman, P., 'Private Goldman exchange officially closes for business', DealBook, *New York Times*, 12 April 2012b.

Lattman, P. and Lichtblau, E., 'E-mails cited to back lawsuit's claim that equity firms colluded on big deals', *New York Times*, 10 November 2012.

Leroy, S., 'Alerte rouge sur le crédit', *L'Agefi*, 26 July 2007.

Lewis, J., 'Ka-ching', *Investment Dealers Digest*, 20 February 2006.

Linley, M., 'SharesPost settles with SEC, gets a slap on the wrist', *Business Insider*, 14 March 2012.

Mackintosh, J. and Arnold, M., 'French probe buy-out collusion', *Financial Times*, 6 July 2007.

Mariathasan, J. and Steward, M., 'Private equity: what are funds of funds for?', *Investment & Pensions Europe*, 1 May 2011.

McCrum, D. and Schäfer, D., 'Investors urge equity funds to reveal budgets', *Financial Times*, 23 January 2012.

Meads, S. and Davies, M., 'Private equity calls big investors in for deals', Reuters, 2011.

Meek, V., 'Funds of funds on trial', RealDeals, 16 May 2012.

Milne, R., 'Chapter 11 might have lent wings to SAS', Inside Business, *Financial Times*, 22 November 2012.

Moseley, S., 'The seven sins of private equity co-investing', *PEI Media*, 18 November 2011.

Moulins, F., 'Daniel Schmidt: "l'Etat doit soutenir le capital-investissement"', *La Lettre Capital Finance*, no. 1021, 6 June 2011, p. 9.

Murray, A., 'LPs concerned about co-investment selection', RealDeals, 11 October 2012.

Natarajan, P., 'China's private equity market sees fewer deal options', *The Wall Street Journal*, 15 October 2012.

Needleman, S., 'Rise in start-ups draws doubters', *The Wall Street Journal*, 15 February 2012.

Patricof, A., 'Another view: VC investing not dead, just different', DealBook, *New York Times*, 9 February 2009.

Pfanner, E., 'Europe aims to encourage young to be entrepreneurs', *New York Times*, 19 September 2012.

Poletti, T., 'Going private starts to make sense', *San Jose Mercury News*, 10 April 2006.

Power, H., 'Is bigger better?', *Private Equity International*, March 2012.

Primack, D., 'Banks bring back bubble-era terms for corporate loans', The Term Sheet, *Fortune*, 9 February 2011a.

Primack, D., 'Random ramblings', The Term Sheet, *Fortune*, 2 March 2011b.

Primack, D., 'Drilling into Oppenheimer', The Term Sheet, *Fortune*, 20 March 2012a.

Primack, D., 'Bain Capital raising USD 8 billion', The Term Sheet, *Fortune*, 30 May 2012b.

Primack, D., 'Breaking down broken venture capital', The Term Sheet, *Fortune*, 11 May 2012c.

Primack, D., 'Private equity recaps (no, not that kind)', The Term Sheet, *Fortune*, 13 August 2012d.

Primack, D., 'Conspiracy theories', The Term Sheet, *Fortune*, 11 October 2012e.

Primack, D., 'Carlyle's Rubenstein: where we're not investing', The Term Sheet, *Fortune*, 12 December 2012f.

Private Equity International, 'Refinancing: a smoother road', *News Analysis*, April 2012a, 20 pp.

Private Equity International, 'When is a flip too quick?', 9 November 2012b.

Private Equity International, 'Limited, not powerless', 23 November 2012c.

Private Equity Online, 'Ban the politicians', 24 April 2009.

Private Equity Online, 'Why the SEC's good intentions may harm investors', 21 January 2011.

Private Equity Wire, 'Direct lending funds offering superior risk/return profile', 17 April 2015.

Quiry, P. and Le Fur, Y., 'Création et partage de valeurs dans les LBO', *La Lettre Vernimmen*, no. 84, February 2010.

Rappaport, L. and Eaglesham, J., 'Private-share trade is probed', Technology, *The Wall Street Journal*, 23 February 2011.

Reuters, 'Internet boom 2.0 is here, starts to look bubbly', *New York Times*, 8 May 2011.

Salter, M., 'Learning from private equity boards', Harvard Business School Working Knowledge, 17 January 2007.

Schneider, D., *'How will the aftermath of the recession impact private equity'*, AltAssets in CapitalEyes, Bank of America Business Capital, July/August, 2010.

Schonfeld, E., 'The lean finance model of venture capital', *TechCrunch*, 4 December 2011.

Schonfeld, E., 'The SEC's crowdfunding conundrum', *TechCrunch*, 5 September 2012.

Schwartz, B., 'Economics made easy: think friction', *New York Times*, 16 February 2012.

Scott, B., 'Private equity defends pre-packs', RealDeals, 30 January 2012a.

Scott, B., 'Solvency II may cause flight to private equity', RealDeals, 14 February 2012b.

Scott, B., 'Pension solvency proposals take more flak', RealDeals, 16 February 2012c.

Scott, B., 'GPs sitting on record 8,000 portfolio companies', RealDeals, 2 April 2012d.

Singer, T., 'Inside an Internet incubator', *Inc. Magazine*, 1 July 2000.

Sorkin, A. R., 'More money than they know what to do with', DealBook, *New York Times*, 1 October 2012.

Sreeharsha, V., 'Brazil steps up investments in overlooked tech start-ups', DealBook, *New York Times*, 5 December 2012.

Stein, B., 'On buyouts, there ought to be a law', *New York Times*, 3 September 2006.

Stewart, M., 'Private equity: let's work together', *Investment & Pensions Europe*, 1 May 2012.

Surowiecki, J., 'Innovative consumption', The Financial Page, *The New Yorker*, 16 May 2011, 42 pp.

Sutton, S., 'Panel: regulation could clarify performance', *Private Equity International*, 8 February 2012.

Tam, P.-W. and Vascelarro, J., 'Restless workers in Silicon Valley seek ways to cash in early', *The Wall Street Journal*, 21 August 2009.

Tett, G., 'Private equity raises "covenant-lite" loans', *Financial Times*, 20 March 2007.

The Economist, 'Hatching a new plan', 10 August 2000.

The Economist, 'Europe's new deal junkies', 18 February 2006.

The Economist, 'The vultures take wing', 31 March 2007.

The Economist, 'Economics focus: Full disclosure', 21 February 2009a.

The Economist, 'Special report on entrepreneurship', 14 March 2009b.

The Economist, 'Big is back', 29 August 2009c.

The Economist, 'Another bubble?', 18 December 2010.

The Economist, 'Another digital gold rush', 14 May 2011.

The Economist, 'The lure of Chilecon Valley', 13 October 2012a.

The Economist, 'CVC's Australian loss – an isolated carcass', 20 October 2012b.

The Economist, 'Something in the air', 27 October 2012c.

The Economist, 'Filling the bank-shaped hole', 15 December 2012d.

The Founding Member, 'VC Open Letters: the year of the start-up default', TheFunded.com, 10 March 2011.

Toll, D., 'Returns scorecard: 10 top funds of funds', PE Hub, 11 January 2012.

Toller, S., 'EU will create single market for VCTs to aid SME funding', *Money Marketing*, 21 April 2011.

Vardi, N., 'Investor sues T.J. Maloney and his USD 1.8 billion private equity firm alleging bogus fees', The Jungle, *Forbes*, 26 April 2011.

Vascellaro, J., 'Some fear a glut in tech "incubators"', *The Wall Street Journal*, 1 December 2011.

Wadhwa, V., 'When it comes to tech entrepreneurs and their successes, legends abound', Boston.com, 2 August 2011.

Waters, R., 'Dotcom boom's shower of gold passes Wall Street by', *Financial Times*, 1 December 2010.

Weiland, D., 'Chinese private equity funding hit by sharp downturn', *Financial Times*, 15 March 2019.

White, S., 'Vulture funds smell blood from Spanish bank woes', *Business & Financial News*, Reuters, 5 June 2012.

Wigglesworth, R., 'Junk bonds gain traction in private equity financing', *Financial Times*, 2 April 2012.

Winfrey, G., 'Mining company sues Castle Harlan', *Private Equity International*, 6 June 2012.

Zuckerman, G., 'Private equity fund in valuation inquiry', *The Wall Street Journal*, 24 February 2012.

Papers and Studies

Acharya, V., Gottschalg, O., Hahn, M. and Kehoe, C. (2009) 'Corporate governance and value creation: evidence from private equity', European Corporate Governance Institute Working Paper 232/2009, 50 pp.

Achleitner, A. K., Lichtner, K. and Diller, C. (2009) 'Value creation in private equity', Centre for Entrepreneurial and Financial Studies and Capital Dynamics, 6 pp.

Aidun, C. and Dandeneau, D. (2005) 'Is it possible to sell a portfolio company for too much?', *Private Equity Alert, Weil, Gotshal & Manges*, **11**, p. 3.

Anderson, J., Gray, E., Browder, J. and Tincher, J. (2019) 'SEC enforcement against private equity firms in 2019: year in review', Willkie Farr & Gallagher, Client Alert, March 1, 7 pp. (www.willkie.com/~/media/Files/Publications/2019/03/SEC_Enforcement_Against_Private_Equity_Firms_in_2018_Year_in_Review.pdf).

Andonov, A., Hochberg, Y. and Rauh, J. (2017) 'Political representation and governance: evidence from the investment decisions of public pension funds', *Journal of Finance*, 73(5), pp. 2041–2086.

Anson, M. (2017) 'Measuring liquidity premiums for illiquid assets', *Journal of Alternative Investments, pp.* 1–12.

Arias, L., El Hedi Arouri, M., Foulquier, P. and Gregoir, S. (2010) 'On the suitability of the calibration of private equity risk in the Solvency II standard formula', EDHEC, 64 pp.

Axelson, U. and Martinovic, M. (2015) 'European venture capital: myths and facts', London School of Economics, 61 pp.

Bain (2018) Global Private Equity Report 2018, 80 pp.

Bain (2019) Global Private Equity Report 2019, 88 pp.

Bain (2019a) India Private Equity Report 2019 (www.bain.com/insights/india-private-equity-report-2019/).

Bain (2019b) Spotlight on private equity in China: the case for caution (www.bain.com/insights/private-equity-china-global-private-equity-report-2019/).

Bank for International Settlements (2008) 'Private equity and leveraged finance markets', Committee on the Global Financial System, CGFS Papers 30, 46 pp.

Barber, B., Morse, A. and Yasuda, A. (2016) 'Impact investing', SSRN Working Paper 2705556, 48 pp.

Bengtsson, O. (2008) 'Relational venture capital financing of serial founders', University of Illinois at Urbana-Champaign, 45 pp.

Bernstein, S., Lerner, J. and Schoar, A. (2009) 'The investment strategies of sovereign wealth funds', Harvard Business School Working Paper 09-112, 53 pp.

Bielesch, F., Brigl, M., Khanna, D., Roos, A. and Schmieg, F. (2012) 'Corporate venture capital – avoid the risk, miss the rewards', BCG.Perspectives, Boston Consulting Group, 12 pp.

Braun, R., Jenkinson, T. and Stoff, I. (2017) 'How persistent is private equity performance? Evidence from deal-level data', *Journal of Financial Economics*, **123**(2), pp. 273–291.

Brigl, M., Herrera, A., Liechtenstein, H., Meerkatt, H., Prats, M. J. and Rose, J. (2008) 'The advantage of persistence – how the best private-equity firms "beat the fade"', Boston Consulting Group and IESE Business School, 28 pp.

Brigl, M., Nowotnik, P., Pelisari, K., Rose, J. and Zwillenberg, P. (2012) 'The 2012 private equity report – engaging for growth', Boston Consulting Group, 26 pp.

Brown, G., Gredil, O. and Kaplan, S. (2017) 'Do private equity funds manipulate reported returns?', *Journal of Financial Economics*, forthcoming [SSRN Working Paper 2271690].

Brown, G., Harris, R., Hu, W., Jenkinson, T., Kaplan, S. and Robinson, T. (2019) 'Can investors time their exposure to private equity?', Kenan Institute of Private Enterprise Research Paper No. 18-26 [SSRN Working Paper 3241102].

Buscombe, T. (2012) 'Real asset investing', in *The Roles of Alternative Investments* (Mercer Management Consulting, New York), pp. 5–9.

Cai, Y., Sevilir, M. and Tian, X. (2014) 'Do entrepreneurs make good VCs?', SSRN Working Paper 2021327, 41 pp.

Cao, J. (2011) 'IPO timing, buyout sponsors' exit strategy and firm performance of RLBOs', *Journal of Financial and Quantitative Analysis*, **46**(4), pp. 1001–1024.

Cao, J. and Lerner, J. (2009) 'The performance of reverse leveraged buyouts', *Journal of Financial Economics*, **91**(2), pp. 139–157.

Cavagnaro, D., Sensoy, B., Wang, Y. and Weisbach, M. (2017) 'Measuring institutional investors' skill at making private equity investments', SSRN Working Paper 2826633.

Chamberlain, T. and Joncheray, F.-X. (2017) 'Reverse leveraged buyout return behaviour: some European evidence', *Eurasian Journal of Economics and Finance*, **5**(4), pp. 142–175.

Chaplinsky, S. (2004) 'Calpers vs. Mercury News – disclosure comes to private equity', Darden Case UVA-F-1438, 20 pp.

Charles River Associates (2010) 'Impact of the proposed AIFM Directive across Europe', 120 pp.

Chen, H., Gompers, P., Kovner, A. and Lerner, J. (2009) 'Buy local? The geography of successful and unsuccessful venture capital expansion', NBER Working Paper 15102, 42 pp.

Cogent Partners (2012) Secondary Pricing Trends & Analysis, July, p. 9.

Cox, D. and Hanson, B. (2018) 'Welcome to the private debt show', Private Equity Analyst Note, PitchBook, Q1, p. 7.

Cumming, D. and Fleming, G. (2012a) 'Barbarians, demons and Hagetaka: a financial history of leveraged buyouts in Asia 1980–2010', SSRN Working Paper 2008513.

Cumming, D. and Fleming, G. (2012b) 'Corporate defaults, workouts and the rise of the distressed asset investment industry', *Business History Review* [SSRN Working Paper 2144912].

Cuny, C. and Talmor, E. (2006) 'A theory of private equity turnarounds', SSRN Working Paper 875823.

Darcy, J., Kreamer-Eis, H., Debande, O. and Guellec, D. (2009) 'Financing technology transfer', European Investment Fund Working Paper 2009/002.

Degeorge, F. and Zeckhauser, R. (1993) 'The reverse LBO decision and firm performance: theory and evidence', *Journal of Finance*, **48**(4), pp. 1323–1348.

Demaria, C. (2015) 'How do co-investments in emerging markets compare with the ones in developed markets?', UBS Chief Investment Office, 22 pp.

Demaria, C. (2017a) 'Is there too much capital in leveraged buyouts?', *Critical Perspectives*, **60**, 10 pp.

Demaria, C. (2017b) 'Private markets secondary investments: no free lunch', *Critical Perspectives*, **61**, 13 pp.

Demaria, C. (2019) 'Measuring private markets risks in practice', *Critical Perspectives*, **72**, 22 pp.

Devine, A. (2015) 'He who dares', *Private Debt Investor*, June, pp. 16–20.

Diamond, D. (1984) 'Financial intermediation and delegated monitoring', *Review of Economic Studies*, **51**, pp. 393–414.

Diller, C. and Herger, I. (2009) 'Assessing the risk of private equity fund investments', Capital Dynamics, in *Private Equity Mathematics*, pp. 29–41.

Dobbs, R., Koller, T., Lund, S., Ramaswamy, S., Harris, J., Krishnan, M. and Duncan K. (2016) 'Diminishing returns: why investors may need to lower their expectations', McKinsey Global Institute, 48 pp.

Doidge, C., Karolyi, A. and Stulz, R. (2017) 'The U.S. listing gap', *Journal of Financial Economics*, **123**(3), pp. 464–487.

Doskeland, T. and Strömberg, P. (2018) 'Evaluating investments in unlisted equity', Norwegian Government Pension Fund Global (GPFG), 154 pp.

EMPEA (2018) 'The shifting landscape for private capital in Brazil', EMPEA Brief, May, 12 pp.

Europe Innova (2008) 'What is the right strategy for more innovation in Europe? Drivers and challenges for innovation performance at the sector level', Synthesis report, 176 pp.

European Commission (2009a) 'European innovation scoreboard 2008 – comparative analysis of innovation performance', Pro-Inno Europe paper 10, 64 pp.

European Commission (2009b) 'Innobarometer 2009 – analytical report', Flash Eurobarometer 267, 166 pp.

European Commission (2012) 'Innovation Union Scoreboard', Pro-Inno Europe, 101 pp.

European Commission (2015) 'Innobarometer 2015 – The Innovation Trends at EU Enterprises Report', Flash Eurobarometer 415, 200 pp.

European Commission (2016) 'Innobarometer 2016 – EU Business Innovation Trends Report', Flash Eurobarometer 433, 209 pp.

European Commission (2017) The 2017 EU Industrial R&D Investment Scoreboard, 118 pp.

EVCA (2002) 'Survey of the economic and social impact of venture capital in Europe', Research Paper, 28 pp.

EVCA (2005) 'Private equity and generational change', 48 pp.

EVCA (2007a) Corporate Venturing 2006 – European Activity Report, 52 pp.

EVCA (2007b) 'Marketing private equity funds to US investors: ERISA issues', EVCA Special Paper, Brussels, 24 pp.

EVCA (2009) 'Annual survey of pan-European private equity and venture capital activity', EVCA Yearbook, Brussels, 624 pp.

EVCA (2010) 'Closing gaps and moving up a gear: the next stage of venture capital evolution in Europe', Venture Capital White Paper, 24 pp.

Ewens, M. and Rhodes-Kropf, M. (2015) 'Is a VC partnership greater than the sum of its partners?', *Journal of Finance*, **70**(3), pp. 1081–1113.

Fairlie, R. (2012) Kauffman Index of Entrepreneurial Activity (1966–2011), Kauffman Foundation, 32 pp.

Fang, L., Ivashina, V. and Lerner, J. (2015) 'The disintermediation of financial markets: direct investing in private equity', *Journal of Financial Economics*, **116**(1), pp. 160–178.

Global Entrepreneurship Monitor (2019) 2018/2019 Global Report, 152 pp.

Goebel, H., Arangua, H., Valadez, A. and Gonzalez, M. (2019) The Private Equity Review, Mexico, 8th edn, June (https://thelawreviews.co.uk/edition/the-private-equity-review-edition-8/1190961/mexico).

Gompers, P. and Xuan, Y. (2006) 'The role of venture capitalists in the acquisition of private companies', SSRN Working Paper 563822.

Gompers, P. and Xuan, Y. (2008) 'Bridge building in venture capital-backed acquisitions', Harvard Business School Working Paper 08-084, 46 pp.

Gompers, P., Kovner, A., Lerner, J. and Scharfstein, D. (2010) 'Performance persistence in entrepreneurship', *Journal of Financial Economics*, **96**, pp. 18–32.

Gottschalg, O. and Kreuter, B. (2007) 'Quantitative private equity due diligence: possible selection criteria and their efficiency', HEC Paris, 13 pp.

Gredil, O., Griffiths, B. and Stucke, R. (2014) 'Benchmarking private equity: the direct alpha method', SSRN Working Paper 2403521.

Guo, S., Hotchkiss, E. and Song, W. (2008) 'Do buyouts (still) create value?', Boston College, University of Cincinnati, 59 pp.

Gust, *Global Accelerator Report 2016* (http://gust.com/accelerator_reports/2016/global/, last accessed 21 April 2019).

Harris, R., Jenkinson, T. and Stucke, R. (2012) 'Are too many private equity funds top quartile?', *Journal of Applied Corporate Finance*, **24**(4), pp. 77–89.

Harris, R., Jenkinson, T. and Kaplan, S. (2014) 'Private equity performance: what do we know?', *Journal of Finance*, **69**(5), pp. 1851–1882.

Hawley, J. and Williams, A. (2007) 'Universal owners: challenges and opportunities', *Corporate Governance: An International Review*, **15**(3), pp. 415–420.

Henzler, F. (2008) 'Alternative routes to liquidity: securitising private equity', in *The Private Equity Secondaries Market – A Complete Guide to its Structure, Operation and Performance*, PEI Media, pp. 35–36.

Higson, C. and Stucke, R. (2012) 'The performance of private equity', Working Paper, Coller Institute of Private Equity, London Business School, 49 pp.

Hochberg, Y. and Rauh, J. (2013) 'Local overweighting and underperformance: evidence from limited partner private equity investments', *Review of Financial Studies*, **26**, pp. 403–451.

Hochberg, Y., Ljungqvist, A. and Lu, Y. (2007) 'Whom you know matters: venture capital networks and investment performance', *Journal of Finance*, **62**(1), pp. 251–301.

Hochberg, Y., Ljungqvist, A. and Vissing-Jorgensen, A. (2014) 'Information hold-up and performance persistence in venture capital', *Review of Financial Studies*, **27**(1), pp. 102–152.

Holthausen, R. and Larcker, D. (1996) 'The financial performance of reverse leveraged buyouts', *Journal of Financial Economics*, **42**, pp. 193–332.

Hsu, D. (2004) 'What do entrepreneurs pay for venture capital affiliation?', *Journal of Finance*, **59**(4), pp. 1805–1844.

Hsu, D. and Kenney, M. (2004) 'Organizing venture capital: the rise and demise of American Research & Development Corporation (1946–1973)', Working Paper 163, 51 pp.

ILPA (2017) Subscription Lines of Credit and Alignment of Interests – Considerations and Best Practices for Limited and General Partners, 7 pp.

Invest Europe, European Private Equity Activity – Statistics on Fundraising, Investments and Divestments, *Annual*.

Jelic, R. (2011) 'Staying power of UK buy-outs', *Journal of Business Finance & Accounting*, **38**(7–8), pp. 945–986.

Jenkinson, T. and Sousa, M. (2009) 'Why SPAC investors should listen to the market', Unpublished Working Paper, University of Oxford [SSRN Working Paper 1331383].

Jenkinson, T., Landsman, W., Rountree, B. and Soonawalla, K. (2016) 'Private equity net asset values and future cash-flows', SSRN Working Paper 2636985.

Jensen, M. (1989, rev. 1997) 'Eclipse of the public corporation', Harvard Business School, 31 pp.

Johan, S. and Zhang, M. (2016) 'Reporting bias in private equity: reporting frequency, endowments and governance', SSRN Working Paper 2826839.

Jones Day (2007) Comparison of Chapter 11 of the United States Bankruptcy Code with the System of Administration in the United Kingdom, the Rescue Procedure in France, Insolvency Proceedings in Germany, and the Extraordinary Administration for Large Insolvent Companies in Italy, 62 pp.

JP Morgan Asset Management (2007) The Alternative Asset Survey 2007, 40 pp.

JP Morgan Asset Management (2010) Alternative Asset Survey 2010, September, 36 pp.

Kaplan, S. and Schoar, A. (2003) 'Private equity performance: returns, persistence and capital flows', *Journal of Finance*, 60(4), pp. 1791–1823.

Katz, S. (2008) 'Earnings quality and ownership structure: the role of private equity sponsors', NBER Working Paper 14085, 53 pp.

Kauffman Foundation (2017) The Kaufffman Index Startup Activity, National Trends, May, 52 pp.

Kedrosky, P. and Stangler, D. (2011) Financialization and Its Entrepreneurial Consequences, Kauffman Foundation, **2011**, 20 pp.

Kelly, R. (2011) 'The performance and prospects of European venture capital', The European Investment Fund Working Paper 2011/09, 22 pp.

Kerr, W., Lerner, J. and Schoar, A. (2011) 'The consequences of entrepreneurial finance: evidence from angel financings', *Review of Financial Studies*, 27(1), pp. 20–55.

Kinlaw, W., Kritzman, M. and Turkington, D. (2013) 'Liquidity and portfolio choice: a unified approach', *Journal of Portfolio Management*, 39(2), pp. 19–27.

Korteweg, A. and Nagel, S. (2016) 'Risk adjusting the returns to venture capital', *Journal of Finance*, 71(3), pp. 1437–1470.

Korteweg, A. and Sorensen, M. (2015) 'Skill and luck in private equity performance', SSRN Working Paper 2419299.

KPMG (2009) 'Turbulent times', *Frontiers in Finance*, 30 pp.

KPMG (2019) Venture Pulse Q4 2018: Global analysis of venture funding, 104 pp.

L'Her, J.-F., Stoyanova, R., Shaw, K., Scott, W. and Lai, C. (2016) 'A bottom-up approach to the risk-adjusted performance of the buyout fund market', *Financial Analysts Journal*, 72(4), pp. 36–48.

LAVCA, Cambridge Associates (2018) Latin American Private Equity Limited Partners Opinion Survey, 12 pp.

Lehmann, A. (2018) 'Risk reduction through Europe's distressed debt market', Bruegel Policy Contribution 2, 13 pp.

Leland, H. and Pyle, D. (1977) 'Informational asymmetries, financial structure and financial intermediation', *Journal of Finance*, 32, pp. 371–387.

Lerner, J., Ledbetter, J., Speen, A., Leamon, A. and Allen, C. (2006) 'Private equity in emerging markets: yesterday, today and tomorrow', *Journal of Private Equity*, 19(3), pp. 8–20.

Lerner, J., Schoar, A. and Wongsunwai, W. (2007) 'Smart institutions, foolish choices: the limited partner performance puzzle', *Journal of Finance*, 62(2), pp. 731–764.

Lerner, J., Schoar, A. and Wang, J. (2008) 'Secrets of the academy: the drivers of university endowment success', Harvard Business School Finance Working Paper 07-066/MIT Sloan Research Paper 4698-08.

Li, Y. (2014) 'Reputation, volatility and performance persistence of private equity', Federal Reserve Board of Governors Working Paper, 56 pp.

Ljungqvist, A. and Richardson, M. (2003) 'The cash flow, return and risk characteristics of private equity', SSRN Working Paper 369600.

Lo, A. (2004) 'The adaptive market hypothesis: market efficiency from an evolutionary perspective', *Journal of Portfolio Management*, 30(5), pp. 15–29.

Lo, A., Petrov, C. and Wiersbicki, M. (2003) 'It's 11 PM – do you know where your liquidity is? The mean–variance–liquidity frontier', *Journal of Investment Management*, 1(1), pp. 55–93.

Longstaff, F. (2018) 'Valuing thinly traded assets', *Management Science*, 64(8), pp. 3469–3970.

Mackewicz & Partners (2004) Institutional Investors and their Activities with Regard to the Alternative Asset Class Private Equity, An Empirical European Survey, 84 pp.

Mariathasan, J. (2011) Private equity: keep a clear head, Investments & Pensions Europe.

McGrady, C. and Heffern, B. (2008) Secondary Pricing Analysis Interim Update, Cogent Partners, Winter 2008, 8 pp.

McKinsey & Company (2012) 'The mainstreaming of alternative investments – fuelling the next wave of growth in asset management', *Financial Services Practice*, 38 pp.

Meerkatt, H. and Liechtenstein, H. (2008) Get ready for the private equity shakeout, BCG-IESE, 11 pp.

Mercer Management Consulting (2012) The roles of alternative investments, 18 pp.

Monitor Group (2010) Paths to Prosperity, 88 pp.

Mooradian, P., Auerbach, A. and Quealy, M. (2013) Growth equity is all grown up, Cambridge Associates, 10 pp.

Mulcahy, D., Weeks, B. and Bradley, H. (2012) We have met the enemy … and he is us, Kauffman Foundation, 52 pp.

Muscarella, C. and Vetsuypens, M. (1990) 'Efficiency and organizational structure: a study of reverse LBOs', *Journal of Finance*, 45(5), pp. 1389–1413.

Nadauld, T., Sensoy, B., Vorkink, K. and Weisbach, M. (2017) 'The liquidity cost of private equity investments: evidence from secondary market transactions', NBER Working Paper 22404, 49 pp.

Nahata, R. (2007) Venture capital reputation and investment performance, Baruch College, 64 pp.

Nielsen, K. (2010) 'The return to direct investment in private firms: new evidence on the private equity premium puzzle', *European Financial Management*, 17(3), pp. 436–463.

Oskarsson, I. and Schläpfer, A. (2008) The performance of spin-off companies at the Swiss Federal Institute of Technology Zurich, ETH Transfer, 40 pp.

Padilla, H. and Arango, P. (2019) *The Private Equity Review, Colombia*, 8th edn, June (https://thelawreviews.co.uk/edition/the-private-equity-review-edition-8/1190924/colombia).

Partners Group (2009) 'The New Buyout: How the financial crisis is changing private equity', Research Flash, November, 15 pp.

PEI Media (2010) Inside the Limited Partner, 237 pp.

Phalippou, L. and Gottschalg, O. (2006) 'The performance of private equity funds', University of Amsterdam, HEC Paris, 50 pp.

PitchBook (2018) 2017 Annual VC Liquidity Report, 12 pp.

PitchBook (2019) 2018 Annual US PE Breakdown, 15 pp.

Preqin (2012) Special Report: LP Appetite for Private Equity Co-investments, 9 pp.

Preqin (2018a) Special Report: Asian Private Equity & Venture Capital, 24 pp.

Preqin (2018b) Special Report: Private Equity in Emerging Markets, May, 16 pp.

Preqin (2019) Preqin Markets in Focus: Private Equity & Venture Capital in India, 12 pp.

PwC, ICF GHK and Ecorys (2014) SMEs' access to public procurement markets and aggregation of demand in the EU, 170 pp.

Rice, B. (2017) 'The upside of the downside of modern portfolio theory', Investment & Wealth Monitor, Investment Management Consultants Association, pp. 13–18, 55.

Robinson, D. and Sensoy, B. (2013) 'Do private equity managers earn their fees? Compensation, ownership and cash flow performance', *Review of Financial Studies* [NBER Working Paper 17942].

Rouvinez, C. (2003) 'Private equity benchmarking with PME+', *Venture Capital Journal*, 43(8), pp. 34–39.

Rouvinez, C. (2007) 'Looking for the premium', Private Equity International, pp. 80–85.

Russell Investment Group (2007) The 2007–2008 Russell Survey on Alternative Investing, 102 pp.

Russell Research (2010) Russell Investments' 2010 Global Survey on Alternative Investing, 16 pp.

Russell Research (2012) Russell Investments' 2012 Global Survey on Alternative Investing, 18 pp.

S&P Global Ratings (2019) 'Global leveraged finance, when the cycle turns', 26 June, 142 pp.

Sallard, D. (1999) Risk-capital markets, a key to job creation in Europe. From fragmentation to integration. Report, Directorate General II, Economic and Financial Affairs, European Commission, Euro papers 32, 36 pp.

Scott, J. (2000) 'Drexel Burnham Lambert: a ten-year retrospective', Austrian Scholar's Conference, Auburn University, 41 pp.

Sensoy, B., Wang, Y. and Weisbach, M. (2014) 'Limited partner performance and the maturing of the private equity industry', *Journal of Financial Economics*, 112(3), pp. 320–343.

Sorensen, M. (2007) 'How smart is smart money? A two-sided matching model of venture capital', *Journal of Finance*, 62(6), pp. 2725–2762.

Sorensen, M. and Jagannathan, R. (2015) 'The public market equivalent and private equity performance', *Financial Analysts Journal*, 71(4), p. 22.

Stafford, E. (2017) 'Replicating private equity with value investing, homemade leverage, and hold-to-maturity accounting', SSRN Working Paper 2720479.

Startup Genome (2018) Global Startup Ecosystem Report 2018 – Succeeding in the New Era of Technology, 242 pp.

Strauss, M. L. and Borenstein, D. (2010) 'Analyzing the Brazilian higher education system using system dynamics', Proceedings of the 45th Annual Conference of the ORSNZ, p. 9.

Strömberg, P. (2008) 'The new demography of private equity', in J. Lerner and A. Gurung (eds), *The Global Impact of Private Equity Report 2008: Globalisation and alternative investments*, World Economic Forum, Vol. 1, pp. 3–26.

Thomas, J. and Pace, L. (2012) 'All in all it was not so much of a maturity wall', Market Commentary, The Carlyle Group, p. 6.

Trinomics (2018) The Entrepreneur's Guide to Growing and Financing Innovative Energy Technology Companies, 45 pp (https://ec.europa.eu/energy/sites/ener/files/documents/building_the_investment_community_for_innovative_energy_entrepreneurss_guide_0.pdf, last accessed 21 April 2019).

United Nations Conference on Trade and Development (2006) World Investment Report, UNCTAD, 372 pp.

Weidig, T. and Mathonet, P.-Y. (2004) 'The risk profile of private equity', QuantExperts/European Investment Fund, 33 pp.

Weild, D. and Kim, E. (2010) 'Market structure is causing the IPO crisis – and more', Grant Thornton, 32 pp.

Weisser, M. and Germano, L. (2006) 'Going . . . Going . . . Going . . . Gone Private', Private Equity Alert, Weil, Gotshal & Manges, August 2006, 4 pp.

Welch, K. and Stubben, S. (2018) 'Private equity's diversification illusion: evidence from fair value accounting', SSRN Working Paper 2379170.

Wilson, E. (2012) 'How to make a region innovative', Strategy + Business, 66 pp.

Data

Preqin
Robert Shiller's online data
StepStone
Thomson Eikon's Cambridge Associates database

White papers

IPEV (2018) International Private Equity and Venture Capital Valuation Guidelines, 57 pp.

Index

Note: Page numbers in *italics* refer to figures and tables.

Printed and bound by CPI Group (UK) Ltd, Croydon, CR0 4YY

16/04/2025

14658509-0002